# Small Arms Today

# Small Arms Today

## *Latest Reports on the World's Weapons and Ammunition*

### 2nd Edition

## Edward Clinton Ezell

with research assistance from
Carlos G. Davila
and
Peter Labbett

STACKPOLE BOOKS, Harrisburg
ARMS AND ARMOUR PRESS, London,
New York, Sydney

Copyright © 1988 by Stackpole Books

Published by
STACKPOLE BOOKS
Cameron and Kelker Streets
P.O. Box 1831
Harrisburg, PA 17105

First published in Great Britain,
by Arms and Armour Press,
Artillery House
Artillery Row
London SW1P 1RT

Distributed in Australia by
Capricorn Link (Australia) Pty. Ltd.
P.O. Box 665
Lane Cove
New South Wales 2066, Australia

Printed in the United States of America

10 9 8 7 6 5 4 3 2 1

**Library of Congress Cataloging-in-Publication Data**

Ezell, Edward Clinton.
    Small arms today : latest reports on the world's weapons and
ammunition / Edward Clinton Ezell : with research assistance of
Carlos G. Davila and Peter Labbett. — 2nd ed.
        p.     cm.
    Bibliography: p.
    Includes index.
    ISBN 0-8117-2280-5 (USA)
    ISBN 0 85368 977 6 (UK)
    1. Firearms—Catalogs.   I. Davila, Carlos G.   II. Labbett, P.
III. Title.
UO380.E94     1988
623.4′42′09047—dc19                                88-21036
                                                        CIP

# Contents

# Contents

# Preface

Any book on military small arms requires access to a variety of information sources. This new book was proof of that statement in many ways. Trying to determine the type of small arms being used by the armies of the world was and continues to be a complicated task. It was rewarding that many people encouraged the compilers of this study and gave freely of the unclassified information at their disposal. We know that this volume is still in its infancy. Cataloging small caliber weapons in use will be a continuing challenge, and we know that many of our readers have information and data that were not at our disposal. The strength of subsequent editions will depend upon help from our established contacts and new information provided by people we have yet to encounter. If you have information that should be included or changes that should be made, please feel free to contact us at the address on the last page of this book.

We want to sincerely thank all who helped in the preparation of this second edition. Not all of the people and organizations who have helped us wish to be identified. Among those who do, the following were very helpful:

United States:   Armex International, Broderick, California
                 Ward Bunyan, Santa Rosa, California
                 Colt Firearms Division, Colt Industries, Hartford, Connecticut
                     Robert E. Roy
                 Chuck de Caro, Washington, D.C.
                 Deep River Armory, Houston, Texas
                     James B. Hughes, Jr.
                 Department of Defense
                     DOD Public Affairs
                     Ed Michalski
                     SP4 Fred Sutter

Defense Intelligence Agency
Defense Logistics Agency
    Defense Logistics Service Center, Battle Creek, Michigan
US Air Force
US Army
    Deputy Chief of Staff for Research, Development and Acquisition
    Foreign Science and Technology Center, Charlottesville, Virginia
    Foreign Military Intelligence Group, Aberdeen Proving Ground, Maryland
        (formerly the 11th Military Intelligence Battalion)
US Marine Corps
    MAJ Richard Jeppesen, Quantico, Virginia
US Navy
    US Naval Sea Systems Command
Department of State
Department of Transportation
    US Coast Guard, Military Capabilities Branch
David Isby, Washington, D.C.
*Journal of Defense & Diplomacy,* McLean, Virginia
    Alan P. Capps, Editor
    Virginia H. Ezell, Assistant Editor
Craig Kristjanson
RAMO, Inc., Nashville, Tennessee
Research Armaments Prototypes, Rogers, Arkansas
Saco Defense Systems Division, Maremont Corporation, Saco, Maine
Smithsonian Institution
    Office of Photographic and Printing Services
        Eric Long, Laurie Minor, and Rick Vargas
*Soldier of Fortune*
    Peter G. Kokalis
    Robert K. Brown, Publisher
Sturm, Ruger and Company, Inc., Southport, Connecticut
Jiri T. Vojta, Syracuse, New York
Winchester International Defense Products, Olin Corporation, East Alton, Illinois


Argentina:    Embassy of Argentina, Washington, D.C.
        COL Raul J. Gomez Sabaini, Office of the Military Attache
    Ignacio J. Osacar, Buenos Aires


Austria:    Bundesministerium für Landesverteidigung, Vienna
    Steyr-Daimler-Puch, Steyr


Belgium:    Embassy of Belgium, Washington, D.C.
        BG L. Van Rafelghem, Defense Attache Office
    Fabrique Nationale, Herstal
    North Atlantic Treaty Organization
        Public Affairs Office


Belize:    WO II J. E. Mahaffy, Weapon Training Warrant Officer, Belize Defence Force

| | |
|---|---|
| Brazil: | Ronaldo S. Olive, Santa Rosa |
| Canada: | Diemaco, Inc., Kitchener, Ontario<br>    Henrik Noesgaard, General Manager<br>Embassy of Canada, Washington, D.C.<br>    Captain K. W. Ferris, Canadian Defence Liaison Staff<br>Jack Krcma, Willowdale, Ontario<br>R. Blake Stevens, Collector Grade Publications, Toronto |
| Czechoslovakia: | MAJ Karel Zeleny, Assistant Military and Air Attache, Embassy of the Czechoslovak Socialist Republic, Washington, D.C. |
| Denmark: | LTC O. Buch, RDAF, Office of the Defense and Armed Forces Attache, Royal Danish Embassy, Washington, D.C. |
| Finland: | LTC Timo Apajakari, MAJ Erkki Nordberg, Finnish Defense Forces, General Headquarters, Helsinki<br>Markku Palokangas, Curator, Sotamuseo, Helsinki |
| France: | Jean Huon, Clairefontaine<br>Manurhin, Mulhouse |
| Germany: | Wilhelm Dietl, Poing<br>Embassy of the Federal Republic of Germany, Washington, D.C.<br>Heckler & Koch GmbH, Oberndorf<br>Masami Tokoi, Dusseldorf |
| Greece: | Embassy of Greece, Washington, D.C.<br>    COL D. Kyriazopolous, Defense Attache<br>Hellenic Arms Industry, SA, Athens |
| Iceland: | Helgi Agustsson, Embassy of Iceland, Washington, D.C. |
| Indonesia: | COL Djarot Supadmo, Defense Attache, Embassy of the Republic of Indonesia, Washington, D.C. |
| Israel: | Electrooptics Industries Ltd., Rehovot<br>Israeli Defense Forces |
| Italy: | COL Sergio Siracusa, Military Attache, Italian Embassy, Washington, D.C. |
| Japan: | Japanese Defense Agency, Tokyo |
| Laos: | Khamsay Sayasane |
| Luxembourg: | Ambassador Paul Peters, Embassy of the Grand Duchy of Luxembourg, Washington, D.C. |

Malaysia:            BG Samsuri Welch bin Abdullah, Defense & Armed Forces Attache, Embassy of
                     Malaysia, Washington, D.C.
                     Public Affairs Office, Ministry of Defence, Kuala Lumpur

New Zealand:         COL P. G. Hotop, Military Attache, MAJ D. R. Wilton, Military Attache, Embassy
                     of New Zealand, Washington, D.C.

Nigeria:             LTC J. O. Williams, Office of the Defense Attache Embassy, Washington, D.C.

Portugal:            COL Carlos Alexandre Leal Machado, Chief of the Armament Department,
                     Ministério do Exército, Lisbon
                     COL Adriano A. Nogueira, Military Attache, Embassy of Portugal

South Africa:        Embassy of South Africa
                         Captain N. S. Vorster, South African Navy
                         Captain H. J. W. Jooste, South African Navy

South Korea:         Daewoo Precision Manufacturing Ltd., Pusan

Sweden:              Embassy of Sweden
                         COL Claes Tamm, Army Attache

Switzerland:         Embassy of Switzerland
                         COL J. Weder, Defense, Military, Naval & Air Attache
                     Heckler & Koch, SA, Neuchatel
                         Wolfhart Fritze
                     Schweizerische Industrie Gesellschaft Neuhausen an Rheinfall
                         Willy Marques
                         Jurg Kueffer

United Kingdom:      *Handgunner*
                         Richard A. I. Munday
                         Jan Stephenson
                     Institute for the Study of Terrorism, London
                         Jillian Becker
                         Ian Geldard
                     Jane's Publishing Company, Ltd., London
                         Christopher Foss
                         Terry Gander
                         Ian Hogg
                         John Weeks, deceased
                     Royal Small Arms Factory, Enfield
                         Office of the Director
                         Pattern Room, Herbert J. Woodend

Uruguay:             GEN Héctor Alvarez, Defense Attache, Embassy of Uruguay, Washington, D.C.
                     Enrique Gomez Haedo, Montevideo

# Introduction

There were three reasons for creating this publication. First, during the recent decade, the tempo of small caliber weapon research, development, and standardization has increased to such an extent that it is difficult to keep current with these advances in a single book such as *Small Arms of the World*. This present publication has allowed your editors to present the latest information in a timely fashion. Second, through its basic format, this book will allow the user to determine which weapons the armies worldwide are using. And where possible and appropriate, data is provided on the weapons being employed by antigovernment and terrorist forces. Lack of such information in an easily accessible format was one of the factors that led the editors to undertake *Small Arms Today*. When possible, information and photographs have been included to aid in the detailed and positive identification of small caliber weapons currently in use. Third, with the proliferation of small caliber ammunition cartridges and projectile types, we have described some of the ammunition that might be found in use. Because older weapons continue in use in many countries, the total number of calibers has increased rather than decreased since the end of World War II.

In the years since World War II, distribution of newly manufactured and obsolete military small arms has become an important adjunct of foreign and military policy for many nations and groups of nations, with the result that the transfer of small caliber weapons has been a dynamic, generally unexamined activity. Most writers, especially academic scholars, have concentrated on larger and more sophisticated weapons and the movement of these items,* or they have dwelt on other

---

*Some typical examples are: Cindy Cannizzo, ed., *The Gun Merchants: Politics and Policies of the Major Arms Suppliers*. New York et al.: Pergamon Press, 1980; Lewis A. Frank, *The Arms Trade in International Relations*. New York et al.: Frederick A. Praeger Publishers, 1969; Stephanie G. Neuman, *Military Assistance in Recent Wars: The Dominance of the Superpowers*. New York et al.: Praeger, 1986; Andrew J. Pierre, *The Global Politics of Arms Sales*. Princeton: Princeton University Press, 1982; and Lewis Sorley, *Arms Transfers under Nixon: A Policy Analysis*. Lexington: The University of Kentucky Press, 1983. One notable exception is Michael T. Klare, *The American Arms Supermarket*. Austin: University of Texas Press, 1984.

issues of importance such as the economic burdens associated with military assistance and military hardware production programs.*

Even casual following of news reports around the globe will underscore the importance of keeping track of where small arms come from and where they go. We have been conservative in our reporting on small arms in use; thus only confirmed reports have been included. Individuals wishing to add to our data are encouraged to correspond with the editors through the publisher's address.

The transfer process for small caliber weapons was deeply influenced by the dissolution of the old colonial empires and the subsequent national and international realignments of power. North Atlantic Treaty Organization (NATO) and Warsaw Pact member states have striven to establish standard patterns of small caliber weapons. Because of their modernity, reliability, and in some cases "sex appeal," those "new" weapons have generally become the most popular among states not aligned with these two major power blocs. Likewise, NATO and Warsaw Pact small arms have been distributed to revolutionary movements around the world as part of the global ebb and flow of power politics.

The following country-by-country checklist is designed to help military personnel, policy planners, and other interested parties understand the types of weapons being used in each country and to help those parties identify the source of the weapons. To facilitate understanding and to establish clarity, we have incorporated two types of identification numbers, where appropriate, into the discussion below. These are NSN and FOM designations. A few words about each are in order.

## NSN

Depending upon one's location, NSN stands for National or NATO stock number. The designation is derived from the former US Federal Stock Numbers (FSNs). The FSN was introduced in 1952 as part of the Defense Cataloging and Standardization Act in an effort to implement the concept of a single-item identification number (e.g., all standard 40-watt light bulbs with the same function, regardless of manufacture, were assigned the same FSN). On September 30, 1974, FSNs were replaced with 13-digit NSNs. The two additional digits identified the nation that originated the item. These digits are called the National Codification Bureau (NCB) Code. The NSN (*Versorgungsnummer* in German) is broken down as follows:

| | |
|---|---|
| Federal Supply Class (FSC) | 1005 |
| National Codification Bureau Code (NCB) | 00 |
| Nonsignificant serial number | 123-4567 |

The NCB + seven digits = National Item Identification Number (NIIN). The FSC + NCB + seven digits = NSN. The last seven digits (nonsignificant serial number) are randomly assigned and have no significance.

In this section we are concerned basically with two ordnance (10 class) federal supply class categories:

1005 — Ordnance materiel through 30mm
1010 — Ordnance materiel 31mm to 75mm

### Examples

7.62 x 51mm NATO *Fusil Automatique Légèr* made by Fabrique Nationale Herstal of Belgium has been assigned the number NSN 1005-13-100-0010.

5.56 x 45mm Rifle, M16A1, made by Colt Firearms Division, Colt Industries of the USA, has been assigned the number NSN 1005-00-073-9421. In this NSN, the -00- means that the number had been assigned prior to the establishment of the NATO country codes.

5.56 x 45mm NATO Rifle, M16A2, made by Colt, has been assigned NSN 1005-01-128-9936.

40 x 53mmSR Machine Gun, Grenade Launching, MK 19 MOD 3 made by Saco Defense Systems Division, Maremont Corporation, US, has been assigned NSN 1010-01-126-9063.

---

*David J. Louscher and Michael D. Salomone, eds., *Marketing Security Assistance: New Perspectives on Arms Sales*. Lexington, Mass.: Lexington Books, 1987; and Michael Brzoska and Thomas Ohlson, eds., *Arms Production in the Third World*. London and Philadelphia: Taylor & Francis, 1986, for the Stockholm International Peace Research Institute.

### NATO NCB Codes

The following are the two-digit codes for the NATO countries and others that adhere to the national codification system. The code designates the country originally cataloging an item of supply.

**NATO Country Codes**

*NATO Members*

| | |
|---|---|
| Belgium | 13 |
| Canada | 21 |
| Denmark | 22 |
| France | 14 |
| Germany, Federal Republic of | 12 |
| Greece | 23 |
| Iceland | 24 |
| Italy | 15 |
| Luxembourg | 28 |
| Netherlands | 17 |
| Norway | 25 |
| Portugal | 26 |
| Spain | 33 |
| Turkey | 27 |
| United Kingdom | 99 |
| United States of America | 00 |
| | 01 |
| | 06 |
| NATO | 11 |

*Other Nations (non-NATO)*

| | |
|---|---|
| Argentina | 29 |
| Austria | 0 |
| Australia | 66 |
| Israel | 31 |
| Japan | 30 |
| Kuwait | ? |
| Malaysia | 34 |
| New Zealand | 98 |
| Saudi Arabia | SA |
| Singapore | 32 |
| South Africa | 18 |
| Thailand | 35 |

### FOM

Foreign Materiel Numbers are assigned to foreign ground-forces materiel for the purpose of standardizing identification of and reporting on equipment being used outside the United States. Roughly derived from the NSN system, FOM numbers are more complex. There are five components to an FOM number:

$$\text{FOM} \quad \underset{\text{1st}}{1005} \quad \underset{\text{2d}}{2} \quad \underset{\text{3d}}{2} \quad \underset{\text{4th}}{7.62} \quad \underset{\text{5th}}{16}$$

1. Federal supply category. Again 10 stands for ordnance and 05 indicates smaller than 31mm.
2. Country designator, which in this case is the Soviet Union.
3. Materiel subcategory, which in this case is a rifle. The categories of interest for this checklist are:

| | |
|---|---|
| Handguns | = 1 |
| Rifles | = 2 |
| Submachine guns | = 3 |
| Machine guns | = 4 |
| Automatic cannon | = 4 |
| Grenade Launchers | = _ |

4. Caliber, which in this case is 7.62mm.
5. Specific item identifier (16 equals the SKS).

To recap: 7.62 x 39mm *Samozaryadiniy karabin Simonova* (SKS) made by Soviet state weapons factories has been assigned the FOM number 1005-2-2-7.62-16.

### FOM Country Designators

| FOM No. | Country Name | Abbreviation |
|---|---|---|
| 073 | Afghanistan | AF |
| 003 | Albania | AL |
| 083 | Algeria | AG |
| xxx | Angola | |
| 026 | Argentina | AR |
| 041 | Australia | AS |
| 027 | Austria | AU |
| xxx | Bahrain | |
| xxx | Bangladesh | |
| xxx | Barbados | |
| 021 | Belgium (NATO) | BE |
| 099 | Benin (formerly Dahomey) | DM |
| 050 | Bolivia | BL |
| 056 | Brazil | BR |
| 004 | Bulgaria (Warsaw Pact) | BU |
| 046 | Burma | BM |
| 106 | Burundi | BY |
| 100 | Cameroons | CM |

| FOM No. | Country Name | Abbreviation | FOM No. | Country Name | Abbreviation |
|---------|--------------|--------------|---------|--------------|--------------|
| 038 | Canada (NATO) | CA | 054 | Iraq | IZ |
| 111 | Central African Republic | CT | 069 | Ireland | EI |
| 116 | Chad | CD | 037 | Israel | IS |
| 063 | Chile | CI | 023 | Italy (NATO) | IT |
| 005 | China, People's Republic of | PRC | xxx | Ivory Coast | |
| 031 | China, Republic of (on Taiwan) | TW | xxx | Jamaica | |
| 057 | Colombia | CO | 030 | Japan | JA |
| 094 | Congo, People's Republic of | CF | 055 | Jordan | JO |
| 077 | Costa Rica | CS | 044 | Kampuchea (formerly Cambodia) | CB |
| 079 | Cuba | CU | 103 | Kenya | KE |
| 101 | Cyprus | CY | 010 | Korea, People's Democratic Republic of (North Korea) | KN |
| 006 | Czechoslovakia (Warsaw Pact) | CZ | | | |
| 033 | Denmark (NATO) | DA | 022 | Korea, Republic of (South Korea) | KS |
| xxx | Djibouti | | xxx | Kuwait | |
| xxx | Dominica | | 043 | Laos | LA |
| 060 | Dominican Republic | DR | 052 | Lebanon | LE |
| 084 | Ecuador | EC | 071 | Liberia | LI |
| 036 | Egypt | EG | 074 | Libya | LY |
| 080 | El Salvador | ES | 081 | Lithuania (not used in this list) | LN |
| 108 | Equatorial Guinea | GV | 025 | Luxembourg (NATO) | LU |
| 066 | Ethiopia | ET | 109 | Madagascar | MA |
| xxx | Fiji | | 092 | Malawi | MI |
| 013 | Finland | FI | 078 | Malaysia | MY |
| 017 | France | FR | 098 | Mali | ML |
| 112 | Gabonese Republic | GB | 117 | Mauritania | MR |
| xxx | The Gambia | | 040 | Mexico | MX |
| 007 | Germany, Democratic Republic of (East Germany — Warsaw Pact) | GC | 120 | Mongolia | MG |
| 016 | Germany, Federal Republic of (West Germany — NATO) | GE | 087 | Morocco | MO |
| | | | 121 | Mozambique | MZ |
| 015 | Germany, pre-1945 | OG | 095 | Nepal | NP |
| 096 | Ghana | GH | 029 | Netherlands | NL |
| 028 | Greece (NATO) | GR | 088 | New Zealand | NZ |
| xxx | Grenada | | 062 | Nicaragua | NU |
| 059 | Guatemala | GT | 110 | Niger | NG |
| xxx | Guinea | | 089 | Nigeria | NI |
| xxx | Guinea-Bisseau | | 020 | Norway (NATO) | NO |
| xxx | Guyana | | xxx | Oman | |
| 061 | Haiti | HA | 045 | Pakistan | PK |
| 085 | Honduras | HO | 058 | Panama | PN |
| 008 | Hungary (Warsaw Pact) | HU | xxx | Papua New Guinea | |
| 070 | Iceland (NATO) | IC | 064 | Paraguay | PA |
| 048 | India | IN | 072 | Peru | PE |
| 049 | Indonesia | ID | 068 | Philippines | RP |
| 053 | Iran | IR | 011 | Poland (Warsaw Pact) | LP |
| | | | 047 | Portugal | PO |

| FOM No. | Country Name | Abbreviation |
|---|---|---|
| xxx | Qatar | |
| 051 | Republic of South Africa | SF |
| 012 | Romania (Warsaw Pact) | RO |
| 105 | Rwanda | RW |
| 076 | Saudi Arabia | SA |
| 097 | Senegal | SG |
| xxx | Seychelles | |
| 113 | Sierra Leone | SL |
| 122 | Singapore | SN |
| 090 | Somalia | SO |
| 024 | Spain (NATO) | SP |
| 104 | Sri Lanka (Ceylon) | CE |
| 082 | Sudan | SU |
| xxx | Swaziland | |
| 019 | Sweden | SW |
| 018 | Switzerland | SZ |
| 032 | Syria | SY |
| 102 | Tanzania | TZ |
| 034 | Thailand | TH |
| 107 | Togo | TO |
| xxx | Tonga | |
| 067 | Tunisia | TS |
| 039 | Turkey (NATO) | TU |
| 115 | Uganda | UG |
| 1A | Unidentified country | UNCO |
| 1B | Unidentified East Bloc country | UCWC |
| 1C | Unidentified Free World country | UFWC |
| 002 | Union of Soviet Socialist Republics (Russia and Soviet Union — Warsaw Pact) | USSR |
| xxx | United Arab Emirates | |
| 035 | United Kingdom (NATO) | UK |
| 000 | United States of America (obsolete, commercial, etc. — NATO) | US |
| 114 | Upper Volta | UV |
| 065 | Uruguay | UY |
| 091 | Venezuela | VE |
| 009 | Vietnam, Socialist Republic of (formerly Democratic Republic of; North Vietnam) | VN |
| 042 | Vietnam, Republic (South Vietnam is now part of the Socialist Republic of Vietnam) | VS |
| xxx | Yemen, Arab Republic of (North) | |
| xxx | Yemen, People's Democratic | |

| FOM No. | Country Name | Abbreviation |
|---|---|---|
| 014 | Yugoslavia | YO |
| 093 | Zaire | ROCL |
| 119 | Zambia | ZA |
| 118 | Zimbabwe | RH |

A few more words are necessary to explain the utility of NSN and FOM identifiers. Since the former numbers are used NATO-wide and the latter are used primarily by the United States, many NATO small caliber weapons will be assigned both identifiers. When both numbers exist, they will be included in the checklist to aid our understanding of the distribution of such weapons. In some instances a single NATO small arm will have multiple NSNs, especially in the case where it has been manufactured in several countries. In other instances, more than one nation may use the same NSN for a basic weapon, but then assign different NSNs for variants.

For example, Fabrique Nationale's 7.62 x 51mm NATO MAG GPMG has been assigned the following identifier: NSN 1005-13-103-2524. The British mark their "Machine Gun 7.62mm L7A2" with this NSN, as in the accompanying photograph. But they have given their "Machine Gun 7.62mm TK L8A1" NSN 1005-99-960-6851, because it is a UK variant developed for use in armored vehicles.

### Status of Weapons

When possible, throughout this checklist, the current status of weapons has been noted. We have indicated if the item is standard (that is, a current issue item), if it is held in reserve for emergency use, if it is obsolescent (i.e., in the process of being withdrawn from service or in the process of being replaced), or if it is obsolete and no longer in use. We have included obsolete weapons, because many of these items are still used by other states (especially if there is a client-state relationship between two governments) or by revolutionary or terrorist organizations. In the section on US small arms, we have employed the Logistics

Receiver markings on FN-manufactured British L7A2 GPMG. Note that this gun is marked with a Belgian NSN 1005-13-103-2524. (RSAF, Enfield)

Receiver markings on Enfield-manufactured L8A1 armor machine gun. Note that this gun is marked with a British NSN 1005-99-960-6851. (RSAF, Enfield)

Control Codes used by the US military. These are as follows:

A    Items that are acceptable for the mission intended, or that can be acceptable during initial production and that will be provided full logistic support until a replacement item is approved or until the requirement for it is phased out.

B    These are secondary standard items in the inventory that may be issued as dictated by a particular mission, but additional manufacture of these items will not be authorized if Standard A items of a like type can be produced in time to satisfy the mission requirement.

F    Items identified by Headquarters, Department of the Army as Mission Essential Contingency Items (MECI) for reserve components only.

O    Obsolete items no longer required or supported for Army operational use.

S    Items no longer acceptable for Army operational use, but that have a residual value for training. Items assigned LCC-S will be supported only from repair parts on hand or by cannibalization.

T    Items produced in limited numbers for final phase of operational testing prior to introduction into the Army's operational inventory.

U    Items not qualified for LCC-A that are procured in limited quantities to satisfy urgent operational requirements.

## The Checklist Format

Some introductory remarks about the checklist format are in order. The format used is as follows:

## COUNTRY NAME

Population (estimate in 1984): __ million. Ground forces: regulars, _____; paramilitary, _____; reserves, _____.

The data for population and size of the ground forces provide a basis for understanding the quantities of small caliber weapons that are required for each country. This is especially helpful because in most instances countries carefully guard the information about the numbers of weapons they have in their inventories.

**HANDGUNS:**
• *Cal.:* Caliber.
  *Official Name:* Name assigned by the country in question (when available).
  *Common Name:* Name generally used in local country and/or worldwide. This is especially useful in identifying imported and/or licensed weapons.

*Remarks:* Data on the current service status; origin or source; FOM or NSN (when available); and other pertinent information.

**SUBMACHINE GUNS:**

**RIFLES:**

**SHOTGUNS:**

**MACHINE GUNS:**

**AUTOMATIC CANNON:**

**GRENADE LAUNCHERS:**

# Abbreviations

| | |
|---|---|
| AA | Antiaircraft. |
| AUG | *Armeeuniversalgewehr* or *Stg 77.* The current Austrian army rifle made by Steyr-Daimler-Puch. |
| AFV | Armored Fighting Vehicle. Term now commonly used to designate tanks and other vehicles that have a 25mm or larger main armament. Distinguished from APC. |
| APC | Armored Personnel Carrier. Generally a vehicle lightly armed with machine guns. |
| B | As a suffix, this letter indicates a belted cartridge case. |
| BAR | Browning Automatic Rifle. |
| ca. | circa, about, or approximately. |
| CETME | Centro de Estudios Tecnios y Materiales Especiales. A division of the Industrias Militares, SA, in Spain. |
| FAL | *Fusil Automatique Légèr.* Developed by Fabrique Nationale and manufactured in several nations. |
| FALO | *Fusil Automatique Lourd.* A heavy barrel FAL. |
| FAL PARA | Paratroop version of FAL with folding stock. |
| FAMAE | Fabricaciones Militares, Santiago, Chile. |
| FAP | *Fusil Automatico Pesado* = FALO. |
| FEG | Femaru es Szerszamgepyar, NV, Budapest, Hungary. |

| | |
|---|---|
| FMS | US foreign military sales—government-to-government sales. |
| FN | Fabrique National Herstal of Herstal-Liège, Belgium. |
| FOM | Foreign Materiel. Used by US to catalog and assign identifiers to foreign ground equipment. |
| FSC | Federal Stock Class. |
| G | *Gewehr*. German for rifle. |
| GAU | Gun Automatic. Prefix used by the US Air Force in designating automatic weapons. |
| HK or HK GmbH | Heckler & Koch, GmbH, Oberndorf/Neckar, West Germany. |
| GIAT | Groupment Industriel des Armements Terrestres. The French government sales organization for their military equipment. |
| GPMG | General Purpose Machine Gun. |
| HMG | Heavy Machine Gun. |
| IAI | Israeli Aircraft Industries. |
| IMI | Israeli Military Industries. |
| LMG | Light Machine Gun. |
| LSN | Local Stock Number. Assigned by US Navy in lieu of an NSN. |
| M | Model. |
| MAB | Manufacture d'Armes de Bayonne (a private company). |
| MAC | Manufacture Nationale d'Armes de Chatellerault. A former division of GIAT. |
| MAG | *Mitrailleuse d'Appui General;* an FN GPMG. |
| MAP | Military Assistance Program |
| MAPF | Manufacture d'Armes des Pyrenees Francaises (a private company). |
| MAS | Manufacture Nationale d'Armes de St. Etienne. A division of GIAT. |
| MAT | Manufacture Nationale d'Armes de Tulle. A division of GIAT. |
| MG | *Maschinengewehr* or Machine Gun. |
| MK MOD | Mark Modification. US Navy system of designating equipment. Mark indicates the basic weapon, while Modification indicates subsequent subtypes of the basic model. |
| Mle. | *Modèle*. French for model. |
| MMG | Medium Machine Gun. |
| MP | *Maschinenpistole*. German for submachine gun or machine pistol. |
| MPi | *Maschinenpistole*. Same as above. Also used by the German Democratic Republic for assault rifles such as the Kalashnikov family. |
| NATO | North Atlantic Treaty Organization. |
| NCB | National Codification Bureau. |
| NSN | NATO or National Stock Number. |
| NTK | Nittoku Metal Industry Company, Ltd., Tokyo, Japan. |

| | |
|---|---|
| P | *Pistole* or Pistol. |
| plc | Public Limited Company. |
| PLO | Palestine Liberation Organization. |
| PRC | People's Republic of China |
| RSAF | Royal Small Arms Factory, Enfield. This UK small arms manufacturer was renamed Royal Ordnance Small Arms (ROSA) in 1984 when the British government privatized several MOD factories as Royal Ordnance Plc. RSAF will be used to designate all small arms made at the Enfield site. |
| SAW | Squad Automatic Weapon. Roughly equivalent to LMG. |
| SD | *Schalldaempfer* or silencer, as in MP5SD. |
| SDP | Steyr-Daimler-Puch |
| SIG | Schweizerische Industrie Gesellschaft/Rheinfalls, Switzerland. |
| SMG | Submachine Gun. |
| SR | Suffix for ammunition, meaning semi-rimmed case. |
| SSG | *Scharfschutzengewehr*, sharpshooter's rifle and a designation used by Steyr-Daimler-Puch of Austria for their sniper rifle. |
| StG | *Sturmgewehr*. German for assault rifle. Also *STG.*, *Stg.*, *Stgw.*, and *StGw*. |
| VADS | Vulcan Air Defense System. |
| vz. | *Vzor*. Czechoslovakian for model. |
| w/ | With. Generally used here to indicate if a weapon was issued with accessories. In German: *mit zub*. |
| w/o | Without. Generally used here to indicate whether a weapon was issued without accessories. In German: *ohne zub*. |
| wz. | *Wzor*. Polish for model. |

# Third World Arms Producers

The number of Third World arms producers continues to expand. The accompanying table shows 36 (non-communist) Third World countries involved in one or more categories of conventional weapons productions. This is almost twice the number of such producers in the early 1970s and about two and a half times the number in the 1960s. Moreover, the industries of Brazil, India, and Israel have grown to encompass the entire range of ground, air, and naval weaponry. Other Third World arms industries are also capable, to a varying extent, of satisfying a significant proportion of domestic and export customers' needs.

A primary reason for the extensive development of Third World arms industries is to provide sources of arms, munitions, and parts that are not subject to embargoes or political shifts by suppliers. The greatest accomplishment of the new producers has been at the lower end of the technological spectrum, in the production of infantry weapons, light vehicles, and munitions. As a result, many of the producers are able to fill their own needs for those arms, and make substantial export sales as well. The arms are usually simple in design and operation, making them attractive to other Third World states.

At the same time, the Third World arms industries have not achieved full independence. Israel, South Africa, and Taiwan, for example, are still heavily reliant on outside financial and technical assistance. The continued development of new arms technologies, moreover, will make it difficult for Third World producers to develop and produce systems that can compete with the most modern Western and Soviet aircraft, missiles, warships, and other high technology arms.

**Arms Production in the Third World, 1982–1987**

| Country | Ground Forces Equipment | | | | Aircraft Tactical Missiles | | | Naval Equipment | |
|---|---|---|---|---|---|---|---|---|---|
| | Small Arms[a] | Artillery[b] | Light Armor | Heavy Armor | Light Aircraft[c] | Jet Fighters | Tactical Missiles | Small Warships | Large[d] Warships |
| Brazil | I M | I M | I | I | I | P | L | I | I[e] |
| Israel | I M | I M | I | I M | I | P | I | I | |
| India | L M | I M | L | L | L | L | L | I | I[e] |
| Argentina | I M | C M | P | P | I | – | C | L | L[e] |
| South Korea | L M | C M | L | P | L | L | – | I | L |
| Taiwan | C M | I M | C | – | I | L | L | C | C |
| South Africa | I M | I M | I | – | C | – | C | L | |
| Egypt | C M | C M | I | – | L | – | C | C | |

## Arms Production in the Third World, 1982–1987 (continued)

| Country | Ground Forces Equipment | | | | Aircraft Tactical Missiles | | | Naval Equipment | |
|---|---|---|---|---|---|---|---|---|---|
| | Small Arms[a] | Artillery[b] | Light Armor | Heavy Armor | Light Aircraft[c] | Jet Fighters | Tactical Missiles | Small Warships | Large[d] Warships |
| Chile | C M | M | I | P | P | | | | |
| Indonesia | I M | M | — | — | L | — | — | L | |
| Mexico | I M | — | C | — | — | — | — | L | |
| Peru | M | M | — | — | — | — | — | L | L |
| Philippines | I M | — | — | — | L | — | — | L | |
| Singapore | I M | M | — | — | — | — | — | I | |
| Thailand | L M | — | — | — | L | — | — | I | |
| Pakistan | L M | M | — | M | L | | | | |
| Turkey | L M | M | — | — | — | — | — | L | L[e] |
| Venezuela | M | — | — | — | — | — | — | I | |
| Nigeria | L M | — | L | | | | | | |
| Malaysia | M | — | — | — | — | — | — | L | |
| Sri Lanka | — | — | — | — | — | — | — | I | |
| Hong Kong | — | — | — | — | — | — | — | I | |
| Iran | L M | | | | | | | | |
| Algeria | — | — | — | — | — | — | — | L | |
| Burma | C M | — | — | — | — | — | — | L | |
| Libya | L | | | | | | | | |
| Saudi Arabia | L M | | | | | | | | |
| Upper Volta | M | | | | | | | | |
| Cameroon | M | | | | | | | | |
| Colombia | M | | | | | | | | |
| Dominican Republic | M | | | | | | | | |
| Iraq | M | | | | | | | | |
| Morocco | M | | | | | | | | |
| Paraguay | M | | | | | | | | |
| Sudan | M | | | | | | | | |
| Syria | M | | | | | | | | |

*Source:* United States Arms Control and Disarmament Agency, *World Military Expenditures and Arms Transfers, 1987* (Washington, DC: Government Printing Office, 1988): 14–15.

*Key:*   I = Independent design/production.     C = Copy or modification.     M = Munitions for system.
              P = Coproduction/codevelopment.     L = Licensed production.     — = Not applicable.

[a] Includes mortars and antitank guns.
[b] Includes multiple rocket launchers.
[c] Includes trainers and helicopters.
[d] With displacement of more than 500 tons.
[e] Also produces submarines under license.

## AFGHANISTAN (Democratic Republic of)

Population (estimate in 1984): 15.54 million. Ground forces: regulars, between 40,000 and 90,000; reserves, ca. 150,000; gendarmerie (a component of the armed forces), ca. 30,000; paramilitary tribal forces, ca. 200,000. Since 1956 the USSR has been the primary supplier of small arms. Some Chinese small caliber weapons are also being used by Afghan government forces. Opposition forces number ca. 90,000 (with 20,000 of that number intermittently active).

**HANDGUNS:**
- *Cal.:* 7.62 x 25mm
  *Common Name:* TT33 Tokarev pistol

  *Remarks:* East Bloc origin.

- *Cal.:* 9 x 29mmR
  *Common Name:* .38 Smith & Wesson revolvers

  *Remarks:* US origin. One sale was licensed by US State Department in mid-1970s for 36 revolvers for police narcotics squad.

**SUBMACHINE GUNS:**
- *Cal.:* 7.62 x 25mm
  *Common Name:* PPSh41 submachine gun

  *Remarks:* Observed in the hands of Afghan Army troops on patrol in Kabul, the capital city.

- *Cal.:* 7.65 x 17mm
  *Common Name:* vz.61 machine pistol

  *Remarks:* Czechoslovakian origin.

- *Cal.:* 9 x 19mm
  *Common Name:* MP5A2 submachine gun

  *Remarks:* Delivered to Afghan police by Heckler & Koch (HK) GmbH as part of a West German police assistance program just prior to Soviet occupation. Quantity delivered was just a few hundred.

**RIFLES:**
- *Cal.:* 7.62 x 39mm
  *Common Name:* SKS rifle

  *Remarks:* East Bloc origin.

- *Cal.:* 7.62 x 39mm
  *Common Name:* AK47 and AKM assault rifles

  *Remarks:* East Bloc origin.

- *Cal.:* 5.45 x 39mm
  *Common Name:* AK74 assault rifle

  *Remarks:* Soviet Army origin. Used by Afghan elite troops only.

- *Cal.:* 7.62 x 54mmR
  *Common Name:* M1944 Mosin Nagant carbine

  *Remarks:* Soviet origin. Used by the militia only.

**SHOTGUNS:**

**MACHINE GUNS:**
- *Cal.:* 7.62 x 39mm
  *Common Name:* RPD LMG

  *Remarks:* East Bloc origin.

- *Cal.:* 7.62 x 39mm
  *Common Name:* RPK LMG

  *Remarks:* East Bloc origin.

- *Cal.:* 5.45 x 39mm
  *Common Name:* RPKS74 LMG

  *Remarks:* Soviet origin for elite units only.

- *Cal.:* 7.62 x 54mmR
  *Common Name:* PK GPMG

  *Remarks:* East Bloc origin.

- *Cal.:* 7.62 x 54mmR
  *Common Name:* SG43 series MGs

  *Remarks:* East Bloc origin. For vehicle and static use.

An Afghan displays two folding stock 7.62 x 39mm Kalashnikov assault rifle variants. In his right hand he holds a German MPiKMS-72; in his left he has a Soviet AKM. (Wilhelm Dietl)

Sayid Hakim of the antigovernment *Jamiat-e-Islami Afghanistan* forces captured this Soviet 5.45 x 39mm AKSU in Kabul province in 1983. (Isby)

• *Cal.:* 7.62 x 54mmR
  *Common Name:* DP/DPM series
  MGs

*Remarks:* Soviet origin.

• *Cal.:* 12.7 x 108mm
  *Common Name:* DShK38/46
  HMG

*Remarks:* Soviet, Czechoslovakian, and Chinese versions. The Czech M53 quad AA mount is commonly employed.

**AUTOMATIC CANNON:**
• *Cal.:* 14.5 x 114mm
  *Common Name:* KPV HMG

*Remarks:* Soviet and Chinese. ZPU-1, ZPU-2, and ZPU-4.

• *Cal.:* 23 x 152mmB
  *Common Name:* ZU23 automatic
  cannon

*Remarks:* East Bloc origin. Ca. 350 23mm AA guns in service. Included in this number is the self-propelled ZSU-23-4 AA system.

### Small Arms Used by Afghan Rebel Forces

Afghan rebel forces, combined into a coalition called the Afghan National Liberation Front, employ a wide variety of small caliber weapons. These include all of the Soviet-type weapons used by the Afghan army and occupying Soviet forces. Other small arms include thousands of British Enfield rifles (of many different patterns), Mauser rifles (of many national origins), and many different machine guns (including the 12.7mm DShK and 14.5mm KPV heavy automatic weapons). Rebel forces are constantly upgrading their small caliber weapons with external assistance. These forces are supported by 15 exile groups, of which 6 are active.

**An Afghan rebel sights his Chinese 7.62 x 39mm Type 56 (SKS) carbine. (Journal of Defense & Diplomacy)**

**Captured Soviet 7.62 x 54mmR SVD. Dragunov sniper rifle in the hands of Panjshri antigovernment forces.** *(Jamiat-e-Islami Afghanistan* **via Isby)**

## ALBANIA (People's Socialist Republic of)

Population (estimate in 1984): 2.91 million. Ground forces: regulars, ca. 43,000; reserves, ca. 150,000; paramilitary: internal security forces (Siguri Shtetet), 5,000; frontier guards, 7,500–8,000. The Albanian armed forces still use many small caliber weapons that date from the Second World War. Those small arms are largely of Soviet origin. In recent years, because of their ideological alignment (joined Warsaw Pact in 1955, withdrew in 1968), the Albanians have acquired substantial quantities of Chinese small arms from the People's Republic of China.

### HANDGUNS:
• *Cal.:* 7.62 x 25mm
  *Common Name:* TT33 Tokarev pistol

*Remarks:* Some older models are of Soviet origin; most recent acquisitions have been from the People's Republic of China (PRC).

### SUBMACHINE GUNS:
• *Cal.:* 7.62 x 25mm
  *Official Name:* M40
  *Common Name:* PPD40 submachine gun

• *Cal.:* 7.62 x 25mm
  *Official Name:* M41
  *Common Name:* PPSh41 submachine gun

• *Cal.:* 9 x 19mm Parabellum
  *Common Name:* MP40 submachine gun

*Remarks:* German World War II vintage submachine guns held in reserve.

### RIFLES:
• *Cal.:* 7.62 x 39mm
  *Common Name:* SKS rifle

*Remarks:* Some older models are of Soviet origin; most recent acquisitions have been from the PRC.

• *Cal.:* 7.62 x 39mm
  *Common Name:* AK47 and AKM assault rifles

*Remarks:* Some older models are of Soviet origin; most recent acquisitions have been from the PRC.

• *Cal.:* 7.62 x 39mm
  *Common Name:* Type 68 rifle

*Remarks:* From the PRC.

• *Cal.:* 7.92 x 57mm
  *Common Name:* M98K Mauser rifles

*Remarks:* German World War II vintage rifles held in reserve.

• *Cal.:* 14.5 x 114mm
  *Common Name:* PTRS antitank rifle

### SHOTGUNS:

### MACHINE GUNS:
• *Cal.:* 7.62 x 39mm
  *Common Name:* RPD LMG

*Remarks:* East Bloc origin.

• *Cal.:* 7.62 x 54mmR
  *Common Name:* SG43 series

*Remarks:* East Bloc origin. For vehicle and static use.

• *Cal.:* 7.62 x 54mmR
  *Common Name:* Type 59T armor MG

*Remarks:* PRC origin. Mounted on Type 62 tank and Type 62 light tank.

• *Cal.:* 7.92 x 57mm
  *Common Name:* MG34 GPMG

*Remarks:* German World War II vintage held in reserve.

- *Cal.:* 7.92 x 57mm
  *Common Name:* MG42 GPMG

  *Remarks:* German World War II vintage held in reserve.

- *Cal.:* 12.7 x 108mm
  *Common Name:* DShK38/46 HMG

  *Remarks:* Soviet and Chinese. PRC Type 54 HMGs mounted on PRC Type 62 tanks and Type 62 light tanks.

**AUTOMATIC CANNON:**
- *Cal.:* 14.5 x 114mm
  *Common Name:* KPV HMG

  *Remarks:* Air defense on some patrol boats. Presumed use as ground air defense also.

- *Cal.:* 25 x 218mm
  *Common Name:* 2-M-3 or 2-M-8 automatic cannon

  *Remarks:* Deck armament for large patrol craft of Soviet S01 class.

## ALGERIA (Democratic and Popular Republic of)

Population (estimate in 1984): 21.35 million. Ground forces: regulars, 110,000 *Armee Nationale Populaire* (ANP); *Gendarmerie Nationale,* 24,000; reserves, up to 100,000. There is also a *Sûreté Nationale* of unknown size. There are several thousand Cuban military troops in country (3,500 divided between Libya and Algeria). The armed forces still use many small arms left behind by the French at the time independence was won. Since the 1960s arms agreements with the Soviet Union, large quantities of Warsaw Pact small arms have been introduced into service.

**HANDGUNS:**
- *Cal.:* 7.65 x 17mm Browning
  *Common Name:* Model 1934/84 pistol

  *Remarks:* Beretta, Italy.

- *Cal.:* 9 x 17mm Browning
  *Common Name:* Beretta M34 pistol

  *Remarks:* Beretta.

- *Cal.:* 9 x 17mm Browning
  *Common Name:* Astra M300 pistol

  *Remarks:* Source unknown.

- *Cal.:* 9 x 18mm
  *Common Name:* Makarov pistol

  *Remarks:* East Bloc origin.

- *Cal.:* 9 x 19mm Parabellum
  *Common Name:* HK P9S pistol

  *Remarks:* Heckler & Koch (HK) origin.

- *Cal.:* 9 x 19mm Parabellum
  *Common Name:* P38 pistol

  *Remarks:* German origin. Source unknown.

- *Cal.:* 9 x 19mm Parabellum
  *Common Name:* MAC Mle. 50 pistol

  *Remarks:* Manufacture Nationale d'Armes de Chatellerault (MAC), France.

- *Cal.:* 9 x 19mm Parabellum
  *Common Name:* Tokagypt 58 pistol

  *Remarks:* Femaru es Szerszamgepyar, NV (FEG), Hungary.

- *Cal.:* 9 x 23
  *Common Name:* Astra M400 pistol

  *Remarks:* Source unknown.

- *Cal.:* 7.62 x 25mm
  *Common Name:* TT33 Tokarev pistol

  *Remarks:* East Bloc origin.

- *Cal.:* 7.62 x 25mm
  *Common Name:* vz.52 pistol

- *Cal.:* 9 x 29mmR
  *Common Name:* .38 Smith &
  Wesson revolver

**SUBMACHINE GUNS:**
- *Cal.:* 7.62 x 25mm
  *Common Name:* PPS43 sub-
  machine gun

- *Cal.:* 9 x 19mm Parabellum
  *Common Name:* Vigneron submachine gun

- *Cal.:* 9 x 19mm Parabellum
  *Common Name:* MAT Mle. 49
  submachine gun

- *Cal.:* 9 x 19mm Parabellum
  *Common Name:* Uzi submachine
  gun

- *Cal.:* 9 x 19mm Parabellum
  *Common Name:* Beretta M1938/
  49 Model 4 submachine gun

- *Cal.:* 9 x 19mm Parabellum
  *Common Name:* Carl Gustav M45
  submachine gun

**RIFLES:**
- *Cal.:* 6.5 x 50.5mmSR
  *Common Name:* M1891 and
  M1891/38 Mannlicher Carcano
  rifles

- *Cal.:* 7.62 x 33mm
  *Common Name:* .30 M2 Carbine

- *Cal.:* 7.62 x 39mm
  *Common Name:* SKS rifle

- *Cal.:* 7.62 x 39mm
  *Common Name:* AK47 and AKM
  assault rifles

- *Cal.:* 7.5 x 54mm
  *Common Name:* MAS Mle. 36
  bolt action rifle

- *Cal.:* 7.5 x 54mm
  *Common Name:* MAS Mle. 49/56
  rifle

- *Cal.:* 7.62 x 51mm NATO
  *Common Name:* BM59 assault
  rifle

- *Cal.:* 7.92 x 33mm
  *Common Name:* Sturmgewehr 44

- *Cal.:* 7.92 x 57mm
  *Common Name:* Mauser 98 bolt
  action rifle

*Remarks:* Czechoslovakian origin.

*Remarks:* US origin. State Department licensed sales for 1,020 revolvers, 1976–77.

*Remarks:* East Bloc origin. Observed being carried by Women's Unit of ANP.

*Remarks:* Société Anonyme Précision Liègeoise, Herstal, Belgium.

*Remarks:* French origin. Manufacture Nationale d'Armes de Tulle (MAT).

*Remarks:* Either Israeli Military Industries (IMI) or FN.

*Remarks:* Beretta.

*Remarks:* Source unknown.

*Remarks:* Italy. OBSOLETE.

*Remarks:* US manufacture acquired through FN.

*Remarks:* East Bloc origin.

*Remarks:* East Bloc origin.

*Remarks:* French origin. Manufacture Nationale d'Armes de St. Etienne (MAS).

*Remarks:* French origin. MAS.

*Remarks:* Beretta manufacture acquired through FN.

*Remarks:* World War II German manufacture. Delivery source unknown. OBSOLETE.

*Remarks:* Source unknown.

**SHOTGUNS:**

**MACHINE GUNS:**
- *Cal.:* 7.5 x 54mm
  *Common Name:* MAC Mle. 1924/29 light machine gun

  *Remarks:* Manufacture Nationale d'Armes de Chatellerault (MAC). France.

- *Cal.:* 7.5 x 54mm
  *Common Name:* AAT 52 GPMG, light machine gun

  *Remarks:* MAC. Mounted on Panhard M3 armored cars.

- *Cal.:* 7.62 x 39mm
  *Common Name:* RPD LMG

  *Remarks:* East Bloc origin.

- *Cal.:* 7.62 x 39mm
  *Common Name:* RPK LMG

  *Remarks:* Reports unconfirmed.

- *Cal.:* 7.62 x 39mm
  *Common Name:* vz.52 LMG

  *Remarks:* Czechoslovakian origin.

- *Cal.:* 7.62 x 54mmR
  *Common Name:* RP46 company machine gun

  *Remarks:* East Bloc origin.

- *Cal.:* 7.62 x 54mmR
  *Common Name:* PKT AMG and PKM GPMG

  *Remarks:* East Bloc origin. On BMP-1 and T62 and T72 armored vehicles.

**Two Algerian soldiers, ca. 1967, clean their 12.7 x 108mm Soviet DShK38/46 heavy machine gun. (East Germany)**

- *Cal.:* 7.62 x 54mmR
  *Common Name:* SGMB and SGMT machine guns

  *Remarks:* East Bloc origin. On BTR-40, BTR-152, and T54 BTR-152, and T54 armored vehicles.

- *Cal.:* 7.62 x 54mmR
  *Common Name:* DP light machine gun

  *Remarks:* East Bloc origin. Presumed OBSOLETE.

- *Cal.:* Unknown
  *Common Name:* MG42/MG3

  *Remarks:* Seen in news photos as recently as 1980; caliber and source unknown. Possibly from Spain.

- *Cal.:* 7.62 x 63mm
  *Common Name:* .30 M1918A2 BAR

  *Remarks:* US origin.

- *Cal.:* 7.62 x 63mm
  *Common Name:* .30 M1919A4 LMG

  *Remarks:* US origin.

- *Cal.:* 7.7 x 56mmR
  *Common Name:* .303 Bren (model unknown)

  *Remarks:* UK origin.

- *Cal.:* 7.92 x 57mm
  *Common Name:* MG34 LMG

  *Remarks:* Source unknown.

- *Cal.:* 12.7 x 99mm
  *Common Name:* .50 M2 HB Browning HMG

  *Remarks:* FN origin. Mounted on Panhard M3 armored car.

- *Cal.:* 12.7 x 108mm
  *Common Name:* DShK38/46 HMG (DShKM)

  *Remarks:* East Bloc origin. Perhaps some DShK38s are still in service.

- *Cal.:* 12.7 x 108mm
  *Common Name:* NSVT HMG

  *Remarks:* Unconfirmed; may be mounted on T72s.

**AUTOMATIC CANNON:**
- *Cal.:* 14.5 x 114mm
  *Common Name:* KPV HMG

  *Remarks:* East Bloc origin. Also used on twin deck AA mounts on patrol boats.

- *Cal.:* 20 x ?mm
  *Common Name:* Model unknown

  *Remarks:* Air defense guns on landing craft acquired in 1983.

- *Cal.:* 23 x 152mmB
  *Common Name:* ZU23 automatic cannon

  *Remarks:* East Bloc origin. Ca. 100 ZSU-23-4 air defense systems in service.

- *Cal.:* 25 x 219mm
  *Common Name:* 2-M-3 or 2-M-8 automatic cannon

  *Remarks:* Deck armament for larger patrol craft and minesweepers of Soviet origin.

## ANGOLA (People's Republic of)

Population (estimate in 1984): 7.77 million. Ground forces: regulars, FAPLA (formerly the MPLA), ca. 80,000; reserves, *Organização de Defesa Popular* (militia), variously estimated between 110,000 and 150,000. There are about 10,000 men in the paramilitary *Policia da Ordem Publicá*. The small arms used by Angola are a mixture. Government forces (evolved from the *Movimento Popular de Libertação de Angola*—MPLA) may still use many Portuguese weapons remaining from the colonial period (e.g., 7.62 x 51mm NATO G3s). Many of these have been replaced by small arms acquired from Soviet and East Bloc sources, with many having been left by Cuban forces previously stationed in Angola. In 1975 in one documented transfer the Soviets supplied 10,000 AK47s, 10,000 AKMs, 10,000 SKSs, 2,000 Tokarev pistols, and 290 belt-fed machine guns of an unidentified type. There are still some 35,000 to 40,000 Cuban soldiers and 5,000 to 10,000 advisers in Angola. There are an additional 3,000 East German technicians and 1,500 Soviet soldiers. There are also between 5,000 and 7,000 SWAPO and 600 ANC troops. FNLA or UNITA after a weapon designation indicates that it is also being used by the rebel *Frente Nacional de Libertação de Angola* or *Uniâo Nacional para a Independência Total de Angola.* UNITA forces also use the South African 5.56mm R4 rifle and R5 carbine, the 9mm L2A3 SMG, the 11.43mm M1928A1 SMG, and the US 40 x 46mmSR M79 grenade launcher.

**HANDGUNS:**

• *Cal.:* 7.65 x 17mm Browning
  *Common Name:* vz.61 machine pistol

*Remarks:* Czechoslovakian origin. (Skorpion)

• *Cal.:* 7.62 x 25mm
  *Common Name:* TT33 Tokarev pistol

*Remarks:* Soviet and East Bloc origin. FNLA.

• *Cal.:* 7.62 x 25mm
  *Common Name:* vz.52 pistol

*Remarks:* Czechoslovakian origin.

• *Cal.:* 7.62 x 25mm
  *Common Name:* Type 67 pistol

*Remarks:* Chinese origin.

• *Cal.:* 9 x 18mm
  *Common Name:* Makarov pistol

*Remarks:* Soviet origin.

• *Cal.:* 9 x 18mm
  *Common Name:* Stechkin machine pistol (APS)

*Remarks:* Soviet origin.

• *Cal.:* 9 x 19mm Parabellum
  *Common Name:* FN Mle. 35 GP pistol

*Remarks:* FN origin. FNLA.

**SUBMACHINE GUNS:**

• *Cal.:* 7.62 x 25mm
  *Common Name:* PPSh41 submachine gun

*Remarks:* Soviet origin.

• *Cal.:* 9 x 19mm Parabellum
  *Common Name:* Uzi submachine gun

*Remarks:* Source unknown; FN?

• *Cal.:* 9 x 19mm Parabellum
  *Common Name:* Star Z45 SMG

*Remarks:* Star-Bonafacio Echeverria y Cia., Spain.

• *Cal.:* 9 x 19mm Parabellum
  *Common Name:* FMBP M948 SMG

*Remarks:* Portuguese origin. Fabrica Militar de Braco de Prata (FMBP); UNITA.

**RIFLES:**

• *Cal.:* 7.62 x 39mm
  *Common Name:* SKS rifle

*Remarks:* Soviet and East Bloc origin.

• *Cal.:* 7.62 x 39mm
  *Common Name:* AK47 and AKM assault rifles

*Remarks:* East Bloc origin. PRC Type 56 and Type 56-1 (AK47 and AKM) are being used by government forces; Hungarian AMD and AMD65 (short AMD) are being used by FNLA. UNITA forces used Bulgarian AKMs, PRC Type 56, East German MPiKMS, and Hungarian AMDs. Romanian AKMs have been observed in news photos illustrating Angolan and UNITA troops.

• *Cal.:* 7.62 x 51mm NATO
  *Common Name:* FAL

*Remarks:* FN FAL ex-Portuguese army. Government, FNLA, and UNITA troops use FAL.

- *Cal.:* 7.62 x 51mm NATO
  *Common Name: Gewehr 3*

- *Cal.:* 7.62 x 54mmR
  *Common Name:* M44 Mosin Nagant bolt action carbines

- *Cal.:* 7.92 x 57mm?
      7.62 x 51mm NATO?
  *Common Name:* M98K bolt
  action rifles

**SHOTGUNS:**

**MACHINE GUNS:**
- *Cal.:* 7.62 x 39mm
  *Common Name:* RPD LMG

- *Cal.:* 7.62 x 39mm
  *Common Name:* RPK LMG

- *Cal.:* 7.62 x 39mm
  *Common Name:* vz.52/57 LMG

- *Cal.:* 7.62 x 51mm
  *Common Name:* MG42/MG3 and
  M53 (Yugo) GPMG

- *Cal.:* 7.62 x 51mm NATO
  *Common Name:* HK21 and HK21
  A1 LMGs

- *Cal.:* 7.62 x 54mmR
  *Common Name:* RP46 company
  machine gun

- *Cal.:* 7.62 x 54mmR
  *Common Name:* PRC Type 67
  GPMG

- *Cal.:* 7.62 x 54mmR
  *Common Name:* SGMT armor
  MG

- *Cal.:* 7.62 x 54mmR
  *Common Name:* PKT armor MG

- *Cal.:* 7.62 x 54mmR
  *Common Name:* DT armor MG

- *Cal.:* 7.7 x 56mmR
  *Common Name:* Bren LMG

- *Cal.:* 7.92 x 57mm
  *Common Name:* MG 13

- *Cal.:* 12.7 x 108mm
  *Common Name:* DShK38/46
  HMG

**AUTOMATIC CANNON:**
- *Cal.:* 14.5 x 114mm
  *Common Name:* KPV HMG

*Remarks:* FMBP. Government and FNLA forces. Some Angolan G3s have found their way to the Caribbean (notably Colombia) via Cuba where they have turned up in the hands of drug traffickers.

*Remarks:* Source unknown. Have been observed (1987) in the hands of UNITA forces.

*Remarks:* Source unknown. Have been observed (1987) in the hands of UNITA forces.

*Remarks:* East Bloc origin.

*Remarks:* East Bloc origin.

*Remarks:* Czechoslovakian origin.

*Remarks:* German and Yugoslavian origin. There may still be 7.92 x 57mm MG42s in service.

*Remarks:* FMBP. Only a few hundred acquired.

*Remarks:* East Bloc origin. UNITA.

*Remarks:* Chinese origin.

*Remarks:* Soviet origin. Mounted on Soviet tanks. Flexible SGMBs seen on armored vehicles such as BTR-152.

*Remarks:* Soviet origin. Mounted on T62 tanks. UNITA has ground versions of PK GPMG.

*Remarks:* Soviet origin. Mounted on T34 tanks. Some DPs may still see service.

*Remarks:* UK origin.

*Remarks:* German origin via Portugal?

*Remarks:* East Bloc origin. Many are mounted on T55 and a variety of other Soviet tanks. Older model DShK38s may also still be in service. Some have been captured by UNITA forces.

*Remarks:* East Bloc origin. ZGU-1 and ZPU-4. Also used on armored personnel carriers and coastal patrol craft.

- *Cal.:* 20 x 110mm
  *Common Name:* M55 automatic
  cannon

*Remarks:* Yugoslavian version of HS804 cannon. Also used on coastal patrol craft.

- *Cal.:* 23 x 152mmB
  *Common Name:* ZU23 automatic
  cannon

*Remarks:* Soviet origin. ZSU-23-2 and ZSU-23-4 air defense systems in service. Some ZSU-23-2 AA systems have been captured by South African forces.

**GRENADE LAUNCHERS:**
- *Cal.:* 30 x 29mm
  *Common Name:* AGS-17 automatic grenade launcher

*Remarks:* Soviet origin. Some have been captured and are being used by South African forces.

### Tribal Breakdown of Contending Groups

There is a tribal complexion to the makeup of the various contending groups in Angola. They are all of Bantu origin. The following is the tribal breakdown: MPLA (established in 1956), mostly Kimbundu; UNITA (established in 1966), mostly Ovimbundu; FNLA (established in 1954), mostly Bakongo.

## ARGENTINA (Republic of)

Population (estimate in 1984): 30.09 million. Ground forces: regulars, 125,000 to 130,000 (with 90,000 conscripts); reserves, 250,000; *Gendarmeria Nacional,* estimated between 12,000 to 16,000; National Guard, 250,000; territorial guards, 50,000; *Infanteria de Marina* (Marines), 6,000; and *Policia Federal,* 22,000.

**HANDGUNS:**
- *Cal.:* 7.65 x 28mm
  *Official Name: Pistola Modelo 1905*
  *Common Name:* M1905 Mannlicher pistol

*Remarks:* OBSOLETE.

- *Cal.:* 9 x 19mm NATO
  *Official Name: Pistola Browning PD*
  *Common Name:* FN Mle. 1935 GP pistol

*Remarks:* Fabrica Militar de Armas Portatiles "Domingo Matheu" (FMAP "DM") at Rosario of Dirección General de Fabricaciones Militares. Handgun production includes several variants of standard model. 184,533 manufactured, 1969–81.

- *Cal.:* 11.43 x 23mm
  *Official Name: Pistola Colt*
  *Common Name:* .45 M1911A1 pistol

*Remarks:* US origin. Colt Firearms.

- *Cal.:* 11.25 x 23mm
  *Official Name: Pistola Sistema Colt Modelo 1927*
  *Common Name:* Variant of US M1911A1 pistol

*Remarks:* FMAP "DM." Secondary standard. Between 1947 and 1966 nearly 74,866 manufactured. Manufacture licensed by Colt Firearms. This weapon will be replaced by *Pistola Browning PD.*

- *Cal.:* 11.25 x 23mm
  *Official Name:* "Ballester-Molina"; "Ballester-Riguad"
  *Common Name:* Variant of US M1911A1 pistol

*Remarks:* OBSOLETE. Made by Hispano Argentina Fabrica de Automoviles, S.A. (HAFDASA). Exported to UK during World War II.

An Argentine-manufactured copy of the 9 x 19mm FN Mle. 1935 GP pistol. This handgun is marked "FABRICA MILITAR DE ARMAS PORTATILES 'D.M.' ROSARIO–D.G.F.M.–LICENCIA F N BROWNING–INDUSTRIA ARGENTINA." (Osacar)

This Argentine marine in Port Stanley at the beginning of the South Atlantic War carries a British 9 x 19mm L34A1 silenced submachine gun. (Osacar)

**Argentine marines disarm British Royal Marines. The Argentine with his hand raised is equipped with a 9 x 19mm British L2A3 submachine gun. (Osacar)**

## SUBMACHINE GUNS:
- *Cal.:* 9 x 19mm NATO
  *Official Name: Pistola Ametralla-
  dora FMK3 and FMK 4.* (FMK
  3 formerly called PA3-DM)
  *Common Name:* Domestic design

  *Remarks:* FMAP "DM." Standard submachine gun (SMG). 39,482 manufactured, 1971–81.

- *Cal.:* 9 x 19mm NATO
  *Official Name: Pistola Ametralla-
  dora PAM 1 and PAM 2*
  *Common Name:* Derivative of US
  M3 series SMG

  *Remarks:* FMAP "DM." Nearly 37,392 made, 1955–72.

- *Cal.:* 11.25 x 23mm
  *Official Name: Pistola Ametralla-
  dora Halcon, Modelo 1943 Gendarmeria Nacional; Modelo
  1946 Aeronautica; Modelo 1949
  Ejercito Argentina*
  *Common Name:* Domestic design

  *Remarks:* Fabrica de Armas Halcon, S.A.T.Y.C. Later called Metalurgica
  Centro S.C.A. Ca. 6,000 made.

- *Cal.:* x 9 x 19mm NATO
  *Official Name: Halcon Modelo
  Livano 57, 60, 62, 63*
  *Common Name:* Domestic design

  *Remarks:* F.A. Halcon. Ca. 12,000 Halcon guns were made.

- *Cal.:* 9 x 19mm NATO
  *Official Name: HAFDASA C-4*
  *Common Name:* Copy of British
  Sten with MP40-type stock

*Remarks:* HAFDASA.

- *Cal.:* 9 x 19mm NATO
  *Official Name: MEMS Pistolas
  Ametralladoras*
  *Common Name:* Domestic design
  in several variants

*Remarks:* Armas & Equipos, S.R.L., of Ciudad de Cordoba. Made in limited numbers.

- *Cal.:* 9 x 19mm NATO
  *Common Name:* Sterling Mark 4
  submachine gun

*Remarks:* Source unknown. Purchased directly from Sterling in the UK. Used by Argentine Marines during South Atlantic War in 1982.

- *Cal.:* 9 x 19mm NATO
  *Common Name:* Sterling Mark 5
  silenced submachine gun

*Remarks:* Same source. Used by Marines as above.

- *Cal.:* 9 x 19mm NATO
  *Common Name:* H&K MP5 submachine gun

*Remarks:* Heckler & Koch (HK), GmbH, West Germany. The Argentine Coast Guard *(Prefectura Naval)* is purchasing MP5A2 and MP5A3 SMGs; *Gendarmeria Nacional* is acquiring MP5A2, MP5A3, and MP5SD.

**RIFLES:**
- *Cal.:* 5.56 x 45mm
  *Common Name:* Steyr AUG rifle

*Remarks:* Steyr-Daimler-Puch (SDP) of Austria. Only 356 of these have been issued to the Army.

- *Cal.:* 5.56 x 45mm
  *Official Name: Fusil Automatico
  del Republica de Argentina*
  *Common Name:* FARA 83

*Remarks:* Domestic design developed by the FMAP "DM." A small number of these rifles were manufactured for field trials; serial production has been delayed until sufficient money is available in the military budget. This rifle has a 1 turn in 229mm (1 in 9 inch) barrel, allowing use of M193 or SS109 ammunition.

- *Cal.:* 7.62 x 51mm NATO
  *Official Name: Fusil Automatico
  Livano (FAL)*
  *Common Name:* FN FAL

*Remarks:* FN and FMAP "DM." Models produced in Argentina include: FAL II = FN 50-00; FAL PARA = FN 50-61; FAL PARA = FN 50-63. About 129,674 manufactured, 1960–81.

**A 1980 vintage 7.62 x 51mm FN FAL as manufactured in Argentina. This rifle is marked with the FN trademark and "FABRICA MILITAR DE ARMAS PORTATILES–ROSARIO INDUSTRIA ARGENTINA." (Osacar)**

**An Argentine infantryman holding his Rosario-made FAL. This photograph was taken during the 1982 South Atlantic War. (Osacar)**

- *Cal.:* 7.62 x 51mm NATO
  *Common Name:* Steyr *Scharf-schutzengewehr* (SSG) sniper rifle

*Remarks:* SDP. The Army has 35 SSGs; 15 are SSG 69s. Most of these rifles are used by Army shooting team. Some were taken to Falklands/Malvinas where a few were captured by British forces during the 1982 war.

- *Cal.:* 7.62 x 51mm NATO
  *Common Name:* BM59 rifle

*Remarks:* Beretta, Italy. Small numbers of BM59s were captured by the British in the 1982 war. News photos showed BM59s being used by Argentine troops during that war.

- *Cal.:* 7.62 x 63mm
  *Common Name:* .30 M1 rifle

*Remarks:* US origin. During the 1950s the US .30 M1 rifle was the standard Navy rifle. When the BM59 was adopted the M1s were converted to use BM59 20-shot magazine. Some M1 rifles are still in the hands of reserve units.

- *Cal.:* 7.62 x 63mm
  *Common Name:* .30 SAFN

*Remarks:* FN origin. Replaced the US M1 rifles; subsequently replaced by FAL. SAFNs were later converted to take FAL 20-shot magazines. Some of these rifles are still in the hands of reserve units.

An Argentine NCO from the 601st
Company during the 9th of July 1987
parade. He is carrying one of the first
Argentine 5.56mm F.A.R.A. 83 assault
rifles made by the small arms factory at
Rosario. (Osacar)

• *Cal.:* 7.65 x 54mm
  *Official Name: Carabina Mauser
  Caballeria Modelo 1909*
  *Common Name:* 7.65mm Mauser
  M1909 carbine

*Remarks:* Made at the FMAP "DM" until 1959. OBSOLETE; some limited
issue. 20,221 M1909 carbines were made, 1942–59. There are also 40,000+
DWM pre–World War I rifles in Army inventory.

**SHOTGUNS:**
• *Cal.:* 18.5 x 59mm
  *Common Name:* 12 gage Moss-
  berg Model 500 shotgun

*Remarks:* US origin. Acquired by Argentine naval units in 1976.

**MACHINE GUNS:**
• *Cal.:* 7.62 x 51mm NATO
  *Official Name: Ametralladora
  MAG*
  *Common Name:* FN MAG

*Remarks:* FN and FMAP "DM." Models in service include MAG *infanterie
Standard* (Model 60-20), T5 (using nondisintegrating link), which is used by
the Army; T12; which is used by the Air Force and Navy and on the Army
Puma helicopter (uses M13 links); and T14, which is used by the Air Force.
MAG *Aviation* (60-30) on the Pucara aircraft; T2 P.800; and the Pod
Marchetti P.904. The MAG *Coaxial* (60-40), T1 is used on several vehicles.
Manufacture at Rosario began in 1980 with 80 guns being assembled that
year.

• *Cal.:* 7.62 x 51mm NATO
*Official Name: Fusil Automatico Pesado (FAP)*
*Common Name:* FN FALO

*Remarks:* FN and FMAP "DM." FN model 50-42. 8,463 of these automatic rifles were manufactured, 1965–81.

• *Cal.:* 7.62 x 51mm NATO
*Common Name:* AAT-52 GPMG

*Remarks:* Groupment Industriel des Armaments Terrestres (GIAT), France. There are 58 Z341 G flexible models and 62 Z341 coaxial models used on army Panchard APCs. A few of these machine guns were captured by British during the 1982 war.

• *Cal.:* 7.62 x 51mm NATO
*Common Name:* MG74 coaxial MG; Austrian MG3

*Remarks:* SDP origin. These guns are mounted on the Army's Kurassier self-propelled antitank guns.

• *Cal.:* 7.62 x 51mm NATO
*Official Name: Ametralladora Browning M3*
*Common Name:* .30 US M3 Browning aircraft gun converted to 7.62mm NATO

*Remarks:* US origin. OBSOLETE.

• *Cal.:* 7.65 x 54mm
*Official Name: Ametralladora Colt Pesada*
*Common Name:* Colt-Browning water-cooled HMG; similar to US 1917 machine gun

*Remarks:* Colt, US. OBSOLETE.

• *Cal.:* 12.7 x 99mm
*Official Name: Ametralladora .50 Browning*
*Common Name:* .50 M2 HB HMG

*Remarks:* US origin.

**AUTOMATIC CANNON:**
• *Cal.:* 20 x 110mm
*Common Name:* KAB-001 (Type 10LA 5TG) automatic cannon on GAI-B01 mount

*Remarks:* Oerlikon-Bührle, Switzerland. MK 7 20mm Oerlikon is also used on ex-British Type 42 destroyers. There are 217 issued to Army units for air defense.

• *Cal.:* 20 x 139mm
*Official Name: Canon Antiaereo 20mm*
*Common Name:* Rheinmetall Rh202

*Remarks:* West German origin. Used by both Army and Navy in twin AA mount. There are also 95 Rh 202 automatic cannon issued with the TAM APC.

**GRENADE LAUNCHERS:**
• *Cal.:* 40 x 46mmSR
*Common Name:* 40mm grenade launcher

*Remarks:* Developed by FMAP "DM."

• *Cal.:* 40 x 46mmSR
*Common Name:* HK69 grenade launcher

*Remarks:* HK GmbH. Argentine *Gendarmeria Nacional* is acquiring initial small quantity of these grenade launchers (ca. 20).

### Other Military Small Arms in Inventory

As with many nations, the Argentine armed forces appear to have made limited purchases of a variety of military small arms. Between 1950 and 1964 the Argentine armed forces acquired 12,621 US 7.62 x 33mm carbines (M1 and M2) and 29,960 rifles (presumably M1 Garands) as military aid from the United States. Other arms in the Argentine inventory include the 9 x 19mm selective fire Star automatic pistol, the

9 x 19mm Uzi submachine gun, the 11.43 x 23mm US M1928A1 and M1A1 submachine guns, the 5.56 x 45mm US M16A1, the Ruger Mini 14, and the Steyr AUG selective fire rifles.

### Small Arms to Central America

Between 1976 and 1984 Argentina became a major supplier of small arms to Central America, especially to El Salvador and Honduras. Many of these weapons were rumored to be destined for *contra* forces fighting the Sandinista government of Nicaragua. The flow of such material ceased after the South Atlantic War of 1982.

## AUSTRALIA (Commonwealth of)

Population (estimate in 1980): 15.46 million. Ground forces: regulars, 32,680; reserves, 30,300; paramilitary, Australian Federal Police, 2,800; State Police Forces, ca. 30,000.

### HANDGUNS:
• *Cal.:* 9 x 19mm NATO
*Official Name:* 9mm Browning L9A1
*Common Name:* FN Mle. 35 GP pistol

*Remarks:* John Inglis of Canada and FN. First GPs were purchased from FN in 1963. The FN pistol w/o tangent sight is NSN 1005-13-010-0795. Also NSN 1005-13-010-0313.

### SUBMACHINE GUNS:
• *Cal.:* 9 x 19mm NATO
*Official Name:* 9mm F1 submachine gun
*Common Name:* Domestic design

*Remarks:* Commonwealth Small Arms Factory, Lithgow. NSN 1005-66-017-3759 w/ equipment; NSN 1005-66-017-2137 w/o equipment. FOM 1005-41-3-9-1. Serial numbers are 7 digits: the first 2 signify year of manufacture; the remaining 5 are weapon serial numbers in that year, starting with 0001. The F1 uses the standard L1A1 rifle bayonet and a magazine that is interoperable with the UK Sterling submachine gun series.

• *Cal.:* 9 x 19mm NATO
*Common Name:* MP5 and MP5SD

*Remarks:* Royal Small Arms Factory (RSAF), Enfield origin.

• *Cal.:* 9 x 19mm NATO
*Common Name:* L34A1 submachine gun

*Remarks:* Sterling Arms Company, UK. This silenced version is used by special operations forces. NSN 1005-99-961-4083.

### RIFLES:
• *Cal.:* 5.56 x 45mm NATO
*Official Name:* 5.56mm F8 rifle
*Common Name:* Steyr AUG

*Remarks:* Late in 1985 the Australian Ministry of Defense announced adoption of the AUG as the new Australian service rifle. Initially, the armed forces will acquire 67,000 AUGs from Lithgow Small Arms Factory. The New Zealanders will purchase 18,000 from Lithgow. Fielding will begin in 1988 and continue through 1996. New Zealand will get rifles simultaneously with the Australians. Production could reach 280,000 AUGs. Australians have export sales rights for the South Pacific region. Models to be employed include: F88 standard rifle w/ 508mm barrel; F88C carbine w/ 407mm barrel; F88S having modified receiver for night vision and other sights; and F88/M203, w/ 621mm barrel and M203 grenade launcher.

• *Cal.:* 7.62 x 51mm NATO
*Official Name:* 7.62mm L1A1 rifle
*Common Name:* FN FAL rifle

*Remarks:* Lithgow. The basis models of this rifle are NSN 1005-66-100-2001 and 1005-66-100-2002. Serial numbers are 7 digits: the first two signify the year of manufacture; the remaining 5 are weapon serial numbers starting with 0001. Will be replaced by AUG.

- *Cal.:* 7.62 x 51mm NATO
  *Official Name:* 7.62mm M82 sniper rifle
  *Common Name:* M82 sniper rifle

  *Remarks:* Parker Hale, UK. NSN 1005-66-097-7479.

- *Cal.:* 7.62 x 51mm NATO
  *Official Name:* 7.62mm M44 sniper rifle
  *Common Name:* Omark M44 sniper rifle

- *Cal.:* 5.56 x 45mm
  *Official Name:* 5.56mm M16 rifle
  *Common Name:* M16A1 rifle

  *Remarks:* Colt, US. Ca. 2,400 M16A1s, with most acquired before 1970. Majority of these rifles are Model 613; a few are 614s (M16) and 653s (M16 Carbines). NSN 1005-00-073-9421.

## SHOTGUNS:

## MACHINE GUNS:

- *Cal.:* 5.56 x 45mm
  *Common Name:* FN Minimi

  *Remarks:* Australia will purchase about 3,420 Minimis to be manufactured at Lithgow. Minimis to be procured over next 20 years will probably total 15,000.

- *Cal.:* 7.62 x 51mm NATO
  *Official Name:* 7.62mm L2A1 automatic rifle
  *Common Name:* FN FALO

  *Remarks:* Lithgow. OBSOLETE. Will be replaced by the Minimi. NSN 1005-66-013-9803.

- *Cal.:* 7.62 x 51mm NATO
  *Official Name:* 7.62mm L4A4 machine gun
  *Common Name:* 7.62mm Bren gun

  *Remarks:* RSAF, Enfield, UK. Will be replaced by the Minimi. NSN 1005-99-961-8595.

- *Cal.:* 7.62 x 51mm NATO
  *Official Name:* 7.62mm M60 GPMG
  *Common Name:* US M60 GPMG

  *Remarks:* Saco-Maremont, US. NSN 1005-00-605-7710.

- *Cal.:* 7.62 x 51mm NATO
  *Official Name:* 7.62mm M60D ACMG
  *Common Name:* US M60D ACMG

  *Remarks:* FMS and Saco-Maremont, US.

- *Cal.:* 7.62 x 51mm NATO
  *Official Name:* 7.62mm L7A2 sustained fire machine gun
  *Common Name:* FN MAG GPMG

  *Remarks:* RSAF. Prior to 1980, the Australians had the Belgian-made MAG *Infanterie Standard* (60-20), T1 in service. Quantities unknown. Ca. 1985 it was decided to acquire from FN 676 MAGs at a price of A$4.15 million. Will replace half of M60 GPMGs; remainder of M60s will be replaced by 5.56mm Minimis. NSN 1005-13-103-2524.

- *Cal.:* 7.62 x 51mm NATO
  *Common Name:* MG3 AMG

  *Remarks:* German MG3s mounted on the Australian Leopard tanks. AA model is NSN 1005-66-101-0352; coaxial model is NSN 1005-66-101-0353.

- *Cal.:* 7.62 x 63mm
  *Official Name:* .30 L3 series
  *Common Name:* US .30 M1919A4 LMG

  *Remarks:* OBSOLETE. In excess of 2,300 were obtained from FMS between 1964 and 1974. L3A3 fixed model is NSN 1005-99-960-5555; L3A4 flexible model is NSN 1005-99-960-5554.

- *Cal.:* 7.7 x 56mmR
  *Common Name:* .303 Vickers MMG

  *Remarks:* Some World War II vintage tripod-mounted Vickers machine guns are still used for overhead fire during indoctrination training of recruits.

• *Cal.:* 12.7 x 99mm
  *Official Name:* .50 M2 HB ma-
  chine gun, Browning
  *Common Name:* US M2 HB
  Browning HMG

*Remarks:* US origin. FMS sales 1964–74 amounted to 685 guns. Some recent purchases (ca. 200) were from Ramo, Inc., US. M2-F1 T50 turret type is NSN 1005-66-036-0435; M2HB flexible is NSN 1005-00-726-5636.

**AUTOMATIC CANNON:**

**GRENADE LAUNCHERS:**
• *Cal.:* 40 x 46mmSR
  *Common Name:* M79 grenade
  launcher

*Remarks:* US origin.

• *Cal.:* 40 x 46mmSR
  *Common Name:* M203 grenade
  launcher attached to M16A1
  rifle.

*Remarks:* US origin. Ca. 100 acquired from Colt in 1981.

# AUSTRIA (Republic of)

Population (estimate in 1984): 7.58 million. Ground forces: regulars, 46,000 (32,500 conscripts); reserves, 158,000 (a total of 900,000 have a reserve commitment); gendarmerie, ca. 12,000.

**HANDGUNS:**
• *Cal.:* 7.65 x 17mm Browning
  *Common Name:* Walther PP

*Remarks:* Manurhin-manufactured Walther pistols. Austrian police have ca. 12,000 7.65mm PPs, which will be replaced by the Glock P80. An additional 2,000 PPKs will be retained for use by policewomen. Customs police also use the PPK.

• *Cal.:* 9 x 19mm NATO
  *Official Name:* Pistole 80
  *Common Name:* Glock pistol

*Remarks:* Glock Ges.m.b.H., Deutsch-Wagram, Austria. Standard for armed forces, federal police, and some special police organizations.

• *Cal.:* 9 x 19mm NATO
  *Official Name:* Pistole 38
  *Common Name:* P38

*Remarks:* German World War II and postwar Walther, Ulm origin. Being replaced by Glock P 80. Starting 1986 the Ministry of Defense *(Bundesminis-terium fur Landesverteidgung)* began to dispose of these P38s at rate of 2,500 per year for next 3 years. NSN 1005-Ö-300-0104.

• *Cal.:* 9 x 19mm NATO
  *Common Name:* FN Mle. 35 GP
  pistol

*Remarks:* FN. OBSOLETE. Formerly used by gendarmerie. These pistols will be kept for the foreseeable future.

• *Cal.:* 11.43 x 23mm
  *Official Name:* Pistole 11
  *Common Name:* .45 M1911A1
  pistol

*Remarks:* US origin. Being replaced by Glock P 80.

**SUBMACHINE GUNS:**
• *Cal.:* 9 x 19mm NATO
  *Official Name:* MPi69
  *Common Name:* MP69

*Remarks:* Steyr-Daimler-Puch (SDP).

• *Cal.:* 9 x 19mm Parabellum
  *Official Name:* MPi40
  *Common Name:* MP40

*Remarks:* German World War II origin; reserve units only; being replaced by the StG77.

• *Cal.:* 7.62 x 25mm
  *Official Name:* MP41
  *Common Name:* PPSh41

*Remarks:* Soviet origin. OBSOLETE. Used by some motorcycle riders; being replaced by the StG77.

**An Austrian soldier with the 9mm MPi 40 submachine gun. (Austrian MOD)**

**RIFLES:**

- *Cal.:* 5.56 x 45mm
  *Official Name:* StG77
  *Common Name:* AUG — *Armee Universalgewehr*

- *Cal.:* 7.62 x 51mm NATO
  *Official Name:* StG58
  *Common Name:* FN FAL

- *Cal.:* 7.62 x 51mm NATO
  *Official Name:* SSG 69 *(Scharf-schutzengewehr)*

- *Cal.:* 7.63 x 63mm
  *Official Name:* GM1
  *Common Name:* US M1 rifle

- *Cal.:* 7.62 x 33mm
  *Official Name:* KM1
  *Common Name:* .30 M1 and M2 carbines

*Remarks:* SDP.

*Remarks:* SDP. Made under license and with cooperation of FN, Herstal, Belgium.

*Remarks:* SDP. Domestic sniper rifle built on a modernized Mannlicher-type action.

*Remarks:* US origin. MAP in early 1960s. Being replaced by StG 77.

*Remarks:* US origin. MAP in early 1960s. Replaced by StG 77.

**SHOTGUNS:**

An Austrian soldier with the 7.62 x 51mm Stgw 58 (FAL) assault rifle. Note the unique muzzle device and the sheet metal front handguards. (Austrian MOD)

An Austrian soldier with the 5.56 x 45mm Stgw 77 assault rifle. Note the synthetic "bull pup" stock assembly and the integral optical sight. (Austrian MOD)

**MACHINE GUNS:**

• *Cal.:* 7.62 x 51mm NATO
  *Official Name:* MG42
  *Common Name:* MG42/59, and
    MG74

*Remarks:* Rheinmetall, Beretta, and SDP. MG74 is manufactured at SDP. Has a heavy bolt to reduce firing rate of weapon.

• *Cal.:* 7.62 x 51mm NATO
  *Official Name:* MG219
  *Common Name:* M73/M219 ar-
    mor MGs

*Remarks:* US origin. Mounted on M60A3 tanks. FMS delivered 123 M219s in 1975. These machine guns are being replaced by MG74.

• *Cal.:* 7.62 x 51mm NATO
  *Official Name:* MG134
  *Common Name:* M134 Minigun

*Remarks:* US origin. FMS sold 12 in 1975 and 9 in 1982. Mounted on OH-58 helicopters.

• *Cal.:* 7.62 x 63mm
  *Official Name:* MG A4
  *Common Name:* .30 M1919A4
    LMG

*Remarks:* US origin. Mounted on M47 tanks and in fixed fortifications. 1,605 provided by the MAP, 1950–63.

• *Cal.:* 12.7 x 99mm
  *Official Name:* US MG M2
  *Common Name:* .50 M2 HB
    Browning machine gun

*Remarks:* US origin. MAP 1950–63 totaled 896 guns. In 1980 FMS delivered 18 new M2 HB HMGs.

**Two views of the Steyr-Daimler-Puch M1974 tripod for the MG74/MG3/MG42 machine gun series. This mount can be used against both ground and aerial targets. (Steyr-Daimler-Puch)**

• *Cal.:* 12.7 x 99mm
*Official Name:* US MG M85
*Common Name:* .50 M85 armor
   MG

*Remarks:* US origin. Mounted on M60A3 tanks. FMS delivered 52 M85s in 1979.

**AUTOMATIC CANNON:**
• *Cal.:* 20 x 128mm
*Official Name:* MK66
*Common Name:* 20mm KAA
   (204GK) automatic cannon

*Remarks:* Oerlikon-Bührle, Switzerland.

• *Cal.:* 20 x 128mm
*Official Name:* FLAK58
*Common Name:* 20mm KAB-001
   (Type 6JLA/5TG) automatic
   cannon on the GAI-B01 mount

*Remarks:* Oerlikon-Bührle. This cannon is designated I/FLAK65/68.

## BAHRAIN (State of)

Population (estimate in 1984): 0.409 million. Ground forces: regulars, 2,550; reserves, none.

**HANDGUNS:**
• *Cal.:* 9 x 29mmR
*Common Name:* .38 Smith &
   Wesson revolvers

*Remarks:* US origin. State Department licensed sales of 280 revolvers to Ministry of Interior, 1976–77.

**SUBMACHINE GUNS:**
• *Cal.:* 9 x 19mm NATO
*Common Name:* Beretta Model 12
   submachine gun

• *Cal.:* 9 x 19mm NATO
*Common Name:* MP5A3 submachine gun

*Remarks:* Heckler & Koch (HK) GmbH design, Enfield origin.

• *Cal.:* 9 x 19mm Parabellum
*Common Name:* MK IV Sterling
   submachine guns

*Remarks:* Sterling Armament Company, UK.

**RIFLES:**
• *Cal.:* 5.56 x 45mm
*Common Name:* Unidentified
   Remington sniper

*Remarks:* US origin. State Department licensed rifle. Sherwood International to deliver 6 rifles and ammunition.

• *Cal.:* 7.62 x 51mm NATO
*Common Name:* FN FAL.

*Remarks:* FN origin. Adopted in 1968.

• *Cal.:* 7.62 x 51mm NATO
*Common Name:* Gewehr 3A3.

*Remarks:* German origin?

• *Cal.:* 7.7 x 56mmR
*Common Name:* .303 No. 1 SMLE
   rifle

*Remarks:* UK origin.

**SHOTGUNS:**

**MACHINE GUNS:**
* *Cal.:* 7.62 x 51mm NATO
  *Common Name:* FN MAG

*Remarks:* Belgian origin. MAG *Infanterie Standard* (60-20), T7 (L7A2), and MAG *Coaxial* (60-40—L7A2), P.806; P.852; and Panhard AML90 (M13 links) are in use. Police use another version.

**AUTOMATIC CANNON:**
* *Cal.:* 20 x ??
  *Common Name:* Unknown Oerlikon

*Remarks:* Automatic cannon mounted on Navy Lurssen FPB-38 fast attack craft and Coast Guard patrol craft.

## BANGLADESH (People's Republic of)

Population (estimate in 1984): 99.59 million. Ground forces: regulars, ca. 80,000; reserves, 66,000; paramilitary: Bangladesh Rifles, 30,000; Armed Police Reserve, 36,000; Bangladesh *Ansans* (security guards), 14,000. Most of the small arms available are of an older British type. These were left behind when the Pakistani army withdrew.

**HANDGUNS:**
* *Cal.:* 9 x 20mmR
  *Common Name:* MK IV Webley .38 S&W revolver

*Remarks:* UK origin.

* *Cal.:* 9 x 19mm NATO
  *Common Name:* L9A1 (FN) pistol

*Remarks:* UK origin.

* *Cal.:* 11.43 x 21.7mmR
  *Common Name:* .455 Webley revolver

*Remarks:* Still possibly in use with some military and police organizations.

**SUBMACHINE GUNS:**
* *Cal.:* 9 x 19mm Parabellum
  *Common Name:* STEN submachine gun

*Remarks:* UK and Indian origin. Older models (MK II, MK III, and MK IV) in use.

* *Cal.:* 9 x 19mm Parabellum
  *Common Name:* L2A3 submachine gun

*Remarks:* Sterling MK IV. Indian made?

**RIFLES:**
* *Cal.:* 7.7 x 56mmR
  *Common Name:* .303 No. 1 and No. 4 Enfield

*Remarks:* UK origin. The No. 1 rifles are still used by the police in Dacca.

* *Cal.:* 7.62 x 51mm NATO
  *Common Name:* L1A1 rifle

*Remarks:* UK origin.

* *Cal.:* 7.62 x 51mm NATO
  *Common Name:* Gewehr 3A2

*Remarks:* Pakistani Ordnance Factory.

* *Cal.:* 7.62 x 51mm NATO
  *Common Name:* Gewehr 3A3

*Remarks:* Heckler & Koch (HK) GmbH origin.

* *Cal.:* 7.62 x 39mm
  *Common Name:* AK47 assault rifles

*Remarks:* Domestic manufacture licensed and technically supported by the People's Republic of China (PRC).

* *Cal.:* 7.62 x 39mm
  *Common Name:* SKS carbines

*Remarks:* Domestic manufacture licensed and technically supported by the PRC.

• *Cal.:* 7.62 x 63mm
  *Common Name:* .30 M1 rifle

*Remarks:* US origin.

**SHOTGUNS:**

**MACHINE GUNS:**
• *Cal.:* 7.62 x 39mm
  *Common Name:* RPD LMG

*Remarks:* Soviet and PRC origin.

• *Cal.:* 7.62 x 51mm NATO
  *Common Name:* L2A1 automatic
  rifle

*Remarks:* Indian origin?

• *Cal.:* 7.62 x 51mm NATO
  *Common Name:* HK11A1

*Remarks:* HK GmbH origin.

• *Cal.:* 7.62 x 51mm NATO
  *Common Name:* HK21A1

*Remarks:* HK GmbH origin.

• *Cal.:* 7.62 x 54mmR
  *Common Name:* SGMT armor
  MG

*Remarks:* East Bloc origin. Mounted on older model Soviet tanks.

• *Cal.:* 7.7 x 56mmR
  *Common Name:* .303 Bren gun

*Remarks:* UK origin.

• *Cal.:* 7.7 x 56mmR
  *Common Name:* .303 Vickers machine gun

*Remarks:* UK origin.

• *Cal.:* 12.7 x 108mm
  *Common Name:* DShKM HMG

*Remarks:* East Bloc origin. China?

**AUTOMATIC CANNON:**
• *Cal.:* 20 x 110mm
  *Common Name:* M55 automatic
  cannon

*Remarks:* Yugoslavian version of HS804 cannon.

• *Cal.:* 25 x 218mm
  *Common Name:* 2-M-3 or 2-M-8
  automatic cannon

*Remarks:* Chinese origin on fast attack craft.

# BARBADOS

Population (estimate in 1984): 0.285 million. Ground forces: regulars, unknown; reserves, unknown; paramilitary, Royal Barbados Police Department, ca. 950.

**HANDGUNS:**
• *Cal.:* 9 x 20mmR
  *Common Name:* MK IV Webley
  .38 S&W revolver

*Remarks:* UK origin.

• *Cal.:* 9 x 20mmR
  *Common Name:* Smith & Wesson
  .38 S&W revolver

*Remarks:* UK surplus.

**SUBMACHINE GUNS:**
• *Cal.:* 9 x 19mm NATO
  *Common Name:* Sterling MK4
  submachine gun

*Remarks:* Sterling Armaments Company, UK.

- *Cal.:* 9 x 19mm NATO
  *Common Name:* MAT49 submachine gun

*Remarks:* Manufacture Nationale d'Armes de Tulle (MAT).

**RIFLES:**
- *Cal.:* 5.56 x 45mm
  *Common Name:* M16A1 rifle

*Remarks:* US origin. Supplied by US government.

- *Cal.:* 5.56 x 45mm
  *Common Name:* M16A2 rifle

*Remarks:* US origin. Barbados acting as purchasing agent for Eastern Caribbean Forces.

- *Cal.:* 7.7 x 56mmR
  *Common Name:* .303 No. 4 Enfield

*Remarks:* UK origin.

- *Cal.:* 7.62 x 51mm NATO
  *Common Name:* L1A1 rifle

*Remarks:* Commonwealth Small Arms Factory, Lithgow, Australia.

**SHOTGUNS:**

**MACHINE GUNS:**
- *Cal.:* 7.7 x 56mmR
  *Common Name:* .303 Bren gun

*Remarks:* UK origin.

- *Cal.:* 7.62 x 51mm NATO
  *Common Name:* L4A3 Bren gun

*Remarks:* Royal Small Arms Factory (RSAF), Enfield.

- *Cal.:* 7.62 x 51mm NATO
  *Common Name:* L7A1 GPMG

*Remarks:* FN origin.

**AUTOMATIC CANNON:**
- *Cal.:* 20 x ???mm
  *Common Name:* Unidentified
  20mm automatic cannon

*Remarks:* Origin unknown. Used on coastal patrol craft.

## BELGIUM (Kingdom of)

Population (estimate in 1984): 9.87 million. Ground forces: regulars, 65,100; reserves, 160,000; paramilitary, *Gendarmerie (Rijkswacht),* ca. 16,000.

**HANDGUNS:**
- *Cal.:* 6.35 x 15mmSR Browning
  *Common Name:* FN Model Baby
  Browning pistol

*Remarks:* FN origin. NSN 1005-13-107-8122 (PB-6-35). Still used by some
military officers.

- *Cal.:* 7.65 x 17mm Browning
  *Common Name:* FN Model 1922
  Browning pistol

*Remarks:* FN origin. NSN 1005-13-100-3601 (FN 3722002606). Still used by
some police organizations.

- *Cal.:* 9 x 19mm NATO
  *Official Name: Pistolet Automa-
  tique Browning Modèle 1935 a
  Grande Puissance*
  *Common Name:* FN Mle. 35 GP
  pistol

*Remarks:* FN origin. Standard Army pistol. The several NSNs for this pistol
include: 1005-13-010-0478 (UK model); 1005-13-010-0313 (GPB151); 1005-13-
010-0325 (GPB156); 1005-13-100-3445 (GPPLB 196; FN 3748110018 Vigilante Model 1001 Belgian). FOM 1005-21-1-9-1. See numbering system below.
Production of this handgun terminated. Machinery shipped to Portugal in
1987.

- *Cal.:* 11.43 x 23mm
  *Common Name:* .45 M1911A1
  pistol

*Remarks:* US origin. Used by the Belgian Navy.

A Belgian infantryman holding a
9 x 19mm FN Mle. 1935 GP pistol.
(FN)

**SUBMACHINE GUNS:**
- *Cal.:* 9 x 19mm NATO
  *Official Name: Mitraillette Uzi*
  *Common Name:* Uzi submachine
  gun

  *Remarks:* FN origin.

- *Cal.:* 9 x 19mm NATO
  *Official Name: Mitraillette MP5*
  *Common Name:* MP5 subma-
  chine gun

  *Remarks:* Heckler & Koch (HK) GmbH origin. Used by Belgian police and
  *Gendarmerie.*

- *Cal.:* 9 x 19mm NATO
  *Official Name: Mitraillete Vigne-
  ron M2*
  *Common Name:* Vigneron submachine gun

  *Remarks:* Société Anonyme Précision, Liègeoise, Herstal, Belgium. NSN
  1005-13-100-8001.

**At the top, the current manufacture 9 x 19mm FN Mle. 1935 GP MK2 pistol. Below, the new FN double action version of the GP series. (FN)**

**This Belgian infantryman holds one FN FAL PARA, with blank firing attachment, and has another PARA slung over his shoulder. In addition he is carrying a belt of 12.7 x 99mm blank ammunition for NATO maneuvers in Turkey during the mid-1970s. (NATO)**

• *Cal.:* 11.43 x 23mm
 *Common Name:* M1A1 submachine gun

*Remarks:* US origin. Reportedly still used by airborne troops.

**RIFLES:**
• *Cal.:* 5.56 x 45mm NATO
 *Official Name:* FN Carabine
 *Common Name:* FNC Model 90.00 and Model 92.00

*Remarks:* FN origin. Used by airborne troops in limited numbers. Model 92.00 is NSN 1005-13-112-4347.

- *Cal.:* 7.62 x 33mm
  *Official Name: Carabine M1*
  *Common Name:* .30 M1 carbine

- *Cal.:* 7.62 x 51mm NATO
  *Official Name: Fusil Automatique
  Légèr*
  *Common Name:* FN FAL

- *Cal.:* 7.62 x 51mm NATO
  *Official Name: FN Sniper*
  *Common Name:* FN Sniper rifle

- *Cal.:* 7.62 x 63mm
  *Common Name:* FN SAFN rifle

- *Cal.:* 7.7 x 56mmR
  *Common Name:* .303 SMLE rifles

*Remarks:* US origin.

*Remarks:* FN origin. The Belgian Army uses models of the FAL, including the short barrel PARA (50-63) M3 NSN 1005-13-103-3387 (FN 3508640007). For the standard FAL M1 (50-00) the NATO identifiers are NSN 1005-13-100-0010 and 1005-13-100-0545; FAL M2 is 1005-13-100-0469 (FN 3508000007). The light automatic weapon, FALO, is NSN 1005-13-100-0470 (FN 3508420030).

*Remarks:* FN origin. Model 30-11. Has a Mauser-type bolt action (made at FN), an Anschutz trigger mechanism, a Kaps 4 x 25 telescope (German), a Delcour barrel, and an FN MAG bipod.

*Remarks:* FN origin. NSN 1005-13-100-3652 (AFAFN). Sniper version has Société Belge d'Optique et d'Instruments de Precision (OIP) telescope; NSN 1005-13-100-3653 (AFAFNTE).

*Remarks:* British origin. Used by Belgian *Gendarmerie.*

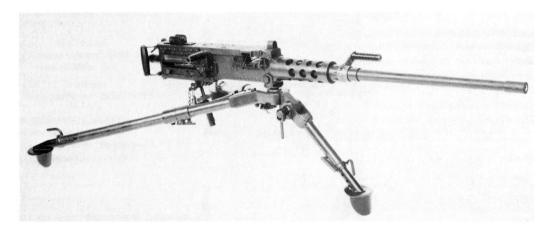

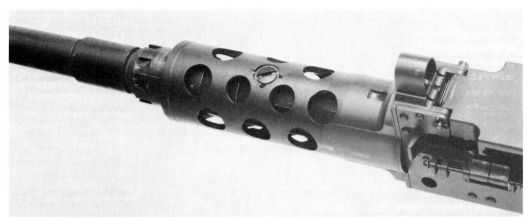

**Two views of FN's new quick change barrel version of the venerable 12.7 x 99mm (.50) M2 HB HMG. (FN)**

### SHOTGUNS:
• *Cal.:* 18.5 x 59mm
*Common Name:* 12 gage FN riot shotgun

*Remarks:* FN origin. NSN 1005-13-112-9560 (FN 3228010002).

• *Cal.:* 18.5 x 59mm
*Common Name:* 12 gage Mossberg Model 500 shotgun

*Remarks:* US origin. Used by *Gendarmerie* and city police forces. Acquired 1983–86.

### MACHINE GUNS:
• *Cal.:* 7.62 x 51mm NATO
*Official Name:* Mitrailleuse a Gaz
*Common Name:* MAG

*Remarks:* FN origin. Redesignated by FN as the *Mitrailleuse d'Appui General;* i.e., GPMG. Among the models used by the Belgian armed forces are: MAG *Infanterie Standard* (60-20), Type BELU M1 (NSN 1005-13-010-0541; Type BELU M2 (NSN 1005-13-103-8140 = FN 3608200434), Type BELU M3 (NSN 1005-13-103-8141 = FN 3608400716); Type BELU M4 (NSN 1005-13-111-3328 = FN 3608400729); MAG *Infanterie Standard Tourelle* (60-20), Type BELU M2; MAG *Coaxe* (60-40 Coaxial), Type M3 Leopard (NSN 1005-13-110-9552 = FN 3608400167); and Type T4 (M4 Ranging machine gun). The AMX-13 coaxial gun is NSN 1005-13-102-7253 (FN 3608400206). The Taurus ARV coaxial gun is NSN 1005-13-110-9553 = FN 3608400221. The NATO identifier for the early infantry model with the wood stock is NSN 1005-13-010-0506. The current plastic version of the MAG is NSN 1005-13-103-2524 (same as L7A2). Type T4 (M4 Ranging machine gun) is NSN 1005-13-111-3328. FOM 1005-21-4-7.62-1.

• *Cal.:* 7.62 x 63mm
*Official Name:* Fusil Mitrailleuse D
*Common Name:* FN Browning automatic rifle Type D; FM D

*Remarks:* FN origin. FN FMD is NSN 1005-13-100-3290. Converted to 7.62mm NATO, it is FN FMDA1 with NSN 1005-13-100-3337.

• *Cal.:* 7.62 x 63mm
*Common Name:* .30 M1917A1 MMG

*Remarks:* US origin. FMS delivered 35 guns in 1971. Earlier 613 unspecified .30 caliber LMGs were delivered by MAP.

• *Cal.:* 7.7 x 56mmR
*Common Name:* .303 Bren gun

*Remarks:* British origin. Used by Belgian *Gendarmerie.*

• *Cal.:* 12.7 x 99mm
*Official Name:* Mitrailleuse Browning
*Common Name:* .50 M2 HB HMG

*Remarks:* FN and US origin. The NATO identifier for the FN-made M2 HB is NSN 1005-13-726-5636. The FN catalog no. is 66-00. MAP delivered 62 guns before 1963. Approx. 60 of the M55 quad AA systems are in the Belgian inventory.

### AUTOMATIC CANNON:
• *Cal.:* 20 x 102mm
*Common Name:* 20mm M168 Vulcan cannon on the M167 Vulcan Air Defense System (VADS)

*Remarks:* US origin. Approximately 25 of the M197s AA systems are in service.

• *Cal.:* 20 x ???mm
*Common Name:* Unidentified 20mm automatic cannon

*Remarks:* Origin unknown. Mounted on Belgian minesweepers.

### FN Internal Catalog Numbers
Fabrique National Herstal assigns internal catalog numbers to their products. Some pertinent ones include:

*Modele 1935 Grande Puissance* pistol:

74-11   Model Vigilante   1001 — phosphated finish plus black lacquer, w/ lanyard loop.
74-12   Model Vigilante   1002 — phosphated finish plus black lacquer, w/o lanyard loop.
74-13   Model Vigilante   1003 — blued finish w/ lanyard loop.
74-14   Model Vigilante   1004 — blued finish w/o lanyard loop.
         Model Capitan     2001 — tangent sight; phosphated finish plus black lacquer, w/ lanyard loop.

# HP MODEL CODE

| 1st DIGIT: SIGHTS | 2nd DIGIT: ENGRAVING | 3rd DIGIT: GRIPS | 4th DIGIT: FINISH |
|---|---|---|---|
| 1 Fixed | 0 None | 0 Checkered black plastic w/lanyard ring cut | 0 Gold |
| 2 Tangent (obsolete) | 1 Hand-engraved (Renaissance) | 1 Checkered black plastic, no lanyard ring cut | 1 Phosphate |
| 3 Sport adjustable | 2 Photo-etched ("Louis XVI") | 2 Lactiplex (Pearlite) | 2 "Old Silver" |
| | | 3 Standard checkered wood | 3 Standard Blue |
| 5 Competition | | 4 Fine-checkered wood | 4 Sandblast/ Blue |
| | | 5 Pachmeyer wrap-around | 5 Matte Chrome |
| | | | 6 Nickel |
| | | | 7 Brilliant Chrome |
| | | | 8 Black anodised (alloy frames) |

**Key to the FN model numbers for Model 1935 GP (high power) pistol. (Collector Grade Publications)**

Model Capitan    2002 – tangent sight; phosphated finish plus black lacquer, w/o lanyard loop.
Model Capitan    2003 – tangent sight; blued finish w/ lanyard loop.
Model Capitan    2004 – tangent sight; blued finish w/o lanyard loop.
Model Sport      3001 – adjustable sight; blued finish.
Model SportLuxe 3002 – adjustable sight; engraved; nickle finish.
Model SportLuxe 3003 – adjustable sight; special blued finish.

*Fusil Automatique Légèr* (FAL):
50-00   Standard FAL w/ fixed butt stock and 533mm barrel.
50-41   FALO heavy barrel automatic rifle version w/ nylon (plastic) butt stock.
50-42   FALO heavy barrel automatic rifle version w/ wood butt stock.
50-61   FAL PARA w/ folding stock and 533mm barrel.
50-63   FAL PARA w/ folding stock, 458mm barrel (to permit attachment of bipod), folding cocking handle, and no carrying handle.
50-63   FAL PARA w/ folding stock, 436mm barrel, folding cocking handle, and no carrying handle.
50-64   FAL PARA w/ folding stock, 533mm barrel, and "hiduminium" alloy lower receiver and magazine.

*FNC 5.56mm rifle:*
90-00   Standard model w/ standard folding stock. FOM 1005-21-2-5.56-2. The CAL, now out of production, was assigned FOM 1005-21-2-5.56-1.
92-00   Shortened barrel model; 449mm vs 363mm barrel.

*Minimi* 5.56mm NATO Squad Automatic Weapon:
FOM 1005-21-4-5.56-2.

*FN Sniper Rifle:*
30-11   Mauser action sniper rifle, caliber 7.62 x 51mm NATO.

*Mitrailleuse d'Appui General:*
60-20   Standard infantry version (MAG *Infanterie Standard*). FOM 1005-21-4-7.62-1.
        Type Belgian/Luxembourg (BELU) M2 for tank turret.
        T1 standard type.
        T2, standard for Israeli Defense Forces.
        T3 (type L7A1) – NSN 1005-13-010-0506
        T4 (M4 ranging machine gun).
        T5 using nondisintegrating belt.
        T6 (L7A2-type) – NSN 1005-13-103-2524.
        T7 (L7A2-type).
        T9 using nondisintegrating belt.
        T11 using nondisintegrating belt.
        T12 using US M13 link.
        T13 using nondisintegrating belt.
        T14 using nondisintegrating belt.
        T15 using nondisintegrating belt.
60-30   Aircraft version *(MAG Aviation).*
        T1, Type M0.32, right and left hand feed.
        T2, Type P 800 Pod P.904, Marchetti.
        M0.32, Pod FN P.935.
        ST450-Mod.06.

60-40   Coaxial version for vehicles *(MAG Coaxe)*.
        Type 1, standard.
        T3, M240 (USA).
        Type M3, Leopard.
        T4 (M4 ranging machine gun). NSN 1005-13-111-3328.
        Type P.806 (L7A2) Shorland and AMX-13.
        Type P.847 on Panhard AML-60.
        Type P.852 on Panhard AML-90.
        Type P.925 (60-417).
        Type P.929, Leopard Canada C1.
        Type Cadillac Gage V150 armored car.
        ST450-Mod.06.
10-10   Jungle version with shorter barrel and buttstock. FOM 1005-21-4-7.62-4.

*12.7mm Mitrailleuse Browning:*
66-00   Standard M2 HB Browning machine gun; NSN 1005-13-726-5636. The M2 w/ Quick Change Barrel (QCB) option does not have an NSN.

## BELIZE (Formerly British Honduras)

Population (estimate in 1984): 0.158 million. Independent in 1973. Ground forces: regulars, still being formed, ca. 500; reserves, unknown, but probably very small. Police force numbers 485, with a 155-person Special Force, which is armed. There is still a British Army regiment in Belize.

**HANDGUNS:**
• *Cal.:* 9 x 19mm Parabellum       *Remarks:* UK origin.
  *Common Name:* Pistol, auto-
    matic, 9mm, L9A1

**SUBMACHINE GUNS:**
• *Cal.:* 9 x 19mm Parabellum       *Remarks:* UK origin.
  *Common Name:* Submachine
  gun, 9mm, L2A3

• *Cal.:* 9 x 29mmR               *Remarks:* US origin. Used by police.
  *Common Name:* .38 Smith & Wes-
  son revolvers

**RIFLES:**
• *Cal.:* 5.56 x 45mm           *Remarks:* Colt M16A1s transferred to Belize out of UK stocks. In 1986 the
  *Common Name:* M16A1 rifle   UK purchased 400 M16A1 rifles for local troops in Belize.
  (Model 613)

• *Cal.:* 7.62 x 51mm NATO      *Remarks:* UK origin.
  *Common Name:* L1A1 rifle

**SHOTGUNS:**

**MACHINE GUNS:**
• *Cal.:* 7.62 x 51mm NATO      *Remarks:* UK origin.
  *Common Name:* L4A4 Bren gun

**Belize Defence Force soldiers prepare for a training exercise. Weapons shown include 5.56mm M16A1s, 7.62mm L1A1s, a 7.62mm L7 Bren gun, and a 7.62mm L7 series GPMG. (Belize Defence Forces)**

- *Cal.:* 7.62 x 51mm NATO
  *Common Name:* L7 series GPMG

*Remarks:* FN origin. MAG Infanterie Standard (60-20), T6 (L7A2) configuration.

**AUTOMATIC CANNON:**

## BENIN (People's Republic of)

Population (estimate in 1984): 3.91 million. Ground forces: regulars, ca. 3,000; reserves, no organized reserves, but 1,200 paramilitary gendarmerie. This is the former state of Dahomey in French West Africa.

**HANDGUNS:**
- *Cal.:* 7.65 x 17mm Browning
  *Common Name:* Walther PP

*Remarks:* Manurhin-made model of Walther PP.

- *Cal.:* 7.62 x 25mm
  *Common Name:* TT33 Tokarev pistol

*Remarks:* East Bloc origin.

**SUBMACHINE GUNS:**
• *Cal.:* 9 x 19mm
  *Common Name:* MAT Mle. 49
  submachine gun

*Remarks:* Manufacture Nationale d'Armes de Tulle (MAT).

**RIFLES:**
• *Cal.:* 7.5 x 54mm
  *Common Name:* MAS 36 bolt
  action rifle

*Remarks:* Manufacture Nationale d'Armes de St. Etienne (MAS).

• *Cal.:* 7.5 x 54mm
  *Common Name:* MAS 49/56 rifle

*Remarks:* MAS

• *Cal.:* 7.62 x 39mm
  *Common Name:* SKS carbine

*Remarks:* Soviet-type, origin unknown.

• *Cal.:* 7.62 x 39mm
  *Common Name:* AK47 and AKM
  assault rifles

*Remarks:* Soviet-type, origin unknown.

**SHOTGUNS:**

**MACHINE GUNS:**
• *Cal.:* 7.5 x 54mm
  *Common Name:* MAC Mle. 24/29
  LMG

*Remarks:* Manufacture Nationale d'Armes de Chatellerault (MAC)

• *Cal.:* 7.5 x 54mm
  *Common Name:* AAT 52 GPMG

*Remarks:* Groupment Industriel des Armements Terrestres (GIAT), France.

• *Cal.:* 7.62 x 54mmR
  *Common Name:* RP46 company
  machine gun

*Remarks:* East Bloc origin.

• *Cal.:* 7.62 x 39mm
  *Common Name:* RPD LMG

*Remarks:* East Bloc origin.

• *Cal.:* 12.7 x 99mm
  *Common Name:* .50 M2 HB
  HMG

*Remarks:* US origin.

• *Cal.:* 12.7 x 108mm
  *Common Name:* DShKM HMG

*Remarks:* Soviet origin. Mounted on Soviet coastal patrol craft. Presumed also to be available in ground versions.

**AUTOMATIC CANNON:**
• *Cal.:* 14.5 x 114mm
  *Common Name:* KPV HMG

*Remarks:* Soviet origin. Mounted on Soviet fast attack craft.

## BOLIVIA (Republic of)

Population (estimate in 1987): 6 million. Ground forces: regulars (composed of 10 divisions), between 28,000 and 30,000; reserves (composed of 27 classes of conscripts who have completed their military service), ca. 10,000 officers; Marine infantry battalion, 600; paramilitary forces, *Carabineros,* 6,000.

**HANDGUNS:**
• *Cal.:* 9 x 19mm Parabellum
  *Common Name:* FN Mle. 35 GP
  pistol

*Remarks:* FN and Argentine origin.

- *Cal.:* 9 x 29mmR
  *Common Name:* .38 Smith & Wesson revolvers

  *Remarks:* US origin. American State Department licensed sale of 50 revolvers for Ministry of Interior and 250 for Customs in 1978.

- *Cal.:* 9 x 29mmR Magnum
  *Common Name:* .357 Magnum Smith & Wesson revolvers

  *Remarks:* US origin. State Department licensed sale of 10 for Ministry of Interior in 1978.

- *Cal.:* 11.43 x 23mm
  *Common Name:* .45 M1911A1 pistol

  *Remarks:* US origin. MAP delivered 1,107 M1911A1 pistols before 1975 and 100 more in 1975.

**SUBMACHINE GUNS:**

- *Cal.:* 9 x 19mm Parabellum
  *Common Name:* Uzi submachine gun

  *Remarks:* FN origin. About 190 were purchased in 1970.

- *Cal.:* 9 x 19mm Parabellum
  *Common Name:* Ingram MAC-10 submachine gun

  *Remarks:* RPB Industries, US. State Department licensed sale of 160 MAC-10 submachine guns for Customs.

- *Cal.:* 9 x 19mm Parabellum
  *Common Name:* MAT Mle. 49 submachine gun

  *Remarks:* MAT. About 2,000 acquired from France in 1984.

- *Cal.:* 9 x 19mm Parabellum
  *Common Name:* Madsen M45 submachine gun

  *Remarks:* Danish origin.

- *Cal.:* 9 x 19mm Parabellum
  *Common Name:* FMK-3 submachine gun

  *Remarks:* Argentine origin.

- *Cal.:* 11.43 x 23mm
  *Common Name:* .45 M3A1 submachine gun

  *Remarks:* US origin. For example, MAP and FMS delivered 77 M3s, 1964–1974.

- *Cal.:* 11.43 x 23mm
  *Common Name:* .45 M1A1 submachine gun (Thompson)

  *Remarks:* US origin.

**RIFLES:**

- *Cal.:* 5.6 x 16mm Long Rifle
  *Common Name:* .22 Remington Nylon 66 semiautomatic rifle

  *Remarks:* US origin. Used by Bolivian police forces.

- *Cal.:* 5.56 x 45mm
  *Common Name:* Galil rifle

  *Remarks:* Israeli Military Industries (IMI), Israel.

- *Cal.:* 5.56 x 45mm
  *Common Name:* M16A1 rifle

  *Remarks:* Source and quantity unknown. About 500 are in inventory.

- *Cal.:* 5.56 x 45mm
  *Common Name:* Steyr AUG

  *Remarks:* Steyr-Daimler-Puch (SDP), of Austria. Only about 500 AUGs have been purchased.

- *Cal.:* 7.62 x 33mm
  *Common Name:* .30 M1 and M2 carbines

  *Remarks:* US origin. MAP delivered 7,583 M1s and 4,084 M2s before 1975.

- *Cal.:* 7.62 x 51mm NATO
  *Common Name:* FN FAL

  *Remarks:* FN origin; models 50-00 and 50-63. In 1971 Bolivia purchased additional FALs from Argentina.

- *Cal.:* 7.62 x 51mm NATO
  *Common Name:* Gewehr 3

  *Remarks:* Heckler & Koch (HK) GmbH origin.

- *Cal.:* 7.62 x 51mm NATO
  *Common Name:* SG510-4 rifle

  *Remarks:* Schweizerische Industrie Gesellschaft/Rheinfalls (SIG) origin. Approx. 5,000 in service.

- *Cal.:* 7.62 x 51mm NATO
  *Common Name:* SG540 rifle

- *Cal.:* 7.62 x 63mm
  *Common Name:* .30 M1 rifle

- *Cal.:* 7.62 x 63mm
  *Common Name:* .30 M1D Sniper
  rifle

- *Cal.:* 7.65 x 53.5mm Mauser
  *Common Name:* FN Mle. 1935
  Mauser rifle and carbine

- *Cal.:* 7.65 x 53.5mm Mauser
  *Common Name:* vz.24 Mauser
  rifle and carbine

- *Cal.:* 7.65 x 53.5mm Mauser
  *Common Name:* Mauser M1908

*Remarks:* SIG design but manufactured by Manurhin of France.

*Remarks:* US origin. MAP delivered 3,992 M1s before 1975. Another 2,014 unspecified rifles delivered before 1963.

*Remarks:* US origin. For example, MAP delivered 12 in 1964 and 36 in 1970.

*Remarks:* FN origin. Reserve only.

*Remarks:* Czechoslovakian origin. Reserve only.

*Remarks:* DWM manufacture (Deutsche Waffen-und Munitions fabriken, pre-1930 Germany). Reserve only.

**SHOTGUNS:**
- *Cal.:* 18.5 x 59mm
  *Common Name:* 12 gage; M37
  Ithaca shotgun

*Remarks:* US origin. MAP delivered 62 riot guns, 1965–66.

**MACHINE GUNS:**
- *Cal.:* 7.62 x 51mm NATO
  *Common Name:* FN MAG

*Remarks:* FN and Argentine origin. In 1971 Bolivia purchased MAGs from Argentina. They have acquired MAG *Infanterie Standard* (60-20), T9 using nondisintegrating link belt.

- *Cal.:* 7.62 x 51mm NATO
  *Common Name:* SG710-3 GPMG

*Remarks:* SIG origin.

- *Cal.:* 7.62 x 51mm NATO
  *Common Name:* M60 GPMG

*Remarks:* US origin. About 500 purchased in 1985 with MAP funds.

- *Cal.:* 7.62 x 51mm NATO
  *Common Name:* M60D aircraft
  door machine gun

*Remarks:* US origin. MAP delivered 8 in 1974; 4 in 1975.

- *Cal.:* 7.62 x 51mm NATO
  *Common Name:* HK21 LMG

*Remarks:* HK design. Made by MAS in France?

- *Cal.:* 7.62 x 51mm NATO
  *Common Name:* AAT 52 GPMG

*Remarks:* French origin.

- *Cal.:* 7.62 x 63mm
  *Common Name:* .30 M1918A1
  BAR

*Remarks:* US origin. MAP delivered 77 in 1964, 9 in 1965, 76 in 1966, 22 in 1968, 122 in 1969, 216 in 1972, 108 in 1973, 598 in 1975.

- *Cal.:* 7.62 x 63mm
  *Common Name:* .30 M1917A1
  MMG

*Remarks:* US origin. MAP delivered 14 in 1971.

- *Cal.:* 7.62 x 63mm
  *Common Name:* .30 M1919A4
  LMG

*Remarks:* US origin. MAP delivered 293 LMGs, 1964–75. Also 121 M1919A6 and 35 M1915A5 in same period.

- *Cal.:* 7.62 x 63mm
  *Common Name:* .30 M37 armor
  MG

*Remarks:* US origin. MAP delivered 40 in 1976.

- *Cal.:* 7.65 x 53.5mm Mauser
  *Common Name:* ZB-30 LMG

*Remarks:* Czechoslovakian origin.

• *Cal.:* 7.65 x 53.5mm Mauser
*Common Name:* Maxim HMG

*Remarks:* German origin. Bought during the 1935 Chaco War.

• *Cal.:* 12.7 x 99mm
*Common Name:* .50 M2 HB
HMG

*Remarks:* US origin. MAP delivered 34 before 1963, 118 in 1967, and 3 in 1974.

**AUTOMATIC CANNON:**

## BOTSWANA (Republic of)

Population (estimate in 1984): 1.04 million. Ground forces: regulars, 2,800; reserves, none; paramilitary, 1,260 police. Former British protectorate of Bechuanaland. Many older British small arms still in use, but Soviet-type small arms increasing in number.

**HANDGUNS:**
• *Cal.:* 9 x 20mmR
*Common Name:* .38 Enfield No.
2, MK 1 pistol

*Remarks:* UK origin.

• *Cal.:* 9 x 19mm NATO
*Common Name:* FN Mle. 35 GP
pistol

*Remarks:* UK origin?

• *Cal.:* 9 x 29mmR
*Common Name:* .38 and .357
Magnum Colt revolvers

*Remarks:* US origin. State Department licensed sale of 13 Colt revolvers for police use in 1976.

**SUBMACHINE GUNS:**
• *Cal.:* 9 x 19mm NATO
*Common Name:* MK IV Sten gun

*Remarks:* UK origin.

**RIFLES:**
• *Cal.:* 5.56 x 45mm
*Common Name:* AR-18 rifle

*Remarks:* Sterling Armaments Corporation, UK.

• *Cal.:* 5.56 x 45mm
*Common Name:* Galil rifle

*Remarks:* Israeli Military Industries (IMI) origin.

• *Cal.:* 7.62 x 51mm NATO
*Common Name:* L1A1 rifle

*Remarks:* UK origin.

• *Cal.:* 7.62 x 51mm NATO
*Common Name:* FN FAL

*Remarks:* FN origin.

• *Cal.:* 7.62 x 39mm
*Common Name:* AK47 assault
rifle

*Remarks:* East Bloc origin. Models observed include Chinese Type 56.

**SHOTGUNS:**

**MACHINE GUNS:**
• *Cal.:* 7.62 x 51mm NATO
*Common Name:* FN MAG (L7A1)

*Remarks:* UK and FN origin. From FN they have acquired MAG *Infanterie Standard* (60-20), T1 model and *Coaxial* (60-40) Cadillac Gage model.

• *Cal.:* 7.62 x 51mm NATO
*Common Name:* L4 series Bren
gun

*Remarks:* UK origin.

- *Cal.:* 7.7 x 53mmR
  *Common Name:* .303 series Bren gun

*Remarks:* UK origin.

- *Cal.:* 7.62 x 54mmR
  *Common Name:* SGMB or PKB flexible machine gun

*Remarks:* East Bloc origin. Mounted on BTR60 APCs.

**AUTOMATIC CANNON:**
- *Cal.:* 14.5 x 114mm
  *Common Name:* KPV HMG

*Remarks:* East Bloc origin. Mounted on BTR60 APCs.

## BRAZIL (Federated Republic of)

Population (estimate in 1984): 134.38 million. Ground forces: regulars, 183,000; reserves, 1,115,000 (400,000 subject to immediate recall) and 225,000 second-line reserves with limited training; paramilitary state militia (also called state military police—*Policia Militar*), ca. 185,000 to 250,000; *Fuzilerios Navais* (Marines), 14,500; police: federal police, 15,000; state civil police *(Policia Civil),* 50,000.

**HANDGUNS:**
- *Cal.:* 11.43 x 23mm
  *Official Name:* Pst 45 M1911A1
  *Common Name:* .45 M1911A1

*Remarks:* Colt origin. Still in use by second-line Navy, Marine Corps, and Air Force units, plus some police forces.

- *Cal.:* 11.43 x 23mm
  *Official Name:* Pst 45 M968
  *Common Name:* .45 Colt Commander

*Remarks:* Fábrica de Itajuba, part of the Industria de Material Belico do Brasil (IMBEL). Version of Colt Commander alloy-frame, shortened .45 pistol. About 200 manufactured.

- *Cal.:* 9 x 19mm Parabellum
  *Official Name:* Pst 9 M973
  *Common Name:* 9mm version of Colt M1911A1

*Remarks:* Fábrica de Itajuba. Some older M1911A1s were converted to 9 x 19mm before new pistols were manufactured. Used by some army units.

- *Cal.:* 9 x 19mm Parabellum
  *Common Name:* 9mm Beretta M92; 9mm Taurus PT92.

*Remarks:* Forjas Taurus, S.A., Brazil. Formerly Industria e Comercio Beretta S.A. Used by Army, Air Force, and Marine Corps.

- *Cal.:* 9 x 29mmR
  *Common Name:* .38 Smith & Wesson revolver

*Remarks:* US origin. State Department licensed sale of 14 revolvers to State Department of Criminal Investigation, Sao Paulo in 1974.

- *Cal.:* 9 x 29mmR
  *Official Name:* Revolver Taurus
  *Common Name:* .38 Taurus revolver

*Remarks:* Forjas Taurus, S.A. These revolvers are used by police organizations.

- *Cal.:* 7.63 x 23mm Mauser
  *Official Name:* PASAM *(Pistola Automatica e Semi-Automatica Mauser)*
  *Common Name:* Mauser 1896 pistol; "broom handle"

*Remarks:* Old German production; selective fire version *(Schnellfeuer-pistole)* of German Mauser C96 pistol. About 500 purchased by Rio de Janeiro's military police in 1930s. About 200 locally modified with frame extension, forward pistol grip, wire stock. Still in service.

**SUBMACHINE GUNS:**
- *Cal.:* 11.43 x 23mm
  *Official Name:* .45 INA M953; .45 INA MB50 also
  *Common Name:* Danish Madsen Model 1953 submachine gun

*Remarks:* Brazilian-made. Used by a few state military police forces and for guard duty by Navy.

- *Cal.:* 11.43 x 23mm
  *Common Name:* .45 M3 submachine gun

  *Remarks:* US origin. MAP delivered 500 M3s in 1964. Used by second-line Marine Corps units.

- *Cal.:* 9 x 19mm Parabellum
  *Official Name:* Mtr M 9 M972
  *Common Name:* Beretta Model 12 and Taurus MT-12 submachine gun

  *Remarks:* Forjas Taurus, S.A. In service with Army, Marine Corps, and some state police forces.

- *Cal.:* 9 x 19mm Parabellum
  *Common Name:* MP5 and MP5SD

  *Remarks:* Heckler & Koch (HK), GmbH. Used by federal police and some state police units.

- *Cal.:* 9 x 19mm Parabellum
  *Common Name:* Walther MP-K submachine gun

  *Remarks:* Walther-made. Police use only.

- *Cal.:* 9 x 19mm Parabellum
  *Common Name:* Mekanika Uru submachine gun

  *Remarks:* Domestic design. Used by some state military forces (including Bahia and Mato Grosso) and reportedly by some Army special units.

In addition, some aging submachine guns are occasionally encountered in police units, including Reisings and US-made Thompsons. Government intelligence and body guard units employ other unidentified types.

**RIFLES:**
- *Cal.:* 5.56 x 45mm
  *Common Name:* HK33 and HK33A1 rifles

  *Remarks:* HK origin. Used only by Air Force, which acquired 15,000 HK33s in 1971.

- *Cal.:* 5.56 x 45mm
  *Common Name:* M16 (Model 614) rifle

  *Remarks:* Purchased less than 500 from Colt, mostly before 1970. Used by Air Force. US State Department licensed sale of 30 M16s in 1976 to both state military police of Sao Paulo and Secretary of Public Security, Alagoas. There are about 1,000 M16A1s in hands of police units.

**Receiver markings on an FN-manufactured 7.62 x 51mm FAL acquired by Brazil. (FN)**

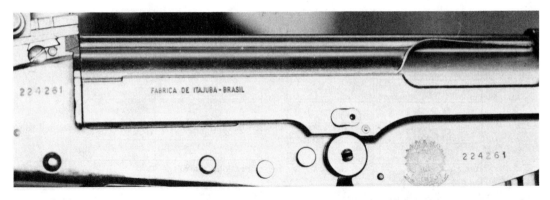

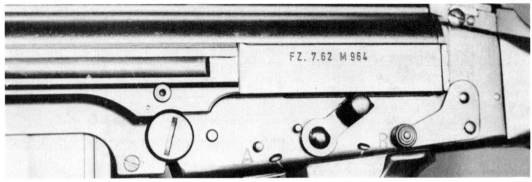

**Receiver markings on an FAL manufactured at the Fábrica de Itajuba. (Stevens)**

- *Cal.:* 5.56 x 45mm
  *Common Name:* M16A2 rifle

- *Cal.:* 7.62 x 51mm NATO
  *Official Name:* 7.62mm M964
  *Common Name:* FN FAL

- *Cal.:* 7.62 x 51mm NATO
  *Official Name:* 7.62mm M969A1
  *Common Name:* FN FAL PARA

- *Cal.:* 7.62 x 51mm NATO
  *Official Name:* Mq 7.62mm M978
  *Common Name:* M1908 Mauser
    bolt action rifle

- *Cal.:* 7.62 x 51mm NATO
  *Common Name:* .30 M1 rifle con-
    verted to 7.62mm NATO

- *Cal.:* 7.62 x 51mm NATO
  *Common Name:* M14 rifle

*Remarks:* Colt, US. The Presidential Guard (antiterrorist force) is equipped with M16A2 rifles.

*Remarks:* Made under license by Fábrica de Itajuba. Ca. 120,000 FALs have been made in Brazil. Used by the Army and Marine Corps. Brazilian FALs are being exported to US for commercial sale by Springfield Armory, Inc. Fábrica de Itajuba also makes a .22LR semiautomatic training rifle that externally looks like the FAL, called the "Falbina," also called MD2. Previously the Brazilian armed forces employed HK .22 LR subcaliber kit with their FAL rifles.

*Remarks:* Fábrica de Itajuba, for the Army and Marine Corps.

*Remarks:* Both older German and more recent Itajuba origin. Some of these modified rifles were built on new shortened actions tailored to 7.62mm NATO cartridge. Held in reserve. These rifles have a G3 drum-type rear sight.

*Remarks:* US origin; converted to the NATO cartridge in Brazil. Uses FAL magazine. Available for export sale.

*Remarks:* US origin. A sample lot of 24 M14s were purchased FMS in 1976.

- *Cal.:* 7.62 x 63mm
  *Official Name:* 7.62mm M949
  *Common Name:* FN SAFN rifle

  *Remarks:* FN origin. Secondary standard for Marine and Navy forces.

- *Cal.:* 7.62 x 63mm
  *Common Name:* .30 M1 rifle

  *Remarks:* US origin. OBSOLETE.

- *Cal.:* 7 x 57mm Mauser
  *Common Name:* M1908 Mauser
  rifle

  *Remarks:* Some unconverted rifles still in the hands of paramilitary units. State police of Sao Paulo has Radom, Poland-made M1908s.

- *Cal.:* 7.62 x 51mm NATO
  *Common Name:* M1908 Mauser
  rifles

  *Remarks:* Fábrica de Itajuba conversion for some state military police forces.

**SHOTGUNS:**
- *Cal.:* 18.5 x 59mm
  *Common Name:* Ithaca M37 shot-
  gun

  *Remarks:* 50 delivered through MAP in 1964.

**MACHINE GUNS:**
- *Cal.:* 7.62 x 51mm NATO
  *Official Name:* 7.62mm M969
  (FAP)
  *Common Name:* FN FALO

  *Remarks:* FN and Fábrica de Itajuba. Used only by marines.

- *Cal.:* 7.62 x 51mm NATO
  *Official Name:* 7.62mm M971
  *Common Name:* FN MAG

  *Remarks:* FN origin. Used by Army, Air Force, and Marines. Models in service include MAG *Infanterie Standard* (60-20), T5 and T9 (nondisintegrating link), T12 (M13 link), MAG *Aviation* (60-30) Pod FN (right and left hand feed versions); MAG *Coaxial* (60-40), 60-413 CHAR M41 P.905), and model for Engesa Cascavel.

- *Cal.:* 7.62 x 51mm NATO
  *Common Name:* Uirapuru GPMG

  *Remarks:* Domestically developed by Mekanika Indústria e Comércio Ltda under contract from army's Instituto Militar de Engenharia. Production expected before 1990.

- *Cal.:* 7.62 x 63mm
  *Common Name:* .30 M1919A4
  LMG

  *Remarks:* MAP and FMS origin.

- *Cal.:* 7.62 x 51mm NATO
  *Common Name:* .30 Madsen
  LMG

  *Remarks:* Denmark. Modified from original 7 x 57mm Mauser by Fábrica de Itajuba. Some 7 x 57mm Mauser caliber Madsen LMGs are still available. Both are held in Army reserve.

- *Cal.:* 7 x 57mm
  *Common Name:* 7mm Hotchkiss
  LMG

  *Remarks:* France. Still held by some paramilitary units.

- *Cal.:* 12.7 x 99m
  *Common Name:* .50 M2 HB
  HMG

  *Remarks:* US origin. Updated US M55 trailer AA mount is made in Brazil. MAP delivered 100, 1950–60. Saco Defense Systems Division of Maremont Corporation delivered ca. 200 M2 HB HMGs in 1986 to AVIBRAS through NAPCO Inc.

- *Cal.:* 12.7 x 99m
  *Common Name:* .30 AN-M3 AC
  MG

  *Remarks:* FMS delivered 100 in 1983.

**AUTOMATIC CANNON:**
- *Cal.:* 20 x 102mm
  *Common Name:* M39A3RH auto-
  matic cannon

  *Remarks:* 2 purchased FMS in 1977.

- *Cal.:* 20 x 110mm
  *Common Name:* HS 404 automatic cannon

  *Remarks:* Oerlikon-Bührle. Mounted on a modified 2-gun version of the US M55 AA mount made in Brazil. Some unidentified 20mm guns being used on Navy patrol craft.

**GRENADE LAUNCHERS:**
• *Cal.:* 40 x 46mmSR                          *Remarks:* MAP and FMS before 1974. Total of 148 units.
  *Common Name:* M79 grenade
  launcher

### Brazilian Arms Industry

During the past decade, Brazilian arms makers have been active in the export market. The Companhia Brasiliera de Cartouchos, S.A. (CBC), Sao Paulo, has supplied Soviet M43-type 7.62 x 39mm cartridges to the government of Iraq in the course of the war with Iran. Other larger caliber artillery ammunition is reported to have been delivered to both Iran and Iraq.

## BRUNEI (Royal Sultanate)

Population (estimate in 1984): 0.218 million. Ground forces: regulars, ca. 3,500; Royal Brunei Police field force, 1,900. There is a Police Special Branch and Department of Security & Intelligence of about 250 people. There is also a 900-man British Gurkha Battalion stationed in Brunei at the Sultan's expense.

**HANDGUNS:**
• *Cal.:* 9 x 19mm Parabellum                  *Remarks:* Origin unknown.
  *Common Name:* FN Mle. 1935 GP
  pistol

**SUBMACHINE GUNS:**
• *Cal.:* 5.56 x 45mm                          *Remarks:* Colt, US. In excess of 240 Colt submachine guns have been ac-
  *Common Name:* XM177E2                       quired.
  (Model 639) submachine gun

**RIFLES:**
• *Cal.:* 5.56 x 45mm                          *Remarks:* Colt, US. Combined total of M16 rifles and carbines in excess of
  *Common Name:* M16A1 (Model                  3,800.
  613) rifle and M16A1 (Model
  653) carbine

• *Cal.:* 7.62 x 51mm NATO                     *Remarks:* Heckler & Koch (HK) GmbH, Germany.
  *Common Name:* Gewehr 3

**SHOTGUNS:**

**MACHINE GUNS:**
• *Cal.:* 5.56 x 45mm                          *Remarks:* Colt, US. Small lot.
  *Common Name:* M16A1 (Model
  611) heavy barrel automatic rifle

• *Cal.:* 5.56 x 45mm                          *Remarks:* HK.
  *Common Name:* HK21 LMG

• *Cal.:* 7.62 x 51mm NATO                     *Remarks:* Schweizerische Industrie Gesellschaft/Rheinfalls (SIG), Switzer-
  *Common Name:* SG710-3 GPMG                  land. In addition to ground guns, this weapon is also found on a twin mount
                                               on patrol boats.

• *Cal.:* 7.62 x 51mm NATO                     *Remarks:* FN origin. MAG *Infanterie Standard* (60-20), T6 (L7A2), and
  *Common Name:* FN MAG                        MAG *Coaxial* (60-40), Type P.806 (L7A2) Shorland.

**Brunei naval patrol craft use the 7.62 x 51mm SIG 710 machine gun on this unique soft recoil dual mount. (SIG)**

**AUTOMATIC CANNON:**
• *Cal.:* 20 x ???mm
  *Common Name:* Hispano Suiza
  automatic cannon

*Remarks:* Unknown origin. Mounted on coastal patrol craft.

**GRENADE LAUNCHERS:**
• *Cal.:* 40 x 46mmSR
  *Common Name:* M203 grenade
  launcher attached to M16A1

*Remarks:* Colt, US. In excess of 200 M203s in service.

## BULGARIA (People's Republic of)

Population (estimate in 1984): 8.97 million. Ground forces: regulars, ca. 105,000 (73,000 conscripts); reserves, ca. 150,000; paramilitary: *Narodna Militsiya* (people's militia or National Police Force), between 125,000 and 150,000; *Komitet Durzhavna Sigurnost* (KDS = State Security Committee), ca. 24,000; frontier guards, between 11,000 and 15,000.

**HANDGUNS:**
• *Cal.:* 9 x 18mm
  *Common Name:* Makarov pistol

*Remarks:* Previously of East Bloc origin; now being made in Bulgaria.

**SUBMACHINE GUNS:**
- *Cal.:* 7.62 x 25mm          *Remarks:* East Bloc origin.
  *Common Name:* PPSh41 SMG

**RIFLES:**
- *Cal.:* 7.62 x 39mm          *Remarks:* East Bloc origin.
  *Common Name:* SKS

- *Cal.:* 7.62 x 39mm          *Remarks:* Polish and domestic Bulgarian manufacture.
  *Common Name:* AK47 and AKM
  assault rifles

- *Cal.:* 7.62 x 54mmR         *Remarks:* Previously the Dragunov was acquired from other countries; now
  *Common Name:* SVD sniper rifle   being made in Bulgaria.

**SHOTGUNS:**

**MACHINE GUNS:**
- *Cal.:* 7.62 x 39mm          *Remarks:* East Bloc origin.
  *Common Name:* RPK LMG

- *Cal.:* 7.62 x 54mmR         *Remarks:* Soviet origin. Mounted on older Soviet tanks and APCs.
  *Common Name:* SGMT armor
  MG

- *Cal.:* 7.62 x 54mmR         *Remarks:* Soviet origin. Mounted on Soviet T62 tanks. PKM version is being
  *Common Name:* PKT armor MG    manufactured domestically in Bulgaria.

- *Cal.:* 7.62 x 54mmR         *Remarks:* Soviet origin. Mounted on older model tanks.
  *Common Name:* DT armor MG

- *Cal.:* 12.7 x 108mm         *Remarks:* Soviet origin. Ground and armored vehicle applications. Also
  *Common Name:* DShK38/46      used on minesweepers.
  HMG

**AUTOMATIC CANNON:**
- *Cal.:* 14.5 x 114mm         *Remarks:* Soviet origin. Ground and naval mounts in service.
  *Common Name:* KPV HMG

- *Cal.:* 23 x 152mmB          *Remarks:* Soviet origin. Versions used include self-propelled ZSU-23-4 AA
  *Common Name:* ZU23 automatic   system.
  cannon

- *Cal.:* 25 x 218mm           *Remarks:* Soviet origin. Mounted on S0-1 large patrol craft.
  *Common Name:* 2-M-3 or 2-M-8
  automatic cannon

## BURMA (Socialist Republic of the Union of)

Population (estimate in 1984): 36.19 million. Ground forces: regulars, ca. 163,000; reserves and home
guard, 73,000; paramilitary: People's Police Force, ca. 38,000; People's Militia, 35,000.

**HANDGUNS:**
- *Cal.:* 9 x 19mm             *Remarks:* FN origin. Post-1962 purchase. A variety of older model .32 and
  *Common Name:* FN Mle. 35 GP    .38 caliber British revolvers are still in service.
  pistol

**SUBMACHINE GUNS:**
- *Cal.:* 9 x 19mm Parabellum  *Remarks:* Locally designed and manufactured. FOM 1005-46-3-9-2.
  *Official Name:* BA 52

## RIFLES:*

- *Cal.:* 5.56 x 45mm
  *Common Name:* M16A1 rifle

- *Cal.:* 7.62 x 33mm
  *Common Name:* M1 and M2 carbines

- *Cal.:* 7.62 x 51mm NATO
  *Common Name:* AR-10 rifle

- *Cal.:* 7.62 x 51mm NATO
  *Common Name:* Gewehr 1

- *Cal.:* 7.62 x 51mm NATO
  *Common Name:* Gewehr 3

*Remarks:* Use of M16 rifles unconfirmed; deduced from FMS sale of 500 M203 grenade launchers.

*Remarks:* MAP, 1950–74, a total of 28,792 carbines were delivered.

*Remarks:* Manufactured by Artillerie Inrichtingen of the Netherlands; acquired through FN of Belgium.

*Remarks:* Surplus West German FALs.

*Remarks:* Heckler & Koch (HK), GmbH design. G3A2 is manufactured domestically by Burmese under a German government license. There is a domestically designed heavy barrel version of this weapon equipped with a new-style bipod.

## SHOTGUNS:

## MACHINE GUNS:

- *Cal.:* 7.62 x 51mm
  *Common Name:* MG3 GPMG

- *Cal.:* 7.62 x 51mm
  *Common Name:* FN MAG

- *Cal.:* 12.7 x 99mm
  *Common Name:* .50 M2 HB HMG

*Remarks:* Source unknown, although Hirtenberger of Austria supplied 100 MG3s in 1985. Possibly from Steyr-Daimler-Puch (SDP).

*Remarks:* FN origin. Models used include: MAG Infanterie Standard (60-20), T1 and MAG Aviation (60-30), Pod Marchetti, P.904.

*Remarks:* Some limited MAP deliveries of .50 M2HB HMGs before 1963.

## AUTOMATIC CANNON:

- *Cal.:* 20 x 110mmRB
  *Common Name:* US MK4 Oerlikon automatic cannon

*Remarks:* US origin. Mounted on ex-US corvettes transferred to Burma.

## GRENADE LAUNCHERS:

- *Cal.:* 40 x 46mmSR
  *Common Name:* M79 grenade launcher

- *Cal.:* 40 x 46mmSR
  *Common Name:* M203 grenade launcher

*Remarks:* MAP delivered 3,000 M79s before 1974. More recently the US provided ammunition for M79 and M203 launchers.

*Remarks:* FMS sale of 500 M203 grenade launchers in 1977.

## Opposition Forces

Burmese Communist Party: 12,000 regulars.
Kachin Independence Army: ca. 8,000.
Karen National Liberation Army: ca. 7,500.
Karenni Army: perhaps 600.
Kawthoolei Muslim Liberation Front: size unestimated.
Kayan New Land Party: perhaps 100.
Mon State Army: ca. 700.
Palaung State Liberation Army, Pa-O National Army, and Wa National Army: reported to have a few hundred fighters each.
Shan State Army: ca. 3,500.

---

*Burma is reported to have purchased 50,000 unspecified-type rifles from Israel in 1954 for a cost of US$700,000.

Shan United Army: ca. 4,000.
Shan United Revolutionary Army: ca. 9,000.

The Karen rebels use 9 x 19mm Uzi submachine guns, 7.62 x 33mm M1 and M2 Carbines, 5.56 x 45mmHK33 rifles, 5.56 x 45mm M16A1 rifles, 7.62 x 39mm PRC AK47s, 7.62 x 39mm PRC SKSs, 7.62 x 51mm NATO M60 GPMGs, and 40 x 46mmSR M79 grenade launchers. US M14s and M1918A2 BARs may also be used.


## BURUNDI (Republic of)

Population (estimate in 1984): 4.69 million. Ground forces: regulars, between 7,000 and 8,000; paramilitary (including gendarmerie), between 1,500 and 2,000. Former Belgian mandate; small arms tend to follow the Belgian pattern.

**HANDGUNS:**
- *Cal.:* 7.65 x 17mm Browning
  *Common Name:* FN Mle. 1910 pistol

  *Remarks:* FN origin.

- *Cal.:* 9 x 19mm Parabellum
  *Common Name:* FN Mle. 1935 GP pistol

  *Remarks:* FN origin.

**SUBMACHINE GUNS:**
- *Cal.:* 9 x 19mm Parabellum
  *Common Name:* Vigneron submachine gun

  *Remarks:* Société Anonyme Précision Liègeoise, Herstal.

- *Cal.:* 9 x 19mm Parabellum
  *Common Name:* MAT Mle. 49 submachine gun

  *Remarks:* Manufacture Nationale d'Armes de Tulle (MAT).

**RIFLES:**
- *Cal.:* 7.62 x 51mm NATO
  *Common Name:* FN FAL

  *Remarks:* Belgian origin.

- *Cal.:* 7.62 x 51mm NATO
  *Common Name: Gewehr 3A3*

  *Remarks:* Heckler & Koch (HK), GmbH design, but of Greek manufacture. Ca. 1,500 have been delivered by the Hellenic Arms Industry.

- *Cal.:* 7.5 x 54mm
  *Common Name:* MAS Mle. 36 bolt action rifle

  *Remarks:* Manufacture Nationale d'Armes de St. Etienne (MAS).

- *Cal.:* 7.5 x 54mm
  *Common Name:* MAS Mle. 49/56 rifle

  *Remarks:* MAS.

- *Cal.:* 7.92 x 57mm
  *Common Name:* Mauser 98K bolt action rifle

  *Remarks:* Source unknown.

**SHOTGUNS:**

**MACHINE GUNS:**
- *Cal.:* 7.62 x 51mm NATO
  *Common Name:* FN FALO

  *Remarks:* FN origin.

- *Cal.:* 7.62 x 51mm NATO
  *Common Name:* FN MAG

  *Remarks:* FN origin. MAG *Infanterie Standard* (60-20), T1.

- *Cal.:* 7.62 x 63mm
  *Common Name:* .30 M1919A4
  LMG

  *Remarks:* US origin.

- *Cal.:* 12.7 x 99mm
  *Common Name:* .50 M2 HB
  HMG

  *Remarks:* US and Belgian origin.

**AUTOMATIC CANNON:**
- *Cal.:* 14.5 x 114mm
  *Common Name:* KPV HMG

  *Remarks:* Soviet origin. About 15 quad 14.5mm AA systems in service.


# CAMEROONS

Population (estimate in 1984): 9.51 million. Ground forces: regulars, ca. 8,500; paramilitary (*Gendarmerie Nationale du Cameroum,* est. at 3,000, and the *Sûreté Nationale* [National Security Police], 2,500), for a total paramilitary strength of ca. 5,500. Small arms generally follow the French colonial pattern. The government of the Cameroons has established a small arms ammunition factory at Garua, where they load 9 x 19mm, 7.62 x 51mm, and 7.5 x 54mm ammunition using French components.


**HANDGUNS:**
- *Cal.:* 7.65 x 17mm Browning
  *Common Name:* Walther PP

  *Remarks:* Walther design. Manurhin of France origin.

- *Cal.:* 9 x 19mm Parabellum
  *Common Name:* FN Mle. 35 GP
  pistol

  *Remarks:* FN origin. In excess of 500 in the inventory.

- *Cal.:* 9 x 29mmR Magnum
  *Common Name:* .357 Manurhin
  MR73 revolvers

  *Remarks:* Manurhin of France origin.

**SUBMACHINE GUNS:**
- *Cal.:* 9 x 19mm
  *Common Name:* MAT Mle. 49
  submachine gun

  *Remarks:* Manufacture Nationale d'Armes de Tulle (MAT), France.

- *Cal.:* 9 x 19mm
  *Common Name:* HK MP5 series
  submachine gun

  *Remarks:* MAT.

**RIFLES:**
- *Cal.:* 5.56 x 45mm
  *Common Name:* M16A1 (Model
  613) rifle

  *Remarks:* Colt, US. Approx. 2,800.

- *Cal.:* 5.56 x 45mm
  *Common Name:* AUG

  *Remarks:* Austrian origin. Steyr-Daimler-Puch. Purchased in 1984 by the armed forces and in 1985 by the Ministry of the Interior.

- *Cal.:* 7.5 x 54mm
  *Common Name:* MAS Mle. 36
  bolt action rifle

  *Remarks:* Manufacture Nationale d'Armes de St. Etienne (MAS), France.

- *Cal.:* 7.5 x 54mm
  *Common Name:* MAS Mle. 49/56
  rifle

  *Remarks:* MAS.

- *Cal.:* 7.62 x 51mm NATO
  *Common Name:* FN FAL

  *Remarks:* Belgian origin. Adopted in 1968. Ca. 7,000 originally acquired.

**SHOTGUNS:**

**MACHINE GUNS:**

- *Cal.:* 7.5 x 54mm
  *Common Name:* MAC Mle. 24/29
  LMG

  *Remarks:* Manufacture Nationale d'Armes de Chatellerault (MAC), France.

- *Cal.:* 7.5 x 54mm
  *Common Name:* AAT 52 GPMG

  *Remarks:* Groupment Industriel des Armements Terrestres (GIAT), France.

- *Cal.:* 7.62 x 51mm NATO
  *Common Name:* HK21 LMG

  *Remarks:* Heckler & Koch (HK) GmbH, Germany. Very small quantities.

- *Cal.:* 7.62 x 51mm NATO
  *Common Name:* FN MAG

  *Remarks:* FN origin. MAG *Infanterie Standard* (60-20), T15 using nondisintegrating link belt, and MAG *Coaxial* (60-40), Cadillac Gage V-150 armored car.

- *Cal.:* 7.62 x 51mm NATO
  *Common Name:* M60 GPMG

  *Remarks:* Saco Defense Systems Division, Maremont. In 1986 the US Navy-assisted Cameroonian Navy obtained 60 additional M60 GPMGs through Military Service Group, Inc. There are two rail MK58 mounted M60s on each new Swift Ships patrol craft.

- *Cal.:* 7.62 x 63mm
  *Common Name:* .30 M1919A4
  LMG

  *Remarks:* US origin.

- *Cal.:* 7.7 x 56mmR
  *Common Name:* .303 Bren gun

  *Remarks:* UK origin.

- *Cal.:* 12.7 x 99mm
  *Common Name:* .50 M2 HB
  HMG

  *Remarks:* U.S. origin. Saco Defense Systems delivered guns 1983–84. In 1986 the US Navy-assisted Cameroonian Navy obtained 60 additional deck-mounted M2s from Military Service Group, Inc. Two MK26 MOD 15 (soft mount) M2s on each Swift Ships patrol craft. Two .50 M2HBs will also be mounted on each of three NAPCO Raider patrol boats purchased early 1987.

**AUTOMATIC CANNON:**

- *Cal.:* 14.5 x 114mm
  *Common Name:* KPV HMG

  *Remarks:* Chinese origin. Largest number of these Type 58 guns appear to be used on twin AA mount version.

- *Cal.:* 20 x 102mm
  *Common Name:* *Modele 621* automatic cannon

  *Remarks:* In 1982 the armed forces acquired four French Gazelle helicopters, each mounting a single GIAT M621 automatic cannon.

**GRENADE LAUNCHERS:**

- *Cal.:* 40 x 46mmSR
  *Common Name:* M203 grenade launcher attached to M16A1

  *Remarks:* Colt, US. Very small quantities.

### Arms Industry in the Cameroons

In 1982, the government of the Cameroons signed an accord with Fritz Werner of West Germany for the delivery of new small arms ammunition manufacturing equipment for the ammunition factory at Garoua in Manucam. In 1986 the government tendered for 9 x 19mm, 5.56 x 45mm, 7.5 x 54mm, 12.7 x 99mm, and 20 x 102mm ammunition.

## CANADA
Population (estimate in 1984): 25.14 million. Ground forces: regulars, ca. 30,000; reserves, 15,000 and 19,000; paramilitary, Royal Canadian Mounted Police *(Gendarmerie Royale Canadienne),* unknown. Two provinces have their own police organizations: Ontario Provincial Police, 5,500; and Quebec Police Force *(Force de Police du Quebec),* 4,850.

**HANDGUNS:**
- *Cal.:* 5.6 x 16mmR
  *Official Name:* Pistol, Caliber .22 Automatic Ruger MK 1
  *Common Name:* .22 LR Sturm Ruger MK 1 pistol

*Remarks:* NSN 1005-21-892-9766 w/ 172mm barrel. NSN 1005-21-884-8316 w/ 175mm barrel.

- *Cal.:* 5.6 x 16mmR
  *Official Name:* Pistol, Caliber .22 Automatic S&W M41
  *Common Name:* .22 LR Smith & Wesson Model 41 pistol

*Remarks:* NSN 1005-00-532-3025.

- *Cal.:* 5.6 x 16mmR
  *Official Name:* Pistol, Caliber .22 Automatic High Standard HD
  *Common Name:* .22 LR High Standard Model HD pistol

*Remarks:* NSN 1005-21-840-5516.

- *Cal.:* 5.6 x 16mmR
  *Official Name:* Revolver, Caliber .22 Colt Police Target
  *Common Name:* .22 LR Colt Police Target revolver

*Remarks:* NSN 1005-21-840-5514.

- *Cal.:* 5.6 x 16mmR
  *Official Name:* Revolver, Caliber .22 S&W M17
  *Common Name:* .22 LR Smith & Wesson Model 17

*Remarks:* NSN 1005-00-831-0234.

- *Cal.:* 7.65 x 17mm Browning
  *Official Name:* Pistol, Caliber .32 Automatic
  *Common Name:* Browning FN Model 1910 pistol

*Remarks:* Belgian origin. NSN 1005-21-894-7301 w/ equipment. NSN 1005-21-860-3669 w/o equipment.

- *Cal.:* 9 x 17mm Browning
  *Official Name:* Pistol, Caliber .380 Automatic, PPK
  *Common Name:* 9mm PPK

*Remarks:* NSN 1005-21-898-7788 w/o equipment.

- *Cal.:* 9 x 19mm NATO
  *Official Name:* Pistol, Browning, FN 9mm HP, No. 1, Mark 1; No. 1, Mark 1*; No. 2, Mark 1; and No. 2, Mark 1*.
  *Common Name:* FN Mle. 1935 GP pistol

*Remarks:* Made by John Inglis Company during World War II. Mark 1* NSN 1005-21-103-5221 w/o equipment; NSN 1005-21-103-5222 w/ equipment. FOM 1005-38-1-9-1. Production totalled ca. 152,000.

- *Cal.:* 9 x 19mm NATO
  *Official Name:* Pistol, 9mm, Automatic, P226
  *Common Name:* SIG P226

*Remarks:* NSN 1005-21-898-7803 w/o equipment.

- *Cal.:* 9 x 19mm NATO
  *Official Name:* Pistol, 9mm, Automatic, P1
  *Common Name:* Walther P1

  *Remarks:* NSN 1005-12-120-6128 w/o equipment.

- *Cal.:* 9 x 19mm NATO
  *Official Name:* Pistol, 9mm, Automatic Glock
  *Common Name:* Glock P80

  *Remarks:* Used by Royal Canadian Mounted Police (RCMP) SWAT teams.

- *Cal.:* 9 x 29mmR
  *Official Name:* Revolver, Caliber .38
  *Common Name:* .38 Smith & Wesson Model 49 Bodyguard revolver with 54mm barrel

  *Remarks:* US origin. NSN 1005-21-900-5798 w/o equipment.

- *Cal.:* 9 x 29mmR
  *Official Name:* Revolver, Caliber .38
  *Common Name:* .38 Smith & Wesson Model 10 revolver with 51mm barrel

  *Remarks:* US origin. NSN 1005-00-937-5840 w/o equipment. Square butt, fixed sights.

- *Cal.:* 9 x 29mmR
  *Official Name:* Revolver, Caliber .38
  *Common Name:* .38 Smith & Wesson Model 10 revolver with 102mm barrel

  *Remarks:* US origin. NSN 1005-00-937-5839 w/o equipment. Round butt, fixed sights.

- *Cal.:* 9 x 29mmR
  *Official Name:* Revolver, Caliber .38
  *Common Name:* .38 Smith & Wesson Model 10 revolver with 127mm barrel

  *Remarks:* US origin. NSN 1005-21-898-7046 w/o equipment. Also NSN 1005-21-894-7294. With butt swivel and grip adapter, NSN 1005-21-884-5654.

- *Cal.:* 9 x 29mmR
  *Official Name:* Revolver, Caliber .38
  *Common Name:* .38 Smith & Wesson Model 10 revolver with 153mm barrel

  *Remarks:* US origin. NSN 1005-21-884-6379 w/o equipment.

- *Cal.:* 9 x 29mmR
  *Official Name:* Revolver, Caliber .38
  *Common Name:* .38 Smith & Wesson Model 14 revolver with 152mm barrel

  *Remarks:* US origin. NSN 1005-00-830-2497 w/o equipment. K38 Masterpiece with adjustable sights.

- *Cal.:* 9 x 29mmR
  *Official Name:* Revolver, Caliber .38
  *Common Name:* .357 Smith & Wesson Model 27 revolver with 89mm barrel

  *Remarks:* US origin. NSN 1005-21-876-6965 w/o equipment.

- *Cal.:* 9 x 29mmR
  *Official Name:* Revolver, Caliber .38
  *Common Name:* .357 Smith & Wesson Model 27 revolver with 213mm barrel

  *Remarks:* US origin. NSN 1005-21-876-6966 w/o equipment.

- *Cal.:* 9 x 29mmR
  *Official Name:* Revolver, Caliber
  .38
  *Common Name:* .357 Smith &
  Wesson Model 28 revolver with
  152mm barrel

*Remarks:* US origin. NSN 1005-21-876-6967 w/o equipment.

- *Cal.:* 9 x 29mmR
  *Official Name:* Revolver, Caliber
  .38
  *Common Name:* .38 Smith &
  Wesson Model 36 revolver with
  76mm barrel

*Remarks:* US origin. NSN 1005-21-871-2046 w/o equipment.

- *Cal.:* 9 x 29mmR
  *Official Name:* Revolver, Caliber
  .38
  *Common Name:* .38 Smith &
  Wesson Model 38 revolver with
  162mm barrel

*Remarks:* US origin. NSN 1005-21-884-6390 w/o equipment.

- *Cal.:* 9 x 29mmR
  *Official Name:* Revolver, Caliber
  .38
  *Common Name:* .38 Ruger Model
  108S revolver with 127mm barrel

*Remarks:* US origin. NSN 1005-21-898-7047 w/o equipment.

- *Cal.:* 9 x 29mmR
  *Official Name:* Revolver, Caliber
  .38
  *Common Name:* .38 Ruger Service Six revolver with 127mm
  barrel

*Remarks:* US origin. NSN 1005-21-898-6313 w/o equipment.

**SUBMACHINE GUNS:**
- *Cal.:* 9 x 19mm NATO
  *Official Name:* Submachine gun,
  9mm, C1
  *Common Name:* Canadian evolu-
  tion of British L2 series

*Remarks:* Canadian Arsenals Ltd. built C1 1958–65. NSN 1005-21-102-8202
w/o equipment. NSN 1005-21-102-8253 w/ equipment. FOM 1005-38-3-9-1.

- *Cal.:* 9 x 19mm NATO
  *Common Name:* MP5A2, A3,
  and K

*Remarks:* Heckler & Koch (HK) GmbH origin. Used by several police forces
including the RCMP.

**RIFLES:** (The US FMS program sold 7,199 unspecified rifles to the Canadian military before 1974.)
- *Cal.:* 5.6 x 16mmR
  *Official Name:* Rifle, Caliber .22
  No. 8, MK 1
  *Common Name:* .22 LR No. 8,
  MK 1 training rifle

*Remarks:* UK origin. With long stock, w/o equipment NSN 1005-99-961-
9008.

- *Cal.:* 5.6 x 16mmR
  *Official Name:* Rifle, Caliber .22
  Match
  *Common Name:* .22 LR Anschutz
  Biathlon rifle

*Remarks:* German Anschutz G34 NSN 1005-12-165-2990 and Anschutz
Model 1403 NSN 1005-12-310-7069.

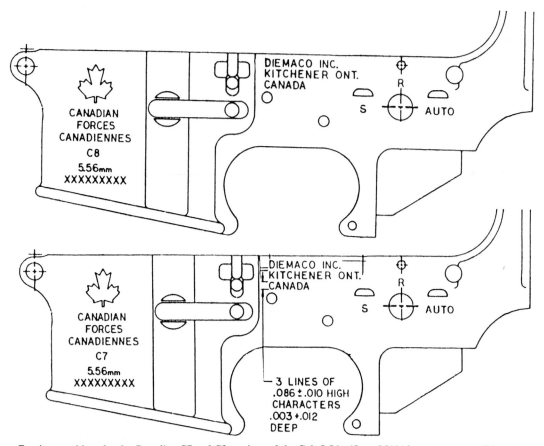

**Receiver markings for the Canadian C7 and C8 versions of the Colt 5.56 x 45mm M16A2-type weapons. (Diemaco)**

• *Cal.:* 5.6 x 16mmR
  *Official Name:* Rifle, Caliber .22
    Target Canadian No. 7, Mark 1
  *Common Name:* .22 LR No. 7,
    Mark 1

*Remarks:* With Bantam stock = NSN 1005-21-103-1331 (w/ equipment); 1005-21-103-1352, and 1005-21-103-1355 (w/o equipment). With long stock = NSN 1005-21-103-1332 (w/ equipment); 1005-21-103-1354 (w/o equipment). With short stock = NSN 1005-21-103-1203 (w/ equipment); 1005-21-103-1356 (w/ equipment). With normal stock = 1005-21-103-1366 (w/ equipment). See also 1005-21-109-2624. The RCMP version is NSN 1005-21-884-8329 for all stock variants.

• *Cal.:* 5.6 x 16mmR
  *Official Name:* Rifle, Caliber .22
    Model 572A rifle
  *Common Name:* .22 LR Reming-
    ton Model 572A Fieldmaster
    rifle

*Remarks:* US origin. NSN 1005-21-884-5654. Used by RCMP. Frame stamped R.C. M. P.

• *Cal.:* 5.56 x 45mm NATO
*Official Name:* Rifle, 5.56mm, automatic, C7
*Common Name:* M16A2 (Model 715) rifle

*Remarks:* The Canadian Armed Forces selected the M16A2 (with a 1 in 7 inch twist barrel) at the end of January 1984. Being made by Diemaco; see note below. 79,935 C7 weapons were ordered in 1984. Combined cost of C7s and C8s was set at C$107 million. The C7 will replace C1 rifles and C1 SMS. NSN 1005-21-898-7044. Blank firing attachment for the C7, C8, and C9 (LMG) is NSN 1005-21-900-9739, which replaces the OBSOLETE 1005-21-898-6319. The C7 bayonet is 1005-21-898-7795; the 30-shot nylon magazine is 1005-21-897-2944.

• *Cal.:* 5.56 x 45mm NATO
*Official Name:* Carbine 5.56mm, automatic, C8
*Common Name:* M16A2 carbine variant

*Remarks:* Being made by Diemaco. 1,565 C8-type weapons were ordered in 1984. Issue of this weapon will be limited to tank crews. NSN 1005-21-898-7045.

• *Cal.:* 5.56 x 45mm
*Official Name:* Rifle, 5.56mm
*Common Name:* AR-15 sporter

*Remarks:* US origin. Colt Firearms. NSN 1005-21-884-6156 w/o equipment.

• *Cal.:* 5.56 x 45mm
*Official Name:* Rifle, 5.56mm
*Common Name:* M16A1 carbine

*Remarks:* US origin. Colt Firearms. NSN 1005-21-884-6533 w/ equipment. Used by RCMP.

• *Cal.:* 7.62 x 51mm NATO
*Official Name:* Rifle, 7.62mm, C1A1
*Common Name:* FN FAL

*Remarks:* Canadian Arsenals, Ltd. made these rifles 1957–68. Control stores census reporting number is NSN 1005-21-842-4334. FOM 1005-38-2-7.62-2. Several variants of this rifle are in service:
C1 w/ long stock (292mm) = NSN 1005-21-150-5294.
C1 w/ normal stock (260mm) = NSN 1005-21-150-5295.
C1 w/ short stock (254mm) = NSN 1005-21-150-5296.
C1A1 w/ extra-long stock w/o equipment = NSN 1005-21-111-1994.
  w/ equipment = NSN 1005-21-111-2000.
C1A1 w/ long stock w/o equipment = NSN 1005-21-111-1995.
  w/ equipment = NSN 1005-21-111-2001.
C1A1 w/ normal stock w/o equipment = NSN 1005-21-111-1996.
  w/ equipment = NSN 1005-21-111-2002.
C1A1 w/ short stock w/o equipment = NSN 1005-21-111-1997.
  w/ equipment = NSN 1005-21-111-2003.
C1D w/ normal stock (Navy) = NSN 1005-21-103-7129.
C1A1D w/ normal stock (Navy) w/o equipment = NSN 1005-21-111-1998.
  w/ equipment = NSN 1005-21-111-2004.
  C1 rifles 01001 to 0L6000 have either short or long stocks; 1L0001 onward have normal butt. C1D series, used by the Royal Canadian Navy, have full automatic change lever assembly (1005-21-102-8349) and plunger, trigger assembly (1005-21-102-8357) permitting automatic fire. Army C1 rifles were semiautomatic only. Bayonets for C1 rifles and SMGs include Bayonet C1 w/ scabbard = NSN 1005-21-150-5293, OBSOLETE; and C1 (chrome-plated for ceremonial purposes) NSN 1005-21-879-0025.

• *Cal.:* 7.62 x 51mm NATO
*Official Name:* Rifle, 7.62mm Canadian No. 4, MK 1*
*Common Name:* .303 No. 4, MK 1* rifle converted

*Remarks:* NSN 1005-21-116-5345. Fitted with Lyman front sight 17A.

• *Cal.:* 7.7 x 56mmR
*Official Name:* Rifle, Caliber .303, Canadian No. 4, MK 1
*Common Name:* .303 No. 4, MK 1 rifle

*Remarks:* Fitted w/ bantam stock = NSN 1005-21-103-1367 (w/ equipment). Fitted w/ normal stock = NSN 1005-21-103-1368 (w/ equipment). Fitted w/ long stock = 1005-21-103-1369 (w/ equipment). Fitted w/ short stock = NSN 1005-21-103-1370 (w/ equipment). Chrome-plated ceremonial spike bayonet for No. 4 rifles is NSN 1005-21-800-3872.

- *Cal.:* 7.7 x 56mmR
  *Official Name:* Rifle, Caliber .303, Canadian No. 4, MK 1
  *Common Name:* .303 No. 4, MK 1 rifle

*Remarks:* With 2-groove barrel = NSN 1005-21-116-7867.

- *Cal.:* 7.7 x 56mmR
  *Official Name:* Rifle, Caliber .303, Canadian No. 4, MK 1, Survival Kit
  *Common Name:* .303 No. 4, MK 1 rifle

*Remarks:* Converted to a sporting rifle for air force survival kit. NSN 1005-21-808-9499.

- *Cal.:* 7.7 x 56mmR
  *Official Name:* Rifle, Caliber .303, Canadian No. 4, MK 1, Drill Purpose
  *Common Name:* .303 No. 4, MK 1 rifle

*Remarks:* NSN 1005-21-116-7861. Deactivated for training.

- *Cal.:* 7.7 x 56mmR
  *Official Name:* Rifle, Caliber .303, Canadian No. 4, MK 1*
  *Common Name:* .303 No. 4, MK 1* rifle

*Remarks:* Fitted w/ bantam stock = NSN 1005-21-103-1237 and 1005-21-103-1341; 1005-21-103-1362 and 1005-21-103-1371 (w/ equipment). Fitted w/ normal stock = NSN 1005-21-103-1329, 1005-21-103-1333, and 1005-21-103-1339; 1005-21-103-1360 and 1005-21-103-1373 (w/ equipment). Fitted w/ long stock = NSN 1005-21-103-1334, 1005-21-103-1340, 1005-21-103-1359, 1005-21-103-1361, and 1005-21-103-1372 (w/ equipment). Fitted w/ short stock = NSN 1005-21-103-1336 (w/ equipment).

The following rifles were DCRA rifles assigned NSNs. Bantam stock w/ equipment 1005-21-842-3818. Long stock 1005-21-842-3819. Short stock 1005-21-842-3820.

The following rifles were Bisley model rifles assigned NSNs. Bantam stock w/o equipment 1005-21-858-1811. Long stock 1005-21-858-1812. Short stock 1005-21-858-1814. Normal stock 1005-12-858-1814.

- *Cal.:* 7.7 x 56mmR
  *Official Name:* Rifle, Caliber .303, Canadian No. 4, MK 1*T
  *Common Name:* .303 No. 4, MK 1*T rifle

*Remarks:* Usually fitted w/ normal stock, but may be fitted w/ bantam, short, or long stock. NSN 1005-21-103-1227.

- *Cal.:* 7.62 x 51mm NATO
  *Official Name:* Rifle, 7.62mm, C3
  *Common Name:* Parker-Hale Model 1200TX

*Remarks:* UK origin. Adopted mid-1970s. NSN 1005-21-871-2317. C3 Sniper rifle is NSN 1005-21-871-2429 w/ equipment. C3 Competition rifle is NSN 1005-21-871-2430 w/ equipment.

- *Cal.:* 7.62 x 51mm NATO
  *Official Name:* Rifle, 7.62mm, Model Sportco 44D, Target
  *Common Name:* Sportco Model 44D single-shot target rifle

*Remarks:* Australian origin. NSN 1005-66-098-4683.

- *Cal.:* 7.62 x 51mm NATO
  *Common Name:* Gewehr 3, or HK91

*Remarks:* Origin unknown; model uncertain. In use by *Surete du Quebec* in 1984.

- *Cal.:* 7.62 x 51mm
  *Official Name:* Rifle, Caliber .308
  *Common Name:* Model 70 Carbine Cal. .308 Winchester

*Remarks:* US origin. Winchester-Olin. Has a 508mm barrel. NSN 1005-21-902-8226. Also Model G7069 is NSN 1005-21-876-6964.

- *Cal.:* 7.62 x 51mm NATO
  *Official Name:* Rifle, 7.62mm Biathlon Model 49

*Remarks:* NSN 1005-21-840-5856.

• *Cal.:* 7.62 x 51mm
*Official Name:* Rifle, Caliber .308 Winchester Ruger M-77
*Common Name:* Model 77 Ruger Rifle Cal. .308

*Remarks:* US origin. Sturm, Ruger Co. Has a 610mm barrel. NSN 1005-21-884-6538. Used by RCMP. Fitted with 25mm scope rings. Both blued and parkerized finishes.

• *Cal.:* 5.56 x 45mm
*Official Name:* Rifle, 5.56mm, Model 700 Remington
*Common Name:* Model 700 Remington Varmint Special rifle

*Remarks:* US origin. Remington Arms Co. NSN 1005-21-884-6369.

• *Cal.:* 5.56 x 48.7
*Official Name:* Rifle, Caliber .22-250 Remington
*Common Name:* Model 77 Ruger Rifle Cal. .22-250

*Remarks:* US origin. Sturm, Ruger Co. Has a 610mm barrel NSN 1005-21-898-6325. Used by RCMP.

• *Cal.:* 5.56 x 48.7
*Official Name:* Rifle, Caliber .22-250 Remington
*Common Name:* Model 70 Winchester Rifle Cal. .22-250

*Remarks:* US origin. Winchester-Olin. Has a 559mm barrel. NSN 1005-21-898-7043. There is also a G7015 model used by the RCMP that has a special nonreflective stock (NSN 1005-21-884-5663).

• *Cal.:* 7.62 x 51mm
*Official Name:* Rifle, Caliber .308 Model 70
*Common Name:* Winchester Model 70 Rifle Cal. .308

*Remarks:* US origin. Winchester-Olin. Several models are used by RCMP. These include Model 70 Featherweight with 559mm barrel (NSN 1005-21-884-5660); Model 70 Featherweight with 559mm barrel and K44 telescope (NSN 1005-21-884-5661); Model 70A with 559mm barrel (NSN 1005-21-884-5662). Featherweight models have a special RCMP stock.

• *Cal.:* 7.62 x 63mm
*Official Name:* Rifle, Caliber .30-06. Model 70
*Common Name:* Winchester Model 70 Rifle Cal. .30-06

*Remarks:* US origin. Winchester-Olin. Has a 521mm barrel. NSN 1005-21-898-7042.

• *Cal.:* 7.62 x 63mm
*Official Name:* Rifle, Caliber .30-06 Model 721
*Common Name:* Model 721 Rifle Cal. .30-06

*Remarks:* NSN 1005-21-876-5484.

• *Cal.:* 6.85 x 63.6mm
*Official Name:* Rifle, Caliber .270 BSA
*Common Name:* BSA Model NC48G Cal. .270

*Remarks:* UK origin. NSN 1005-21-889-3562.

• *Cal.:* 7.62 x 51.8mm
*Official Name:* Rifle, Caliber .30-30 Winchester, Model 94
*Common Name:* Winchester Model 94 .30-30 lever action rifle

*Remarks:* US origin. Winchester-Olin. Has a 508mm barrel. NSN 1005-21-864-6848. Used by RCMP and other police organizations.

• *Cal.:* 7.62 x 51.8mm
*Official Name:* Rifle/Shotgun Caliber .30-30/20 gage Model 24V
*Common Name:* .30-30/ 20 gage Model 24V Savage over-under combination gun

*Remarks:* US origin. Savage Industries. NSN 1005-21-884-6522.

## SHOTGUNS:

- *Cal.:* 18.5 x 59mm
  *Official Name:* Shotgun, 12 gage, Riot type
  *Common Name:* 12 gage Winchester Model 1200 pump shotgun

- *Cal.:* 18.5 x 59mm
  *Official Name:* Shotgun, 12 gage
  *Common Name:* 12 gage Winchester Model 12 pump shotgun

- *Cal.:* 18.5 x 59mm
  *Official Name:* Shotgun, 12 gage
  *Common Name:* 12 gage Winchester Model 2400 shotgun

- *Cal.:* 18.5 x 59mm
  *Official Name:* Shotgun, 12 gage
  *Common Name:* 12 gage Winchester Model 2200 shotgun

- *Cal.:* 18.5 x 59mm
  *Official Name:* Shotgun, 12 gage
  *Common Name:* 12 gage Remington Model 1100 pump shotgun

- *Cal.:* 18.5 x 59mm
  *Official Name:* Shotgun, 12 gage
  *Common Name:* 12 gage Remington Model 1100 pump shotgun

- *Cal.:* 18.5 x 59mm
  *Official Name:* Shotgun, 12 gage
  *Common Name:* 12 gage Remington Model 870 pump shotgun

- *Cal.:* 18.5 x 59mm
  *Official Name:* Shotgun, 12 gage
  *Common Name:* 12 gage Remington Model 870 pump shotgun

- *Cal.:* 18.5 x 59mm
  *Official Name:* Shotgun, 12 gage
  *Common Name:* 12 gage Remington Model 870 pump shotgun

- *Cal.:* 18.5 x 59mm
  *Official Name:* Shotgun, 12 gage, Model 870-4800.
  *Common Name:* 12 gage Remington Model 870 pump shotgun

- *Cal.:* 18.5 x 59mm
  *Official Name:* Shotgun, 12 gage, Model 870-5032.
  *Common Name:* 12 gage Remington Model 870 pump shotgun

- *Cal.:* 18.5 x 59mm
  *Common Name:* 12 gage Mossberg Model 500 shotgun

*Remarks:* US origin. Winchester-Olin. Has a 457mm barrel. Folding stock model w/ sling swivels is NSN 1005-21-903-8262; wood stock model is NSN 1005-21-877-5856.

*Remarks:* US origin. Winchester-Olin. Has a 750mm barrel. NSN 1005-21-897-0696 w/o equipment.

*Remarks:* US origin. Winchester-Olin. Has a 711mm barrel. NSN 1005-21-885-9091 w/o equipment. Used by RCMP.

*Remarks:* US origin. Winchester-Olin. Has a 762mm barrel. NSN 1005-21-885-9092 w/o equipment. Used by RCMP.

*Remarks:* US origin. Remington Arms Co. Has a 660mm barrel. NSN 1005-21-895-9070 w/o equipment.

*Remarks:* US origin. Remington Arms Co. Has a 406mm barrel. Used w/ Remote Control Handling Equipment, Tracked, MK 6. NSN 1005-21-902-8209. The 558mm barrel version is NSN 1005-21-872-8157.

*Remarks:* US origin. Remington Arms Co. Has a 508mm barrel and wood stock. NSN 1005-21-884-6388 w/o equipment. RCMP use a version w/ NSN 1005-21-884-5657. There is also a 711mm barrel model used by RCMP and other police organizations = NSN 1005-21-884-5658.

*Remarks:* US origin. Remington Arms Co. Has a 508mm barrel, parkerized finish, and folding stock. NSN 1005-21-895-9492 w/o equipment. M870P-4796 with 457mm barrel; folding stock is 1005-21-884-6384. M870P-4798 w/ 508mm barrel, blue finish, and folding stock is 1005-21-884-6386.

*Remarks:* US origin. Remington Arms Co. Has a 406mm barrel. NSN 1005-21-902-8227 w/ equipment.

*Remarks:* US origin. Remington Arms Co. Has a 508mm barrel. NSN 1005-21-884-5668 w/o equipment.

*Remarks:* US origin. Remington Arms Co. Has a 457mm barrel and wood stock. NSN 1005-21-884-6378 w/o equipment. M870P-5030 w/ 508mm barrel is NSN 1005-21-884-6380.

*Remarks:* US origin. Quebec Provincial prison guards and police forces. Acquired 1982–85.

- *Cal.:* 18.5 x 59mm
  *Official Name:* Shotgun, 12 gage
  *Common Name:* 12 gage Lion double barrel, over-under

*Remarks:* NSN 1005-21-900-5805 w/o equipment. NSN 1005-21-808-9656 w/ equipment.

- *Cal.:* 18.5 x 59mm
  *Official Name:* Shotgun, 12 gage
  *Common Name:* 12 gage Cooey Model 84, single-shot shotgun

*Remarks:* NSN 1005-21-898-7785.

**MACHINE GUNS:**
- *Cal.:* 5.56 x 45mm NATO
  *Official Name:* Machine gun, 5.56mm, Light, C9
  *Common Name:* FN Minimi SAW

*Remarks:* FN origin. 6,750 C9-type weapons were ordered in 1984. There are both FN guns (NSN 1005-13-112-5092) and Canadian models (NSN 1005-21-897-0690). This squad automatic weapon will replace C2 series weapons.

- *Cal.:* 7.62 x 51mm NATO
  *Official Name:* Machine gun, 7.62mm, C2A1, Drill Purpose
  *Common Name:* Canadian version of FN FALO

*Remarks:* Canadian Arsenals Ltd. Deactivated for training. NSN 1005-21-112-3482.

- *Cal.:* 7.62 x 51mm NATO
  *Official Name:* Machine gun, 7.62mm, C2A1
  *Common Name:* Canadian version of FN FALO

*Remarks:* Canadian Arsenals Ltd. FOM 1005-38-2-7.62-3. NSN 1005-21-111-1999 w/o equipment; NSN 1005-21-111-2005 w/ equipment.

- *Cal.:* 7.62 x 51mm NATO
  *Official Name:* Machine gun, 7.62mm, C1
  *Common Name:* Canadian adaptation of US of .30 M1919A4 chambered to fire 7.62mm NATO cartridge

*Remarks:* US origin. FMS delivered 1,000 guns in 1979. The Canadians still list M1919A4 (flexible) in their stock listing: NSN 1005-00-714-2393 and NSN 1005-00-672-1643. The M1919A4 (fixed) is NSN 1005-00-714-2392. The C1 is NSN 1005-21-872-5569 w/ equipment. The C1 (flexible) is NSN 1005-21-841-6505 and 1005-21-854-2793; C1 (fixed) is NSN 1005-21-842-4583; C1A1 (flexible) is NSN 1005-21-844-3358; C1A1 (flexible w/ equipment) is NSN 1005-21-842-4583. M2 tripod for this series is NSN 1005-00-650-7052.

C1 MG mount for the Lynx command and reconnaissance vehicle is NSN 1005-21-845-7184. C1 MG coaxial mount for the Centurion tank is NSN 1005-21-852-1634. C1 No. 5, MK 1 mount for the Centurion tank is NSN 1005-99-812-6162. C1 No. 8, MK 1 for the Ferret Scout Car is NSN 1005-99-812-6173.

- *Cal.:* 7.62 x 51mm NATO
  *Official Name:* Machine gun, 7.62mm, C1 and C5
  *Common Name:* Canadian adaptation of US of .30 M1919A4 chambered to fire 7.62mm NATO cartridge

*Remarks:* US origin. The C5 series is a product improvement of the C1 series. The C5A1 (fixed) is NSN 1005-21-875-9061 w/o equipment; C1 (fixed w/ equipment) is NSN 1005-21-875-9064; C1 (flexible w/o equipment) is NSN 1005-21-875-9062; C5A1 (flexible w/ equipment) is NSN 1005-21-875-9063.

- *Cal.:* 7.62 x 63mm
  *Official Name:* Machine, Gun, Caliber .30 M1919A4 Drill Purpose
  *Common Name:* .30 M1919A4 LMG

*Remarks:* NSN 1005-21-107-3164. Deactivated for training.

- *Cal.:* 7.62 x 63mm
  *Official Name:* Machine Gun, Caliber .30, M37
  *Common Name:* .30 M37 AMG

*Remarks:* US origin. NSN 1005-00-716-2946 with sights.

• *Cal.:* 7.62 x 51mm NATO
  *Official Name:* Machine gun, 7.62mm, C6
  *Common Name:* FN MAG coaxial and flexible

*Remarks:* FN origin. Models in service include MAG *Coaxial* (60-40), T3, Leopard CADA C1 Mod. P.929, and US-type M240. The coaxial model is NSN 1005-21-902-8207 w/ equipment. The flexible model is NSN 1005-13-112-5223 w/o equipment and NSN 1005-21-902-8231 w/ equipment. NSN 1005-12-310-1668 designated a German-made mount for the C6. The L7A1 tripod mount for the C6 is NSN 1005-99-960-4473; the cradle assembly is 1005-99-960-4474.

Blank firing attachments: Used w/ Leopard Tank C1, is NSN 1005-13-010-0613.

• *Cal.:* 7.62 x 51mm NATO
  *Official Name:* Machine Gun, 7.62mm, GAU2B/A (M134)
  *Common Name:* M134 high rate of fire Minigun

*Remarks:* US origin. FMS delivered 6 in 1975. NSN 1005-00-903-0751.

• *Cal.:* 12.7 x 99mm
  *Official Name:* Machine Gun, Caliber .50, L6A1
  *Common Name:* Ranging MG for 105mm tank gun

*Remarks:* UK origin. NSN 1005-21-840-5647 and 1005-99-960-6173.

• *Cal.:* 12.7 x 99mm
  *Official Name:* Machine gun, .50, M2 HMG
  *Common Name:* .50 M2 HB HMG

*Remarks:* US origin. Models used include M2 HB TT (NSN 1005-00-13-6944); M2 HB Flexible (NSN 1005-00-322-9715); M2 HB Flexible Vehicular (NSN 1005-00-726-5636); M2 HB Fixed Vehicular (NSN 1005-00-726-5637); mechanical trigger-fired M2 flexible M2 for Grizzly LAV (NSN 1005-21-880-2405); solenoid-fired M2 flexible M2 for Grizzly LAV (NSN 1005-21-879-2958); M2 fixed used on Lynx command and reconnaissance vehicle (NSN 1005-21-880-0459). The Canadians employ tripod mounts M2 (NSN 1005-00-322-9718) and M3 (NSN 1005-00-322-9716) and M31C pedestal gun mounts (NSN 1005-00-317-2442 and 1005-00-706-9767). They also use M63 AA mount (NSN 1005-00-714-2396 and 1005-00-673-3246), Mount M49A1 (NSN 1005-00-732-3017), and swing-a-way mount for .50 machine gun on M113A1 w/ TOW (NSN 1005-00-836-7286). M2HB blank firing attachment is NSN 1005-21-900-5819 (PN 7975784-1) and 1005-21-884-8322 (PN 7975525).

• *Cal.:* 12.7 x 99mm
  *Official Name:* Machine gun, .50, AN-M2
  *Common Name:* .50 AN-M2 ACMG

*Remarks:* US origin. NSN 1005-00-726-5644.

• *Cal.:* 12.7 x 99mm
  *Official Name:* Machine gun, .50, AN-M3
  *Common Name:* .50 AN-M3 ACMG

*Remarks:* US origin. NSN 1005-00-726-5650.

• *Cal.:* 12.7 x 99mm
  *Official Name:* Machine gun, .50, XM218
  *Common Name:* XM218

*Remarks:* US origin. XM218 is variant of AN-M2 for use on CH-135 helicopter. NSN 1005-00-165-4561.

**MISCELLANEOUS MACHINE GUN MOUNTS:**
Mount Machine Gun Model 106A1 for .50 Cal. MG NSN 1005-00-704-6650.
Mount Machine Gun Model for Cal. .30 and .50 Cal. MGs NSN 1005-00-706-8880.
Mount, Machine Gun, Ball Assembly for Machine Gun on ARV Taurus NSN 1005-12-7502.
Mount, Machine Gun, Ball Assembly for Machine Gun on ARV Taurus NSN 1005-12-7503.
Mount, Kit, Door, Machine Gun. 7.62mm, Left Hand for CH-135 Helicopter NSN 1005-21-871-2044 (C72E50076-1).
Mount, Kit, Door, Machine Gun. 7.62mm, Right Hand for CH-135 Helicopter NSN 1005-21-871-2045 (C72E50076-2).

**AUTOMATIC CANNON:**

• *Cal.:* 20 x 102mm
  *Common Name:* M39A2LH & RH; M39A3RH & LH automatic cannon

*Remarks:* US origin. FMS delivered 4 M39A2s in 1978 and 4 M39A3s in 1984. M39A2 RH is NSN 1005-00-566-0044; M39A2 LH is NSN 1005-00-566-0045; M39A3 RH is NSN 1005-00-930-7786; M39A3 LH is NSN 1005-00-930-7787. A3 models are used in CF-5 fighter.

• *Cal.:* 20 x 102mm
  *Official Name:* Gun System, 20mm
  *Common Name:* 20mm automatic cannon with cannon M61A1 (NSN 1005-00-056-6753)

*Remarks:* This gun system is used on CF-18 fighter aircraft. NSN 1005-21-890-7022.

**GRENADE LAUNCHERS:**

• *Cal.:* 18mm
  *Official Name:* Launcher, Grenade, Shotgun
  *Common Name:* Grenade launcher attachment

*Remarks:* Attachment for shotguns. Used by RCMP. Used with Type 518CS and 118CN tear gas grenades. Launched with Type 455 cartridge. NSN 1005-21-894-7610.

• *Cal.:* 20mm
  *Official Name:* Launcher, Grenade
  *Common Name:* Grenade launcher

*Remarks:* Attachment for C1 rifles. NSN 1005-99-960-0263.

## Canadian Small Arms Manufacture

In 1976 the Canadian government decided to close Canadian Arsenals, Ltd., a Crown Corporation. This act left their armed forces without a domestic source of spare parts, in-service repair, or production. In March 1976 the government entered into a 10-year contract with a private sector manufacturer, Diemaco, Inc., a subsidiary of Devtek Corporation, in Kitchener, Ontario, for the manufacture of spare parts and in-service maintenance of current small arms. Diemaco manufactures the newly adopted C7 rifle and C8 carbine (Canadian versions of the US Army/US Marine Corps M16A2 rifle), at a new production facility for that project, which started production in 1985. Some assemblies of these new rifles will be obtained from Colt Industries in the United States for the initial guns assembled by Diemaco. Government schedules established the following delivery dates: Preproduction C7/C8s delivered in August 1985. Production in Canada started in December 1985. Canadian troops stationed in Germany to receive first rifles and carbines in autumn of 1986. Troops in Canada to begin receiving guns in spring of 1987. First 100 percent Canadian-manufactured guns were delivered in September 1987. Reequipping of the Canadian forces to be completed by 1989. Production to continue until July 1992 for reserve and replacement stocks.

## CAPE VERDE (Republic of)

Population (estimate in 1984): 0.350 million. Ground forces: regulars, 2,000; reserves, unknown. The People's Revolutionary Armed Forces (FARP) are divided into an army, navy and air force. Paramilitary forces include the *Policia da Ordem Publicá,* the *Departmento de Seguranca Nacional,* and the *Milicia Popular.* The latter militia organization has about 650 people.

**HANDGUNS:**

**SUBMACHINE GUNS:**

• *Cal.:* 9 x 19mm Parabellum
  *Common Name:* M948 submachine gun

*Remarks:* Portuguese origin. Made at Fabrica Militar de Braco de Prata (FMBP) in Lisbon, Portugal.

**RIFLES:**
- *Cal.:* 7.62 x 39mm          *Remarks:* East Bloc origin.
  *Common Name:* SKS carbine

- *Cal.:* 7.62 x 39mm          *Remarks:* East Bloc origin.
  *Common Name:* AK47 and AKM
  assault rifles

**SHOTGUNS:**

**MACHINE GUNS:**
- *Cal.:* 7.62 x 39mm          *Remarks:* East Bloc origin.
  *Common Name:* RPD LMG

- *Cal.:* 7.62 x 39mm          *Remarks:* East Bloc origin.
  *Common Name:* RPK LMG

- *Cal.:* 7.62 x 51mm NATO     *Remarks:* Origin unknown.
  *Common Name:* MG3 GPMG

- *Cal.:* 7.62 x 54mmR         *Remarks:* East Bloc origin.
  *Common Name:* PK GPMG

- *Cal.:* 7.62 x 54mmR         *Remarks:* East Bloc origin.
  *Common Name:* SG43 series of
  MG

- *Cal.:* 7.62 x 54mmR         *Remarks:* East Bloc origin.
  *Common Name:* RP46 and DP
  series of MG

- *Cal.:* 12.7 x 108mm         *Remarks:* East Bloc origin.
  *Common Name:* DShK HMG

**AUTOMATIC CANNON:**
- *Cal.:* 14.5 x 114mm         *Remarks:* Origin unknown.
  *Common Name:* Soviet-type KPV


# CENTRAL AFRICAN REPUBLIC

Population (estimate in 1984): 2.58 million. Ground forces: regulars, ca. 2,000; reserves, none; *Gendarmerie Centrafricaine,* ca. 1,500. Small arms generally follow the French colonial pattern.

**HANDGUNS:**
- *Cal.:* 9 x 29mmR            *Remarks:* French origin.
  *Common Name:* .38 Special
  Manurhin M73 revolver

- *Cal.:* 9 x 17mm Browning    *Remarks:* Manurhin-made Walther design.
  *Common Name:* PP automatic
  pistol

- *Cal.:* 7.65 x 20mm          *Remarks:* Manufacture Nationale d'Armes de St. Etienne (MAS).
  *Common Name:* MAS Mle. 1935S
  pistol

- *Cal.:* 9 x 19mm Parabellum  *Remarks:* Manufacture Nationale d'Armes de Chatellerault (MAC).
  *Common Name:* MAC Mle. 1950
  pistol

## SUBMACHINE GUNS:
- *Cal.:* 9 x 19mm Parabellum
  *Common Name:* MAT 49 submachine gun

  *Remarks:* Manufacture Nationale d'Armes de Tulle (MAT).

- *Cal.:* 9 x 19mm Parabellum
  *Common Name:* Uzi submachine gun

  *Remarks:* Israeli Military Industries (IMI), Israel.

## RIFLES:
- *Cal.:* 5.56 x 45mm
  *Common Name:* SG540 rifle

  *Remarks:* Manurhin-made SIG rifle. Ca. 200 rifles in the inventory.

- *Cal.:* 5.56 x 45mm
  *Common Name:* M16A1 rifle

  *Remarks:* Reported, but not confirmed. Not as the result of direct sale from Colt.

- *Cal.:* 7.62 x 39mm
  *Common Name:* AK47 and AKM assault rifles

  *Remarks:* East Bloc origin.

- *Cal.:* 7.5 x 54mm
  *Common Name:* MAS Mle. 36 bolt action rifle

  *Remarks:* MAS.

- *Cal.:* 7.5 x 54mm
  *Common Name:* MAS Mle. 49/56 rifle

  *Remarks:* MAS.

## SHOTGUNS:

## MACHINE GUNS:
- *Cal.:* 5.56 x 45mm
  *Common Name:* M16A1 heavy barrel automatic rifle

  *Remarks:* Reported, but not confirmed.

- *Cal.:* 7.62 x 39mm
  *Common Name:* RPD LMG

  *Remarks:* East Bloc origin.

- *Cal.:* 7.62 x 39mm
  *Common Name:* RPK LMG

  *Remarks:* East Bloc origin.

- *Cal.:* 7.62 x 54mmR
  *Common Name:* RP46 company and DP machine guns

  *Remarks:* East Bloc origin.

- *Cal.:* 7.62 x 54mmR
  *Common Name:* SGMT armor MG

  *Remarks:* Soviet origin. Mounted on older Soviet tanks.

- *Cal.:* 7.5 x 54mm
  *Common Name:* MAC Mle. 24/29 LMG

  *Remarks:* MAC.

- *Cal.:* 7.5 x 54mm
  *Common Name:* AAT52 GPMG

  *Remarks:* MAT, Groupment Industriel des Armements Terrestres (GIAT), France.

- *Cal.:* 12.7 x 108mm
  *Common Name:* DShK38/46 HMG

  *Remarks:* Soviet origin. Ground and armored vehicle applications.

## AUTOMATIC CANNON:

## CHAD (Republic of)

Population (estimate in 1984): 5.12 million. Ground forces: regulars, *Forces Armees Nationales Tchadiennes* (FANT), between 14,000 and 15,000; paramilitary, *Gendarmerie Nationale Tchadienne,* between 5,000 and 6,000. This nation's armed forces employ a wide variety of small caliber weapons, but French patterns predominate. Antigovernment forces consist of the *Forces Armee Populaire* (Goukouni), which is allied with Libya. The FAP has an effective strength of about 10,000 and has been supported by as many as 7,000 Libyans. The FAN (Forces Armees du Nord—Habre) has about 7,000 men. The FAT (Forces Armees du Tchad) has about 5,000. The French support the government forces with about 1,400 troops. Zaire and some other African states have supported the Chadian armed forces with men and materiel. The FAN was led by H. Habre, the current president. It attacked the FAP led by the former president Goukouni and won. The latter is now living in Libyan exile. FAN became the FANT.

### HANDGUNS:
- *Cal.:* 7.65 x 17mm Browning  
  *Common Name:* PP automatic pistol

  *Remarks:* Manurhin-licensed production of the Walther PP.

- *Cal.:* 7.65 x 20mm  
  *Common Name:* MAS Mle. 1935S pistol

  *Remarks:* Manufacture Nationale d'Armes de St. Etienne (MAS).

- *Cal.:* 7.62 x 25mm  
  *Common Name:* vz.52 pistol

  *Remarks:* Czechoslovakian origin.

- *Cal.:* 9 x 19mm Parabellum  
  *Common Name:* P38/P1

  *Remarks:* Walther, West Germany.

- *Cal.:* 9 x 19mm Parabellum  
  *Common Name:* MAC Mle. 1950 pistol

  *Remarks:* Manufacture Nationale d'Armes de Chatellerault (MAC).

- *Cal.:* 9 x 19mm Parabellum  
  *Common Name:* MAB PA-15S

  *Remarks:* Manufacture d'Armes de Bayonne (MAB).

- *Cal.:* 9 x 19mm Parabellum  
  *Common Name:* Tokagypt pistol

  *Remarks:* Femaru es Szerszamgepyar (FEG), Hungary.

- *Cal.:* 9 x 19mm Parabellum  
  *Common Name:* FN Mle. 1935 GP pistol

  *Remarks:* Belgian origin.

- *Cal.:* 9 x 29mmR  
  *Common Name:* .38 Special Manurhin MR73 revolver

  *Remarks:* French origin.

- *Cal.:* 11.43 x 23mm  
  *Common Name:* .45 M1911A1 pistol

  *Remarks:* US origin.

- *Cal.:* 11.43 x 23mm  
  *Common Name:* .45 M1917 revolver

  *Remarks:* Colt, US.

### SUBMACHINE GUNS:
- *Cal.:* 9 x 19mm Parabellum  
  *Common Name:* MP38 and MP40

  *Remarks:* World War II Germany.

- *Cal.:* 9 x 19mm NATO  
  *Common Name:* MAT49 submachine gun

  *Remarks:* Manufacture Nationale d'Armes de Tulle (MAT).

- *Cal.:* 9 x 19mm Parabellum
  *Common Name:* Mark II Sten gun

  *Remarks:* UK origin.

- *Cal.:* 9 x 19mm Parabellum
  *Common Name:* M38/49 submachine gun (Model 4)

  *Remarks:* Beretta, Italy.

- *Cal.:* 9 x 19mm Parabellum
  *Common Name:* M12 submachine
  gun

  *Remarks:* Beretta.

- *Cal.:* 9 x 19mm Parabellum
  *Common Name:* Uzi submachine
  gun

  *Remarks:* Israeli Military Industries (IMI), Israel.

- *Cal.:* 9 x 19mm Parabellum
  *Common Name:* vz.23 and vz.25
  submachine guns

  *Remarks:* Czechoslovakian origin.

**RIFLES:**
- *Cal.:* 6.5 x 52.5
  *Common Name:* M 1891 and M
  1891/38  Mannlicher-Carcano
  rifles

  *Remarks:* Italian origin. OBSOLETE.

- *Cal.:* 7.62 x 39mm
  *Common Name:* SKS carbine

  *Remarks:* East Bloc origin.

- *Cal.:* 7.62 x 39mm
  *Common Name:* AK47 and AKM
  assault rifles

  *Remarks:* East Block origin. These Kalashnikov-type weapons include the Yugoslav Model 64A (Mod 70), Chinese Type 56, Romanian, and the East German MPiKMS72.

- *Cal.:* 7.62 x 39mm
  *Common Name:* vz.58 assault rifle

  *Remarks:* Czechoslovakian origin.

- *Cal.:* 7.5 x 54mm
  *Common Name:* MAS Mle. 36
  bolt action rifle

  *Remarks:* French origin. MAS.

- *Cal.:* 7.5 x 54mm
  *Common Name:* MAS Mle. 49/56
  rifle

  *Remarks:* French origin. MAS.

- *Cal.:* 7.62 x 51mm NATO
  *Common Name:* SG542 rifle

  *Remarks:* Manurhin-made Schweizerische Industrie Gesellschaft/Rheinfalls (SIG) rifle. Reported to be used by French Foreign Legion troops assigned to Chad.

- *Cal.:* 7.62 x 51mm NATO
  *Common Name:* FN FAL

  *Remarks:* FN origin.

- *Cal.:* 7.62 x 51mm NATO
  *Common Name:* Modelo 58 assault rifle

  *Remarks:* Centro de Estudios Tecnics y Materiales Especiales (CETME), Spain.

- *Cal.:* 7.62 x 51mm NATO
  *Common Name:* Gewehr 3

  *Remarks:* Heckler & Koch (HK) GmbH, Germany.

- *Cal.:* 7.62 x 51mm NATO
  *Common Name:* M14A1 rifle

  *Remarks:* US origin. MAP delivered 2,003 M14A1s in 1983.

**SHOTGUNS:**

**MACHINE GUNS:**
- *Cal.:* 7.62 x 39mm
  *Common Name:* RPD LMG

  *Remarks:* East Bloc origin.

- *Cal.:* 7.62 x 39mm
  *Common Name:* RPK LMG

  *Remarks:* East Bloc origin.

- *Cal.:* 7.62 x 39mm
  *Common Name:* Mod. 70B1 LMG

  *Remarks:* Yugoslavian origin.

- *Cal.:* 7.62 x 39mm
  *Common Name:* vz.52 LMG

  *Remarks:* Czechoslovakian Bloc origin.

- *Cal.:* 7.62 x 51mm NATO
  *Common Name:* FN FALO

  *Remarks:* FN origin?

- *Cal.:* 7.62 x 51mm NATO
  *Common Name:* FN MAG

  *Remarks:* FN origin?

- *Cal.:* 7.62 x 51mm NATO
  *Common Name:* AAT52 GPMG

  *Remarks:* MAT, Groupment Industriel des Armements Terrestres (GIAT).

- *Cal.:* 7.5 x 54mm
  *Common Name:* Mle. 24/29 LMG

  *Remarks:* MAC.

- *Cal.:* 7.62 x 54mmR
  *Common Name:* SGM series of MGs

  *Remarks:* Soviet origin. Older SG43s included.

- *Cal.:* 7.62 x 54mmR
  *Common Name:* RP46 and DP series of MGs

  *Remarks:* Soviet origin.

- *Cal.:* 7.62 x 54mmR
  *Common Name:* PK GPMG

  *Remarks:* Soviet origin.

- *Cal.:* 7.62 x 63mm
  *Common Name:* .30 M1919A4 LMG

  *Remarks:* US guns, probably via France.

- *Cal.:* 7.7 x 56mmR
  *Common Name:* .303 Bren guns

  *Remarks:* UK origin.

- *Cal.:* 7.92 x 57mm
  *Common Name:* vz.53 GPMG

  *Remarks:* Czechoslovakian origin.

- *Cal.:* 8.5 x 59mmRB
  *Common Name:* M37 Breda machine gun

  *Remarks:* Italian origin.

- *Cal.:* 12.7 x 99mm
  *Common Name:* .50 M2 HB HMG

  *Remarks:* US origin. MAP delivered 21 M2 HBs in 1981.

- *Cal.:* 12.7 x 108mm
  *Common Name:* DShK38/46 HMG

  *Remarks:* Soviet origin. Some older DShK38 HMGs may still be in service.

**AUTOMATIC CANNON:**

- *Cal.:* 14.5 x 114mm
  *Common Name:* KPV HMG

  *Remarks:* Soviet origin. Four AA versions—ZGU-1, ZPU-1, ZPU-2, and ZPU-4—in service. Many are mounted on French 420VPC and Toyota trucks.

- *Cal.:* 20 x 139mm
  *Common Name:* M621 20mm automatic cannon

  *Remarks:* Used by FANT in their Panhard AMLs and Cascavel EE9s and by the French *Force d'Action Rapide* on their ACMAT VLRA light trucks.

- *Cal.:* 23 x 152mmB
  *Common Name:* ZU23 automatic cannon

  *Remarks:* Soviet origin. The twin gun version has been seen in news photos.

**GRENADE LAUNCHERS:**

- *Cal.:* 30 x 29mm
  *Common Name:* AGS17 grenade launcher

  *Remarks:* Soviet origin. Reported, but not confirmed.

- *Cal.:* 40 x 46mmSR
  *Common Name:* M79 grenade launcher

  *Remarks:* US origin. MAP delivered 100 M79s in 1983.

## CHILE (Republic of)

Population (estimate in 1984): 11.65 million. Ground forces: regulars, ca. 53,000 (30,000 conscripts); reserves, ca. 240,000; paramilitary forces, 27,000 *Carabineros* (this organization controls all police forces); *Infanteria de Marina* (Marines), ca. 5,000.

**HANDGUNS:**

- *Cal.:* 8 x 18mm
  *Common Name:* Roth-Steyr pistol

  *Remarks:* OBSOLETE.

- *Cal.:* 9 x 22.7mm
  *Common Name:* Steyr-Hahn 1912 pistol

  *Remarks:* OBSOLETE, but still in limited service.

- *Cal.:* 9 x 19mm Parabellum
  *Common Name:* FN Mle. 1935 GP pistol

  *Remarks:* Belgian origin.

- *Cal.:* 9 x 19mm Parabellum
  *Common Name:* P38

  *Remarks:* Walther, West Germany.

- *Cal.:* 9 x 19mm Parabellum
  *Common Name:* Beretta Model 92 pistol

  *Remarks:* Beretta, Italy, and the state arms industry (Fabricaciones Militares (FAMAE), Santiago. FAMAE makes the M92 type with the frame-mounted safety.

- *Cal.:* 9 x 19mm Parabellum
  *Common Name:* SIG-Sauer pistol

  *Remarks:* Schweizerische Industrie Gesellschaft/Rheinfalls (SIG), Sauer, West Germany. Of P220 series, but exact model is unknown.

- *Cal.:* 9 x 23mm
  *Common Name:* .38 Colt Super pistol

  *Remarks:* Received from Cuba during the Allende years. Carried by the *Grupo Amigos del Presidente.*

- *Cal.:* 9 x 29mmR
  *Common Name:* .38 Special FAMAE revolver

  *Remarks:* Made by the state arms industry (FAMAE). These revolvers are used by army and air force officers.

- *Cal.:* 11.43 x 23mm
  *Common Name:* .45 M1911A1 pistol

  *Remarks:* US origin. MAP delivered 10 in 1964. Another 175 unspecified pistols were delivered before 1964.

**SUBMACHINE GUNS:**

- *Cal.:* 9 x 19mm Parabellum
  *Common Name:* Domestic design

  *Remarks:* Made by the state arms industry (FAMAE).

- *Cal.:* 9 x 19mm Parabellum
  *Common Name:* Uzi submachine gun

  *Remarks:* Origin unknown.

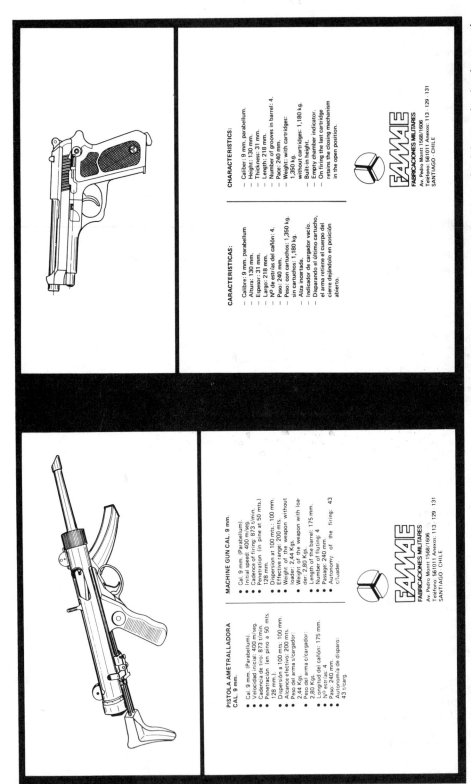

PISTOLA AMETRALLADORA CAL. 9 mm.

- Cal. 9 mm. (Parabellum).
- Velocidad inicial: 400 m/seg.
- Cadencia de tiro: 873 t/min.
- Penetración (en pino a 50 mts.) 128 mm.).
- Dispersión a 100 mts: 100 mm.
- Alcance efectivo: 200 mts.
- Peso del arma s/cargador: 2,44 Kgs.
- Peso del arma c/cargador: 2,80 Kgs.
- Longitud del cañón: 175 mm.
- N° estrías: 4
- Paso: 240 mm.
- Autonomía de disparo: 43 t/carg.

MACHINE GUN CAL. 9 mm.

- Cal. 9 mm. (Parabellum).
- Initial speed: 400 m/seg.
- Cadence of firing: 873 t/min.
- Penetration (in pine at 50 mts.) 128 mm.).
- Dispersion at 100 mts.: 100 mm.
- Effective range: 200 mts.
- Weight of the weapon without loader: 2,44 Kgs.
- Weight of the weapon with loader: 2,80 Kgs.
- Length of the barrel: 175 mm.
- Number of fluting: 4
- Passage: 240 mm.
- Autonomy of the firing: 43 c/loader.

FAMAE
FABRICACIONES MILITARES
Av. Pedro Montt 1568/1606
Teléfono: 561011 Anexos: 113 · 129 · 131
SANTIAGO · CHILE

CARACTERISTICAS:

- Calibre: 9 mm. parabellum
- Altura: 130 mm.
- Espesor: 31 mm.
- Largo: 218 mm.
- N° de estrías del cañón: 4.
- Paso: 240 mm.
- Peso: con cartuchos: 1,350 kg. sin cartuchos: 1,180 kg.
- Alza incertada.
- Indicador de cargador vacío.
- Disparando el último cartucho, el arma retiene el cuerpo del cierre dejándolo en posición abierto.

CHARACTERISTICS:

- Caliber: 9 mm. parabellum.
- Height: 130 mm.
- Thickness: 31 mm.
- Length: 218 mm.
- Number of grooves in barrel: 4.
- Pace: 240 mm.
- Weight: with cartridges: 1,350 kg. without cartridges: 1,180 kg.
- Built-in height.
- Empty chamber indicator.
- On firing the last cartridge retains the closing mechanism in the open position.

FAMAE
FABRICACIONES MILITARES
Av. Pedro Montt 1568/1606
Teléfono: 561011 Anexos: 113 · 129 · 131
SANTIAGO · CHILE

Two current products of the Chilean FAMAE factory in Santiago. *Left,* Pistola Ametralladora (rapid fire pistol); *right,* Pistola Semi-Automatica (semi automatic pistol). (FAMAE)

- *Cal.:* 9 x 19mm Parabellum
  *Common Name:* HK MP5 submachine gun

  *Remarks:* Origin unknown.

- *Cal.:* 9 x 19mm Parabellum
  *Common Name:* M12S submachine gun

  *Remarks:* Beretta, Italy.

- *Cal.:* 9 x 19mm Parabellum
  *Common Name:* Madsen Model 1953 submachine gun

  *Remarks:* Danish origin. OBSOLETE.

- *Cal.:* 9 x 19mm Parabellum
  *Common Name:* Star Z45 submachine gun

  *Remarks:* Star-Bonifacio Echeverria, Spain.

- *Cal.:* 9 x 19mm Parabellum
  *Common Name:* MAC-10 submachine gun

  *Remarks:* Military Armaments Corp., US.

- *Cal.:* 9 x 19mm Parabellum
  *Common Name:* L34A1 silenced submachine gun

  *Remarks:* UK origin.

- *Cal.:* 9 x 19mm Parabellum
  *Common Name:* MP-40 Schmeisser

  *Remarks:* World War II Germany. Received from Cuba during the Allende years.

- *Cal.:* 9 x 19mm Parabellum
  *Common Name:* vz.25 submachine gun

  *Remarks:* Czechoslovakian origin. Received from Cuba during the Allende years.

- *Cal.:* 11.43 x 23mm
  *Common Name:* .45 M3 submachine gun

  *Remarks:* US origin. MAP delivered 37 in 1964; 70 unspecified SMGs were delivered before 1964. FMS sold 80 unspecified SMGs before 1963.

**RIFLES:**

- *Cal.:* 5.56 x 45mm
  *Common Name:* M16A1 (Model 613) rifle

  *Remarks:* Colt Industries, ca. 5,000 purchased 1976–77. FMS delivered 470 in 1974. The *Infanteria de Marina* appears to have nearly all of these weapons.

- *Cal.:* 5.56 x 45mm
  *Common Name:* Galil rifle

  *Remarks:* Israeli Military Industries (IMI), Israel. The air force has 8,000 Galils.

- *Cal.:* 7.62 x 51mm NATO
  *Common Name:* SIG 540

  *Remarks:* Schweizerische Industrie Gesellschaft/Rheinfalls, Switzerland (SIG) design made under license in Chile since 1986.

- *Cal.:* 5.56 x 45mm
  *Common Name:* HK33 rifle

  *Remarks:* Heckler & Koch (HK) GmbH. Ca. 500 in 1975.

- *Cal.:* 7.62 x 33mm
  *Common Name:* .30 M1 and M2 carbines

  *Remarks:* US origin. MAP delivered 977 carbines before 1974; FMS sold 1,900 M2s in 1971.

- *Cal.:* 7.62 x 39mm
  *Common Name:* AK47 and AKM assault rifles

  *Remarks:* Acquired via Cuba during the Allende years by *Grupo Amigos del Presidente* (GAP).

- *Cal.:* 7.62 x 51mm NATO
  *Common Name:* FN FAL

  *Remarks:* Chilean Model 50-00. Adopted in 1960.

- *Cal.:* 7.62 x 51mm NATO
  *Common Name:* SG510-4 rifle

  *Remarks:* SIG. Government acquired ca. 14,500 in the early 1960s from SIG. Reported being manufactured by FAMAE in Chile.

- *Cal.:* 7.62 x 63mm
  *Common Name:* .30 M1 rifle

  *Remarks:* US origin. MAP delivered 1,191 M1s before 1976. An additional 1,048 unspecified type rifles were delivered by MAP before 1964.

**Receiver markings on an FN-manufactured 7.62 x 51mm FAL acquired by Chile. (FN)**

Saddle sabbard for the Chilean 7.62 x 51mm SIG-4 assault rifle. (SIG)

- *Cal.:* 7.62 x 63mm
  *Common Name:* .30 M1C sniper
  rifle

- *Cal.:* 7 x 57mm
  *Common Name:* Mauser M95 and
  M1904 bolt action rifle

- *Cal.:* 7 x 57mm
  *Common Name:* Steyr Model 1912
  rifles

*Remarks:* US origin. MAP delivered 45 sniper M1s before 1976.

*Remarks:* Ludwig Loewe, Berlin. Some of these rifles and carbines have been converted to 7.62 x 51mm (NATO) by FAMAE. Used for ceremonial purposes only.

*Remarks:* Used for ceremonial purposes only.

**SHOTGUNS:**
- *Cal.:* 18.5 x 59mm
  *Common Name:* 12 gage Winchester Model 1200 shotgun

- *Cal.:* 18.5 x 59mm
  *Common Name:* 12 gage Winchester Model 12 shotgun

- *Cal.:* 18.5 x 59mm
  *Common Name:* 12 gage Ithaca M37 shotgun

- *Cal.:* 18.5 x 59mm
  *Common Name:* 12 gage Remington shotgun

*Remarks:* US origin. FMS delivered 200 M1200s in 1971. NSN 1005-00-921-5483.

*Remarks:* US origin. MAP delivered 240 M12s in 1966. NSN 1005-00-677-9150.

*Remarks:* US origin. MAP delivered 40 M37s in 1966. NSN 1005-00-973-2138.

*Remarks:* US origin.

**MACHINE GUNS:**
- *Cal.:* 7.62 x 51mm NATO
  *Common Name:* FN FALO

- *Cal.:* 7.62 x 51mm NATO
  *Common Name:* MG42/59

- *Cal.:* 7.62 x 51mm NATO
  *Common Name:* M60 GPMG

- *Cal.:* 7.62 x 63mm
  *Common Name:* .30 M1918A2 BAR

- *Cal.:* 7.62 x 63mm
  *Common Name:* .30 M1919A4 LMG

- *Cal.:* 12.7 x 99mm
  *Common Name:* .50 M2 HB HMG

*Remarks:* Chilean Model 50-42.

*Remarks:* Rheinmetall, West Germany. Were acquired in early 1960s.

*Remarks:* US origin. Used by naval forces.

*Remarks:* US origin. MAP delivered 139 before 1976.

*Remarks:* US origin. MAP delivered 28 before 1975. An additional unspecified 183 .30 caliber LMGs were delivered before 1975.

*Remarks:* US origin. MAP delivered 107 M2 HBs before 1975. Used as a ground gun, in the M55 quad AA mount, and on a twin liquid cooled antiaircraft mount. The latter mount is a local design, and the AN-M2s have a special small-diameter cooling jacket through which the coolant is circulated by a 12-volt battery-operated pump.

**AUTOMATIC CANNON:**
- *Cal.:* 20 x 139mm
  *Common Name:* HS820 automatic cannon. (KAD-B13-3 type HS820 L85; HS820-SL7⁰A3-3)

- *Cal.:* 20 x 139mm
  *Common Name:* Rheinmetall Rh202

*Remarks:* SOGEO — Sociedad General de Comercio, S.A. — of Chile uses this gun on the Oerlikon GAI-CO1 single AA mount.

*Remarks:* Rheinmetall origin. Are mounted on other Chilean naval craft.

Twin liquid-cooled .50 (12.7 x 99mm) Browning antiaircraft system developed locally in Chile. (Gander)

# CHINA (People's Republic of)

Population (estimate in 1984): 1,035 million. Ground forces: regulars, ca. 3,760,000; reserves, armed militia ca. 7,000,000; unarmed civil militia, 75,000,000–100,000,000.

## HANDGUNS:

- *Cal.:* 7.62 x 25mm
  *Official Name:* Type 54
  *Common Name:* TT33 Tokarev pistol; also called Type 51

  *Remarks:* State factories. An export model of this pistol was called the Model 20. FOM 1005-5-1-7.62-1. Several variants of this pistol are offered for export sale by China North Industries Corporation, Beijing (NORINCO).

- *Cal.:* 9 x 18mm
  *Official Name:* Type 59
  *Common Name:* Makarov pistol

  *Remarks:* State factories. Export sales by NORINCO.

- *Cal.:* 7.62 x 17mm
  *Official Name:* Type 64

  *Remarks:* State factories. Domestic silenced pistol. Called a survival pistol by PRC officials.

- *Cal.:* 7.62 x 16mm
  *Official Name:* Type 64 pistol
  *Common Name:* Domestic design of blowback pistol

  *Remarks:* NORINCO.

- *Cal.:* 7.65 x 17mm
  *Official Name:* Type 67

  *Remarks:* State factories. Domestically created silenced pistol.

- *Cal.:* 7.62 x 16mm
  *Official Name:* Type 77 self-defense pistol
  *Common Name:* Domestic design of blowback pistol

  *Remarks:* NORINCO. This pocket-size pistol has a trigger guard, which can be squeezed to cock the pistol.

## SUBMACHINE GUNS:

- *Cal.:* 7.62 x 25mm
  *Official Name:* Type 43
  *Common Name:* PPS43 submachine gun

  *Remarks:* State factories. FOM 1005-5-3-7.62-2.

- *Cal.:* 7.62 x 25mm
  *Official Name:* Type 50
  *Common Name:* PPSh41 submachine gun

  *Remarks:* State factories. FOM 1005-5-3-7.62-1.

- *Cal.:* 7.62 x 25mm
  *Official Name:* Type 64
  *Common Name:* Type 64 micro-sound submachine gun

  *Remarks:* State factories. Domestic silenced submachine gun. FOM 1005-5-3-7.62-3. Fires Type 64 subsonic cartridge or regular Type 51 cartridge. Weighs 3.4kg; is 843mm overall with stock extended; 635mm with stock folded. Has a 30-shot box magazine.

- *Cal.:* 7.62 x 25mm
  *Official Name:* Type 85
  *Common Name:* Type 85 micro-sound submachine gun

  *Remarks:* State factories. Domestic silenced submachine gun. A variant of Type 64 but having a receiver/operating mechanism similar to Type 85 SMG. Weighs 2.5kg; is 869mm overall with stock extended; 631mm with stock folded. Has a 30-shot box magazine.

- *Cal.:* 7.62 x 25mm
  *Official Name:* Type 79 light submachine gun
  *Common Name:* Domestic design

  *Remarks:* NORINCO. This pistol caliber submachine gun has external styling similar to the Soviet Kalashnikov assault rifles. It weighs 1.9kg; is 740mm overall with stock extended; 470mm with stock folded. Has a 20-shot box magazine.

- *Cal.:* 7.62 x 25mm
  *Official Name:* Type 80 automatic pistol
  *Common Name:* Domestic design

  *Remarks:* NORINCO. A classic-type machine pistol with an external configuration similar to the Mauser C96 broom handle pistol. It weighs 1.1kg; has a removable shoulder stock; w/ stock attached the weapon is 300mm overall. Magazine capacity is believed to be 20 cartridges.

| FACTORY | COUNTRY |
|---|---|
| [symbol] 1954 г. | USSR |
| [symbol] 56 -1 | PRC |
| [symbol] | PRC |
| M-7 & M-22 | PRC |
| [symbol] 58 | N. KOREA |
| [symbol] | BULGARIA |
| [symbol] 1962 | POLAND |
| [symbol] [symbol] ② | RUMANIA |
| [symbol] | E. GERMANY |
| ⅃Ӿ 1951 г. | USSR |
| [symbols] | PRC |
| ○ △ ★ | PRC |
| [symbols] ③ ⑦ | PRC |
| [symbols] ③⑦ [symbol] | PRC |
| [symbol] | E. GERMANY |
| [symbol] | PRC |
| [symbol] 216 | PRC |
| [symbol] ☆ | USSR |
| [symbol] [symbol] | USSR |
| She [symbol] | CZECH |
| ② [symbols] 45 43 | HUNGARY |
| ☆ VN | N. VIETNAM |
| N R | YUGOSLAVIA |
| ① ⑪ ⑬ Z/14 | CZECH |
| [symbol] 63 | E. GERMANY |
| [symbol] [symbol] | N. KOREA |
| [symbols] | PRC |

Typical receiver markings found on East Bloc small arms. Variations will be encountered. (US Army)

- *Cal.:* 7.62 x 25mm
  *Official Name:* Type 85 light submachine gun
  *Common Name:* Type 85 light submachine gun

*Remarks:* State factories. Domestic submachine gun. A variant of Type 79 but has a simplified tubular receiver/operating mechanism. Weighs 1.9kg; is 628mm overall with stock extended; 444mm with stock folded. Has a 30-shot box magazine.

**RIFLES:**
- *Cal.:* 7.62 x 54mmR
  *Official Name:* Type 53 carbine
  *Common Name:* Soviet M1944 bolt action carbine

*Remarks:* State factories. FOM 1005-5-2-7.62-1.

- *Cal.:* 7.62 x 39mm
  *Official Name:* Type 56 semiautomatic rifle
  *Common Name:* SKS carbine

*Remarks:* State factories. Export model called the M21.

- *Cal.:* 7.62 x 39mm
  *Official Name:* Type 56 submachine gun
  *Common Name:* AK47 assault rifle

*Remarks:* State factories. The Type 56-1 assault rifle is the folding stock model. The PRC also has manufactured a wood stock version and a folding stock version of AKM; FOM 1005-5-2-7.62-4. Those weapons are also designated Type 56 submachine gun. An export version of AK47 is called M22; Type 56-1 is FOM 1005-5-2-7.62-3.

- *Cal.:* 7.62 x 39mm
  *Official Name:* Type 56-2 submachine gun
  *Common Name:* AKM-type assault rifle

*Remarks:* NORINCO. This most recent version of Type 56 has a side-folding metal stock of domestic design. Can be identified by reddish plastic cheekpiece on the folding stock assembly.

**Two Chinese 7.62 x 25mm silenced ("micro sound") submachine guns; Type 85 *(left)* and Type 64 *(right)*. (Gander)**

- *Cal.:* 7.62 x 39mm
  *Official Name:* Type 63
  *Common Name:* Domestic design; also called Type 68

  *Remarks:* State factories. FOM 1005-5-2-7.62-5. This design combines features of the SKS self-loading rifle, the AK assault rifle, and some unique features. This selective fire rifle has a 20-shot magazine with a follower that operates a bolt hold-open feature that is missing from the Type 56 (Kalashninov) assault rifles. Both wood and synthetic stocks were produced for this weapon. A reported 6,000,000 were manufactured. Reportedly these are used for the People's Militia and will be replaced by the Type 81.

- *Cal.:* 7.62 x 39mm
  *Official Name:* Type 68
  *Common Name:* Improved Type 63

  *Remarks:* State factories. Sheet metal receiver only?

- *Cal.:* 7.62 x 39mm
  *Official Name:* Type 73
  *Common Name:* Further improved version of Type 63/68

  *Remarks:* State factories. Design work credited to Tang Wenlie.

- *Cal.:* 7.62 x 39mm
  *Official Name:* Type 81
  *Common Name:* Domestic design

  *Remarks:* State factories. Version of Type 68/73. Has a three-shot burst capability; comes in both fixed stock (Type 81) and folding stock (Type 81-1) versions.

- *Cal.:* 7.62 x 39mm
  *Official Name:* Type 84 semiautomatic rifle
  *Common Name:* SKS carbine, w/ standard AK magazine

  *Remarks:* State factories.

- *Cal.:* 7.62 x 54mmR
  *Official Name:* Type 85 semiautomatic sniping rifle
  *Common Name:* Copy of Soviet SVD

  *Remarks:* Offered for export sale by NORINCO.

**SHOTGUNS:**

**MACHINE GUNS:**
- *Cal.:* 7.62 x 39mm
  *Official Name:* Type 74 LMG
  *Common Name:* Domestic design of RPK type

  *Remarks:* NORINCO. This squad automatic weapon is a PRC design similar to the Soviet RPK. It is built around an AKM receiver, but has a new Chinese-designed gas system, buttstock assembly, and 101-shot drum magazine. Type 74 weighs 6.5kg; is 1,070mm overall.

- *Cal.:* 7.62 x 39mm
  *Official Name:* Type 81 LMG
  *Common Name:* Domestic design

  *Remarks:* NORINCO. This squad automatic weapon is a variant of Type 81 rifle. It is built around a Type 81 receiver. It uses a 75-shot drum magazine. Type 81 weighs 5.15kg; is 1,004mm overall.

- *Cal.:* 7.62 x 54mmR
  *Official Name:* Type 53
  *Common Name:* Soviet DPM

  *Remarks:* State factories. FOM 1005-5-4-7.62-3.

- *Cal.:* 7.62 x 39mm
  *Official Name:* Type 56
  *Common Name:* Soviet RPD; third model of Soviet design

  *Remarks:* State factories. FOM 1005-5-4-7.62-1.

- *Cal.:* 7.62 x 39mm
  *Official Name:* Type 56-1
  *Common Name:* Soviet RPD; fifth model of Soviet design

  *Remarks:* State factories. FOM 1005-5-4-7.62-1.

- *Cal.:* 7.62 x 54mmR
  *Official Name:* Type 57
  *Common Name:* Soviet SGM

  *Remarks:* State factories. FOM 1005-5-4-7.62-6. The SGM is exported as the M18. The SG43 is FOM 1005-5-4-7.62-5 and is called Type 53 HMG.

China's new lightweight 12.7 x 108mm Type 77 antiaircraft machine gun. (NORINCO)

- *Cal.:* 7.62 x 54mmR
  *Official Name:* Type 58
  *Common Name:* Soviet RP46

  *Remarks:* State factories. FOM 1005-5-4-7.62-2.

- *Cal.:* 7.62 x 54mmR
  *Official Name:* Type 59T
  *Common Name:* Soviet SGMT

  *Remarks:* State factories. Offered for export sale by NORINCO.

- *Cal.:* 7.62 x 54mmR
  *Official Name:* Type 67
  *Common Name:* Domestic design

  *Remarks:* State factories. FOM 1005-5-4-7.62-8.

- *Cal.:* 7.62 x 54mmR
  *Official Name:* Type 67-1
  *Common Name:* Domestic design

  *Remarks:* NORINCO. Product-improved Type 67 weighs 11.5kg and measures 1345mm overall.

- *Cal.:* 7.62 x 54mmR
  *Official Name:* Type 67-2
  *Common Name:* Domestic design

  *Remarks:* NORINCO. Product-improved Type 67-1 GPMG weighs 10kg and is 1250mm overall. New Type 67-1 tripod weighs 5.6kg vs 13.5kg.

- *Cal.:* 7.62 x 54mmR
  *Official Name:* Type 67-2C
  *Common Name:* Domestic design

  *Remarks:* NORINCO. Variant of Type 67-2.

*This page and facing page:* **The new Chinese 35mm W87 automatic grenade launching machine gun. (NORINCO** courtesy of *Soldier of Fortune*)

*Top:* **Firing the Type W87 with 6-round box magazine from the tripod. Right-side view clearly shows the optical sight unit.** *Bottom:* **Firing the Type W87 35mm automatic grenade launcher with 9-round drum from the prone position off its integral bipod. Weight in this configuration is an amazing 26.5 pounds, empty.**

• *Cal.:* 12.7 x 108mm
*Official Name:* Type 54
*Common Name:* Soviet DShKM HMG

*Remarks:* State factories. Export model called M17.

• *Cal.:* 12.7 x 108mm
*Official Name:* Type 59
*Common Name:* Soviet DShKM HMG

*Remarks:* State factories. Has slightly larger interior diameter in the muzzle brake to allow the use of special sabotted AP ammunition.

• *Cal.:* 12.7 x 108mm
*Official Name:* Type 77 AA MG
*Common Name:* Domestic design

*Remarks:* NORINCO. Much modified Degtyarev-type mechanism. Weight of empty gun is 56.1kg. Has an overall length of 2150mm and cyclic rate of fire of 650–750 shots per minute.

• *Cal.:* 12.7 x 108mm
*Official Name:* Type 85 AMG
*Common Name:* Domestic design

*Remarks:* NORINCO. Vehicle version of Type 77. Slightly lighter than Type 77.

Firing the Type W87 with 9-round drum from its tripod, which weighs only 17.7 pounds. Note flared muzzle device with four cross-cuts on top. Recoil impulse of the W87 is reputed to be no greater than that of the Goryunov medium machine gun.

**AUTOMATIC CANNON:**

- *Cal.:* 14.5 x 114mm
  *Official Name:* Type 56
  *Common Name:* Soviet KPV HMG

*Remarks:* NORINCO. There are two PRC versions similar to Soviet ZPU-1; Type 75 and Type 75-1. The first has wheels for towing; the latter does not. It is intended for man or animal packing. The PRC version of the ZPU-2 AA mount is Type 58; the ZPU-4 is Type 56.

- *Cal.:* 23 x 152mmB
  *Common Name:* 23mm Gatling cannon

*Remarks:* NORINCO. Chinese version of US M61 Gatling (Vulcan) in 23mm.

- *Cal.:* 25 x 218mm
  *Common Name:* 2-M-3 or 2-M-8 automatic cannon

*Remarks:* Source unknown; assumed to be of Chinese origin. Used on minesweepers and other naval craft.

**GRENADE LAUNCHERS:**

- *Cal.:* 20mm
  *Official Name:* Type 67

*Remarks:* This muzzle attachment for Type 56-1 series of AKs is designed to allow the launching 70mm antitank rifle grenades.

- *Cal.:* 30 x 29mm
  *Common Name:* AGS-17 grenade launcher

*Remarks:* Under development in the PRC. NORINCO introduced this weapon at the Cairo International Defence Equipment exhibition in November 1987.

- *Cal.:* 35 x ??mm
  *Common Name:* Type W87 automatic grenade launcher

*Remarks:* Domestic-designed self-loader. This selective fire launcher when loaded and tripod mounted weighs 23kg. NORINCO introduced the W87 at the Cairo International Defence Equipment exhibition in November 1987. It has a cyclic rate of 400 spm and is fed by 6-, 9-, and 12-shot magazines.

## REPUBLIC OF CHINA (on Taiwan)

Population (estimate in 1984): 19.11 million. Ground forces: regulars, ca. 400,000; reserves, 100,000 active with another 1,500,000 militia. The ROC Marines are about 90,000 strong. There are about 25,000 police officers on Taiwan. Paramilitary forces number about 100,000.

**HANDGUNS:**

- *Cal.:* 9 x 19mm Parabellum
  *Common Name:* Browning Mle. 35 GP pistol

  *Remarks:* Manufactured by John Inglis of Canada during World War II. Licensed copy of FN Mle. 1935 GP. Also direct purchase from FN after 1958.

- *Cal.:* 9 x 29mmR
  *Common Name:* .38 Smith & Wesson revolvers

  *Remarks:* State Department licensed sales for 3,600 revolvers in both 1976 and 1978 for the Ministry of the Interior. These handguns are used by police organizations.

- *Cal.:* 11.43 x 23mm
  *Common Name:* .45 M1911A1 pistol

  *Remarks:* US origin through MAP and FMS 1950–74. More than 39,000 M1911A1s delivered.

**SUBMACHINE GUNS:**

- *Cal.:* 11.43 x 23mm
  *Common Name:* .45 M1921 Thompson

  *Remarks:* Copy made in China.

- *Cal.:* 11.43 x 23mm
  *Official Name:* Type 36
  *Common Name:* .45 M3A1 submachine gun

  *Remarks:* Copy made in China. US Military Assistance Program delivered about 1,000 M3A1s in 1970.

- *Cal.:* 9 x 19mm Parabellum
  *Official Name:* Type 37
  *Common Name:* 9mm version of M3A1

  *Remarks:* Copy made in China. A silenced version of this SMG was created during the 1960s by the PRC and the North Vietnamese — FOM 1005-5-3-9-1.

**RIFLES:**

- *Cal.:* 5.56 x 45mm
  *Common Name:* M16A1 (Model 613)

  *Remarks:* US origin. Ca. 47,000 of M16A1 rifle purchased from Colt before 1976.

- *Cal.:* 5.56 x 45mm
  *Official Name:* Type 65

  *Remarks:* Domestic version of the M16 rifle made in Taiwan.

- *Cal.:* 5.56 x 45mm
  *Official Name:* Type 68

  *Remarks:* Domestic 5.56mm rifle designed and made on Taiwan. Similar to the M16A1 rifle with a piston-type gas system.

- *Cal.:* 7.62 x 33mm
  *Common Name:* .30 M1 and M2 carbines

  *Remarks:* US origin. OBSOLETE. Nearly 180,000 M1 and M2 carbines were delivered through FMS and MAP 1950–74.

- *Cal.:* 7.62 x 51mm NATO
  *Official Name:* Type 57
  *Common Name:* M14 rifle

  *Remarks:* US M14-type rifle made on American production machinery sent to Taiwan. More than one million ROC Type 57 rifles have been made in Taiwan. Prior to start of manufacture, the US also delivered about 8,000 M14s via FMS and 165,729 M14s via MAP (i.e., before 1977).

- *Cal.:* 7.62 x 63mm
  *Common Name:* .30 M1 rifle

  *Remarks:* US origin. Before 1964 more than 114,000 M1 rifles were delivered by MAP.

- *Cal.:* 7.62 x 63mm
  *Common Name:* .30 M1C sniper rifle

  *Remarks:* US origin. MAP delivered 217 in 1969 and 1971.

- *Cal.:* 7.62 x 63mm
  *Common Name:* .30 M1D sniper rifle

  *Remarks:* US origin. MAP delivered 782 in 1970.

Taiwanese 5.56 x 45mm Type 68 rifle, a piston-operated design derived from the US M16A1 rifle. (ARMEX)

**SHOTGUNS:**
• *Cal.:* 18.5 x 59mm
  *Common Name:* 12 gage Winchester Model 12 shotgun

*Remarks:* US origin. FMS delivered 29,981 in 1973.

**MACHINE GUNS:**
• *Cal.:* 7.62 x 51mm NATO
  *Official Name:* Type 57
  *Common Name:* M60 GPMG

*Remarks:* US M60 is manufactured on Taiwan with US machinery.

• *Cal.:* 7.62 x 63mm
  *Official Name:* Type 41
  *Common Name:* Chinese version of Canadian 7.92mm Bren LMG

*Remarks:* Chinese manufacture. FOM 1005-31-4-7.62-1.

• *Cal.:* 7.62 x 63mm
  *Common Name:* .30 M1919A4 LMG

*Remarks:* US origin. Ca. 51,000 Browning machine guns were provided by the US before 1974.

• *Cal.:* 7.92 x 57mm Mauser
  *Official Name:* Type 24
  *Common Name:* Maxim MG 08 MMG

*Remarks:* Chinese-made Maxim machine gun. FOM 1005-31-4-7.92-4. OBSOLETE.

• *Cal.:* 12.7 x 99mm
  *Common Name:* .50 M2 HB HMG

*Remarks:* US origin. More than 200 M2 HB Browning machine guns were provided before 1974; an additional 60 M2s for the tank M1 Cupola were sold by FMS in 1974.

**AUTOMATIC CANNON:**
• *Cal.:* 20 x 110mmRB
  *Common Name:* US Mk4 Oerlikon (Type S) automatic cannon

*Remarks:* US origin on ship mounts.

## COLOMBIA (Republic of)

Population (estimate in 1984): 28.25 million. Ground forces: regulars, ca. 57,000 (28,500 conscripts); marines, 1,500; reserves, 70,000; secondary reserves, ca. 230,000; paramilitary: National Police (Policia Nacional), 45,000 to 50,000; *Carabineros, 37,000.*

**HANDGUNS:**

- *Cal.:* 9 x 19mm Parabellum
  *Common Name:* FN Mle. 35 GP pistol

  *Remarks:* FN origin. Purchased from FN before 1950 and again after 1958.

- *Cal.:* 9 x 29mmR
  *Common Name:* .38 Smith & Wesson revolver

  *Remarks:* US origin. The US State Department licensed delivery of 1,500 .38 caliber revolvers and 1,500 .32 caliber revolver kits to be assembled in Colombia. Part of a 1979 contract with the Ministry of Defense. Shipments also licensed for National Police in 1977 (3,900) and 1978 (1,000). In 1985 the police bought 20,000 S&W M10 .38 caliber revolvers. Annually, the Colombians are purchasing 15,000 kits of revolver parts to be assembled in-country.

- *Cal.:* 9 x 29mmR
  *Common Name:* .38 Ruger revolver

  *Remarks:* US origin. The Colombians are purchasing about 5,000 Ruger revolvers each year.

- *Cal.:* 11.43 x 23mm
  *Common Name:* .45 M1911A1 pistol

  *Remarks:* US origin. MAP provided 220 M1911A1s 1964–66. An additional 2,700 handguns were delivered by MAP and FMS before 1964.

**SUBMACHINE GUNS:**

- *Cal.:* 9 x 19mm Parabellum
  *Common Name:* Madsen M46, M50, and M53 submachine guns

  *Remarks:* Danish origin. FOM 1005-33-3-9-2.

- *Cal.:* 9 x 19mm Parabellum
  *Common Name:* Walther MP-K

  *Remarks:* Walther, West Germany.

- *Cal.:* 9 x 19mm Parabellum
  *Common Name:* HK MP5A3 and MP5K

  *Remarks:* Origin unknown.

- *Cal.:* 9 x 19mm Parabellum
  *Common Name:* Uzi submachine gun

  *Remarks:* Israeli Military Industries (IMI) origin. The Mini-Uzi has also been reported.

- *Cal.:* 9 x 19mm Parabellum
  *Common Name:* Ingram MAC-10 submachine gun

  *Remarks:* RPB Industries, US. The US State Department licensed sale of 395 M10s in 1977 for the National Police.

- *Cal.:* 11.43 x 23mm
  *Common Name:* .45 M3A1 submachine gun

  *Remarks:* US origin. MAP delivered over 570 M3-type SMGs before 1967. FMS provided 90-some odd unspecified SMGs before 1964.

**RIFLES:**

- *Cal.:* 5.56 x 45mm
  *Common Name:* Galil rifle

  *Remarks:* IMI.

- *Cal.:* 7.62 x 51mm NATO
  *Common Name:* Galil rifle

  *Remarks:* IMI. About 10,000 purchased from IMI.

- *Cal.:* 7.62 x 33mm
  *Common Name:* .30 M1 and M2 carbines

  *Remarks:* US origin. MAP and FMS programs delivered more than 7,500 M1 and M2 carbines before 1968.

- *Cal.:* 7.62 x 51mm NATO
  *Common Name:* Gewehr 3

  *Remarks:* Heckler & Koch (HK) GmbH origin. Ca. 30,000 G3s acquired in the early 1970s. Now the basic infantry rifle. Some units still use the FAL. Portuguese-made G3s, from Angola via Cuba, are being used by drug traffickers.

- *Cal.:* 7.62 x 51mm NATO
  *Common Name:* FAL

  *Remarks:* Origin unknown; some have arrived in country via drug traffickers.

- *Cal.:* 7.62 x 51mm NATO
  *Common Name:* SL7 semiautomatic rifle

  *Remarks:* HK origin. Between 20,000 and 30,000 were ordered for the police; they were not delivered.

- *Cal.:* 7.62 x 51mm NATO
  *Common Name:* M14 rifle

  *Remarks:* US origin. FMS delivered 4,000 M14s in 1974 and 2,478 more in 1980.

- *Cal.:* 7.62 x 51mm NATO?
  *Common Name:* MAS 49/56 rifle

  *Remarks:* Unconfirmed reports of this weapon being used.

- *Cal.:* 7.62 x 63mm
  *Common Name:* .30 M1 rifle

  *Remarks:* US origin. Nearly 19,000 rifles delivered MAP and FMS before the mid-1960s.

- *Cal.:* 7.62 x 63mm
  *Common Name:* FN SAFN rifle

  *Remarks:* FN origin.

- *Cal.:* 7.62 x 63mm
  *Common Name:* Mauser Model
  1898

  *Remarks:* OBSOLETE. FN origin. Made in the early 1950s.

- *Cal.:* 7.65 x 53.5mm Mauser
  *Common Name:* Mauser Model
  1891 and 1898 rifles

  *Remarks:* OBSOLETE. Most of these Mauser 1898 rifles have been converted to 7.62 x 63mm.

**SHOTGUNS:**
- *Cal.:* 18.5 x 59mm
  *Common Name:* 12 gage High
  Standard riot shotguns

  *Remarks:* US origin. The US State Department licensed the sale of 30 shotguns in 1976 for the Military Industry Security Police.

- *Cal.:* 18.5 x 59mm
  *Common Name:* 12 gage Mossberg Model 500 shotguns

  *Remarks:* US origin. Acquired by Military Police and National Police forces 1982–86.

**MACHINE GUNS:**
- *Cal.:* 7.62 x 51mm NATO
  *Common Name:* M60 GPMG

  *Remarks:* US origin. Saco Defense Systems sold first M60s in 1985. Reports circulated in 1983 that the Colombians had purchased 1,000 M60s and 1,500 M60E3s were not based in fact.

- *Cal.:* 7.62 x 51mm NATO
  *Common Name:* M60D aircraft
  gun

  *Remarks:* US origin. FMS delivered 24 M60Ds in 1982.

- *Cal.:* 7.62 x 51mm NATO
  *Common Name:* HK21E1 LMG

  *Remarks:* HK origin.

- *Cal.:* 7.62 x 51mm NATO
  *Common Name:* FN MAG

  *Remarks:* FN origin. Seen mounted on Brazilian EE-11 APCs.

- *Cal.:* 7.62 x 63mm
  *Common Name:* M1918A2 BAR

  *Remarks:* US origin. MAP delivered 318 BARs in 1964 and 1965.

- *Cal.:* 7.62 x 63mm
  *Common Name:* .30 M1919A4
  LMG

  *Remarks:* US origin. A small number of M1919A6 LMGs were also provided by the US. Quantities unknown.

- *Cal.:* 12.7 x 99mm
  *Common Name:* .50 M2 HB
  HMG

  *Remarks:* US origin.

**AUTOMATIC CANNON:**
- *Cal.:* 20 x ???mm
  *Common Name:* Unidentified
  20mm automatic cannon

  *Remarks:* Mounted on naval craft.

**GRENADE LAUNCHERS:**
• *Cal.:* 40 x 46mmSR
  *Common Name:* M79 grenade
  launcher

*Remarks:* US origin. FMS delivered 75 M79s in 1979.

### Colombian Arms Industry

The Industria Militar (INDUMIL) produces 7.62 x 51mm NATO caliber ball ammunition and assembles the G3A3 rifle from parts supplied by HK GmbH. INDUMIL manufactures some less-complicated components of the G3A3.

## COMOROS (Federal Islamic Republic of)

Population (estimate in 1984): 0.455 million. Ground forces: regulars, unknown; reserves: unknown; paramilitary (*Force de Police Nationale,* 400).

**HANDGUNS:**

**SUBMACHINE GUNS:**
• *Cal.:* 9 x 19mm Parabellum
  *Common Name:* MAT Mle. 49
  submachine gun

*Remarks:* French origin. Manufacture Nationale d'Armes de Tulle (MAT).

**RIFLES:**
• *Cal.:* 7.5 x 54mm
  *Common Name:* MAS Mle. 36
  bolt action rifle

*Remarks:* French origin. Manufacture Nationale d'Armes de St. Etienne (MAS).

• *Cal.:* 7.62 x 39mm
  *Common Name:* SKS carbine

*Remarks:* East Bloc origin or Type 56?

• *Cal.:* 7.62 x 39mm
  *Common Name:* AK47 assault
  rifle

*Remarks:* East Bloc origin.

**SHOTGUNS:**

**MACHINE GUNS:**
• *Cal.:* 7.5 x 54
  *Common Name:* AAT 52 GPMG

*Remarks:* Groupment Industriel des Armements Terrestres (GIAT), France.

• *Cal.:* 7.62 x 39
  *Common Name:* RPD LMG

*Remarks:* East Bloc origin.

• *Cal.:* 7.62 x 39
  *Common Name:* RPK LMG

*Remarks:* East Bloc origin.

• *Cal.:* 7.62 x 54mmR
  *Common Name:* Type 58 GPMG

*Remarks:* People's Republic of China (PRC) origin.

• *Cal.:* 7.62 x 54mmR
  *Common Name:* RP46 LMG

*Remarks:* East Bloc origin.

• *Cal.:* 7.62 x 54mmR
  *Common Name:* S6M series
  MMG

*Remarks:* East Bloc origin.

**AUTOMATIC CANNON:**

## CONGO (People's Republic of)

Population (estimate in 1984): 1.75 million. Ground forces: regulars, *Armee Populaire Nationale,* between 6,500 and 8,000; paramilitary *Gendarmerie Nationale,* 1,400; militia 2,500. In excess of 2,000 Cuban troops in residence.

**HANDGUNS:**
- *Cal.:* 7.65 x 17mm Browning
  *Common Name:* Walther PP

  *Remarks:* Manurhin-made.

- *Cal.:* 9 x 19mm Parabellum
  *Common Name:* MAC Mle. 50 pistol

  *Remarks:* Manufacture Nationale d'Armes de Chatellerault (MAC).

- *Cal.:* 7.62 x 25mm
  *Common Name:* TT33 Tokarev pistol

  *Remarks:* East Bloc origin.

**SUBMACHINE GUNS:**
- *Cal.:* 9 x 19mm Parabellum
  *Common Name:* Vigneron submachine gun

  *Remarks:* Société Anonyme de Précision Liègeoise.

- *Cal.:* 9 x 19mm Parabellum
  *Common Name:* MAT 49 submachine gun

  *Remarks:* Manufacture Nationale d'Armes de Tulle (MAT).

- *Cal.:* 9 x 19mm Parabellum
  *Common Name:* LF-57 submachine gun

  *Remarks:* L. Franchi, Italy.

- *Cal.:* 9 x 19mm Parabellum
  *Common Name:* Sola Super submachine gun

  *Remarks:* Société Luxembourgeoise d'Armes, S.A., Ettelbruk, Luxembourg.

- *Cal.:* 7.62 x 25mm
  *Common Name:* PPSh41 submachine gun

  *Remarks:* Soviet origin?

**RIFLES:**
- *Cal.:* 7.62 x 39mm
  *Common Name:* AK47 and AKM assault rifles

  *Remarks:* East Bloc origin.

- *Cal.:* 7.5 x 54mm
  *Common Name:* MAS Mle. 36 bolt action rifle

  *Remarks:* French origin. Manufacture Nationale d'Armes de St. Etienne (MAS).

- *Cal.:* 7.5 x 54mm
  *Common Name:* MAS Mle. 49/56 rifle

  *Remarks:* French origin. MAS.

- *Cal.:* 7.62 x 51mm NATO
  *Common Name:* Modelo 58 CETME assault rifle

  *Remarks:* Centro de Estudios Tecnios y Materiales Especiales (CETME), Spain.

- *Cal.:* 7.62 x 51mm NATO
  *Common Name:* FN FAL

  *Remarks:* FN origin.

- *Cal.:* 7.62 x 63mm
  *Common Name:* FN SAFN rifle

  *Remarks:* FN origin.

**SHOTGUNS:**

**MACHINE GUNS:**
- *Cal.:* 7.5 x 54mm
  *Common Name:* AAT52 GPMG

  *Remarks:* Groupment Industriel des Armements Terrestres (GIAT), France.

- *Cal.:* 7.5 x 54mm
  *Common Name:* Chatellerault M24/29 LMG

  *Remarks:* MAC.

- *Cal.:* 7.62 x 54mmR
  *Common Name:* RP46 company machine gun

  *Remarks:* East Bloc origin. Including the PRC Type 58 LMG. Some older DP LMGs are still in service.

- *Cal.:* 7.62 x 54mmR
  *Common Name:* PK GPMG

  *Remarks:* East Bloc origin.

- *Cal.:* 7.62 x 54mmR
  *Common Name:* Type 58 machine gun

  *Remarks:* People's Republic of China (PRC) origin.

- *Cal.:* 7.62 x 54mmR
  *Common Name:* Type 67 machine gun

  *Remarks:* PRC origin.

- *Cal.:* 7.62 x 54mmR
  *Common Name:* Type 76 machine gun

  *Remarks:* PRC origin.

- *Cal.:* 7.62 x 54mmR
  *Common Name:* SGMT armor MG

  *Remarks:* Soviet origin. Mounted on older Soviet tanks and APCs.

- *Cal.:* 7.62 x 39mm
  *Common Name:* RPD LMG

  *Remarks:* East Bloc origin.

- *Cal.:* 7.62 x 39mm
  *Common Name:* RPK LMG

  *Remarks:* East Bloc origin.

- *Cal.:* 12.7 x 108mm
  *Common Name:* DShK HMG

  *Remarks:* East Bloc origin. Both the DShK38 and the DShK38/46 (Chinese Type 54) are in use. Employed on ground, armor, and naval mounts.

**AUTOMATIC CANNON:**
- *Cal.:* 14.5 x 114mm
  *Common Name:* KPV HMG

  *Remarks:* East Bloc origin. Used on several different ground and sea mounts. Some 16 ZPU-4 AA systems are reported to be in service.

- *Cal.:* 20 x ???mm
  *Common Name:* 20mm automatic cannon

  *Remarks:* Unknown type used on the on "Pirana" class fast attack craft.

- *Cal.:* 23 x 152mmB
  *Common Name:* 23mm ZU automatic cannon

  *Remarks:* Both the towed twin gun AA mount and the self-propelled ZSU-23-4 AA system are in use.

- *Cal.:* 25 x 118mm
  *Common Name:* Chinese 2-M-3 or 2-M-8 automatic cannon

  *Remarks:* PRC origin. Twin guns mounted on "Shanghai" class fast attack craft.

**Small Arms Used by Anti-government Forces**

The MPLC (*Mouvement pour la liberation du Congo*—"Katangais") have the 7.92 x 57mm MG42, 7.62 x 51mm NATO M60 GPMG, 7.62 x 54mmR DP and RP46 machine guns, 12.7 x 99mm M2HB HMG, 12.7 x 108mm DShK HMG, and 14.5 x 114mm HMG.

## COOK ISLANDS

Population (estimate in 1984): 0.016 million. Ground forces: regulars, unknown; reserves: unknown. Self-governing islands in "free association" with New Zealand, which provides for the defense needs of the islands.

**HANDGUNS:**

**SUBMACHINE GUNS:**

**RIFLES:**

**SHOTGUNS:**

**MACHINE GUNS:**

**AUTOMATIC CANNON:**

## COSTA RICA (Republic of)

Population (estimate in 1984): 2.69 million. Ground forces: regulars, none (army abolished in 1949); *Guardia Civil* (including police and border guards) 7,000. Enough small caliber weapons on hand to equip a force of 10,000 men.

**HANDGUNS:**
- *Cal.:* 9 x 29mmR                     *Remarks:* Wide variety of US .38 Special revolvers.

- *Cal.:* 11.43 x 23mm                  *Remarks:* US origin. Small numbers delivered in 1964 as part of MAP.
  *Common Name:* .45 M1911A1
  pistol

**SUBMACHINE GUNS:**
- *Cal.:* 9 x 19mm Parabellum           *Remarks:* Beretta, Italy.
  *Common Name:* Beretta M38/49,
  Model 4 submachine gun

- *Cal.:* 11.43 x 23mm                  *Remarks:* US origin. FMS program delivered before 1963. Silenced versions
  *Common Name:* .45 M3 series          also reported.
  submachine gun

**RIFLES:**
- *Cal.:* 5.56 x 45mm                   *Remarks:* Israeli Military Industries (IMI) origin.
  *Common Name:* Galil rifle

- *Cal.:* 5.56 x 45mm                   *Remarks:* US origin?
  *Common Name:* M16A1 rifle

- *Cal.:* 5.56 x 45mm                   *Remarks:* Taiwan (ROC) origin.
  *Common Name:* Type 68 rifle

- *Cal.:* 7.62 x 33mm                   *Remarks:* US origin. FMS delivered 6,000 carbines in 1975.
  *Common Name:* .30 M1 and M2
  carbines

- *Cal.:* 7.62 x 51mm NATO              *Remarks:* US origin.
  *Common Name:* M14 rifle

**Costa Rican Border Guard force at Penas Blancas ca. 1984. Their rifles include a 7.62 x 51mm FAL center, 5.56 x 45mm IMI Galils, and a 7.62 x 51mm US M14 on the lower left. (DeCaro)**

- *Cal.:* 7.62 x 51mm NATO
  *Common Name:* FN FAL

  *Remarks:* FN origin. Received from Venezuela at the time of the Sandinista war against Somoza in Nicaragua.

- *Cal.:* 7 x 57mm Mauser
  *Common Name:* FN Mauser

  *Remarks:* Belgian origin.

- *Cal.:* 7.62 x 63mm
  *Common Name:* .30 M1 rifle

  *Remarks:* US origin.

- *Cal.:* 7.62 x 63mm
  *Common Name:* .30 M1903A3
    rifle

  *Remarks:* US origin.

**SHOTGUNS:**

**MACHINE GUNS:**
- *Cal.:* 7.62 x 51mm NATO
  *Common Name:* M60 GPMG

  *Remarks:* US origin.

- *Cal.:* 7.62 x 63mm
  *Common Name:* .30 M1918A2
    BAR

  *Remarks:* US origin.

- *Cal.:* 7.62 x 63mm
  *Common Name:* .30 M1919A4
    LMG

  *Remarks:* US origin. FMS delivered 35 guns before 1964. Some older commercial models of the Browning light machine gun are still in service.

**AUTOMATIC CANNON:**
• *Cal.:* 20 x 138mm
　*Common Name:* 20mm Breda
　automatic cannon

*Remarks:* Some of these 1930 vintage Breda automatic cannon may still be in service as AA guns.

**GRENADE LAUNCHERS:**
• *Cal.:* 40 x 46mmSR
　*Common Name:* M79 grenade
　launcher

*Remarks:* US origin.


## CUBA (Republic of)

Population (estimate in 1984): 9.99 million. Ground forces: regulars, variously estimated between 150,000 and 190,000; reserves, between 90,000 and 190,000; paramilitary: State Ministry of Interior—Security Forces, 15,000; Frontier Guards, 3,500. Ministry of Defense—Youth Labor Army, 100,000, Civil Defense Force, 100,000, and Territorial Militia, 530,000.


**HANDGUNS:**
• *Cal.:* 9 x 18mm
　*Common Name:* Makarov pistol

*Remarks:* East Bloc origin.

• *Cal.:* 9 x 19mm Parabellum
　*Common Name:* FN Mle. 1935 GP
　pistol

*Remarks:* FN origin. Purchased after 1962.

**SUBMACHINE GUNS:\***
• *Cal.:* 9 x 19mm Parabellum
　*Common Name:* FN Uzi subma-
　chine gun

*Remarks:* FN origin. Ca. 15,000 were purchased from FN. A few with the Cuban Army coat of arms (escudo) obliterated were found by US and Caribbean forces during Operation "Urgent Fury" in Grenada.

• *Cal.:* 9 x 19mm Parabellum
　*Common Name:* Beretta subma-
　chine guns

*Remarks:* Beretta, Italy. Ca. 1,000 purchased 1959–60.

• *Cal.:* 9 x 19mm Parabellum
　*Common Name:* vz.23 and vz.25
　submachine guns

*Remarks:* Czechoslovakian origin. Many were disposed of as military aid (e.g., to Grenada).

• *Cal.:* 9 x 19mm Parabellum
　*Common Name:* Star Z45 subma-
　chine gun

*Remarks:* Star-Bonifacio Echeverria, Spain.

**RIFLES:**
• *Cal.:* 7.62 x 33mm
　*Common Name:* .30 M1 and M2
　carbines

*Remarks:* US origin,* probably obsolete.

• *Cal.:* 7.62 x 33mm
　*Common Name:* .30 Cristobal
　MK2 carbines

*Remarks:* Dominican Republic origin. Ca. 3,500 acquired 1959–60. OBSOLETE.

• *Cal.:* 7.62 x 39mm
　*Common Name:* AK47, AKM,
　and AKMS assault rifles

*Remarks:* Soviet and Warsaw Pact models.

*All US origin weapons delivered prior to the defeat of General Batista's army in 1959. All Belgian weapons delivered prior to the arms embargo against Castro's government in 1960.

- *Cal.:* 7.62 x 45mm
  *Common Name:* vz.52 rifle

  *Remarks:* Czechoslovakian origin. Most of these rifles have been passed on to client states as military aid. Many recovered in Grenada.

- *Cal.:* 7.62 x 51mm NATO
  *Common Name:* FN FAL

  *Remarks:* FN origin. Many of these FALs have been shipped to Central and South America as aid to revolutionary groups. Most have had Cuban coat of arms removed by drilling a hole. Cuba purchased in excess of 35,000 FALs from FN, 1958–59. Some have been recovered from antigovernment forces in Chile, Colombia, and El Salvador.

- *Cal.:* 7.62 x 63mm
  *Common Name:* .30 M1 rifle

  *Remarks:* US origin.* OBSOLETE.

- *Cal.:* 7.62 x 63mm
  *Common Name:* .30 M1903A3 rifle

  *Remarks:* US origin.* OBSOLETE.

- *Cal.:* 7.7 x 56mmR
  *Common Name:* .303 Lee Enfield

  *Remarks:* UK origin, route of delivery unknown. Ca. 10,000 acquired 1959–60. OBSOLETE. May have been disposed of as military aid.

**SHOTGUNS:**

**MACHINE GUNS:**
- *Cal.:* 7.62 x 39mm
  *Common Name:* RPD LMG

  *Remarks:* Soviet origin.

- *Cal.:* 7.62 x 39mm
  *Common Name:* RPK LMG

  *Remarks:* Soviet origin.

- *Cal.:* 7.62 x 45mm
  *Common Name:* vz.52 LMG

  *Remarks:* Czechoslovakian origin. The Cubans have distributed these guns as military aid.

- *Cal.:* 7.62 x 51mm NATO
  *Common Name:* FN MAG

  *Remarks:* Belgian origin.

- *Cal.:* 7.62 x 54mmR
  *Common Name:* DPM and RP46 LMGs

  *Remarks:* East Bloc origin. OBSOLETE. These machine guns are only used by militia units. Some DT armor machine guns may still be held in reserve.

- *Cal.:* 7.62 x 54mmR
  *Common Name:* SG43/SGM MG series

  *Remarks:* East Bloc origin.

- *Cal.:* 7.62 x 54mmR
  *Common Name:* PK MG series

  *Remarks:* East Bloc origin.

- *Cal.:* 12.7 x 99mm
  *Common Name:* .50 M2 HB HMG

  *Remarks:* US origin.*

- *Cal.:* 12.7 x 108mm
  *Common Name:* DShK38 and DShK38/46 (DShKM) HMG

  *Remarks:* East Bloc origin. The quad AA mount M53 is held in Cuban inventory. Some may be of Czech origin, since Czech quad mounts are found on BTR-152 APCs used by Cubans.

- *Cal.:* 12.7 x 108mm
  *Common Name:* NSVT armor machine gun

  *Remarks:* Soviet origin. Mounted on T72 tanks.

**AUTOMATIC CANNON:**
- *Cal.:* 14.5 x 114mm
  *Common Name:* KPV HMG

  *Remarks:* East Bloc origin. ZPU-1, ZPU-2, and ZPU-4 mounts.

---

*All US origin weapons delivered prior to the defeat of General Batista's army in 1959. All Belgian weapons delivered prior to the arms embargo against Castro's government in 1960.

- *Cal.:* 23 x 152mmB
  *Common Name:* ZU23 automatic
  cannon

  *Remarks:* Soviet origin. Both the towed and self-propelled AA systems using this cannon are in service.

- *Cal.:* 25 x 218mm
  *Common Name:* 2-M-3 or 2-M-8
  automatic cannon

  *Remarks:* Soviet origin. Mounted on patrol craft and fast attack craft.

## CYPRUS (Republic of)

Population (estimate in 1984): 0.664 million. Ground forces: regulars, Greek-Cypriot National Guard, between 12,000 and 13,000, of which ca. 10,000 are readily available; regulars, Turkish-Cypriot Security Force *(Kirbis Turk Emniyet Kuvvetleri),* between 3,500–4,500; reserves, Greek, between 50,000 and 60,000 (about 30,000 ready for immediate service); Turkish, ca. 15,500 (5,000 immediately available); paramilitary, Greek police 3,000. In addition there are between 22,000 and 35,500 Turkish mainland forces and 2,500 Greek mainland forces on the island. The "Turkish Federated States of Cyprus" was established in February 1975. This divided island nation has a mixture of small arms of the type found in the Greek and Turkish armies. There are also some East Bloc small arms in use.

**HANDGUNS:**
- *Cal.:* 9 x 29mmR
  *Common Name:* .38 Smith & Wesson revolvers

  *Remarks:* US origin. Small quantities delivered to Nicosia Police via State Department licensed sale in 1976.

**SUBMACHINE GUNS:**
- *Cal.:* 9 x 19mm Parabellum
  *Common Name:* L2A3 submachine gun

  *Remarks:* UK origin.

**RIFLES:**
- *Cal.:* 7.62 x 39mm
  *Common Name:* vz.58 assault rifle

  *Remarks:* Czechoslovakian origin.

- *Cal.:* 7.62 x 51mm NATO
  *Common Name:* Gewehr 3

  *Remarks:* Of German, Greek, and Turkish origin.

- *Cal.:* 7.62 x 51mm NATO
  *Common Name:* Gewehr 1

  *Remarks:* Of German origin. These rifles were provided to the Turkish military as aid from the German government.

- *Cal.:* 7.62 x 51mm NATO
  *Common Name:* FN FAL

  *Remarks:* Origin unknown. Purchasing spare parts in 1987.

- *Cal.:* 7.62 x 63mm
  *Common Name:* .30 M1 (Garand) rifle

  *Remarks:* Origin unknown. Purchasing space parts in 1987.

**SHOTGUNS:**

**MACHINE GUNS:**
- *Cal.:* 7.62 x 51mm NATO
  *Common Name:* FN MAG

  *Remarks:* FN origin. Both the MAG *Infanterie Standard* (60-20), T1, and the MAG *Coaxial* (60-40) on the Shorland armored car are in service. Purchasing spare parts in 1987.

- *Cal.:* 7.62 x 54mmR
  *Common Name:* DT armor MG

  *Remarks:* Soviet origin. Mounted on older Soviet tanks.

- *Cal.:* 7.62 x 54mmR
  Common Name: SGMT armor
  MG

  *Remarks:* Soviet origin. Mounted on older Soviet tanks.

- *Cal.:* 7.62 x 63mm
  Common Name: .30 M1919A6
  LMG

  *Remarks:* Origin unknown. Purchasing spare parts in 1987.

- *Cal.:* 12.7 x 99mm
  Common Name: .50 M2 HB
  HMG

  *Remarks:* Origin unknown. Purchasing spare parts in 1987.

- *Cal.:* 12.7 x 108mm
  Common Name: DShK38/46
  HMG

  *Remarks:* East Bloc origin.

**AUTOMATIC CANNON:**
- *Cal.:* 20 x 110mm
  Common Name: M55 automatic
  cannon

  *Remarks:* Yugoslavian origin.


## CZECHOSLOVAKIA (Socialist Republic of)

Population (estimate in 1984): 15.47 million. Ground forces: regulars, reduced in recent years, variously estimated 120,000 to 180,000 (except for senior NCOs and officers, all are conscripts) (*Československá Lidová Armáda* [CSLA] – Čzechoslovakian People's Army); reserves, 350,000 (200,000 active); paramilitary: *Pohranicini straz* (border troops), 11,000; *Livodá Milice* (people's militia) of about 25,000 drawn from members of the Communist Party. The *LM* has special insignia on standard Army uniforms. *Svazu pro Spolupraci Armadou* or SVAZARM = "Association for Cooperation with the Army or Czechoslovakian National Rifle Association, in effect, 120,000; Public Security service (uniform police or *Verejna Bezpecnost* or *VB*), 24,000; the *Federalni Sprava Zpravodajskych Sluzba* (Federal Information Service Department or FSZS) that replaced the *Statni Tajna Bezpecnost* (STB) in 1968 is the Czech equivalent of the KGB), 7,000.


**HANDGUNS:**
- *Cal.:* 7.62 x 17mm Browning
  Official Name: Pistole vz.50 and
  vz.50/70
  Common Name: Model 50 pistol

  *Remarks:* Personal defense weapon for police officers and the STB. This pistol replaced the vz.27 pistol in the early 1960s. Many of the vz.27s were sent to Vietnam and other compatible countries.

- *Cal.:* 7.62 x 25mm
  Official Name: Pistole vz.52
  Common Name: Model 52 pistol

  *Remarks:* This is the standard Army issue pistol. FOM 1005-6-1-7.62-1. Will be replaced by the 9 x 18mm Makarov caliber vz.82 pistol.

**SUBMACHINE GUNS:**
- *Cal.:* 7.65 x 17mm Browning
  Official Name: Samopal vz.61
  Common Name: Skorpion ma-
  chine pistol Model 61

  *Remarks:* Standard issue for tank crews, some police, and the STB. Expected it will be replaced with a 9 x 18mm version. FOM 1005-6-1-7.65-3.

- *Cal.:* 9 x 17mm Browning
  Official Name: Samopal vz.64
  Common Name: Skorpion Model
  64

  *Remarks:* Export model.

**Receiver markings from Czechoslovakian submachine guns.** *Left,* **markings from the 7.62 x 25mm vz.24;** *right,* **markings from the 9 x 19mm vz.25. (US Army)**

• *Cal.:* 9 x 18mm Makarov
*Official Name: Samopal vz.65*
Common Name: Skorpion Model 65

*Remarks:* Export model.

• *Cal.:* 9 x 19mm Parabellum
*Official Name: Samopal vz.68*
Common Name: Skorpion Model 68

*Remarks:* Export model.

• *Cal.:* 9 x 19mm Parabellum
*Official Name: Samopal vz.23*
Common Name: Model 23 sub-machine gun, with wood stock

*Remarks:* OBSOLETE. About 100,000 of these vz.23 and vz.25 submachine guns were built, and subsequently most were exported to the Middle East, Africa, and Cuba. They have been used by revolutionary groups such as the PLO and the former government of Grenada.

• *Cal.:* 9 x 19mm Parabellum
*Official Name: Samopal vz.25*
Common Name: Model 25 sub-machine gun with folding stock

*Remarks:* OBSOLETE as above for vz.23. Supplied to Israel, Syria, and Egypt to name a few countries. FOM 1005-6-3-9-1.

• *Cal.:* 7.62 x 25mm
*Official Name: Samopal vz.24*
Common Name: Model 24 sub-machine gun with wood stock

*Remarks:* OBSOLETE in Czech Army service since mid-1960s. Was used by *Livodá Milice* until 1970. Many exported to Vietnam, Cuba, Angola, Mozambique, and others.

• *Cal.:* 7.62 x 25mm
*Official Name: Samopal vz.26*
Common Name: Model 26 sub-machine gun with folding stock

*Remarks:* OBSOLETE as vz.26. Used by the Czech airborne until ca. 1970. Exported as military aid as above.

**RIFLES:**
• *Cal.:* 7.62 x 45mm
*Official Name: Samonabíjejicí puška vz.52*
Common Name: Model 52 semi-automatic rifle

*Remarks:* OBSOLETE. Used only for ceremonial Presidential Guard at the Prague Castle. Most vz.52 rifles were subsequently converted to fire the 7.62 x 39mm Soviet cartridge; redesignated vz.52/57. Large numbers in both calibers have been exported to the Middle East (e.g., Syria), Africa, and Cuba. Cuba sent many of these weapons to Nicaragua, which supplied antigovernment forces in Honduras with them. Some of these rifles were found in Grenada. FOM 1005-6-2-7.62-1.

• *Cal.:* 7.62 x 39mm
*Official Name: Samonabíjejicí puška vz.52/57*
Common Name: Model 52/57 semiautomatic rifle

*Remarks:* OBSOLETE. See above FOM 1005-6-2-7.62-3. Most are retained as weapons to be used in the event of military mobilization.

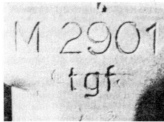

Additional receiver markings from Czechoslovakian small arms. *Top,* marking from the 7.62 x 39mm vz.58 assault rifle; *second,* marking from 7.62 x 54mmR SGM LMG; *third,* marking typical of that on both the 7.62 x 45mm vz.52 and the 7.62 x 39mm vz.52/57 LMG; *bottom,* marking on 7.62 x 54mmR vz.59 GPMG. (US Army)

- *Cal.:* 7.62 x 39mm
  *Official Name: Samopal vz.58P*
  *Common Name:* Model 58 automatic or assault rifle

- *Cal.:* 7.62 x 39mm
  *Official Name: Samopal vz.58V*
  *Common Name:* Model 58 with folding stock

- *Cal.:* 7.62 x 54mmR
  *Official Name: Odstřelovací puška vz.54*
  *Common Name:* Model 54 sniper rifle

*Remarks:* Standard issue. Conventional stock can be found made from plastic or less frequently wood. This unique weapon has a magazine that will not interchange with that of the Soviet Kalashnikov weapons. FOM 1005-6-2-7.62-2-1.

*Remarks:* Standard issue for artillery, airborne, communications, and truck drivers. FOM 1005-6-2-7.62-2.

*Remarks:* Standard; built on Mosin Nagant bolt action with free floating barrel.

## SHOTGUNS:

## MACHINE GUNS:

- *Cal.:* 7.62 x 45mm
  *Official Name: Lehký kulomet vz.52*
  *Common Name:* Model 52 LMG

- *Cal.:* 7.62 x 39mm
  *Official Name: Lehký kulomet vz.52/57*
  *Common Name:* Model 52/57 LMG

- *Cal.:* 7.62 x 54mmR
  *Official Name: Univerzálaní kulomet vz.59*
  *Common Name:* Model 59 GPMG

- *Cal.:* 7.62 x 54mm R
  *Official Name: Univerzálaní kulomet vz.59L*
  *Common Name:* Model 59 GPMG with light barrel

- *Cal.:* 7.62 x 64mmR
  *Official Name: Kulomet vz.59T*
  *Common Name:* Model 59 AFV/APC MG

- *Cal.:* 7.62 x 51mm NATO
  *Official Name: Kulomet vz.59N*
  *Common Name:* Model 59 GPMG

- *Cal.:* 7.62 x 54mmR
  *Common Name:* PKT armor MG

- *Cal.:* 7.62 x 54mmR
  *Official Name: Těžký kulomet Gurjanov vz.43*
  *Common Name:* Copy of SG43

- *Cal.:* 7.62 x 54mmR
  *Official Name: Těžký kulomet Degtyarev*
  *Common Name:* Soviet DT armor machine gun

*Remarks:* OBSOLETE. Widely exported as military aid. FOM 1005-6-4-7.62-1.

*Remarks:* OBSOLETE. Converted to 7.62 x 39mm. Formerly used by the *Livodá Milice.* Widely exported as military aid. Frequently encountered in Central America. FOM 1005-6-4-7.62-2.

*Remarks:* Now the standard machine gun. FOM 1005-6-4-7.62-3. Called the *Univerzalani Kulomet vz.59 na dvojnozce* when mounted on bipod; weighs 8.67kg w/ empty magazine. Called the *UK vz.59 na pdostavci* when it is mounted on the tripod with its 4 x 8 Meopta telescope. A loaded 50-round magazine weighs 1.98kg.

*Remarks:* Standard.

*Remarks:* Standard.

*Remarks:* NATO caliber version of vz.59 for export. Some of these guns are being used in the Middle East.

*Remarks:* Soviet origin. Mounted on Soviet T62 and T72 tanks.

*Remarks:* OBSOLETE, but held by reserve troops and the *Livodá Milice.* Replaced the 7.92mm MG42s used immediately after World War II. Licensed copy of the Soviet SG43 vehicular-mounted machine guns. Licensed production began about 1952.

*Remarks:* Long OBSOLETE. Soviet DT tank machine gun.

## Czechoslovakia

- *Cal.:* 7.92 x 57mm
*Official Name: Kulomet vz.26*
*Common Name:* ZB26 machine gun

*Remarks:* Long OBSOLETE in Czechoslovakia. These were provided to the Vietnamese during the 1950s. Still occasionally used by some revolutionary groups in the Middle East and Africa.

- *Cal.:* 7.92 x 57mm
*Official Name: Kulomet vz.37*
*Common Name:* ZB37 BESA machine gun

*Remarks:* Long OBSOLETE in Czechoslovakia. These were provided to the Vietnamese during the 1950s; 4,000 went to Israel in 1949. They are still used by some revolutionary groups in the Middle East and Africa.

- *Cal.:* 12.7 x 54mmR
*Official Name: Kulomet DŠK vz.54*
*Common Name:* Model 54 HMG

*Remarks:* Licensed copy of Soviet 12.7mm DShK38/46 HMG. Licensed for manufacture in 1952. Quad mount version has been given FOM 1005-6-4-12.7-7-1-A.

- *Cal.:* 12.7 x 108mm
*Common Name:* NSVT armor machine gun

*Remarks:* Soviet origin? Mounted on T72 and newer tanks.

### AUTOMATIC CANNON:
- *Cal.:* 14.5 x 114mm
*Common Name:* KPV HMG

*Remarks:* Licensed copy of the Soviet KPV. ZPU-4 version is in common usage.

- *Cal.:* 15 x 105mm
*Common Name:* Domestic design; essentially a scaled-up BESA

*Remarks:* Export gun.

- *Cal.:* 23 x 152mmB
*Common Name:* ZU23 automatic cannon

*Remarks:* Uncertain as to manufacturing source. The self-propelled ZSU-23-4 AA system is a standard service item.

### Czechoslovakian Small Arms Manufacture

The Czechoslovakian state arms industry, Česká Zbrojovka A. S. Strakonice or CZ, ceased producing small arms in the mid-1950s. Handguns are manufactured at Zavody Preshneho Strojirenstvi v Uherskem Brode (Factory for precision machining at Uhersky Brod). Rifles, machine guns, sporting arms, and related firearms are manufactured at the Československá Zbrojovka N. P. Brno. The sporting arms are made at Brno, and military production is located at several locations such as Povazske Strjirny and Dubnica Nad Vahom. The Czech small arms manufacturing industry has also been engaged in the distribution of small arms in support of the foreign and military goals of the East Bloc for most of the post–World War II era.

## DENMARK (Kingdom of)

Population (estimate in 1984): 5.12 million. Ground forces: regulars, ca. 22,000 (9,000 conscripts); reserves, Field Army reserve, 45,000+; Regional Defense Force, ca. 24,000; Home Guard, ca. 60,400; paramilitary state police force *(Rigspolitiet),* about 7,500–8,000.

### HANDGUNS:
- *Cal.:* 9 x 17mm
*Common Name:* Walther PP

*Remarks:* Walther origin. Used by Danish police organizations.

- *Cal.:* 9 x 19mm Parabellum
*Official Name:* 9 x 19mm P M/40(S)
*Common Name:* Swedish Model 40 Lahti pistol

*Remarks:* Limited issue. Made in Sweden.

- *Cal.:* 9 x 19mm Parabellum
  *Official Name:* 9 x 19mm P M/46
  *Common Name:* FN Mle. 1935 GP pistol

  *Remarks:* FN origin. Standard. Purchased before 1950 and from 1958 to 1961.

- *Cal.:* 9 x 19mm Parabellum
  *Official Name:* 9 x 19mm P M/49
  *Common Name:* SIG 47/8 pistol

  *Remarks:* Swiss origin. SIG Model P-210/2.

**SUBMACHINE GUNS:**

- *Cal.:* 9 x 19mm Parabellum
  *Official Name:* 9 x 19mm Mp M49 Hovea
  *Common Name:* Husqvarna submachine gun

  *Remarks:* Swedish origin.

- *Cal.:* 9 x 19mm Parabellum
  *Official Name:* 9 x 19mm Mp M/41
  *Common Name:* Finnish Suomi submachine gun

  *Remarks:* Finnish origin. OBSOLETE.

- *Cal.:* 9 x 19mm Parabellum
  *Official Name:* 9 x 19mm Mp M/44
  *Common Name:* Swedish Model 37-39 submachine gun

  *Remarks:* Swedish origin. OBSOLETE.

- *Cal.:* 9 x 19mm Parabellum
  *Common Name:* MP5A2 and MP5A3 submachine gun

  *Remarks:* Heckler & Koch (HK) GmbH origin. Used by Danish police organizations.

**RIFLES:**

- *Cal.:* 5.56 x 45mm
  *Common Name:* M16A1 rifle

  *Remarks:* US origin. Used by some Danish police forces. A few hundred of these were declared surplus late in 1987 and disposed of in 1988.

- *Cal.:* 7.62 x 51mm NATO
  *Official Name:* 7.62mm NATO G M/66
  *Common Name:* Gewehr 3

  *Remarks:* Rheinmetall-made G3s designated M/66. These M/66s are used by Home Guard; are semiautomatic only. Can be converted to selective fire with a special key. Standard.

- *Cal.:* 7.62 x 51mm NATO
  *Official Name:* 7.62mm NATO G M/75
  *Common Name:* Gewehr 3

  *Remarks:* HK origin. Standard for front-line army units. Designated G3A5 by HK with a catalog identification number 224038. Leased from West German government. Selective fire.

- *Cal.:* 7.62 x 51mm NATO
  *Official Name:* 7.62mm NATO G M/50
  *Common Name:* M1 rifle converted to 7.62mm NATO

  *Remarks:* Converted to 7.62mm NATO caliber by Beretta, Italy. These rifles are still carried by artillery troops. MAP provided 69,808 M1 rifles before 1964.

- *Cal.:* 7.62 x 63mm
  *Official Name:* 7.62mm G M/53
  *Common Name:* .30 M1917 – Enfield rifle

  *Remarks:* US origin. OBSOLETE.

**SHOTGUNS:**

**MACHINE GUNS:**

- *Cal.:* 7.62 x 51mm NATO
  *Official Name:* 7.62mm NATO Mg M/42/59
  *Common Name:* MG42/59

  *Remarks:* Rheinmetall of West Germany. Standard. Also called MG 62.

- *Cal.:* 7.62 x 63mm
  *Official Name:* 7.62mm Mg M/48
  *Common Name:* Basically same as
  Madsen Model 50 LMG

  *Remarks:* OBSOLETE. Some still held by the Home Guard.

- *Cal.:* 7.62 x 63mm
  *Official Name:* 7.62mm Mg M/51
  *Common Name:* SIG Model 50

  *Remarks:* Swiss origin. OBSOLETE.

- *Cal.:* 7.62 x 63mm
  *Official Name:* 7.62mm Mg M/
  52-1
  *Common Name:* .30 M1919A4
  LMG

  *Remarks:* US origin. OBSOLETE. Less than 300 provided by MAP and FMS, 1950–74.

- *Cal.:* 7.62 x 63mm
  *Official Name:* 7.62mm Mg M/52-
  11
  *Common Name:* .30 M1919A5
  LMG

  *Remarks:* US origin. OBSOLETE.

- *Cal.:* 12.7 x 99mm
  *Official Name:* 12.7mm Mg M/50
  *Common Name:* .50 M2HB HMG

  *Remarks:* US origin. Standard. Used on ground, vehicle, and M55 Quad AA mounts.

**AUTOMATIC CANNON:**
- *Cal.:* 20 x ???mm
  *Common Name:* 20mm automatic
  cannon

  *Remarks:* Unknown 20mm guns mounted on large patrol and coastal patrol craft.

## DJIBOUTI (Republic of)

Population (estimate in 1984): 0.289 million. Ground forces: regulars, ca. 3,600; paramilitary *(Gendarmerie* and *Sûreté Nationale),* 10,000; French Foreign Legionnaires, ca. 7,000. A former French colony whose small arms continue to follow the French pattern.

**HANDGUNS:**
- *Cal.:* 9 x 19mm Parabellum
  *Common Name:* MAC Mle. 50
  pistol

  *Remarks:* Manufacture Nationale d'Armes de Chatellerault (MAC).

- *Cal.:* 9 x 19mm NATO
  *Common Name:* MAB P-15S

  *Remarks:* Manufacture d'Armes de Bayonne (MAB).

- *Cal.:* 9 x 17mm
  *Common Name:* MAB *Modele D*

  *Remarks:* MAB.

**SUBMACHINE GUNS:**
- *Cal.:* 9 x 19mm Parabellum
  *Common Name:* MAT Mle. 49
  submachine gun

  *Remarks:* Manufacture Nationale d'Armes de Tulle (MAT).

**RIFLES:**
- *Cal.:* 5.56 x 45mm
  *Common Name:* SG540 rifle

  *Remarks:* Manurhin-made SIG rifle used by French Foreign Legion.

- *Cal.:* 5.56 x 45mm
  *Common Name:* FAMAS rifle

  *Remarks:* Manufacture Nationale d'Armes de St. Etienne (MAS), Groupment Industriel des Armements Terrestres (GIAT), France. Ca. 400 acquired through end of 1984.

- *Cal.:* 7.62 x 39mm
  *Common Name:* AK47-type rifles

  *Remarks:* East Bloc origin.

- *Cal.:* 7.62 x 51mm NATO
  *Common Name:* CETME Modelo
  58 assault rifle

  *Remarks:* Centro de Estudios Tecnios Y Materiales Especiales (CETME), Spain.

- *Cal.:* 7.62 x 51mm NATO
  *Common Name: Gewehr 3*

  *Remarks:* Heckler & Koch (HK) design made by (MAS).

- *Cal.:* 7.62 x 51mm NATO
  *Common Name:* FN FAL

  *Remarks:* Origin unknown.

- *Cal.:* 7.5 x 54mm
  *Common Name:* MAS Mle. 36
  bolt action rifle

  *Remarks:* MAS, GIAT, France.

- *Cal.:* 7.5 x 54mm
  *Common Name:* MAS 49/56 rifle

  *Remarks:* MAS, GIAT, France.

**SHOTGUNS:**

**MACHINE GUNS:**
- *Cal.:* 7.5 x 54mm
  *Common Name:* AAT 52 GPMG

  *Remarks:* MAS, GIAT, France.

- *Cal.:* 7.5 x 54mm
  *Common Name:* Chatellerault
  Mle. 24/29 LMG.

  *Remarks:* MAC, France.

- *Cal.:* 7.62 x 39mm
  *Common Name:* RPD LMG.

  *Remarks:* East Bloc origin.

- *Cal.:* 7.62 x 39mm
  *Common Name:* RPK LMG.

  *Remarks:* East Bloc origin.

- *Cal.:* 7.62 x 51mm
  *Common Name:* FN MAG.

  *Remarks:* FN origin. MAG *Infanterie Standard* (60-20), T2.

- *Cal.:* 12.7 x 99mm
  *Common Name:* .50 M2 HB
  HMG.

  *Remarks:* US origin, via France.

**AUTOMATIC CANNON:**


# DOMINICA (Commonwealth of)

Population (estimate in 1980): 0.074 million. Ground forces: regulars, unknown; reserves, unknown; Dominica police force, ca. 280. Former British colony whose small arms follow the older British pattern.

**HANDGUNS:**

**SUBMACHINE GUNS:**

**RIFLES:**
- *Cal.:* 7.62 x 51mm NATO
  *Common Name:* UK L1A1 rifle

  *Remarks:* UK origin?

**SHOTGUNS:**

**MACHINE GUNS:**

**AUTOMATIC CANNON:**

# DOMINICAN REPUBLIC

Population (estimate in 1984): 6.42 million. Ground forces: regulars, ca. 14,000; reserves (paramilitary gendarmerie), 10,000 national police *(Policia Nacional Dominicana).*

**HANDGUNS:**
- *Cal.:* 11.43 x 23mm
  *Common Name:* .45 M1911A1 pistol

  *Remarks:* US origin.

- *Cal.:* 9 x 19mm Parabellum
  *Common Name:* FN Mle. 1935 GP pistol

  *Remarks:* Belgian origin. Purchased after 1962.

- *Cal.:* 9 x 29mmR
  *Common Name:* Smith & Wesson revolvers; a variety

  *Remarks:* US origin.

**SUBMACHINE GUNS:**
- *Cal.:* 9 x 19mm Parabellum
  *Common Name:* Model 38/49 submachine gun

  *Remarks:* Beretta, Italy, and the Armeria San Cristobal, Dominican Republic.

- *Cal.:* 9 x 19mm Parabellum
  *Common Name:* Uzi submachine gun

  *Remarks:* Israeli Military Industries (IMI) or FN origin. The government acquired 225 in 1975; another 200 in 1979.

- *Cal.:* 9 x 19mm Parabellum
  *Common Name:* MAC M10 submachine gun

  *Remarks:* Source uncertain. Probably made locally at the Armeria San Cristobal, Dominican Republic.

**RIFLES:**
- *Cal.:* 5.56 x 45mm
  *Common Name:* M16A1 rifle

  *Remarks:* US origin. MAP delivered 1,060 in 1982. Colt, US. Delivered ca. 5,000 Model 613s rifles.

- *Cal.:* 7.62 x 51mm NATO
  *Common Name:* M14 rifle

  *Remarks:* US origin. MAP delivered 670 in 1982; 980 in 1983.

- *Cal.:* 7.62 x 51mm NATO
  *Common Name:* Gewehr 3

  *Remarks:* Heckler & Koch (HK) GmbH origin.

- *Cal.:* 7.62 x 51mm NATO
  *Common Name:* FN FAL

  *Remarks:* Belgian origin.

- *Cal.:* 7.62 x 51mm NATO
  *Common Name:* CETME Modelo 58 assault rifle

  *Remarks:* Centro de Estudios Tecnios y Materiales Especiales (CETME), Spain.

- *Cal.:* 7.62 x 33mm
  *Common Name:* MK3 Cristobal Carbine

  *Remarks:* Armeria San Cristobal, Dominican Republic. FOM 1005-60-2-7.62-1.

- *Cal.:* 7.62 x 33mm
  *Common Name:* .30 M1 carbine

  *Remarks:* US origin.

**SHOTGUNS:**
- *Cal.:* 18.5 x 59mm
  *Common Name:* 12 gage Winchester Model 1200 shotgun

  *Remarks:* US origin. MAP delivered 120 in 1966, 67 in 1969, and 37 in 1970. NSN 1005-00-921-5483.

- *Cal.:* 18.5 x 59mm
  *Common Name:* 12 gage Mossberg Model 500 shotgun

  *Remarks:* US origin. Police and Customs Department acquired 1979–83.

**MACHINE GUNS:**

- *Cal.:* 7.62 x 51mm NATO
  *Common Name:* M60 GPMG

  *Remarks:* Saco, Maremont, US. MAP delivered 27 in 1966, 27 in 1967, 4 in 1968, 28 in 1969, and 12 in 1970. FMS sold 162 in 1981.

- *Cal.:* 7.62 x 51mm NATO
  *Common Name:* MAG GPMG.

  *Remarks:* FN origin.

- *Cal.:* 7.62 x 63mm
  *Common Name:* .30 M11918A2 BAR

  *Remarks:* US origin. Some of FN origin.

- *Cal.:* 7.62 x 63mm
  *Common Name:* .30 M1917A1 MMG

  *Remarks:* US origin.

- *Cal.:* 7.62 x 63mm
  *Common Name:* .30 M1919A4 LMG

  *Remarks:* US origin.

- *Cal.:* 12.7 x 99mm
  *Common Name:* .30 M2 HB HMG

  *Remarks:* US origin. The Dominican army has also locally converted AN-M2 aircraft machine guns altered to the M2HB configuration.

**AUTOMATIC CANNON:**

- *Cal.:* 20 x ???mm
  *Common Name:* 20mm automatic cannon

  *Remarks:* Unknown 20mm guns on various naval craft.

**GRENADE LAUNCHERS:**

- *Cal.:* 40 x 46mmSR
  *Common Name:* M79 grenade launcher

  *Remarks:* US origin. MAP delivered 30 in 1970. FMS sold 81 in 1982.

Some older weapons that may be held in reserve include 9 x 19mm Lanchester, 9 x 19mm M37/39 Suomi, 9 x 19mm MK II Sten, 11.43 x 23mm M50/M55 Reising, 9 x 19mm M50 Madsen, 11.43 x 23mm M3A1, and 11.43 x 23mm M1928A1 submachine guns; 7.62 x 63mm M1 and M1903A3 rifles; and 7.62 x 63mm Lewis machine guns.

# ECUADOR (Republic of)

Population (estimate in 1984): 9.09 million. Ground forces: regulars, ca. 30,000; reserves, 50,000; Marines, 1,000; paramilitary, variously estimated between 5,800 and 35,000 (includes the national civil police—Policia Nacional).

**HANDGUNS:**

- *Cal.:* 9 x 19mm Parabellum
  *Common Name:* FN Mle. 1935 GP pistol

  *Remarks:* Belgian origin.

- *Cal.:* 9 x 29mmR
  *Common Name:* .38 Smith & Wesson revolvers

  *Remarks:* US origin. State Department licensed sales of 464 to the National Police in 1978; 550 to Police General Command in 1978; 600 to Quito prison guards in 1979. The *Banco Internacional* acquired 100 .32 S&W revolvers in 1978 also.

- *Cal.:* 11.43 x 23mm
  *Common Name:* .45 M1911A1 pistol; reserve stocks only

  *Remarks:* US origin. MAP delivered 65 M1911A1s before 1968.

**SUBMACHINE GUNS:**
- *Cal.:* 9 x 19mm Parabellum
  *Common Name:* Uzi submachine gun

  *Remarks:* FN and Israeli Military Industries (IMI), Israel. Over 5,000 acquired.

- *Cal.:* 11.43 x 23mm
  *Common Name:* .45 M3 submachine gun

  *Remarks:* US origin. MAP delivered 30 in 1967.

**RIFLES:**
- *Cal.:* 5.56 x 45mm
  *Common Name:* Steyr AUG

  *Remarks:* Steyr-Daimler-Puch (SDP), Austria. First AUGs were delivered prior to the end of 1987, with completion of deliveries by 1989.

- *Cal.:* 5.56 x 45mm
  *Common Name:* Ruger Mini-14 rifle

  *Remarks:* Sturm, Ruger Co., US. A few hundred purchased for police use only.

- *Cal.:* 5.56 x 45mm
  *Common Name:* SG540 rifle

  *Remarks:* Manurhin-made SIG design.

- *Cal.:* 5.56 x 45mm
  *Common Name:* M16A1 (Model 653) carbine

  *Remarks:* Small quantity acquired directly from Colt, US. This weapon is used by the Ecuadorian Special Forces. One marketing service has reported that between 25,000 and 35,000 have been delivered; probably incorrect.

- *Cal.:* 7.62 x 33mm
  *Common Name:* .30 M1 and M2 carbines

  *Remarks:* US origin. MAP delivered 576 before 1968. Several hundred already in service.

- *Cal.:* 7.62 x 51mm NATO
  *Common Name:* FN FAL

  *Remarks:* Belgian origin. About 60,000 delivered 1960–80.

- *Cal.:* 7.62 x 51mm NATO
  *Common Name:* M14 rifle

  *Remarks:* US origin. FMS sold 12 in 1977.

- *Cal.:* 7.62 x 51mm NATO
  *Common Name:* M14 National Match rifle

  *Remarks:* US origin. FMS sold 12 in 1975. Acquired for International Military Rifle competition.

- *Cal.:* 7.63 x 63mm
  *Common Name:* .30 M1 rifle

  *Remarks:* US origin. MAP delivered 585 before 1964, added to several thousand provided 1950–60.

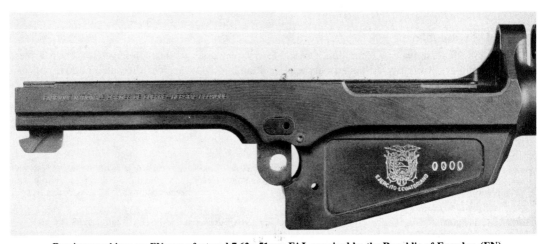

**Receiver markings on FN-manufactured 7.62 x 51mm FAL acquired by the Republic of Ecuador. (FN)**

- *Cal.:* 7.65 x 53.5mm Mauser
  *Common Name:* Mauser M1891
  bolt action rifle

  *Remarks:* German origin. Also later FN-Mauser models.

- *Cal.:* 7.92 x 57mm
  *Common Name:* vz.24 rifle

  *Remarks:* Czechoslovakian origin. Purchased in 1939; employed in the 1940 war with Peru.

**SHOTGUNS:**
- *Cal.:* 18.5 x 59mm
  *Common Name:* 12 gage Moss-
  berg Model 500 shotgun

  *Remarks:* US origin. Police Anticrime Strike Forces, 1985.

**MACHINE GUNS:**
- *Cal.:* 7.62 x 51mm NATO
  *Common Name:* FN MAG

  *Remarks:* FN origin. Models used include the MAG *Infanterie Standard* (60-20), T5 with nondisintegrating belt feed, used by both army and air force. The Infantry T14 is used by both army and navy. The MAG Coaxial (60-40) Std. 1 and the AMX-13 turret model are also in service.

- *Cal.:* 7.62 x 51mm NATO
  *Common Name:* 7.62mm NATO
  M1919A4 LMG

  *Remarks:* US origin. Converted to 7.62mm NATO by FN.

- *Cal.:* 7.62 x 51mm NATO
  *Common Name:* M134 high rate
  of fire gun (Minigun)

  *Remarks:* US origin. FMS sold 32 in 1981.

- *Cal.:* 7.62 x 63mm
  *Common Name:* .30 M1919A4
  LMG

  *Remarks:* US origin.

- *Cal.:* 7.92 x 57mm
  *Common Name:* MG42 GPMG

  *Remarks:* Zavodi Crvena Zastava, Kragujevac, Yugoslavia. *Mitrajez M53.*

- *Cal.:* 7.92 x 57mm
  *Common Name:* ZB-30 LMG

  *Remarks:* Czechoslovakian origin. Purchased before World War II.

- *Cal.:* 12.7 x 99mm
  *Common Name:* .50 M2 HB
  HMG

  *Remarks:* US origin. RAMO sold direct 100 M2HBs on M63 AA mounts in 1981. Ecuadorian armed forces also use the M55 quad mount .50 antiaircraft system.

**AUTOMATIC CANNON:**
- *Cal.:* 20 x 102mm
  *Common Name:* 20mm M168 Vul-
  can automatic cannon

  *Remarks:* General Electric, US. At least 44 M163 self-propelled Vulcan Air Defense System were in service as of 1979. Ca. 28 M167A2 towed VADS were in service as of 1979.

- *Cal.:* 20 x ???mm
  *Common Name:* 20mm automatic
  cannon

  *Remarks:* Unknown 20mm guns mounted on smaller naval craft.

**GRENADE LAUNCHERS:**
- *Cal.:* 40 x 46mmSR
  *Common Name:* M203 grenade
  launcher attached to M16A1

  *Remarks:* Between 40 and 50 from Colt. Rifles may have been purchased directly from US government.

# EGYPT (Arab Republic of)

Population (estimate in 1984): 47.05 million. Ground forces: regulars, ca. 350,000 (180,000 conscripts); reserves, ca. 500,000; paramilitary, 139,000 (national guard, 60,000; frontier corps, 12,000; static defense and security forces, 60,000; coast guard, 7,000).

**HANDGUNS:**

• *Cal.:* 9 x 19mm Parabellum
*Official Name:* 9mm Helwan
*Common Name:* Beretta 9mm
M951 Brigadier pistol

*Remarks:* Beretta and the domestic concern Military Factories General Organization at Maadi Military & Civil Industries Co. FOM 1005-36-1-9-1.

• *Cal.:* 9 x 19mm Parabellum
*Common Name:* Tokagypt pistol

*Remarks:* Femaru es Szerszamgepyar (FEG), Hungary; manufactured for Egyptian police use.

• *Cal.:* 9 x 29mmR
*Common Name:* .38 Smith & Wesson revolvers

*Remarks:* US origin. State Department licensed the sale of 2,380 revolvers in 1977–78 for the UAR police. An additional 23 .38 caliber revolvers and 16 .357 revolvers were obtained by the Security Department of the Presidency in 1977–79.

• *Cal.:* 9 x 29mmR
*Common Name:* .357 MR-73 Manurhin revolvers

*Remarks:* Manurhin, France.

**SUBMACHINE GUNS:**

• *Cal.:* 7.65 x 17mm
*Common Name:* M61 Skorpion SMG

*Remarks:* Czechoslovakian origin. Carried by security guards.

• *Cal.:* 9 x 19mm Parabellum
*Official Name:* 9mm Port Said
*Common Name:* Carl Gustav M45 submachine gun

*Remarks:* Copy of Swedish Model 45 SMG, made at the Maadi Military & Civil Industries Co.

• *Cal.:* 9 x 19mm Parabellum
*Common Name:* Carl Gustav M45 submachine gun

*Remarks:* Made by FFV Ordnance Division, Sweden.

• *Cal.:* 9 x 19mm Parabellum
*Official Name:* 9mm Akaba
*Common Name:* Simplified (?) Port Said submachine gun

*Remarks:* Maadi Military & Civil Industries Co.

• *Cal.:* 9 x 19mm Parabellum
*Common Name:* Beretta M12S submachine gun

*Remarks:* Beretta, Italy.

• *Cal.:* 9 x 19mm Parabellum
*Common Name:* Beretta M38/49 (Model 4) submachine gun

*Remarks:* Beretta.

**Slide markings in Egyptian-manufactured Beretta 9 x 19mm M951 pistol. The trademark between the English and Arabic is the logo of the Maadi Military & Civil Industries Co. (Krcma)**

**An American paratrooper of the 82d Airborne examines an Egyptian-made 7.62 x 39mm AKM in the presence of Egyptian airborne troops during "Bright Star 82" exercises in the Middle East. (DOD–USAF)**

- *Cal.:* 9 x 19mm Parabellum
  *Common Name:* Beretta M34 sub-machine gun

  *Remarks:* Beretta.

- *Cal.:* 9 x 19mm Parabellum
  *Common Name:* Star Z-45 submachine gun

  *Remarks:* Star, Bonafacio Echeverria, Spain.

**RIFLES:**
- *Cal.:* 5.56 x 45mm
  *Common Name:* M16A1 rifle

  *Remarks:* US origin. FMS sold 40 to the Egyptians for evaluation in 1981.

- *Cal.:* 7.62 x 39mm
  *Official Name:* 7.62mm Misr
  *Common Name:* AKM assault rifle

  *Remarks:* USSR and Maadi Military & Civil Industries Co.

- *Cal.:* 7.62 x 39mm
  *Common Name:* AK47 assault rifle

  *Remarks:* Soviet origin.

- *Cal.:* 7.62 x 39mm
  *Common Name:* SKS carbine

  *Remarks:* Soviet origin.

**Egyptian infantrymen receive familiarization training with US 5.56 x 45mm M16A1 rifles during "Bright Star 83." The soldier in the foreground is shooting an M16A1 with an M203 grenade launcher attached. (DOD)**

- *Cal.:* 7.62 x 39mm
  *Official Name:* 7.62mm Raschid
  *Common Name:* Scaled-down version of the Hakim rifle

- *Cal.:* 7.62 x 54mmR
  *Common Name:* SVD sniping rifle

- *Cal.:* 7.92 x 57mm
  *Official Name:* 7.92mm Hakim
  *Common Name:* Copy of Model 42 Ljungman rifle

- *Cal.:* 7.92 x 57mm
  *Common Name:* FN SAFN rifle

- *Cal.:* 7.62 x 39mm
  *Common Name:* vz.52/57 rifle

- *Cal.:* 7.92 x 33mm
  *Common Name:* Stg. 44 assault rifle

*Remarks:* Locally made by the Maadi; Military & Civil Industries Co. Obsolescent; use limited to static units. Some sold as surplus in 1986 to Western arms dealers.

*Remarks:* Domestic copy of the Soviet Dragunov sniper rifle.

*Remarks:* Locally made by the Maadi Military & Civil Industries Co. Obsolescent; use limited to static units. Many sold as surplus in 1986 to Western arms dealers.

*Remarks:* FN origin. Purchased during King Farouk's reign.

*Remarks:* Czechoslovakian origin. OBSOLETE.

*Remarks:* World War II German manufacture (possible with post-war spares and magazines from East Germany). About 4,000 offered for sale by the Egyptians in 1985–86.

**SHOTGUNS:**
- *Cal.:* 18.5 x 59mm
  *Common Name:* 12 gage Moss-berg Model 500 shotgun

  *Remarks:* Police use only.

- *Cal.:* 18.5 x 59mm
  *Common Name:* Franchi SPAS-12 riot-type shotgun, with folding metal stock

  *Remarks:* Franchi of Italy. Acquired by the Military Police.

- *Cal.:* 18.5 x 59mm
  *Common Name:* Franchi PA3 riot-type shotgun, with wooden stock

  *Remarks:* Franchi of Italy. Acquired by the Military Police.

**MACHINE GUNS:**
- *Cal.:* 7.62 x 39mm
  *Official Name:* 7.62mm Suez
  *Common Name:* Copy of RPD LMG

  *Remarks:* USSR and Maadi Military & Civil Industries Co.

- *Cal.:* 7.62 x 39mm
  *Common Name:* vz.52 and vz.52/57 LMGs

  *Remarks:* Czechoslovakian origin.

- *Cal.:* 7.62 x 51mm NATO
  *Common Name:* M60 GPMG

  *Remarks:* US origin. FMS sold 52 in 1981.

- *Cal.:* 7.62 x 51mm NATO
  *Common Name:* M73 armor MG

  *Remarks:* US origin. Mounted on M60A3 tanks.

- *Cal.:* 7.62 x 51mm NATO
  *Common Name:* FN MAG

  *Remarks:* FN origin. This weapon reportedly has been adopted by the Egyptian Army. Its production at the Maadi Military & Civil Industries Co. has been licensed by FN.

- *Cal.:* 7.62 x 51mm NATO
  *Common Name:* M240 armor MG

  *Remarks:* US origin. Copy of the FN MAG made by FN Manufacturing, Inc. of Columbia, S.C., US. FMS sold 219 in 1982 for use on M60 tanks. There was a reported sale of 551 more in 1985.

- *Cal.:* 7.62 x 54mmR
  *Official Name:* 7.62mm Asswan
  *Common Name:* Copy of SGM MG

  *Remarks:* USSR and Maadi Military & Civil Industries Co.

- *Cal.:* 7.62 x 54mmR
  *Common Name:* SG43 MG series

  *Remarks:* Soviet origin. Nearly all variants used.

- *Cal.:* 7.62 x 54mmR
  *Common Name:* PKT armor machine gun

  *Remarks:* Soviet origin. Mounted on T62 tanks.

- *Cal.:* 7.7 x 56mmR
  *Common Name:* .303 Bren gun

  *Remarks:* UK origin.

- *Cal.:* 7.7 x 56mmR
  *Common Name:* .303 Vickers gun

  *Remarks:* UK origin.

- *Cal.:* 12.7 x 99mm
  *Common Name:* .50 M2 HB HMG

  *Remarks:* US origin. FMS sold 1,028 between 1979 and 1981. Flexible mount on M60A3 tanks. Saco Defense Systems Division of Maremont Corp. delivered additional M2s in 1986 through NAPCO Inc.

- *Cal.:* 12.7 x 99mm
  *Common Name:* .50 M85 armor MG

  *Remarks:* US origin. Mounted on M60A3 tanks. FMS sold an additional 93 guns in 1982.

- *Cal.:* 12.7 x 108mm
  *Common Name:* DShK38 and DShK38/46

  *Remarks:* Soviet origin. Single HMGs. Ground mount, vehicular mount, and the Czech M53 quad AA mount.

**AUTOMATIC CANNON:**

- *Cal.:* 14.5 x 114mm
  *Common Name:* KPV HMG

  *Remarks:* Soviet origin. 1-, 2-, and 4-gun antiaircraft mounts. Also used as a vehicular gun.

- *Cal.:* 20 x ???mm
  *Common Name:* 20mm automatic cannon

  *Remarks:* Unknown 20mm guns on several naval craft.

- *Cal.:* 20 x 102mm
  *Common Name:* 20mm Vulcan M61 cannon

  *Remarks:* General Electric provided 40 Vulcan cannon in 1982/83.

- *Cal.:* 23 x 152mmB
  *Common Name:* ZU23 automatic cannon

  *Remarks:* Soviet origin. 2- and 4-gun antiaircraft mounts. Approx. 350 ZSU-23-4 SP AA systems are in service with the Egyptian Army. Reportedly these guns have been refurbished and overhauled by a US company.

- *Cal.:* 25 x 218mm
  *Common Name:* 2-M-3 or 2-M-8 automatic cannon

  *Remarks:* Soviet origin. Mounted on "S0-1" class patrol craft.

## Egyptian Small Arms Manufacture

Since the mid-1950s, the Egyptian armed forces have been working toward self-sufficiency in military weapons from small arms to aircraft. During that era, the Egyptians have received technical assistance from Swedish and Soviet technicians. Most of their small caliber weapons are manufactured by the Maadi Military & Civil Industries Co. at a production facility that was formerly called "Factory 54." Maadi is a subdivision of the larger state-operated enterprise called the Military Factories General Organization. Most of the current Egyptian small arms are variants of the Soviet arms they first purchased in large numbers in the early 1950s. The Egyptians also manufacture quality ammunition for their small caliber weapons. Since the mid-1970s the Egyptian defense industries have sought to export their products whenever possible. Egypt sent unspecified arms to Morocco in 1979 and has been supporting Iraq during the course of the Iran-Iraq war.

## EL SALVADOR (Republic of)

Population (estimate in 1984): 4.88 million. Ground forces: regulars, ca. 39,000; reserves, ca. 30,000; paramilitary, ca. 11,500 effective (national guard, 2,500 to 4,000; national police *[Policía Nacional]* 3,000 to 4,500; treasury police *[Policía de la Hacienda],* 2,000 to 2,500; *Orden* — territorial civil defense corps of 70,000, of which 2,000 are effectives).

**HANDGUNS:**

- *Cal.:* 9 x 19mm Parabellum
  *Common Name:* Fn Mle. 35 GP pistol

  *Remarks:* FN origin. Purchased before 1950 and again 1958–61. During the last 10 years the Salvadorans have been buying this handgun from the Argentine factory (FMAP), at Rosario.

- *Cal.:* 11.43 x 23mm
  *Common Name:* .45 M1911A1 pistol

  *Remarks:* US origin. MAP grant before 1964. FMS delivery of 225 M1911A1s in 1982.

**SUBMACHINE GUNS:**

- *Cal.:* 9 x 19mm Parabellum
  *Common Name:* M46/53 submachine gun

  *Remarks:* Madsen/Dansk Industri Syndikat, Denmark.

- *Cal.:* 9 x 19mm NATO
  *Common Name:* MP5 submachine gun

  *Remarks:* Heckler & Koch (HK) GmbH. A very small number provided.

- *Cal.:* 9 x 19mm NATO
  *Common Name:* FMK submachine gun

  *Remarks:* Fabrica Militar de Armas Portatiles "Domingo Matheu" (FMAP "DM"), Rosario, Argentina.

## RIFLES:
- *Cal.:* 7.62 x 33mm
  *Common Name:* .30 M2 carbine

  *Remarks:* US origin. MAP delivered 156 before 1964.

- *Cal.:* 5.56 x 45mm
  *Common Name:* M16A1 rifle

  *Remarks:* Colt, US. MAP delivered 11,886 in 1981–82, and FMS delivered 20,743 1982–84. Previously this rifle was issued only to elite units such as the Atlacati Battalion; it is now the standard infantry rifle.

- *Cal.:* 5.56 x 45mm
  *Common Name:* HK 33 rifle

  *Remarks:* HK GmbH origin, but means of delivery unknown. Between 2,000 and 3,000 are reported in country.

- *Cal.:* 7.62 x 51mm NATO
  *Common Name:* Gewehr 3

  *Remarks:* HK origin. These G3s may have been acquired from Indonesia, although this is denied by the Indonesians. Many G3s have been seen in the hands of antigovernment rebels.

- *Cal.:* 7.62 x 63mm
  *Common Name:* .30 M1D sniper
  rifle

  *Remarks:* US origin. MAP delivered 211 1982–84.

- *Cal.:* 7.62 x 63mm
  *Common Name:* .30 M1 rifle

  *Remarks:* US origin. MAP delivered 1,365 before 1965.

- *Cal.:* 7 x 57mm
  *Common Name:* 7mm Mauser
  rifle

  *Remarks:* Used by *Hacienda Policía* (Treasury), National Police, National Guard, and Static Defense Forces.

## SHOTGUNS:

## MACHINE GUNS:
- *Cal.:* 7.62 x 51mm NATO
  *Common Name:* M60 GPMG

  *Remarks:* Saco, Maremont, US. MAP delivered 542 1981–83.

- *Cal.:* 7.62 x 51mm NATO
  *Common Name:* M60D aircraft
  gun

  *Remarks:* Saco, Maremont, US. MAP delivered 46 1982–83.

- *Cal.:* 7.62 x 51mm NATO
  *Common Name:* GAU-2A1B
  minigun

  *Remarks:* General Electric, US.

- *Cal.:* 7.62 x 51mm NATO
  *Common Name:* Madsen-Saetter
  LMG

  *Remarks:* Dansk Industri Syndikat design converted from 7.92 x 57mm Mauser to 7.62mm NATO. FOM 1005-33-4-7.62-1.

- *Cal.:* 7.62 x 63mm
  *Common Name:* .30 Madsen-
  Saetter

  *Remarks:* Indonesian surplus? This source of origin is denied by the Indonesians.

- *Cal.:* 7.62 x 63mm
  *Common Name:* .30 M1919A6
  LMG

  *Remarks:* US origin. MAP before 1977. About 100 guns.

- *Cal.:* 12.7 x 99mm
  *Common Name:* .50 M2 HB
  HMG

  *Remarks:* US origin. MAP delivered 72 before 1964 and 90 1982–83. RAMO delivered 27 in 1983–84 with M3 mounts.

In late January 1981, Honduran authorities seized a refrigerated trailer truck, which was being used to smuggle arms to Salvadoran guerrillas. Approximately 100 M16A1 rifles, some of which were traceable to Vietnam, along with large quantities of 5.56mm ammunition and mortar bombs, were discovered in the hollowed-out insulation on the top of the truck. (US Department of State)

**Two views of the Cuban FAL. The first one illustrates the Cuban crest applied by the FN factory. The second shows the hole drilled to "sanitize" the FALs before they were shipped to El Salvador. (FN and Kokalis)**

**AUTOMATIC CANNON:**
- *Cal.:* 20 x 110mm
  *Common Name:* M55 automatic cannon

*Remarks:* Yugoslavian origin. Variant on the Hispano-Suiza (now Oerlikon) HS804 cannon. The Salvadorans use the 3-gun HS630-3-type antiaircraft mount.

**GRENADE LAUNCHERS:**
- *Cal.:* 40 x 46mmSR
  *Common Name:* M79 grenade launcher

*Remarks:* US origin. FMS delivered 645 in 1981–82 and MAP delivered 995 1981–84.

- *Cal.:* 40 x 46mmSR
  *Common Name:* M203 grenade launcher

*Remarks:* US origin. Mounted on M16A1 rifle. MAP delivered 224 in 1983.

## Military Aid to El Salvador

In recent years the United States has been supplying small caliber weapons to the armed forces of El Salvador as indicated by the above inventory. At the same time, the governments of Nicaragua and Cuba have been supplying a mixture of Soviet and Czechoslovakian small arms to the antigovernment guerrillas in El Salvador. Government forces have also recovered Cuban FALs with the Cuban army markings removed. The Cubans failed to remove the serial numbers that identify them as being made for the Cuban government in the late 1950s and early 1960s. US M16A1 rifles that were left behind in Vietnam in 1975 at the time the South Vietnamese government fell have also been taken from killed Salvadorian rebels. Other M16A1s of the same origin have been confiscated by Honduran government personnel before the rifles could be smuggled into El Salvador.

The following quantities of arms were captured and lost by Salvadoran armed forces during the period 1 January 1981 through August 1984.

|  | *Captured* | *Lost* |
|---|---|---|
| Rifles: | 2,149 (including 1,620 M16A1s) | 3,426 |
| Machine Guns: | 15 | 98 |
| Grenade Launchers: | 70 | 141 |
| Recoilless Rifles: | 3 | 37 |
| Mortars: | 5 | 47 |

See entry on Vietnam for more information on US materiel abandoned there in 1975.

## Government Opposition Forces (totals ca. 10,000)

*Direccion Revolucionaria Unificada* (DRU) — political wing is *Frente Democratico Revolucionario* (FDR) and military wing is *Frente Farabundo Marti para la Liberacion Nacional* (FMLN): ca. 8,000 plus 6,000 claimed as reserves. These troops have been seen with FALs and G3s. There are four other smaller antigovernment forces active in El Salvador.

## EQUATORIAL GUINEA (Republic of)

Population (estimate in 1984): 0.35 million. Ground forces: regulars, variously estimated 1,400 to 8,600; paramilitary (Guardia Civil), 2,000 to 8,000. Former Spanish colony, but majority of small arms currently appear to be of East Bloc origin. Cuba has about 240 troops in-country.

**HANDGUNS:**
- *Cal.:* 7.62 x 25mm
  *Common Name:* TT33 Tokarev pistol

  *Remarks:* East Bloc origin.

- *Cal.:* 9 x 17mm
  *Common Name:* .380 Astra 300 pistol

  *Remarks:* Spanish origin?

**SUBMACHINE GUNS:**
- *Cal.:* 9 x 19mm Parabellum
  *Common Name:* MAT Mle. 49 submachine gun

  *Remarks:* Manufacture Nationale d'Armes de Tulle (MAT).

- *Cal.:* 9 x 19mm Parabellum
  *Common Name:* vz.23 and vz.25 submachine guns

  *Remarks:* Czechoslovakian origin.

- *Cal.:* 7.62 x 25mm
  *Common Name:* PPSh41 submachine gun

  *Remarks:* Soviet origin.

- *Cal.:* 7.62 x 25mm
  *Common Name:* PPS43 submachine gun

  *Remarks:* Soviet origin.

**RIFLES:**
- *Cal.:* 7.62 x 39mm
  *Common Name:* SKS carbine

  *Remarks:* East Bloc origin.

- *Cal.:* 7.62 x 39mm
  *Common Name:* AK47 and AKM assault rifles

  *Remarks:* East Bloc origin.

- *Cal.:* 7.62 x 39mm
  *Common Name:* vz.58 assault rifle

  *Remarks:* Czechoslovakian origin.

- *Cal.:* 7.62 x 51mm NATO
  *Common Name:* CETME assault rifle

  *Remarks:* Fabrica de Armas de Oviedo of the Empresa Nacional Santa Barbara de Industrias Militares, of Spain.

- *Cal.:* 7.92 x 33mm
  *Common Name:* STG. 44

  *Remarks:* World War II Germany. Unconfirmed reports.

**SHOTGUNS:**

**MACHINE GUNS:**
- *Cal.:* 7.62 x 39mm
  *Common Name:* RPD LMG

  *Remarks:* East Bloc origin.

- *Cal.:* 7.62 x 39mm
  *Common Name:* RPK LMG

  *Remarks:* East Bloc origin.

- *Cal.:* 7.62 x 54mmR
  *Common Name:* PK GPMG

  *Remarks:* East Bloc origin.

- *Cal.:* 7.62 x 54mmR
  *Common Name:* SG43 and SGM MG series

  *Remarks:* East Bloc origin. Including SGMT on older Soviet tanks.

- *Cal.:* 7.62 x 54mmR
  *Common Name:* Type 67 GPMG

  *Remarks:* PRC origin.

- *Cal.:* 7.62 x 54mmR
  *Common Name:* RP46 LMG

  *Remarks:* East Bloc origin.

- *Cal.:* 7.62 x 54mmR
  *Common Name:* DT armor machine gun

  *Remarks:* Soviet origin. Mounted on older Soviet tanks.

- *Cal.:* 12.7 x 108mm
  *Common Name:* DShK 38/46 HMG

  *Remarks:* East Bloc origin.

**AUTOMATIC CANNON:**
- *Cal.:* 14.5 x 114mm
  *Common Name:* KPV HMG

  *Remarks:* Soviet origin. Both ground and naval mounted guns are in service.

- *Cal.:* 25 x 218mm
  *Common Name:* 2-M-3 or 2-M-8 automatic cannon

  *Remarks:* Soviet origin. Mounted on Soviet "P6" class patrol craft.


## ETHIOPIA

Population (estimate in 1984): 31.99 million. Ground forces: regulars, about 60,000, plus ca. 150,000 "People's Militia; reserves, ca. 20,000; paramilitary, ca. 169,000 including a mobile emergency police force of about 9,000 effectives and a frontier guard force of about 2,500. Approximately 1,400 Soviet technicians, about 11,000 Cuban "advisory" troops and 250 East German technicians were stationed in Ethiopia (as of early 1984) to ensure that insurgents in Eritrea and the clash with Somalia over the Ogaden region do not get out of hand. There may be some South Yemeni troops in Ethiopia as well. While Ethiopian small arms previously were of German and US types, they are primarily of the East Bloc pattern. Many of these weapons have been provided by the Libyans. Rebel forces have been supplied by the Somalia government with Kalashnikovs and other East Bloc weapons. Rebels also use older Ethiopian small caliber weapons.


**HANDGUNS:**
- *Cal.:* 5.6 x 16mmR
  *Common Name:* .22 Long Rifle Smith & Wesson K22 Masterpiece revolver

  *Remarks:* US origin. FMS delivered 60 in 1972.

- *Cal.:* 7.65 x 17mm
  *Common Name:* Beretta M34/84 pistol

  *Remarks:* Beretta, Italy.

- *Cal.:* 7.65 x 17mm
  *Common Name:* vz.27 pistol

  *Remarks:* Czechoslovakian origin.

- *Cal.:* 9 x 18mm
  *Common Name:* Makarov pistol

  *Remarks:* East Bloc origin.

- *Cal.:* 9 x 19mm Parabellum
  *Common Name:* Smith & Wesson M39 pistol

  *Remarks:* US origin.

- *Cal.:* 9 x 29mmR
  *Common Name:* .38 Colt Detective Special revolver

  *Remarks:* US origin. FMS delivered 88 in 1972. NSN 1005-00-726-5655.

- *Cal.:* 9 x 29mmR
  *Common Name:* .38 Smith & Wesson M10 revolver

  *Remarks:* US origin. MAP delivered 8 in 1971. NSN 1005-00-937-5840.

• *Cal.:* 9 x 29mmR
*Common Name:* .38 Smith & Wesson M10 revolver

*Remarks:* US origin. MAP delivered 50 in 1970. NSN 1005-00-937-5839.

• *Cal.:* 11.43 x 23mm
*Common Name:* .45 M1911A1 pistol

*Remarks:* US origin. MAP delivered 917 between 1969 and 1971.

**SUBMACHINE GUNS:**
• *Cal.:* 7.62 x 25mm
*Common Name:* PPSh41 submachine gun

*Remarks:* Soviet origin? As late as 1977, the People's Militia had PPSh41 SMGs with the 71-shot drum magazines.

• *Cal.:* 7.62 x 25mm
*Common Name:* Model 1943/52 submachine gun

*Remarks:* Polish origin.

• *Cal.:* 9 x 19mm Parabellum
*Common Name:* M 38/42 submachine gun

*Remarks:* Beretta.

• *Cal.:* 9 x 19mm Parabellum
*Common Name:* M 38/49 (Model 4) submachine gun

*Remarks:* Beretta.

• *Cal.:* 9 x 19mm Parabellum
*Common Name:* Uzi submachine gun

*Remarks:* Source unknown.

• *Cal.:* 11.43 x 23mm
*Common Name:* .45 M3 and M3A1 submachine guns

*Remarks:* US origin. MAP delivered 567 SMGs before 1972, including 142 M3s and 135 M3A1s.

**RIFLES:**
• *Cal.:* 7.62 x 33mm
*Common Name:* .30 M1 and M2 carbines

*Remarks:* US origin. MAP delivered 16,416 before 1973.

• *Cal.:* 7.62 x 39mm
*Common Name:* Type 56 (AK47) assault rifle

*Remarks:* People's Republic of China (PRC).

• *Cal.:* 7.62 x 39mm
*Common Name:* Type 56 or SKS carbine

*Remarks:* PRC? Oromo Liberation Front have been seen using this weapon.

• *Cal.:* 7.62 x 39mm
*Common Name:* AKM

*Remarks:* Source unknown. Oromo Liberation Front have been seen using this weapon.

• *Cal.:* 7.62 x 39mm
*Common Name:* vz.52/57 rifle

*Remarks:* Czechoslovakian origin, via Cuba?

• *Cal.:* 7.62 x 39mm
*Common Name:* vz.58 rifle

*Remarks:* Czechoslovakian origin, via Cuba? Oromo Liberation Front have been seen using this weapon.

• *Cal.:* 7.62 x 39mm
*Common Name:* Type 68 rifle

*Remarks:* PRC.

• *Cal.:* 7.62 x 39mm
*Common Name:* vz.58 assault rifle

*Remarks:* Czechoslovakian origin.

• *Cal.:* 7.62 x 39mm
*Common Name:* M64A or M70 assault rifle

*Remarks:* Zavodi Crvena Zastava, Kragujevac, Yugoslavia.

- *Cal.:* 7.62 x 51mm NATO
  *Common Name:* M14 rifle

- *Cal.:* 7.62 x 51mm NATO
  *Common Name:* BM59 (MK IV)
  rifle

- *Cal.:* 7.62 x 51mm NATO
  *Common Name:* Gewehr 3

- *Cal.:* 7.62 x 51mm NATO
  *Common Name:* FAL

- *Cal.:* 7.5 x 54mm
  *Common Name:* MAS Mle 36 bolt
  action rifle

- *Cal.:* 7.62 x 54mmR
  *Common Name:* M44 Mosin-
  Nagant carbines

- *Cal.:* 7.62 x 63mm
  *Common Name:* .30 M1 rifle

- *Cal.:* 7.62 x 63mm
  *Common Name:* .30 M1C sniper
  rifle

- *Cal.:* 7.62 x 63mm
  *Common Name:* .30 M1D sniper
  rifle

- *Cal.:* 7.7 x 56mmR
  *Common Name:* .303 SMLE

- *Cal.:* 7.92 x 33mm
  *Common Name:* STG. 44

- *Cal.:* 7.92 x 57mm
  *Common Name:* Mauser 98k rifle

- *Cal.:* 6.5 x 52.5mm
  *Common Name:* M1891 and
  M1891/38 Mannlicher Carcano
  bolt action rifles

*Remarks:* US origin. MAP delivered 3,949 in 1971, 5,005 in 1972, 4,723 in 1973, 4,516 in 1974, and 5,260 in 1975. Oromo Liberation Front have been seen using this weapon.

*Remarks:* Beretta.

*Remarks:* Source unknown.

*Remarks:* Source unknown. Some marked EdC.

*Remarks:* Manufacture Nationale d'Armes de Chatellerault (MAC).

*Remarks:* Soviet origin. Oromo Liberation Front have been seen using this weapon.

*Remarks:* US origin. Before 1964 MAP delivered 19,823 rifles, of which at least 200 were M1s. Before 1975 an additional 1,880 were delivered.

*Remarks:* US origin. In 1966 MAP delivered 3.

*Remarks:* US origin. In 1967 MAP delivered 6.

*Remarks:* Source and specific models unknown.

*Remarks:* World War II German. These weapons continue to be seen in the hands of antigovernment rebels. Some are said to have been received from Czechoslovakia.

*Remarks:* World War II German and M48 Yugoslav. These weapons continue to be seen in the hands of antigovernment rebels. Some are said to have been received from Czechoslovakia.

*Remarks:* Italian origin. OBSOLETE. Oromo Liberation Front (OLF) have been seen using this weapon.

**SHOTGUNS:**

**MACHINE GUNS:**
- *Cal.:* 7.62 x 39mm
  *Common Name:* vz.52/57 LMG

- *Cal.:* 7.62 x 39mm
  *Common Name:* RPD LMG

- *Cal.:* 7.62 x 39mm
  *Common Name:* RPK LMG

- *Cal.:* 7.62 x 39mm
  *Common Name:* M70B1 LMG

*Remarks:* Czechoslovakian origin.

*Remarks:* East Bloc origin. Some in hands of OLF forces.

*Remarks:* East Bloc origin.

*Remarks:* Zavodi Crvena Zastava, Kragujevac, Yugoslavia.

- *Cal.:* 7.62 x 54mmR
  *Common Name:* RP46 company machine gun

  *Remarks:* Soviet origin. Some older DP LMGs may still be in service.

- *Cal.:* 7.62 x 54mmR
  *Common Name:* SG43 MG series

  *Remarks:* East Bloc origin.

- *Cal.:* 7.62 x 54mmR
  *Common Name:* Type 67 GPMG

  *Remarks:* PRC origin.

- *Cal.:* 7.62 x 54mmR
  *Common Name:* PK GPMG and PKT AMG

  *Remarks:* Soviet origin. Mounted on Soviet T62 tanks.

- *Cal.:* 7.62 x 51mm NATO
  *Common Name:* BM59 (MK IV) LMG version of the BM59 rifle

  *Remarks:* Beretta.

- *Cal.:* 7.62 x 51mm NATO
  *Common Name:* M60 GPMG

  *Remarks:* US origin. MAP delivered 132 in 1972, 244 in 1973, 128 in 1974, and 132 in 1975.

- *Cal.:* 7.62 x 63mm
  *Common Name:* .30 M1918A2 BAR

  *Remarks:* US origin. MAP delivered 64 between 1967 and 1969.

- *Cal.:* 7.62 x 63mm
  *Common Name:* .30 M1919A1 LMG

  *Remarks:* US origin.

- *Cal.:* 7.62 x 63mm
  *Common Name:* .30 M1919A4 LMG

  *Remarks:* US origin. MAP delivered 72 before 1971.

- *Cal.:* 7.62 x 63mm
  *Common Name:* .30 M1919A6 LMG

  *Remarks:* US origin. MAP delivered 42 before 1971.

- *Cal.:* 7.92 x 57mm
  *Common Name:* M50 Madsen LMG

  *Remarks:* Madsen/Dansk Industri Syndikat, Denmark. In addition the Ethiopian armed forces previously had 7.92mm M1907, M1910, M1934, and M1935 Madsen LMGs. Just how many are still serviceable and used is unknown.

- *Cal.:* 7.92 x 57mm
  *Common Name:* FN BAR Type D

  *Remarks:* Belgian origin.

- *Cal.:* 7.92 x 57mm
  *Common Name:* MG34 GPMG

  *Remarks:* Origin and manufacturer unknown.

- *Cal.:* 7.92 x 57mm
  *Common Name:* MG42 GPMG

  *Remarks:* Origin and manufacturer unknown.

- *Cal.:* 7.7 x 53mmR
  *Common Name:* .303 Bren guns

  *Remarks:* UK origin.

- *Cal.:* 7.7 x 53mmR
  *Common Name:* .303 Vickers guns

  *Remarks:* UK origin. OBSOLETE.

- *Cal.:* 7.62 x 63mm
  *Common Name:* .30 Lewis gun

  *Remarks:* OBSOLETE. Origin unknown. May be used by rebel forces.

- *Cal.:* 8.5 x 59mmRB
  *Common Name:* M37 Breda HMG

  *Remarks:* Italian origin. OBSOLETE.

- *Cal.:* 12.7 x 99mm
  *Common Name:* .50 M2 HB HMG

  *Remarks:* US origin. MAP and FMS delivered 110 before 1976. An additional 16 M2s for the M1 Cupola were delivered before 1975, as were 16 M55 quad AA systems.

- *Cal.:* 12.7 x 99mm
  *Common Name:* .50 M85 armor MG

  *Remarks:* US origin. FMS delivered 22 in 1974 and 1975.

- *Cal.:* 12.7 x 108mm
  *Common Name:* DShK38/46 HMG

  *Remarks:* Soviet origin.

**AUTOMATIC CANNON:**
- *Cal.:* 14.5 x 114mm
  *Common Name:* KPV HMG in ZPU-4

  *Remarks:* East Bloc origin. Also mounted on naval craft.

- *Cal.:* 20 x 110mm
  *Common Name:* M55 automatic cannon

  *Remarks:* Yugoslavian origin. Mounted on coastal patrol craft.

- *Cal.:* 20 x 139mm
  *Common Name:* 20mm French automatic cannon

  *Remarks:* French origin. Mounted on French "Edic" class landing craft.

- *Cal.:* 23 x 152mmB
  *Common Name:* ZU23 automatic cannon.

  *Remarks:* East Bloc origin. Used by Tigre People's Liberation Front (TPLF) forces.

**GRENADE LAUNCHERS:**
- *Cal.:* 40 x 46mmSR
  *Common Name:* M79 grenade

  *Remarks:* US origin. MAP delivered 1,008 1971–73.

**Small Arms Used by Antigovernment Forces**

The major Ethiopian antigovernment forces include the Tigre People's Liberation Front (TPLF) (ca. 5,000 effectives), which uses arms of the type listed above and G3 and FAL assault rifles. The Eritrean Liberation Front (ELF) has some 6,500 effectives; the *Front de Liberation de l'Erythree—Conseil de la Révolution* (FLE-CR) has ca. 10,000 effectives; People's Liberation Front Revolutionary Guards (PLFG) has ca. 5,000 effectives; *Front Populaire de Liberation de l'Erythree* (FPLE) People's Liberation Front (EPLF) has ca. 12,000 effectives; Oromo Liberation Front (OLF) made up of Nilotic tribesmen; Ethiopian People's Revolutionary Party (EPRP); Ethiopian People's Democratic Movement (EPDM); Ethiopian Democratic Union (EDU); Afar Liberation Front (ALF); Gambela People's Liberation Movement (GPLM); and the Western Somali Liberation Front, which has an unknown strength, also use the FAL, M14, and other captured Soviet pattern infantry weapons. Other common weapons in the hands of antigovernment forces include the 7.62 x 39mm AKM, 7.62 x 51mm NATO FN MAG, 7.62 x 54mmR PK GPMG, the 7.7 x 56mmR (.303) Bren guns, 7.92 x 57mm MG34, the 12.7 x 108mm DShK HMG, and the 14.5 x 114mm KPV HMG.

# FIJI (Dominion of)

Population (estimate in 1980): 0.686 million. Ground forces: regulars, ca. 2,500; reserves, ca. 900. Royal Fiji Police have about 1,480 officers. Fiji supports United Nations peacekeeping activities in the Middle East with units attached to UNIFIL in Lebanon (626 men). Fijian troops are also assigned to the Multi-national Force and Observers (MFO) in the Sinai (469 men). Fijian small arms follow the British pattern, but specifics are not available.

**HANDGUNS:**
- *Cal.:* 11.43 x 23mm
  *Common Name:* .45 M1911A1 pistol

*Remarks:* US origin. FMS delivered 57 in 1981.

**SUBMACHINE GUNS:**

**RIFLES:**
- *Cal.:* 5.56 x 45mm
  *Common Name:* M16A1 rifle

*Remarks:* US origin. FMS delivered 743 in 1981.

- *Cal.:* 5.56 x 45mm
  *Common Name:* M16A2 rifle

*Remarks:* US origin. Colt Firearms made a direct sale of about 750 in 1984. The US government has transferred between 400 and 700.

- *Cal.:* 7.62 x 51mm NATO
  *Common Name:* L1A1 rifle

*Remarks:* UK origin?

**SHOTGUNS:**

**MACHINE GUNS:**
- *Cal.:* 7.62 x 51mm NATO
  *Common Name:* M60 GPMG

*Remarks:* US origin. FMS delivered 66 in 1981.

**AUTOMATIC CANNON:**

**GRENADE LAUNCHERS:**
- *Cal.:* 40 x 46mmSR
  *Common Name:* M79 grenade launcher

*Remarks:* US origin. FMS delivered 103 in 1981.

### Arms Purchases

Following the May 14, 1987, military coup, led by COL Sitiveni Rabuka, Australia and New Zealand placed an embargo on military aid. The Fijian forces lack sufficient modern weapons for their reserve units. An army team is investigating acquisition of 5.56mm rifles from South Korea and Taiwan in an effort to supplement their existing stocks of M16 rifles.

## FINLAND (Republic of)

Population (estimate in 1984): 4.87 million. Ground forces: regulars, between 30,900 and 35,000 (22,300 to 28,000 conscripts); reserves (all services), 700,000 (30,000 assist with conscript training; 42,000 do 40–100 days annual reserve training; and some 210,000 would be deployed with regulars to form a "fast deployment force" in the event of national mobilization). There is a border guard force of about 3,700 effectives.

**HANDGUNS:**
- *Cal.:* 9 x 19mm Parabellum
  *Official Name:* 9,00 Pistooli Malli 35
  *Common Name:* Lahti M35 pistol; 9,00 PIST 35

*Remarks:* Made at Valtion Kivaaritehdas (VKT, the State Rifle Factory). This state-owned enterprise is now called Valmet. Only about 9,000 were manufactured. OBSOLETE.

• *Cal.: 9 x 19mm Parabellum*
*Official Name: 9,00 Pistooli Malli 40*
*Common Name:* FN Mle. 1935 GP pistol; 9,00 PIST FN

*Remarks:* FN origin. The pistols have tangent rear sights and were originally fitted with stocks. These were used by the Finnish air force. OBSOLETE.

• *Cal.: 7.65 x 21mm Parabellum*
*Official Name: 7.65 Pistooli Malli 23*
*Common Name:* Parabellum M23 pistol (Luger); 9,00 PIST 23

*Remarks:* Reworked DWM P08s. OBSOLETE in the regular army, but still in hands of reservists. Police units still use the Luger.

• *Cal.: 9 x 19mm Parabellum*
*Official Name: 9,00 Pistooli Malli 08*
*Common Name:* Parabellum M08 pistol (Luger); 9,00 PIST 08

*Remarks:* DWM P08s. OBSOLETE.

• *Cal.: 9 x 19mm Parabellum*
*Official Name: 9,00 Pistooli Malli 38*
*Common Name:* P38; 9,00 PIST WAL

*Remarks:* Wartime-captured P38s. These pistols are currently issued to Finnish forces assigned to United Nations peacekeeping missions. It was the only double action pistol available prior to the adoption of the M80.

• *Cal.: 9 x 19mm Parabellum*
*Official Name: 9,00 Pistooli Malli 80*
*Common Name:* Developed from FN Mle. 1935 GP pistol; 9,00 PIST 80

*Remarks:* FN origin. About 10,000 have been purchased from FN Herstal.

• *Cal.: 9 x 19mm Parabellum*
*Official Name: 9,00 Pistooli Malli MAB PA-15*
*Common Name:* MAB PA-15; 9,00 PIST SEK

*Remarks:* French origin. Manufacture d'Armes de Bayonne (MAB). A few were purchased for army trials. Subsequently issued to Finnish border guard forces.

**SUBMACHINE GUNS:**
• *Cal.: 9 x 19mm Parabellum*
*Official Name: 9,00 Konepistooli Malli 31*
*Common Name:* Model 31 submachine gun (Suomi); 9,00 KP 31

*Remarks:* Domestic design. OBSOLETE. Replaced by assault rifles.

• *Cal.: 9 x 19mm Parabellum*
*Official Name: 9,00 Konepistooli Malli 44 and 44/46*
*Common Name:* Model 44 and 44/46 submachine guns; 9,00 KP 44

*Remarks:* Design derived from the Soviet PPS43. OBSOLETE. Note that this weapon is 9mm Parabellum, not 7.62 x 25mm, and that it uses Suomi or Carl Gustav magazines. Replaced by assault rifles. Made by OY Tikkakoski AB.

• *Cal.: 9 x 19 Parabellum*
*Official Name: 9,00 Konepistooli Malli 42*
*Common Name:* Model 42 (Mark II) Sten guns; 9,00 KP STEN II

*Remarks:* UK manufacture. Obtained from Interarms in the mid-1950s. OBSOLETE. Not in use. Only a few in reserve.

• *Cal.: 9 x 19mm Parabellum*
*Official Name: 9,00 Konepistooli Malli 43*
*Common Name:* Model 43 (Mark III) Sten guns; 9,00 KP STEN III

*Remarks:* UK manufacture. Obtained from Interarms in the mid-1950s. OBSOLETE. Some few thousand held in reserve.

**Two Finnish soldiers in winter camouflage uniforms armed with 7.62 x 39mm RK 62 assault rifles. (Finnish Ministry of Defense)**

**RIFLES:**
• *Cal.:* 7.62 x 39mm
  *Official Name: 7,62 Rynnakko-kivääri Malli 54*
  *Common Name:* Model 54 assault rifle; Soviet AK47; 7,62 RK 54

*Remarks:* These Soviet-made AK47s are held in reserve. The folding stock version (RK54TP) was used by paratroops and military police. Withdrawn from service in 1985.

- *Cal.:* 7,62 x 39mm
  *Official Name: 7,62 Rynnakko-kivääri Malli 60*
  *Common Name:* Model 60 assault rifle; 7,62 RK 60

- *Cal.:* 7,62 x 39mm
  *Official Name: 7,62 Rynnakko-kivääri Malli 62*
  *Common Name:* Model 62 assault rifle; 7,62 RK 62

- *Cal.:* 7,62 x 39mm
  *Official Name: 7,62 Rynnakko-kivääri Malli 62/76*
  *Common Name:* Model 62/76 assault rifle; 7,62 RK 62/76

- *Cal.:* 7,62 x 39mm
  *Official Name: 7,62 Rynnakko-kivääri Malli 71*
  *Common Name:* Model 71 assault rifle; 7,62 RK 71

- *Cal.:* 7.62 x 54mmR
  *Official Name: 7,62 Kivääri Malli 39*
  *Common Name:* Ukkopekka M 39 rifle; 7,62 KIV 39

- *Cal.:* 7.62 x 54mmR
  *Official Name: 7,62 Kivääri Malli 85*
  *Common Name:* Model 85 sniper rifle; 7,62 KIV 85

*Remarks:* Finnish rifle derived from the Soviet AK47. Made by Valmet and Sako. Withdrawn from service. FOM 1005-13-2-7.62-3.

*Remarks:* Finnish rifle derived from the M60. Made by Valmet and Sako. FOM 1005-13-2-7.62-4. Original model without night sights was redesignated M62PT when later production M62s were equipped with tritium night sights. In fall of 1985, the Finnish Ministry of Defense allocated 76 million Finnish marks to purchase more Model 62 rifles with machined steel receivers having decided that sheet metal receiver rifles were not sufficiently robust. Production of these weapons was to have been shared by Valmet and Sako. Since that time those firms have merged. It is estimated that new production will total between 39,000 and 45,000 rifles. These rifles will be the TP (folding stock) variant.

*Remarks:* Finnish version of AKM. Valmet and Sako. Stamped sheet metal receiver. FOM 1005-13-2-7.62-5. In fall of 1985, the Defense Ministry decided to return to the RK 62 version; see previous entry. Also a side folding stock model designated RK 62/76TP.

*Remarks:* Finnish version of AKM. Very small series of rifles having a Kalashnikov-type front sight assembly. These weapons were experimental only; they are held in storage.

*Remarks:* Finnish version of M1891 Russian Mosin-Nagant rifle. This and all earlier versions of the Mosin-Nagant are now OBSOLETE. Although no longer used, still held in reserve stocks, and many privately held by reservists. FOM 1005-13-2-7.62-2. Some original Soviet 1891 rifles are also held in reserve.

*Remarks:* Finnish sniper rifle based on the Mosin-Nagant mechanism. New barrels and other parts by Valmet. Stocks made at army facilities. 4X telescopes by Schmidt & Bender, MSW, and Zeiss.

**SHOTGUNS:**

**MACHINE GUNS:**

- *Cal.:* 7.62 x 39mm
  *Official Name: 7,62 Konekivääri Malli 54*
  *Common Name:* Model 54 LMG; the Soviet RPD; 7,62 KK 54

- *Cal.:* 7.62 x 39mm
  *Official Name: 7,62 Konekivääri Malli 62*
  *Common Name:* Model 62 LMG; 7,62 KK 62

- *Cal.:* 7.62 x 39mm
  *Official Name: 7,62 Automaatti-kivääri Malli 78*
  *Common Name:* Model 78 LMG

*Remarks:* Soviet-made RPD belt-fed machine guns.

*Remarks:* Finnish design influenced by the Czech vz.52 LMG. Made by Valmet. Some of the earlier KK60s are still in use.

*Remarks:* RPK-type weapon built on the Model 62/76 receiver by Valmet. Only test samples were acquired by the Finnish forces.

- *Cal.:* 7.62 x 54mmR
  *Official Name: 7,62 Konekivääri Malli SGMT*
  *Common Name:* SGMT armor MG; 7,62KK SGMT

*Remarks:* Soviet origin. Mounted on older Soviet tanks.

- *Cal.:* 7.62 x 54mmR
  *Official Name: 7,62 Konekivääri Malli PKT*
  *Common Name:* PKT armor MG; 7,62KK PKT

*Remarks:* Soviet origin. Mounted on Soviet T72 tanks and retrofitted to older armored vehicles. Ground model not used.

- *Cal.:* 7.62 x 54mmR
  *Official Name: 7,62 Pikakivääri Malli 27*
  *Common Name:* DP ground MG; 7,62 PK 27

*Remarks:* Soviet origin. OBSOLETE, no longer in use.

- *Cal.:* 7.62 x 54mmR
  *Official Name: 7,62 Pikakivääri Malli 26*
  *Common Name:* Lahti Saloranta PK26 LMG; 7,62 PK 26

*Remarks:* Finnish LMG designed by Aimo Lahti and made by Valmet. OBSOLETE, no longer in use.

- *Cal.:* 7.62 x 54mmR
  *Official Name: 7,62 Konekivääri Malli 32/33 Maxim*
  *Common Name:* Maxim Model 32/33 medium machine gun; 7,62 KK 32/33

*Remarks:* These KK32/33 Maxims are held in reserve, but not used. They have a selective fire rate for either 450–500 spm or 800 spm.

- *Cal.:* 12.7 x 108mm
  *Official Name: 12,7 Panssari-vaunukonekivääri DShKM*
  *Common Name:* DShKM HMG; 12,7 PSVKK DShKM

*Remarks:* Believed to be of Soviet origin. Often seen on T62 tanks and other armored vehicles.

- *Cal.:* 12.7 x 108mm
  *Official Name: 12,7 Panssari-vaunukonekivääri NSVT*
  *Common Name:* NSVT HMG; 12,7 PSVKK NSVT

*Remarks:* Soviet-made. Mounted on Soviet T72 series. Being retrofitted to some older armored vehicles. Ground model not used.

## AUTOMATIC CANNON:

- *Cal.:* 14.5 x 114mm
  *Official Name: 14,5 Panssari-vaunukonekivääri KPVT*
  *Common Name:* KPVT HMG; 14,5 PSVKK KPVT

*Remarks:* Soviet origin. Tank machine gun.

- *Cal.:* 20 x 138Bmm
  *Official Name: 20 Ilmatorjunta Kanuua*
  *Common Name:* Flak 30; 20 ITK 30

*Remarks:* Pre-1945 German antiaircraft guns. OBSOLETE, no longer in service.

- *Cal.:* 20 x 138Bmm
  *Official Name: 20 Ilmatorjunta Kanuua*
  *Common Name:* Flak 38 (BSW); 20 ITK 30

*Remarks:* Pre-1945 German antiaircraft guns built by Mauser. OBSOLETE, no longer in service.

- *Cal.:* 20 x 138Bmm
  *Official Name: 20 Ilmatorjunta Kanuua*
  *Common Name:* Flak BREDA; 20 ITK 35 BREDA

  *Remarks:* Pre-1945 Italian antiaircraft guns built by Mauser. OBSOLETE, no longer in service.

- *Cal.:* 20 x 128mm
  *Official Name: 20 Ilmatorjunta Kanuua*
  *Common Name:* KAB-001 (Type 10La/5TG); 20 ITK OERLI-KON

  *Remarks:* Oerlikon-Bührle. Tested, but not in service.

- *Cal.:* 20 x 120mm
  *Official Name: 20 Ilmatorjunta Kanuua*
  *Common Name:* Madsen automatic cannon; 20 ITK MAD-SEN

  *Remarks:* Madsen-made antiaircraft cannon.

- *Cal.:* 23 x 152mmB
  *Official Name: 23 Ilmatorjunta Kanuua Malli 61*
  *Common Name:* ZU23 automatic cannon; 20 ITK 61

  *Remarks:* Soviet origin. Used on both ground and naval mounts.

- *Cal.:* 30 x 170mmB
  *Official Name: 30 Ilmatorjunta Kanuua Malli 62*
  *Common Name:* 30mm HS831 automatic cannon; 30 ITK 62

  *Remarks:* Hispano Suiza cannon, which became the Oerlikon KCB.

## Finnish Small Arms Industry

During 1986–87, the Finnish small arms industry underwent significant changes. The two major manufacturers SAKO (Noika) and Valmet were merged in 1987. Previously both companies had expressed the desire to cease producing small arms, but the Defense Ministry refused to allow this on the grounds that such action would reduce the mobilization capabilities of the armed forces. In the summer of 1987 about 200 workers (out of a total of about 1,000) were scheduled for layoff; announcement of these plans triggered two days of work stoppages. Corporate studies of further nationalization continue, with the SAKO factory at Tikkakoski being scheduled for closing in July 1988. Other changes may follow.

## Finnish Weapon Terminology

| | | |
|---|---|---|
| *Pistooli* | = PIST | = Pistol. |
| *Konepistooli* | = KP | = Submachine gun. |
| *Rynnakkokivääri* | = RK | = Assault rifle. |
| *Konekikivääri* | = KK | = Belt-fed machine gun prior to 1954, now used for all machine guns. |
| *Pikakivääri* | = PK | = Magazine-fed machine guns. Used prior to 1945. |
| *Panssarivaunukonekivääri* | = PSVKK | = Panzer (tank) machine gun. |
| *Ilmatorjuntakannuna* | = ITK | = Antiaircraft cannon. |
| *Päivätahtäimillä* | = PT | = Day sight. |
| *Taittopera* | = TP | = Folding stock version. |
| *Sekalainen* | = SEK | = Miscellaneous. |

## FRANCE (Republic of)

Population (estimate in 1985): 55.06 million. Ground forces: regulars, 338,668 in 1987 (185,678 conscripts); reserves, ca. 400,000; paramilitary: *Gendarmerie Nationale,* about 87,497 (58,566 conscripts); *Compagnies Republicaines de Sécurité* (C.R.S.), 14,581.

### HANDGUNS:

• *Cal.:* 7.65 x 17mm Browning
*Official Name: Pistolet Automatique Unique Rr 51*
*Common Name:* Rr 51 police pistol

*Remarks:* Manufacture d'Armes des Pyrenees Françaises (MAPF). Still used by municipal police forces and the Customs police.

• *Cal.:* 7.65 x 17mm Browning
*Official Name: Pistolet Automatique Unique Bcf-66*
*Common Name:* Bcf-66 pistol

*Remarks:* MAPF. Export sales.

• *Cal.:* 7.65 x 17mm Browning
*Official Name: Pistolet Automatique Walther-Manurhin*
*Common Name:* PP pistol

*Remarks:* Matra-Manurhin. Still used by the Paris municipal police force.

• *Cal.:* 7.65 x 17mm Browning
*Official Name: Pistolet Automatique Mod D*
*Common Name:* MAB Mod. D pistol

*Remarks:* Manufacture d'Armes de Bayonne (MAB). Still used by Customs and border police units.

• *Cal.:* 9 x 19mm NATO
*Official Name: Pistolet Automatique MAB PA-15*
*Common Name:* PA-15 pistol

*Remarks:* MAB. Made for export. Never officially adopted.

• *Cal.:* 9 x 19mm NATO
*Official Name: Pistolet Automatique Précision F1*
*Common Name:* F1 target pistol

*Remarks:* MAB. Target version of PA-15. This model is used by army and air force.

• *Cal.:* 9 x 19mm NATO
*Official Name: Pistolet Automatique MAC Modèle 1950*
*Common Name:* Model 1950 pistol; P.A. 50

*Remarks:* Manufacture Nationale d'Armes de Chatellerault (MAC) (1953–63) and the Manufacture Nationale d'Armes de St. Etienne (MAS) Groupment Industriel des Armements Terrestres (GIAT) (1963–78). FOM 1005-17-1-9-1. Currently used by all the armed forces and the C.R.S.; will be replaced by Beretta Model 92F.

• *Cal.:* 9 x 19mm NATO
*Official Name: Pistolet Automatique MAS 9mm G 1*
*Common Name:* Beretta Model 92F pistol

*Remarks:* The *Gendarmerie Nationale* announced the adoption of Model 92F on 7 July 1987 and will acquire 110,000 1987–95. The pistols will be manufactured in France under license from Beretta. They will be assembled at MAS. Matra-Manurhin, the other competitor in the handgun trials, will share some in the production of 40% of the components for these pistols. Model 92F will replace the MAC 50 pistols used by the *Gendarmerie.* The MAS G1 does not have a mechanical safety; the slide-mounted lever only decocks the hammer.

• *Cal.:* 9 x 19mm Parabellum
*Official Name: Pistol Automatique P38*
*Common Name:* P38 pistol

*Remarks:* Mauser Werke (Code "SVW"). Manufactured 1945–46. OBSOLETE. Used by the *Gendarmerie* until the 1980s.

• *Cal.:* 9 x 29mmR Magnum
*Official Name: Revolver Manurhin MR-73*
*Common Name:* .357 Magnum Manurhin MR-73 revolver

*Remarks:* Manurhin-made revolver, with a milled frame, used by various police organizations and the *Groupe d'Intervention de la Gendarmerie Nationale* (GIGN, a SWAT-type unit).

- *Cal.:* 9 x 29mmR Magnum
  *Official Name: Revolver Ruger-Manurhin RMR*
  *Common Name:* .357 Magnum RMR Special Police revolver

  *Remarks:* Manurhin-made revolver with an investment cast frame provided by Sturm, Ruger, and Co.; 18,000 were made for the Police Nationale and the C.R.S.

- *Cal.:* 9 x 29mmR Magnum
  *Official Name: Revolver Manurhin MR F1*
  *Common Name:* .357 Magnum Manurhin MR Special police revolver F 1

  *Remarks:* Manurhin-made revolver, with an investment cast frame. Will replace all other handguns used by police organizations and the C.R.S.

- *Cal.:* 9 x 29mmR
  *Official Name: Revolver Colt Detective Special "Douanes Francaises"*
  *Common Name:* .38 Colt revolver with 76mm barrel

  *Remarks:* Colt-made. Specially built for the Customs Office.

- *Cal.:* 7.65 x 20mm
  *Official Name: Pistolet Automatique Modèle 1935A*
  *Common Name:* S.A.C.M. Model 1935A pistol

  *Remarks:* OBSOLETE. Used until 1970s by motorcycle policemen in Paris. Still carried by some gendarmes. FOM 1005-17-1-7.65-3.

- *Cal.:* 7.65 x 20mm
  *Official Name: Pistolet Automatique Modèle 1935S*
  *Common Name:* MAS Model 1935S and 1935 SM1 pistols

  *Remarks:* OBSOLETE. Used until the 1970s by motorcycle policemen in Paris.

- *Cal.:* 11.43 x 23mm
  *Official Name: Pistolet Automatique Colt .45*
  *Common Name:* Colt .45 M1911A1 pistol

  *Remarks:* US origin. OBSOLETE.

*Note on Manurhin Self-loading pistol production:* When the first edition of *Small Arms Today* was being prepared, the Manufacture de Machines du Haut-Rhin (Manurhin) of Mulhouse advised the editors that they had been "the *only* post-war European producer of 'Walther' PP, PPK, and PPK/S pistols. Manurhin has had the *exclusive* European production license from Carl Walther since 1952. Manurhin produces the pistols *for* Walther in Germany today and has done so for 31 years. [Until 1987,] there were *NO* PP, PPK, or PPK/S Walthers *produced* in Germany (even though they may be stamped 'made in Germany'). Manurhin ships the pistols to Walther, where they are stamped, proof-fired in the German proof house, boxed, and shipped onward for sale in the US and other countries worldwide." Since 1987, Walther has been producing their pocket pistols as well as their larger 9 x 19mm caliber pistols in their factory in West Germany.

*Note:* The French Army is also currently conducting separate trials of candidate 9mm pistols. The candidates include the Beretta M92S, the SIG P226, the HK P7M13, the Glock 17, and the Walther P88 pistol.

**SUBMACHINE GUNS:**
- *Cal.:* 9 x 19mm NATO
  *Official Name: Pistolet Mitrailleur MAT Modèle 1949*
  *Common Name:* MAT 1949 submachine gun

  *Remarks:* Manufacture Nationale d'Armes de Tulle (MAT) and MAS, GIAT. FOM 1005-17-3-9-1. Still used by crews of armored vehicles, the *Gendarmerie,* reserve troops, and some police organizations.

- *Cal.:* 9 x 19mm NATO
  *Official Name: Pistolet Mitrailleur MAT Modele 1949/54*
  *Common Name:* MAT 1949/54 submachine gun

  *Remarks:* MAT, GIAT. Variation of the MAT 49 with a longer barrel and selector; some models have a fixed wooden stock. Used by the Paris municipal police.

- *Cal.:* 9 x 19mm NATO
  *Official Name: Pistolet Mitrailleur Gevarm D.4*
  *Common Name:* Gevarm D.4 submachine gun

*Remarks:* Manufactured by Gevarm, a subsidiary company of Gevelot cartridge factory. OBSOLETE. Formerly used by C.R.S. and the Customs office.

- *Cal.:* 9 x 19mm NATO
  *Official Name: Pistolet Mitrailleur Uzi 4*
  *Common Name:* FN Uzi submachine gun

*Remarks:* FN origin. These were weapons recovered during the Algerian war. OBSOLETE, but still used by some police organizations.

- *Cal.:* 11.43 x 23mm
  *Official Name: Pistolet Mitrailleur Thompson*
  *Common Name:* Thompson M1 and M1A1 submachine guns

*Remarks:* US origin. OBSOLETE.

- *Cal.:* 7.65 x 20mm
  *Official Name: Pistolet Mitrailleur MAS Modele 1938*
  *Common Name:* P.M. 38 submachine gun

*Remarks:* OBSOLETE.

- *Cal.:* 9 x 19mm NATO
  *Official Name: Pistolet Mitrailleur Heckler & Koch MP5 SD*
  *Common Name:* HK MP5 SD submachine gun

*Remarks:* Heckler & Koch (HK) GmbH origin. Limited issue to GIGN and some paratroop, commando, and other elite units. Some MP5 A2, A3, and K are also used by these special units.

**A French Marine special operations Commando on exercise with his 5.56 x 45mm FAMAS assault rifle. (Huon)**

## RIFLES:

- *Cal.*: 7.5 x 54mm
  *Official Name: Fusil MAS Modele
  1936*
  Common Name: MAS 36 rifle

- *Cal.*: 7.5 x 54mm
  *Official Name: Fusil MAS Modele
  1936 M 51*
  Common Name: MAS 36/51 rifle

- *Cal.*: 7.5 x 54mm
  *Official Name: Fusil MAS Modele
  1949*
  Common Name: MAS 49 rifle

- *Cal.*: 7.5 x 54mm
  *Official Name: Fusil MAS Modele
  49/56*
  Common Name: MAS 49/56 rifle

- *Cal.*: 5.56 x 45mm
  *Official Name: Fusil Automatique
  F1 MAS*
  Common Name: FAMAS.
  "Clairon"

- *Cal.*: 5.56 x 45mm
  *Official Name: Fusil Automatique
  SIG-Manurhin SG 540*
  Common Name: SG540 rifle

- *Cal.*: 5.56 x 45mm
  *Official Name: Fusil Automatique
  SIG-Manurhin SG 543*
  Common Name: SG543 rifle

- *Cal.*: 7.62 x 51mm NATO
  *Official Name: Fusil Automatique
  SIG-Manurhin SG 542*
  Common Name: SG542 rifle

- *Cal.*: 5.56 x 45mm
  *Official Name: Mousqueton AMD
  5.56*
  Common Name: AMD rifle

*Remarks:* MAS. 5-shot, bolt action rifle. Still used by the *Gendarmerie* for law enforcement.

*Remarks:* MAS. Same as above with a 22mm launcher attachment for grenades. Still used by the *Gendarmerie* for law enforcement.

*Remarks:* MAS. 10-shot, self-loading rifle, no bayonet. OBSOLETE.

*Remarks:* MAS, GIAT. Same as above, but has integral grenade launcher and can mount a bayonet. Still in service with the French Navy.

*Remarks:* MAS, GIAT. Adopted by the French Armed Forces in 1977. FOM 1005-17-2-5.56-1. Total acquisition for the French forces was originally set at 317,000, but this number was reduced to 280,000 due to financial problems. Delivery of the initial complement of 148,000 rifles was completed in April 1983 — (54K in 1981; 43K in 82; 51K in 83). The SG540 was used as an interim 5.56mm rifle (in Lebanon and Chad) while deliveries of the FAMAS were underway. The FAMAS is now standard with all frontline units (including Air Force Base protection units, Marine Commandos, and the *Gendarmerie* Mobile). The standard model FAMAS was the first 5.56 x 45mm NATO rifle adopted by the NATO test centers for testing 5.56 x 45mm NATO ammunition. There are also a shorter Commando version w/ 405mm barrel instead of the 488mm barrel; a standard model w/ an integrated optical sight; a standard model w/ NATO scope mount; a standard model w/o grenade launcher; a standard model w/ a 1 in 180mm twist barrel instead of the regular 1 in 305mm twist. Any of these can be furnished w/ black, olive green, or sand yellow plastic stock. Two commercial models of the FAMAS have been introduced. Both are semiautomatic fire only. For the domestic French market the rifle is sold in .222 Remington caliber with a 570mm barrel; 800mm overall. For export in 5.56 x 45mm (.223 Remington) w/ 488mm barrel and 757mm over-all.

*Remarks:* Used by French Foreign Legion, Paratroops, and overseas troops in several African and Asian assignments. SIG design made by Manufacture de Machines du Haut-Rhin (Manurhin), Mulhouse. FOM 1005-18-2-5.56-1.

*Remarks:* Same as above with shorter barrel. Made for export sales. Used by some police organizations.

*Remarks:* Made for export.

*Remarks:* French variation of the Ruger AC-556, mounted and finished by Humbert at St. Etienne (the importer). Used by the C.R.S. in replacement for the venerable Lebel-Berthier M 1892 carbine. Use began in the early 1980s.

• *Cal.:* 7.5 x 54mm
*Official Name: Fusil a Répétition
Modèle F1, pour Tireur d'Elite*
*Common Name:* FR F1 sniper rifle

*Remarks:* MAS, GIAT. Officially adopted in 1967. The French army acquired 150 in 1964 and 5,150 in 1967. Other proposed models (not made) included the *Tir Sportif* (target model) and the *Grande Chasse* (hunting model). These weapons are being converted to 7.62mm NATO FOM 1005-17-2-7.5-7.

• *Cal.:* 7.62 x 51mm NATO
*Official Name: Fusil a Répétition
Modèle F2, pour Tireur d'Elite*
*Common Name:* FR F2 sniper rifle

*Remarks:* MAS, GIAT. This rifle resembles the FR F1 but is chambered for the 7.62mm NATO cartridge. It is also fitted w/ a new, heavier barrel, which is covered by a plastic thermal sleeve to reduce the heat haze emanating from a hot barrel. The FR F1 wood fore-end has been replaced by a plastic one, and the bipod is attached to a saddle mounted over the barrel and has a quick adjustment system. The weapon can be fitted w/ wood or plastic buttstocks. The FR F2 has standard NATO scope mounts for optical or night vision scopes.

• *Cal.:* 7.62 x 51mm NATO
*Official Name: Fusil a Répétition
Steyr-Mannlicher SSG pour Ti-
reur d'Elite*
*Common Name:* Steyr SSG rifle

*Remarks:* Steyr-Daimler-Puch (SDP). Used by some SWAT units.

• *Cal.:* 7.62 x 33mm
*Official Name: Carabine U.S.*
*Common Name:* .30 M1 and M2 carbines

*Remarks:* US origin. OBSOLETE. MAP provided 155,356 carbines before 1964. Some are still used for police work; e.g., during 1985 riots in New Caledonia.

• *Cal.:* 7.62 x 63mm
*Official Name: Garand*
*Common Name:* .30 M1 rifle

*Remarks:* US origin. MAP provided 232,499 before 1964. OBSOLETE.

## SHOTGUNS:

Shotguns are not popular with police organizations. Some of them (American models) are used by GIGN and other SWAT units.

## MACHINE GUNS:

• *Cal.:* 7.5 x 54mm
*Official Name: Fusil-mitrailleur
Modele 1924 M 29*
*Common Name:* F.M.24/29

*Remarks:* MAC. Still used by the *Gendarmerie.*

• *Cal.:* 7.5 x 54mm
*Official Name: Mitrailleuse Mo-
dele 1931*
*Common Name:* MAC 31 machine gun

*Remarks:* Many variations exist (tank, infantry, fortress). OBSOLETE. The last of these guns were withdrawn from service when the E.B.R. armored vehicle was discarded in 1985.

• *Cal.:* 7.5 x 54mm
*Official Name: Arme Automa-
tique Modele 1952 version fusil-
mitrailleur*
*Common Name:* A. A. 52 or MAT 52 light machine gun

*Remarks:* MAC and MAT, GIAT. Still used by reserve troops.

• *Cal.:* 7.5 x 54mm
*Official Name: Arme Automa-
tique Modele 1952 version
mitrailleuse*
*Common Name:* A. A. 52 or MAT 52 GPMG

*Remarks:* MAC and MAT, GIAT. Still used by reserve troops. Heavier barrel version.

- *Cal.:* 7.62 x 51mm NATO
  *Official Name: Arme Automatique* de 7.62mm N — *Modele* F 1, version *fusil-mitrailleur*
  *Common Name:* A. A. 7.62mm N-F 1 light machine gun

*Remarks:* MAC and MAT, GIAT. Used by front line troops.

- *Cal.:* 7.62 x 51mm NATO
  *Official Name: Arme Automatique de 7.62mm N — Modele F 1, version mitrailleuse*
  *Common Name:* A. A. 7.62mm N-F 1 GPMG

*Remarks:* MAC and MAT, GIAT. Used by front-line troops. Heavier barrel version. The heavy barrel armor machine gun version is used by NATO ammunition manufacturers and NATO Test Centers to acceptance-test 7.62mm NATO ammunition. The US military uses MCN 1005-00-X90-9245 for these test guns. Also FOM 1005-17-4-7.62-3-1 for the heavy barrel armor gun.

- *Cal.:* 7.62 x 51mm NATO
  *Official Name: Arme Automatique de 7.62mm N — Modele F 1, version char N⁰ 1*
  *Common Name:* A. A. 7.62mm N-F 1 tank machine gun, No. 1

*Remarks:* MAC and MAT, GIAT. Used in turrets; has a manual trigger or an electric trigger. (Type A is not waterproof; Type B is waterproof.) No stock.

- *Cal.:* 7.62 x 51mm NATO
  *Official Name: Arme Automatique de 7.62mm N — Modele F 1, version char N⁰ 2*
  *Common Name:* A. A. 7.62mm N-F 1 tank machine gun, No. 2

*Remarks:* MAC and MAT, GIAT. Used as an external flexible gun on armored vehicles. Has a manual trigger and a shoulder stock.

- *Cal.:* 7.62 x 51mm NATO
  *Official Name: Arme Automatique de 7.62mm N — Modele F 1, version avion N⁰ 2*
  *Common Name:* A. A. 7.62mm N-F 1 aircraft machine gun, No. 2

*Remarks:* MAC and MAT, GIAT. No sights and manual trigger.

- *Cal.:* 7.62 x 51mm NATO
  *Official Name: Arme Automatique de 7.62mm N — Modele F 1, version avion N⁰ 3*
  *Common Name:* A. A. 7.62mm N-F 1 aircraft machine gun, No. 3

*Remarks:* MAC and MAT, GIAT. Very similar to tank machine gun No. 1. No sights.

- *Cal.:* 7.62 x 51mm NATO
  *Official Name: Arme Automatique de 7.62mm N — Modele F 1, version avion N⁰ 4*
  *Common Name:* A. A. 7.62mm N-F 1 aircraft machine gun, No. 4

*Remarks:* MAC and MAT, GIAT. Very similar to tank machine gun No. 1. Has sights.

- *Cal.:* 7.62 x 51mm NATO
  *Common Name:* FN MAG

*Remarks:* FN origin. MAG *Infanterie Standard* (60-20), T1 and MAG *Co-axial* (60-40). Mounted on armored vehicles for export sales.

- *Cal.:* 7.62 x 63mm
  *Official Name: Fusil-mitrailleur BAR Modele 1918 A2*
  *Common Name:* M1918 BAR

*Remarks:* US origin. OBSOLETE.

- *Cal.:* 7.62 x 63mm
  *Official Name: Mitrailleuse Browning Modele 1919 A4*
  *Common Name:* .30 M1919A4 LMG

*Remarks:* US origin. MAP and FMS delivered 8,932 unspecified .30 caliber LMGs before the mid-1960s. OBSOLETE.

- *Cal.:* 7.62 x 63mm
  *Official Name: Mitrailleuse Browning Modele 1919 A5*
  *Common Name:* .30 M1919A5 LMG

  *Remarks:* US origin. OBSOLETE.

- *Cal.:* 7.62 x 63mm
  *Official Name: Mitrailleuse Browning Modele 1919 A6*
  *Common Name:* .30 M1919A6 LMG

  *Remarks:* US origin. OBSOLETE.

*Note:* The French Army is conducting trials in search of a new machine gun. Candidates include a new variation of the A.A. 7.62mm N F 1 with reversible feed and a 7.62mm NATO version of the FN Minimi machine gun.

- *Cal.:* 12.7 x 99mm
  *Official Name: Mitrailleuse de 12.7mm Modele M 2 HB*
  *Common Name:* .50 M2 HB HMG

  *Remarks:* Still used as an antiaircraft weapon on many vehicles. Also mounted coaxially with the 105mm main gun on the AMX 30 tank. Most M2 HBs are of US origin, with many spare parts subsequently fabricated in French arms factories. More than 580 were provided by the US before the mid-1960s, including 200 for M1 Cupolas.

- *Cal.:* 12.7 x 99mm
  *Official Name: Mitrailleuse de 12.7mm pour avion*
  *Common Name:* .50 AN M2 AMG

  *Remarks:* OBSOLETE. US origin.

**AUTOMATIC CANNON:**
- *Cal.:* 20 x 81mm
  *Official Name: Canon mitrailleur de 20mm Type MG 151*
  *Common Name:* MG151/20 automatic cannon

  *Remarks:* Variation of the MG151/20 gun altered by the French with a selector and produced by EFAB and MAT, GIAT. Formerly used on vehicles, ground mounts (Model 53 T or M 53 T1), and helicopters. OBSOLETE.

- *Cal.:* 20 x 102mm
  *Official Name: Modèle 621*
  *Common Name:* Domestic design

  *Remarks:* MAT, GIAT. Used in a variety of vehicular applications, including Puma, Alouette III, and Gazelle helicopters. Also available in pod mounted versions.

- *Cal.:* 20 x 139mm
  *Official Name: Canon Mitrailleur 20 F1 (CN-MIT-20 F1)*
  *Common Name:* Variant of M621

  *Remarks:* MAT, GIAT. Vehicular mountings of several types. Twin *Cerbere* 76 T2 AA mount is rework of the FRG Rh 202 twin AA mount. Three hundred on order in 1984.

- *Cal.:* 20 x 139mm
  *Official Name: Canon Mitrailleur 20 F2 (CN-MIT-20-F2)*
  *Common Name:* Variant of F1

  *Remarks:* MAT, GIAT. Commercial designation is M693. The *Tarasque,* single gun on Model 53 T 2 mount; *Centaure* 76 T1 twin AA mount is made by CETME of Spain.

# GABON

Population (estimate in 1985): 0.958 million. Ground forces: regulars, variously estimated as being between 1,000 and 3,900; paramilitary: *Gendarmerie Nationale Gabonaise,* ca. 1,700; Forces Nationales de Police, ca. 1,000. Total paramilitary forces are about 5,300. This former French colony still receives French military support and aid. Small arms generally follow the French pattern.

**HANDGUNS:**
- *Cal.:* 9 x 29mmR
  *Common Name:* Manurhin MR 73 revolver

  *Remarks:* Manurhin, France.

- *Cal.:* 9 x 19mm NATO
  *Common Name:* MAC Mle. 1950
  pistol

  *Remarks:* Manufacture Nationale d'Armes de Chatellerault (MAC).

- *Cal.:* 9 x 19mm NATO
  *Common Name:* MAB P-15S
  pistol

  *Remarks:* Manufacture d'Armes de Bayonne (MAB).

**SUBMACHINE GUNS:**

- *Cal.:* 9 x 19mm NATO
  *Common Name:* MAT Mle. 49
  submachine gun

  *Remarks:* Manufacture Nationale d'Armes de Tulle (MAT).

- *Cal.:* 9 x 19mm NATO
  *Common Name:* M12S submachine gun

  *Remarks:* Beretta, Italy.

- *Cal.:* 9 x 19mm NATO
  *Common Name:* Uzi submachine
  gun

  *Remarks:* Israeli Military Industries (IMI), Israel.

- *Cal.:* 9 x 19mm NATO
  *Common Name:* Sterling Mark 4
  submachine gun

  *Remarks:* Sterling Armament Co., UK.

**RIFLES:**

- *Cal.:* 5.56 x 45mm
  *Common Name:* M16A1 (Model
  613) rifle and M16A1 (Model
  653) carbine

  *Remarks:* Acquired directly from Colt in 1983; ca. 2,000.

- *Cal.:* 5.56 x 45mm
  *Common Name:* SG540 rifle

  *Remarks:* Manurhin-made SIG design used by French Foreign Legionnaires in Gabon.

- *Cal.:* 5.56 x 45mm
  *Common Name:* FAMAS rifle

  *Remarks:* Groupment Industriel des Armement Terrestres (GIAT), France. Some 800 of these rifles were acquired in 1982–83. Total in service may be 5,000.

- *Cal.:* 5.56 x 45mm
  *Common Name:* FN CAL

  *Remarks:* FN origin.

- *Cal.:* 7.62 x 39mm
  *Common Name:* Type 56 (AK47)
  assault rifle

  *Remarks:* People's Republic of China (PRC).

- *Cal.:* 7.62 x 51mm NATO
  *Common Name:* SG542 rifle

  *Remarks:* Manurhin-made SIG design. Reported use is unconfirmed.

- *Cal.:* 7.62 x 51mm NATO
  *Common Name:* Gewehr 3

  *Remarks:* Manufacture Nationale d'Armes de St. Etienne (MAS), GIAT, France.

**SHOTGUNS:**

**MACHINE GUNS:**

- *Cal.:* 7.5 x 54mm
  *Common Name:* AAT52 GPMG

  *Remarks:* MAT, GIAT.

- *Cal.:* 7.5 x 54mm
  *Common Name:* Mle. 1924/29
  LMG

  *Remarks:* MAC.

- *Cal.:* 7.62 x 51mm NATO
  *Common Name:* FN MAG

  *Remarks:* FN origin. MAG *Coaxial* (60-40) on Cadillac Gage and Engesa Cascaval armored cars.

- *Cal.:* 7.62 x 63mm
  *Common Name:* .30 M1919A4
  LMG

  *Remarks:* US origin.

- *Cal.:* 7.62 x 63mm
  *Common Name:* .30 M1917A1
  MMG

  *Remarks:* US origin.

- *Cal.:* 12.7 x 99m
  *Common Name:* .50 M2 HB
  HMG

  *Remarks:* US origin. FMS provided 4 in 1975.

**AUTOMATIC CANNON:**

**GRENADE LAUNCHERS:**
- *Cal.:* 40 x 46mmSR
  *Common Name:* M203 grenade
  launcher for M16A1

  *Remarks:* Colt, US, has delivered about 25.

# THE GAMBIA (Republic of)

Population (estimate in 1984): 0.725 million. Ground forces: regulars, 400; reserves, unknown. There was a paramilitary Police Field Force of about 200, which was disbanded when the Confederation Pact with Senegal was signed. Small arms follow the British pattern. In December 1981 The Gambia and Senegal signed a Confederation Pact to combine their armed forces. See also Senegal.

**HANDGUNS:**
- *Cal.:* 9 x 20mmR
  *Common Name:* .38 Webley Mark
  IV revolver

  *Remarks:* UK surplus.

**SUBMACHINE GUNS:**
- *Cal.:* 9 x 19mm Parabellum
  *Common Name:* Sterling Mark 4
  submachine gun and L2A3 submachine gun

  *Remarks:* Sterling Armament Co., UK, and Lithgow Small Arms Factory in Australia.

**RIFLES:**
- *Cal.:* 7.62 x 39mm
  *Common Name:* AK-47 type as-
  sault rifles

  *Remarks:* Origin unknown.

- *Cal.:* 7.62 x 51mm NATO
  *Common Name:* FN FAL

  *Remarks:* FN origin.

- *Cal.:* 7.62 x 51mm NATO
  *Common Name:* L1A1 rifle

  *Remarks:* Royal Small Arms Factory (RSAF), Enfield.

- *Cal.:* 7.7 x 56mmR
  *Common Name:* .303 Enfield
  No. 4 rifle

  *Remarks:* RSAF.

**SHOTGUNS:**

**MACHINE GUNS:**
- *Cal.:* 7.62 x 51mm NATO
  *Common Name:* 7.62mm L4A4
  Bren

  *Remarks:* RSAF.

- *Cal.:* 7.62 x 51mm NATO
  *Common Name:* 7.62mm FN
  MAG

  *Remarks:* Origin unknown.

• *Cal.:* 7.62 x 51mm NATO
  *Common Name:* 7.62mm FN
  FALO

*Remarks:* Origin unknown.

• *Cal.:* 12.7 x 99mm
  *Common Name:* .50 M2 HB
  HMG

*Remarks:* Origin presumed to be US. Source unknown.

**AUTOMATIC CANNON:**

## GERMANY (Democratic Republic—East)

Population (estimate in 1984): 16.71 million. Ground forces: regulars, the *Nationale Volksarmee* (NVA), is variously estimated as being between 107,000 to 120,000 (ca. 71,500 conscripts); reserves: the Home Guard (*Betriebskampfgruppen*—Worker's Combat Group) 15,000 active and 500,000 in reserve controlled by the *Volkspolizei; Gesellschaft fur Sport und Technik* (GST) premilitary training for ca. 450,000 youth, which explains the existence of the KKMPi69 .22 LR rifle. Men have a reserve commitment until the age of 50 for ranks and 60 for officers. Paramilitary organizations include the *Wachtregiment Felix Dzierzynski,* which is a 6,200-man riot control unit named for the first leader of the Soviet secret police; *Volkspolizei* (VOPO), about 25,000; and the *Grenzschutztruppen* (Border Guards), about 50,000. The NVA was first equipped with World War II vintage Soviet small arms in 1956; some newer weapons were introduced in 1957; and in 1959 the Kalashnikov assault rifle became the basic infantry weapon replacing older rifles and submachine guns. Since that time, the NVA has continued to receive newer models of Soviet weapons, most of which are manufactured in Germany.

**HANDGUNS:**
• *Cal.:* 9 x 18mm
  *Official Name: Pistole M*
  *Common Name:* Makarov pistol

*Remarks:* German copy of the Soviet Makarov pistol. Introduced into the NVA in 1958.

• *Cal.:* 9 x 19mm
  *Common Name:* Radom pistol

*Remarks:* OBSOLETE; formerly used by police.

• *Cal.:* 7.62 x 25mm
  *Official Name: Pistole TT*
  *Common Name:* Tokarev TT
  pistol

*Remarks:* Soviet origin. Introduced into the NVA in 1956; replaced by the *Pistole M;* OBSOLETE.

*Note:* In 1985 the *Volkspolizei* began disposing of the Walther PP and P38 pistols (made after 1945 in East Germany under Soviet supervision), as well as the P 08 (Luger) pistols that also had been used until recently. These PP and P38 pistols are marked with the factory code "2/1001." That marking has also been seen on replacement P 08 and Stg. 44 magazines.

**SUBMACHINE GUNS:**
• *Cal.:* 7.62 x 25mm
  *Official Name: Maschinenpistole 41 MPi 41*
  *Common Name:* PPSh 41

*Remarks:* Soviet origin. Introduced into the NVA in 1956; replaced by the MPiK; OBSOLETE.

*Note:* The *Nationale Volksarmee* (NVA) does not currently use pistol caliber submachine guns, having substituted the Kalashnikov assault rifle for both the rifle and the submachine gun. Some older Soviet and German submachine guns may still be held in reserve.

**Post-1945 German Democratic Republic-made 7.65 x 17mm PPK-type pistol with factory code 1001-0. (Fritze)**

**RIFLES:** (Rifles manufactured at the Volkseigener Betrieb [VEB] Ernst-Thälmann-werk, Suhl, Thuringia, the pre-1945 J. P. Sauer & Sohn factory.)

- *Cal.:* 5.45 x 39mm
  *Common Name:* AK74 assault rifle

  *Remarks:* The NVA has begun the fielding of their own version of the Soviet 5.45 x 39mm AK74-type assault rifles.

- *Cal.:* 7.62 x 39mm
  *Official Name: Selbstladekarabiner S*
  *Common Name:* Simonov SKS carbine

  *Remarks:* German copy. Introduced into the NVA in 1957; replaced by the *MPiK* and now obsolete except for ceremonial activities.

- *Cal.:* 7.62 x 39mm
  *Official Name: MPiK – Maschinenpistole Kalashnikow*
  *Common Name:* AK47 assault rifle

  *Remarks:* German copy. Introduced into the NVA in 1957; replaced by the *MPiKM* series starting in 1959 and now obsolescent.

- *Cal.:* 7.62 x 39mm
  *Official Name: MPiKS – mit Schulterstutze*
  *Common Name:* AK47 with folding stock

  *Remarks:* German copy. FOM 1005-7-2-7.62-1.

- *Cal.:* 5.6 x 16mmR
  *Official Name: KKMPi69 (or Kleinkaliber Maschinenpistole Kalashnikow-69)*
  *Common Name:* .22 long rifle; training rifle configured to look like AKM

  *Remarks:* German design.

- *Cal.:* 7.62 x 39mm
  *Official Name: MPiKMS-72*
  *Common Name:* AKM w/ side folding stock

  *Remarks:* German variant.

**SHOTGUNS:**

**MACHINE GUNS:**
- *Cal.:* 7.62 x 39mm
  *Official Name: LMG-K*
  *Common Name:* RPK LMG

  *Remarks:* German copy.

- *Cal.:* 7.62 x 54mmR
  *Official Name: PKi*
  *Common Name:* PK GPMG

  *Remarks:* German copy.

- *Cal.:* 7.62 x 54mmR
  *Official Name: PKB*
  *Common Name:* PKB

  *Remarks:* German copy.

- *Cal.:* 7.62 x 54mmR
  *Official Name: PKS*
  *Common Name:* PKS

  *Remarks:* German copy.

- *Cal.:* 7.62 x 54mmR
  *Official Name: PKT*
  *Common Name:* PKT

  *Remarks:* German copy.

- *Cal.:* 7.62 x 54mmR
  *Common Name:* SGMT

  *Remarks:* Soviet origin.

- *Cal.:* 7.62 x 54mmR
  Common Name: DT

  *Remarks:* Soviet origin.

- *Cal.:* 12.7 x 108mm
  Common Name: DShK38/46
  HMG

  *Remarks:* Soviet origin.

- *Cal.:* 12.7 x 108mm
  Common Name: NSVT armor
  HMG

  *Remarks:* Soviet origin. On newer tanks.

**AUTOMATIC CANNON:**
- *Cal.:* 14.5 x 114mm
  Common Name: KPV HMG

  *Remarks:* Soviet origin.

- *Cal.:* 23 x 152mmB
  Common Name: ZU23 automatic
  cannon

  *Remarks:* Soviet origin. ZPU-1, ZPU-2, and ZPU-4.

## GERMANY (Federal Republic—West)

Population (estimate in 1984): 61.39 million. Ground forces: regulars, ca. 335,600 (181,200 conscripts; including territorial army, 44,200); reserves, 615,000; border police *(Bundesgrenzschutz),* ca. 22,000; *Bundesbahnpolizei,* ca. 3,500.

**HANDGUNS:**
- *Cal.:* 9 x 19mm NATO
  Official Name: Pistole 1—P1
  Common Name: Walther P38

  *Remarks:* Post-1945 designation for the P38, the standard pistol of the *Bundeswehr.* Some are marked Manurhin. Assembled from Walther parts shipped to France. Issued to the police in Berlin, not permitted to have German-made guns after WWII. NSN 1005-12-120-0440 w/ equipment; 1005-12-120-6168 w/o equipment. FOM 1005-15-1-9-2.

- *Cal.:* 9 x 19mm NATO
  Official Name: Pistole 2—P2
  Common Name: SIG SP47/8

  *Remarks:* OBSOLETE. About 800 P210-4 pistols are still in use; 480 are conversions to .22 long rifle for training. Each company *(Hundertschaft)* of the *Bereitschaftpolizei* (Police Field Force Reserve) and the *Bundesgrenzschutz* has two of these .22 pistols. Lower Saxony *(Niedersachsen)* uses the designation P2 for the Walther PP.

- *Cal.:* 9 x 19mm NATO
  Official Name: Pistole 3—P3
  Common Name: Astra 600/43

  *Remarks:* NSN 1005-12-134-3793 w/o equipment. OBSOLETE.

- *Cal.:* 9 x 19mm NATO
  Official Name: Pistole 4—P4
  Common Name: P1, w/ short
  barrel

  *Remarks:* Walther origin. This 110mm barrel pistol (P1 has 125mm barrel) developed for the police market was produced 1975–81. NSN 1005-12-169-8553. Supplied to the *Bundesgrenzschutz,* ca. 6,500. Declared surplus in 1987 and sold. The P38K version was made in even smaller numbers and supplied to GSG9; no stock number assigned.

- *Cal.:* 9 x 19mm NATO
  Official Name: Pistole 5—P5
  Common Name: Walther P5

  *Remarks:* Adopted by the state police *(Landespolizei)* in Rhineland-Palatinate and in Baden-Wurttemberg.

- *Cal.:* 9 x 19mm NATO
  Official Name: Pistole 6—P6
  Common Name: SIG-Sauer P225

  *Remarks:* Used by *Bundesgrenzschutz, Bereitschaftpolizei, Bundeszollpolizei* (Federal Customs Police), *Bundesbahnpolizei* (Federal Railway Police), *Bundespostpolizei* (Federal Postal Police), Berlin police, and the state police in Schleswig-Holstein, Hansestadt-Hamburg, Bremen, North Rhine-Westphalia, and Hessen.

- *Cal.:* 9 x 19mm NATO
  Common Name: SIG-Sauer P220

  *Remarks:* NSN 1005-12-184-3621 w/o equipment.

- *Cal.:* 9 x 19mm NATO
  *Official Name: Pistole 7* — P7
  *Common Name:* Heckler & Koch
  P7. Originally called *Poli-zeiselbstlade-pistole* — PSP

- *Cal.:* 9 x 19mm NATO
  *Official Name: Pistole 9* — P9S
  *Common Name:* Heckler & Koch
  P9S

- *Cal.:* 7.65 x 17mm Browning
  *Official Name: Pistole 11* — P11
  *Common Name:* Heckler & Koch
  HK4

- *Cal.:* 7.65 x 17mm Browning
  *Official Name: Pistole 21* — P21
  *Common Name:* Walther PPK

- *Cal.:* 7.65 x 17mm Browning
  *Official Name: Pistole 22* — P22
  *Common Name:* Walther PP

- *Cal.:* 5.6 x 16mmR
  *Official Name: Pistole 31* — P31
  *Common Name:* Hammerli-Walther M200

- *Cal.:* 9 x 19mm NATO
  *Common Name:* FN Mle. 35GP
  pistol

- *Cal.:* 9 x 29mmR
  *Common Name:* .357 Smith &
  Wesson Model 19 revolver

- *Cal.:* 11.43 x 23mm
  *Common Name:* .45 M1911A1
  pistol

**SUBMACHINE GUNS:**
- *Cal.:* 9 x 19mm NATO
  *Official Name: Maschinenpistole
  1* — MP1
  *Common Name:* Beretta Model
  38/49 submachine gun

- *Cal.:* 9 x 19mm NATO
  *Official Name: Maschinenpistole
  2* — MP2
  *Common Name:* IMI Uzi sub-machine gun

- *Cal.:* 9 x 19mm NATO
  *Official Name: Maschinenpistole 5*
  *Common Name:* Heckler & Koch
  HK54 submachine gun

*Remarks:* Adopted by the *Bundesgrenzschutzgruppe* 9 (GSG9) antiterrorist force, and the *Bundeskriminalamt* (BKA; the West German equivalent of the US Federal Bureau of Investigation), and state police in Lower Saxony, Baden Wurttemberg, and Bavaria. NSN 1005-12-186-5059.

*Remarks:* Adopted by Saarland state police and the GSG9. NSN 1005-12-175-9631.

*Remarks:* Police use. OBSOLETE. Berlin police formerly used HK4s marked MAS, assembled in France, to get around the restriction on German-made guns.

*Remarks:* Police officers and pilots of the *Luftwaffe* and the *Marine* (Navy) use the PPK. NSN 1005-12-120-6118 w/ belt holster; 1005-12-133-4912 w/ shoulder-hung holster; 1005-12-133-4911 w/ shoulder holster. NSN 1005-12-120-0893. Obsolescent. Until recently many Walther PPs were also used by German police forces. Most were made by Manurhin in France.

*Remarks:* NSN 1005-12-159-3025 w/o equipment.

*Remarks:* Hammerli target pistol with 190mm barrel. NSN 1005-12-127-2774. The Walther .22 Short OSP is NSN 1005-12-185-2108. The Walther GSP is NSN 1005-12-190-8650.

*Remarks:* Belgian origin. OBSOLETE. All purchased before 1962 and disposed of by 1969. Used by State Police forces; e.g., North Rhine-Westphalia.

*Remarks:* US origin. Used by the GSG9.

*Remarks:* US origin. OBSOLETE; formerly used by the *Bundesmarine* (Navy).

*Remarks:* OBSOLETE.

*Remarks: Bundeswehr* standard. Used in both the fixed wood stock *(Holz-schaft)* (MP2 w/ equipment NSN 1005-12-130-1258; 1005-12-130-1257 w/o equipment) and metal folding stock *(Klappschaft)* (MP2A1 w/ equipment NSN 1005-12-127-6701; 1005-12-127-6700 w/o equipment) versions.

*Remarks: Bundesgrenzschutz. Bundeswehr* has used the MP5 series since 1985. Berlin police have MP5s marked MAS from France to avoid restrictions on German-made guns. NSN 1005-12-158-2289 for MP5 A2 w/ standard buttstock; 1005-12-196-3766 for MP5 A4 (MP5 A3 in USA), w/ retractable stock. Retractable stock alone is NSN 1005-12-169-8554. MP5 SD2 silenced SMG is NSN 1005-12-170-1828. MP5K (short SMG) is NSN 1005-12-185-1371. MP5KA1 (w/o sights) is NSN 1005-12-175-3641. The *Zielpunkt-projektor* (spot projecting sighting device) for MP5 is NSN 1240-12-175-4049. MP5 SD and MP5K are used by border police, GSG9, and some state police.

Member of the *Bundeswehr* armed with a folding stock 9 x 19mm **MP2A2 (Uzi)** submachine gun. (Gander)

• *Cal.:* 9 x 19mm NATO
  *Common Name:* Walther MPK and MPL submachine guns

*Remarks:* German-made weapons used by Berlin police; marked Manurhin to avoid restrictions on German guns in West Berlin.

• *Cal.:* 9 x 19mm NATO
  *Common Name:* Carl Gustav submachine gun

*Remarks:* Swedish origin. NSN 1005-12-910-0122 w/ equipment. Only small quantities in store.

• *Cal.:* 11.43 x 23mm
  *Common Name:* .45 M1 and M1A1 submachine guns

*Remarks:* US origin. OBSOLETE. Formerly used by the *Bundesmarine* (Navy).

• *Cal.:* 5.56 x 45mm
  *Common Name:* HK 53 submachine gun

*Remarks:* Heckler & Koch (HK) GmbH. Used by some police forces. NSN 1005-12-307-0120.

**RIFLES:**

• *Cal.:* 7.62 x 51mm NATO
*Official Name: Gewehr 1* – G1
*Common Name:* FN FAL

*Remarks:* Obsolescent. Originally 100,000 rifles purchased for the *Bundes-grenzschutz*. Most have been sold as surplus or provided as military aid (i.e., Turkey). Some still used in sniper version by some state police forces and the *Bereitschaftpolizei*. Gradually being replaced by the G8 and G8A1. NSN 1005-12-124-2305 w/ equipment. NSN 1005-13-100-0010 w/o equipment. The sniper version (G1ZF-Z4B) is NSN 1005-12-124-3155 w/o equipment.

• *Cal.:* 7.62 x 51mm NATO
*Official Name: Gewehr 2* – G2
*Common Name:* SIG StG57

*Remarks:* Acquired for trials only.

• *Cal.:* 7.62 x 51mm NATO
*Official Name: Gewehr 3* – G3
*Common Name:* G3 rifle

*Remarks:* The original G3, as received from Centro de Estudios Technios y Materiales Especiales (CETME), w/ wooden stock and III/61 *Klapvisier* (folding sight) is NSN 1005-12-930-0444 w/ equipment; 1005-12-930-0375 w/o equipment. Standardized July, 1960. G3 w/ *Drehvisier* (drum sight) is NSN 1005-12-124-7413. Standard July 1961. The basic G3 has gone through numerous minor changes but is still *Bundeswehr* standard with new furniture. Made by HK and in smaller numbers by Rheinmetall. G3s are used by NATO ammunition manufacturers and NATO test centers to acceptance-test 7.62mm NATO ammunition. Berlin police have G3s marked MAS and France to avoid restrictions on German-made guns in Berlin. This model was standard until June 1962.

• *Cal.:* 7.62 x 51mm NATO
*Official Name: Gewehr 3A1* – G3A1
*Common Name:* G3A1

*Remarks:* Standard from October 1963. Retractable metal stock *(Schulter-stutze)* NSN 1005-12-141-1623 w/ equipment, and NSN 1005-12-140-5194 w/o equipment.

• *Cal.:* 7.62 x 51mm NATO
*Official Name: Gewehr 3A2* – G3A2
*Common Name:* G3A2

*Remarks:* Standard from June 1962. NSN 1005-12-124-7412 w/ equipment and NSN 1005-12-124-7413 w/o equipment. G3 A2ZF is NSN 1005-12-124-7418.

• *Cal.:* 7.62 x 51mm NATO
*Official Name: Gewehr 3A3* – G3A3
*Common Name:* G3A3

*Remarks:* Standard since December 1964. Synthetic plastic solid buttstock w/ equipment is NSN 1005-12-144-0627; NSN 1005-12-140-9436; 1005-12-187-3009 (phosphated finish); and 1005-12-187-3010 w/o equipment. The G3 A3ZF w/ equipment is NSN 1005-12-145-2928, NSN 1005-12-145-2929 w/o equipment. FOM 1005-15-2-7.62-2.

• *Cal.:* 7.62 x 51mm NATO
*Official Name: Gewehr 3A4* – G3A4
*Common Name:* G3A4

*Remarks:* Standard since December 1964. G3 A4 w/ retractable buttstock w/ equipment NSN 1005-12-143-8615 and NSN 1005-12-140-9437 w/o equipment.

• *Cal.:* 7.62 x 51mm NATO
*Official Name: Gewehr 3A5* – G3A5
*Common Name:* G3A5

*Remarks:* NSN 1005-12-146-2826 w/o equipment. The Danish model.

• *Cal.:* 7.62 x 51mm NATO
*Official Name: Gewehr 3A6* – G3A6
*Common Name:* G3A6

*Remarks:* NSN 1005-12-159-3609 w/o equipment. The Iranian model.

• *Cal.:* 7.62 x 51mm NATO
*Official Name: Gewehr 3A7* – G3A7
*Common Name:* G3A7

*Remarks:* NSN 1005-12-159-3608 w/o equipment. The Turkish model.

• *Cal.:* 7.62 x 51mm NATO
*Official Name: Gewehr 3 SG1*
*Common Name:* G3 sniper rifle

*Remarks:* HK GmbH. NSN 1005-12-181-2400.

Two views of the receiver markings on the *Gewehr 3*. The left side markings indicate that this G3 was made in April 1962 by Heckler & Koch. The "FS" indicates that the rifle has been modified to have the free-swinging barrel of the later production rifles. The right side markings record that this weapon has been through the *Bundeswehr* rebuild program five times. This rifle was reworked in March 1963, November 1969, March 1975, July 1980, and May 1983. Each rebuild was certified by a government inspector. As the result of this rebuild program, the *Bundeswehr* has one of the most reliable small arms inventories in the world. (Heckler & Koch)

*Bundeswehr* **member armed with a retracting stock 7.62 x 51mm NATO G3A4 assault rifle. (US Army; Sutter)**

• *Cal.:* 7.62 x 51mm NATO
  *Official Name: Gewehr 4 — G4*
  *Common Name:* Armalite AR-10

*Remarks:* Acquired for trials only.

• *Cal.:* 7.62 x 51mm NATO
  *Official Name: Gewehr 5*
  *Common Name:* SSG sniper rifle

*Remarks:* Steyr-Daimler-Puch (SDP), Austria. A version of the SSG w/ iron sights. Without equipment, NSN 1005-12-158-8533. Regular SSG w/ synthetic stock, NSN 1005-12-186-6285; and 1005-12-186-6285 w/ wood stock.

• *Cal.:* 7.62 x 51mm NATO
  *Official Name: Gewehr 7*

*Remarks:* NSN 1005-12-162-4607 w/ equipment and adjustable stock.

• *Cal.:* 7.62 x 51mm NATO
  *Official Name: Gewehr 8*
  *Common Name:* Police sniper rifle

*Remarks:* HK GmbH. NSN 1005-12-194-0948. Used only by the *Bundesgrenzschutz.* Built on the HK11 machine gun. Can be converted to belt feed. Selective fire.

• *Cal.:* 7.62 x 51mm NATO
  *Official Name: Gewehr 8 A1*

*Remarks:* HK GmbH. NSN 1005-12-194-0949. Used by state police forces. Only feeds from standard 20 shot G3 magazines and special drum magazines.

• *Cal.:* 7.62 x 51mm NATO
  *Official Name: Prazisionschutzen-*
  *gewehr 1 — PSG-1*
  *Common Name:* PSG-1 sniper
  rifle

*Remarks:* HK GmbH. NSN 1005-120194-7555. This sniper rifle is used by most German state police forces.

- *Cal.:* 4.92 x 34mmOH
  *Official Name: Gewehr 11* — G11
  *Common Name:* Developmental
  rifle by Heckler & Koch and
  Dynamit Nobel

*Remarks:* Caseless ammunition/rifle R&D project being conducted for the *Bundeswehr.* Another version is being developed for the US as part of the Advanced Combat Rifle program.

- *Cal.:* 7.92 x 57mm
  *Official Name: Gewehr 21*
  *Common Name:* Mauser 98K

*Remarks:* World War II rifles. Still used for some ceremonial drill activities. NSN 1005-12-134-3790 w/o equipment; 1005-12-137-0194 w/ equipment.

- *Cal.:* 5.6 x 16mmR
  *Official Name: Gewehr 31* — G31

*Remarks:* Erma-Werke, Dachau. .22 LR training rifle. NSN 1005-12-120-0900 w/ equipment. The G31A1 is NSN 1005-12-120-2860 w/o equipment; 1005-12-120-7715 w/ equipment.

- *Cal.:* 5.6 x 16mmR
  *Official Name: Gewehr 32* — G32
  *Common Name:* Walther KKJ
  rifle

*Remarks:* Walther, Ulm. .22 LR training rifle. NSN 1005-12-120-8966 w/o equipment. NSN 1005-12-120-6020.

- *Cal.:* 5.6 x 16mmR
  *Official Name: Gewehr 33* — G33

*Remarks:* J. G. Anchuetz, GmbH, Ulm. .22 LR training rifle. NSN 1005-12-120-5391 w/o equipment; 1005-12-120-7592 w/ equipment.

- *Cal.:* 5.6 x 16mmR
  *Official Name: Gewehr 34* — G34

*Remarks:* J. G. Anchuetz, GmbH, Ulm. .22 LR target rifle. NSN 1005-12-165-2990 w/o sight; 1005-12-162-4439 w/ sight. Also 1005-12-162-4608 w/ equipment, and 1005-12-165-2990 w/o equipment.

- *Cal.:* 5.6 x 16mmR

*Remarks:* HK origin. .22 LR target rifle. NSN 1005-12-187-8541. HK catalog no. 220 262.

- *Cal.:* 5.6 x 16mmR

*Remarks:* Ministry of the Interior. .22 LR target rifle. NSN 1005-12-191-4439. HK catalog no. 220 262.

- *Cal.:* 5.56 x 45mm
  *Official Name:* Gewehr 41 — G41
  *Common Name:* Heckler & Koch
  variant of HK33 to meet NATO
  STANAG 4172

*Remarks:* Not standard German weapon despite "G" designator and NSN identifier. The G41 is being offered for export and is currently being tested by the Italian Army. NSN 1005-12-185-4755. G41A2 is NSN 1005-12-306-1292 w/o equipment.

- *Cal.:* 7.62 x 51mm NATO
  *Common Name:* HK 81 sniper
  rifles

*Remarks:* HK origin. Selective fire sniper weapon with set trigger, telescope, and bipod is NSN 1005-12-184-0395. HK catalog no. 222 934. Same weapon with burst fire feature NSN 1005-12-184-5592.

- *Cal.:* 7.62 x 63mm
  *Common Name:* .30 M1 rifle

*Remarks:* US origin. Before mid-1960s FMS provided 46,754 M1 rifles.

**A custom 7.62 x 33mm (.30) M1 Carbine as used by the Hessian State Police in West Germany. The stock was made by Messrs Wolfe, a noted sporting stock manufacturing company. The scope is a Zeiss-Diavari 1.5 to 6 power variable telescope. About thirty of these special rifles were made. (Fritze)**

- *Cal.:* 7.62 x 33mm
  *Common Name:* .30 M1 carbine

- *Cal.:* 7.62 x 33mm
  *Common Name:* .30 M1 carbine
  police sniper weapons

**SHOTGUNS:**
- *Cal.:* 18.5 x 59mm
  *Common Name:* 12 gage HK502
  shotgun

- *Cal.:* 18.5 x 59mm
  *Common Name:* 12 gage HK512
  shotgun

**MACHINE GUNS:**
- *Cal.:* 7.92 x 57mm
  *Official Name: Maschinengewehr
  42-1* MG42-1
  *Common Name:* MG42/58

- *Cal.:* 7.92 x 57mm
  *Official Name: Maschinengewehr
  42-1* MG42-2
  *Common Name:* MG42/59

*Remarks:* US origin. Before 1964 MAP provided 34,192 carbines.

*Remarks:* Used by Hessian state police. Other police units and prison guards used the M1 carbine as well.

*Remarks:* Franchi autoloading shotgun used by German police as an antiriot weapon.

*Remarks:* Franchi autoloading shotgun used by German police as an antiriot weapon. NSN 1005-12-308-5059 w/o equipment.

*Remarks:* NSN-1005-12-040-0012.

*Remarks:* NSN-1005-12-040-0013.

*Bundeswehr* **soldier armed with a standard 7.62 x 51mm NATO MG3 GPMG. (US Army; Sutter)**

• *Cal.:* 7.62 x 51mm NATO
*Official Name: Maschinengewehr 1*
MG1
*Common Name:* Post-1945 model
of MG42

*Remarks:* The first postwar machine guns used by West Germany were wartime MG42s (FOM 1005-15-4-7.92-1) acquired from Norway in 7.92 x 57mm and reworked by Rheinmetall. Primarily used by the *Bundesgrenzschutz.* These MG1s were rebarreled MG42/59s (NSN 1005-12-121-1507 w/o equipment; 1005-12-121-6672 w/ equipment). FOM 1005-15-4-7.62-1. These guns were 1,224mm overall; had 550g bolt assembly and nonchrome bore. Used feed belt similar to World War II *Patronengurt.*

• *Cal.:* 7.62 x 51mm NATO
*Official Name: Maschinengewehr 1A1* MG1A1
*Common Name:* Post-1945 model
of MG42

*Remarks:* This machine gun fired the 7.62mm NATO cartridge, with sights properly calibrated for that cartridge. Overall length 1,230mm; chrome bore; modified trigger assembly. Used DM1 nondisintegrating feed belt. NSN 1005-12-139-6145 w/o equipment; 1005-12-140-3789 w/ equipment.

• *Cal.:* 7.62 x 51mm NATO
*Official Name: Maschinengewehr 1A2* MG1A2
*Common Name:* MG1A2

*Remarks:* This machine gun had a longer ejection port, heavier bolt (959g), and friction ring buffer — slower rate of fire 700–900 s.p.m. Overall length 1,230mm; chrome bore. Used DM1 nondisintegrating feed belt as well as DM6 and US M13 disintegrating links. NSN 1005-12-139-6145 w/o equipment; 1005-12-140-3789 w/ equipment.

• *Cal.:* 7.62 x 51mm NATO
*Official Name: Maschinengewehr 1A3* MG1A3
*Common Name:* MG1A3

*Remarks:* The gun (NSN 1005-12-140-7539 w/o equipment; 1005-12-140-9789 w/ equipment) was a further modification to the MG1A1 with changes to the bolt, barrel, feed mechanism, bolt, stock recoil booster, and flash suppressor. Current *Bundeswehr* plans call for conversion of all MG1A3s to MG3 configuration. Rheinmetall still does the final assembly of MG3, but many components are subcontracted to firms such as HK GmbH. Uses DM1, DM6, and M13 feed links.

• *Cal.:* 7.62 x 51mm NATO
*Official Name: Maschinengewehr 1A4* MG1A4
*Common Name:* MG1A4

*Remarks:* This gun is a shortened version of the MG1; 1000mm overall. NSN 1005-12-140-9134 w/o equipment.

• *Cal.:* 7.62 x 51mm NATO
*Official Name: Maschinengewehr 1A5* MG1A4
*Common Name:* MG1A5

*Remarks:* This gun is a shortened armor version of the MG1. No butt stock. Overall length 1090mm. NSN 1005-12-140-9133 w/o equipment; 1005-12-148-6856 w/ equipment.

• *Cal.:* 7.62 x 51mm NATO
*Official Name: Maschinengewehr 2* MG2
*Common Name:* MG2

*Remarks:* Designation subsequently given to wartime MG42s converted 7.62mm NATO. Overall length 1230mm. NSN 1005-12-123-9965 w/o equipment; 1005-12-123-9964 w/ equipment.

• *Cal.:* 7.62 x 51mm NATO
*Official Name: Maschinengewehr 3*

*Remarks: Bundeswehr* standard. Differs in minor details such as addition of antiaircraft rear sight, shape of barrel booster-flash suppressor and uses DM1, DM6, or M13 links. With equipment it is NSN 1005-12-145-2484; 1005-12-145-2485 w/o equipment. In addition to integral bipod, the MG1 and MG3 are mounted on tripod (*Feldlafette*, MG DM1A2), w/ equipment NSN 1005-12-147-6680; 1005-12-230-4970 w/o equipment.

Other MG mounts are:

| | | |
|---|---|---|
| BLAF | MG DM1 | — NSN 1005-12-133-0078 |
| BLAF | MG DM2 | — NSN 1005-12-133-0090 |
| DRLAF | MG DM2 | — NSN 1005-12-135-6089 |
| BLAF | MG DM2A1 | — NSN 1005-12-139-6674 |
| BLAF | MG DM3 | — NSN 1005-12-133-0087; 1005-12-149-5298 w/ equipment |
| BLAF | MG DM4 | — NSN 1005-12-137-1258 |
| BLAF | MG DM5 | — NSN 1005-12-142-8064 |
| DRLAF | MG DM7 | — NSN 1005-12-149-5307 |
| BLAF | MG DM7 | — NSN 1005-12-305-6795 |
| BLAF | MG DM9 | — NSN 1005-12-149-5026 |
| BLAF | MG DM48 | — NSN 1005-12-195-1289 for Turkey |

- *Cal.:* 7.62 x 51mm NATO
  *Official Name: Maschinengewehr 3A1* MG3A1
  *Common Name:* MG3A1

- *Cal.:* 7.62 x 51mm NATO
  *Common Name:* HK21 GPMG

- *Cal.:* 7.62 x 51mm NATO
  *Common Name:* M60D door machine gun

- *Cal.:* 7.62 x 63mm
  *Common Name:* .30 Browning M1919A4 machine guns

- *Cal.:* 12.7 x 99mm
  *Common Name:* .50 M2HB HMG

*Remarks:* Armor/vehicle version of the MG3. No buttstock. Overall length 1090mm. NSN 1005-12-147-9925 w/o equipment; 1005-12-147-9926 w/ equipment.

*Remarks:* HK origin. The Portuguese version is NSN 1005-12-308-6280 w/o equipment.

*Remarks:* US origin. FMS provided 35 in 1978.

*Remarks:* US origin. MAP and FMS provided 2,590 before the mid-1960s. Were used in US M42 tanks. OBSOLETE. These machine guns were sold to Merex, who in turn sold them to the Saudi Arabian military.

*Remarks:* US origin. Used on OBSOLETE US vehicles, such as M48 series tanks. Being replaced by MG3 on AFVs.

## AUTOMATIC CANNON:

- *Cal.:* 20 x 139mm
  *Official Name: Feldkanone 20 DM1 und DM1A1*
  *Common Name:* Rheinmetall HS820

- *Cal.:* 20 x 139mm
  *Official Name: Feldkanone 20 DM2*

- *Cal.:* 20 x 139mm
  *Official Name: Feldkanone 20 DM3*

- *Cal.:* 20 x 139mm
  *Official Name: Feldkanone 20 DM4*

- *Cal.:* 20 x 139mm
  *Official Name: Feldkanone 20 DM5*
  *Common Name:* Rheinmetall Rh202

- *Cal.:* 20 x 139mm
  *Official Name: Feldkanone 20 DM6*
  *Common Name:* Rheinmetall Rh202

*Remarks:* Production licensed by Hispano-Suiza/Oerlikon. DM1 is NSN 1005-12-132-1285 w/o equipment; 1005-12-124-3156 w/ equipment. FOM 1005-18-4-20-1. DM1A1 is NSN 1005-12-147-3024 w/o equipment; 1005-12-146-3639.

*Remarks:* DM2 is NSN 1005-12-150-7434 w/o equipment; 1005-12-150-7454 w/ equipment.

*Remarks:* DM3 is NSN 1005-12-150-7457 w/ equipment.

*Remarks:* DM4 is NSN 1005-12-150-7458 w/o equipment; 1005-12-150-7460 w/ equipment.

*Remarks:* Domestic design. Standard since 1968. With equipment the DM5 is NSN 1005-12-150-7462; NSN 1005-12-150-7461 and 1005-12-152-3744 w/o equipment. When mounted on the single gun Norwegian AA mount *(Kanone, Feld-, 20MM, Flugabwehr; 20mm x 139 Kongsberglafette, FK-FLA20-2ZUB)* it is NSN 1005-12-152-3744, while the mount *(Lavett, 20MM Luftvern [Lafette, Feld, Feld-, Maschinenkanone] HS669N)* is NSN 1005-25-114-4069. There was an earlier DM4 that had 5-degree rifling as opposed to the 6-degree rifling of DM5. Both DM4 and DM5 auto cannon have right, left, and top belt feed.

*Remarks:* Domestic design. This is a variant of DM5 that has a barrel with a 6-degree rifling twist and right and left feed. With equipment this gun is NSN 1005-12-171-9416; w/o equipment it is 1005-12-171-9417. Mount EG-IIA1 for the DM6 is 1005-12-306-8769.

## GRENADE LAUNCHERS:

- *Cal.:* 40 x 46mmSR
  *Official Name: Granatpistole 40mm*
  *Common Name:* HK69A1 grenade launcher

*Remarks:* Domestic design. Standard since 1979. By early 1986 the *Bundeswehr* had acquired 10,000 of these grenade launchers. Their total requirement is 12,000 launchers. NSN 1010-12-177-7637. The *Bundesgrenzschutz* uses a slightly different model called the MZPI.

**SIGNAL PISTOLS:**
* *Cal.:* 26.5mm
  *Official Name: P2 A1 Signalpistole*
  *Common Name:* P2 A1 signal pistol

  *Remarks:* HK origin. NSN 1095-12-162-2332.

* *Cal.:* 19mm
  *Official Name: Notsignalgerat*
  *Common Name:* Emergency flare launcher

  *Remarks:* HK origin. NSN 1370-12-170-5771.

**LINE-THROWING RIFLES:**
* *Cal.:* 7.92mm
  *Official Name: Leinenschiessgewher*
  *Common Name:* 7.92mm line throwing rifle

* *Cal.:* 11.43mm
  *Official Name: Leinenschiessgewher*
  *Common Name:* .45 cal. line throwing rifle

# GHANA (People's Revolutionary Republic of)

Population (estimate in 1984): 13.08 million. Ground forces: regulars, variously estimated as being between 10,000 and 15,000; reserves, 1,000 to 1,500; paramilitary: Army auxilliary force used as border guards, 5,000.

**HANDGUNS:**
* *Cal.:* 9 x 20mmR
  *Common Name:* .38 Enfield No. 2 Mark I revolver

  *Remarks:* Royal Small Arms Factory (RSAF), Enfield.

* *Cal.:* 9 x 19mm Parabellum
  *Common Name:* FN Mle. 35 GP pistol

  *Remarks:* FN origin.

**SUBMACHINE GUNS:**
* *Cal.:* 9 x 19mm Parabellum
  *Common Name:* Sterling Mark 4 submachine gun

  *Remarks:* Sterling Armament Co., UK.

* *Cal.:* 9 x 19mm Parabellum
  *Common Name:* MP5 submachine

  *Remarks:* Heckler & Koch (HK), GmbH.

**RIFLES:**
* *Cal.:* 5.56 x 45mm
  *Common Name:* M16A1 (Model 613) rifle

  *Remarks:* Acquired from Colt in 1976–77; ca. 2,000. Total in service estimated at 6,000.

* *Cal.:* 5.56 x 45mm
  *Common Name:* HK 33 rifle

  *Remarks:* Origin unknown.

- *Cal.:* 7.7 x 56mmR
  *Common Name:* .303 No. 4 Enfield rifle

  *Remarks:* RSAF.

- *Cal.:* 7.62 x 39mm
  *Common Name:* AK47 and AKM assault rifles

  *Remarks:* Origin unknown. Some may be from East Germany. Folding stock versions are in service.

- *Cal.:* 7.62 x 51mm NATO
  *Common Name:* Gewehr 3

  *Remarks:* HK origin. Total in service estimated at 12,000.

- *Cal.:* 7.62 x 51mm NATO
  *Common Name:* FN FAL and L1A1

  *Remarks:* FN and UK origin. Still a major weapon.

**SHOTGUNS:**
- *Cal.:* 18.5 x 59mm
  *Common Name:* 12 gage Mossberg Model 500 shotgun

  *Remarks:* US origin. Used by Ghana Prison Department guard force. Acquired in 1981.

**MACHINE GUNS:**
- *Cal.:* 7.62 x 51mm NATO
  *Common Name:* FN MAG

  *Remarks:* FN origin. MAG *Infanterie Standard* (60-20), T1 and MAG *Coaxial* (60-40) ranging machine gun on the Scimitar armored car. Also mounted on the MOWAG Piranha APC.

- *Cal.:* 7.7 x 56mmR
  *Common Name:* .303 Bren LMG

  *Remarks:* RSAF.

- *Cal.:* 12.7 x 99mm
  *Common Name:* .50 M2 HB HMG

  *Remarks:* Origin unknown.

- *Cal.:* 12.7 x 108mm
  *Common Name:* DShK 38/46 HMG

  *Remarks:* Soviet origin.

**AUTOMATIC CANNON:**
- *Cal.:* 14.5 x 114mm
  *Common Name:* KPV HMG

  *Remarks:* East Bloc origin.

# GREECE (Hellenic Republic)

Population (estimate in 1984): 9.98 million. Ground forces: regulars, variously estimated as being between 135,000 and 165,000 (ca. 99,500 to 125,000 conscripts); gendarmerie (Khorofylaki) 25,000 to 30,000; national guard, 70,000; reserves, between 250,000 and 350,000.

**HANDGUNS:**
- *Cal.:* 9 x 19mm NATO
  *Common Name:* P7 pistol

  *Remarks:* Greek Air Force receiving German police type from Heckler and Koch (HK), GmbH.

- *Cal.:* 11.43 x 23mm
  *Common Name:* .45 M1911A1 pistol

  *Remarks:* US origin. More than 5,800 M1911A1 pistols were provided through MAP and FMS before 1974.

- *Cal.:* 9 x 29mmR
  *Common Name:* .38 Smith & Wesson revolvers—various models

  *Remarks:* US origin. For example, 300 S&W M10 51mm barrel revolvers were delivered as MAP aid in 1970.

**SUBMACHINE GUNS:**
- *Cal.:* 9 x 19mm NATO
  *Common Name:* MPi69 submachine gun

- *Cal.:* 9 x 19mm NATO
  *Common Name:* UZI submachine gun

- *Cal.:* 9 x 19mm NATO
  *Official Name:* EMP5
  *Common Name:* HK MP5A3 submachine gun

- *Cal.:* 9 x 19mm Parabellum
  *Common Name:* Ingram M10 submachine gun

- *Cal.:* 11.43 x 23mm
  *Common Name:* .45 M1A1 Thompson submachine gun

- *Cal.:* 11.43 x 23mm
  *Common Name:* .45 M3A1 submachine gun

**RIFLES:**
- *Cal.:* 5.56 x 45mm NATO
  *Common Name:* M16A2 rifle (Model 701)

- *Cal.:* 7.62 x 33mm
  *Common Name:* .30 M1 carbine

- *Cal.:* 7.62 x 51mm NATO
  *Common Name:* FN FAL

*Remarks:* Steyr-Daimler-Puch (SDP), Austria.

*Remarks:* Origin unknown.

*Remarks:* Originally MP5s were purchased directly from HK GmbH. Hellenic Arms Industry of Athens is now licensed by HK to manufacture their weapons. Not determined if it will be used by Greek Army.

*Remarks:* Origin unknown. Used by airport police.

*Remarks:* US origin. MAP delivered to the Greeks in excess of 2,900 Thompsons before 1963. Presumed OBSOLETE.

*Remarks:* US origin. MAP delivered in excess of 1,400 M3A1s and about 20 M3s prior to 1974.

*Remarks:* Ca. 300 purchased from Colt for use by the Greek Special Forces. Some Model 723s (M16A2 carbine) also included in this order.

*Remarks:* US origin. MAP delivered 30,002 M1 carbines and 250 M2 carbines before 1975.

*Remarks:* Belgian origin. Also acquired the PARA model in the early 1970s.

The *Gewehr 3* receiver markings as currently made by the Hellenic Arms Industry for the Greek Army. This weapon was made in September 1981. Note the stylized logo for the Hellenic Arms Industry in front of the selector lever. (Hellenic Arms Industry)

- *Cal.:* 7.62 x 51mm NATO
  *Common Name:* Gewehr 3

  *Remarks:* Hellenic Arms Industry (HAI), Athens, licensed by HK, which identifies this model with the catalog number 224043. HAI will make 200,000 G3s for the Greek Army at the rate of 2,000 per month.

- *Cal.:* 7.62 x 63mm
  *Common Name:* .30 M1 rifle

  *Remarks:* US origin. MAP delivered in excess of 185,800 M1 rifles before 1975. An additional 1,085 were purchased through FMS.

- *Cal.:* 7.62 x 63mm
  *Common Name:* .30 M1C sniper rifle

  *Remarks:* US origin. MAP delivered 1,780 in 1970.

- *Cal.:* 7.62 x 63mm
  *Common Name:* .30 M1D sniper rifle

  *Remarks:* US origin. MAP delivered 104 in 1970.

**SHOTGUNS:**
- *Cal.:* 18.5 x 59mm
  *Common Name:* 12 gage Winchester Model 12 shotgun

  *Remarks:* US origin. MAP delivered 300 M12s before 1970. NSN 1005-00-677-9150. Other unknown shotgun models delivered earlier in 1963.

**MACHINE GUNS:**
- *Cal.:* 7.62 x 51mm NATO
  *Common Name:* MG3 GPMG

  *Remarks:* HAI is assembling the MG3 under license from Rheinmetall. There is some local manufacture of parts.

- *Cal.:* 7.62 x 51mm NATO
  *Common Name:* HK11A1 GPMG

  *Remarks:* HAI is assembling the HK11 under license from HK GmbH with some local manufacture of parts. Unclear if this MG is to be used by the Greek military.

- *Cal.:* 7.62 x 51mm NATO
  *Common Name:* FN MAG

  *Remarks:* Belgian origin. Models in service include: MAG *Infanterie Standard* (60-20) T1, MAG *coaxial* (60-40) T3 (MAG 58), MAG *coaxial* P.806, and MAG US M240.

- *Cal.:* 7.62 x 51mm NATO
  *Common Name:* M60 GPMG

  *Remarks:* US origin. Starting in 1977 the Greek Army has purchased through FMS 726 M60s.

- *Cal.:* 7.62 x 63mm
  *Common Name:* .30 M1918A2 BAR

  *Remarks:* US origin. MAP delivered 1780 BARs before 1975 and an additional 150 BARs in 1975.

- *Cal.:* 7.62 x 63mm
  *Common Name:* .30 M1919A4 LMG

  *Remarks:* US origin. MAP delivered 1,367 before 1975. Another 87 M1919A6 LMGs were also given. Before 1963 MAP provided 2,450 unspecified .30 caliber LMGs.

- *Cal.:* 7.62 x 63mm
  *Common Name:* .30 M37 AMG

  *Remarks:* US origin. FMS delivered 198 M37 armor machine guns before 1975.

- *Cal.:* 12.7 x 99mm
  *Common Name:* .50 M2 HB HMG

  *Remarks:* US origin. During the past decade MAP delivered 774 M2HBs and FMS delivered 19 flexible M2s; 517 M2s for the M1 cupola and 71 for the M55 Quad AA systems. Latter two deliveries were through MAP.

**AUTOMATIC CANNON:**
- *Cal.:* 20 x 102mm
  *Common Name:* M39A3RH automatic cannon

  *Remarks:* US origin. FMS delivered 41 guns in 1977.

- *Cal.:* 20 x 102mm
  *Common Name:* M61 automatic cannon

  *Remarks:* US origin. FMS 16; MAP 18 in 1977.

- *Cal.:* 20 x 110mmRB
  *Common Name:* US MK4 Oerlikon (Type S) automatic cannon

  *Remarks:* US origin. On naval craft.

- *Cal.:* 20 x 139mm
  *Common Name:* M693 automatic cannon

  *Remarks:* French origin.

- *Cal.:* 20 x 139mm
  *Common Name:* Rh202 automatic
  cannon

*Remarks:* Some guns are of German origin, but this cannon is also being made under license from *Mauser* at HAI. Used in the twin antiaircraft version. HAI also has license to manufacture the 30mm Mauser auto cannon.

**GRENADE LAUNCHERS:**
- *Cal.:* 40 x 46mmSR
  *Common Name:* M79 grenade
  launcher

*Remarks:* US origin. MAP delivered 2,666 M79s before 1975.

- *Cal.:* 40 x 46mmSR
  *Common Name:* M203 grenade
  launcher

*Remarks:* US origin. FMS delivered 100 M203s 1979-80.

## Greek Small Arms Industry

The Hellenic Arms Industry (*Elleniki Biomichania Oplon* — EBO or "EVO" in Greek), a state-owned corporation established in 1977, located at Aiyion west of Corinth, has licensed the production of several Heckler & Koch small caliber weapons — G3A3, G3A4, MP5, HK11, and HK21. A major rearmament program for the Greek armed forces was announced in May 1987, with EVO being one of the major beneficiaries. It is still not clear which of these besides the *Gewehr* 3 will be used by the Greek armed forces. To support its factory operations, the Hellenic Arms Industry is seeking export sales. Some weapons have been exported to Africa, notably Burundi. In December 1984 the Greeks signed an arms export agreement with the Libyans for the sale of US$500 million in arms by the year 1988. There are unconfirmed reports of transfer of G3s to Libya in exchange for credits for petroleum products. This agreement was later publicly renounced by the Greek government.

Greek weapons production by 1985 had expanded beyond its original purpose of domestic production of defense equipment to being a source of hard currency through exports.

## GRENADA (State of)

Population (estimate in 1984): 0.113 million. Ground forces: regulars, apparently will be about 100 effectives, as the United States Army Special Forces 30-man team was, in mid-1985, training two 40-man "Special Service Units" (platoons) for each of the following eastern Caribbean countries: Grenada, St. Vincent, St. Lucia, Dominica, and St. Kitts.

**HANDGUNS:**

**SUBMACHINE GUNS:**

**RIFLES:**
- *Cal.:* 5.56 x 45mm
  *Common Name:* M16A1 rifle

*Remarks:* US origin. Supplied as part of above Special Service Unit (SSU) training program.

**SHOTGUNS:**

**MACHINE GUNS:**
- *Cal.:* 7.62 x 51mm NATO
  *Common Name:* M60 GPMG

*Remarks:* US origin. Supplied as part of above SSU training program.

- *Cal.:* 12.7 x 99mm
  *Common Name:* .50 M2 HB
  HMG

*Remarks:* US origin. Supplied as part of above SSU training program.

A trooper of the 82d Airborne Division stands guard over stacked cases of 7.62 x 39mm ammunition made in the Soviet Union. This ammunition cache was discovered in Grenada after the October 1983 visit to the island. (DOD)

A case of 7.62 x 39mm ammunition marked with Cuban identification marks. (DOD)

**AUTOMATIC CANNON:**

**GRENADE LAUNCHERS:**
• *Cal.:* 40 x 46mmSR
　*Common Name:* M203 grenade
　launcher on M16A1

*Remarks:* US origin. Supplied as part of above SSU training program.

Prior to 25 October 1983, regular strength was estimated to have been 1,200+ ; reserves, unknown. Small arms followed the British pattern until 1979, when the Cuban government began to supply the Grenadian People's Revolutionary Army. The items listed below were captured by the United States and Caribbean forces in October 1983. Most of the arms were "hand-me-downs" from Cuba.

**HANDGUNS:**
Miscellaneous pistols, not further
　identified

*Remarks:* 300.

**SUBMACHINE GUNS:**
• *Cal.:* 11.43 x 23mm
　*Common Name:* M3A1 subma-
　chine gun

*Remarks:* 32.

• *Cal.:* 9 x 19mm Parabellum
　*Common Name:* vz.23 and vz.25
　submachine guns

*Remarks:* 55.

• *Cal.:* 9 x 19mm Parabellum
　*Common Name:* FN made Uzi
　submachine guns

*Remarks:* 1, with Cuban Army markings removed.

• *Cal.:* 7.62 x 25mm
　*Common Name:* PPS43

*Remarks:* 180.

• *Cal.:* 9 x 19mm Parabellum
　*Common Name:* MK II Sten gun

*Remarks:* 17.

• *Cal.:* 9 x 19mm Parabellum
　*Common Name:* Sterling MK 4
　submachine gun

*Remarks:* 7.

**RIFLES:**
• *Cal.:* 7.62 x 39mm
　*Common Name:* SKS carbines

*Remarks:* 4,074.

• *Cal.:* 7.62 x 39mm
　*Common Name:* AK47 assault
　rifle (no AKMs)

*Remarks:* 1,626.

• *Cal.:* 7.62 x 45mm?
　*Common Name:* vz.52 rifle

*Remarks:* 1,120.

• *Cal.:* 7.62 x 54mmR
　*Common Name:* M1944 Mosin-
　Nagant carbines

*Remarks:* 2,432.

• *Cal.:* 7.7 x 56mmR
　*Common Name:* .303 Enfields

*Remarks:* 58.

**SHOTGUNS:**
Miscellaneous models

*Remarks:* 300.

Two US Army Rangers hold weapons captured in Grenada. The Ranger on the right has a 7.62 x 37mm vz.52/57 LMG resting against his chest. The other weapons are 7.62 x 39mm AK47 assault rifles. (DOD)

**MACHINE GUNS:**
- *Cal.:* 7.62 x 54mmR             *Remarks:* 9.
  *Common Name:* PK GPMG

- *Cal.:* 7.7 x 56mmR             *Remarks:* 2.
  *Common Name:* .303 Bren gun

- *Cal.:* 12.7 x 108mm             *Remarks:* At least 2 quad antiaircraft mounts.
  *Common Name:* DShK38/46 HMG

**AUTOMATIC CANNON:**
- *Cal.:* 14.5 x 114mm             *Remarks:* No numbers given.
  *Common Name:* KPV HMG

- *Cal.:* 23 x 152mmB             *Remarks:* 12 twin antiaircraft mounts; exact numbers not given.
  *Common Name:* ZU23 automatic cannon

Caribbean soldiers gathering their equipment during operations on Grenada in October 1983. The soldier in the foreground has a British 7.62 x 51mm L1A1. (DOD)

# GUATEMALA (Republic of)

Population (estimate in 1984): 7.96 million. Ground forces: regulars, 38,000; reserves (paramilitary forces), ca. 9,500 *Policia National* and ca. 2,100 Treasury Police (Border Guards); territorial militia, 500,000, of which 70,000 may be armed.

## HANDGUNS:
- *Cal.:* 9 x 19mm Parabellum
  *Common Name:* FN Mle. 1935 GP pistol

  *Remarks:* Belgian origin.

- *Cal.:* 9 x 19mm Parabellum
  *Common Name:* Star, various models

  *Remarks:* Spanish origin.

- *Cal.:* 9 x 19mm Parabellum
  *Common Name:* CZ 75 pistol

  *Remarks:* Czechoslovakian origin. Privately purchased by Army officers.

- *Cal.:* 9 x 29mmR
  *Common Name:* .38 Colt Detective Special revolver

  *Remarks:* US origin. MAP provided 644 1968–74. NSN 1005-00-726-5786. Unspecified Colt revolvers (675) licensed for delivery to the National Police in 1977.

- *Cal.:* 9 x 29mmR
  *Common Name:* .38 Smith & Wesson revolvers

  *Remarks:* US origin. State Department licensed sale of 200 unspecified models in 1978.

- *Cal.:* 9 x 29mmR
  *Common Name:* .38 Smith & Wesson M10 revolvers

  *Remarks:* US origin. MAP provided 8 in 1970.

- *Cal.:* 11.43 x 23mm
  *Common Name:* .45 M1911A1 pistol

  *Remarks:* US origin. MAP and FMS provided 1,694 pistols prior to 1974, including 709 specifically identified as M1911A1s.

## SUBMACHINE GUNS:
- *Cal.:* 9 x 19mm Parabellum
  *Common Name:* M46/53 submachine gun

  *Remarks:* Madsen/Dansk Industri Syndikat.

- *Cal.:* 9 x 19mm Parabellum
  *Common Name:* Model 12 submachine gun

  *Remarks:* Beretta, Italy.

- *Cal.:* 9 x 19mm Parabellum
  *Common Name:* Uzi submachine gun

  *Remarks:* Israeli Military Industries (IMI), Israel. Some mini-Uzi submachine guns still in use.

- *Cal.:* 9 x 19mm Parabellum
  *Common Name:* Ingram MAC-10 submachine gun

  *Remarks:* Military Armaments Co., US. Also acquired in 9 x 17mm Browning (ACP).

- *Cal.:* 11.43 x 23mm
  *Common Name:* .45 M1A1 submachine gun

  *Remarks:* US origin. FMS provided 223 in 1974.

- *Cal.:* 11.43 x 23mm
  *Common Name:* .45 M3A1 submachine gun

  *Remarks:* US origin. FMS provided 300 in 1971. Another 470 unspecified SMGs were also provided before 1974.

## RIFLES:
- *Cal.:* 5.56 x 45mm
  *Common Name:* Galil rifle

  *Remarks:* IMI. The first order was for 35,000, with a follow-on order of 15,000 more.

- *Cal.:* 5.56 x 45mm
  *Common Name:* M16A1 rifle

  *Remarks:* US origin. Not the result of direct sale from Colt or MAP.

- *Cal.:* 7.62 x 33mm
  *Common Name:* .30 M1 and M2
  carbines

*Remarks:* US origin. FMS provided 342 M2s in 1971. MAP delivered 700 M2s 1950–67. MAP provided 5,000 M1s in 1974. An additional 121 were delivered through MAP before 1964.

- *Cal.:* 7.62 x 51mm NATO
  *Common Name:* CETME assault
  rifle

*Remarks:* Fabrica de Armas de Oviedo of the Empresa Nacional Santa Barbara de Industrias Militares, of Spain. Most of these rifles were disposed of in 1981.

- *Cal.:* 7.62 x 63mm
  *Common Name:* .30 M1 rifle

*Remarks:* US origin. MAP provided 81 before 1964, 561 in 1964, 291 in 1965, 281 in 1965, and 172 in 1968. FMS provided 1,145 in 1971–72. An additional 3,108 unspecified rifles were delivered by FMS before 1968.

- *Cal.:* 7.62 x 63mm
  *Common Name:* .30 M1C sniper
  rifle

*Remarks:* US origin. MAP provided 50 before 1967.

- *Cal.:* 7.62 x 63mm
  *Common Name:* .30 M1D sniper
  rifle

*Remarks:* US origin. FMS provided 9 M1Ds in 1971 and again in 1972.

**SHOTGUNS:**

**MACHINE GUNS:**
- *Cal.:* 7.62 x 51mm NATO
  *Common Name:* FN MAG

*Remarks:* FN origin. Models in service include: MAG *Infanterie Standard* (60-20) T9 (nondisintegrating link belt), MAG *Aviation* (60-30) P.935 (right-hand feed).

- *Cal.:* 7.62 x 63mm
  *Common Name:* .30 M1918A2
  BAR

*Remarks:* US origin. FMS delivered 72 in 1971. MAP provided 212 1964–68 and 300 in 1975.

- *Cal.:* 7.62 x 63mm
  *Common Name:* .30 M1919A4
  LMG

*Remarks:* US origin. MAP provided 33 between 1967 and 1974. An additional 32 unspecified LMGs were delivered through MAP before 1964.

- *Cal.:* 7.62 x 63mm
  *Common Name:* .30 M1919A6
  LMG

*Remarks:* US origin. FMS provided 46 in 1971. MAP provided 81 1964–70.

- *Cal.:* 7.62 x 63mm
  *Common Name:* .30 M37 AMG

*Remarks:* US origin. FMS provided 7 in 1971. NSN 1005-00-856-7528 (w/o sights).

- *Cal.:* 12.7 x 99mm
  *Common Name:* .50 M2 HB
  HMG

*Remarks:* US origin. MAP provided 19 unspecified .50 caliber MGs before 1964 and 27 more 1964–71. FMS provided 20 in 1971–72, plus 7 guns in M1 cupolas in 1972.

**AUTOMATIC CANNON:**

**GRENADE LAUNCHERS:**
- *Cal.:* 40 x 46mmSR
  *Common Name:* M79 grenade
  launcher

*Remarks:* US origin. MAP provided 7 in 1970.

Some additional older small arms still in reserve may include: 9 x 19mm Parabellum M37/39 Suomi, 9 x 19mm Parabellum MP40, 11.43 x 23mm M50 Reising submachine guns; 7.7 x 56mmR (.303) No. 4 Enfield rifles; 7.92 x 57mm vz.24 Mauser rifles; 7.92 x 57mm Kar 43 rifles; 7.92 x 57mm MG34 light machine guns; and 7.62 x 63mm M1917 water-cooled Browning machine guns.

## GUINEA (People's Revolutionary Republic of)

Population (estimate in 1984): 5.58 million. Ground forces: regulars, between 5,000 and 8,500; reserves (paramilitary forces) 9,000+ (People's militia 7,000; *Gendarmerie,* 1,000; *Garde Republicaine,* 1,600); *Service de Securite* [National Police], ca. 1,500. The latter has been trained by Czechoslovakian advisers. Some older pattern French small arms may still be held in reserve.

**HANDGUNS:**
• *Cal.:* 7.62 x 25mm                    *Remarks:* Soviet origin.
  *Common Name:* TT33 Tokarev
  pistol

**SUBMACHINE GUNS:**
• *Cal.:* 9 x 19mm Parabellum            *Remarks:* Manufacture Nationale d'Armes de Tulle (MAT).
  *Common Name:* MAT Mle. 49
  submachine gun

• *Cal.:* 9 x 19mm Parabellum            *Remarks:* Czechoslovakian origin.
  *Common Name:* vz.23 and vz.25
  submachine guns

• *Cal.:* 7.62 x 25mm                    *Remarks:* East Bloc origin.
  *Common Name:* PPSh41 subma-
  chine gun

• *Cal.:* 7.62 x 25mm                    *Remarks:* East Bloc origin.
  *Common Name:* PPS43 subma-
  chine gun

**RIFLES:**
• *Cal.:* 7.62 x 39mm                    *Remarks:* East Bloc origin.
  *Common Name:* SKS carbine

• *Cal.:* 7.62 x 39mm                    *Remarks:* East Bloc origin.
  *Common Name:* AK47 and AKM
  assault rifles

• *Cal.:* 7.62 x 39mm                    *Remarks:* East Bloc origin.
  *Common Name:* vz.58 assault rifle

• *Cal.:* 7.5 x 54mm                     *Remarks:* Manufacture Nationale d'Armes de Chatellerault (MAC).
  *Common Name:* MAS Mle. 36
  bolt action rifle

• *Cal.:* 7.5 x 54mm                     *Remarks:* MAC.
  *Common Name:* MAS Mle. 49/56
  rifle

**SHOTGUNS:**

**MACHINE GUNS:**
• *Cal.:* 7.62 x 39mm                    *Remarks:* East Bloc origin.
  *Common Name:* RPD LMG

• *Cal.:* 7.62 x 39mm                    *Remarks:* East Bloc origin.
  *Common Name:* RPK LMG

• *Cal.:* 7.62 x 39mm                    *Remarks:* Czechoslovakian origin.
  *Common Name:* vz.52 LMG

• *Cal.:* 7.62 x 54mmR                   *Remarks:* East Bloc origin.
  *Common Name:* PK GPMG

- *Cal.:* 7.62 x 54mmR
  *Common Name:* SGM series MGs

  *Remarks:* East Bloc origin. SGMTs on Soviet armored vehicles.

- *Cal.:* 7.62 x 54mmR
  *Common Name:* DT armor MGs

  *Remarks:* Soviet origin. DT mounted on older models of Soviet armored vehicles.

- *Cal.:* 7.62 x 54mmR
  *Common Name:* RP46 GPMG

  *Remarks:* Soviet origin.

- *Cal.:* 12.7 x 108mm
  *Common Name:* DShK38/46 HMG

  *Remarks:* East Bloc origin.

**AUTOMATIC CANNON:**
- *Cal.:* 14.5 x 114mm
  *Common Name:* KPV HMG

  *Remarks:* East Bloc origin. Models in service include the towed quad gun ZPU-4.

- *Cal.:* 20 x ???mm
  *Common Name:* 20mm French automatic cannon

  *Remarks:* French origin on patrol boats made by Chantiers Navals de "Esterel."

- *Cal.:* 25 x 218mm
  *Common Name:* 2-M-3 or 2-M-8 automatic cannon

  *Remarks:* Soviet origin. Mounted on minesweepers.

## GUINEA-BISSEAU (Republic of)

Population (estimate in 1984): 0.842 million. Ground forces: regulars, ca. 6,000; reserves (paramilitary forces), ca. 5,000. Some limited quantities of older Portuguese small arms may still be used by the paramilitary forces.

**HANDGUNS:**
- *Cal.:* 7.62 x 25mm
  *Common Name:* TT33 Tokarev pistol

  *Remarks:* Soviet origin.

- *Cal.:* 7.62 x 25mm
  *Common Name:* vz.52 pistol

  *Remarks:* Czechoslovakian origin.

**SUBMACHINE GUNS:**
- *Cal.:* 7.62 x 25mm
  *Common Name:* PPSh41 submachine gun

  *Remarks:* Soviet origin.

- *Cal.:* 7.62 x 25mm
  *Common Name:* PP543 submachine gun

  *Remarks:* Soviet origin.

- *Cal.:* 9 x 19mm Parabellum
  *Common Name:* vz.23 and vz.25 submachine guns

  *Remarks:* Czechoslovakian origin.

- *Cal.:* 9 x 19mm Parabellum
  *Common Name:* FMBP M948 submachine gun

  *Remarks:* Portuguese origin.

**RIFLES:**
- *Cal.:* 7.62 x 39mm
  *Common Name:* vz.52/57 rifle

  *Remarks:* Czechoslovakian origin.

- *Cal.:* 7.62 x 39mm
  *Common Name:* SKS carbine

  *Remarks:* East Bloc origin.

- *Cal.:* 7.62 x 39mm
  *Common Name:* AK47 and AKM
  assault rifles

  *Remarks:* East Bloc origin.

**SHOTGUNS:**

**MACHINE GUNS:**

- *Cal.:* 7.62 x 39mm
  *Common Name:* RPD LMG

  *Remarks:* East Bloc origin.

- *Cal.:* 7.62 x 39mm
  *Common Name:* RPK LMG

  *Remarks:* East Bloc origin.

- *Cal.:* 7.62 x 51mm NATO
  *Common Name:* MG3 GPMG

  *Remarks:* Rheinmetall, West Germany.

- *Cal.:* 7.62 x 54mmR
  *Common Name:* PK GMPG

  *Remarks:* Soviet origin.

- *Cal.:* 7.62 x 54mmR
  *Common Name:* RP46 LMG

  *Remarks:* Soviet origin.

- *Cal.:* 7.62 x 54mmR
  *Common Name:* SG43 series of
  MGs

  *Remarks:* Soviet origin. SGMTs mounted on Soviet armored vehicles.

- *Cal.:* 7.62 x 54mmR
  *Common Name:* DTM GPMG

  *Remarks:* Soviet origin. Mounted on older models of Soviet armored vehicles.

- *Cal.:* 7.62 x 54mmR
  *Common Name:* DP and RP46
  LMGs

  *Remarks:* Soviet origin. Very limited use.

- *Cal.:* 12.7 x 108mm
  *Common Name:* DShK38/46
  HMG

  *Remarks:* Soviet origin.

**AUTOMATIC CANNON:**

- *Cal.:* 14.5 x 114mm
  *Common Name:* KPV HMG

  *Remarks:* Soviet origin. Several models may be in service, but the ZPU-1 single gun AA mount has been directly observed.

- *Cal.:* 23 x 152mmB
  *Common Name:* ZU23 automatic
  cannon

  *Remarks:* East Bloc origin.

# GUYANA (Cooperative Republic of)

Population (estimate in 1984): 0.837 million. Ground forces: regulars, ca. 6,000; reserves, ca. 10,000, including 5,000 paramilitary forces (which include the Guyana Police—Mounted Branch, Rural Constabulary, and Special Constabulary [Reserve]).

**HANDGUNS:**

- *Cal.:* 7.65 x 17mm Browning
  *Common Name:* Walther PPK

  *Remarks:* Manurhin, France.

- *Cal.:* 9 x 19mm Parabellum
  *Common Name:* Smith & Wesson
  Model 39 pistol

  *Remarks:* US origin.

- *Cal.:* 9 x 29mmR
  *Common Name:* .38 Caliber revolvers, models unknown

*Remarks:* Origin unknown.

**SUBMACHINE GUNS:**
- *Cal.:* 9 x 19mm Parabellum
  *Common Name:* M12 Beretta sub-
  machine gun

*Remarks:* Beretta origin.

- *Cal.:* 9 x 19mm Parabellum
  *Common Name:* Sterling submachine guns, models unknown

*Remarks:* UK origin.

**RIFLES:**
- *Cal.:* 7.62 x 39mm
  *Common Name:* SKS carbines

*Remarks:* Origin unknown.

- *Cal.:* 7.62 x 39mm
  *Common Name:* AK47 assault
  rifles

*Remarks:* Origin unknown.

- *Cal.:* 7.62 x 51mm NATO
  *Common Name:* L1A1 rifle

*Remarks:* Royal Small Arms Factory (RSAF), Enfield.

- *Cal.:* 7.62 x 51mm NATO
  *Common Name:* Gewehr 3

*Remarks:* Heckler & Koch (HK) origin?

- *Cal.:* 7.7 x 56mmR
  *Common Name:* .303 No. 4
  Enfield rifles

*Remarks:* UK origin.

**SHOTGUNS:**

**MACHINE GUNS:**
- *Cal.:* 7.62 x 51mm NATO
  *Common Name:* L4A3 Bren gun

*Remarks:* RSAF.

- *Cal.:* 7.62 x 51mm NATO
  *Common Name:* L7A2 GPMG

*Remarks:* RSAF.

**AUTOMATIC CANNON:**

## HAITI (Republic of)

Population (estimate in 1984): 5.80 million. Ground forces: regulars, ca. 7,000; reserves (paramilitary forces), *Volontaires de la Securite Nationale* (replacement for the *Tontons Macoute* abolished in early 1986), ca. 15,000.

**HANDGUNS:**
- *Cal.:* 9 x 19mm
  *Common Name:* FN Mle. 35 GP
  pistol

*Remarks:* FN origin?

- *Cal.:* 9 x 19mm
  *Common Name:* Beretta M951
  pistol

*Remarks:* Beretta origin.

- *Cal.:* 9 x 29mmR
  *Common Name:* .38 Colt revolvers, various models

*Remarks:* US origin.

- *Cal.:* 9 x 29mmR
  *Common Name:* .38 Smith & Wesson revolvers

- *Cal.:* 11.43 x 23mm
  *Common Name:* .45 M1911A1 pistol

*Remarks:* US origin. State Department licensed sale of 20 S&W revolvers to the Haitian armed forces in 1976.

*Remarks:* US origin. FMS provided 100 in 1974. MAP provided 460 1966–69. An additional 195 pistols were provided before 1975.

**SUBMACHINE GUNS:**
- *Cal.:* 9 x 17mm
  *Common Name:* MAC-11 submachine gun

- *Cal.:* 9 x 19mm
  *Common Name:* Mini-Uzi submachine gun

- *Cal.:* 11.43 x 23mm
  *Common Name:* .45 M1928A1 and M1A1 (Thompson) submachine guns

- *Cal.:* 11.43 x 23mm
  *Common Name:* .45 M3 submachine guns

*Remarks:* Military Armaments Corp, US.

*Remarks:* Israeli Military Industries (IMI), Israel.

*Remarks:* US origin.

*Remarks:* US origin.

**RIFLES:**
- *Cal.:* 5.56 x 45mm
  *Common Name:* M16A1 (Model 613) rifle

- *Cal.:* 5.56 x 45mm
  *Common Name:* IMI Galil rifle

- *Cal.:* 7.62 x 33mm
  *Common Name:* .30 M1 and M2 carbines

- *Cal.:* 7.62 x 51mm NATO
  *Common Name:* Gewehr 3A4

- *Cal.:* 7.62 x 51mm NATO
  *Common Name:* M14 rifle

- *Cal.:* 7.62 x 51mm NATO
  *Common Name:* FN FAL

- *Cal.:* 7.62 x 63mm
  *Common Name:* .30 M1 rifle

- *Cal.:* 7.62 x 63mm
  *Common Name:* FN Mle. 24/30 rifle

*Remarks:* Acquired few hundred (ca. 500) from Colt in 1974.

*Remarks:* Israeli origin.

*Remarks:* US origin.

*Remarks:* Heckler & Koch (HK), West Germany.

*Remarks:* US origin. MAP provided 1,250 in 1976.

*Remarks:* FN origin?

*Remarks:* US origin. MAP provided 799 before 1964.

*Remarks:* FN origin.

**SHOTGUNS:**

**MACHINE GUNS:**
- *Cal.:* 7.62 x 51mm NATO
  *Common Name:* FN FALO

- *Cal.:* 7.62 x 51mm NATO
  *Common Name:* M60 GPMG

- *Cal.:* 7.62 x 51mm NATO
  *Common Name:* FN MAG

*Remarks:* FN origin?

*Remarks:* US origin. Source not known.

*Remarks:* FN origin? UK? The L7A2 version is found mounted on the Cadillac Gage V150 armored cars.

- *Cal.:* 7.62 x 63mm
  *Common Name:* .30 M1919A4
  LMG

  *Remarks:* US origin.

- *Cal.:* 7.62 x 63mm
  *Common Name:* .30 M1918A2
  BAR

  *Remarks:* US origin. There are also some FN Type D BARs reported as well.

- *Cal.:* 12.7 x 99mm
  *Common Name:* .50 M2 HB
  HMG

  *Remarks:* US origin. At least 15 provided by Israeli sources.

**AUTOMATIC CANNON:**
- *Cal.:* 20 x 128mm
  *Common Name:* KAA (204GK)
  automatic cannon

  *Remarks:* Oerlikon-Bührle design but made in the UK by British Research and Manufacture Company, Ltd. Received, mounted on their Cadillac Gage V-150 APC.

- *Cal.:* 20 x 110mm
  *Common Name:* TCM-20 AA
  systems

  *Remarks:* Israeli origin. Twin AA systems from Ramta, IAI, Israel. Delivered in September, 1984. HS 404 automatic cannon.

## HONDURAS (Republic of)

Population (estimate in 1984): 4.42 million. Ground forces: regulars, ca. 15,500; reserves (paramilitary), *Cuerpo Especial de Seguridad* (Public Security Forces), ca. 4,500.

**HANDGUNS:**
- *Cal.:* 9 x 19mm Parabellum
  *Common Name:* FN Mle. 1935 GP
  pistol

  *Remarks:* Belgian origin.

- *Cal.:* 9 x 29mmR
  *Common Name:* .38 Smith & Wesson revolvers

  *Remarks:* US origin. State Department licensed sale of 50 revolvers to Customs Police in 1977.

- *Cal.:* 11.43 x 23mm
  *Common Name:* .45 Smith & Wesson revolvers

  *Remarks:* US origin. State Department licensed sale of 7 revolvers to Public Security Force (Tegucigalpa) in 1977.

- *Cal.:* 11.43 x 23mm
  *Common Name:* .45 M1911A1
  pistol

  *Remarks:* US origin. Ca. 750 acquired through US aid program before 1975. An additional 41 were provided by FMS in 1980 and 13 in 1983.

**SUBMACHINE GUNS:**
- *Cal.:* 9 x 19mm Parabellum
  *Common Name:* HK MP5 and
  MP5SD (silenced version) submachine guns

  *Remarks:* Origin unknown. Heckler & Koch (HK), GmbH did not supply these weapons. Acquired in 1983.

- *Cal.:* 9 x 19mm Parabellum
  *Common Name:* FN Uzi submachine gun

  *Remarks:* Belgian origin. Also have some Israeli Military Industries- (IMI) made Uzi SMGs.

- *Cal.:* 9 x 19mm Parabellum
  *Common Name:* IMI Mini-Uzi
  submachine gun

  *Remarks:* Israeli origin.

- *Cal.:* 9 x 19mm Parabellum
  *Common Name:* Ingram MAC-10
  submachine gun

  *Remarks:* Military Armaments Co., US.

**Salvadoran troops firing with the 5.56 x 45mm M16A1 rifle during training sessions at the Regional Military Training Center operated by personnel from the 1st Battalion, 7th Special Forces Group in Honduras (August, 1983). (US Army; Spec. 5 Herbert Johnson)**

- *Cal.:* 9 x 19mm Parabellum
  *Common Name:* Beretta Model 93R machine pistol

  *Remarks:* Beretta origin — 1984.

**RIFLES:**
- *Cal.:* 5.56 x 45mm
  *Common Name:* M16A1 (Model 613) rifle

  *Remarks:* Colt, US. Approx. 9,500 purchased directly from Colt; FMS delivered 164 in 1980 and 118 in 1983.

- *Cal.:* 5.56 x 45mm
  *Common Name:* M16A1 (Model 653) carbine

  *Remarks:* Colt, US. Approx. 1,700 purchased.

- *Cal.:* 5.56 x 45mm
  *Common Name:* Ruger Mini-14 rifle

  *Remarks:* Sturm, Ruger and Company, US.

- *Cal.:* 5.56 x 45mm
  *Common Name:* IMI Galil rifle

  *Remarks:* Israeli origin.

- *Cal.:* 7.62 x 33mm
  *Common Name:* .30 M1 and M2 carbines

  *Remarks:* US origin. FMS and MAP provided 1,914 before 1975. In 1977 another 5,000 carbines were delivered.

- *Cal.:* 7.62 x 51mm NATO
  *Common Name:* M14 rifle

  *Remarks:* US origin. FMS provided 1,500 in 1974, 1,000 in 1976, and 8 in 1980.

**This 5.56mm M16A1 rifle (#1039301), shipped to Cam Ranh Bay, South Vietnam, on 2 May 1968, was captured by the Honduran armed forces in 1983 during counter-insurgency operations. While the exact path this and other M16s traveled is unknown, they probably went to Honduras via Nicaragua and Cuba. (Smithsonian; Vargas)**

These 5.56mm M16A1 rifles, shipped to South Vietnam between 1967 and 1970, were captured by the Honduran armed forces in 1983 during counter-insurgency operations. (Smithsonian; Minor)

• *Cal.:* 7.62 x 51mm NATO
  *Common Name:* FN FAL

*Remarks:* Of both Belgian and Argentine origin. The FN and Rosario-made FALOs are employed as a sniper weapon rather than as a squad automatic weapon.

• *Cal.:* 7.62 x 63mm
  *Common Name:* .30 M1 rifle

*Remarks:* US origin. Ca. 3,500 acquired FMS and MAP 1950–74. In 1976, 200 were obtained from unknown sources; in 1979, 2,000 more were acquired.

• *Cal.:* 7.62 x 63mm
  *Common Name:* .30 M1D sniper

*Remarks:* US origin. FMS delivered 1,300 M1Ds in 1973.

**SHOTGUNS:**
• *Cal.:* 18.5 x 59mm
  *Common Name:* 12 gage Winchester Model 1200 riot shotgun

*Remarks:* US origin. FMS sold 3 in 1980. NSN 1005-00-921-5483.

**MACHINE GUNS:**
• *Cal.:* 5.56 x 45mm
  *Common Name:* M16A1 (Model 611) heavy barrel automatic rifle

*Remarks:* Colt, US. Approx. 1,000 purchased.

• *Cal.:* 5.56 x 45mm
  *Common Name:* Ultimax 100 SAW

*Remarks:* Chartered Industries of Singapore. Purchased in October 1984.

• *Cal.:* 7.62 x 51mm NATO
  *Common Name:* M60 GPMG

*Remarks:* US origin. FMS sold 9 in 1980 and 5 in 1983.

• *Cal.:* 7.62 x 51mm NATO
  *Common Name:* FN MAG

*Remarks:* US origin. FMS sold 9 in 1980 and 5 in 1983.

• *Cal.:* 7.62 x 51mm NATO
  *Common Name:* M134 high rate of fire machine gun

*Remarks:* US origin. FMS sold 10 in 1981 and 5 in 1983.

• *Cal.:* 7.62 x 51mm NATO
  *Common Name:* FN MAG

*Remarks:* FN origin. MAG *Infanterie Standard* (60-20), T5 using nondisintegrating link belt. Used by Army and Air Force.

• *Cal.:* 7.62 x 63mm
  *Common Name:* .30 M1918A2 BAR

*Remarks:* US origin.

• *Cal.:* 7.62 x 63mm
  *Common Name:* .30 M1919A4, M1919A6, and other variants of the Browning LMG

*Remarks:* US origin.

• *Cal.:* 7 x 57mm
  *Common Name:* Madsen Model 37 LMG

*Remarks:* Danish origin.

• *Cal.:* 12.7 x 99mm
  *Common Name:* .50 M2 HB HMG

*Remarks:* US origin. Most recent deliveries were made by FMS in 1967 and 1983 (NSN 1005-00-322-9715) Ramo, Inc. provided 102 M2 HB HMGs with spares, accessories, and mounts in 1978.

**AUTOMATIC CANNON:**

**GRENADE LAUNCHERS:**
• *Cal.:* 40 x 46mmSR
  *Common Name:* M79 grenade launcher

*Remarks:* US origin. MAP provided 108 before 1975 and 720 between 1975 and 1979.

• *Cal.:* 40 x 46mmSR
  *Common Name:* M203 grenade launcher attached to M16A1 rifle

*Remarks:* Colt, US. Approx. 1,000. FMS provided 122 in 1980 and 18 in 1983.

**A Salvadoran soldier practices assembly of his 7.62 x 51mm M60 GPMG during training at the RMTC in Honduras. (US Army; Johnson)**

## HUNGARY (People's Republic of)

Population (estimate in 1984): 10.68 million. Ground forces: regulars, ca. 84,000 (50,000 conscripts); reserves, ca. 143,000 (all services); border guards, 15,000; worker's militia, variously estimated between 60,000 and 250,000. Paramilitary forces include: *Rendorseg* (People's Police), which is under the Ministry of the Interior, and the State Security Police (BKH), or about 30,000. About half of the BKH are border guards. The BKH also trains the Worker's Militia.

### HANDGUNS:

• *Cal.:* 7.62 x 17mm Browning
*Official Name: Pisztoly 48 Minta*
*Common Name:* Walam M48 pistol

*Remarks:* Copy of Walther PPK by Femaru es Szerszamgepyar, NV, (FEG, Ferunion) Budapest. The factory is also called Temergyarto, NV (National Manufacturing Plant). OBSOLETE. Formerly used by the Hungarian police. FOM 1005-8-1-7.65-2-A.

• *Cal.:* 9 x 18mm Makarov
*Common Name:* Makarov pistol

*Remarks:* Soviet-type. Origin unknown. Limited numbers believed to be in service with troops assigned to Warsaw Pact mobilization units.

• *Cal.:* 7.62 x 25mm
*Official Name: Pisztoly 48 Minta*
*Common Name:* Model 48 pistol

*Remarks:* Copy of Tokarev pistol made by FEG. The grip plates have a monogram containing a star, sheaf of wheat, and hammer enclosed within a wreath. A 9 x 19mm version, developed under the direction of Egyptian Army General Haamdi, head of Army research and development at the time, was exported to Egypt as the Tokagypt. Only a few Tokagypt pistols were actually delivered to Egypt; most were sold in Canada, Europe, and elsewhere. Both models are obsolescent in their respective armies.

• *Cal.:* 9 x 17mm Browning
*Official Name:* PA-63

*Remarks:* Design derived from the Walther PP. Officer's sidearm. Also made in 7.65 Browning.

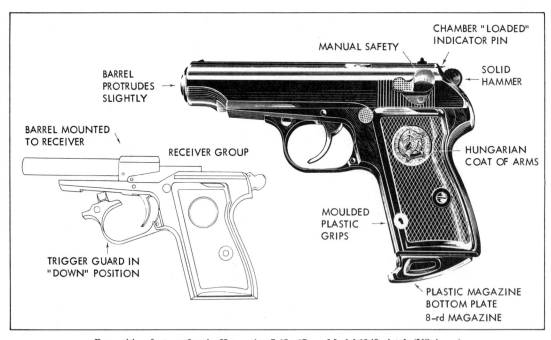

**Recognition features for the Hungarian 7.65 x 17mm Model 1948 pistol. (US Army)**

The 7.62 x 39mm Hungarian AMD-65 grenade-launching rifle, which is equipped with a shock absorber in the folding stock, a forestock that reciprocates as the rifle is fired, and an optical sight for aiming the weapon when grenades are being fired. Below the rifle are the antipersonnel PGR grenade and the antiarmor PGK grenade. Both are equipped with exhaust nozzles, indicating that they are rocket-boosted versions. (US Army)

**SUBMACHINE GUNS:**

• *Cal.:* 7.62 x 25mm
  *Official Name: Gepisztoly 53 Minta*
  *Common Name:* Spigon subma-chine gun

*Remarks:* Domestic design, manufacturer unknown. These submachine guns have been used by Palestine Liberation Organization (PLO) forces during recent Middle East wars.

• *Cal.:* 7.62 x 25mm
  *Official Name: Gepisztoly 48 Minta*
  *Common Name:* Model 48 sub-machine gun

*Remarks:* Copy of Soviet PPSh41. OBSOLETE.

**RIFLES:**

• *Cal.:* 7.62 x 39mm
  *Common Name:* AK47 assault rifle

*Remarks:* Soviet and Hungarian origin.

• *Cal.:* 7.62 x 39mm
  *Common Name:* AKM with wood stock

*Remarks:* Hungarian origin. Believed to be made at FEG.

• *Cal.:* 7.62 x 39mm
  *Common Name:* AKM with plas-tic stock

*Remarks:* Hungarian origin. The butt stocks of these rifles have also been made from a light blue, light gray, and dark gray nylon-type material. FOM 1005-8-2-7.62-2-A.

• *Cal.:* 7.62 x 39mm
  *Common Name:* AMD-65 with side folding stock

*Remarks:* Shortened airborne version of the AKM with a large muzzle brake device and folding stock.

• *Cal.:* 7.62 x 39mm
  *Common Name:* AMD65 grenade launching model

*Remarks:* Special grenade launching version of the AKM with a special stock and handguard that allows the gun to recoil without the shooter losing a good grip on the weapon when firing rifle grenades. The folding buttstock has a shock absorber to attenuate the recoil associated with firing grenades. Also has a special optical sight.

• *Cal.:* 7.62 x 54mmR
  *Common Name:* M44 Mosin Nagant carbine

*Remarks:* Based on the Soviet M1944 Mosin-Nagant carbine. This weapon was manufactured until the mid-1950s. Although long OBSOLETE in the Hungarian service, it has been exported widely to many client countries.

• *Cal.:* 7.62 x 54mmR
  *Common Name:* M48 sniper rifle

*Remarks:* Based on the M1891/30 Mosin-Nagant sniper rifle. This weapon was manufactured until the mid-1950s. Although long OBSOLETE in the Hungarian service, it has been exported widely to many client countries.

• *Cal.:* 7.62 x 54mmR

*Remarks:* Copy of Soviet SVD sniper rifle.

**SHOTGUNS:**

**MACHINE GUNS:**

• *Cal.:* 7.62 x 39mm
  *Common Name:* RPD LMG

*Remarks:* Hungarian origin.

• *Cal.:* 7.62 x 39mm
  *Common Name:* RPK LMG

*Remarks:* Hungarian origin.

• *Cal.:* 7.62 x 54mmR
  *Common Name:* PK series of MGs

*Remarks:* Hungarian versions of PK, PKT, and PKS.

• *Cal.:* 7.62 x 54mmR
  *Common Name:* SGM and SGMT AMG

*Remarks:* Soviet and Hungarian origin. The Hungarians have developed their own variant of the SGM, which is used in a GPMG role. This weapon has a RPD-type buttstock, is fired from a bipod, and resembles the PK in external configuration. The SGMT is mounted on older tanks and APCs.

• *Cal.:* 12.7 x 108mm
  *Common Name:* DShK38 and DShKM HMGs

*Remarks:* Soviet and Hungarian origin.

• *Cal.:* 12.7 x 108mm
  *Common Name:* NSVT heavy armor machine gun

*Remarks:* Soviet origin. Mounted on T72 main battle tanks in Hungarian service?

**AUTOMATIC CANNON:**

• *Cal.:* 14.5 x 114mm
  *Common Name:* KPV HMG

*Remarks:* Hungarian origin?

• *Cal.:* 23 x 152mmB
  *Common Name:* ZU23 automatic cannon

*Remarks:* Origin unknown.

*Note on commercial FEG handguns:* The Femaru es Szerszamgepyar, NV, Budapest, was established in the nineteenth century as the Metallwaren, Waffen und Maschinenfabrik (Metal wares, Weapons and Machine Factory). After Hungarian independence in 1919 it was renamed the Fegyver es Gepgyar Reszvenytarsasag (Small Arms and Machine Factory Limited). Since its establishment the factory has manufactured a number of handguns. Some of the models include the 7.65mm Frommer Stop pistol (which had the official designation *19 Minta Pisztoly* — Model 19 Pistol), the 9 x 17mm (*29 Minta Pisztoly* — Model 29 Pistol), which was made as the 37M during World War II by the German occupying forces. In addition to the pistols listed at the beginning of this section, the state factory has also manufactured four pistols for commercial sale in recent years:

• *Cal.:* 7.65 x 17mm
  *Common Name:* FEG Model R pistol

*Remarks:* This double action pistol is marked on the left side of the slide: "Cal 7,65mm Browning MADE IN HUNGARY FEG BUDAPEST."

- *Cal.:* 9 x 19mm Parabellum
  *Common Name:* FEG Model EP-9
  pistol

  *Remarks:* This single action pistol, an unauthorized copy of the FN Mle. 35 GP pistol, is marked on the left side of the slide: "PARABELLUM MADE IN HUNGARY FEG BUDAPEST." Cal 9mm. This pistol differs from its Belgium predecessor by having a ventilated sight rib and in the location of the lanyard ring.

- *Cal.:* 9 x 19mm Parabellum
  *Common Name:* FEG Model P9R
  pistol

  *Remarks:* This double action pistol, a modification of the FN Mle. 35 GP pistol, has a steel frame.

- *Cal.:* 9 x 19mm Parabellum
  *Common Name:* FEG Model
  P9RA pistol

  *Remarks:* This double action pistol, a modification of the FN Mle. 35 GP pistol, has an aluminum alloy frame.

## ICELAND (Republic of)

Population (estimate in 1984): 0.239 million. Ground forces: regulars, none (there is only a police force and a coast guard); reserves, none. There is a national police force of about 250 personnel. Small arms used by those forces follow current US pattern, with the small arms and ammunition being provided by the US NAVSEASYSCOM.

**HANDGUNS:**

**SUBMACHINE GUNS:**
- *Cal.:* 9 x 19mm Parabellum
  *Common Name:* MP5 subma-
  chine gun

  *Remarks:* Heckler & Koch- (HK) type MP5s in the hands of the Icelandic Harbor Police.

**RIFLES:**

**SHOTGUNS:**

**MACHINE GUNS:**

**AUTOMATIC CANNON:**

## INDIA (Republic of)

Population (estimate in 1984): Ca. 745.39 million. Ground forces: regulars, ca. 960,000; reserves, ca. 200,000; territorial army, ca., 50,000; paramilitary: Border Security Force, 85,000; other organizations, 175,000.

**HANDGUNS:**
- *Cal.:* 9 x 19mm Parabellum
  *Common Name:* FN Mle. 1935 GP
  pistol

  *Remarks:* FN origin.

- *Cal.:* 9 x 19mm Parabellum
  *Common Name:* Glock P80

  *Remarks:* Glock origin. Special Protection Group, National Security Guard.

- *Cal.:* 9 x 19.7mmR
  *Common Name:* Ruger Service-
  Six revolver with 102mm barrel

  *Remarks:* Sturm, Ruger and Company has supplied their Service-Six in .38 S&W (i.e., .38-200 or .380 Rim.) Purchased ca. 1978–79.

- *Cal.:* 9 x 19mm Parabellum
  *Common Name:* CZ75 pistol

*Remarks:* Merkuria of Czechoslovakia were to have supplied 55,000 (for 62 rupees) for use by police and other internal security organizations. In the fall of 1987 the Ministry of Home Affairs announced cancellation of the contract due to struggle between local Indian agent (William Jacks Pvt. Ltd.), Merkuria, and the government.

- *Cal.:* 11.43 x 21.7mmR
  *Common Name:* .455 Webley revolver

*Remarks:* UK origin. Still used by police organizations.

**SUBMACHINE GUNS:**
- *Cal.:* 9 x 19mm Parabellum
  *Common Name:* Sterling MK 4 submachine gun

*Remarks:* Indian-made at the government factory at Crawnpore.

- *Cal.:* 9 x 19mm Parabellum
  *Common Name:* Lanchester submachine gun

*Remarks:* Indian-made at the government factory at Crawnpore.

- *Cal.:* 9 x 19mm NATO
  *Common Name:* MP5K submachine gun

*Remarks:* Heckler & Koch (HK) GmbH design. Origin unknown. Prime Minister Rajiv Gandhi's bodyguard carries this weapon.

**RIFLES:**
- *Cal.:* 7.62 x 51mm NATO
  *Official Name:* 1ASL
  *Common Name:* L1A1/FAL

*Remarks:* Indian-made at the Government Rifle Factory, Ishapore.

- *Cal.:* 7.62 x 63mm
  *Common Name:* .30 M1 rifle

*Remarks:* US origin. FMS provided 8,000 before 1964.

- *Cal.:* 7.7 x 56mmR
  *Common Name:* .303 No. 4 Enfield rifle

*Remarks:* UK origin.

**SHOTGUNS:**

**MACHINE GUNS:**
- *Cal.:* 7.7 x 56mm
  *Common Name:* .303 Vickers Berthier LMG

*Remarks:* UK origin. FOM 1005-48-4-7.7-1.

- *Cal.:* 7.62 x 51mm NATO
  *Common Name:* L4A4 Bren LMG

*Remarks:* Royal Small Arms Factory (RSAF), Enfield. Also made at Ishapore.

- *Cal.:* 7.62 x 51mm NATO
  *Common Name:* FN MAG

*Remarks:* Belgian origin. MAG *Infanterie Standard* (60-20), T4. Some L7A1s from UK. Also MAG *Aviation* (60-30), T1 (Mod.032RH) is in service. Indian government is making MAG and UK MAG tripod under license at Ishapore.

- *Cal.:* 7.62 x 54mmR
  *Common Name:* SGMT armor MG

*Remarks:* Soviet origin. Mounted on older Soviet tanks and APCs.

- *Cal.:* 12.7 x 99mm
  *Common Name:* .50 M2 HB HMG

*Remarks:* World War II vintage of US origin and some newly manufactured M2s purchased from FN. The previously reported sale from Saco Defense Division, Maremont Corp. was never consumated. Ishapore is planning to manufacture M2HB flexible HMG.

- *Cal.:* 12.7 x 99mm
  *Common Name:* .50 L21A1 ranging machine gun

*Remarks:* UK origin. Mounted on the Vickers MBT.

- *Cal.:* 12.7 x 108mm
  *Common Name:* DShKM armor machine gun

*Remarks:* Soviet origin. Mounted on Soviet MBTs.

**AUTOMATIC CANNON:**
- *Cal.:* 23 x 152mmB
  *Common Name:* ZU23 automatic cannon

*Remarks:* Soviet origin. The Indian Army employs a substantial number of the Soviet ZSU-23-4 SP AA system.

- *Cal.:* 25 x 208mm
  *Common Name:* 2-M-3 or 2-M-8 automatic cannon

*Remarks:* The "Nataya-1" class ocean-going minesweepers mount both 25mm and 30mm automatic cannon in twin antiaircraft mounts.

# INDONESIA (Republic of)

Population (estimate in 1984): 169.44 million. Ground forces: regulars, ca. 180,000 to 210,000; reserves, ca. 35,000; *Tentara Nasional – Polisi* (TNI-PO), 110,000; police mobile brigade (paramilitary gendarmerie), ca. 12,000; militia, ca. 70,000 to 100,000. In the years since Indonesia gained independence in 1949, the armed services have acquired a wide variety of small caliber weapons. The weapons listed below are ones likely to be encountered in active service or held in active reserve. Dozens of World War II weapons-types are still held in government storage facilities. Those weapons include bolt action rifles, submachine guns, and a host of obsolete machine gun models.

**HANDGUNS:**
- *Cal.:* 9 x 29mmR
  *Common Name:* .38 Colt revolvers

*Remarks:* US origin. Indonesia was the recipient of large numbers of US revolvers. Before 1963, 56,322 unspecified handguns were delivered. Commercial sale for 1,326 revolvers was licensed in 1979 by the US State Department.

- *Cal.:* 9 x 29mmR
  *Common Name:* .38 Colt Detective Special revolvers

*Remarks:* US origin. MAP provided 604 in 1974. NSN 1005-00-726-5786.

- *Cal.:* 9 x 29mmR
  *Common Name:* .38 Smith & Wesson M10 revolvers with 102mm barrels

*Remarks:* US origin. MAP provided 1,332 in 1971, 3,943 in 1972. NSN 1005-00-937-5839.

- *Cal.:* 9 x 29mmR
  *Common Name:* .38 Smith & Wesson M15 revolvers with 102mm barrels

*Remarks:* US origin. MAP provided 316 in 1974. NSN 1005-00-835-9773.

- *Cal.:* 9 x 29mmR
  *Common Name:* .38 Smith & Wesson M15 revolvers with 51mm barrels

*Remarks:* US origin. MAP provided 2,000 in 1972. NSN 1005-00-973-2058.

- *Cal.:* 11.43 x 23mm
  *Common Name:* .45 M1911A1 pistol

*Remarks:* US origin. OBSOLETE. These may be the 56,322 pistols noted above that were provided by MAP before 1964.

- *Cal.:* 9 x 19mm Parabellum
  *Official Name:* Pindad P1A9mm
  *Common Name:* FN Mle. 1935 GP pistol

*Remarks:* Unlicensed copy of FN. Made by Fabrik Sendjata Ringan Pindad. About 30,000 of these pistols were made. Some Mle.35s were purchased from FN.

- *Cal.:* 9 x 19mm Parabellum
  *Common Name:* Model 92S pistol

*Remarks:* Copy licensed by Beretta. Made at Pindad factory.

- *Cal.:* 7.62 x 25mm
  *Common Name:* TT33 Tokarev pistol

*Remarks:* Soviet origin. OBSOLETE.

## SUBMACHINE GUNS:
- *Cal.:* 9 x 19mm Parabellum
  *Official Name:* PM Mod. VII
  *Common Name:* Domestic design, with design features from US M3A1 and Beretta Model 38/49

*Remarks:* Developed and manufactured by the Fabrik Sendjata dan Meisu, Bandung. Introduced ca. 1957, this SMG is no longer made. Limited issue.

- *Cal.:* 9 x 19mm Parabellum
  *Common Name:* Model 38/49 submachine gun

*Remarks:* Beretta and Indonesian origin. Indonesian copies of this SMG date from the 1960s "confrontation" conflict with the UK.

- *Cal.:* 9 x 19mm Parabellum
  *Common Name:* Model 12 submachine gun

*Remarks:* Beretta design made under license in Indonesia. Standard issue.

- *Cal.:* 9 x 19mm Parabellum
  *Common Name:* Model 45 (Carl Gustav) submachine gun

*Remarks:* Swedish origin. OBSOLETE.

- *Cal.:* 9 x 19mm Parabellum
  *Common Name:* Model 46/53 Madsen submachine gun

*Remarks:* Danish origin. OBSOLETE.

- *Cal.:* 11.43 x 23mm
  *Common Name:* .45 caliber SMGs, unspecified model

*Remarks:* US origin. MAP provided 179 SMGs before 1974.

## RIFLES:
- *Cal.:* 5.56 x 45mm
  *Common Name:* M16A1 (Model 613) rifle

*Remarks:* Colt, US. Indonesia was an early purchaser of ArmaLite AR-15 rifles in 1960s. Between 1978 and 1981 the Indonesian armed forces acquired in excess of 50,000 M16A1s directly from Colt. In addition, they acquired the following quantities from MAP sources: 15,000 in 1971; 90 in 1972; 1,618 in 1973; 1,148 in 1975; 1,148 in 1976; 3,153 in 1977; 6,314 in 1978. Police acquired an undisclosed quantity from an undisclosed source in 1979.

- *Cal.:* 5.56 x 45mm
  *Common Name:* SG540 rifle

*Remarks:* Manurhin-made SIG design.

- *Cal.:* 5.56 x 45mm
  *Common Name:* FNC

*Remarks:* FN origin. This weapon appears to be the new standard rifle for Indonesian forces. The Indonesian Air Force ordered 10,000 FNCs in 1982. On April 26, 1984, the Indonesian government signed an agreement with FN that permits manufacture of the FNC in Indonesia. The Indonesians have begun assembly and some manufacture at a government arsenal.

- *Cal.:* 5.56 x 45mm
  *Common Name:* Ruger Mini-14 rifle

*Remarks:* Sturm, Ruger and Co., US.

- *Cal.:* 7.62 x 33mm
  *Common Name:* .30 M1 and M2 carbines

*Remarks:* US origin. A total of 21,000 carbines were provided through MAP before 1964.

- *Cal.:* 7.62 x 39mm
  *Common Name:* vz.52/57 rifle

*Remarks:* Czechoslovakian origin. Static guard details only.

- *Cal.:* 7.62 x 39mm
  *Common Name:* AK47 and AKM assault rifles

*Remarks:* East Bloc origin.

- *Cal.:* 7.62 x 39mm
  *Common Name:* SKS carbine

*Remarks:* East Bloc origin.

**Indonesian Army soldier with 5.56 x 45mm M16A1 rifle and Mecar bullet trap antipersonnel rifle grenade. (Mecar)**

- *Cal.:* 7.62 x 51mm NATO
  *Common Name:* FN FAL

*Remarks:* Adopted in 1958. Indonesian FALs are marked with initials indicating specific branches of the service: A.B.R.I = *Angakan Bersenjata Republik Indonesia* for Forces Armed Republic of Indonesia; A.L.R.I = *Laut* for Navy; A.U.R.I. = *Udara* for Air Force.

- *Cal.:* 7.62 x 51mm NATO
  *Common Name:* BM59 rifle

*Remarks:* Beretta assault rifle evolved from US M1 rifle, with 20-shot magazine. Made under license at Indonesian weapons factory at Bandung during the 1960s.

- *Cal.:* 7.62 x 51mm NATO
  *Common Name:* Gewehr 3

*Remarks:* Rheinmetall origin.

- *Cal.:* 7.62 x 51mm NATO
  *Common Name: Gewehr 3SG1* sniper

*Remarks:* Heckler & Koch (HK) origin. About 1,000 were acquired in the late 1970s.

- *Cal.:* 7.62 x 51mm NATO
  *Common Name:* FN Mauser 98 carbine

*Remarks:* FN origin. Some Indonesian police organizations use these bolt action rifles in 7.62mm NATO caliber with 460mm barrels. About 10,000 are still in service.

- *Cal.:* 7.62 x 63mm
  *Common Name:* FN SAFN 49 rifle

*Remarks:* FN origin. OBSOLETE.

- *Cal.:* 7.62 x 63mm
  *Common Name:* .30 M1 rifle

*Remarks:* US origin. OBSOLETE. MAP provided 21,418 before 1964 and 3,000 in 1971. In addition, 53,388 unspecified .30 caliber rifles were delivered through MAP and FMS before 1964.

- *Cal.:* 7.62 x 63mm
  *Common Name:* .30 M1C sniper rifle

*Remarks:* US origin. OBSOLETE. MAP provided 10 before 1964.

**SHOTGUNS:**
- *Cal.:* 18.5 x 59mm
  *Common Name:* 12 gage Mossberg Model 500 shotgun

*Remarks:* Acquired in 1982 from Mossberg by the National Police for riot use.

- *Cal.:* 18.5 x 59mm
  *Common Name:* 12 gage Winchester Model 1200 shotgun

*Remarks:* US origin. MAP provided 45 before 1974. Acquired for police riot use.

**MACHINE GUNS:**
- *Cal.:* 5.56 x 45mm
  *Common Name:* FN Minimi SAW

*Remarks:* FN origin. Indonesian armed forces have begun purchasing this weapon from FN.

- *Cal.:* 7.62 x 51mm NATO
  *Common Name:* M60 GPMG

*Remarks:* US origin. MAP provided 284 before 1975; 135 in 1975; 24 in 1976; and 272 in 1978. FMS provided 57 in 1975.

- *Cal.:* 7.62 x 51mm NATO
  *Common Name:* M60C MG

*Remarks:* US origin. FMS provided 52 in 1975.

- *Cal.:* 7.62 x 51mm NATO
  *Common Name:* FN MAG

*Remarks:* FN origin. MAG *Infanterie Standard* (60-20), T1; MAG *Aviation* (60-30), P.935 (left-hand feed) and *Aviation,* T2 (P.800); MAG *Coaxial* (60-40), on their Cadillac Gage armored cars.

- *Cal.:* 7.62 x 51mm NATO
  *Common Name:* Madsen-Saetter GPMG

*Remarks:* Danish origin. FOM 1005-33-4-7.62-1.

- *Cal.:* 7.62 x 54mmR
  *Common Name:* DP, RP46, SG43, and other Soviet models

*Remarks:* Soviet origin. All of these machine guns are OBSOLETE.

- *Cal.:* 7.62 x 63mm
  *Common Name:* .30 Browning M1919 series machine guns

*Remarks:* US origin. MAP provided 432 before 1964.

- *Cal.:* 12.7 x 99mm
  *Common Name:* .50 M2 HB
  HMG

*Remarks:* US origin. MAP provided 371 before 1964, and FMS delivered 24 in 1976. An additional 300 were purchased in 1980 from Ramo, Inc. with spares, accessories, and mounts.

- *Cal.:* 12.7 x 108mm
  *Common Name:* DShK38/46
  HMG

*Remarks:* East Bloc origin.

**AUTOMATIC CANNON:**
- *Cal.:* 20 x 110mmRB
  *Common Name:* US Mark 4
  Oerlikon automatic cannon

*Remarks:* US origin. Other data not determined.

- *Cal.:* 20 x ???mm
  *Common Name:* 20mm automatic
  cannon

*Remarks:* Unknown model mounted on French patrol boats delivered by Chantiers Navals de "Esterel."

- *Cal.:* 25 x 218mm
  *Common Name:* 2-M-3 or 2-M-8
  automatic cannon

*Remarks:* Mounted on Soviet minesweepers.

**GRENADE LAUNCHERS:**
- *Cal.:* 40 x 46mmSR
  *Common Name:* M79 grenade
  launcher

*Remarks:* US origin. MAP provided 24 in 1971.

- *Cal.:* 40 x 46mmSR
  *Common Name:* M203 grenade
  launcher mounted on M16A1
  rifle

*Remarks:* US origin. MAP provided 66 in 1975; 66 in 1976; 72 in 1977; and 350 in 1978.

## IRAN (Islamic Republic of)

Population (estimate in 1984): 43.82 million. Ground forces: regulars, uncertain, but probably between 150,000 and 300,000 (over 100,000 conscripts); reserves, between 300,000 and 400,000; gendarmerie and police, ca. 70,000; Islamic revolutionary guard (Pasdaran), ca. 250,000.

**HANDGUNS:**
- *Cal.:* 9 x 19mm Parabellum
  *Common Name:* SIG P220 pistol

*Remarks:* Iran acquired about 5,000 P220s in 1982 via Portugal.

- *Cal.:* 9 x 19mm Parabellum
  *Common Name:* Beretta M92
  pistol

*Remarks:* News photos released in 1987 illustrated chador-clad women being trained with M92 pistols.

- *Cal.:* 11.43 x 23mm
  *Common Name:* .45 M1911A1
  pistol

*Remarks:* US origin. Iran acquired large numbers of US handguns prior to the fall of the Shah. MAP and FMS provided 28,267 before 1975. FMS provided 7,668 in 1975 and 1,106 in 1976.

- *Cal.:* 9 x 29mmR
  *Common Name:* .38 Colt Detective Special revolvers

*Remarks:* US origin. MAP provided 96 in 1967. NSN 1005-00-726-5786.

- *Cal.:* 9 x 29mmR
  *Common Name:* .38 Smith & Wesson Model 10 revolvers

*Remarks:* US origin. FMS provided 3,021 in 1975 (NSN 1005-00-937-5839) and 800 in 1975–76 (NSN 1005-00-937-5840). State Department licensed direct sale of 3,000 S&W revolvers to Tehran Police in 1977, but they had such revolvers since 1974 or earlier. Some Model 15s also purchased.

**SUBMACHINE GUNS:**

- *Cal.:* 9 x 19mm Parabellum
  *Common Name:* IMI Uzi submachine gun

  *Remarks:* FN origin. The Uzi was the standard SMG before the Islamic revolution, and it was acquired in large quantities.

- *Cal.:* 9 x 19mm Parabellum
  *Common Name:* HK MP5A2 and MP5A3 submachine gun

  *Remarks:* Heckler & Koch (HK) delivered sizeable numbers (ca. 5,000) MP5s to Iran before the fall of the Shah. Includes some MP5A3s.

- *Cal.:* 9 x 19mm Parabellum
  *Common Name:* M12 Beretta submachine gun

  *Remarks:* Beretta origin.

- *Cal.:* 7.62 x 25mm
  *Common Name:* PPSh41 submachine gun

  *Remarks:* Manufactured for several years after 1943 at Mosalsalsasi weapons factory. Called the Model 22 after the Persian year 1322 (1943). OBSOLETE. FOM 1005-53-3-7.62-1.

- *Cal.:* 11.43 x 23mm
  *Common Name:* .45 M3A1 submachine gun

  *Remarks:* US origin. OBSOLETE. Before 1964 MAP provided 2,072 unspecified .45 caliber submachine guns. MAP and FMS delivered 3,297 M3s before 1977 and 194 M3A1s in 1975–76.

- *Cal.:* 11.43 x 23mm
  *Common Name:* .45 M1928A1 and M1A1 (Thompson) submachine guns

  *Remarks:* US origin. OBSOLETE. May be the unspecified SMGs listed above.

**RIFLES:**

- *Cal.:* 7.62 x 51mm NATO
  *Common Name: Gewehr 3*

  *Remarks:* Heckler & Koch (HK) and Iranian manufacture. The Iranian model of the G3 is designated G3A6 by HK, with an identification no. 224039. The G3 production line was damaged during the early stages of the Islamic revolution, was rebuilt and currently is manufacturing G3s. Before the revolution the factory was making about 145,000 G3s per year. Since then the production rate has been about 50,000 per year. NSN 1005-12-146-3609.

- *Cal.:* 7.62 x 33mm
  *Common Name:* M1 and M2 carbines

  *Remarks:* US origin. OBSOLETE. MAP delivered 10,000 before 1964.

- *Cal.:* 7.62 x 39mm
  *Common Name:* AKM assault rifle

  *Remarks:* Origin unknown. May be from East Germany, Romania, and the PRC. Have been seen in news photographs illustrating both Islamic Guards (progovernment) and Muhjadeen forces (antigovernment).

- *Cal.:* 7.62 x 63mm
  *Common Name:* .30 M1 rifle

  *Remarks:* US origin. MAP delivered 165,493 M1s before 1963. Until recently presumed to be obsolete, but (summer 1987) news photos have shown Iranian troops carrying M1s.

- *Cal.:* 7.62 x 63mm
  *Common Name:* .30 M1D sniper rifle

  *Remarks:* US origin. OBSOLETE. MAP provided 32 before 1964 and 2 in 1976.

- *Cal.:* 7.62 x 54mmR
  *Common Name:* SVD sniper rifle

  *Remarks:* Origin unknown.

- *Cal.:* 7.92 x 57mm
  *Official Name:* Model 30
  *Common Name:* Persian Mauser rifle

  *Remarks:* OBSOLETE. FOM 1005-53-2-7.92-1.

**SHOTGUNS:**

- *Cal.:* 18.5 x 59mm
  *Common Name:* 12 gage Ithaca Model 37 shotgun w/o bayonet lug

  *Remarks:* Police riot use. MAP provided 2 in 1967. NSN 1005-00-973-2183.

• *Cal.:* 18.5 x 59mm
*Common Name:* 12 gage Winchester Model 12 riot shotgun

*Remarks:* US origin. MAP provided 2 before 1964. Acquired for police riot use. NSN 1005-00-677-9150.

• *Cal.:* 18.5 x 59mm
*Common Name:* 12 gage Mossberg Model 500 riot gun

*Remarks:* US origin. Provided by Mossberg for the Presidential Guard in 1977.

## MACHINE GUNS:
• *Cal.:* 7.62 x 39mm
*Common Name:* RPK LMG.

*Remarks:* Origin unknown.

• *Cal.:* 7.62 x 51mm NATO
*Common Name:* MG3 GPMG (MG42)

*Remarks:* Manufactured under license of the West German government. See note below.

• *Cal.:* 7.62 x 51mm NATO
*Common Name:* M73 armor MG

*Remarks:* US origin. Mounted on US M60A3 tanks.

• *Cal.:* 7.62 x 51mm NATO
*Common Name:* 7.62mm machine gun TK, L8A1

*Remarks:* UK origin. Mounted on MK3/3P Chieftan MBT. These machine guns were made at the Royal Small Arms Factory (RSAF), Enfield.

• *Cal.:* 7.62 x 51mm NATO
*Common Name:* 7.62mm machine gun TK, L37A1

*Remarks:* UK origin. Mounted on MK3/3P Chieftan MBT. RSAF.

• *Cal.:* 7.62 x 54mmR
*Common Name:* PK GPMG

*Remarks:* Origin unknown.

• *Cal.:* 7.62 x 54mmR
*Common Name:* RP-46 company machine gun

*Remarks:* Origin unknown.

• *Cal.:* 7.92 x 57mm
*Official Name:* Model 1934
*Common Name:* ZB26/30 LMG

*Remarks:* Czechoslovakian design made under license. OBSOLETE. FOM 1005-53-4-7.92-1.

• *Cal.:* 7.62 x 63mm
*Common Name:* .30 M1919A4 LMG

*Remarks:* US origin. OBSOLETE. MAP and FMS delivered 4,419 before 1976.

• *Cal.:* 7.62 x 63mm
*Common Name:* .30 M1919A6 LMG

*Remarks:* US origin. MAP delivered 1,858 in 1975, and FMS delivered 45 in 1975.

• *Cal.:* 12.7 x 99mm
*Common Name:* .50 M2 HB HMG

*Remarks:* US origin. MAP delivered 544 before 1064, and FMS and MAP provided an additional 1,464 prior to 1975.

• *Cal.:* 12.7 x 99mm
*Common Name:* .50 M85 armor MG

*Remarks:* US origin. Mounted on US M60A3 tanks.

• *Cal.:* 12.7 x 99mm
*Common Name:* .50 ranging machine gun, L21A1

*Remarks:* UK origin. Mounted on MK3/3P Chieftan MBT.

• *Cal.:* 12.7 x 108mm
*Common Name:* DshKM heavy machine gun

*Remarks:* Origin unknown.

## AUTOMATIC CANNON:
• *Cal.:* 14.5 x 114mm
*Common Name:* KPV HMG

*Remarks:* East Bloc origin. At least 600 of the ZPU-1 single towed AA units are in service. Other versions also in service.

- *Cal.:* 23 x 152mmB
  *Common Name:* ZU23 automatic
  cannon

*Remarks:* Soviet origin. About 100 23mm ZSU/23-4 self-propelled antiaircraft units in service.

**GRENADE LAUNCHERS:**
- *Cal.:* 30 x 29mm
  *Common Name:* AGS17 grenade
  launcher

*Remarks:* Soviet origin?

- *Cal.:* 40 x 46mmSR
  *Common Name:* M79 grenade
  launcher

*Remarks:* US origin. MAP provided 20 in 1966 and 84 in 1967; FMS provided 2,802 in 1975.

### Iranian Small Arms Industry

The production facilities for the G3 rifle and the MG3 general purpose machine gun at the Mosalsalsasi weapons factory were arranged for in a government-to-government deal between the Federal Republic of Germany and the Shah's government of Iran. The actual management of the program was supervised by Fritz Werner, a German company that was owned and controlled by the government of West Germany since the mid-1960s. It is through this firm that spare parts, production tooling, and raw materials are believed to still be provided to Iran.

## IRAQ (Republic of)

Population (estimate in 1984): 15 million. Ground forces: regulars, ca. 600,000; reserves, ca. 75,000, paramilitary: Frontier guards, ca. 4,800; Ministry of Defense security troops, ca. 6,000; People's Army, a militia force variously estimated between 100,000 and 650,000; and ca. 10,000 volunteers from other Arab countries.

**HANDGUNS:**
- *Cal.:* 7.62 x 25mm
  *Common Name:* TT33 Tokarev
  pistol

*Remarks:* East Bloc origin.

- *Cal.:* 9 x 19mm Parabellum
  *Common Name:* Beretta, model
  unknown

*Remarks:* The Iraquis are reportedly making a Beretta-type automatic pistol (Brigadier?).

- *Cal.:* 9 x 19mm Parabellum
  *Common Name:* FN Mle. 35 GP
  pistol

*Remarks:* FN. Purchased 1958–61.

- *Cal.:* 9 x 19mm Parabellum
  *Common Name:* CZ 75 pistol

*Remarks:* Czechoslovakian origin.

- *Cal.:* 9 x 19mm Parabellum
  *Common Name:* Smith & Wesson
  automatic pistol, model unknown

*Remarks:* US origin. State Department licensed sale of pistols in 1976.

- *Cal.:* 9 x 29mmR
  *Common Name:* .357 Smith &
  Wesson revolvers, model un-
  known

*Remarks:* US origin. State Department licensed sale of 100 revolvers to the Baghdad police in 1976 and 100 to the Ministry of the Interior in 1976.

- *Cal.:* 9 x 29mmR
  *Common Name:* .38 Smith & Wesson revolvers, model unknown

*Remarks:* US origin. State Department licensed sale of 110 revolvers to the Ministry of the Interior in 1976.

An Iraqui boy soldier holds his 7.62 x 39mm East German MPIKM over his head. (Dietl)

**SUBMACHINE GUNS:**
- *Cal.:* 9 x 19mm Parabellum
  *Common Name:* L2A1 subma-
  chine gun

*Remarks:* Sterling Armament Co., UK.

**RIFLES:**
- *Cal.:* 7.62 x 39mm
  *Common Name:* AK47 and AKM
  assault rifles

*Remarks:* East Bloc origin: East German and Romanian. The Iraqi armed
forces domestically manufacture the AKM with technical assistance from the
Yugoslavian and West German arms industries.

- *Cal.:* 7.62 x 39mm
  *Common Name:* SKS carbine

*Remarks:* East Bloc origin.

- *Cal.:* 7.62 x 54mmR
  *Common Name:* Dragunov-type
  sniper rifle

*Remarks:* The Iraqi armed forces manufacture a Dragunov-type sniper rifle
with technical assistance from the Yugoslavian arms industry.

**SHOTGUNS:**

**MACHINE GUNS:**
- *Cal.:* 7.62 x 39mm
  *Common Name:* RPD LMG

*Remarks:* East Bloc origin.

- *Cal.:* 7.62 x 39mm
  *Common Name:* RPK LMG

*Remarks:* East Bloc origin.

- *Cal.:* 7.5 x 54mm
  *Common Name:* AAT52 GPMG

*Remarks:* Manufacture Nationale d'Armes de St. Etienne (MAS), GIAT.

• *Cal.:* 7.62 x 51mm NATO
  *Common Name:* FN MAG

*Remarks:* Belgian origin. MAG *Infanterie Standard* (60-20), T1; MAG *Aviation* (60-30), P.935 (left-hand feed) and MAG *Coaxial* (60-40) on their Engesa Cascaval APCs.

• *Cal.:* 7.62 x 54mmR
  *Common Name:* PKT armor MG

*Remarks:* Soviet origin. Mounted on Soviet T62 tanks.

• *Cal.:* 7.62 x 54mmR
  *Common Name:* SG43/SGM
  series MGs

*Remarks:* East Bloc origin.

• *Cal.:* 7.62 x 54mmR
  *Common Name:* Type 59T series
  AMGs

*Remarks:* People's Republic of China (PRC) armor machine gun on Type 69 tanks.

• *Cal.:* 12.7 x 108mm
  *Common Name:* DShK38/46
  HMG

*Remarks:* East Bloc origin, including PRC Type 54s on PRC Type 69 tanks. This DShKm is also reported to be manufactured in Iraq.

• *Cal.:* 12.7 x 108mm
  *Common Name:* NSVT HMG

*Remarks:* Soviet origin, mounted on Soviet T72 tanks? Type 69 tanks.

**AUTOMATIC CANNON:**
• *Cal.:* 14.5 x 114mm
  *Common Name:* KPV HMG

*Remarks:* East Bloc origin.

• *Cal.:* 23 x 152mmB
  *Common Name:* ZU automatic
  cannon

*Remarks:* East Bloc origin. Both the ZSU23-2 and the ZSU23-4 versions are in service. Iraq has more than 4,000 air defense guns in its inventory.

• *Cal.:* 25 x 218mm
  *Common Name:* 2-M-3 or 2-M-8
  automatic cannon

*Remarks:* Soviet origin. Mounted on Soviet S01 class patrol craft.

# IRELAND (Republic)

Population (estimate in 1984): 3.58 million. Ground forces: regulars, ca. 12,200; reserves, between 15,000 and 15,500 (954 first-line and 14,377 second-line). The volunteer reserves is called *Force Cosanta Aitiuil.*

**HANDGUNS:**
• *Cal.:* 9 x 19mm Parabellum
  *Common Name:* FN Mle. 1935 GP
  pistol

*Remarks:* Belgian origin.

**SUBMACHINE GUNS:**
• *Cal.:* 9 x 19mm Parabellum
  *Common Name:* Model 1945
  (Carl Gustav) submachine gun

*Remarks:* Swedish origin.

• *Cal.:* 9 x 19mm Parabellum
  *Common Name:* Uzi submachine
  gun

*Remarks:* Origin uncertain.

• *Cal.:* 5.56 x 45mm
  *Common Name:* HK53 submachine gun

*Remarks:* Heckler & Koch (HK).

A member of the Irish armed forces aims his 9 x 19mm Carl Gustav sub-machine gun. (Foss/Gander)

**RIFLES:**

• *Cal.:* 5.56 x 45mm
  *Common Name:* Steyr AUG

*Remarks:* Steyr-Daimler-Puch (SDP), Austria. Adoption announced in January, 1988. The first of these rifles were delivered in 1988. Other rifles tested included the US M16A2, HK G41, SIG 550-2, Beretta AR70/90, FN FNC, French F3 FAMAS, Israeli Military Industres (IMI) Galil 377, and the Enfield L85A1.

• *Cal.:* 5.56 x 45mm
  *Common Name:* HK33 rifles

*Remarks:* HK.

• *Cal.:* 7.62 x 51mm NATO
  *Common Name:* FN FAL

*Remarks:* Belgian origin. Because of the 1987 defense budget cuts the selection of a 5.56mm rifle to replace the FALs was delayed. In January 1988 it was announced that the new rifle would be the Steyr AUG.

- *Cal.:* 7.7 x 56mmR
  *Common Name:* .303 No. 4
  Enfield rifles

*Remarks:* UK origin. Sold off 10,000 of these rifles in the early 1980s, but the Volunteer reservists are still armed with the .303 caliber rifles, BRENs, and Vickers machine guns.

**SHOTGUNS:**

**MACHINE GUNS:**
- *Cal.:* 7.62 x 51mm NATO
  *Common Name:* FN MAG

*Remarks:* Belgian origin. In addition to the infantry models, the Irish forces have the following: MAG *Aviation* (60-30), Pod Marchetti (P.904); MAG *Coaxial* (60-40), ST-450 (M.06) in both right- and left-hand feed versions; MAG *Coaxial* (60-40), P.847 on the Panhard AML 60 (nondisintegrating link belt) and the P.852 on the Panhard AML 90 (nondisintegrating link belt).

- *Cal.:* 7.7 x 56mmR
  *Common Name:* .303 Brens

*Remarks:* UK origin. Reserve forces only.

- *Cal.:* 7.7 x 56mmR
  *Common Name:* .303 Vickers
  MMG

*Remarks:* UK origin. Reserve forces only.

- *Cal.:* 12.7 x 99mm
  *Common Name:* .50 M2 HB
  HMG

*Remarks:* US origin. The Browning .50 M2 HB began to be introduced in 1982 on a scale of 4 to each battalion to fill the requirement for a heavy infantry support machine gun that had emerged as a result of UN peacekeeping activities. In 1986 the Irish Army acquired 11 M2 HB HMGs from Saco Defense Systems through NAPCO Inc. of the US. Because of 1987 defense budget cuts, the equipping of all 11 regular infantry battalions has been slowed.

**AUTOMATIC CANNON:**
- *Cal.:* 20 x ???mm
  *Common Name:* 20mm Hispano
  auto cannon

*Remarks:* These 20mm cannon were taken from Vampire T.11 trainer aircraft and used to arm old landsverk armored cars. These vehicles are employed as escort for explosives convoys.

## ISRAEL (State of)

Population (estimate in 1984): 3.855 million. Ground forces: regulars, ca. 104,000; reserves, 460,000—immediately available for mobilization, ca. 600,000 including civil defense units. There is also the Israel Police Force estimated at 20,000 officers, 5,000 of whom are assigned to the Frontier Guard force.

**HANDGUNS:**
- *Cal.:* 9 x 19mm Parabellum
  *Common Name:* Model 951

*Remarks:* Beretta, Italy.

- *Cal.:* 9 x 29mmR
  *Common Name:* .38 and .357
  Magnum Smith & Wesson revolvers

*Remarks:* US origin. State Department licensed sale of 72 S&W .357 Magnum caliber revolvers to Israeli police 1978–79 and 20 .38 caliber S&W revolvers in 1979. Also licensed the delivery of 10 .44 Magnum revolvers and 44 9mm pistols.

- *Cal.:* 11.43 x 23mm
  *Common Name:* .45 M1911A1
  pistol

*Remarks:* US origin. FMS delivered 200 in 1976.

**SUBMACHINE GUNS:**
- *Cal.:* 9 x 19mm Parabellum
  *Common Name:* Uzi submachine
  gun

*Remarks:* Israeli Military Industries (IMI). Catalog number 00-039. FOM 1005-37-3-9-1.

° *Cal.:* 9 x 19mm Parabellum
*Common Name:* Mini-Uzi submachine gun

*Remarks:* IMI. Not standard. Catalog no. 00-046.

## RIFLES:

• *Cal.:* 5.56 x 45mm
*Common Name:* Galil rifle

*Remarks:* IMI. Standard infantry rifle. Catalog no. for standard ARM w/ bipod 00-354. AR w/o bipod 00-362. SAR w/ short barrel 00-365. For the nonstandard 7.62mm NATO Galils the catalog no. are: ARM: 00-336; AR: 00-337; SAR: 00-338. FOM for the basic 5.56mm Galil is 1005-37-2-5.56-1.

• *Cal.:* 5.56 x 45mm
*Common Name:* M16A1 (Model 613) rifle and M16A1 (Model 653) carbine

*Remarks:* Colt; US government. The Colt sales to Israel total approx. 150,000 − 65,000 rifles and 45,000 carbines. FMS provided 77,124 before 1975 and an additional 20,000 in 1977.

• *Cal.:* 7.62 x 33mm
*Common Name:* .30 M1 and M2 carbines

*Remarks:* US origin. FMS provided 10,000 carbines in 1978. Issued to Civil Defense school guards.

• *Cal.:* 7.62 x 39mm
*Common Name:* AKM assault rifle

*Remarks:* East Bloc origin. Used by some first-line units and by some police reserve units.

• *Cal.:* 7.62 x 51mm NATO
*Common Name:* FN FAL

*Remarks:* FN-made and IMI assembled versions. OBSOLETE. Many have been sold as surplus.

• *Cal.:* 7.62 x 51mm NATO
*Common Name:* M14 rifle

*Remarks:* US origin. FMS provided 22,501 before 1975. A small quantity were captured from PLO. Currently issued to Civil Defense Guards.

• *Cal.:* 7.62 x 51mm NATO
*Common Name:* Galil sniper rifle

*Remarks:* IMI.

• *Cal.:* 7.62 x 51mm NATO
*Common Name:* Mauser M1898 rifle

*Remarks:* World War II M98s converted to 7.62mm NATO and new rifles from FN in the 1950s. OBSOLETE. Many have been sold as surplus.

• *Cal.:* 7.62 x 63mm
*Common Name:* .30 US rifles of unspecified model

*Remarks:* US origin. FMS delivered 80,000 in 1975 and 45,609 in 1978.

## SHOTGUNS:

## MACHINE GUNS:

• *Cal.:* 7.62 x 51mm NATO
*Common Name:* FN MAG

*Remarks:* FN origin. MAG Infanterie Standard (60-20), T2.

• *Cal.:* 7.62 x 51mm NATO
*Common Name:* FN FALO

*Remarks:* FN origin. OBSOLETE.

• *Cal.:* 7.62 x 51mm NATO
*Common Name:* M73 and M219 armor MG

*Remarks:* US origin. OBSOLETE. FMS delivered 170 spare M219 guns for US tanks before 1975.

• *Cal.:* 7.62 x 51mm NATO
*Common Name:* M34 high rate of fire gun (Minigun)

*Remarks:* US origin. FMS delivered 12 of these General Electric Miniguns before 1975.

• *Cal.:* 7.62 x 63mm
*Common Name:* .30 M1919A4 LMG

*Remarks:* US origin. FMS delivered 18,500 in 1977. It is believed that these guns have been converted to 7.62 x 51mm NATO caliber. An additional 4,939 .30 caliber Browning machine guns were delivered by MAP before 1975.

• *Cal.:* 7.62 x 63mm
*Common Name:* .30 M1919A6 LMG

*Remarks:* US origin. FMS delivered 1,090 in 1981. It is believed that these guns have been converted to 7.62 x 51mm NATO caliber.

**Typical Israeli receiver markings.** *Top,* markings on an Israeli 7.62 x 51mm FAL; *bottom,* markings on an IMI 5.56 x 45mm Galil SAR. (Stevens and IMI)

**Israeli Defense Forces personnel sighting in a 7.62 x 51mm FN MAG using the Eliraz Dry Zeroing Device. The work is being done on an APC. Note the 12.7 x 99mm M2 HB HMG to the right. (Electrooptics Industries Ltd.)**

• *Cal.:* 12.7 x 99mm
  *Common Name:* M2 HB HMG

*Remarks:* US origin. FMS delivered 1217 M2 flexible, 24 XM26 Cupola guns, 75 M1 cupola guns, and 250 AN M3 AC MGs before 1975.

• *Cal.:* 12.7 x 99mm
  *Common Name:* M85 Armor MG

*Remarks:* US origin. FMS delivered 720 spare M85s for US tanks before 1975.

• *Cal.:* 12.7 x 108mm
  *Common Name:* DShKM HMG

*Remarks:* East Bloc origin.

**AUTOMATIC CANNON:**
• *Cal.:* 20 x 110mm
  *Common Name:* TCM-20 twin antiaircraft gun (HS404 automatic cannon)

*Remarks:* Israeli Aircraft Industries (IAI). Two 20mm guns on a modified US M55 trailer-type AA gun mount. Some of the early versions used US M3A1 and M3 aircraft cannon. As of March 1983, 700 of these TCM-20 AA systems had been manufactured. Some have been exported.

• *Cal.:* 20 x 102mm
  *Common Name:* 20mm M168 Vulcan automatic cannon on M163 and M167 Vulcan Air Defense Systems (VADS)

*Remarks:* US origin. Combined total of about 80 Vulcan Air Defense System (VADS) family AA systems in service.

• *Cal.:* 20 x 102mm
  *Common Name:* 20mm H39A3RH

*Remarks:* US origin. FMS delivered 3 guns in 1978.

**GRENADE LAUNCHERS:**

- *Cal.:* 40 x 46mmSR
  Common Name: M79 grenade launcher

  *Remarks:* US origin. FMS delivered 1,240 before 1976.

- *Cal.:* 40 x 46mmSR
  Common Name: M203 grenade launcher mounted on M16A1

  *Remarks:* US origin. FMS delivered 10,280 before 1976.

- *Cal.:* 40 x 53mmSR
  Common Name: MK19 MOD 1 grenade launcher

  *Remarks:* IMI manufacture. Ca. 600 in service.

- *Cal.:* 40 x 53mmSR
  Common Name: M129 aircraft grenade launcher

  *Remarks:* US origin. FMS delivered 12 between 1975 and 1976.

## ITALY (Republic of)

Population (estimate in 1984): 56.99 million. Ground forces: regulars, ca. 260,000 (160,000 conscripts); reserves, ca. 550,000, with 250,000 available for immediate mobilization; paramilitary, *Carabinieri* (Italian Army), 84,500. Other police units include the *Polizia di Stato* (National Police), 67,500; the *Corpo Vigili Urbani* (Municipal Police), size unknown; and the *Guardia di Finanze,* 45,000. Counterterrorist units include: *Gruppi per Interventi Speciali* (G.I.S.) of the *Carabinieri,* the *Nuclei Operaitivi Centrali di Sicurezza* (N.O.C.S.) of the *Polizia di Stato* (Ministry of the Interior), N.O.D. *(Nucleo Operativo Diretto),* the 9th Battalion ("Col. Moschin") of the *Brigata Folgore,* and the *Comando subacquei e incursori (Comsubin)* of the *Marina militare* (Italian Navy).

**HANDGUNS:**

- *Cal.:* 9 x 19mm NATO
  *Official Name: Pistola mod.51*
  Common Name: M951 pistol; Brigadier

  *Remarks:* Defense Division, Pietro Beretta, SA, Val Trompia, Brescia, Italy. FOM 1005-23-1-9-1. Use limited.

- *Cal.:* 9 x 19mm NATO
  *Official Name: Pistola mod.92*
  Common Name: M92 and M92S pistols

  *Remarks:* Beretta. FOM 1005-23-1-9-6. Used by *Polizia di Stato.*

- *Cal.:* 9 x 17mm Browning
  *Official Name: Pistola mod.34*
  Common Name: M34 pistol

  *Remarks:* Beretta. Still widely used by Italian Army officers, the police officers of the *Polizia di Stato,* and other military and police organizations.

- *Cal.:* 9 x 19mm NATO
  *Official Name: Pistola mod. P-018*
  Common Name: Bernardelli M P-018

  *Remarks:* Vincenzo Bernadelli, Val Trompia, Brescia.

- *Cal.:* 9 x 19mm NATO
  *Official Name: Pistola mod. CB.M2 tipo 80*
  Common Name: Benelli CB.M2

  *Remarks:* Paolo Benelli, Urbino.

- *Cal.:* 9 x 17mm Browning
  *Official Name: Pistola mod. 85/B*
  Common Name: M 85/B pistol

  *Remarks:* Beretta. Used by the *Polizia di Stato.*

- *Cal.:* 9 x 17mm Browning
  *Official Name: Pistola mod. 84*
  *Common Name:* M 84 pistol

*Remarks:* Beretta. There is also a model 84/B.

**SUBMACHINE GUNS:**

- *Cal.:* 9 x 19mm NATO
  *Official Name: Pistola Mitragli-trice mod. 12;* PM12 and PM12S
  *Common Name:* M12 submachine gun

*Remarks:* Beretta. In addition to use by the Army (notably special operations forces and paratroops), the PM12 is used by a number of police organizations *(Polizia di Stato* and *Carabinieri)* and counterterrorist groups such as the N.O.C.S., *Comsubin,* and Italian Airport Police.

- *Cal.:* 9 x 19mm NATO
  *Official Name: Pistola Mitragli-trice mod. 57*
  *Common Name:* PM57 submachine gun

*Remarks:* Luigi Franchi, Brescia. Limited use.

- *Cal.:* 9 x 19mm NATO
  *Common Name:* MP5A3 and MP5SD submachine guns

*Remarks:* Heckler & Koch (HK) GmbH origin. Used by the *Carabinieri,* G.I.S., and *Polizia di Stato* N.O.C.S. antiterrorist units.

- *Cal.:* 9 x 19mm NATO
  *Official Name: Pistola Mitragli-trice* mod. 38/49; PM38/49
  *Common Name:* M38/49, Models 4 and 5 submachine guns

*Remarks:* Beretta.

- *Cal.:* 9 x 19mm NATO
  *Official Name: Pistola mod.93R*
  *Common Name:* Model 93R Machine pistol

*Remarks:* Beretta. Used by the *Carabinieri* antiterrorist units.

**RIFLES:**

- *Cal.:* 7.62 x 33mm
  *Common Name:* .30 M1 Carbine

*Remarks:* MAP delivered 156,863 before 1965.

- *Cal.:* 7.62 x 33mm
  *Common Name:* Beretta P-30 Carbine

*Remarks:* Beretta design. Used by various Italian police units.

- *Cal.:* 7.62 x 51mm NATO
  *Official Name: Fucile Automatico Beretta Modello 59* (BM 59); also called the *Fucile Automatico Leggero* (FAL)
  *Common Name:* BM59 rifle series

*Remarks:* Standard Army rifle developed by Beretta based upon the basic design of the US .30 M1 rifle: The basic model is the BM59 Mark Ital, which has a wood stock, 20-shot magazine, and bipod. FOM 1005-23-2-7.62-4-1. The BM59 Mark Ital TA *(Truppe Alpine)* is used by Alpine troops. The BM59 Mark Ital TP *(Truppe Paracadutiste)* is used by airborne troops. Both have folding stocks. Also in use is the BM59 Mark II w/ pistol grip, winter trigger, and bipod, and the BM59 Mark E. Approximately 100,000 BM59 series weapons are in service.

- *Cal.:* 7.62 x 63mm
  *Official Name: Garand tipo 2*
  *Common Name:* .30 M1 rifle

*Remarks:* MAP provided 132,185 M1s before 1964 and FMS provided another 100,000 M1s before 1974. Large quantities were also manufactured by Beretta. Both versions are still widely used in the Italian Army, especially by organizations such as the Artillery.

- *Cal.:* 5.56 x 45mm
  *Official Name: Fucile d'assalto Beretta Modelo 70*
  *Common Name:* AR70 Mod SC/ .223 assault rifle

*Remarks:* Beretta. Used by special operations troops and the Air Force. The latter has more than 1,200 in inventory and has ordered more. FOM 1005-23-2-5.56-1. Folding stock version is FOM 1005-23-2-5.56-1-1. LMG version is FOM 1005-23-2-5.56-1-2. LM70/78 LMG is FOM 1005-23-3-5.56-1.

• *Cal.:* 7.62 x 51mm NATO
*Official Name: Gewehr 3 SG1*
*Common Name: Gewehr 3 SG1*
sniper

*Remarks:* HK. Used by the Rome police and by the *Carabinieri*. Also used by counterterrorist groups such as the N.O.C.S. and *Comsubin*.

• *Cal.:* 7.62 x 51mm NATO
*Common Name:* Mauser M66
sniper

*Remarks:* Mauser, West Germany. Used by police units of the Ministry of the Interior.

### SHOTGUNS:
• *Cal.:* 18.5 x 59mm
*Official Name: Fucile automatico*
*per scopi speciali cal. 12*
*Common Name:* SPAS 12 shotgun

*Remarks:* Luigi Franchi.

### MACHINE GUNS:
• *Cal.:* 7.62 x 51mm NATO
*Official Name: Mitraglitrice MG*
*Common Name:* MG42/59
GPMG

*Remarks:* Beretta and Whitehead-Motofides. Both licensed by Rheinmetall. Whitehead (in Livorno) made the receiver body. Beretta made the bolt (heavy one for slow fire) and other parts. Franchi made barrels, trigger assemblies and other parts. Bernadelli made the tripod. Called the *Fucile Mitragliatore* when used with bipod; the *Mitragliatrice* when used with tripod.

• *Cal.:* 7.62 x 51mm NATO
*Common Name:* M73 armor MG

*Remarks:* US origin.

• *Cal.:* 7.62 x 63mm
*Common Name:* .30 M1919A4
LMG

*Remarks:* MAP delivered in excess of 2,275 before 1965.

• *Cal.:* 12.7 x 99mm
*Official Name: Mitraglitrice .50*
*Common Name:* .50 M2 HB
HMG

*Remarks:* US origin. In addition to their use of the M2 as a flexible vehicle gun, the Italian Army also uses this gun in the quad M55 trailer antiaircraft configuration. About 109 of these quad AA systems in service.

• *Cal.:* 12.7 x 99mm
*Official Name: Mitraglitrice M 85*
*Common Name:* .50 M85 armor
MG

*Remarks:* US origin.

### AUTOMATIC CANNON:
• *Cal.:* 20 x 110mmRB
*Common Name:* US MK4 Oerli-
kon automatic cannon

*Remarks:* US Navy.

• *Cal.:* 20 x 139mm
*Official Name: RH 202*
*Common Name:* Rh202 automatic
cannon

*Remarks:* Origin unknown.

• *Cal.:* 25 x 137
*Official Name: KBA*
*Common Name:* Oerlikon KBA
B02 automatic cannon

*Remarks:* Oerlikon-Bürhle, Switzerland. Mounted as a single weapon on an IFV version of the M113 and as a quad mounted antiaircraft system on OTO Melara's SIDAM version of the M113A1 APC.

## IVORY COAST (Republic of)

Population (estimate in 1984): 9.16 million. Ground forces: regulars, ca. 4,500; paramilitary *(Gendarmerie Nationale de Cote d'Ivorie),* between 2,000 and 3,000. There is also a paramilitary youth organization called the *Service Civique* of about 1,000 members. Most of the small arms follow the French pattern.

## HANDGUNS:
- *Cal.:* 9 x 18mm Browning
  *Common Name:* Walther PP

  *Remarks:* Manurhin, France.

- *Cal.:* 9 x 19mm Parabellum
  *Common Name:* MAB PA15

  *Remarks:* Manufacture d'Armes de Bayonne (MAB).

- *Cal.:* 9 x 19mm Parabellum
  *Common Name:* MAS Mle. 1950 pistol

  *Remarks:* Manufacture Nationale d'Armes de St. Etienne (MAS).

- *Cal.:* 9 x 29mmR Magnum
  *Common Name:* .357 Magnum MR73 revolver

  *Remarks:* Manuhrin.

## SUBMACHINE GUNS:
- *Cal.:* 9 x 19mm Parabellum
  *Common Name:* MAS Mle. 49 submachine gun

  *Remarks:* MAS.

## RIFLES:
- *Cal.:* 5.56 x 45mm
  *Common Name:* SG540 rifle

  *Remarks:* Manuhrin-made SIG design. About 6,000 reported to be in the inventory as of 1981, with perhaps another 1,000 added by 1985.

- *Cal.:* 5.56 x 45mm
  *Common Name:* M16A1 rifle

  *Remarks:* Colt, US. About 50 M16A1 rifles were acquired in the late 1970s.

- *Cal.:* 7.5 x 54mm
  *Common Name:* MAS Mle. 36 rifle

  *Remarks:* MAS origin.

- *Cal.:* 7.5 x 54mm
  *Common Name:* MAS Mle. 49/56 rifle

  *Remarks:* MAS origin.

- *Cal.:* 7.62 x 51mm NATO
  *Common Name:* Gewehr 3

  *Remarks:* Heckler & Koch (HK) design. Made by MAS.

- *Cal.:* 7.62 x 51mm NATO
  *Common Name:* FN 30-11 Sniper rifle

  *Remarks:* FN origin. About 200 acquired in 1984.

## SHOTGUNS:
- *Cal.:* 18.5 x 59mm
  *Common Name:* 12 gage FN riot shotgun

  *Remarks:* FN origin.

## MACHINE GUNS:
- *Cal.:* 7.5 x 54mm
  *Common Name:* MAC Mle. 24/29 LMG

  *Remarks:* Manufacture Nationale d'Armes de Chatellerault (MAC).

- *Cal.:* 7.5 x 54mm
  *Common Name:* AAT 52 GPMG

  *Remarks:* Manufacture Nationale d'Armes de Tulle. (MAT) origin.

- *Cal.:* 12.7 x 99mm
  *Common Name:* .50 M2 HB HMG

  *Remarks:* US origin.

## AUTOMATIC CANNON:
- *Cal.:* 20 x 139mm
  *Common Name:* HS820 (L85) automatic cannon

  *Remarks:* Oerlikon-Bührle HS820-SL7°A3-3 cannon mounted on the French self-propelled AA vehicle, M3VDA. At least 6 units in service. There are also about a dozen unspecified towed 20mm AA guns in the inventory.

## JAMAICA

Population (estimate in 1984): 2.31 million. Ground forces: regulars, ca. 3,500; reserves, ca. 2,000; paramilitary (Jamaica Constabulary), estimated at between 5,000 and 6,000.

**HANDGUNS:**
- *Cal.:* 9 x 19mm NATO
  *Common Name:* L9A1 pistol

*Remarks:* UK origin.

- *Cal.:* 9 x 29mmR
  *Common Name:* .38 Smith & Wesson revolvers

*Remarks:* US origin. State Department licensed the sale of 750 S&W revolvers for the police.

**SUBMACHINE GUNS:**
- *Cal.:* 9 x 19mm NATO
  *Common Name:* Sterling MK 4 submachine gun

*Remarks:* Sterling Armament Corp., UK.

**RIFLES:**
- *Cal.:* 5.56 x 45mm
  *Common Name:* M16A1 (Model 613) rifle and M16A1 (Model 653) carbine

*Remarks:* Acquired from Colt between 1980 and 1982. Between 500 and 600 in service. The Defence Forces will acquire more through the FMS program.

- *Cal.:* 7.62 x 51mm NATO
  *Common Name:* L1A1 rifle

*Remarks:* Commonwealth Small Arms Factory, Lithgow, Australia.

- *Cal.:* 7.7 x 56mmR
  *Common Name:* .303 No. 4 Enfield rifle

*Remarks:* UK origin.

**SHOTGUNS:**

**MACHINE GUNS:**
- *Cal.:* 7.62 x 51mm NATO
  *Common Name:* L1A2 SAW

*Remarks:* Lithgow-made.

- *Cal.:* 7.62 x 51mm NATO
  *Common Name:* L7A1 GPMG

*Remarks:* Royal Small Arms Factory (RSAF), Enfield, and FN, Herstal, Belgium. From FN they have purchased MAG *Infanterie Standard* (60-20), L7A2 version.

- *Cal.:* 7.62 x 63mm
  *Common Name:* .30 M1919A4 LMG

*Remarks:* MAP provided 12 before 1965.

- *Cal.:* 12.7 x 99mm
  *Common Name:* .50 M2 HB Browning heavy machine gun

*Remarks:* US origin on patrol craft.

**AUTOMATIC CANNON:**
- *Cal.:* 20 x ???mm
  *Common Name:* 20mm automatic cannon

*Remarks:* Mounted on patrol craft.

## JAPAN

Population (estimate in 1980); 116.78 million. Ground forces: regulars, 155,000; reserves, 40,000. Japanese police personnel are estimated at 245,000.

### HANDGUNS:
• *Cal.:* 9 x 19mm NATO
  *Common Name:* P220

*Remarks:* Schweizerische Industrie Gesellschaft/Rheinfalls (SIG)-Sauer design. Early issue pistols were delivered from Germany. Japanese are manufacturing the P220 under license.

• *Cal.:* 9 x 29mmR
  *Common Name:* .38 Special Model 60 revolver

*Remarks:* Shin Chuo Kogo K.K., Tokyo.

### SUBMACHINE GUNS:
• *Cal.:* 9 x 19mm Parabellum
  *Common Name:* MP5 and MP5K submachine guns

*Remarks:* Heckler & Koch (HK) GmbH origin. In service with Japanese special police units.

• *Cal.:* 9 x 19mm Parabellum
  *Common Name:* SCK Model 66 submachine guns

*Remarks:* Shin Chuo Kogo K.K. About 6,000 manufactured.

• *Cal.:* 11.43 x 23mm
  *Common Name:* .45 M3A1 submachine gun

*Remarks:* US origin.

**A soldier of the Japanese Ground Self Defense Forces aims his 7.62 x 51mm Type 64 rifle. (Tokoi)**

## RIFLES:
- *Cal.:* 7.62 x 51mm NATO
  *Official Name:* Type 64 rifle (64 Shiki Jidoju)
  *Common Name:* Type 64 rifle

*Remarks:* Howa Machinery Company, Ltd. FOM 1005-30-2-7.62-6. The reduced-power Japanese 7.62mm cartridge is FOM 1005-30-1-7.62-3. About 250,000 manufactured since 1964.

- *Cal.:* 7.62 x 33mm
  *Common Name:* .30 M1 and M2 carbines

*Remarks:* US origin.

- *Cal.:* 7.62 x 63mm
  *Common Name:* .30 M1 rifle

*Remarks:* US origin.

## SHOTGUNS:
- *Cal.:* 18.5 x 59mm
  *Common Name:* 12 gage Mossberg Model 500 shotgun

*Remarks:* Police riot use.

## MACHINE GUNS:
- *Cal.:* 7.62 x 51mm NATO
  *Official Name:* Type 62 GPMG. (62 Shiki Kikanju)
  *Common Name:* Type 62 GPMG

*Remarks:* Nittoku Metal Industry Company, Ltd. (NTK), Tokyo. FOM 1005-30-3-7.62-1. About 3,500 manufactured.

**A Japanese GSDF trooper sights his 7.62 x 51mm Type 62 GPMG, which is mounted on an improvised ski mount for winter warfare. (Japanese Defense Agency)**

• *Cal.:* 7.62 x 51mm NATO
*Official Name:* Type 74 armor MG
*Common Name:* Type 74 armor
MG

*Remarks:* NTK. FOM 1005-30-3-7.62-2.

• *Cal.:* 12.7 x 99mm
*Common Name:* .50 M2 HB
HMG

*Remarks:* US origin. In 1984–85 the Japanese purchased about 900 M2 HB HMGs. About 280 M55 AA systems are still in service with the Japanese Self Defense Forces.

**AUTOMATIC CANNON:**
• *Cal.:* 20 x 102mm
*Official Name:* Type JM61 auto-
matic cannon
*Common Name:* M61 Vulcan
automatic cannon

*Remarks:* NTK-made, under license from General Electric.

• *Cal.:* 20 x 139mm
*Common Name:* Rh202 automatic
cannon

*Remarks:* NTK-made, under license from Rheinmetall.

## JORDAN (Hashemite Kingdom of)

Population (estimate in 1984): 2.69 million. Ground forces: regulars, ca. 68,000; reserves, all services 35,000; Mobile Police Force, 3,550; Civil Militia (actually the gendarmerie), between 8,500 and 11,500.

**HANDGUNS:**
• *Cal.:* 9 x 19mm Parabellum
*Common Name:* FN Mle. 35GP
pistol

*Remarks:* FN origin.

• *Cal.:* 9 x 19mm Parabellum
*Common Name:* Glock P80

*Remarks:* Glock origin. Special guard forces.

• *Cal.:* 9 x 20mmR
*Common Name:* .380 Webley and
Enfield revolvers

*Remarks:* UK origin.

• *Cal.:* 9 x 29mmR
*Common Name:* .38 Smith & Wesson M10 108mm barrel revolver

*Remarks:* US origin. FMS delivered 121 in 1970. Another 3,000 unspecified S&W revolvers were sold under State Department license in 1976. Some model 15s are also in use.

• *Cal.:* 11.43 x 21.7mmR
*Common Name:* .455 Webley revolver

*Remarks:* UK origin. Some still in service, but OBSOLETE.

• *Cal.:* 11.43 x 23mm
*Common Name:* .45 M1911A1
pistol

*Remarks:* US origin.

**SUBMACHINE GUNS:**
• *Cal.:* 9 x 19mm Parabellum
*Common Name:* MP5K

*Remarks:* Origin unknown.

• *Cal.:* 9 x 19mm Parabellum
*Common Name:* L34A1 silenced
submachine gun

*Remarks:* Sterling, UK.

• *Cal.:* 9 x 19mm Parabellum
*Common Name:* Sten guns

*Remarks:* UK origin. Various models.

## RIFLES:

- *Cal.:* 5.45 x 39mm
  *Common Name:* AK74 assault rifle

  *Remarks:* Soviet origin. Quantities small.

- *Cal.:* 5.56 x 45mm
  *Common Name:* M16A1 rifle

  *Remarks:* US origin. After an original 20 were delivered through MAP in 1967, the following deliveries were made: 21,000 in 1971, 24,000 in 1972, 700 in 1973 via MAP, and 4,500 in 1974 and 18,000 in 1975 FMS.

- *Cal.:* 5.56 x 45mm NATO
  *Common Name:* M16A2 rifle without 3-shot burst control feature

  *Remarks:* Colt Firearms, US direct sale in the spring of 1985 of 7,000 M16A2s.

- *Cal.:* 5.56 x 45mm
  *Common Name:* SG540 rifle

  *Remarks:* Manurhin-made Schweizerische Industrie Gesellschaft/Rheinfalls (SIG) design.

- *Cal.:* 5.56 x 45mm
  *Common Name:* **AR**70/.223 rifle

  *Remarks:* Beretta, Italy.

- *Cal.:* 5.56 x 45mm
  *Common Name:* Mini-14 rifle

  *Remarks:* Sturm, Ruger, and Co.

- *Cal.:* 7.62 x 33mm
  *Common Name:* .30 M2 carbine

  *Remarks:* US origin. MAP delivered 10,166 before 1965. FMS delivered 1,802 in 1968 and 361 in 1970.

- *Cal.:* 7.62 x 51mm NATO
  *Common Name:* M14 rifle

  *Remarks:* US origin. FMS delivered 1,700 in 1970.

- *Cal.:* 7.62 x 51mm NATO
  *Common Name:* Gewehr 3

  *Remarks:* Origin uncertain.

- *Cal.:* 7.62 x 51mm NATO
  *Common Name:* FN FAL

  *Remarks:* Reported, but not confirmed.

- *Cal.:* 7.62 x 63mm
  *Common Name:* .30 M1 rifle

  *Remarks:* US origin. Before 1964 MAP delivered 17,857 rifles, of which 5,601 are identified as M1s. MAP also delivered 1,000 in 1964 and 5,000 in 1967. FMS delivered 7,105 in 1968.

- *Cal.:* 7.62 x 63mm
  *Common Name:* .30 M1D sniper rifles

  *Remarks:* US origin. MAP delivered 121 in 1968.

## SHOTGUNS:

- *Cal.:* 18.5 x 59mm
  *Common Name:* 12 gage Mossberg Model 500 shotgun

  *Remarks:* Used by Jordanian Army and police units.

## MACHINE GUNS:

- *Cal.:* 7.62 x 51mm NATO
  *Common Name:* M60 GPMG

  *Remarks:* US origin. MAP delivered 1,000 in 1974 and 323 in 1977.

- *Cal.:* 7.62 x 51mm NATO
  *Common Name:* HK21E GPMG

  *Remarks:* Heckler & Koch (HK), GmbH origin. Delivered 1987?.

- *Cal.:* 7.62 x 51mm NATO
  *Common Name:* M219 AMG

  *Remarks:* US origin. FMS delivered 21 in 1982. Others are mounted on the US M60 MBTs.

- *Cal.:* 7.62 x 51mm NATO
  *Common Name:* FN MAG

  *Remarks:* FN origin. From FN they have purchased MAG *Infanterie Standard* (60-20), T1 version.

- *Cal.:* 7.62 x 51mm NATO
  *Common Name:* L8A2 AMG

  *Remarks:* UK origin. Mounted on the Khalid main battle tank.

- *Cal.:* 7.62 x 51mm NATO
  *Common Name:* L37A2 AMG

  *Remarks:* UK origin. Mounted on the Khalid main battle tank.

- *Cal.:* 7.62 x 63mm
  *Common Name:* .30 M1918A2
  BAR

*Remarks:* US origin. MAP delivered 200 in 1964 and FMS delivered 1,303 in 1968.

- *Cal.:* 7.62 x 63mm
  *Common Name:* .30 M1919A4
  LMG

*Remarks:* US origin. MAP delivered 20 in 1964.

- *Cal.:* 7.62 x 63mm
  *Common Name:* .30 M1919A6
  LMG

*Remarks:* US origin. MAP delivered 900 in 1967 and 87 in 1971. FMS delivered 732 in 1968 and 50 in 1970.

- *Cal.:* 12.7 x 99mm
  *Common Name:* .50 M2 HB
  HMG

*Remarks:* US origin. A total of 1,161 .50 caliber Brownings of all types were delivered via FMS and MAP. These included: 135 (1005-00-693-4854) in 1974; 694 (1005-00-726-5636) 1971–74; 250 (1005-00-606-8412) in 1967; 20 (1005-00-322-9175) in 1964; 31 (1005-00-602-2105) in 1974. There are also about 36 towed M55 AA systems in service.

- *Cal.:* 12.7 x 99mm
  *Common Name:* .50 M85 AMG

*Remarks:* US origin. FMS delivered 2 in 1973 and 12 in 1982. Others are mounted on the US M60 MBTs.

**AUTOMATIC CANNON:**
- *Cal.:* 20 x 102mm
  *Common Name:* 20mm M168 Vulcan automatic cannon on the M163 and the M167 Vulcan Air Defense Systems (VADS)

*Remarks:* US origin. About 100 M163 AA systems in service.

- *Cal.:* 23 x 152mmB
  *Common Name:* ZU23 antiaircraft cannon

*Remarks:* Soviet origin. About 20 ZSU-23-4 SP AA systems delivered by the Soviets in 1982. There are about 40 of these systems in service.

**GRENADE LAUNCHERS:**
- *Cal.:* 40 x 46mmSR
  *Common Name:* M79 grenade launcher

*Remarks:* US origin. MAP delivered 500 in 1971.

- *Cal.:* 40 x 46mmSR
  *Common Name:* M203 grenade launcher

*Remarks:* US origin. MAP delivered 900 in 1972–73. FMS delivered 200 in 1980.

Older weapons that may still be in service include: 9 x 19mm vz.23 and vz.25, 9 x 19mm MP40, 9 x 19mm Port Said, 9 x 19mm Carl Gustav M45, and 11.43 x 23mm M1928A1 and M1 submachine guns. Older rifles include 7.62 x 39mm AK47s, SKSs, and vz.52s.

# KAMPUCHEA

Population (estimate in 1980): 8.87 million. Ground forces: regulars, numbers uncertain following the Vietnamese invasion of 1978 (Hen Samrin Army estimated at 30,000); reserves, no data. Until recently there have been between 200 and 300,000 Vietnamese troops in Kampuchea. The small caliber weapons situation in Kampuchea is equally uncertain. Toward the end of the active United States presence in Southeast Asia, in the mid-1970s, there was a mixture of Western (US) and East Bloc equipment in what was formerly Cambodia. See discussion under Vietnam for more data on 1945–75 era.

**HANDGUNS:**
- *Cal.:* 7.62 x 25mm
  *Common Name:* Tokarev pistol

  *Remarks:* East Bloc and PRC origin.

- *Cal.:* 9 x 19mm Parabellum
  *Common Name:* FN Mle. 35 GP
    pistol

  *Remarks:* FN. Post-1958 purchase and again after 1962.

- *Cal.:* 9 x 29mmR
  *Common Name:* .38 Smith & Wes-
    son revolvers

  *Remarks:* Models uncertain, but such weapons have been observed in news photographs in the mid-1980s.

**SUBMACHINE GUNS:**
- *Cal.:* 9 x 19mm Parabellum
  *Common Name:* vz.23 and vz.25
    series submachine guns

  *Remarks:* Czechoslovakian origin. Such weapons have been observed in news photographs in the mid-1980s.

**RIFLES:**
- *Cal.:* 5.56 x 45mm
  *Common Name:* M16A1 (Model
    603) rifle

  *Remarks:* Local militia forces have been observed carrying the M16A1 rifle. Presumably these are rifles formerly belonging to South Vietnamese (ARVN) or earlier Cambodian forces.

- *Cal.:* 7.62 x 39mm
  *Common Name:* AKM assault
    rifle

  *Remarks:* In 1982 news reports indicated that the anti-government forces were using Soviet-made AKMs, which they had captured from the Vietnamese invaders.

- *Cal.:* 7.62 x 39mm
  *Common Name:* Type 68 rifle

  *Remarks:* PRC origin.

- *Cal.:* 7.62 x 51mm NATO
  *Common Name:* FN FAL

  *Remarks:* Adopted the FAL in 1960.

**SHOTGUNS:**

**MACHINE GUNS:**
- *Cal.:* 7.62 x 51mm NATO
  *Common Name:* M60 GPMG

  *Remarks:* Former US weapons.

- *Cal.:* 7.62 x 54mmR
  *Common Name:* Type 59T AMG

  *Remarks:* PRC origin on Chinese Type 62 tanks.

- *Cal.:* 12.7 x 108mm
  *Common Name:* Type 54 HMG

  *Remarks:* PRC origin on Chinese Type 62 tanks.

**AUTOMATIC CANNON:**
- *Cal.:* 14.5 x 114mm
  *Common Name:* KPV HMG

  *Remarks:* East Bloc origin. ZPU-1, ZPU-2, and ZPU-4 mounts.

**Antigovernment Forces in Kampuchea:**

There are three main, separate resistance forces. Khmer Rouge (25,000 to 40,000), supported by the PRC; Khmer People's National Liberation Front (KPNLF—15,000 to 20,000), supported by noncommunist factions; Sikhanouist Army (ca. 9,000 armed fighters), supported by the PRC and ASEAN. The latter has received a few thousand rifles from Singapore. Khmer Rouge uses among other weapons the PRC Type 68 rifle. Khmer People's National Liberation Front forces use the 9 x 19mm MP5, 5.56 x 45mm HK53 and the 5.56 x 45mm M16A1. Politically these three resistance groups are tied together as the Coalition Government of Democratic Kampuchea, but militarily they operate independently.

## KENYA (Republic of)

Population (estimate in 1980); 16.4 million. Ground forces: regulars, between 8,000 and 13,000; paramilitary, 2,000 police. There appears to be no organized reserves. There is a close continuing relationship between the armies of Kenya and the United Kingdom. This relationship is reflected in the equipment of the Army. In addition to the small caliber weapons listed below, older weapons (such as the 9mm Sten gun) may still be in service.

**HANDGUNS:**
- *Cal.:* 9 x 19mm Parabellum
  *Common Name:* FN Mle. 35 GP pistol

  *Remarks:* FN origin?

- *Cal.:* 9 x 20mmR
  *Common Name:* .38 Webley MKIV revolvers

  *Remarks:* UK origin.

**SUBMACHINE GUNS:**
- *Cal.:* 9 x 19mm Parabellum
  *Common Name:* MP5 submachine gun

  *Remarks:* Heckler & Koch (HK), GmbH, West Germany.

- *Cal.:* 9 x 19mm Parabellum
  *Common Name:* Sterling MK 4 submachine gun

  *Remarks:* Sterling Arms Company, Ltd., UK. 500 acquired in 1984 and another 1,500 are on order.

- *Cal.:* 9 x 19mm Parabellum
  *Common Name:* Uzi submachine gun

  *Remarks:* Origin unknown.

**RIFLES:**
- *Cal.:* 7.62 x 51mm NATO
  *Common Name:* L1A1 (FN FAL) rifle

  *Remarks:* Kenya adopted the UK version of the FAL in 1966.

- *Cal.:* 7.62 x 51mm NATO
  *Common Name:* Gewehr 3A3

  *Remarks:* Enfield-made, under license from HK. There have been reports that 200,000 were purchased, but this number is seriously exaggerated.

- *Cal.:* 7.7 x 56mmR
  *Common Name:* .303 Enfields

  *Remarks:* Both World War II MK III and No. 4 issue British Enfields are still in service.

**SHOTGUNS:**

**MACHINE GUNS:**
- *Cal.:* 7.62 x 51mm NATO
  *Common Name:* AA 52 GPMG

  *Remarks:* Groupment Industriel des Armements Terrestres (GIAT), France.

- *Cal.:* 7.62 x 51mm NATO
  *Common Name:* FN MAG

  *Remarks:* FN origin. MAG *Infanterie Standard* (60-20), L7A2 model.

- *Cal.:* 7.62 x 51mm NATO
  *Common Name:* M60 GPMG

  *Remarks:* US origin. FMS provided 17 in 1979.

- *Cal.:* 7.62 x 51mm NATO
  *Common Name:* HK21A1 LMG

  *Remarks:* Enfield-made, under license from Heckler & Koch.

- *Cal.:* 7.62 x 51mm NATO
  *Common Name:* L4A4 Bren guns

  *Remarks:* UK origin.

- *Cal.:* 7.7 x 56mmR
  *Common Name:* .303 Bren guns

  *Remarks:* UK origin.

- *Cal.:* 12.7 x 99mm
  *Common Name:* L21A2 ranging MG

  *Remarks:* UK origin. Mounted on British Vickers MBT.

- *Cal.:* 12.7 x 99mm
  *Common Name:* .50 M2 HB HMMG

  *Remarks:* US origin. Some towed M55 AA systems in service.

**AUTOMATIC CANNON:**
- *Cal.:* 20 x 110mm
  *Common Name:* TCM-20 twin AA mount (HS404 automatic cannon)

  *Remarks:* Israeli Aircraft Industries (IAI).

**GRENADE LAUNCHERS:**
- *Cal.:* 40 x 46mmSR
  *Common Name:* M79 grenade launcher

  *Remarks:* US origin.

# KOREA, NORTH (Democratic People's Republic of)

Population (estimate in 1984): 19.63 million. Ground forces: regulars, ca. 700,000; reserves, Home Guard variously estimated at 260,000, 400,000, 1,000,000, and 1,500,000. The Public Security Department is supplemented by public security troops and border guards totalling about 39,000. The North Korean Type designation usually indicates the year manufacture was started in-country.

**HANDGUNS:**
- *Cal.:* 7.65 x 17mm Browning
  *Official Name:* Type 64
  *Common Name:* Copy of FN Browning Mle. 1900 pistol

  *Remarks:* Korean origin. Also manufactured in a silenced version.

- *Cal.:* 7.65 x 17mm Browning
  *Official Name:* Type 64, new model
  *Common Name:* New Korean design

  *Remarks:* Korean origin. Marked 7.62mm but is actually 7.65 x 17mm.

- *Cal.:* 7.62 x 25mm
  *Official Name:* Type 68
  *Common Name:* TT33 Tokarev pistol variant

  *Remarks:* Korean origin. Internally modified to such an extent that it should be considered as a derivative design.

**SUBMACHINE GUNS:**
- *Cal.:* 7.62 x 25mm
  *Official Name:* Type 49
  *Common Name:* PPSh41 submachine gun

  *Remarks:* Korean origin. OBSOLETE.

**RIFLES:**
- *Cal.:* 7.62 x 39mm
  *Official Name:* Type 58
  *Common Name:* AKM assault rifle

  *Remarks:* Korean origin. Production of this weapon began in 1958 at Arms Factory 65. At present, this type weapon is made at factories 61 and 65 at a rate of about 154,000 per year.

**Receiver markings on a North Korean 7.62 x 39mm Type 58 (AK47) assault rifle. (Tokoi)**

- *Cal.:* 7.62 x 39mm
  *Official Name:* Type 63
  *Common Name:* SKS carbine

  *Remarks:* Korean origin. Made at Factory 67.

- *Cal.:* 7.62 x 39mm
  *Official Name:* Type 68
  *Common Name:* AKM assault rifle w/ either wood or folding stock

  *Remarks:* Korean origin.

- *Cal.:* 7.62 x 54mmR
  *Official Name:* Type 1891/30
  *Common Name:* Korean version of Soviet sniper rifle

  *Remarks:* Korean origin. FOM 1005-18-2-7.62-3.

**SHOTGUNS:**

**MACHINE GUNS:**
- *Cal.:* 7.62 x 54mmR
  *Official Name:* Type 64
  *Common Name:* RP46 company machine gun

  *Remarks:* Soviet origin.

- *Cal.:* 7.62 x 39mm
  *Official Name:* Type 62
  *Common Name:* RPD LMG

  *Remarks:* Soviet and North Korean origin. Most of the Korean RPDs are copies of the fifth Soviet model.

- *Cal.:* 7.62 x 39mm
  *Common Name:* Domestic version of RPK LMG

  *Remarks:* Korean origin. Made at Factory 67.

- *Cal.:* 7.62 x 54mmR
  *Common Name:* PK series of GPMG

  *Remarks:* Soviet PK, PKB, PKS, and likely other versions.

- *Cal.:* 7.62 x 54mmR
  *Common Name:* SGM series of
    MGs

*Remarks:* Soviet origin, being supplanted by PK series. Made at Factory 67.

- *Cal.:* 7.62 x 54mmR
  *Common Name:* Type 59T AMG

*Remarks:* PRC origin on Type 62 tank.

- *Cal.:* 12.7 x 108mm
  *Common Name:* DShK38/46
    HMG

*Remarks:* Soviet and PRC origin. Mounted on Soviet T72 and Chinese Type 62 tanks.

**AUTOMATIC CANNON:**
- *Cal.:* 14.5 x 114mm
  *Common Name:* KPV HMG

*Remarks:* Soviet and Korean origin. Made at Factory 67; domestic production began ca. 1963. ZPU-2 and ZPU-4 AA systems in service.

- *Cal.:* 23 x 152mmB
  *Common Name:* ZU23 automatic
    cannon

*Remarks:* East Bloc origin.

- *Cal.:* 25 x 218mm
  *Common Name:* 2-M-3 or 2-M-8
    automatic cannon

*Remarks:* Soviet origin on S0-1 class patrol craft.

**Arms Sales by North Korea**

There are at least eight factories in North Korea that manufacture infantry weapons: No. 26 (3,000 employees) makes mortars, machine guns, and heavier weapons; No. 61 makes automatic rifles; No. 65 (12,000 employees) makes automatic rifles, mortars, etc.; No. 66 makes automatic weapons; No. 67 (7,500 employees) makes automatic rifles and a variety of light, medium, and heavy machine guns; No. 81 (2,500 employees) makes recoilless rifles and related munitions; No. 82 (2,500) makes mortars and munitions; No. 93 (10,000 employees) makes rifles, grenades, and artillery. Ammunition, grenades, and other explosive munitions are made at factories No. 13, 17, 26, 32, 42, 61, 65, 66, 67, 81, 82, 93, 101, 191, Yongpung, Yongampo, Kyongwon, Jongsong, and Hwangchoi. As a consequence of having this domestic armament-making capacity, with very little fanfare the North Korean defense industries, which date back to 1946, have become major international suppliers of military equipment. Substantial quantities of North Korean hardware have been sold to Iran, Libya, Nicaragua, Syria, and other nations. These sales provide North Korea with much-needed foreign currency and political clout. In addition, smaller states such as Malta have received North Korean weapons as military assistance gifts. North Korean weapons (small arms through artillery) have turned up in the hands of antigovernment forces in Africa and the Middle East. The Palestine Liberation Organization (PLO) was a major recipient of such materiel via Libya.

## KOREA, SOUTH (Republic of)

Population (estimate in 1984): 41.99 million. Ground forces: regulars, ca. 540,000; reserves, 1,400,000; Homeland Reserve Defense Force, 3,300,000. The Republic of Korea Police total some 90,000.

**HANDGUNS:**
- *Cal.:* 11.43 x 23mm
  *Common Name:* .45 M1911A1
    pistol

*Remarks:* US origin. MAP provided 9,370 M1911A1 pistols prior to 1975.

- *Cal.:* 9 x 29mmR
  *Common Name:* .38 Smith & Wes-
    son M10 revolver

*Remarks:* US origin. MAP provided 1,106 before 1975. NSN 1005-00-937-5839. In 1978 the US State Department licensed the delivery of 201 unspecified .38 caliber S&W revolvers for police use.

- *Cal.:* 9 x 29mmR
  *Common Name:* .38 Smith & Wesson M10 revolver

- *Cal.:* 9 x 29mmR
  *Common Name:* .38 Smith & Wesson M15 revolver

- *Cal.:* 9 x 29mmR
  *Common Name:* .38 Colt Detective Special revolver

**SUBMACHINE GUNS:**
- *Cal.:* 11.43 x 23mm
  *Common Name:* .45 M3 and M3A1 submachine gun

**RIFLES:**
- *Cal.:* 5.56 x 45mm
  *Common Name:* M16A1 (Model 603K) rifle

- *Cal.:* 5.56 x 45mm
  *Common Name:* K1 rifle

- *Cal.:* 7.62 x 33mm
  *Common Name:* .30 M1 and M2 carbines

- *Cal.:* 7.62 x 51mm NATO
  *Common Name:* M14 rifle

*Remarks:* US origin. FMS provided 500 in 1976. NSN 1005-00-937-5840.

*Remarks:* US origin. MAP provided 30 before 1975. NSN 1005-00-835-9773.

*Remarks:* US origin. MAP provided 405 before 1975. NSN 1005-00-726-5786.

*Remarks:* US origin. MAP provided 86,192 M3s from 1964 to 1974 and 1,235 M3A1s in the same period.

*Remarks:* Manufactured under license from Colt Industries at Pusan Arsenal until January 1983 when the production was transferred to Daewoo Precision Industries Ltd. of Pusan. It is estimated that as many as 590,000 M16A1 rifles have been manufactured in South Korea. Prior to the start of domestic manufacture, MAP delivered 26,810 M16A1 rifles.

*Remarks:* Domestic rifle manufactured at Daewoo Precision Industries Ltd. of Pusan. A carbine version, the K2, is also being manufactured.

*Remarks:* US origin. OBSOLETE? MAP provided 43,849 M1 carbines before 1964 and 954,138 in the decade 1964–74. Another 19,742 M2 carbines were provided by MAP in that same decade. FMS delivered 72,000 more M1s 1964–74. 1976–78 the US State Department licensed the delivery of 374 commercially made M2 carbines by the Plainfield Manufacturing Company for use by the Korean police.

*Remarks:* US origin. Only small numbers.

**Daewoo Precision Industries, Ltd. of South Korea has developed several new 5.56 x 45mm weapons. The first of these is the K1A1 submachine gun illustrated here. Building on their experience with production of the M16A1 rifle, they have created a weapon that embodies design features from the M16A1, the Kalashnikov, and several other contemporary weapons. Empty, without the magazine, the K1A1 weighs 2.87 kg (6.3 pounds). This weapon has selective single, 3-shot burst and full automatic fire. The front sight has a tritium element for night shooting. (Daewoo)**

The K2 rifle has many features of the K1A1, but its barrel is 465mm compared to 263mm. The K2 also has a side-folding stock instead of a retractable metal stock. As with the K1A1, the K2 employs the M16A1 20- and 30-shot magazines. In addition to the K1A1 and the K2, Daewoo has created a light machine gun, the K3, which bears a strong external resemblance to the FN Minimi. (Daewoo)

• *Cal.:* 7.62 x 63mm
*Common Name:* .30 M1 rifle

*Remarks:* US origin. OBSOLETE? MAP delivered 296,422 M1 rifles between 1964 and 1974. In addition, about 109 M1D and 15 M1C sniper rifles were also provided.

**SHOTGUNS:**
• *Cal.:* 18.5 x 59mm
*Common Name:* Ithaca M37 shotgun, 12 gage

*Remarks:* US origin.

• *Cal.:* 18.5 x 59mm
*Common Name:* Winchester M1200. shotgun, 12 gage

*Remarks:* US origin. MAP provided 1,390 shotguns 1964–74.

**MACHINE GUNS:**
• *Cal.:* 5.56 x 45mm
*Common Name:* K3 LMG (SAW)

*Remarks:* Domestic squad automatic weapon manufactured at Daewoo Precision Industries Ltd. of Pusan. Significantly modified variant of FN Minimi.

• *Cal.:* 7.62 x 51mm NATO
*Common Name:* M60 GPMG

*Remarks:* US origin. MAP provided 7,693 M60s 1964–74.

• *Cal.:* 7.62 x 51mm NATO
*Common Name:* M60D ACMG

*Remarks:* US origin. FMS provided small numbers of M60Ds in the early 1980s for use in the M48 tank cupola.

• *Cal.:* 7.62 x 51mm NATO
*Common Name:* FN MAG

*Remarks:* FN origin. MAG *Infanterie Standard* (60-20), T1 model.

• *Cal.:* 7.62 x 51mm NATO
*Common Name:* M134 high rate of fire machine guns

*Remarks:* US origin. FMS provided 75 M134s in 1976.

• *Cal.:* 7.62 x 63mm
*Common Name:* .30 M1918A2 LMG

*Remarks:* US origin. MAP provided 950 1964–74.

• *Cal.:* 7.62 x 63mm
*Common Name:* .30 M1919A4 LMG

*Remarks:* US origin. MAP provided 4,412 M1919A4s before 1965. In addition, they provided small numbers of 1919A1s.

- *Cal.:* 12.7 x 99mm
  *Common Name:* .50 M2 HB
  HMG

*Remarks:* US origin. MAP and FMS provided 750 M2 HB HMGs before 1975. In addition, they provided 20 M2s for the M1 Cupola in 1975 and 35 M55 quad gun AA systems.

**AUTOMATIC CANNON:**
- *Cal.:* 20 x 102mm
  *Common Name:* 20mm M39A2
  automatic cannon

*Remarks:* US origin. FMS provided 10 in 1980. In addition 13 M39A3RH and 12 M39A3LH automatic cannon were provided by MAP before 1975.

- *Cal.:* 20 x 102mm
  *Common Name:* 20mm M167
  automatic cannon

*Remarks:* US origin. FMS provided 88 before 1975.

- *Cal.:* 20 x 102mm
  *Common Name:* 20mm M168 Vulcan automatic cannon on the M163 and M167 Vulcan Air Defense System (VADS)

*Remarks:* US origin. They also have domestically made the versions of the M163 system in service. About 66 M163 Vulcan Air Defense System (VADS) in service.

**GRENADE LAUNCHERS:**
- *Cal.:* 40 x 46mmSR
  *Common Name:* M79 grenade
  launcher

*Remarks:* US and Korean origin. Prior to 1975, MAP provided 8,886 M79s.

- *Cal.:* 40 x 46mmSR
  *Common Name:* M203 grenade
  launcher

*Remarks:* US and Korean origin.

## South Korean Small Arms Industry

Daewoo Precision Industries Ltd. of Pusan offers for export sale their K1 rifle, M2 carbine, and K3 squad automatic weapon; the 40mm M79 and M203 grenade launchers; and the 20mm M167 Vulcan Air Defense System.

# KUWAIT

Population (estimate in 1984): 1.76 million. Ground forces: regulars, ca. 10,000; paramilitary (National Guard, Palace Guard, and Border Guards), ca. 3,000. The Public Security Department is estimated to have about 18,000 men.

**HANDGUNS:**
- *Cal.:* 9 x 29mmR
  *Common Name:* .38 Smith & Wesson revolvers

*Remarks:* US origin. The US State Department licensed the sale of 4,450 S&W revolvers in 1983.

- *Cal.:* 9 x 29mmR
  *Common Name:* .38 Colt Detective Special revolver

*Remarks:* US origin.

**SUBMACHINE GUNS:**
- *Cal.:* 9 x 19mm NATO
  *Common Name:* Sterling MK 4 (L2A3) submachine gun

*Remarks:* Sterling Armament Corp. of the UK provided chrome-plated MK 4s for the king's Palace Guard in 1982–83.

- *Cal.:* 9 x 19mm NATO
  *Common Name:* Sterling Mark 5 silenced submachine gun (L34A1)

  *Remarks:* Sterling provided gold plated MK 5s for the king's personal body-guards in 1982–83.

- *Cal.:* 9 x 19mm NATO
  *Common Name:* HK MP5, MP5K, and MP5SD

  *Remarks:* Royal Small Arms Factory (RSAF), Enfield, made Heckler & Koch (HK) submachine guns.

**RIFLES:**
- *Cal.:* 7.62 x 51mm NATO
  *Common Name:* FAL and FAL PARA (50.63)

  *Remarks:* FN origin. Adopted in 1957 and still in service.

- *Cal.:* 7.62 x ??mm
  *Common Name:* .30 Winchester sniper rifle

  *Remarks:* US origin. Ca. 15 in service.

- *Cal.:* 7.62 x 51mm NATO
  *Common Name:* FN M80 sniper rifle

  *Remarks:* FN origin.

**SHOTGUNS:**

**MACHINE GUNS:**
- *Cal.:* 7.62 x 51mm NATO
  *Common Name:* FN MAG

  *Remarks:* FN origin MAG *Infanterie Standard* (60-20), T1, or L7A2 models are in service. In addition, the British L8A1 and L37A1 AMGs are used on the MK3 Chieftan MBTs.

- *Cal.:* 7.62 x 63mm
  *Common Name:* .30 M1919A4 LMG

  *Remarks:* US origin.

- *Cal.:* 12.7 x 99mm
  *Common Name:* .50 M2 HB HMG

  *Remarks:* US origin. RAMO, Inc. sold 151 M2 HBs and mounts, which were delivered on M113 APCs in 1978. MAP delivered 74 in 1980. In addition, the British L2A1 ranging machine gun is used on the MK3 Chieftan MBTs.

**AUTOMATIC CANNON:**
- *Cal.:* 23 x 152mmB
  *Common Name:* KPV HMG

  *Remarks:* East Bloc origin.

### Submachine Guns Recovered

Following a 1978–79 terrorist attack on the Iraqi embassy, Kuwaiti authorities recovered Enfield-made HK MP5K submachine guns, which were marked with the Yugoslavian Federal Police Crest.

## LAOS (People's Democratic Republic of)

Population (estimate in 1984): 3.73 million. Ground forces: regulars, ca. 65,450; reserves, Area forces 9,900; reserves 111,000; civilian forces ca. 5,000. Very little is known in the West about the People's Liberation Army of Laos. The same is true for the nature of the small caliber weapons in use. There are a wide variety of small arms of United States, French, and East Bloc origin in the country. The following are known to be currently in active service. See discussion under Vietnam for more data on 1945–75 era. It is reported that about 60,000 Vietnamese troops are stationed in Laos.

**HANDGUNS:**
- *Cal.:* 9 x 17mm Browning
  *Official Name:* M70 (CP)
  *Common Name:* cz 70 pistol

  *Remarks:* Czechoslovakian origin.

- *Cal.:* 9 x 18mm
  *Official Name:* Type 59 (Ka 59)
  *Common Name:* Makarov pistol

  *Remarks:* East Bloc origin.

- *Cal.:* 7.62 x 25mm
  *Official Name:* Type 57 (Ka 57)
  *Common Name:* TT33 Tokarev pistol

  *Remarks:* East Bloc origin.

- *Cal.:* 7.62 x 25mm
  *Official Name:* Type 54 (Ka 54)
  *Common Name:* TT33 Tokarev pistol

  *Remarks:* East Bloc origin.

**SUBMACHINE GUNS:**
- *Cal.:* 7.62 x 25mm
  *Official Name:* 1943g
  *Common Name:* PPS43 submachine gun

  *Remarks:* East Bloc origin.

- *Cal.:* 7.62 x 25mm
  *Official Name:* KA 49
  *Common Name:* MAT49 submachine gun

  *Remarks:* East Bloc origin.

- *Cal.:* 7.62 x 25mm
  *Official Name:* Type 50 (Ka 50)
  *Common Name:* PPSh41 submachine gun

  *Remarks:* East Bloc origin.

**RIFLES:**
- *Cal.:* 7.62 x 54mmR
  *Official Name:* Type 53
  *Common Name:* M44 carbine

  *Remarks:* East Bloc origin.

- *Cal.:* 7.62 x 39mm
  *Official Name:* Type 56
  *Common Name:* PRC SKS carbine

  *Remarks:* People's Republic of China origin.

- *Cal.:* 7.62 x 39mm
  *Official Name:* SKS 45
  *Common Name:* Soviet SKS carbine

  *Remarks:* Soviet or East Bloc origin.

- *Cal.:* 7.62 x 39mm
  *Official Name:* AKM
  *Common Name:* AKM assault rifle

  *Remarks:* East Bloc origin.

- *Cal.:* 7.62 x 39mm
  *Official Name:* AK47
  *Common Name:* AK47 assault rifle

  *Remarks:* East Bloc origin.

**SHOTGUNS:**
Not used by Lao forces.

**MACHINE GUNS:**
- *Cal.:* 7.62 x 54mmR            *Remarks:* East Bloc origin.
  *Official Name:* Rotniy Pulemet
  *Common Name:* RP46

- *Cal.:* 7.62 x 39mm            *Remarks:* East Bloc origin.
  *Official Name:* RPD
  *Common Name:* RPD

- *Cal.:* 12.7 x 108mm           *Remarks:* People's Republic of China.
  *Official Name:* Type 54
  *Common Name:* Chinese DShKM

**AUTOMATIC CANNON:**
- *Cal.:* 14.5 x 114mm           *Remarks:* People's Republic of China.
  *Official Name:* Type 56
  *Common Name:* Chinese KPV
    HMG

- *Cal.:* 23 x 152mmB           *Remarks:* East Bloc origin.
  *Official Name:* ZU
  *Common Name:* ZU23 Automatic
    Cannon

# LEBANON

Population (estimate in 1984): 2.60 million. Ground forces: regulars, between 30,000 and 35,000; paramilitary supporting the central government, ca. 5,000+. The figures for the Lebanese army vary widely because of the state of political flux in that country. There are about 25,000 Syrian troops of the Arab Legion stationed in Lebanon. The *Direction General de Forces de Securite Interieure* has four departments: the Beruit Police; the Judicial Police; the *Gendarmerie* (est. at 5,000); and the Internal Security Forces Joint Training Unit. The chaos of the current political situation — a consequence of the post-1975 civil war and the Syrian/PLO/Israeli interventions in the domestic affairs of this nation — also has produced a wide variety of Western and East Bloc small arms, many of which continue to circulate in Lebanon. In addition to the official government small arms listed below, some data is presented at the end of this listing on the other small arms likely to be encountered in this country.

**HANDGUNS:**
- *Cal.:* 9 x 19mm Parabellum    *Remarks:* Belgian origin.
  *Common Name:* FN Mle. 1935 GP
    pistol

- *Cal.:* 9 x 19mm Parabellum    *Remarks:* West German origin.
  *Common Name:* Walther P38/P1

- *Cal.:* 9 x 19mm Parabellum    *Remarks:* Walther-licensed pistol made in France.
  *Common Name:* Manurhin P1

- *Cal.:* 9 x 19mm Parabellum    *Remarks:* US origin.
  *Common Name:* Colt Commander 9mm pistol

- *Cal.:* 9 x 19mm Parabellum    *Remarks:* US origin. State Department licensed sale of 70 in 1978–79.
  *Common Name:* 9mm Smith &
    Wesson pistol; model not identified

- *Cal.:* 9 x 29mmR
  *Common Name:* .38 Smith & Wesson revolvers

- *Cal.:* 9 x 29mmR Magnum
  *Common Name:* .357 Magnum Smith & Wesson revolvers

**SUBMACHINE GUNS:**
- *Cal.:* 9 x 19mm Parabellum
  *Common Name:* MAT 49 submachine gun

- *Cal.:* 9 x 19mm Parabellum
  *Common Name:* Sterling Mark 4 submachine gun

**RIFLES:**
- *Cal.:* 5.56 x 45mm
  *Common Name:* M16A1 (Model 613) rifle

- *Cal.:* 5.56 x 45mm
  *Common Name:* FN CAL

- *Cal.:* 5.56 x 45mm
  *Common Name:* SG540 rifle

- *Cal.:* 5.56 x 45mm
  *Common Name:* FAMAS rifle

- *Cal.:* 5.56 x 45mm
  *Common Name:* HK33 rifle

- *Cal.:* 7.62 x 33mm
  *Common Name:* .30 M1 carbine

- *Cal.:* 7.62 x 51mm NATO
  *Common Name:* FAL

- *Cal.:* 7.62 x 51mm NATO
  *Common Name:* M14 rifle

- *Cal.:* 7.62 x 51mm NATO
  *Common Name:* Gewehr 3

- *Cal.:* 7.62 x 63mm
  *Common Name:* .30 M1 rifle

**SHOTGUNS:**

**MACHINE GUNS:**
- *Cal.:* 7.5 x 54mm
  *Common Name:* MAC Mle. 24/29 LMG

*Remarks:* US origin. State Department licensed sale of 158 in 1978; 30 in 1979 to the Director General for National Security. The Internal Security Forces acquired 4,500 .38 S&W revolvers in 1978. A mixture of 400 .38 and .357 S&W revolvers were sold to Lebanon in 1979.

*Remarks:* US origin. State Department licensed the sale of 30 in 1978; 10 in 1979 to the Director General for National Security.

*Remarks:* Manufacture Nationale d'Armes de Tulle (MAT).

*Remarks:* Sterling Armament Co., UK.

*Remarks:* Approx. 50,000 have been acquired since the 1960s, which gives some indication of the use and loss rate for Lebanese small arms. These M16 rifles have been purchased by the government from the US government and directly from Colt Firearms. The Colt M16s carry an AL prefix for their serial number, and they have either the cedar tree of Lebanon or the crest of the F.S.I. = *Force de Securite Interieur.* AL in turn stands for *Armee Libanaise* (Army of Lebanon). Colt supplied about 20,000 M16A1s 1972–82. FMS and MAP provided 1,400 before 1975. FMS delivered 8,000 in 1978; 17,000 in 1980; and 21,000 in 1983.

*Remarks:* Belgian origin. Quantities unknown, but probably small. Not likely to be in widespread use.

*Remarks:* Manurhin-made Schweizerische Industrie Gesellschaft/Rheinfalls (SIG) design.

*Remarks:* Manufacture Nationale d'Armes de St. Etienne (MAS), Groupment Industriel des Armements Terrestres (GIAT).

*Remarks:* MAS and Enfield-made. Used only by the police and the Presidential Guard.

*Remarks:* US origin. FMS provided 900 before 1975.

*Remarks:* FN origin. Adopted in 1956.

*Remarks:* US origin. Purchased from US government.

*Remarks:* Most made by Manufacture Nationale d'Armes de St. Etienne (MAS) under license from Heckler & Koch (HK). Marked with Lebanese army crest. Royal Small Arms Factory (RSAF), Enfield-marked G3s have been captured from PLO. These are believed to have been shipped originally to the Lebanese government via Saudi Arabia.

*Remarks:* US origin. FMS provided 5,000 before 1965.

*Remarks:* Manufacture Nationale d'Armes de Chatellerault (MAC).

- *Cal.:* 7.5 x 54mm
  *Common Name:* AAT52 GPMG; standard and heavy barrel versions

  *Remarks:* MAT.

- *Cal.:* 7.62 x 51mm NATO
  *Common Name:* FN MAG

  *Remarks:* FN origin. MAG *Infanterie Standard* (60-20), T1 are in service. Also used are MAG *Coaxial* (60-40), ST450-M06 for the *Auto Blinde Chaimite* Portuguese Armored Personnel Carrier (left-hand feed, solenoid-fired) machine guns.

- *Cal.:* 7.62 x 51mm NATO
  *Common Name:* M60 GPMG

  *Remarks:* US origin. FMS delivered 68 in 1983.

- *Cal.:* 7.62 x 51mm NATO
  *Common Name:* M219 AMG

  *Remarks:* US origin. FMS delivered 3 in 1979 and 34 in 1983.

- *Cal.:* 7.62 x 63mm
  *Common Name:* .30 M1919A4 Browning and related models

  *Remarks:* US origin.

- *Cal.:* 7.7 x 56mm
  *Common Name:* .303 Bren LMG

  *Remarks:* UK origin.

- *Cal.:* 7.92 x 57mm
  *Common Name:* MG34 LMG

  *Remarks:* German origin. OBSOLETE.

- *Cal.:* 7.92 x 57mm
  *Common Name:* Besa MMG

  *Remarks:* UK origin. OBSOLETE.

- *Cal.:* 12.7 x 99mm
  *Common Name:* .50 M2 HB HMG

  *Remarks:* US origin. MAP provided 159 before 1975; 120 in 1978; 69 in 1980; 76 in 1981; 435 in 1983; 252 in 1984.

**AUTOMATIC CANNON:**
- *Cal.:* 20 x 110mm
  *Common Name:* M55 automatic cannon

  *Remarks:* Yugoslavian origin.

- *Cal.:* 20 x 128mm
  *Common Name:* KAB-001 (Type 10La/5TG) automatic cannon

  *Remarks:* Oerlikon Bührle, Switzerland.

- *Cal.:* 23 x 152mmB
  *Common Name:* ZU23 automatic cannon

  *Remarks:* Soviet origin.

**GRENADE LAUNCHERS:**
- *Cal.:* 40 x 46mmSR
  *Common Name:* M79 grenade launcher

  *Remarks:* US origin. FMS procured 111 in 1979.

- *Cal.:* 40 x 46mmSR
  *Common Name:* M203 grenade launcher attached to M16A1 rifle

  *Remarks:* US origin. MAP procured 254 before 1975; 208 in 1981. A small number have been acquired directly from Colt.

### Small Caliber Weapons Used by the PLO and Other Sectarian Militia Units in Lebanon

The post-1975 disintegration of the Lebanese Army and the subsequent turmoil led to the dispersal of Lebanese Army weapons, which was accompanied by the importation of large quantities of new weapons by the warring factions. In addition to the legally constituted Army of Lebanon and *Force de Securite Interieur* (Police Field Force), there are six loose coalitions: *Maronite Christian Lebanese Front* – Phalange Party, National Liberal Party, Guardians of the Cedars, Tanzim, Kaslik Front (Maronite Clergy) (This faction has the support of the remaining Army and F.S.I. personnel); *National Salvation Front* (Syrian-supported) — Progressive Socialist Party (Druze), Zgharta Front (Marda Brigade), Nasserite Organization, National Confrontation Front; Arab Democratic Party; Lebanese Arab Army (former members of the Army of Lebanon), Syrian Socialist National Party, Lebanese Communist Party, Communist Action Organization, Murabitun, Baath Party; *Radical Muslim Factions* — Islamic Amal, Union of Islamic Ulema, Union of Islamic Students, Dawa Party, Hussein Suicide Commandos, Dissident Amal Faction, Islamic Unification Movement, Popular Resistance, Lebanese Arab Movement, Jundallah, Mujahidin Organization, 24 October Movement; *Israel supported Militias in Southern Lebanon* — Army of Free Lebanon, Ansar, Tyre Port Guard, Village Guards (for several different villages), Druze guard, Ayn al-Hilwah, Rashidiyah Guard; *Independent Muslim Factions* — Al Amal, Islamic Coalition, Islamic Grouping, Democratic Socialist Party, Nassirite Corrective Movement, Popular Nasserist Organization, Arab Socialist Union, Baath Party Iraqi Wing, Lebanese National Resistance Union; *Independent Christian Factions* — Independent Parliamentary Bloc, Maronite League, National Bloc. There are another dozen or so factions that were active as late as 1982, but which were not active in 1983. Also operating in Lebanon are the various factions of the Palestine Liberation Organization (PLO), which is itself a fragile and often divided coalition of at least the following: al-Fatah; Popular Front for the Liberation of Palestine; Democratic Front for the Liberation of Palestine; Arab Liberation Front; and the Popular Struggle Front. During the 1982 Israeli "Operation Peace in Galilee," the Israeli Defense Forces captured large quantities of small caliber weapons, the inventory of which provides some limited insight into the variety of materiel that has been introduced into Lebanon:

**HANDGUNS:**

• *Cal.:* 7.65 x 17mm Browning
  *Common Name:* Walther PP copy

*Remarks:* These pistols, marked "Mauser Oberaudorf and Berlin," are made by the firm G. S. Mauser, which should not be confused with the Mauserwerke in Oberndorf an Neckar. They were fitted with silencers.

• *Cal.:* 9 x 17mm Browning
  *Common Name:* Walther PP copy

*Remarks:* Made by Makina ve Kimya Endustrsi Kurumu (MKE) in Turkey.

• *Cal.:* 9 x 19mm Parabellum
  *Common Name:* M951 Brigadier pistol

*Remarks:* Beretta.

• *Cal.:* 7.62 x 25mm
  *Common Name:* TT33 Tokarev pistol

*Remarks:* East Bloc origin.

**SUBMACHINE GUNS:**

• *Cal.:* 7.62 x 25mm
  *Common Name:* PPS43

*Remarks:* Soviet origin.

• *Cal.:* 7.62 x 25mm
  *Common Name:* Hungarian Spigon Model 53 submachine gun

*Remarks:* Hungarian origin.

• *Cal.:* 9 x 19mm Parabellum
  *Common Name:* vz.23 and vz.25 submachine guns

*Remarks:* Czechoslovakian origin.

• *Cal.:* 9 x 19mm Parabellum
  *Common Name:* Carl Gustav and Port Said submachine guns

*Remarks:* Swedish and Egyptian origin.

• *Cal.:* 11.43 x 23mm
  *Common Name:* .45 M1928A1 and M1 (Thompson) submachine guns

*Remarks:* US origin.

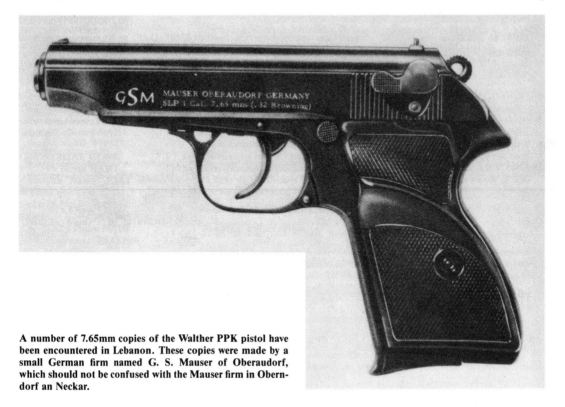

A number of 7.65mm copies of the Walther PPK pistol have been encountered in Lebanon. These copies were made by a small German firm named G. S. Mauser of Oberaudorf, which should not be confused with the Mauser firm in Oberndorf an Neckar.

**RIFLES:**

- *Cal.:* 5.56 x 45mm
  *Common Name:* M16A1 rifle

  *Remarks:* US origin. Supplied to the Lebanese government and subsequently pilfered from government depots.

- *Cal.:* 7.62 x 51mm NATO
  *Common Name:* M14 rifle

  *Remarks:* US origin. Supplied to Lebanese government and pilfered from government depots.

- *Cal.:* 7.62 x 51mm NATO
  *Common Name:* Gewehr 3

  *Remarks:* MAS and Enfield-made G3s and a handful of HK21 LMGs from the same factories.

- *Cal.:* 7.62 x 51mm NATO
  *Common Name:* CETME Modelo 58 assault rifle

  *Remarks:* Spanish origin.

- *Cal.:* 7.62 x 51mm NATO
  *Common Name:* FN FAL

  *Remarks:* FN origin. FALs made for Libya.

- *Cal.:* 7.62 x 39mm
  *Common Name:* SKS carbine

  *Remarks:* Soviet, East German, Chinese, and North Korean origin.

- *Cal.:* 7.62 x 39m
  *Common Name:* AK47 and AKM assault rifles; called "abu kornein" by Arab soldiers (i.e., "possessor of two horns," which refers to the curves of the magazine and pistol grip)

  *Remarks:* 20-some different types of the Kalashnikov assault rifle (from a wide variety of countries including the USSR, Poland, East Germany, Bulgaria, Romania, Hungary, People's Republic of China [PRC], and North Korea) have turned up in Lebanon. Many of these weapons were in very good to unused condition. While some dated from the earliest production types (1948–51), the majority had dates ranging from the early 1970s to 1980.

# PACKING LIST_____

Package No. **I354/I848**

Gross weight _____ *93* ___ kg

Net weight _____ *62* ___ kg

Consignee _____ *Sea Port for Chief Engineering Department* _____
(to be filled in as per order)

Description_____ *Automatic rifles, mod. AKMC cal. 7.62 mm* _____

Narjad No. _____ **80/4635I-I8355** _____

| Description of items packed<br>(type, model, mark) | Unit of measure<br>(kg, pieces,<br>meters, etc.) | Quantity | Marking |
|---|---|---|---|
| 1. Automatic rifles, mod. AKMC<br>    cal. 7.62 mm, Nos: | pcs. | 10 | Marking<br>according<br>to narjad |
|     324 04       268914 | | | |
|     254930     31733 | | | |
|     324I3I     3I6695 | | | |
|     323597     3I5020 | | | |
|     276I90     3I8767 | | | |
| 2. Knife-bayonet 6X4 | pcs. | 10 | |
| 3. Steel magazine $\frac{\text{assy 7}}{\text{56-A-212}}$ | pcs. | 40 | |
| 4. Case, compl. with accessories $\frac{\text{assy}}{6\text{IO4}}$ | pcs. | 10 | |
| 5. Plastic oil can 6IO5 | pcs. | 10 | |
| 6. Bag for 3 magazines, 56-Ш-212 | pcs. | 10 | |
| 7. Rifle sling, unified 6Ш5 | pcs. | 10 | |
| 8. Case for article, 6Ш21 | pcs. | 10 | |

Corrosion-proofing period till _____ **09** . **I979** _____

Packed by _____
(signature)

Inspected by _____
(signature)

**Soviet packing list for AKMS assault rifles, which accompanied weapons shipped by the Soviets to Libya, and which Libya in turn shipped to the PLO. Note combination of English and Russian terminology. Apparently, the Soviets prepack weapons for export, and then they can withdraw sufficient crates to meet export requirements when they arise.**

Two views of the receiver markings on a Lebanese Army *Gewehr 3A3* manufactured by the Manufacture Nationale d'Armes de St. Etienne. This was one of many G3A3s captured from the PLO by the Israeli Defense Forces during the 1982 "Operation Peace in Galilee." (Smithsonian; Eric Long)

**Receiver markings on a G3A3 manufactured by the UK Royal Small Arms Factory, Enfield, which was taken from the PLO by the Israeli Defense Forces during "Operation Peace in Galilee." (Smithsonian; Eric Long)**

• *Cal.:* 7.7 x 56mm
  *Common Name:* .303 Enfield
  rifles of various models

*Remarks:* Favored by all forces as a sniping weapon.

**SHOTGUNS:**
Wide variety of commercial shotguns numbering in the thousands; mostly of European and East Bloc origin.

**MACHINE GUNS:**
• *Cal.:* 7.92 x 57mm
  *Common Name:* MG34 GPMG

*Remarks:* World War II, Germany.

• *Cal.:* 7.92 x 57mm
  *Common Name:* MG42 GPMG

*Remarks:* World War II, Germany.

• *Cal.:* 7.62 x 54mmR
  *Common Name:* RPD, RP46,
  SGM, and PK machine guns

*Remarks:* East Bloc origin.

• *Cal.:* 12.7 x 99mm
  *Common Name:* M2 HB HMG

*Remarks:* US origin.

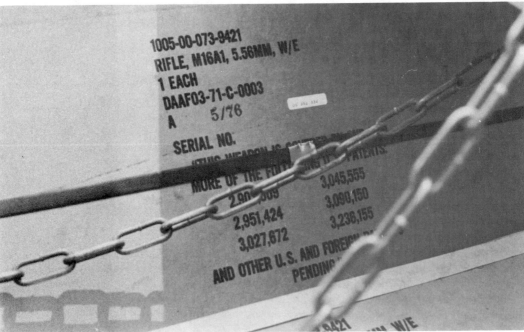

1005-00-073-9421
RIFLE, M16A1, 5.56MM, W/E
1 EACH
DAAF03-71-C-0003
A      5/76

SERIAL NO.

MORE OF THE FO

2,9        3,045,555
2,951,424    3,090,150
3,027,872    3,238,155

AND OTHER U.S. AND FOREIGN
PENDING

9421      W/E

**Two views of cartons containing American M16A1 rifles. These rifles were captured during "Operation Peace in Galilee," and the serial numbers indicate that the rifles were shipped to US Army depots in the summer of 1976. They may have been provided as aid or sold to the Lebanese army by the US government. (DOD)**

- *Cal.:* 12.7 x 108mm
  *Common Name:* DShK 38 and
  DShK 38/46 HMG

*Remarks:* Soviet and Chinese origin.

**AUTOMATIC CANNON:**
- *Cal.:* 14.5 x 114mm
  *Common Name:* KPV HMG

*Remarks:* Soviet and Chinese origin. Dozens on single gun trailer mounts of Chinese origin. All models of all manufacturers are in service.

- *Cal.:* 20 x 110mm
  *Common Name:* M55 automatic
  cannon

*Remarks:* Yugoslavian origin. Several of these 3-gun mounts were captured by Israeli Defense Forces in the 1982 "Operation Peace in Galilee." This was a favored weapon of many factions when mounted on the bed of a truck. The 20mm and the 23mm AA guns proved very effective for wall breaching in street fighting.

- *Cal.:* 23 x 152mmB
  *Common Name:* ZU23 automatic
  cannon, often truck mounted

*Remarks:* Soviet and Yugoslavian origin. Single, twin, and quad mounts. In service with many factions.

**Materiel Captured from PLO**

   The following numbers will give some idea of the aggregate quantities of materiel captured as of the end of 1982 from the PLO in the south of Lebanon by the Israeli Defense Forces during "Operation Peace in Galilee."

| | | | |
|---|---|---|---|
| Small caliber weapons | 33,303 | | |
| Antitank weapons | 1,352 | | |
| Mortars | 215 | Mortar bombs (60, 81, 82, 120, and 160mm) | 51,637 |
| Rocket launchers | 62 | Rockets | 7,507 |
| Field guns | 82 | Artillery shells | 15,445 |
| Antiaircraft weapons | 196 | | |
| Armored combat vehicles | 420 | | |
| Soft-skinned vehicles | 636 | | |
| Mines | 16,371 | | |
| Hand grenades | 19,200 | | |

*Note:* For general background on the fighting in Lebanon and the effects of various weapons see: US Army Human Engineering Laboratory, *Military Operations in Selected Lebanese Built-up Areas, 1975–1978,* by Paul A. Jureidini, R. D. McLaurin, and James M. Price. Technical Memorandum 11-79 (Human Engineering Laboratory: Aberdeen Proving Ground, Maryland, June 1979), 165 pp.

## LESOTHO (Kingdom of)

Population (estimate in 1980): 1.47 million. Ground forces: regulars, no data; reserves, no data. Once called Basutoland, this small country is an enclave inside the Republic of South Africa (RSA); most weapons are provided by the RSA defense establishment.

**HANDGUNS:**
- *Cal.:* 9 x 20mmR
  *Common Name:* .38 Enfield No. 2
  revolver

*Remarks:* UK origin.

**SUBMACHINE GUNS:**
- *Cal.:* 7.62 x 25mm
  *Common Name:* PPSh41 submachine gun

  *Remarks:* East Bloc origin. Ex-ANC?

- *Cal.:* 7.62 x 25mm
  *Common Name:* PPS43 submachine gun

  *Remarks:* East Bloc origin.

- *Cal.:* 9 x 19mm Parabellum
  *Common Name:* Sterling MK 4 submachine gun

  *Remarks:* Sterling Armaments Co., UK.

**RIFLES:**
- *Cal.:* 5.56 x 45mm
  *Common Name:* M16A1 rifle and M16A1 carbine

  *Remarks:* Colt, US. Initial orders for a few hundred placed in 1981 (Model 613 and Model 653).

- *Cal.:* 5.56 x 45mm
  *Common Name:* Beretta AR70/ .223 rifle

  *Remarks:* Italian origin. Used by the Police Mobile Unit.

- *Cal.:* 5.56 x 45mm
  *Common Name:* IMI Galil rifle

  *Remarks:* Israeli Military Industries (IMI)? May be South African R4s.

- *Cal.:* 7.62 x 39mm
  *Common Name:* AK47 assault rifle

  *Remarks:* Some Chinese models; the origin of the others is unknown.

- *Cal.:* 7.62 x 51mm NATO
  *Common Name:* FN FAL

  *Remarks:* FN origin?

**SHOTGUNS:**

**MACHINE GUNS:**
- *Cal.:* 7.62 x 51mm NATO
  *Common Name:* L7A1 and L7A2 GPMGs

  *Remarks:* UK origin.

- *Cal.:* 7.62 x 51mm NATO and 7.7 x 56mmR
  *Common Name:* Bren guns

  *Remarks:* UK origin. More recent models include the L4A1 and the L4A4.

- *Cal.:* 7.62 x 54mmR
  *Common Name:* SGM GPMG

  *Remarks:* East Bloc origin.

**AUTOMATIC CANNON:**

# LIBERIA (Republic of)

Population (estimate in 1980): 2.16 million. Ground forces: regulars, ca. 5,200; paramilitary, between 7,000 and 10,000.

**HANDGUNS:**
- *Cal.:* 9 x 29mmR
  *Common Name:* .38 Smith & Wesson revolvers of various models

  *Remarks:* US origin. FMS and MAP have provided small numbers of S&W M10 revolvers (NSN 1005-00-937-5839).

- *Cal.:* 9 x 29mmR
  *Common Name:* .38 Colt revolvers of various models

*Remarks:* US origin. The Liberian Bureau of Immigration and Naturalization acquired 17 in 1977; 235 in 1979. The National Police acquired 350 in 1979, and the Director of Special Security Services acquired a mix of 60 .38 and .357 Magnum Colt revolvers in 1979. The Ministry of Justice bought 320 .38 caliber Colt revolvers, 110 .357 Magnum revolvers, and 59 mixed .38 and .357 Magnum revolvers in 1979.

- *Cal.:* 9 x 19mm Parabellum
  *Common Name:* FN Browning Mle. 35 GP pistols

*Remarks:* FN via Fargo International of the US. Fargo delivered 13,000 High-Powers 1976–77.

- *Cal.:* 11.43 x 23mm
  *Common Name:* .45 M1911A1 pistol

*Remarks:* US origin. FMS and MAP delivered more than 350 before 1975.

### SUBMACHINE GUNS:
- *Cal.:* 9 x 19mm Parabellum
  *Common Name:* Uzi submachine gun

*Remarks:* Source unknown.

- *Cal.:* 9 x 19mm Parabellum
  *Common Name:* MAC-10 submachine gun

*Remarks:* Source unknown.

- *Cal.:* 11.43 x 23mm
  *Common Name:* .45 M3 series submachine guns

*Remarks:* US origin.

### RIFLES:
- *Cal.:* 5.56 x 45mm
  *Common Name:* M16A1 (Model 613) rifle

*Remarks:* At least 1,000 purchased directly from Colt. US to Liberia government aid unknown.

- *Cal.:* 5.56 x 45mm
  *Common Name:* M16A2 rifle

*Remarks:* At least 100 purchased directly from Colt.

- *Cal.:* 7.62 x 33mm
  *Common Name:* .30 M1 and M2 carbines

*Remarks:* US origin. MAP and FMS provided 186 before 1975. Fargo International delivered 10 Plainfield M2 carbines to the National Police in 1978.

- *Cal.:* 7.62 x 51mm NATO
  *Common Name:* FN FAL

*Remarks:* FN origin. Adopted in 1962. Current condition and status unknown.

- *Cal.:* 7.62 x 63mm
  *Common Name:* .30 M1 rifle

*Remarks:* US origin. MAP provided 1,973 before 1975. FMS delivered 3,000 in that same period.

### SHOTGUNS:
- *Cal.:* 18.5 x 59mm
  *Common Name:* 12 gage Ithaca Model 37 riot shotgun

*Remarks:* US origin. National Police purchased 10 in 1978. Previously, the US government had delivered small numbers of this weapon to the Liberians.

- *Cal.:* 18.5 x 59mm
  *Common Name:* 12 gage Winchester Model 1200 riot shotgun

*Remarks:* US origin. Small numbers.

### MACHINE GUNS:
- *Cal.:* 5.56 x 45mm
  *Common Name:* M16A1 (Model 611) heavy barrel AR

*Remarks:* Colt, US. Ca. 150.

- *Cal.:* 7.62 x 51mm NATO
  *Common Name:* FN FALO

*Remarks:* FN origin?

- *Cal.:* 7.62 x 51mm NATO
  *Common Name:* SIG 710-3 GPMG

- *Cal.:* 7.62 x 51mm NATO
  *Common Name:* M60 GPMG
                      *Remarks:* Reported, but not confirmed.

- *Cal.:* 7.62 x 63mm
  *Common Name:* .30 M1918A2 BAR
      *Remarks:* US origin. MAP provided 57 before 1975, while FMS delivered 3,000 before 1975.

- *Cal.:* 7.62 x 63mm
  *Common Name:* .30 M1917A1 LMG
      *Remarks:* US origin.

- *Cal.:* 7.62 x 63mm
  *Common Name:* .30 M1919A4 LMG
      *Remarks:* US origin. FMS and MAP delivered 112 before 1975.

- *Cal.:* 12.7 x 99mm
  *Common Name:* .50 M2 HB HMG
      *Remarks:* US origin. MAP provided 33 before 1975.

**AUTOMATIC CANNON:**

**GRENADE LAUNCHERS:**
- *Cal.:* 40 x 46mmSR
  *Common Name:* M203 grenade launcher mounted on M16A1
      *Remarks:* Colt, US. Ca. 275.

## LIBYA (Socialist People's Libyan Arab Jamahiriya)

Population (estimate in 1980): 3.68 million. Ground forces: regulars, between 45,000 and 60,000; reserves, 40,000-strong People's Militia. Cuba stations fewer than 3,000 military troops as advisers and trainers in Libya. Prior to the 1 September 1969 coup in which Colonel Mu'ammar Abu Minyar al-Qadhafi and his fellow officers ousted King Idriss, the Libyan ground forces consisted of less than 5,000 men. Since Qadhafi seized power, he has used his nation's enormous petroleum-derived wealth to build one of the most highly militarized states in terms of per capita expenditure and quantities of hardware, in the world. He has also used that wealth to purchase small arms from the Soviet, East Bloc, and other arms-producing countries in an attempt to make Libya the "Arsenal of Islam." The weapons thus acquired have been distributed to a variety of terrorist and revolutionary organizations ranging from the Palestine Liberation Organization and Irish Republican Army to Chadian, Corsican, Basque, Eritrean, and Moroccan (Polisario) revolutionaries, to mention but a few. Recently, Qadhafi has provided arms and financial support in the hundreds of millions of dollars to antigovernment forces in Upper Volta and El Salvador. In mid-April 1983, Brazilian government officials discovered that four aircraft (three IL-76s and one C-130), ostensibly loaded with humanitarian supplies, were carrying small arms, ammunition, and related hardware to the Sandinista government of Nicaragua. In a like manner, many of the weapons captured by the Israelis during their 1982 operations in southern Lebanon were still in shipping crates having Tripoli and Benghazi marked as their destination. In the spring of 1983, a military mission from Libya visited Argentina to inquire as to the possibility of acquiring Argentine small arms, including Argentine-made FALs. (See Lebanon for additional data.) During the first four months of 1987, Libya lost great quantities of military equipment to Chadian Defense Forces.

**HANDGUNS:**
- *Cal.:* 7.65 x 17mm
  *Common Name:* Beretta Mle. 34/ 84 pistol

  *Remarks:* Beretta, Italy.

- *Cal.:* 7.62 x 25mm
  *Common Name:* Tokarev pistol

  *Remarks:* East Bloc origin.

- *Cal.:* 9 x 18mm
  *Common Name:* Makarov pistol

  *Remarks:* East Bloc origin.

- *Cal.:* 9 x 18mm
  *Common Name:* Stechkin machine pistol

  *Remarks:* East Bloc origin.

- *Cal.:* 9 x 20mmR
  *Common Name:* .38 Enfield No. 2 revolver

  *Remarks:* UK origin.

- *Cal.:* 9 x 29mmR
  *Common Name:* .38 Smith & Wesson revolver

  *Remarks:* US origin.

**SUBMACHINE GUNS:**
- *Cal.:* 7.65 x 17mm
  *Common Name:* vz.61 Czech Skorpion machine pistol

  *Remarks:* Czechoslovakian origin.

- *Cal.:* 9 x 19mm Parabellum
  *Common Name:* Mle. 38A submachine gun

  *Remarks:* Beretta, Italy.

- *Cal.:* 9 x 19mm Parabellum
  *Common Name:* PM12 submachine gun

  *Remarks:* Beretta, Italy, and FN, Herstal, Belgium, have provided between 40,000 and 50,000 of these SMGs.

- *Cal.:* 9 x 19mm Parabellum
  *Common Name:* vz.23 and 25 submachine gun

  *Remarks:* Czechoslovakian origin.

- *Cal.:* 9 x 19mm Parabellum
  *Common Name:* L2A1 submachine gun

  *Remarks:* UK origin. Silenced version.

- *Cal.:* 9 x 19mm Parabellum
  *Common Name:* L34A1 submachine gun

  *Remarks:* UK origin. Silenced version.

- *Cal.:* 9 x 19mm Parabellum
  *Common Name:* Sten submachine gun

  *Remarks:* UK origin.

**RIFLES:**
- *Cal.:* 7.62 x 39mm
  *Common Name:* SKS carbine

  *Remarks:* East Bloc origin.

- *Cal.:* 7.62 x 39mm
  *Common Name:* AK47 and AKM assault rifles

  *Remarks:* East Bloc origin. Including the Hungarian AMD, the Romanian wood and folding stock models, and the East German MiPKMS. The latter is often seen in the hands of Qadhafi's female militia.

- *Cal.:* 7.62 x 39mm
  *Common Name:* vz.58 assault rifles

  *Remarks:* Czechoslovakian origin.

- *Cal.:* 7.62 x 51mm NATO
  *Common Name:* FAL

  *Remarks:* FN origin. Adopted in 1955. Many of the more recently acquired FALs have been provided to elements of the PLO.

- *Cal.:* 7.62 x 51mm NATO
  *Common Name:* BM59 MK IV rifle

*Remarks:* Beretta, Italy. The squad automatic weapon (FM) is also in service.

- *Cal.:* 7.62 x 51mm NATO
  *Common Name: Gewehr 3*

*Remarks:* Hellenic Arms Industry, Greece. Reported to have been delivered as part of an arms for oil deal.

- *Cal.:* 6.5 x 52.5mm
  *Common Name:* M1891 and M1891/38 Mannlicher Carcano bolt action rifles

*Remarks:* Italian origin. OBSOLETE, but still may be held in reserve stocks.

- *Cal.:* 7.7 x 56mmR
  *Common Name:* .303 MK III and No. 4 Lee Enfield bolt action rifles

*Remarks:* UK origin. OBSOLETE.

**SHOTGUNS:**

**MACHINE GUNS:**
- *Cal.:* 7.62 x 39mm
  *Common Name:* RPD LMG

*Remarks:* East Bloc origin.

- *Cal.:* 7.62 x 39mm
  *Common Name:* RPK LMG

*Remarks:* East Bloc origin.

- *Cal.:* 7.62 x 51mm NATO
  *Common Name:* FN MAG

*Remarks:* FN origin. Models in service include MAG *Infanterie Standard* (60-20), T6 (L7A2); MAG *Aviation* (60-30), Pod Marchetti, P.904; and MAG *Coaxial* (60-40), Type P.806 (L7A2) and Panhard AML 90 using M13 links.

- *Cal.:* 7.62 x 51mm NATO
  *Common Name:* FN FALO

*Remarks:* FN origin.

- *Cal.:* 7.62 x 51mm NATO
  *Common Name:* MG3 GPMG

*Remarks:* Italian origin. Believed to have been made by Beretta. Mounted on M113 APCs delivered by OTO Melara.

- *Cal.:* 7.62 x 54mmR
  *Common Name:* RP46 company machine gun

*Remarks:* East Bloc origin.

- *Cal.:* 7.62 x 54mmR
  *Common Name:* DP machine gun

*Remarks:* East Bloc origin.

- *Cal.:* 7.62 x 54mmR
  *Common Name:* PKT armor MG

*Remarks:* Soviet origin. Mounted on Soviet T62 and T72 tanks. Infantry version also in service.

- *Cal.:* 7.62 x 54mmR
  *Common Name:* SGMT armor MG

*Remarks:* Soviet origin. Mounted on older generation Soviet tanks. Some SG43 ground mount and flexible vehicle-mounted machine guns are also in service.

- *Cal.:* 7.62 x 54mmR
  *Common Name:* vz.53 GPMG

*Remarks:* Czechoslovakian origin.

- *Cal.:* 7.62 x 51mm NATO
  *Common Name:* vz.59N GPMG

*Remarks:* Czechoslovakian origin.

- *Cal.:* 7.7 x 56mmR
  *Common Name:* .303 Bren guns

*Remarks:* UK origin. Believed to be OBSOLETE. May still be held in reserve stocks. Some 7.62mm NATO L4A4s may be in the Libyan inventory.

- *Cal.:* 7.92 x 57mm
  *Common Name:* MG34 LMG

*Remarks:* World War II German manufacture. OBSOLETE. May still be held in reserve stocks.

- *Cal.:* 8 x 59mmRB
  *Common Name:* Breda M37 MMG

*Remarks:* Italian origin. OBSOLETE. May still be held in reserve stocks.

• *Cal.:* 12.7 x 99mm
  *Common Name:* .50 M2 HB
  HMG

*Remarks:* US origin? Mounted on OTO Melara delivered M113A1 APCs.

• *Cal.:* 12.7 x 108mm
  *Common Name:* DShK38/46
  HMG

*Remarks:* East Bloc origin.

**AUTOMATIC CANNON:**
• *Cal.:* 14.5 x 114mm
  *Common Name:* KPV HMG

*Remarks:* East Bloc origin.

• *Cal.:* 23 x 152mmB
  *Common Name:* ZU23

*Remarks:* East Bloc origin. Several versions including the self-propelled ZSU-23-4 AA system.

### US Infantry Weapons Provided to Libya, 1964–1967

|                                       | 1951–63 | 1964 | 1965 | 1966 | 1967 | Total |
|---------------------------------------|---------|------|------|------|------|-------|
| .30 M1 carbine:                       | 106     | · · · | · · · | · · · | · · · | 106   |
| .30 M1 rifle                          | 663     | · · · | · · · | · · · | · · · | 663   |
| .30 M1919A6 LMG:                      | 52      | 22   | 14   | 22   | · · · | 110   |
| .50 M2 HB HMG:                        | 5       | 5    | 5    | 7    | · · · | 22    |
| M63 Antiaircraft mount for M2 HMG:    | 5       | · · · | · · · | 5    | 12   | 22    |
| 3.5-inch M20A1B1 rocket launcher:     | 13      | 13   | 19   | 12   | 54   | 111   |
| 60mm M2 mortar:                       | 12      | 9    | 9    | 9    | 26   | 65    |
| 60mm M19 mortar:                      | 9       | · · · | · · · | · · · | · · · | 9     |

*Source:* Defense Security Assistance Agency, Grant Aid Data for Military Assistance Program.

## LUXEMBOURG (Grand Duchy)

Population (estimate in 1984): 0.366 million. Ground forces: regulars, 720; reserves (gendarmerie), 470.

**HANDGUNS:**
• *Cal.:* 9 x 17mm NATO
  *Common Name:* FN DA .380
  pistol

*Remarks:* Belgian origin. Acquired 900 for the gendarmerie, which in 1986 replaced them with S&W revolvers.

• *Cal.:* 9 x 19mm NATO
  *Common Name:* FN Mle. 1935 GP
  pistol

*Remarks:* FN origin. Purchased between 1958 and 1961.

• *Cal.:* 9 x 29mmR
  *Common Name:* .38 Smith & Wesson revolvers

*Remarks:* The gendarmerie, in 1986, acquired 900 S&W revolvers to replace their Browning DA High Power pistols.

• *Cal.:* 11.43 x 23mm
  *Common Name:* .45 M1911A1
  pistol

*Remarks:* US origin. FMS provided 41 before 1975.

**SUBMACHINE GUNS:**
• *Cal.:* 9 x 19mm NATO
  *Common Name:* Uzi submachine
  gun

*Remarks:* FN origin?

- *Cal.:* 9 x 19mm NATO
  *Common Name:* MP5

*Remarks:* Heckler & Koch (HK) origin. Initial purchases made in 1986.

**RIFLES:**
- *Cal.:* 7.62 x 63mm
  *Common Name:* FN SAFN Mle.
  49 rifle

*Remarks:* FN origin. OBSOLETE.

- *Cal.:* 7.62 x 51mm NATO
  *Common Name:* FN FAL

*Remarks:* FN origin.

**SHOTGUNS:**

**MACHINE GUNS:**
- *Cal.:* 7.62 x 51mm NATO
  *Common Name:* FN MAG

*Remarks:* FN origin.

- *Cal.:* 7.62 x 63mm
  *Common Name:* .30 M1919A4
  LMG

*Remarks:* US origin. MAP provided 246 before 1965.

- *Cal.:* 12.7 x 99mm
  *Common Name:* M2 HB HMG

*Remarks:* US origin. Ramo, Inc. delivered 90 M2 HBs w/ accessories in 1980.

**AUTOMATIC CANNON:**

## MADAGASCAR (Democratic Republic)

Population (estimate in 1984): 9.64 million. Ground forces: regulars, ca. 20,000; Presidential Security Regiment, 1,200; National Gendarmerie *(Gendarmerie Malgache),* 8,000; National Police, 3,000. Both East German and North Korean teams of military advisors reside in Madagascar. The Koreans have trained the elite Presidential Security Regiment.

**HANDGUNS:**
- *Cal.:* 7.65 x 17mm Browning
  *Common Name:* Walther PP

*Remarks:* Manuhrin-made.

- *Cal.:* 7.65 x 20mm
  *Common Name:* MAC Mle. 1935
  pistol

*Remarks:* Manufacture Nationale d'Armes de Chatellerault (MAC)

- *Cal.:* 7.62 x 25mm
  *Common Name:* TT33 Tokarev
  pistol

*Remarks:* East Bloc origin.

- *Cal.:* 7.62 x 25mm
  *Common Name:* vz.52 pistol

*Remarks:* Czechoslovakian origin.

- *Cal.:* 9 x 19mm Parabellum
  *Common Name:* MAB P-15 pistol

*Remarks:* Manufacture d'Armes de Bayonne (MAB).

**SUBMACHINE GUNS:**
- *Cal.:* 9 x 19mm Parabellum
  *Common Name:* MAT 49 subma-
  chine gun

*Remarks:* Manufacture Nationale d'Armes de Tulle (MAT).

**RIFLES:**
- *Cal.:* 7.62 x 39mm
  *Common Name:* SKS carbine

  *Remarks:* People's Republic of China (PRC) and East Bloc origin.

- *Cal.:* 7.62 x 39mm
  *Common Name:* AK47 and AKM
  assault rifles

  *Remarks:* PRC and East Bloc origin.

- *Cal.:* 7.62 x 39mm
  *Common Name:* Type 68 rifle

  *Remarks:* PRC origin.

- *Cal.:* 7.5 x 54mm
  *Common Name:* MAS Mle. 36
  bolt action rifle

  *Remarks:* Manufacture Nationale d'Armes de St. Etienne (MAS)

- *Cal.:* 7.5 x 54mm
  *Common Name:* MAS Mle. 49/56
  rifle

  *Remarks:* MAS

**SHOTGUNS:**

**MACHINE GUNS:**
- *Cal.:* 7.5 x 54mm
  *Common Name:* MAC Mle. 24/29
  LMG

  *Remarks:* MAC, France.

- *Cal.:* 7.5 x 54mm
  *Common Name:* AAT52 GPMG

  *Remarks:* MAT, Groupment Industriel des Armements Terrestres (GIAT).

- *Cal.:* 12.7 x 99mm
  *Common Name:* .50 M2 HB
  HMG

  *Remarks:* US origin.

- *Cal.:* 12.7 x 108mm
  *Common Name:* DShK38/46
  HMG

  *Remarks:* East Bloc origin, including PRC Type 54 HMG.

**AUTOMATIC CANNON:**
- *Cal.:* 14.5 x 114mm
  *Common Name:* KPV HMG

  *Remarks:* East Bloc origin. Approx. 100 ZPU-4 AA systems are in service.

- *Cal.:* 23 x 152mmB
  *Common Name:* ZU23 automatic
  cannon

  *Remarks:* East Bloc origin. Approx. 20 AA systems of this caliber in service. Specific models not known.

# MALAWI (Republic of)

Population (estimate in 1984): 6.83 million. Ground forces: regulars, ca. 5,000; paramilitary, ca. 1,000.

**HANDGUNS:**
- *Cal.:* 9 x 19mm NATO
  *Common Name:* L9A1 pistol

  *Remarks:* UK origin.

- *Cal.:* 9 x 20mmR
  *Common Name:* .38 Enfield No. 2
  revolver

  *Remarks:* UK origin.

**SUBMACHINE GUNS:**
- *Cal.:* 9 x 19mm NATO
  *Common Name:* L2A3 submachine gun

  *Remarks:* UK origin.

**RIFLES:**
- *Cal.:* 5.56 x 45mm
  *Common Name:* CETME Modelo L rifle

  *Remarks:* Centro de Estudios Tecnios y Materiales Especiales (CETME), Spain.

- *Cal.:* 7.62 x 51mm NATO
  *Common Name:* FN FAL

  *Remarks:* FN origin. Adopted 1974.

- *Cal.:* 7.62 x 51mm NATO
  *Common Name:* Gewehr 3

  *Remarks:* Heckler & Koch (HK) design.

- *Cal.:* 7.7 x 56mmR
  *Common Name:* .303 No. 4 SMLE rifle

  *Remarks:* UK origin.

**SHOTGUNS:**

**MACHINE GUNS:**
- *Cal.:* 7.62 x 51mm NATO
  *Common Name:* FN FALO

  *Remarks:* Belgian origin.

- *Cal.:* 7.62 x 51mm NATO
  *Common Name:* L7A1 GPMG

  *Remarks:* UK origin (Royal Small Arms Factory [RSAF], Enfield) and FN MAG *Infanterie Standard* (60-20), T7 (L7A2).

**AUTOMATIC CANNON:**
- *Cal.:* 14.5 x 114mm
  *Common Name:* KPV HMG

  *Remarks:* East Bloc origin.

# MALAYSIA

Population (estimate in 1980): 15.33 million. Ground forces: regulars, ca. 100,500; reserves, 45,000 in the Territorial Army, 15,000 in the Local Defence Corps. Paramilitary forces include the 12,000-man Police Field Force and the People's Volunteer Corps (RELA) of 350,000+ men. The *Polis Jabatan Diraja Malaysia* (Royal Malaysian Police Department) has about 19,000 officers.

**HANDGUNS:**
- *Cal.:* 9 x 19mm NATO
  *Common Name:* L9A1 pistol

  *Remarks:* UK origin.

- *Cal.:* 9 x 19mm NATO
  *Common Name:* P9S pistol

  *Remarks:* Heckler & Koch (HK), GmbH. Several thousand ordered with lanyard loop. HK catalog no. 210409.

- *Cal.:* 9 x 29mmR
  *Common Name:* .38 Smith & Wesson revolver

  *Remarks:* US origin. State Department licensed sale of 17,828 revolvers 1976–78 for the Royal Malay Police. During that same period the National Bureau of Investigation bought 20 revolvers; the Customs service bought 63; and the Selangor State Government bought 10.

**SUBMACHINE GUNS:**
- *Cal.:* 9 x 19mm NATO
  *Common Name:* L2A3 submachine gun

  *Remarks:* UK origin.

**Malaysian army soldiers on exercise in 1980 (Gonsales II) with 5.56 x 45mm M16A1 rifles. (Malaysian MOD)**

**RIFLES:**

• *Cal.:* 5.56 x 45mm
  *Common Name:* M16A1 (Model 613) rifle and M16A1 (Model 653) carbine

*Remarks:* Colt, US. Most widely used 5.56mm rifle in Malaysia. Approx. 200,000 M16A1 rifles are in service; 5,000 are the carbine version.

• *Cal.:* 5.56 x 45mm
  *Common Name:* HK33 rifle

*Remarks:* HK, West Germany. Ca. 50,000 have been purchased.

• *Cal.:* 5.56 x 45mm
  *Common Name:* AR70/.223 rifle

*Remarks:* Beretta, Italy. Ca. 5,000 have been purchased.

• *Cal.:* 7.62 x 51mm NATO
  *Common Name:* L1A1 rifle

*Remarks:* Commonwealth Small Arms Factory, Lithgow, Australia.

• *Cal.:* 7.62 x 51mm NATO
  *Common Name:* G3SG1 sniper rifle

*Remarks:* HK GmbH.

**SHOTGUNS:**
- *Cal.:* 18.5 x 59mm
  *Common Name:* 12 gage Moss-
  berg Model 500 shotgun

  *Remarks:* Acquired for the Army in September–November, 1980.

- *Cal.:* 18.5 x 59mm
  *Common Name:* 12 gage Winchester Model 12 shotgun

  *Remarks:* US origin. FMS delivered 29,981 before 1975.

**MACHINE GUNS:**
- *Cal.:* 5.56 x 45mm
  *Common Name:* AR70/223 LMG

  *Remarks:* Beretta, Italy.

- *Cal.:* 7.62 x 51mm NATO
  *Common Name:* HK11A1 LMG

  *Remarks:* HK GmbH. Used by the Police Field Forces. Very large numbers purchased.

- *Cal.:* 7.62 x 51mm
  *Common Name:* L4A4 Bren LMG

  *Remarks:* Royal Small Arms Factory (RSAF), Enfield.

- *Cal.:* 7.62 x 51mm NATO
  *Common Name:* L2A1 (FAL) SAW

  *Remarks:* Commonwealth Small Arms Factory.

- *Cal.:* 7.62 x 51mm NATO
  *Common Name:* L7A1 GPMG

  *Remarks:* RSAF. Version of FN MAG.

- *Cal.:* 7.62 x 51mm NATO
  *Common Name:* FN MAG

  *Remarks:* FN origin. Models in service include MAG *Infanterie Standard* (60-20), T3 (L7A2); MAG *Coaxial* (60-40), ST 450-M06 (right- and left-hand feed); Type P.806 (L7A2); (60-417) P.925 w/ L7A2 barrel; Sankey CAN L7A2; and Cadillac Gage armored car L7A2 version.

- *Cal.:* 7.62 x 51mm NATO
  *Common Name:* HK21E GPMG

  *Remarks:* HK.

- *Cal.:* 12.7 x 99mm
  *Common Name:* M2 HB HMG

  *Remarks:* US origin. Ramo, Inc. have delivered an unspecified number of guns since 1979 for Navy patrol craft.

**AUTOMATIC CANNON:**
- *Cal.:* 20 x 128mm
  *Common Name:* KAA (204GK) automatic cannon

  *Remarks:* Oerlikon Bührle.

**GRENADE LAUNCHERS:**
- *Cal.:* 40 x 46mmSR
  *Common Name:* M79 grenade launcher

  *Remarks:* US origin. FMS delivered 225 M79s before 1975.

- *Cal.:* 40 x 46mmSR
  *Common Name:* M203 grenade launcher attached to M16A1 rifle

  *Remarks:* US origin. More than 8,500 acquired from Colt.

**Weapons Used by Antigovernment Forces**

During the 1980s the small Communist Terrorist (CT) forces have lost a variety of small arms to Malaysian and Thai security forces. Included in these captures have been 9mm Ingram M10 and M11 submachine guns, 5.56mm M16 rifles, M26 and M76 hand grenades, and a few grenade cartridges for the M79/M203 grenade launchers.

## MALDIVES

Population (estimate in 1984): 0.173 million. Ground forces: regulars, unknown; reserves, unknown; paramilitary, unknown.

**HANDGUNS:**
- *Cal.:* 7.65 x 17mm Browning
  *Common Name:* Walther PPK

  *Remarks:* Walther design; source unknown.

- *Cal.:* 9 x 29mmR
  *Common Name:* .38 revolvers

  *Remarks:* Types and source unknown.

**SUBMACHINE GUNS:**

**RIFLES:**
- *Cal.:* 5.56 x 45mm
  *Common Name:* M16A1 rifles

  *Remarks:* Reported but not confirmed.

- *Cal.:* 7.62 x 39mm
  *Common Name:* AK47 assault rifle

  *Remarks:* There are supposed to be 400 government men armed with AK47s of unknown origin.

**SHOTGUNS:**

**MACHINE GUNS:**
- *Cal.:* 7.62 x 51mm NATO
  *Common Name:* 7.62mm GPMGs

  *Remarks:* Such weapons reported but specific models and types not known.

**AUTOMATIC CANNON:**

## MALI (Republic of)

Population (estimate in 1984): 7.56 million. Ground forces: regulars, ca. 4,600; paramilitary, ca. 5,500 (including the *Gendarmerie Nationale* of 1,500 men).

**HANDGUNS:**
- *Cal.:* 7.65 x 17mm Browning
  *Common Name:* Walther PP and PPK pistols

  *Remarks:* Manurhin-made. Ammunition still being purchased in 1987 for these pistols.

- *Cal.:* 7.65 x 20mm
  *Common Name:* MAC Mle. 1935 pistol

  *Remarks:* Manufacture Nationale d'Armes de Chatellerault (MAC).

**SUBMACHINE GUNS:**
- *Cal.:* 7.62 x 25mm
  *Common Name:* PPSh 41 submachine gun

  *Remarks:* East Bloc origin.

- *Cal.:* 9 x 19mm Parabellum
  *Common Name:* MAT 49 submachine gun

  *Remarks:* Manufacture Nationale d'Armes de Tulle (MAT).

**RIFLES:**
- *Cal.:* 7.62 x 39mm
  *Common Name:* AK47 assault rifle

  *Remarks:* East Bloc origin.

- *Cal.:* 7.5 x 54mm
  *Common Name:* MAS 36 bolt action rifle

  *Remarks:* Manufacture Nationale d'Armes de St. Etienne (MAS), Groupment Industriel des Armements Terrestres (GIAT).

- *Cal.:* 7.5 x 54mm
  *Common Name:* MAS 49/56 rifle

  *Remarks:* MAS.

**SHOTGUNS:**

**MACHINE GUNS:**
- *Cal.:* 7.5 x 54mm
  *Common Name:* AAT52 GPMG

  *Remarks:* MAS, GIAT.

- *Cal.:* 7.62 x 39mm
  *Common Name:* RPK LMG

  *Remarks:* East Bloc origin.

- *Cal.:* 7.62 x 39mm
  *Common Name:* RPK LMG

  *Remarks:* East Bloc origin.

- *Cal.:* 7.62 x 54mmR
  *Common Name:* PK series GPMGs

  *Remarks:* East Bloc origin.

- *Cal.:* 7.62 x 54mmR
  *Common Name:* SGM and SGMT series MGs

  *Remarks:* East Bloc origin.

- *Cal.:* 7.62 x 54mmR
  *Common Name:* Type 59T AMGs

  *Remarks:* People's Republic of China (PRC) origin on Type 62 light tanks.

- *Cal.:* 7.62 x 54mmR
  *Common Name:* DTM MGs

  *Remarks:* East Bloc origin. On older Soviet tanks.

- *Cal.:* 12.7 x 99mm
  *Common Name:* DShKM HMG

  *Remarks:* East Bloc origin.

**AUTOMATIC CANNON:**
- *Cal.:* 14.5 x 114mm
  *Common Name:* KPV HMG

  *Remarks:* East Bloc origin.

# MALTA

Population (estimate in 1984): 0.356 million. Ground forces: regulars, 1,000; reserves, 800 *(Id Dejna)*; paramilitary, ca. 3,000. Limited data on small arms in use. Items followed by an asterisk have been deduced from 1986 ammunition tenders.

**HANDGUNS:**
- *Cal.:* 7.62 x 25mm
  *Common Name:* TT33 Tokarev pistol*

  *Remarks:* Source unknown.

- *Cal.:* 9 x 17mm
  *Common Name:* Beretta Model 34 and Model 38 pistols*

  *Remarks:* Source unknown.

- *Cal.:* 9 x 18mm
  *Common Name:* Makarov pistol*

  *Remarks:* Source unknown, likely North Korea.

- *Cal.:* 9 x 29mmR
  *Common Name:* .38 Smith & Wesson revolver

  *Remarks:* US origin. State Department licensed sale of 100 S&W revolvers in 1977.

**SUBMACHINE GUNS:**
- *Cal.:* 9 x 19mm Parabellum
  *Common Name:* Model unknown*

- *Cal.:* 9 x 19mm Parabellum
  *Common Name:* MP5K

  *Remarks:* Origin unknown.

- *Cal.:* 9 x 19mm Parabellum
  *Common Name:* L2A1 submachine gun

  *Remarks:* Origin unknown.

- *Cal.:* 9 x 19mm Parabellum
  *Common Name:* Uzi submachine gun

  *Remarks:* Unconfirmed.

**New hardware in Malta. North Korean quad 14.5mm ZPU-4 towed antiaircraft system provided to Malta as a consequence of the 1982 arms transfer agreements between the two countries. (Gander)**

**RIFLES:**
- *Cal.:* 7.62 x 39mm
  *Common Name:* Type 58 AKM

  *Remarks:* North Korean origin.

- *Cal.:* 7.62 x 51mm NATO
  *Common Name:* Model unknown*

  *Remarks:* FAL?

**SHOTGUNS:**

**MACHINE GUNS:**

**AUTOMATIC CANNON:**
- *Cal.:* 14.5 x 114mm
  *Common Name:* KPV HMG

  *Remarks:* North Korean origin. At least 50 North Korean-made ZPU-4 quad antiaircraft systems are in service as a result of the 1982 arms agreement.

- *Cal.:* 20 x ???mm
  *Common Name:* Model unknown*

  *Remarks:* Believed to be Oerlikon type.

### Weapons Acquired from North Korea

During the Labor government, in power 1982–86, two major secret arms agreements (March 1982 and July 1982) were signed by the Maltese and North Korean governments. As a consequence, in 1983 the Maltese received small caliber automatic weapons and a variety of antiaircraft weapons.

# MARTINIQUE

Population (estimate in 1980): 0.330 million. Ground forces: regulars, unknown; paramilitary (police), unknown.

**HANDGUNS:**

**SUBMACHINE GUNS:**

**RIFLES:**

**SHOTGUNS:**

**MACHINE GUNS:**

**AUTOMATIC CANNON:**

# MAURITANIA (Islamic Republic of)

Population (estimate in 1980): 1.63 million. Ground forces: regulars, ca. 9,000; paramilitary (police), ca. 6,000. Former French colony. Small arms probably still follow the French pattern.

**HANDGUNS:**
- *Cal.:* 9 x 19mm Parabellum
  *Common Name:* MAC Mle. 50 pistol

  *Remarks:* Manufacture Nationale d'Armes de Chatellerault (MAC), France.

- *Cal.:* 9 x 19mm Parabellum
  *Common Name:* MAB P15S pistol

  *Remarks:* Manufacture Nationale d'Armes de Bayonne (MAB), France.

- *Cal.:* 7.65 x 20mm
  *Common Name:* MAS1935 pistol

  *Remarks:* Manufacture Nationale d'Armes de St. Etienne (MAS), France.

- *Cal.:* 7.62 x 25mm
  *Common Name:* Tokarev pistol

  *Remarks:* East Bloc origin.

**SUBMACHINE GUNS:**
- *Cal.:* 9 x 19mm Parabellum
  *Common Name:* Star Z45 sub-machine gun

  *Remarks:* Star Bonafacio Echeverria, Spain.

- *Cal.:* 9 x 19mm Parabellum
  *Common Name:* MAT 49 sub-machine gun

  *Remarks:* Manufacture Nationale d'Armes de Tulle (MAT), France.

- *Cal.:* 7.62 x 25mm
  *Common Name:* PPSh41 submachine gun

  *Remarks:* East Bloc origin.

**RIFLES:**
- *Cal.:* 7.62 x 39mm
  *Common Name:* AK47 and AKM assault rifle

  *Remarks:* East Bloc origin.

- *Cal.:* 7.5 x 54mm
  *Common Name:* MAS Mle. 36 boltaction rifle

  *Remarks:* MAS origin.

- *Cal.:* 7.5 x 54mm
  *Common Name:* MAS 49/56 rifle

  *Remarks:* MAS origin.

- *Cal.:* 7.5 x 54mm
  *Common Name:* FR-F1 sniper rifle

  *Remarks:* Groupment Industriel des Armement Terrestres (GIAT) origin.

- *Cal.:* 7.62 x 51mm NATO
  *Common Name:* MAS *Gewehr 3*

  *Remarks:* MAS origin.

- *Cal.:* 7.62 x 51mm NATO
  *Common Name:* FN FAL

  *Remarks:* Unknown origin.

- *Cal.:* 7.62 x 51mm NATO
  *Common Name:* CETME *Modelo 58* rifle

  *Remarks:* Spanish origin.

- *Cal.:* 7.92 x 57mm
  *Common Name:* Mauser 98K rifle

  *Remarks:* Unknown origin.

- *Cal.:* 7.62 x 54mmR
  *Common Name:* Mosin-Nagant M1891/30 rifle

  *Remarks:* Unknown origin.

**SHOTGUNS:**

**MACHINE GUNS:**
- *Cal.:* 7.5 x 54mm
  *Common Name:* MAC Mle. 24/29 LMG

  *Remarks:* MAC.

- *Cal.:* 7.62 x 51mm NATO
  *Common Name:* AAT 52 GPMG

  *Remarks:* GIAT, France.

- *Cal.:* 7.62 x 51mm NATO
  *Common Name:* MG42/59
  GPMG

  *Remarks:* Empressa Nacional Santa Barbara, Spain.

- *Cal.:* 7.62 x 51mm NATO
  *Common Name:* FN MAG

  *Remarks:* FN origin. FN MAG *Coaxial* (60-40), Mod. Panhard AML 90 w/ nondisintegrating link, and Panhard AML 90 13 w/ US M13 disintegrating links.

- *Cal.:* 12.7 x 99mm
  *Common Name:* M2 HB HMG

  *Remarks:* US origin.

- *Cal.:* 12.7 x 108mm
  *Common Name:* DShK HMG
  series

  *Remarks:* East Bloc origin.

**AUTOMATIC CANNON:**

- *Cal.:* 14.5 x 114mm
  *Common Name:* KPV HMG

  *Remarks:* East Bloc origin. ZPU-1 and ZPU-2 versions.

- *Cal.:* 23 x 153mmB
  *Common Name:* ZU23 automatic
  cannon

  *Remarks:* East Bloc origin. ZU-23-2 AA system.

## MAURITIUS

Population (estimate in 1984): 1.02 million. Ground forces: regulars (Police Special Mobile Force, which is an embryo army; there are no other armed forces, technical aid being provided by India and France), 800; reserves (Mauritius Police Force), ca. 4,100.

**HANDGUNS:**

- *Cal.:* 9 x 29mmR
  *Common Name:* Manurhin .38
  Special MR73 revolver

  *Remarks:* French origin.

- *Cal.:* 7.65 x 17mm Browning
  *Common Name:* Walther PP

  *Remarks:* Manurhin-made.

**SUBMACHINE GUNS:**

- *Cal.:* 9 x 19mm Parabellum
  *Common Name:* MP5A2

  *Remarks:* Origin unknown.

**RIFLES:**

- *Cal.:* 5.56 x 45mm
  *Common Name:* SIG 540 assault
  rifle

  *Remarks:* Manurhin-made Schweizerische Industrie Gesellschaft/Rheinfalls (SIG) design.

- *Cal.:* 7.62 x 51mm NATO
  *Common Name:* L1A1 rifle

  *Remarks:* UK origin?

- *Cal.:* 7.7 x 56mm
  *Common Name:* .303 No. 4 Enfield rifle

  *Remarks:* Royal Small Arms Factory (RSAF), Enfield.

**SHOTGUNS:**

**MACHINE GUNS:**
- *Cal.:* 7.62 x 51mm NATO
  *Common Name:* L4A4 Bren LMG

  *Remarks:* RSAF, Enfield. Also L4A1?

- *Cal.:* 7.7 x 56mm
  *Common Name:* .303 MK 1 Bren
  LMG

  *Remarks:* UK origin.

- *Cal.:* 7.5 x 54mm
  *Common Name:* AAT52 GPMG

  *Remarks:* Manufacture Nationale d'Armes de Tulle (MAT), Groupment Industrie Armement Terrestres (GIAT).

**AUTOMATIC CANNON:**

# MEXICO (United States of)

Population (estimate in 1984): 77.66 million. Ground forces: regulars, Army, ca. 94,500; Marine Corps, 3,810; reserves, ca. 250,000; paramilitary, federal police 23,000; Rural Defense Corps *(Rurales),* 120,000.

**HANDGUNS:**
- *Cal.:* 9 x 19mm NATO
  *Common Name:* HK P7 M13
  pistol

  *Remarks:* Heckler & Koch (HK) design. Will be manufactured in Mexico.

- *Cal.:* 11.23 x 23mm
  *Common Name:* .45 M1911A1
  pistol

  *Remarks:* US origin. FMS delivered 200 M1911A1 pistols in 1976. State Department licensed sale of 1,100 pistols from Colt in 1978.

- *Cal.:* 9 x 19mm Parabellum
  *Common Name:* 9mm Smith &
  Wesson pistol

  *Remarks:* US origin. State Department licensed sale of 10 to the Direccion General de Policia y Transport in 1978.

- *Cal.:* 9 x 29mmR
  *Common Name:* .38 Smith & Wesson revolver

  *Remarks:* US origin. State Department licensed sale of 140 to the Direccion General de Policia y Transport in 1978.

- *Cal.:* 9 x 29mmR Magnum
  *Common Name:* .357 Magnum
  Smith & Wesson revolver

  *Remarks:* US origin. State Department licensed sale of 9 to the Inspector General of Police for the State of Chihuahua in 1978.

- *Cal.:* 9 x 29mmR
  *Common Name:* .38 Colt revolver

  *Remarks:* US origin. State Department licensed sale of 12 revolvers to the Inspector General of Police for the State of Chihuahua in 1976 through Interarms.

- *Cal.:* 11.43 x 23mm
  *Common Name:* .45 Colt police
  revolver

  *Remarks:* US origin. State Department licensed sale of 450 revolvers to the Inspector General of Police for the State of Chihuahua in 1977.

**SUBMACHINE GUNS:**
- *Cal.:* 11.43 x 23mm
  *Common Name:* .45 M3A1 submachine gun

  *Remarks:* US origin. FMS delivered 174 submachine guns before 1975.

- *Cal.:* 9 x 19mm NATO
  *Common Name:* MP5 submachine gun

  *Remarks:* HK origin; now being manufactured under license from HK.

- *Cal.:* 9 x 19mm NATO
  *Common Name:* MP-K submachine gun

  *Remarks:* Walther origin. Used by the Navy only.

- *Cal.:* 9 x 19mm Parabellum
  *Common Name:* HM-3 submachine gun

  *Remarks:* Domestic design by Mendoza; status unknown.

- *Cal.:* 5.56 x 45mm
  *Common Name:* HK53 submachine gun

  *Remarks:* HK.

**RIFLES:**

- *Cal.:* 7.62 x 51mm NATO
  *Common Name: Gewehr 3* (G3A3 and G3A4)

  *Remarks:* HK origin; also currently being manufactured in Mexico under license. First G3s acquired in 1979. HK catalog no. for the Mexican G3s is 224001.

- *Cal.:* 7.62 x 51mm NATO
  *Common Name:* FN FAL

  *Remarks:* Formerly assembled in Mexico from FN-supplied parts.

- *Cal.:* 5.56 x 45mm
  *Common Name:* M16A1 rifle

  *Remarks:* US origin. State Department licensed sale of 500 M16 rifles and 25 M16 carbines to the Inspector General of Police for the State of Chihuahua in 1977. Other police organizations also have small quantities for special units.

- *Cal.:* 7.62 x 33mm
  *Common Name:* .30 M1 and M2 carbines

  *Remarks:* US origin. FMS delivered 768 M1 carbines before 1975. In 1976 the State Department licensed the sale of 4 M2 carbines to the police of the State of Chihuahua.

- *Cal.:* 7.62 x 63mm
  *Official Name:* M1954
  *Common Name:* Mexican-made Mauser rifle

  *Remarks:* Mexico.

- *Cal.:* 7 x 57mm
  *Common Name:* Mexican Mauser rifle

  *Remarks:* OBSOLETE; some may still be in service.

**SHOTGUNS:**

- *Cal.:* 18.5 x 59mm
  *Common Name:* 12 gage Mossberg Model 500 shotgun

  *Remarks:* Federal police and state police forces for urban police and riot use. Acquired 1977–86.

- *Cal.:* 18.5 x 59mm
  *Common Name:* 12 gage HK510 single-shot shotgun

  *Remarks:* HK.

**MACHINE GUNS:**

- *Cal.:* 5.56 x 45mm
  *Common Name:* Ameli SAW

  *Remarks:* Empresa Nacional, Santa Barbara, Spain.

- *Cal.:* 7.62 x 51mm NATO
  *Common Name:* FN MAG

  *Remarks:* Belgian origin. The Mexican armed forces use both the Standard Infantry Model (60-20) and the Aviation (60-30) P.935 variant in both left- and right-hand feed.

- *Cal.:* 7.62 x 51mm NATO
  *Common Name:* HK21A1 LMG

  *Remarks:* HK.

- *Cal.:* 7.62 x 63mm
  *Common Name:* .30 M1919A4 LMG

  *Remarks:* US origin. FMS provided 1,123 before 1964.

- *Cal.:* 7.62 x 63mm
  *Common Name:* .30 RM-2 LMG

  *Remarks:* Domestic design; Mendoza-made LMG. Status unknown.

- *Cal.:* 12.7 x 99mm
  *Common Name:* .50 M2 HB HMG

  *Remarks:* US origin. Used individually and in the M55 quad AA trailer mount.

**AUTOMATIC CANNON:**
- *Cal.:* 20 x 102mm
  *Common Name:* M693 automatic
  cannon

*Remarks:* French origin.


# MONGOLIA (People's Republic of)

Population (estimate in 1980): 1.86 million. Ground forces: regulars, between 25,000 and 33,000; Ministry of Public Security paramilitary frontier guards, ca. 18,000; People's Militia (national police) 30,000; reserves, ca. 40,000. Limited data on small arms, but reported to follow the Soviet pattern.

**HANDGUNS:**

**SUBMACHINE GUNS:**

**RIFLES:**

**SHOTGUNS:**

**MACHINE GUNS:**
- *Cal.:* 7.62 x 54mmR
  *Common Name:* PKT armor MG

*Remarks:* Soviet origin. Mounted on Soviet T62 tanks.

- *Cal.:* 7.62 x 54mmR
  *Common Name:* SGMT armor
  MG

*Remarks:* Soviet origin. Mounted on older Soviet tanks and APCs.

- *Cal.:* 7.62 x 54mmR
  *Common Name:* DTM armor MG

*Remarks:* Soviet origin. Mounted on older Soviet tanks and APCs.

- *Cal.:* 12.7 x 108mm
  *Common Name:* DShKM HMG

*Remarks:* Soviet origin.

**AUTOMATIC CANNON:**


# MOROCCO (Kingdom of)

Population (estimate in 1984): 23.56 million. Ground forces: regulars, ca. 125,000; paramilitary, *Gendarmerie Royale Morocaine,* ca. 30,000, including 11,000 *Surete Nationale.*

**HANDGUNS:**
- *Cal.:* 7.65 x 17mm
  *Common Name:* HK4 pistol

*Remarks:* Heckler & Koch (HK) GmbH origin. Ca. 2,000 pistols acquired in 1977.

- *Cal.:* 7.65 x 17mm
  *Common Name:* Walther PP

*Remarks:* Manuhrin-made PP.

- *Cal.:* 9 x 19mm NATO
  *Common Name:* HK VP70M machine pistol

*Remarks:* HK origin.

- *Cal.:* 9 x 19mm Parabellum
  *Common Name:* MAS Mle. 1950
  pistol

*Remarks:* Manufacture Nationale d'Armes de St. Etienne (MAS), France.

- *Cal.:* 9 x 19mm Parabellum
  *Common Name:* MAB P-15 pistol

  *Remarks:* Manufacture d'Armes de Bayonne (MAB).

- *Cal.:* 9 x 29mmR
  *Common Name:* .38 Smith & Wesson M10 revolvers

  *Remarks:* US origin. MAP delivered 20 before 1975. NSN 1005-00-937-5839.

- *Cal.:* 9 x 29mmR
  *Common Name:* .38 Colt Detective Special revolvers

  *Remarks:* US origin. MAP delivered 96 before 1975. NSN 1005-00-726-5786.

**SUBMACHINE GUNS:**
- *Cal.:* 9 x 19mm Parabellum
  *Common Name:* Beretta M38/49 (M4) submachine gun

  *Remarks:* Beretta, Italy.

- *Cal.:* 9 x 19mm Parabellum NATO
  *Common Name:* MP 5 submachine gun

  *Remarks:* HK design manufactured at the Royal Small Arms Factory (RSAF), Enfield.

- *Cal.:* 9 x 19mm Parabellum
  *Common Name:* MAT 49 submachine gun

  *Remarks:* Manufacture Nationale d'Armes de Tulle (MAT).

- *Cal.:* 9 x 19mm Parabellum NATO
  *Common Name:* L2A3 submachine gun

  *Remarks:* UK origin.

- *Cal.:* 9 x 19mm Parabellum
  *Common Name:* MAC-10 submachine gun

  *Remarks:* Military Armaments Corporation.

- *Cal.:* 11.43 x 23mm
  *Common Name:* .45 M3 submachine gun

  *Remarks:* US origin. MAP delivered 1,172 before 1975. NSN 1005-00-726-5786.

**RIFLES:**
- *Cal.:* 7.62 x 33mm
  *Common Name:* .30 M1 and M2 carbines

  *Remarks:* US origin. The Moroccans have also acquired Beretta-made M2 carbines (Model 1957) for their forces. This weapon has also been licensed for production at the Manufacture d'Armes de Fes.

- *Cal.:* 5.56 x 45mm
  *Common Name:* M16A1 (Model 613) rifle and M16A1 (Model 653) carbines

  *Remarks:* Colt, US. Approx. 3,500 rifles and 100 carbines acquired directly from Colt in the mid-1970s. FMS delivered 122 before 1975. Used by several organizations including the National Security Police *(Surete Nationale)*.

- *Cal.:* 5.56 x 45mm
  *Common Name:* Beretta Mod. 70/223 rifle

  *Remarks:* Italian design delivered by FN.

- *Cal.:* 5.56 x 45mm
  *Common Name:* FN CAL

  *Remarks:* Reported to have been purchased but not confirmed.

- *Cal.:* 7.5 x 54mm
  *Common Name:* MAS 36 rifle

  *Remarks:* MAS.

- *Cal.:* 7.5 x 54mm
  *Common Name:* MAS 49/56 rifle

  *Remarks:* MAS.

- *Cal.:* 7.62 x 39mm
  *Common Name:* AK47 and AKM assault rifles

  *Remarks:* East Bloc origin, including the Romanian-made version.

- *Cal.:* 7.62 x 39mm
  *Common Name:* M76 assault rifle

  *Remarks:* Valmet, Finland. At least 600 in service.

- *Cal.:* 7.62 x 51mm NATO
  *Common Name:* FN FAL

  *Remarks:* FN origin. Adopted 1963. An additional 10,000 ordered from FN in 1982.

- *Cal.:* 7.62 x 51mm NATO
  *Common Name:* BM59 Mark IV rifle

  *Remarks:* Beretta, Italy.

- *Cal.:* 7.62 x 51mm NATO
  *Common Name:* Gewehr 3

  *Remarks:* HK design made at MAS in France.

- *Cal.:* 7.62 x 51mm NATO
  *Common Name:* M14 rifle

  *Remarks:* US origin. FMS delivered 44 National Match versions before 1975 and 48 standard M14s in 1982.

**SHOTGUNS:**

**MACHINE GUNS:**

- *Cal.:* 7.5 x 54mm
  *Common Name:* MAC Mle. 24/29 LMG

  *Remarks:* Manufacture Nationale d'Armes de Chatellerault (MAC).

- *Cal.:* 7.5 x 54mm
  *Common Name:* AAT52 GPMG

  *Remarks:* MAT.

- *Cal.:* 7.62 x 39mm
  *Common Name:* RPD LMG

  *Remarks:* East Bloc and Egyptian origin.

- *Cal.:* 7.62 x 51mm NATO
  *Common Name:* BM59 Mark IV automatic rifle version

  *Remarks:* Beretta, Italy.

- *Cal.:* 7.62 x 51mm NATO
  *Common Name:* FN FALO

  *Remarks:* FN origin.

- *Cal.:* 7.62 x 51mm NATO
  *Common Name:* HK11 LMG

  *Remarks:* HK origin.

- *Cal.:* 7.62 x 51mm NATO
  *Common Name:* FN MAG

  *Remarks:* FN received order for 1,000 of the MAG Standard Infanterie (Model 60-20), T1 in 1982.

- *Cal.:* 7.62 x 51mm NATO
  *Common Name:* M60 GPMG

  *Remarks:* US origin. FMS delivered 157 in 1975.

- *Cal.:* 7.62 x 51mm NATO
  *Common Name:* M60D ACMG

  *Remarks:* US origin. FMS delivered 52 in 1980 and 56 in 1982.

- *Cal.:* 7.62 x 51mm NATO
  *Common Name:* M73 and M219 AMGs

  *Remarks:* US origin. Mounted on US M60A3 tanks. FMS delivered 26 in 1980 and 28 in 1982.

- *Cal.:* 7.62 x 51mm NATO
  *Common Name:* MG74 (MG3) AMG

  *Remarks:* Austrian origin. Reported to be mounted on the Steyr-Daimler-Puch (SDP) *Jagdpanzer SK 105.*

- *Cal.:* 7.62 x 51mm NATO
  *Common Name:* M134 high rate of fire MG (Minigun)

  *Remarks:* US origin.

- *Cal.:* 7.62 x 63mm
  *Common Name:* M37 AMG

  *Remarks:* US origin. FMS delivered 26 before 1975 and 197 in 1976. Some M1919A4 and M1917A1 machine guns of US origin are reported still to be in the inventory.

- *Cal.:* 7.62 x 54mmR
  *Common Name:* SGMT armor MG

  *Remarks:* Soviet origin. Mounted on older Soviet tanks.

- *Cal.:* 7.62 x 63mm
  *Common Name:* .30 M1918A2 BAR

  *Remarks:* US origin.

- *Cal.:* 7.62 x 63mm
  *Common Name:* .30 M1919A4
  LMG

*Remarks:* US origin. There also may be some M1917A1 water-cooled medium machine guns still in the inventory.

- *Cal.:* 12.7 x 99mm
  *Common Name:* .50 M2 HB
  HMG

*Remarks:* US and FN origin. FMS delivered 537 in 1975 and 132 for the M1 tank cupola in 1976. FN received an order for 250 in 1982. Saco Defense Division of Maremont Corporation sold an unspecified number of M2s to Morocco in 1986. NAPCO sold 375 Saco M2 HBs in 1987.

- *Cal.:* 12.7 x 108mm
  *Common Name:* DShK38/46
  HMG

*Remarks:* Soviet origin. Mounted on older Soviet tanks.

**AUTOMATIC CANNON:**
- *Cal.:* 14.5 x 114mm
  *Common Name:* KPV HMG

*Remarks:* East Bloc origin. The common versions, which were captured from Polisario rebels, are the ZPU-2 and the ZPU-4. Other versions may be in service.

- *Cal.:* 20 x 102mm
  *Common Name:* 20mm M168 Vulcan cannon on the M167 and the M163 SP Vulcan Air Defense System (VADS)

*Remarks:* US origin. Exact number unknown. In 1979 40 of the M163A1 SP systems and 40 of the M167A1 towed versions were made available as part of a Carter administration aid package.

- *Cal.:* 20 x 102mm
  *Common Name:* M621 automatic cannon

*Remarks:* Groupment Industriel des Armements Terrestres (GIAT), France. In April 1983 Moroccan armed forces received 12 Gazelle helicopters, and each one mounted a single GIAT M621 cannon. The Moroccans also have the VAB 6 x 6 vehicle with the twin AA system.

### Weapons Used by Antigovernment Forces

The basic antigovernment armed force is the group known as POLISARIO (Front Populaire pour la Libération du Sakiet al-Hamra et du Rio de Oro); i.e., the Western Sahara. This organization, with about 4,000 regulars, is recognized by the Ethiopian government and is aligned with Mauritania. Weapons used by POLISARIO troops include: 7.62 x 39mm AK47 and AKM assault rifles (specifically the Romanian model); 7.62 x 51mm NATO French NF 1 (AAT 52) GPMGs; 7.62 x 54mmR RP46 and PK series machine guns; 12.7 x 99mm M2 HB and 12.7 x 108mm DShK HMGs; and 14.5 x 114mm KPV automatic cannon. MG42-type machine guns of an unspecified caliber are also in service.

## MOZAMBIQUE (People's Republic of)

Population (estimate in 1984): 13.41 million. Ground forces: Forças Populares de Libertação de Moçambique—FPLM regulars, variously estimated between 24,000 and 50,000; reserves, People's militia, ca. 30,000; paramilitary border guards, ca. 6,000. There is a national police *(Serviço Nacional de Segurança Popular)* of unspecified size. The revolutionary Marxist government (it grew out of the *Frente de Libertação de Moçambique*—FRELIMO), which came to power in 1975, still employs many Portuguese small arms. Soviet, East German, North Korean, Czechoslovakian, and Cuban (ca. 2,500) advisors are active in Mozambique, thus it is possible that newer pattern East Bloc small arms may be in use. Military aid has been received from Libya, Ethiopia, and the People's Republic of China. Those weapons listed are confirmed. There may be as many as 12,000 friendly troops from Zimbabwe.

**HANDGUNS:**

• *Cal.:* 7.62 x 25mm
*Common Name:* Tokarev pistol

*Remarks:* East Bloc origin.

• *Cal.:* 7.62 x 25mm
*Common Name:* vz.25 pistol

*Remarks:* Czechoslovakian origin.

• *Cal.:* 9 x 18mm
*Common Name:* APS (Stechkin)
machine pistol

*Remarks:* East Bloc origin.

• *Cal.:* 9 x 18mm
*Common Name:* Makarov pistol

*Remarks:* East Bloc origin.

• *Cal.:* 9 x 19mm Parabellum
*Common Name:* FN Mle. 35 GP
pistol

*Remarks:* FN origin.

• *Cal.:* 9 x 19mm Parabellum
*Common Name:* Walther P38
pistol

*Remarks:* Source unknown — Manurhin?

**SUBMACHINE GUNS:**

• *Cal.:* 7.65 x 17mm
*Common Name:* vz.61 Skorpion
submachine gun

*Remarks:* Czechoslovakian origin.

• *Cal.:* 7.62 x 25mm
*Common Name:* PPSh 41 submachine gun

*Remarks:* Soviet origin? Also used by RENAMO.

• *Cal.:* 9 x 19mm Parabellum
*Common Name:* vz.23 and vz.25
submachine guns

*Remarks:* Czechoslovakian origin.

• *Cal.:* 9 x 19mm Parabellum
*Common Name:* Star Z-45 submachine gun

*Remarks:* Star Bonafacio Echeverria, Spain.

• *Cal.:* 9 x 19mm Parabellum
*Common Name:* FMBP M48 submachine gun

*Remarks:* Portuguese origin. Nearly 100 were seized from antigovernment forces in 1984.

**RIFLES:**

• *Cal.:* 7.62 x 51mm NATO
*Common Name:* FN FAL

*Remarks:* Belgian origin. First adopted in 1959.

• *Cal.:* 7.62 x 39mm
*Common Name:* AK47/AKM assault rifles

*Remarks:* East Bloc origin. Variants used include the Hungarian AMD, East German MPiKMS72, and the Yugoslavian M64A (Mod 70AB2). Romanian folding stock AKMs have also been observed. Many of these weapons are equipped with the newer synthetic-type orange color magazines.

• *Cal.:* 7.62 x 39mm
*Common Name:* vz.58 assault rifle

*Remarks:* Czechoslovakian origin.

• *Cal.:* 7.62 x 39mm
*Common Name:* SKS carbine

*Remarks:* East Bloc origin.

• *Cal.:* 7.62 x 51mm NATO
*Common Name:* M1961 rifle (G3)

*Remarks:* FMBP origin, Portugal.

**SHOTGUNS:**

**MACHINE GUNS:**
- *Cal.:* 7.62 x 39mm
  *Common Name:* RPD LMG

  *Remarks:* East Bloc origin.

- *Cal.:* 7.62 x 39mm
  *Common Name:* RPK LMG

  *Remarks:* East Bloc origin.

- *Cal.:* 7.62 x 39mm
  *Common Name:* vz.52/57 LMG

  *Remarks:* Czechoslovakian origin.

- *Cal.:* 7.62 x 51mm NATO
  *Common Name:* vz.59N GPMG

  *Remarks:* Czechoslovakian origin.

- *Cal.:* 7.62 x 51mm NATO
  *Common Name:* FN FALO

  *Remarks:* Belgian origin. First adopted in 1959.

- *Cal.:* 7.62 x 51mm NATO
  *Common Name:* MG3 GPMG

  *Remarks:* Source unknown, probably Portugal. May actually be the MG42/59 model.

- *Cal.:* 7.62 x 54mmR
  *Common Name:* vz.53 GPMG

  *Remarks:* Czechoslovakian origin.

- *Cal.:* 7.62 x 54mmR
  *Common Name:* RP46 company machine gun

  *Remarks:* East Bloc origin. The older Soviet DP and DTM models of the Degtyarev machine guns are also still in service.

- *Cal.:* 7.62 x 54mmR
  *Common Name:* PKT armor MG

  *Remarks:* Soviet origin. Mounted on older Soviet tanks. Infantry PKs are also reported to be in service.

- *Cal.:* 7.62 x 54mmR
  *Common Name:* SGM vehicle MGs

  *Remarks:* East Bloc origin.

- *Cal.:* 7.62 x 54mmR
  *Common Name:* M1910 Maxim HMG

  *Remarks:* Soviet origin. Presumed to be OBSOLETE.

- *Cal.:* 12.7 x 108mm
  *Common Name:* DShK38/46 HMG

  *Remarks:* East Bloc origin.

**AUTOMATIC CANNON:**
- *Cal.:* 14.5 x 114mm
  *Common Name:* KPV HMG

  *Remarks:* East Bloc origin. Several different AA mounts employed.

- *Cal.:* 20 x 110mm
  *Common Name:* M55 automatic cannon

  *Remarks:* Yugoslavian origin. The M55/B1 20/3 three-gun AA system is in service.

- *Cal.:* 23 x 152mmB
  *Common Name:* ZU23 automatic cannon

  *Remarks:* East Bloc origin. Including the ZSU-23-4 self-propelled AA system.

**GRENADE LAUNCHERS:**
- *Cal.:* 30 x 29mm
  *Common Name:* AGS17 automatic granade launcher

  *Remarks:* Soviet Union origin.

### Weapons Used by Antigovernment Forces

The main antigovernment force is the Mozambican National Resistance (*Resistência Nacional Moçam-bicana — RENAMO — RNM*). The strength of the RNM (or MNR) resistance movement is variously esti-mated. One source indicates that in 1985 it had about 6,000 trained fighters and about 3,000 men in reserve. Another source estimated its fighting strength at about 12,000 in 1983–84. Yet another source in 1987 said that RENAMO numbered about 22,000 full-time guerrillas and about 7,000 part-time fighters. Some supplies in the early 1980s came from the South African government. Recent photographs have shown a large representation of Romanian small arms including the AKM assault rifle, FPK sniper rifle, and the RPK with 75-round drum-type magazine. Some Portuguese G3s are still in use, as are older weapons such as the PPSh41.

## NAMIBIA

Population (estimate in 1984): 1.11 million. Ground forces: regulars, unknown; paramilitary, unknown. Army units are equipped with small arms following the pattern of those used by the South African Army, and many are acquired directly from South Africa. Young members of the antigovernment forces of SWAPO (South West Africa People's Organization) have been shown in mid-1986 news photographs carrying 7.62 x 25mm PPSh41-type submachine guns (country of manufacture and origin unknown). The South West African Territory Forces (SWATF) have also captured East German MPiKMs from SWAPO units and caches on several occasions in 1986–87. The troops of the People's Liberation Army of Namibia (PLAN) also carry AKMs, but their origin is unknown.

**HANDGUNS:**
• *Cal.:* 9 x 20mmR                          *Remarks:* UK origin.
  *Common Name:* .38 Enfield No. 2
  revolver

**SUBMACHINE GUNS:**
• *Cal.:* 9 x 19mm Parabellum                *Remarks:* UK origin.
  *Common Name:* L2A3 subma-
  chine gun

**RIFLES:**
• *Cal.:* 7.62 x 51mm NATO                   *Remarks:* FN origin.
  *Common Name:* FN FAL

• *Cal.:* 7.62 x 39mm                         *Remarks:* Source unknown. The South African 32nd Battalion stationed
  *Common Name:* AK47 and AKM                 in Namibia is equipped almost exclusively with Soviet AKs and other
  assault rifles                             equipment.

**SHOTGUNS:**

**MACHINE GUNS:**
• *Cal.:* 7.62 x 51mm NATO                   *Remarks:* UK origin?
  *Common Name:* L4A4 Bren LMG

**AUTOMATIC CANNON:**

## NEPAL (Kingdom of)

Population (estimate in 1984): 16.58 million. Ground forces: regulars, ca. 25,000; paramilitary, ca. 15,000 police. Nepalese Army units are equipped with small arms following the pattern of those used by the Indian Army, and many are acquired directly from India.

**HANDGUNS:**
* *Cal.:* 9 x 19mm NATO           *Remarks:* Origin uncertain.
  *Common Name:* FN Mle. 1935 GP
  pistol

**SUBMACHINE GUNS:**
* *Cal.:* 9 x 19mm NATO           *Remarks:* Indian origin.
  *Common Name:* L2A3 subma-
  chine gun

**RIFLES:**
* *Cal.:* 7.62 x 51mm NATO         *Remarks:* Indian origin.
  *Common Name:* L1A1 rifle

**SHOTGUNS:**

**MACHINE GUNS:**
* *Cal.:* 7.62 x 51mm NATO         *Remarks:* UK origin via India?
  *Common Name:* L4A4 Bren LMG

* *Cal.:* 7.62 x 51mm NATO         *Remarks:* UK origin via India?
  *Common Name:* L7A1 GPMG

**AUTOMATIC CANNON:**

## NETHERLANDS (Kingdom of)

Population (estimate in 1980): 14.37 million. Ground forces: regulars, 75,000 (conscripts, 43,000); reserves, 140,000+; paramilitary, 3,855 in the *Koninklijke Marechausse* (Royal Military Constabulary); the state police *(Rijkspolitie)* is about 6,300 strong; and the municipal police *(Gemeentepolitie)* has about 19,500 personnel.

**HANDGUNS:**
* *Cal.:* 9 x 19mm NATO           *Remarks:* Walther, West Germany. Between 30,000 and 50,000 purchased for
  *Common Name:* Walther P5     the gendarmerie.

* *Cal.:* 9 x 19mm NATO           *Remarks:* Heckler & Koch (HK), GmbH. Used by Dutch special forces.
  *Common Name:* HK P9S

* *Cal.:* 9 x 19mm NATO           *Remarks:* Belgian and Canadian origin. FN high-powers purchased before
  *Common Name:* FN Mle. 1935 GP   1950 and again 1958–61.
  pistol

* *Cal.:* 9 x 29mmR Magnum       *Remarks:* US origin. Have been replaced by HK P9S. NSN 1005-17-600-
  *Common Name:* .357 Magnum   3378?
  Smith & Wesson Model 19 re-
  volvers

- *Cal.:* 9 x 29mmR Magnum
  *Common Name:* .357 Magnum Colt Python revolvers, with 102mm barrels

*Remarks:* US origin. Will be replaced by HK P9S.

- *Cal.:* 11.43 x 23mm
  *Common Name:* .45 M1911A1 pistols

*Remarks:* US origin. MAP provided 1,200 before 1965. OBSOLETE.

- *Cal.:* 7.65 x 17mm and 9 x 17mm
  *Common Name:* FN Model 1910 pistol

*Remarks:* FN origin. NSN for the 7.65mm version is 1005-17-028-2878. OBSOLETE; formerly used by the police.

- *Cal.:* 7.65 x 17mm
  *Common Name:* FN Model 1910/22 pistol

*Remarks:* FN origin. OBSOLETE; formerly used by the police.

**SUBMACHINE GUNS:**
- *Cal.:* 9 x 19mm NATO
  *Official Name: Pistoolmitrailleur Uzi*
  *Common Name:* Uzi submachine gun

*Remarks:* Israeli Military Industries (IMI) origin. NSN 1005-17-054-7823 w/ wood stock? NSN 1005-17-031-8948 w/ metal folding stock. Also NSN 1005-17-005-7111; 1005-17-660-1211 (M61); 1005-17-660-1212 (M61 *Exercitie*); and 1005-17-060-2616.

**A Royal Netherlands Marine stands guard during winter exercises armed with a 9 x 19mm Uzi submachine gun. (NATO)**

• *Cal.:* 9 x 19mm NATO
*Common Name:* MP5 submachine gun

*Remarks:* HK origin. All variants.

**RIFLES:**
• *Cal.:* 7.62 x 51mm NATO
*Official Name:* 7,62mm *Het licht automatisch geweer* (Fal) Model 2
*Common Name:* FN FAL

*Remarks:* Belgian origin. Adopted in 1961. NSNs 1005-17-660-2617; 1005-17-660-2615 (BN 507).

The exercise models *(Geweer Exercitie)* are NSN 1005-17-023-9395 and 1005-17-640-0147.

• *Cal.:* 7.62 x 51mm NATO
*Official Name:* 7,62mm *Het scherpschuttersgeweer* (Fal) Model 2, *met kijker OIP/Fal*
*Common Name:* FN FAL sniper rifle

*Remarks:* Belgian origin. Adopted in 1961. These rifles are fitted with OIP telescope; i.e., Belgian Army telescope made by Société Belge d'Optique et d'Instruments de Precision (OIP).

• *Cal.:* 7.62 x 51mm NATO
*Common Name:* 7.62mm FN Mauser sniper rifle

*Remarks:* Belgian origin. Used by the Dutch police. Began surplussing these rifles in 1987–88. Being replaced by the HK PSG1 sniper rifle.

• *Cal.:* 7.62 x 51mm NATO
*Common Name:* 7.62mm HK PSG1 sniper rifle

*Remarks:* West German origin. Used by the Dutch police. Acquired late 1987–early 1988.

• *Cal.:* 7.62 x 51mm NATO
*Common Name:* 7.62mm SSG

*Remarks:* Steyr-Daimler-Puch (SDP). NSN 1005-17-055-9546.

• *Cal.:* 5.56 x 45mm
*Common Name:* HK33SG1 sniper rifle

*Remarks:* HK origin. Used by police snipers.

• *Cal.:* 7.62 x 33mm
*Common Name:* .30 M1 and M2 carbine

*Remarks:* US origin. MAP and FMS provided nearly 170,000 before 1965. Many of these have been declared surplus and sold. They are still in service with police organizations.

• *Cal.:* 6.5 x 54mmR
*Official Name:* 6,5mm *Geweer No. 1*
*Common Name:* 6.5mm M95 Dutch Mannlicher rifle

*Remarks:* Domestic rifle. NSN 1005-17-049-3800 and 1005-17-053-7529.

• *Cal.:* 7.62 x 63mm
*Official Name: Geweer, M1*
*Common Name:* .30 M1 rifle

*Remarks:* US origin. MAP and FMS provided nearly 91,000 M1 rifles before 1975. These are presumed to be OBSOLETE. Some M1D sniper rifles may still be in service. The M1 *Exercitie* (exercise) is NSN 1005-17-049-4533 and 1005-17-051-4070.

• *Cal.:* 7.7 x 56mmR
*Common Name:* .303 Enfield rifle

*Remarks:* UK origin. NSN 1005-17-614-5322. OBSOLETE.

• *Cal.:* 7.92 x 57mm
*Common Name:* Model 98 Mauser rifle with short barrel

*Remarks:* OBSOLETE; formerly used by the gendarmerie. Made by FN in 1947–48.

**SHOTGUNS:**
• *Cal.:* 18.5 x 59mm
*Official Name:* Jachtgeweer Kal. 12
*Common Name:* 12 gage shotgun SKB 500

*Remarks:* NSN 1005-17-050-7318.

- *Cal.:* 18.5 x 59mm
  *Official Name:* Jachtgeweer Kal.
  12
  *Common Name:* 12 gage Magnum
  shotgun

  *Remarks:* NSN 1005-17-802-4672.

- *Cal.:* 18.5 x 59mm
  *Official Name:* Jachtgeweer Kal.
  12
  *Common Name:* 12 gage Mondial
  Model 1204 Mod 107 shotgun

  *Remarks:* NSN 1005-17-804-2310.

- *Cal.:* 18.5 x 59mm
  *Official Name:* Jachtgeweer Kal.
  12; Leswapen
  *Common Name:* 12 gage training
  shotgun

  *Remarks:* NSN 1005-17-608-3285.

**MACHINE GUNS:**

- *Cal.:* 7.62 x 51mm NATO
  *Official Name:* 7,62mm *Het zwarr
  automatisch geweer* (Falo)
  *Common Name:* FN FALO

  *Remarks:* Belgian origin. Adopted in 1961.

- *Cal.:* 7.62 x 51mm NATO
  *Official Name:* 7,62mm *Mitrailleur*
  *Common Name:* FN MAG

  *Remarks:* Belgian origin. MAG (AN 606) with equipment is NSN 1005-17-033-6259; w/o equipment 1005-17-033-6258. The MAG coaxial (Mod. KM) is NSN 1005-17-046-9992. Coax is also 1005-17-029-1264 and 1005-17-029-1265. The drill purpose MAG (MADV2-*Leswapen*) is NSN 1005-17-052-9757. Also NSN 1005-17-640-0312 (AN 528); 1005-17-640-0317; AN 528.

- *Cal.:* 7.62 x 63mm
  *Common Name:* .30 M1919A4
  LMG

  *Remarks:* US origin. MAP provided 791 before 1965.

- *Cal.:* 7.7 x 56mmR
  *Common Name:* .303 MK 2 Bren
  gun

  *Remarks:* UK origin. NSN 1005-17-611-5463 (AN-095MK2). Also NSN 1005-17-049-3973.

- *Cal.:* 12.7 x 99mm
  *Common Name:* .50 M2 HB
  HMG

  *Remarks:* US origin. The Dutch have several models in service. The M2 HB is NSN 1005-17-608-4074. Other models include 1005-17-027-2947 (AN 537); 1005-17-042-2978 (AN 059, left-hand hand feed) 1005-17-042-2979 (AN 059, right-hand hand feed); 1005-17-046-9936 (KLUM02-1-1-1-003B1); 1005-17-804-2356 (KLUM02-1-1-1-003B2); 1005-17-600-3225 AN 059); 1005-17-600-3227 (AN 059); 1005-17-605-1610 (AN 358); 1005-17-702-8090; 1005-17-710-4321; 1005-17-710-3422 (AN 540). MAP provided 80 M2s prior to 1965. Presently the Dutch army has about 90 of the M55 AA systems in service. In the early 1980s Ramo, Inc. delivered 800 kits for the M2 HB that allow the gun to fire plastic training ammunition.

**AUTOMATIC CANNON:**

- *Cal.:* 20 x 110mm RB
  *Official Name: Kanon, 20mm*
  *Common Name:* 20mm MK16
  automatic cannon

  *Remarks:* US Navy origin. NSN 1005-17-029-5946. The electrical training model *(Electrischdemonstratiemodell)* 1005-17-029-4819.

- *Cal.:* 25 x 137mm
  *Common Name:* KBA (TRW
  6425) automatic cannon

  *Remarks:* Oerlikon-Buhrle. NSN 1005-17-045-5339 (AN 517). With equipment NSN 1005-17-048-5377. Also NSN 1005-17-046-2566 (KBA); 1005-17-051-8295; and 1005-17-051-8296.

**SIGNAL GUNS:**
- *Cal.:* 26.5mm (?)
  *Official Name:* Lucht Pistool
  *Common Name:* Walther P53 signal pistol

*Remarks:* Carl Walther, Ulm, West Germany. NSN 1005-17-608-3337.

## Nederlandsche Wapen Munitiefabriek N.V. (NWM)

NWM, a private sector small arms manufacturer, has offered several small caliber weapons for international sale in the past twenty years. These have been licensed designs. Included in their licensed offerings were the 7.62mm NATO CETME Modelo 58—FOM 1005-29-2-7.62-2; and the 5.56mm Galil—FOM 1005-29-2-5.56-1—called the MN1 by the Dutch. NWM also offered for sale the 5.56mm Stoner 63 weapons family. Artillerie-Inrichtingen, a government-owned enterprise, marketed the Armalite AR-10 assault rifle internationally in the mid-1960s and early 1970s after an unsuccessful bid to equip the Dutch army with this rifle.

# NEW ZEALAND

Population (estimate in 1984): 3.24 million. Ground forces: regulars, ca. 5,600; reserves, 1,500; territorial army, 6,000.

**HANDGUNS:**
- *Cal.:* 9 x 19mm NATO
  *Official Name:* 9mm Pistol Automatic
  *Common Name:* L9A1 pistol

*Remarks:* FN origin via UK. Introduced 1964.

- *Cal.:* 9 x 19mm NATO
  *Official Name:* 9mm Pistol Automatic No. 2, MK 1
  *Common Name:* Canadian No. 2, Mark 1

*Remarks:* Canadian Inglis Browning GP.

**SUBMACHINE GUNS:**
- *Cal.:* 9 x 19mm NATO
  *Official Name:* 9mm Submachine Gun L9A1
  *Common Name:* L2A3 submachine gun

*Remarks:* UK origin. Issued to armored fighting vehicle crews.

- *Cal.:* 9 x 19mm NATO
  *Common Name:* MP5 submachine gun

*Remarks:* Heckler & Koch (HK) GmbH.

**RIFLES:**
- *Cal.:* 5.56 x 56mm
  *Common Name:* .220 Model 70? sniper rifle

- *Cal.:* 5.56 x 45mm NATO
  *Common Name:* Steyr AUG A1

*Remarks:* Steyr, Austria. Early in 1987 the New Zealand Army announced standardization of the AUG. This weapon will be produced in Australia with some participation of New Zealand manufacturers. The initial procurement will be 18,000 rifles. Major reason for selecting this over the M16A2 rifle was to maintain compatibility of infantry weapons with those of the Australian armed forces.

The 9 x 19mm FN Browning High Power (GP) pistol has been standard with New Zealand forces since 1964. (New Zealand MOD)

• *Cal.:* 7.62 x 51mm NATO
  *Official Name:* 7.62mm Rifle, L1A1
  *Common Name:* L1A1 rifle

*Remarks:* Commonwealth Small Arms Factory, Lithgow, Australia.

• *Cal.:* 7.62 x 51mm NATO
  *Official Name:* 7.62mm Rifle, M82
  *Common Name:* M82 sniper rifle

*Remarks:* Parker-Hale, UK.

• *Cal.:* 7.62 x 63mm
  *Common Name:* .30 M1 rifle

*Remarks:* US origin. FMS delivered 1,998 before 1975.

• *Cal.:* 5.56 x 45mm
  *Official Name:* 5.56mm Rifle, M16A1
  *Common Name:* M16A1 rifle

*Remarks:* Colt, US. Limited issue to special troops. Introduced in 1967.

**SHOTGUNS:**

**The US 5.56 x 45mm M16A1 rifle with 40 x 46 M203 grenade launcher has been a standard weapon in New Zealand since 1968. It will be replaced by Australian-made Steyr AUGs. (New Zealand MOD)**

**As with many Commonwealth nations, the 7.62 x 51mm NATO FN MAG (L7 series) has been the standard GPMG since 1964. (New Zealand MOD)**

**MACHINE GUNS:**
- *Cal.:* 7.62 x 51mm NATO
  *Official Name:* 7.62mm Rifle Automatic L2A1
  *Common Name:* L2A1 automatic rifle

  *Remarks:* Lithgow, Australia.

- *Cal.:* 7.62 x 51mm NATO
  *Official Name:* 7.62mm Light Machine Gun, L4A4
  *Common Name:* L4A4 Bren LMG

  *Remarks:* Royal Small Arms Factory (RSAF), Enfield.

- *Cal.:* 7.62 x 51mm NATO
  *Official Name:* 7.62mm General Purpose Machine Gun, L7A1
  *Common Name:* L7A1 series GPMG

  *Remarks:* RSAF. Introduced 1964. The L7A2 has been purchased from **FN.**

- *Cal.:* 12.7 x 99mm
  *Official Name:* Machine Gun 0.5 inch M2
  *Common Name:* .50 M2 HB HMG

  *Remarks:* US origin. Used on armored vehicles only. FMS delivered 12 in 1973.

**AUTOMATIC CANNON:**

**GRENADE LAUNCHERS:**
- *Cal.:* 40 x 46mmSR
  *Official Name:* 40mm Grenade Launcher M79
  *Common Name:* M79 grenade launcher

  *Remarks:* US origin.

- *Cal.:* 40 x 46mmSR
  *Official Name:* 40mm Grenade Launcher M203
  *Common Name:* M203 grenade launcher mounted on M16A1

  *Remarks:* US origin. Introduced 1968.

# NICARAGUA (Republic of)

Population (estimate in 1984): 2.91 million. Ground forces: regulars, ca. 60,000; border guards, 5,000; paramilitary "Sandinista" militia, ca. 50,000+ ; reserves, 12,000 on active duty. The number of East Bloc small arms has increased during the past several years.

**HANDGUNS:**
- *Cal.:* 9 x 18mm Makarov
  *Common Name:* PM

  *Remarks:* East Bloc origin.

- *Cal.:* 9 x 19mm NATO
  *Common Name:* FN Mle. 35 GP pistol

  *Remarks:* FN. Purchased 1958–61.

- *Cal.:* 9 x 29mmR
  *Common Name:* .38 Colt Detective Special revolver

  *Remarks:* US origin. MAP provided 604 in 1974 and FMS provided 431 in 1976. NSN 1005-00-726-5786.

- *Cal.:* 9 x 29mmR
  *Common Name:* .38 Smith & Wesson revolver

  *Remarks:* US origin.

- *Cal.:* 11.43 x 23mm
  *Common Name:* .45 M1911A1 pistol

  *Remarks:* US origin.

**SUBMACHINE GUNS:**
- *Cal.:* 7.62 x 25mm
  *Common Name:* PPSh41 submachine gun

  *Remarks:* East Bloc origin.

- *Cal.:* 9 x 19mm Parabellum
  *Common Name:* vz.23 and vz.25 submachine guns

  *Remarks:* Czechoslovakian origin.

- *Cal.:* 9 x 19mm Parabellum
  *Common Name:* Uzi submachine gun

  *Remarks:* Origin uncertain.

- *Cal.:* 9 x 19mm Parabellum
  *Common Name:* Madsen M50 submachine gun

  *Remarks:* Dansk Industri Syndikat, Denmark.

**RIFLES:**
- *Cal.:* 5.56 x 45mm
  *Common Name:* M16A1 (Models 603 and 613) rifles

  *Remarks:* Colt sold approx. 6,000 Model 613s in 1976 to the Nicaraguan National Guard. Since the Sandinista revolution thousands of Colt Model 603s have been illicitly acquired. Although originally from the US, these rifles have come to Central America from the M16A1s left behind in Vietnam by the US military.

- *Cal.:* 5.56 x 45mm
  *Common Name:* Galil rifle

  *Remarks:* Israeli Military Industries (IMI), Israel. About 10,000 obtained in 1978.

- *Cal.:* 5.56 x 45mm
  *Common Name:* SG540 rifle

  *Remarks:* Manurhin-made SIG rifle.

- *Cal.:* 7.62 x 33mm
  *Common Name:* .30 M1 and M2 carbines

  *Remarks:* US origin. MAP provided 121 before 1963.

- *Cal.:* 7.62 x 39mm
  *Common Name:* AK47 and AKM assault rifles

  *Remarks:* East Bloc origin via Cuba and Libya. Several variants are used, including Soviet AKMS and East German MPiKMS-72.

- *Cal.:* 7.62 x 39mm
  *Common Name:* SKS carbine

  *Remarks:* East bloc origin. Ceremonial purposes.

- *Cal.:* 7.62 x 39mm
  *Common Name:* vz.52/57 rifle

  *Remarks:* Czechoslovakian origin. Probably some 7.62 x 45mm versions as well.

- *Cal.:* 7.62 x 51mm NATO
  *Common Name:* AR-10 rifle

  *Remarks:* Armalite, Inc., US, or Artillerie-Inrichtingen, Netherlands during Somoza era.

- *Cal.:* 7.62 x 51mm NATO
  *Common Name:* FN FAL

  *Remarks:* FALs are former Cuban issue delivered to Nicaragua.

- *Cal.:* 7.62 x 54mmR
  *Common Name:* M44 Mosin bolt action rifle

  *Remarks:* East Bloc origin. Militia units only.

- *Cal.:* 7.62 x 54mmR
  *Common Name:* SVD sniper rifle

  *Remarks:* East Bloc origin.

**A member of the force led by former Contra leader Eden Pastore (Commander Zero) ca. 1983 holds a US 7.62 x 51mm M14 fitted with an ART-type scope. (De Caro)**

**SHOTGUNS:**
- *Cal.:* 18.5 x 59mm
  *Common Name:* Model 12 Winchester shotgun

  *Remarks:* US origin. MAP provided 32 in 1970. NSN 1005-00-677-9150.

- *Cal.:* 18.5 x 59mm
  *Common Name:* Model 500 Mossberg shotgun

  *Remarks:* US origin. Acquired in 1977–79.

**MACHINE GUNS:**
- *Cal.:* 7.62 x 39mm
  *Common Name:* RPD LMG

  *Remarks:* Soviet origin.

- *Cal.:* 7.62 x 39mm
  *Common Name:* RPK LMG

  *Remarks:* East Bloc origin.

- *Cal.:* 7.62 x 51mm NATO
  *Common Name:* M60 GPMG

  *Remarks:* US origin.

- *Cal.:* 7.62 x 51mm NATO
  *Common Name:* MAG GPMG

  *Remarks:* FN origin. MAG turret mount (60-30), T9 using nondisintegrating links.

- *Cal.:* 7.62 x 54mmR
  *Common Name:* DP and RP46 LMG

  *Remarks:* Soviet origin.

- *Cal.:* 7.62 x 54mmR
  *Common Name:* SGMT armor MG

  *Remarks:* Soviet origin. Mounted on older Soviet tanks.

- *Cal.:* 7.62 x 54mmR
  *Common Name:* PKT armor MG

  *Remarks:* Soviet origin. Mounted on Soviet tanks.

- *Cal.:* 7.62 x 63mm
  *Common Name:* .30 M1919A4/AG Browning machine gun

  *Remarks:* US origin. MAP provided 26 before 1964.

- *Cal.:* 12.7 x 99mm
  *Common Name:* .50 M2 HB HMG

  *Remarks:* US origin.

- *Cal.:* 12.7 x 108mm
  *Common Name:* DShK38/46 HMG

  *Remarks:* Soviet origin. Mounted on older Soviet tanks.

**AUTOMATIC CANNON:**
- *Cal.:* 14.5 x 114mm
  *Common Name:* KPV HMG

  *Remarks:* East Bloc origin. Some 120 ZPU-1 AA mounts and an unknown quantity of ZPU-4 AA mounts. Other versions probably in service.

- *Cal.:* 23 x 152mmB
  *Common Name:* ZU23 automatic

  *Remarks:* East Bloc origin. ZSU-2 cannon and other versions used for antiaircraft artillery.

**GRENADE LAUNCHERS:**
- *Cal.:* 30 x 29mm
  *Common Name:* AGS-17 grenade launcher

  *Remarks:* Soviet automatic grenade launcher.

- *Cal.:* 40 x 46mmR
  *Common Name:* M79 grenade launcher

  *Remarks:* US origin. MAP delivered 64 in 1967.

**Small Arms Used by Antigovernment *(Contra)* Forces**

Small arms seen in news and television photographs include:

Con esta arma se puede efectuar el tiro
directo o indirecto (parabólico), tanto
por ráfagas cortas de hasta 5 disparos,
como por ráfagas largas de hasta 10
disparos ininterrumpidamente.

## DATOS BALISTICOS Y ESTRUCTURALES

| | | |
|---|---|---|
| Fabricación | : | Soviética |
| Calibre | : | 30 mm. |
| Peso | : | Aprox. 40 lbs. (sin trípode). Aprox. 68 lbs. (con trípode). |
| Longitud | : | 84 cms. |
| Distancia del tiro de puntería | : | 1,700 mts. |
| Cadencia de fuego: | | 350-400 (máximo por minuto). 50-100 (mínimo por minuto). |
| Capacidad de la caja de municiones | : | 29 granadas |
| Radio de destrucción masiva | : | 7 mts. (mínimo) |

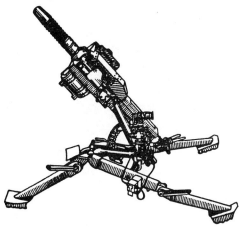

Vista general del lanzagranadas automático de 30 mm.,
AGS-17

### DESARME Y ARME DE CAMPAÑA

Este tipo de desarme se realiza para
limpiar, engrasar e inspeccionar el lan-

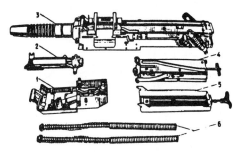

PIEZAS Y MECANISMOS PRINCIPALES:

1- Receptor; 2- Mecanismo disparador a percusión; 3-
Tubo; 4- Cierre; 5- Tapa del cajón de mecanismos con
mecanismos de recarga; 6- Muelles recuperadores.

zagranadas. El desarme excesivamente fre-
cuente es perjudicial ya que acelera el
desgaste de las piezas y mecanismos.

El desarme y arme debe realizarse sobre
una mesa o superficie limpia, empleando
las herramientas propias del arma. Al
separar o acoplar las piezas no se deben
aplicar esfuerzos excesivos ni golpes
bruscos.

Antes del desarme es necesario:

- Separar el aparato de puntería, gi-
  rando la manija excéntrica de iz-
  quierda a derecha y desplazando
  el aparato de puntería a la izquier-
  da.

- Separar la caja de municiones, apre-
  tando por abajo el trinquete y ele-
  vando la caja por el asa.

- Cerciorarse que la recámara esté
  vacía.

### ORDEN DEL DESARME

1.-Separar el receptor del cajón de mecanismos. Presionar sobre los trin-
   quetes y abrir el receptor, girándo-
   lo hacia adelante hasta ponerlo en
   los fijadores: girar el transporta-
   dor con el eje del receptor aproxi-
   madamente a 45º y, balanceando sua-
   vemente el receptor y el transporta-

**RIFLES:**
• *Cal.:* 5.56 x 45mm
  *Common Name:* M16 rifle

• *Cal.:* 7.62 x 33mm
  *Common Name:* M1 and M2 carbines

• *Cal.:* 7.62 x 39mm
  *Common Name:* AKM assault rifle

• *Cal.:* 7.62 x 51mm NATO
  *Common Name:* M14 rifle

• *Cal.:* 7.62 x 51mm NATO
  *Common Name:* FAL rifle

**MACHINE GUNS:**
• *Cal.:* 7.62 x 39mm
  *Common Name:* RPD LMG

• *Cal.:* 7.62 x 51mm NATO
  *Common Name:* M60 GPMG

• *Cal.:* 12.7 x 108mm
  *Common Name:* DShKM HMG

*Remarks:* Both rifles and the Model 653 carbine.

*Remarks:* Romanian models have been seen in news reports.


# NIGER (Republic of)

Population (estimate in 1984): 6.28 million. Ground forces: regulars, ca. 2,150; paramilitary, *Gendarmerie Nationale du Niger,* 1,500; *Garde Republicaine,* 1,100; *Garde Presidentielle,* 160; plus the *Surete Nationale* (national police) of unspecified size, 1,800.

**HANDGUNS:**
• *Cal.:* 7.65 x 17mm Browning
  *Common Name:* Walther PP pistol

• *Cal.:* 9 x 19mm NATO
  *Common Name:* MAB PA-15 pistol

• *Cal.:* 9 x 29mmR
  *Common Name:* .357 Manurhin MR 73 revolver

**SUBMACHINE GUNS:**
• *Cal.:* 9 x 19mm NATO
  *Common Name:* MAT 49 submachine gun

• *Cal.:* 9 x 19mm NATO
  *Common Name:* MP5 submachine gun

• *Cal.:* 9 x 19mm Parabellum
  *Common Name:* Uzi submachine gun

*Remarks:* Walther design made by Manurhin in France.

*Remarks:* Manufacture d'Armes de Bayonne (MAB).

*Remarks:* Made by Manurhin in France.

*Remarks:* Manufacture Nationale d'Armes de Tulle (MAT).

*Remarks:* Heckler & Koch (HK), Germany.

*Remarks:* Origin unknown.

## RIFLES:

• *Cal.:* 7.5 x 54mm
*Common Name:* MAS36 bolt action rifle

*Remarks:* Manufacture Nationale d'Armes de St. Etienne (MAS).

• *Cal.:* 7.5 x 54mm
*Common Name:* MAS49/56 rifle

*Remarks:* MAS.

• *Cal.:* 7.62 x 51mm NATO
*Common Name: Gewehr 3*

*Remarks:* HK design produced by MAS.

• *Cal.:* 7.62 x 51mm NATO
*Common Name:* M14 rifle

*Remarks:* US origin. FMS program provided 172 in 1983.

## SHOTGUNS:

## MACHINE GUNS:

• *Cal.:* 7.5 x 54mm
*Common Name:* MAC Mle. 24/29 LMG

*Remarks:* Manufacture Nationale d'Armes de Chatellerault (MAC).

• *Cal.:* 7.5 x 54mm
*Common Name:* AA 52 GPMG

*Remarks:* Groupment Industriel des Armement Terrestres (GIAT), France.

• *Cal.:* 7.62 x 51mm NATO
*Common Name:* HK11 LMG

*Remarks:* HK?

• *Cal.:* 7.62 x 51mm NATO
*Common Name:* HK21 LMG

*Remarks:* HK?

• *Cal.:* 12.7 x 99mm
*Common Name:* .50 M2 HB HMG

*Remarks:* US origin.

## AUTOMATIC CANNON:

• *Cal.:* 20 x 139mm
*Common Name: Canon Mitrailleur 20 F2* (M693)

*Remarks:* GIAT, France. These 20mm guns are mounted on the M3 VDA SP AA system. About 10 of these vehicles are in service with Niger forces.

# NIGERIA (Federal Republic of)

Population (estimate in 1984): 88.15 million. Ground forces: regulars, ca. 180,000; reserves, limited number, ca. 10,000. A wide variety of Western and East Bloc small arms are still left over from the Nigerian civil war of 1967–70. Current standard small arms held in the inventory (not all are actually issued to troops) include the following:

## HANDGUNS:

• *Cal.:* 7.65 x 17mm Browning
*Common Name:* FN Model 1910 pistol

*Remarks:* FN-made pistols still used by officials of the Nigerian National Intelligence Agency.

• *Cal.:* 9 x 19mm Parabellum
*Common Name:* FN Mle. 1935 GP pistol

*Remarks:* Belgian origin. Licensed by FN to manufacture this pistol. It is not known if they have actually made this weapon.

• *Cal.:* 9 x 19mm Parabellum
*Common Name:* Beretta M951 pistol

*Remarks:* Italian origin.

- *Cal.:* 9 x 19mm Parabellum
  *Common Name:* P220 pistol

- *Cal.:* 9 x 19mm Parabellum
  *Common Name:* P38 pistol

- *Cal.:* 7.62 x 25mm
  *Common Name:* vz.52 pistol

- *Cal.:* 9 x 20mmR
  *Common Name:* .38 Enfield No. 2
  revolvers

- *Cal.:* 9 x 20mmR
  *Common Name:* .38 Webley MK
  IV revolvers

**SUBMACHINE GUNS:**
- *Cal.:* 9 x 19mm Parabellum
  *Common Name:* Sterling Mark 4
  submachine gun

- *Cal.:* 9 x 19mm Parabellum
  *Common Name:* Beretta M12 submachine gun

- *Cal.:* 9 x 19mm Parabellum
  *Common Name:* Beretta M38/48
  (Model 4) submachine gun

- *Cal.:* 9 x 19mm Parabellum
  *Common Name:* MP5A3 submachine guns

- *Cal.:* 9 x 19mm Parabellum
  *Common Name:* Uzi submachine
  guns

- *Cal.:* 9 x 19mm Parabellum
  *Common Name:* vz.23 and vz.25
  submachine guns

- *Cal.:* 9 x 19mm Parabellum
  *Common Name:* LF57 submachine gun

- *Cal.:* 9 x 19mm Parabellum
  *Common Name:* British Sten guns

**RIFLES:**
- *Cal.:* 5.56 x 45mm
  *Common Name:* SG540 rifle

- *Cal.:* 5.56 x 45mm
  *Common Name:* M16A1 rifle

- *Cal.:* 5.56 x 45mm
  *Common Name:* AR-18 rifle

- *Cal.:* 5.56 x 45mm
  *Common Name:* AR70/223 rifle

- *Cal.:* 5.56 x 45mm
  *Common Name:* FNC rifle

*Remarks:* Sauer-made SIG pistol.

*Remarks:* In March of 1986 Walther of West Germany was holding 6,000 P38s they had manufactured for Nigeria. The Nigerians were refusing to accept these handguns. Probably lacked hard currency to pay for the pistols.

*Remarks:* Czechoslovakian origin via Romania.

*Remarks:* UK origin.

*Remarks:* UK origin.

*Remarks:* Sterling Armament Co., UK.

*Remarks:* Italian origin. The Nigerians have a license to assemble this weapon at the Kaduna Ordnance Factory of the Defence Industries Corporation (DICON). Many seen in service with parkerized refinished exterior.

*Remarks:* Italian origin. Used by the Nigerian police.

*Remarks:* Heckler & Koch (HK) origin. These appear to be the newest submachine guns in the Nigerian inventory.

*Remarks:* Origin unknown.

*Remarks:* Czechoslovakian origin.

*Remarks:* Luigi Franchi, Italy.

*Remarks:* OBSOLETE; may still be held in reserve.

*Remarks:* Manurhin-made SIG rifle.

*Remarks:* South Korean origin. Being acquired by the Nigerian police.

*Remarks:* In use by police forces, especially around Lagos, but source is unknown.

*Remarks:* Beretta, Italy. In use with the Nigerian police forces.

*Remarks:* FN. Used by the Nigerian army and police forces.

- *Cal.:* 7.62 x 51mm NATO
  *Common Name:* BM59 rifle, Nigerian model. Called the Beretta

- *Cal.:* 7.62 x 51mm NATO
  *Common Name: Gewehr 3* (G3)

- *Cal.:* 7.62 x 51mm NATO
  *Common Name:* FN FAL and L1A1; also called SLR

- *Cal.:* 7.62 x 51mm NATO
  *Common Name:* Parker Hale Model 82 sniper rifle

- *Cal.:* 7.62 x 51mm NATO
  *Common Name:* Steyr SSG sniper rifle

- *Cal.:* 7.5 x 54mm
  *Common Name:* MAS 36 bolt action rifle

- *Cal.:* 7.5 x 54mm
  *Common Name:* MAS 49 rifle

- *Cal.:* 7.62 x 39mm
  *Common Name:* AK47 and AKM assault rifles

- *Cal.:* 7.62 x 39mm
  *Common Name:* vz.58 assault rifles

- *Cal.:* 7.62 x 33mm
  *Common Name:* .30 M1 carbine

- *Cal.:* 7.7 x 56mmR
  *Common Name:* .303 Enfield

*Remarks:* Beretta, Italy. The Nigerians have a license to assemble this weapon at the Kaduna Ordnance Factory of the Defence Industries Corporation.

*Remarks:* HK design assembled by the Royal Ordnance Factory at Enfield.

*Remarks:* Belgian origin. Adopted 1967. Also British L1A1s. The Nigerians have had a license to assemble this weapon since 1977 at the Kaduna Ordnance Factory of the Defence Industries Corporation but they apparently have not built any.

*Remarks:* These weapons have been introduced recently by the British SAS advisors who are training Nigerian troops in their use. About a dozen are in service.

*Remarks:* These weapons are the older version of the Steyr-Daimler-Puch (SDP) SSG with the double set trigger.

*Remarks:* Manufacture Nationale d'Armes de Guerre (MAS).

*Remarks:* MAS.

*Remarks:* Soviet and East Bloc origin. Most Kalashnikovs appear to have been removed from service. It is reported that those weapons have been given to Afghan rebel forces.

*Remarks:* Czechoslovakian origin. These were used by Biafran troops during the Civil War in the mid-1960s. There may still be some in country.

*Remarks:* US origin. FMS program delivered 100 in 1975.

*Remarks:* A variety of British Enfield rifles are still in service, including Mark IIIs, No. 4 rifles, and No. 5 carbines.

*Note:* There are reports that the 5.56mm Steyr AUG and the 7.62mm NATO CETME Model 58 rifles are also in use by Nigerian forces. This has not been confirmed.

**SHOTGUNS:**

**MACHINE GUNS:**
- *Cal.:* 5.56 x 45mm
  *Common Name:* AUG LMG

- *Cal.:* 7.62 x 39mm
  *Common Name:* RPD LMG

- *Cal.:* 7.62 x 39mm
  *Common Name:* RPK LMG

- *Cal.:* 7.62 x 51mm NATO
  *Common Name:* BM59 rifle squad automatic weapon version of the BM59 rifle

- *Cal.:* 7.62 x 51mm NATO
  *Common Name:* L4A1 and L4A4 Bren LMGs

- *Cal.:* 7.62 x 51mm NATO
  *Common Name:* HK21 LMG

*Remarks:* SDP heavy barrel squad automatic version of the AUG.

*Remarks:* East Bloc origin.

*Remarks:* East Bloc origin.

*Remarks:* Beretta, Italy.

*Remarks:* UK origin.

*Remarks:* HK design, but assembled by the Royal Ordnance Factory, Enfield. Approx. 6,000 in the inventory.

- *Cal.:* 7.62 x 51mm NATO
  *Common Name:* FN MAG

  *Remarks:* Belgium origin.

- *Cal.:* 7.62 x 51mm NATO
  *Common Name:* MG1 and MG74

  *Remarks:* West German (Rheinmetall) and Austrian (Steyr) origin. Mounted on Steyr Jagdpanzer SK 105 and other police armored vehicles. There may be some older MG42/59 still in service as well.

- *Cal.:* 7.62 x 54mmR
  *Common Name:* RP46 company machine gun

  *Remarks:* East Bloc origin.

- *Cal.:* 7.62 x 54mmR
  *Common Name:* SGMT armor MG

  *Remarks:* Soviet and Czechoslovakian origin.

- *Cal.:* 7.7 x 56mmR
  *Common Name:* .303 Bren guns

  *Remarks:* UK origin.

- *Cal.:* 12.7 x 99mm
  *Common Name:* .50 M2 HB HMG

  *Remarks:* US origin. Acquired M2s from Saco Defense Systems in 1982. Reportedly the Nigerians sought to purchase 1,000 M2 HBs. This has not been confirmed.

- *Cal.:* 12.7 x 108mm
  *Common Name:* DShK38/46 HMG

  *Remarks:* Soviet origin.

**AUTOMATIC CANNON:**
- *Cal.:* 14.5 x 114mm
  *Common Name:* KPV HMG

  *Remarks:* East Bloc origin.

- *Cal.:* 23 x 152mmB
  *Common Name:* ZU23 automatic cannon

  *Remarks:* East Bloc origin. ZSU-23-4 self-propelled AA system. 30-plus units in service.

### Nigerian Small Arms Industry

In an effort to establish a small arms and small arms ammunition manufacturing capability at the Kaduna Ordnance Factory of the Defence Industries Corporation (DICON), the Nigerian government has acquired technical assistance and licenses for the production of weapons and ammunition. From Fabrique Nationale (FN) they obtained (in 1977) a license to make the FAL. From Beretta they acquired licenses for the production of the M12 submachine gun and the BM59 rifle. Nigeria has manufactured 7.62mm NATO and 9mm NATO cartridges (cartridge headstamp is OFN = Ordnance Factory, Nigeria, near Lagos) since 1970. During the last couple of years technicians from FN, Beretta, and the West German ammunition machinery maker Fritz Werner have been employed at the arms factory providing technical assistance to and training for the Nigerian factory staff.

## NORWAY (Kingdom of)

Population (estimate in 1984): 4.15 million. Ground forces: regulars, ca. 20,000 (conscripts, 17,500); reserves, between 120,000 and 165,000. (These figures include about 90,000 Home Guard troops that can be called to duty very rapidly.)

**HANDGUNS:**
- *Cal.:* 9 x 19mm NATO
  *Official Name:* M38
  *Common Name:* P38/P1

  *Remarks:* World War II and postwar Walther manufacture.

- *Cal.:* 9 x 19mm NATO
  *Common Name:* Glock P80 pistol

- *Cal.:* 9 x 19mm NATO
  *Common Name:* P7 M8 pistol

- *Cal.:* 11.43 x 23mm
  *Official Name: M1912 and M1914*
  *Common Name:* Copy of .45
  M1911 pistol

**SUBMACHINE GUNS:**
- *Cal.:* 9 x 19mm NATO
  *Official Name: Maskin M40*
  *Common Name:* German MP40

- *Cal.:* 9 x 19mm NATO
  *Common Name:* British Sten guns

- *Cal.:* 9 x 19mm NATO
  *Common Name:* MP5A2 and
  MP5A3

*Remarks:* Glock, Austria. NSN 1005-25-133-7665.

*Remarks:* Heckler & Koch (HK), GmbH, Germany.

*Remarks:* Made in Norway. OBSOLETE.

*Remarks:* Pre-1945 manufacture. Current issue for armor crews.

*Remarks:* Pre-1945 manufacture. Exact models not known. Still current issue for armor crews.

*Remarks:* HK GmbH. Norway ordered 12,500 from Germany in 1985. The armed forces are still short of submachine guns.

**A Norwegian tank driver equipped with a 9 x 19mm MP40. (NATO)**

- *Cal.:* 9 x 19mm NATO
  *Common Name:* Suomi-37/39
  submachine gun

*Remarks:* Husqvarna, Sweden. Used by Norwegian Marine commandos.

**RIFLES:**
- *Cal.:* 7.62 x 51mm NATO
  *Official Name: Gevaer, Auto-matisk AG3*
  *Common Name: Gewehr 3*

*Remarks:* Kongsberg Vapenfabrikk-made under license from HK. There was still a shortage of these weapons in 1987.

- *Cal.:* 7.62 x 51mm NATO
  *Common Name:* Mauser 98K
  rifles

*Remarks:* World War II manufacture. Kongsberg converted 4,000 to 7.62 x 51mm NATO in the postwar period.

- *Cal.:* 7.62 x 63mm
  *Common Name:* .30 M1 rifles

*Remarks:* US origin. MAP provided 72,801 before 1964.

- *Cal.:* 7.62 x 33mm
  *Common Name:* .30 M1 and M2
  carbines

*Remarks:* US origin. MAP provided 98,267 before 1964. OBSOLETE?

**SHOTGUNS:**

**MACHINE GUNS:**
- *Cal.:* 7.62 x 51mm NATO
  *Official Name: Maskin Gevaer MG3*
  *Common Name:* MG3 GPMG

*Remarks:* Rheinmetall, Germany. MG1A1 GPMGs are also in service.

- *Cal.:* 7.62 x 51mm NATO
  *Common Name:* MG34 LMG

*Remarks:* World War II manufacture. Kongsberg converted these to 7.62mm NATO for use by the Home Guard. Still in service as of 1986 when Kongsberg was seeking vendors for spare parts such as barrels, bolts, etc.

- *Cal.:* 7.62 x 63mm
  *Common Name:* .30 M1919A4
  LMG

*Remarks:* US origin. The US delivered 1,403 guns before 1975; FMS delivered 557 in 1975.

- *Cal.:* 12.7 x 99mm
  *Common Name:* .50 M2 HB
  HMG

*Remarks:* US origin. MAP provided 10 before 1964 and 1 in 1981; 73 were obtained from FMS 1964–75. More recently the Norwegians have purchased the FN-made HB M2 with the quick change heavy barrel (QCHB). The American M55 AA mount is still used by Norwegian forces.

**AUTOMATIC CANNON:**
- *Cal.:* 20 x 139mm
  *Common Name:* Rh202 automatic
  cannon

*Remarks:* Rheinmetall, Germany. Norway purchased 300 in 1974. Used on the FK-20-2 AA twin mount built by Kongsberg. The single Norwegian AA mount is called the *Lavett, 20mm Luftvern HS669N* and has the NSN 1005-25-1145-4069.

**GRENADE LAUNCHERS:**
- *Cal.:* 40 x 46mmSR
  *Common Name:* HK79 grenade
  launcher

*Remarks:* West German origin. HK GmbH has delivered substantial quantities of these grenade launchers to the Norwegian armed forces for mounting on their AG3 assault rifles. Total acquisition anticipated to be about 3,250.

# OMAN (Sultanate)

Population (estimate in 1980): 1.01 million. Ground forces: regulars, between 16,500 and 20,000; paramilitary (Home Guard or Firqat, 3,500; Royal Guard, ca. 1,200).

**HANDGUNS:**
• *Cal.:* 9 x 19mm Parabellum
  *Common Name:* FN Mle. 1935 GP
     pistol

*Remarks:* Belgian origin.

**SUBMACHINE GUNS:**
• *Cal.:* 9 x 19mm Parabellum
  *Common Name:* Sterling Mark 4
     submachine gun

*Remarks:* Sterling Armament Co., UK.

**RIFLES:**
• *Cal.:* 5.56 x 45mm
  *Common Name:* AUG

*Remarks:* Steyr-Daimler-Puch (SDP), Austria. Between 30 and 32 thousand AUGs have been acquired. The first AUGs were issued to the Royal Guard in 1982 and then to the armed forces in 1983.

**An Omani soldier equipped with a Steyr 5.56 x 45mm AUG stands guard at Thumrait, SOAF Base in Oman, 1983. (DOD)**

**Omani troops armed with the RPG-7 antitank rocket launcher (foreground) and the 7.62 x 51mm NATO FALs defend a position during 1981 exercises. (Omani Embassy via JODD)**

- *Cal.:* 5.56 x 45mm
  *Common Name:* M16A1 (Model 613) rifle

  *Remarks:* US origin. Approx. 3,000 acquired directly from Colt. These rifles are used by the Sultan's Royal Guard, the Royal Omani Police, and the Sultan's Special Forces.

- *Cal.:* 5.56 x 45mm
  *Common Name:* M16A2 rifle

  *Remarks:* US origin. Acquired directly from Colt. Using units unknown.

- *Cal.:* 5.56 x 45mm
  *Common Name:* SG540 rifle

  *Remarks:* Manurhin-made SIG rifle.

- *Cal.:* 7.62 x 51mm NATO
  *Common Name:* FN FAL

  *Remarks:* FN origin.

- *Cal.:* 7.62 x 51mm NATO
  *Common Name:* G3

  *Remarks:* Reported but unconfirmed.

**SHOTGUNS:**

**MACHINE GUNS:**
- *Cal.:* 7.62 x 51mm NATO
  *Common Name:* FN FALO

  *Remarks:* FN origin.

- *Cal.:* 7.62 x 51mm NATO
  *Common Name:* FN MAG

- *Cal.:* 12.7 x 99mm
  *Common Name:* .50 M2 HB
  HMG

- *Cal.:* 12.7 x 99mm
  *Common Name:* .50 L21A1 ranging machine gun

- *Cal.:* 12.7 x 99mm
  *Common Name:* .50 M85 AMG

**AUTOMATIC CANNON:**
- *Cal.:* 20 x 139mm
  *Common Name:* HS820 automatic cannon

- *Cal.:* 20 x 139mm
  *Common Name:* Canon Mitrailleur 20 F2 (M693)

*Remarks:* FN origin. Oman has both the MAG Infanterie Standard (60-20), T 7 (or L7A2) type, and the coaxial (60-40) type in service. From the UK, Oman has 7.62mm armor machine guns L8A1 and L37A1 mounted on the UK chieftan MK7/2C main battle tank.

*Remarks:* Presumed to be of both US and Belgian origin. One M2 HB was purchased from FMS in 1980.

*Remarks:* UK origin. Mounted on the UK Chieftan MK7/2C main battle tank.

*Remarks:* US origin. Mounted on the US M60A1 main battle tank.

*Remarks:* Origin uncertain. These may be BMARCO, UK-made guns. This model is believed to be used on board Omani Coast Guard patrol craft.

*Remarks:* Groupment Industriel des Armements Terrestres (GIAT), France. These 20mm guns are mounted on the VAB 6 x 6 APC. About 8 of these vehicles are in service with Omani forces.

**An Omani soldier mans a 7.62 x 51mm NATO MAG during 1981 exercises. (Omani Embassy via JODD)**

**Esad Tariq Taimur, an Omani tank commander, stands behind a cupola-mounted 7.62 x 51mm NATO MAG during armor exercises. (Omani Embassy via JODD)**

• *Cal.:* 23 x 152mmB
  *Common Name:* ZU23 automatic
  cannon

*Remarks:* East Bloc origin. ZSU-23-4 self-propelled AA system.

**GRENADE LAUNCHERS:**
• *Cal.:* 40 x 46mmSR
  *Common Name:* M79 grenade
  launcher

*Remarks:* US origin.

• *Cal.:* 40 x 46mmSR
  *Common Name:* M203 grenade
  launcher attached to M16A1

*Remarks:* Approximately 350 acquired directly from Colt.

### Small Arms Used by Antigovernment Forces

Weapons used include 7.62 x 39mm PRC Type 56 rifles (AK and SKS), Czechoslovakian vz.58 rifles, and 7.62 x 39mm RPDs and 12.7 x 108mm DShKMs.

## PAKISTAN (Islamic Republic of)

Population (estimate in 1980): 81.5 million. Ground forces: regulars, ca. 400,000; reserves, ca. 500,000.

**HANDGUNS:**
• *Cal.:* 9 x 19mm Parabellum
  *Common Name:* P38/P1

*Remarks:* Walther, West Germany.

- *Cal.:* 9 x 20mmR
  *Common Name:* .38 Webley MK IV revolvers

*Remarks:* UK origin.

- *Cal.:* 9 x 29mmR
  *Common Name:* .38 Smith & Wesson Model 36 square butt revolver

*Remarks:* US origin. Airport and other police. In 1976 the Karachi Airport security police purchased 970 S&W .38 caliber revolvers of unspecified model directly from the factory.

- *Cal.:* 11.43 x 21.7mmR
  *Common Name:* .455 Webley Revolver

*Remarks:* UK and local manufacture.

- *Cal.:* 11.43 x 23mm
  *Common Name:* .45 M1911A1 pistol

*Remarks:* US origin. Acquired 66 M1911A1s from MAP in 1975.

**SUBMACHINE GUNS:**
- *Cal.:* 9 x 19mm Parabellum
  *Common Name:* Mark V Sten gun

*Remarks:* UK origin.

- *Cal.:* 9 x 19mm NATO
  *Common Name:* MP5A2 submachine gun

*Remarks:* Heckler & Koch (HK) design. Some acquired directly from HK GmbH and currently being completely fabricated under HK license at the Pakistan Ordnance Factory (POF) Weapon Factory at Wah. Locally manufactured MP5 are marked "POF" on the top of the receiver. The POF MP5s have new style broad front handguard.

- *Cal.:* 9 x 19mm NATO
  *Common Name:* MP5K submachine gun

*Remarks:* HK design. Acquired directly from HK.

- *Cal.:* 11.43 x 23mm
  *Common Name:* .45 M3A1 SMG

*Remarks:* US origin. Acquired 103 M3A1s from MAP before 1975.

**RIFLES:**
- *Cal.:* 7.62 x 51mm NATO
  *Common Name:* Gewehr 3, G3A2, G3A3 rifle series

*Remarks:* Pakistani-made at POF Wah under license from HK. Production of wood-stocked G3A2 rifles phased out at end of 1986. G3A3 production began mid-1986. Rifles are of latest HK "export version" including the broad "tropical" handguard and bipod. Latter is made by a POF subcontractor. A special bayonet of combined HK and Enfield features is made locally. Both rifle and current magazines are phosphated and lacquered (earlier magazines were phosphated only). POF will use a brown speckled finish plastic material for the stocks of the G3A3s, because the Army does not like the standard Oberndorf green. Brown color is similar to older German MG34 and MG42 stocks.

- *Cal.:* 7.62 x 39mm
  *Common Name:* PRC Type 56 (SKS)

*Remarks:* PRC or Bangladesh origin?

- *Cal.:* 7.62 x 39mm
  *Common Name:* PRC Type 56 (AK47)

*Remarks:* Believed to be of PRC origin.

- *Cal.:* 7.62 x 33mm
  *Common Name:* .30 M1 and M2 carbines

*Remarks:* US origin. MAP delivered about 100 carbines before 1975.

- *Cal.:* 7.62 x 63mm
  *Common Name:* .30 M1 rifle

*Remarks:* US origin. Acquired 118,627 M1 rifles from MAP before 1975. Another 70,699 unspecified rifles were obtained prior to 1975 from MAP. M1 rifles are still used by some static guards.

- *Cal.:* 7.62 x 63mm
  *Common Name:* .30 M1C and M1D sniper rifles

*Remarks:* US origin. 12 acquired from MAP before 1975.

- *Cal.:* 7.7 x 56mmR
  *Common Name:* .303 Enfield No.
  1 and No. 4 rifles

*Remarks:* UK origin. Some jungle carbines (No. 5) are still used by airport and other static guard forces.

**SHOTGUNS:**
- *Cal.:* 18.5 x 59mm
  *Common Name:* 12 gage Mossberg Model 500 shotgun

*Remarks:* National Guard (Punjab Province) and Karachi police for antiriot use.

- *Cal.:* 18.5 x 59mm
  *Common Name:* 12 gage Savage Model 69E shotgun

*Remarks:* Karachi police acquired ca. 600 for antiriot use.

**MACHINE GUNS:**
- *Cal.:* 7.62 x 51mm NATO
  *Common Name:* MG1A3P and MG3

*Remarks:* Pakistani at POF Wah under license from Rheinmetall. Reportedly some major unfinished assemblies for these machine guns are imported from Santa Barbara in Spain. These MGS are found with both phosphated and black lacquered finishes. Stock and grip plates are of same brown plastic material as used on new G3A3s.

- *Cal.:* 7.62 x 51mm NATO
  *Common Name:* FN MAG

*Remarks:* FN origin. Pakistani armed forces use the following models of the FN MAG: MAD Infanterie Standard (60-20) T1 and T9 (latter used nondisintegrating links) and the coaxial model for tanks (60-40).

- *Cal.:* 7.62 x 51mm NATO
  *Common Name:* M73 and M219 AMGs

*Remarks:* US origin. Mounted on M48A5 tanks. FMS program provided 100 M219s in 1982.

- *Cal.:* 7.62 x 39mm
  *Common Name:* Type 56 (RPD) LMG

*Remarks:* Chinese origin.

- *Cal.:* 7.62 x 54mmR
  *Common Name:* SGMT armor MG

*Remarks:* Soviet or Chinese origin. Mounted on older models of Soviet-type tanks.

- *Cal.:* 7.62 x 54mmR
  *Common Name:* Type 59T AMG

*Remarks:* PRC origin. Mounted on PRC Type 62 tank.

- *Cal.:* 7.62 x 63mm
  *Common Name:* .30 M1918A2 BAR

*Remarks:* US origin. MAP delivered 2,500 before 1975.

- *Cal.:* 7.62 x 63mm
  *Common Name:* .30 M1919A4E1 AMG

*Remarks:* US origin. Mounted on US M47 series tanks. MAP delivered 1,285 before 1964.

- *Cal.:* 7.62 x 63mm
  *Common Name:* .30 M1919A6 LMG

*Remarks:* US origin.

- *Cal.:* 7.7 x 56mmR
  *Common Name:* .303 Mark 2 and Mark 3 Bren LMG

*Remarks:* UK origin.

- *Cal.:* 12.7 x 99mm
  *Common Name:* .50 M2 HB HMG

*Remarks:* US origin. About 50 of the M55 quad AA mount are still in service. Most of these have come from MAP.

- *Cal.:* 12.7 x 108mm
  *Common Name:* PRC Type 54 HMG

*Remarks:* PRC origin. Some Soviet DShKMs are also believed to be used on Soviet tanks. Type 54 HMGs are used in ground configuration and mounted on PRC Type 62 tanks. In addition, in November 1985 the POF Wah established a new factory to manufacture this gun. Of the 421 components that make up this weapon, 416 will be made at the Wah facility and 5 will be subcontracted. Type 54 HMG is being built with the technical assistance of the Chinese.

**AUTOMATIC CANNON:**
- *Cal.:* 23 x 152mmB
  *Common Name:* 23mm ZU auto-
  matic cannon

*Remarks:* Soviet origin.

## Small Arms Manufacture in Pakistan

As of 1986 the Pakistan Ordnance Factory (POF) Ammunition Factory at Wah was producing the following types of small caliber ammunition: 9 x 19mm NATO ball; 7.62 x 51mm NATO (L2A2 Ball, L5A3 Tracer, Blank, High Pressure, Drill, Rifle Grenade Blank). In 1988 the POF began manufacturing 12.7 x 108mm ball ammunition for the PRC HMG. The factory also produces DM1 nondisintegrating belts and DM6/M13 links for their machine guns.

## PANAMA (Republic of)

Population (estimate in 1984): 2.10 million. Ground forces: regulars, Guardia Nacional (National Guard, which serves as both a police and military force), ca. 11,000; reserves, unknown; paramilitary, 7,500.

**HANDGUNS:**
- *Cal.:* 9 x 19mm Parabellum
  *Common Name:* FN Mle. 1935 GP
  pistol

*Remarks:* FN origin.

- *Cal.:* 11.43 x 23mm
  *Common Name:* .45 M1911A1
  pistol

*Remarks:* US origin. FMS and MAP provided 227 M1911A1s before 1975.

- *Cal.:* 9 x 29mmR
  *Common Name:* Mixture of Colt
  and Smith & Wesson .38 caliber
  revolvers

*Remarks:* US origin. S&W delivered 218 .38 caliber revolvers in 1977.

**SUBMACHINE GUNS:**
- *Cal.:* 9 x 19mm Parabellum
  *Common Name:* Uzi submachine
  gun

*Remarks:* Believed to be from FN. Mini-Uzi reported, but not confirmed.

- *Cal.:* 11.43 x 23mm
  *Common Name:* M1928A1 and
  M1A1 (Thompson) submachine
  guns

*Remarks:* US origin. Mainly used by police organizations.

**RIFLES:**
- *Cal.:* 7.62 x 33mm
  *Common Name:* .30 M1 and M2
  carbines

*Remarks:* US origin. MAP delivered 138 M1 carbines before 1964 and 809 M2 carbines 1964–75.

- *Cal.:* 5.56 x 45mm
  *Common Name:* M16A1 (Model
  613) rifle

*Remarks:* US origin. Approx. 1,650 acquired directly from Colt. Sherwood International delivered 650 M16s to Panamanian police units in 1978.

- *Cal.:* 5.56 x 45mm
  *Common Name:* Type 65 rifle

*Remarks:* Republic of China. The Taiwanese delivered their new rifle in 1986. Quantities unknown.

- *Cal.:* 7.62 x 63mm
  *Common Name:* .30 M1 rifle

*Remarks:* US origin. MAP delivered 213 before 1975.

**SHOTGUNS:**
- *Cal.:* 18.5 x 59mm
  *Common Name:* 12 gage Ithaca Model 37 shotgun

  *Remarks:* US origin. MAP delivered 36 before 1975.

- *Cal.:* 18.5 x 59mm
  *Common Name:* 12 gage Stevens Model 77E shotgun

  *Remarks:* US origin. MAP delivered 6 before 1975.

- *Cal.:* 18.5 x 59mm
  *Common Name:* 12 gage Remington Model 870P shotgun

  *Remarks:* US origin.

- *Cal.:* 18.5 x 59mm
  *Common Name:* 12 gage Winchester Model 1200 shotgun

  *Remarks:* US origin.

**MACHINE GUNS:**
- *Cal.:* 5.56 x 45mm
  *Common Name:* M16A1 (Model 611) heavy barrel automatic rifle

  *Remarks:* Colt, US. Approx. 200.

- *Cal.:* 7.62 x 51mm NATO
  *Common Name:* FN MAG

  *Remarks:* Belgian origin.

- *Cal.:* 7.62 x 51mm NATO
  *Common Name:* M60 GPMG

  *Remarks:* US origin on Cadillac Gage V-150 APCs.

- *Cal.:* 7.62 x 63mm
  *Common Name:* .30 M1918A2 BAR

  *Remarks:* US origin. MAP delivered 18 before 1975.

- *Cal.:* 7.62 x 63mm
  *Common Name:* .30 M1919A4 LMG

  *Remarks:* US origin.

- *Cal.:* 12.7 x 99mm
  *Common Name:* .50 M2 HB HMG

  *Remarks:* US origin.

**AUTOMATIC CANNON:**

**GRENADE LAUNCHERS:**
- *Cal.:* 40 x 46mmSR
  *Common Name:* M203 grenade launcher attached to M16A1

  *Remarks:* Colt, US. Approx. 200.

# PAPUA NEW GUINEA

Population (estimate in 1984): 3.35 million. Ground forces: regulars, ca. 2,850; reserves, unknown; paramilitary, 4,600 police. Small arms follow the pattern of the Australian army, with most weapons being acquired directly from Australia.

**HANDGUNS:**

**SUBMACHINE GUNS:**

**RIFLES:**
- *Cal.:* 5.56 x 45mm
  *Common Name:* AUG

*Remarks:* The Papua New Guinea armed forces contracted early in 1988 with Australia for 5,000 Australian-made AUG rifles. These weapons will be used to arm the infantry. The overall size of the PNG armed forces will be doubled by the year 2000 if current plans are followed.

- *Cal.:* 5.56 x 45mm
  *Common Name:* M16A1 rifle

*Remarks:* US origin. In the fall of 1986 it was reported that the US government will provide 300 reconditioned M16A1 rifles.

- *Cal.:* 7.62 x 51mm NATO
  *Common Name:* L1A1F1 rifle

*Remarks:* Shortened L1A1 from the Commonwealth Small Arms Factory, Lithgow, Australia.

**SHOTGUNS:**

**MACHINE GUNS:**

**AUTOMATIC CANNON:**

# PARAGUAY (Republic of)

Population (estimate in 1984): 3.12 million. Ground forces: regulars, ca. 12,500 (9,000 of whom are conscripts); paramilitary, National Police force of 8,000; reserves (regular), 60,000; unorganized reserves, ca. 400,000.

**HANDGUNS:**
- *Cal.:* 9 x 19mm Parabellum
  *Common Name:* FN Mle. 35 GP
  pistol

*Remarks:* FN origin.

- *Cal.:* 9 x 19mm Parabellum
  *Common Name:* HK P9S pistol

*Remarks:* Heckler & Koch (HK), GmbH, Germany.

- *Cal.:* 9 x 19mm Parabellum
  *Common Name:* HK VP70Z pistol

*Remarks:* HK GmbH.

- *Cal.:* 11.43 x 23mm
  *Common Name:* .45 M1911A1
  pistol

*Remarks:* US origin. MAP provided 138 before 1975.

**SUBMACHINE GUNS:**
- *Cal.:* 9 x 19mm Parabellum
  *Common Name:* Madsen M46,
  M50, and M53 submachine
  guns

*Remarks:* Danish origin. FOM 1005-33-3-9-2.

- *Cal.:* 9 x 19mm Parabellum
  *Common Name:* Uzi submachine
  gun

*Remarks:* Origin unknown.

- *Cal.:* 9 x 19mm Parabellum
  *Common Name:* Carl Gustav submachine gun

*Remarks:* Origin unknown.

- *Cal.:* 11.43 x 23mm
  *Common Name:* .45 M3A1 submachine gun

*Remarks:* US origin.

**RIFLES:**
- *Cal.:* 5.56 x 45mm
  *Common Name:* SG540 rifle

  *Remarks:* Manurhin-made SIG rifle.

- *Cal.:* 7 x 57mm Mauser
  *Common Name:* M1907 and later
  Mauser bolt action rifles

  *Remarks:* Mauser and FN origin. OBSOLETE.

- *Cal.:* 7.62 x 33mm
  *Common Name:* .30 M1 and M2
  carbines

  *Remarks:* US origin.

- *Cal.:* 7.62 x 51mm NATO
  *Common Name: Gewehr 3* (G3)

  *Remarks:* HK GmbH, Germany.

- *Cal.:* 7.62 x 51mm
  *Common Name:* FN FAL

  *Remarks:* FN origin. Adopted 1956.

- *Cal.:* 7.62 x 63mm
  *Common Name:* .30 M1 rifle

  *Remarks:* US origin. The US provided 30,749 before 1975.

**SHOTGUNS:**
- *Cal.:* 18.5 x 59mm
  *Common Name:* 12 gage Smith &
  Wesson police shotguns

  *Remarks:* US origin. Purchased directly from S&W for police use in 1976.

**MACHINE GUNS:**
- *Cal.:* 7.62 x 51mm NATO
  *Common Name:* FN FALO

  *Remarks:* FN origin.

- *Cal.:* 7.62 x 63mm
  *Common Name:* .30 M1918A2
  BAR

  *Remarks:* US origin. MAP provided 54 before 1975.

- *Cal.:* 7.62 x 63mm
  *Common Name:* .30 M1917 MMG

  *Remarks:* US origin.

- *Cal.:* 7.62 x 63mm
  *Common Name:* .30 M1919A4
  LMG

  *Remarks:* US origin. MAP provided 338 before 1975.

- *Cal.:* 7.65 x 57mm
  *Common Name:* 7.65 Model 1924
  LMG

  *Remarks:* Madsen Denmark.

- *Cal.:* 12.7 x 99mm
  *Common Name:* .50 M2 HB
  HMG

  *Remarks:* US origin.

**AUTOMATIC CANNON:**

**GRENADE LAUNCHERS:**
- *Cal.:* 40 x 46mmR
  *Common Name:* M79 grenade
  launcher

  *Remarks:* US origin. MAP provided 24 before 1974.

# PERU (Republic of)

Population (estimate in 1984): 19.16 million. Ground forces: regulars, ca. 75,000 (ca. 50,000 conscripts); reserves, ca. 300,000; paramilitary *(Guardia Civil),* 25,000; Republican Guard *(Guardia Republicana—*gendarmerie), 5,000; Investigative Police *(Policia de Investigaciones),* 5,000.

**HANDGUNS:**
- *Cal.:* 6.35 x 15.5mmSR Browning
  *Common Name:* .25 FN baby pistol

  *Remarks:* FN origin. Carried by military officers.

- *Cal.:* 9 x 17mm Browning
  *Common Name:* Walther PP

  *Remarks:* Walther design made by Manurhin. Carried by military officers.

- *Cal.:* 9 x 17mm Browning
  *Common Name:* Walther PPK

  *Remarks:* Walther design made by Manurhin. Carried by military officers.

- *Cal.:* 9 x 17mm Browning
  *Common Name:* FN Model 1910

  *Remarks:* FN. Carried by military officers.

- *Cal.:* 9 x 19mm Parabellum
  *Common Name:* FN Mle. 1935 GP pistol

  *Remarks:* Belgian origin.

- *Cal.:* 9 x 19mm Parabellum
  *Common Name:* Star pistol

  *Remarks:* Spanish origin. OBSOLETE. Air Force.

- *Cal.:* 9 x 19mm Parabellum
  *Common Name:* Star Model 30M pistol

  *Remarks:* Spanish origin. Star Bonifacio Echeverria y Cia has delivered 10,000 of these pistols to the Peruvian armed forces (in 1987?).

- *Cal.:* 9 x 29mmR
  *Common Name:* Variety of Llama, Colt, and Smith & Wesson .38 caliber revolvers

  *Remarks:* US and Spanish origin. Some recent acquisitions include: 90 .38 Colt Detective Special (1005-00-726-5786) from MAP before 1975; 12,506 .38 Colt revolvers from Colt for the *Guardia Civil* 1977–79; 2,526 .38 S&W revolvers from S&W for the *Guardia Civil* 1976–78; 2,581 .38 S&W revolvers from S&W for the *Policia de Investigaciones* 1978–79; 30,000 .38 S&W M10 revolvers from S&W in 1986 for the *Policia de Investigaciones* 1978–79; 40,000 .38 S&W revolvers ordered in 1987 for the reorganized police forces.

- *Cal.:* 11.43 x 23mm
  *Common Name:* .45 M1911A1 pistol

  *Remarks:* US origin. OBSOLETE. MAP delivered 10 before 1975.

**SUBMACHINE GUNS:**
- *Cal.:* 9 x 19mm Parabellum
  *Official Name:* MGP-79
  *Common Name:* Domestic design

  *Remarks:* Made by the Servicio Industrial de la Marina (SIMA) of the Centro de Fabrication de Armas (MGP = Marina de Guerra). The design team was led by Juan Erquiaga in 1979.

- *Cal.:* 9 x 19mm Parabellum
  *Common Name:* FMK submachine gun

  *Remarks:* Argentine origin.

- *Cal.:* 9 x 19mm Parabellum
  *Common Name:* Uzi submachine gun

  *Remarks:* FN origin. Used by all armed forces.

- *Cal.:* 9 x 19mm Parabellum
  *Common Name:* Madsen submachine gun

  *Remarks:* Madsen, Denmark. Used exclusively by the *Policia de Investigaciones*.

- *Cal.:* 9 x 19mm Parabellum
  *Common Name:* vz.25 submachine gun

  *Remarks:* Czechoslovakian origin. Used by the Air Force.

- *Cal.:* 9 x 19mm Parabellum
  *Common Name:* Star Z45 and Z62 submachine guns

  *Remarks:* Star Bonafacio Echeverria, S.A., Spain.

**RIFLES:**
- *Cal.:* 5.56 x 45mm
  *Common Name:* M16A1 rifle

  *Remarks:* US origin. The Police Emergency Brigade has 50 of these rifles. Some M16A1 carbines may also be in use.

- *Cal.:* 7.62 x 33mm
  *Common Name:* .30 M1 and M2 carbine

*Remarks:* US origin. OBSOLETE. MAP provided 811 M1s before 1964 and 10 M2s between 1964 and 1975.

- *Cal.:* 7.62 x 39mm
  *Common Name:* AK47 folding stock assault rifle

*Remarks:* East Bloc origin. Previously used exclusively by Air Force airborne troops only. This may change since in 1986 the Peruvian paramilitary forces acquired 20,000 North Korean-made AKMs (Type 68) at a unit price of US$97, an obvious political price. In 1988, 20,000 more Type 68s were acquired; of these, 4,000 are for the Civil Guard, 1,640 for the Investigative Police, 1,860 for the Police Training Directorate, and 2,500 for the Police Special Operations Directorate.

- *Cal.:* 7.62 x 51mm NATO
  *Common Name:* FN FAL

*Remarks:* FN and DGFM, Argentine, origin. Both the standard and Para models are in service. In 1986, there were several news reports that the Peruvian armed forces had signed a contract for 198,000 FALs from Argentina's Fabricaciones Militares. These reports are unconfirmed.

- *Cal.:* 7.62 x 51mm NATO
  *Common Name:* Gewehr 3A3

*Remarks:* Heckler & Koch (HK), GmbH, Germany.

- *Cal.:* 7.62 x 51mm NATO
  *Common Name:* SSG sniper rifle

*Remarks:* Steyr-Daimler-Puch (SDP), Austria. Purchased after the 1965 communist/APRA uprising in the Andes.

- *Cal.:* 7.62 x 63mm
  *Common Name:* .30 M1 rifle

*Remarks:* US origin. MAP delivered 10,000 between 1964 and 1975.

**SHOTGUNS:**
- *Cal.:* 18.5 x 59mm
  *Common Name:* 12 gage Mossberg Model 500 shotgun

*Remarks:* US origin. Sold direct by Mossberg for use by paramilitary and security forces.

**MACHINE GUNS:**
- *Cal.:* 7.62 x 51mm NATO
  *Common Name:* FN MAG

*Remarks:* FN origin. MAG Infanterie Standard (60-20) T14 using nondisintegrating link belt and Coaxial (60-40) T1.

- *Cal.:* 7.62 x 51mm NATO
  *Common Name:* M60 GPMG

*Remarks:* US origin. US provided 7 in 1980.

- *Cal.:* 7.62 x 54mmR
  *Common Name:* SGMT armor MG

*Remarks:* Soviet origin. Mounted on older model Soviet tanks.

- *Cal.:* 7.62 x 63mm
  *Common Name:* .30 M1919A4 LMG

*Remarks:* US origin. MAP and FMS delivered 525 of these LMGs before 1964.

- *Cal.:* 7.62 x 63mm
  *Common Name:* .30 M1917A1 MMG

*Remarks:* US origin.

- *Cal.:* 7.65 x 54mm
  *Common Name:* Czech ZB30 LMG

*Remarks:* Czechoslovakian origin. Some of these guns were converted to 7.62mm NATO by Ing. Juan Erquiaga.

- *Cal.:* 12.7 x 99mm
  *Common Name:* .50 M2 HB HMG

*Remarks:* US and FN origin. US sources delivered 162 before 1964 and 167 1964–75.

- *Cal.:* 12.7 x 108mm
  *Common Name:* DShk38/46 HMG

*Remarks:* East Bloc origin. Mounted on T55 tanks and other Soviet vehicles.

**AUTOMATIC CANNON:**
- *Cal.:* 23 x 152mmB
  *Common Name:* ZU23 automatic

*Remarks:* Soviet origin. ZSU-cannon. Peru began receiving the 23-4 self-propelled AA system in 1973. 23 of these systems are reported to be in the inventory.

## PHILIPPINES (Republic of)

Population (estimate in 1984): 55.53 million. Ground forces: regulars, ca. 60,000; reserves, ca. 20,000 (an additional 70,000 have a part-time commitment). Paramilitary Philippine Constabulary, ca. 43,500. There exists a variety of Western small arms, especially weapons from the United States. In the past five years the armed forces have taken steps to limit the different models in service.

### HANDGUNS:
• *Cal.:* 9 x 19mm Parabellum
  *Common Name:* FN Mle. 35 GP
  Pistol

*Remarks:* FN origin.

• *Cal.:* 9 x 19mm Parabellum
  *Common Name:* Glock P80

*Remarks:* Glock origin. Presidential Guards.

• *Cal.:* 11.43 x 23mm
  *Common Name:* .45 M1911A1 pistol

*Remarks:* US origin.

### SUBMACHINE GUNS:
• *Cal.:* 9 x 19mm Parabellum
  *Common Name:* Uzi submachine
  gun

*Remarks:* Origin unknown. (Mini-Uzi also reportedly in use.)

• *Cal.:* 11.43 x 23mm
  *Common Name:* .45 M3A1 submachine gun

*Remarks:* US origin.

• *Cal.:* 11.43 x 23mm
  *Common Name:* .45 M1A1
  Thompson submachine gun

*Remarks:* US origin. Used by paramilitary forces only.

### RIFLES:
• *Cal.:* 5.56 x 45mm
  *Common Name:* M16A1 (Model
  613) rifle and M16A1 (Model
  653) carbine

*Remarks:* Made by Elisco Tool Co. under license from Colt. FMS delivered 4,000 M16A1s before 1975 and 35 in 1975. MAP delivered 22,991 in 1975. Aprox. 45,000 Model 613 rifles were acquired directly from Colt before 1976. No data on the number of M16s manufactured by Elisco Tool has been located.

• *Cal.:* 5.56 x 45mm
  *Common Name:* Galil rifle

*Remarks:* Israeli Military Industries. AR, ARM and SAR versions used.

• *Cal.:* 7.62 x 33mm
  *Common Name:* M1 and M2 carbines

*Remarks:* US origin. MAP delivered 8,831 M1 carbines before 1965 and 15 in 1975. An additional 40 M2 carbines were delivered in 1975.

• *Cal.:* 7.62 x 51mm NATO
  *Common Name:* M14 rifle

*Remarks:* US origin. MAP provided 4,000 before 1975 and 100,000 in 1978.

• *Cal.:* 7.62 x 51mm NATO
  *Common Name:* Gewehr 3

*Remarks:* Origin uncertain.

• *Cal.:* 7.62 x 63mm
  *Common Name:* .30 M1 rifle

*Remarks:* US origin. FMS delivered 22,205 in 1975 and another 11,594 unidentified rifles (presumed to be M1s) before 1964. OBSOLETE.

• *Cal.:* 7.62 x 63mm
  *Common Name:* .30 M1D sniper
  rifle

*Remarks:* US origin. FMS delivered 2,629 in 1975.

### SHOTGUNS:
• *Cal.:* 18.5 x 59mm
  *Common Name:* Winchester
  M1200 12 gage shotgun

*Remarks:* US origin. FMS delivered 263 before 1975.

**MACHINE GUNS:**

- *Cal.:* 5.56 x 45mm
  *Common Name:* Ultimax 100 SAW

  *Remarks:* Chartered Industries of Singapore.

- *Cal.:* 7.62 x 51mm NATO
  *Common Name:* M60 GPMG

  *Remarks:* US origin. MAP delivered 1,253 in 1975; 603 in 1976; 122 in 1977; 50 in 1978; 25 in 1979; 200 in 1980.

- *Cal.:* 7.62 x 51mm NATO
  *Common Name:* M60D ACMG

  *Remarks:* US origin. MAP delivered 1,914 in 1975; 26 in 1976.

- *Cal.:* 7.62 x 51mm NATO
  *Common Name:* FN MAG

  *Remarks:* FN origin. MAG Infanterie Standard (60-20), T1 and T9 (latter uses nondisintegrating link belt); Aviation MAG (60-30) in Pod Marchetti, P.904; and Coaxial MAG (60-40) for the Cadillac Gage turret, for the turret of the Portuguese APC Chaimite; and the Dutch type for the AIFV 60-417 (p. 92S) with standard barrel 1005-17-640-0312. Also seen in hands of antigovernment forces.

- *Cal.:* 7.62 x 63mm
  *Common Name:* .30 M1918A2 BAR

  *Remarks:* US origin. FMS delivered 5 in 1975; 4,595 in 1976.

- *Cal.:* 7.62 x 63mm
  *Common Name:* .30 M1919A4 LMG

  *Remarks:* US origin. FMS delivered 19,261 before 1975. Another 215 unidentified .30 LMGs were delivered by MAP before 1965. Also M1916A6 LMGs in service.

- *Cal.:* 12.7 x 99mm
  *Common Name:* .50 M2 HB HMG

  *Remarks:* US origin. FMS delivered 20 in 1975; 96 in 1977. Ramo, Inc. delivered 97 guns in 1984.

- *Cal.:* 12.7 x 99mm
  *Common Name:* .50 AN M3 ACMG

  *Remarks:* US origin. MAP delivered 100 before 1975; 42 in 1978.

**AUTOMATIC CANNON:**

- *Cal.:* 20 x 102mm
  *Common Name:* Gun, automatic 20mm M168

  *Remarks:* US origin. FMS is providing 24 M167A1 towed Vulcan Air Defense Systems (VADS) to the Philippine armed forces.

**GRENADE LAUNCHERS:**

- *Cal.:* 40 x 46mmSR
  *Common Name:* M79 grenade launcher

  *Remarks:* US origin. MAP provided 609 before 1975. FMS provided 1,000 in 1976.

- *Cal.:* 40 x 46mmSR
  *Common Name:* M203 grenade launcher attached to M16A1

  *Remarks:* US origin. MAP provided 1,606 before 1975; 229 in 1976; 500 in 1977. FMS provided 375 before 1975; 1,500 in 1976. Colt delivered directly approx. 3,000 in the late 1970s.

### Antigovernment Forces

There are two major antigovernment rebel forces—the Philippine Democratic Revolution (Muslim and Marxist, first reported in 1985) and the older New People's Army (Communist). The latter has about 3,000 fighters. In addition to weapons taken from the government, they have received much assistance from outside the Philippines.

## POLAND (People's Republic of)

Population (estimate in 1984): 36.89 million. Ground forces: regulars, ca. 210,000 (conscripts, ca. 153,000); reserves, ca. 500,000 (for all services). In addition there are about 218,000 paramilitary Ministry of the Interior border guards.

## HANDGUNS:

• *Cal.:* 9 x 18mm
*Official Name: Pistolet wz.64*
*Common Name:* P-64 pistol

*Remarks:* Evolution from the Walther PP design. FOM 1005-11-1-9-2.

• *Cal.:* 9 x 18mm
*Official Name: Pistolet wz.65*
*Common Name:* P-65 pistol

*Remarks:* Polish version of Soviet Makarov.

## SUBMACHINE GUNS:

• *Cal.:* 9 x 18mm
*Official Name: Pistolet Maszynow wzor 63 – PM wz.63*
*Common Name:* Model 63 machine pistol

*Remarks:* Polish design and manufacture. FOM 1005-11-1-9-3.

## RIFLES:

• *Cal.:* 7.62 x 39mm
*Official Name:* PMK
*Common Name:* Polish version of AK47 assault rifle

*Remarks:* Polish manufacture. Now only issued to reserves.

• *Cal.:* 7.62 x 39mm
*Official Name:* PMK-DGN-60
*Common Name:* Grenade launching version of PMK

*Remarks:* Polish manufacture. FOM 1005-11-2-7.62-2. This weapon launches the PGN-60 antitank grenade FOM 1330-11-2-2 and the F-1/N 60 antipersonnel grenade FOM 1330-11-2-1.

• *Cal.:* 7.62 x 39mm
*Official Name:* PMKM
*Common Name:* Polish version of AKM assault rifle

*Remarks:* Polish manufacture.

• *Cal.:* 7.62 x 54mmR
*Common Name:* Polish version of Dragunov sniper rifle

*Remarks:* Polish manufacture?

• *Cal.:* 7.62 x 54mmR
*Common Name:* Polish version of Soviet M1891/30 sniper rifle

*Remarks:* Polish manufacture. Appear to have been made as late as 1956? Probably an export weapon.

• *Cal.:* 7.62 x 54mmR
*Common Name:* Polish version of Soviet M44 bolt rifle

*Remarks:* Polish manufacture. Appear to have been made as late as 1956? Probably an export weapon.

## SHOTGUNS:

## MACHINE GUNS:

• *Cal.:* 7.62 x 39mm
*Common Name:* RPD LMG

*Remarks:* Soviet origin. Reserves.

• *Cal.:* 7.62 x 39mm
*Common Name:* RPK LMG

*Remarks:* Polish manufacture.

• *Cal.:* 7.62 x 54mmR
*Common Name:* PK GPMG series (PKB PKS, PKT)

*Remarks:* Polish manufacture.

• *Cal.:* 7.62 x 54mmR
*Common Name:* SGMT armor MG

*Remarks:* Soviet origin. Mounted on older models of Soviet tanks.

• *Cal.:* 12.7 x 108mm
*Common Name:* DShK38/46 HMG

*Remarks:* Soviet origin? M53 quad antiaircraft mount in service.

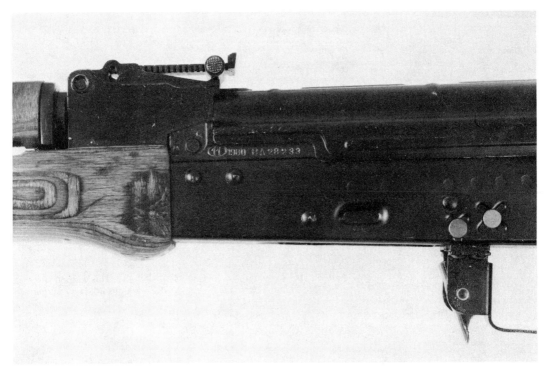

Receiver markings on a Polish AKM captured by the Israeli Defense Forces during "Operation Peace in Galilee." The markings include the Polish Factory 11 in an oval, plus the date 1980, and the serial number BA28233. Most of the weapons taken from the PLO were of very recent manufacture. (Smithsonian; Eric Long)

• *Cal.:* 12.7 x 108mm
  *Common Name:* NSVT HMG

**AUTOMATIC CANNON:**
• *Cal.:* 14.5 x 114mm
  *Common Name:* KPV HMG

• *Cal.:* 23 x 152mmB
  *Common Name:* ZU23 automatic
  cannon

• *Cal.:* 25 x 218mm
  *Common Name:* 2-M-3 or 2-M-8
  automatic cannon

*Remarks:* Soviet origin? Mounted on T72 model main battle tanks.

*Remarks:* Soviet origin? ZPU-2 and ZPU-4 versions in service.

*Remarks:* Soviet origin? The towed ZSU-23-2 AA system and the ZSU-23-4 self-propelled AA system are both in service.

*Remarks:* Soviet origin? Mounted on coastal mine sweepers.

## PORTUGAL (Republic of)

Population (estimate in 1984): 10.05 million. Ground forces: regulars, ca. 39,000; paramilitary: *Guarda Nacional Republicana* (gendarmerie), 14,600; *Policia de Seguranca Publica;* 15,300; *Guarda Fiscal,* 7,350.

**HANDGUNS:**

• *Cal.:* 7.65 x 17mm
 *Official Name: Pistola Walther
   7.65mm*
 *Common Name:* Walther PP.P1

*Remarks:* Walther design. Made by Manurhin of France.

• *Cal.:* 9 x 19mm NATO
 *Official Name: Pistola Walther
   9mm M/61*
 *Common Name:* P1

*Remarks:* Walther design. Made by Walther. Standard handgun.

• *Cal.:* 9 x 19mm Parabellum
 *Common Name:* FN Mle. 35 GP
   pistol

*Remarks:* FN origin. FN provided Portugal with machinery to manufacture this handgun in 1987.

• *Cal.:* 9 x 19mm NATO
 *Common Name:* VP70M

*Remarks:* Heckler & Koch (HK) GmbH, West Germany.

**SUBMACHINE GUNS:**

• *Cal.:* 9 x 19mm NATO
 *Official Name: Pistola Metralha-
   dora Beretta 9mm*
 *Common Name:* Beretta M12S
   submachine gun

*Remarks:* Beretta, Italy. *Policia de Seguranca Publica* acquired 150 of these submachine guns in 1984.

• *Cal.:* 9 x 19mm NATO
 *Official Name: Pistola Metralha-
   dora Vigneron 9mm M/61*
 *Common Name:* Vigneron submachine gun

*Remarks:* Societe Anonyme Precision Liegeoise, Herstal, Belgium. Now OBSOLETE?

• *Cal.:* 9 x 19mm NATO
 *Official Name: Pistola Metralha-
   dora Uzi 9mm M/61*
 *Common Name:* Uzi submachine
   gun – MP2

*Remarks:* Israeli Military Industries (IMI). Acquired 10,000 Uzis from the Federal Republic of Germany in 1961.

• *Cal.:* 9 x 19mm NATO
 *Official Name: Pistola Metralha-
   dora Sterling 9mm MK4*
 *Common Name:* Sterling MK4
   submachine gun

*Remarks:* Sterling Arms Company, UK.

• *Cal.:* 9 x 19mm NATO
 *Official Name: Pistola Metralha-
   dora FPB 9mm M/63*
 *Common Name:* Domestic design
   FMBP M/963 submachine gun

*Remarks:* Fabrica Militar de Braco de Prata (FMBP), Lisbon. FMBP is a subdivision of Industrias Nacionais de Defesa, de Portugal (INDEP). This weapon has been made in relatively small quantities.

• *Cal.:* 9 x 19mm NATO
 *Official Name: Pistola Metralha-
   dora FPB 9mm M/76*
 *Common Name:* FMBP M/976
   submachine gun

*Remarks:* FMBP origin. This weapon has been made in relatively small quantities.

• *Cal.:* 9 x 19mm NATO
 *Common Name:* Ingram M10 submachine gun

*Remarks:* Military Armaments Co., US.

• *Cal.:* 9 x 19mm NATO
 *Common Name:* Star Z-45 submachine gun

*Remarks:* Spanish origin.

• *Cal.:* 9 x 19mm NATO
*Common Name:* Franchi LF-57
submachine gun

*Remarks:* Luigi Franchi, Italy. Called the "Santa Luisa" locally.

**RIFLES:**
• *Cal.:* 5.56 x 45mm
*Common Name:* Galil-type rifle

*Remarks:* Source unknown. Portuguese airborne troops have been seen in news photographs since early 1985 armed with a Galil-type 5.56mm rifle.

• *Cal.:* 5.56 x 45mm
*Common Name:* HK33 rifle

*Remarks:* Small quantities in use. Assembled in Portugal?

• *Cal.:* 7.62 x 51mm NATO
*Official Name: Espingarda Auto-
matica G3 7,62mm M63*
*Common Name: Gewehr 3*

*Remarks:* FMBP production in Portugal licensed by HK. Produced in both the fixed stock and retractable stock versions. Standard service rifle.

• *Cal.:* 7.62 x 51mm NATO
*Common Name:* FN FAL

*Remarks:* FN origin. Used during wars in Angola and Mozambique. Now retired, sold, or given away.

• *Cal.:* 7.62 x 51mm NATO
*Common Name:* AR-10 rifle

*Remarks:* Artillerie-Inrichtingen, Netherlands. Only a few thousand procured; now OBSOLETE.

**SHOTGUNS:**

**MACHINE GUNS:**
• *Cal.:* 7.62 x 51mm NATO
*Official Name: Metralhadora M/
960 7,62mm*
*Common Name:* MG42/59
GPMG

*Remarks:* Rheinmetall origin.

• *Cal.:* 7.62 x 51mm NATO
*Official Name: Metralhadora M/
968 7,62mm*
*Common Name:* HK21 GPMG

*Remarks:* FMBP production in Portugal licensed by HK. Standard service GPMG.

• *Cal.:* 7.62 x 51mm NATO
*Official Name: Metralhadora
MAG FN 7,62mm*
*Common Name:* FN MAG
GPMG

*Remarks:* FN.

• *Cal.:* 7.62 x 51mm NATO
*Official Name: Metralhadora
M60D 7,62mm C-EMTRIPE*
*Common Name:* M60D ACMG

*Remarks:* US origin.

• *Cal.:* 7.62 x 51mm NATO
*Official Name: Metralhadora
M219 7,62mm Coaxial*
*Common Name:* M219 AMG

*Remarks:* US origin. FMS delivered 43 in 1984 as spare coaxial guns for US tanks being used by Portugal.

• *Cal.:* 12.7 x 99mm
*Official Name: Metralhadora
Browning M2 HB 12,7mm*
*Common Name:* .50 M2 HB
HMG

*Remarks:* US origin. The Portuguese use several versions of the M2 HB HMG: the ground model *(terrestre)*, the M1 turret *(torre M1)*, and the M45 turret *(torre M45)*. MAP delivered 25 .50 M2 HB Brownings in 1979. There are also approx. 20 M55 quad gun AA systems *(Metralhadora Quadrupla AA M55 12,7mm M53)* in service.

**AUTOMATIC CANNON:**
• *Cal.:* 20 x 102mm
*Common Name:* Gun, automatic,
20mm M168 (Vulcan)

*Remarks:* US origin. The Portuguese government ordered 10 US M163A1 self-propelled Vulcan Air Defense Systems (VADS) in 1987 directly from General Electric.

- *Cal.:* 20 x 139mm
  *Official Name: Metralhadora Bi-tubo AA 20mm M81*
  *Common Name:* Rh 202 20mm automatic cannon

*Remarks:* Rheinmetall, West Germany. These twin gun systems were acquired in the early 1980s and are currently used for close-in AA defense.

**GRENADE LAUNCHERS:**
- *Cal.:* 40 x 46mmSR
  *Common Name:* M79 grenade launchers

*Remarks:* US origin. MAP provided 104 in 1977 and 300 in 1978.

### Further Notes on Portuguese Small Arms

For many years the Portuguese have had a wide variety of older weapons in reserve. Early in 1984 they began offering many of these weapons for sale. Included in that offering were the following:

| | |
|---|---|
| **HANDGUNS:** | 368 pistols of various types (Savage M/915; Parabellums M/908 and M/943, etc.). |
| **SUBMACHINE GUNS:** | 8,786 submachine guns of various types (FMBP M/948; Vigneron M/961; Sten; PPSh41; and Madsen). |
| **RIFLES AND CARBINES:** | 10,595 shoulder weapons of various types (Mauser M/904 and M/937; US Enfield M/917; Mosin-Nagant; etc.). |
| **MACHINE GUNS:** | 5,444 machine guns of various types (Lewis; Vickers Berthier; Bren; Dreyse; Madsen; Breda; Besa; Browning; etc.). |

### Portuguese Small Arms Manufacturing

The Fabrica Militar de Braco de Prata, located in suburban Lisbon, is the major ordnance factory of the Portuguese War Office. Established on 1 June 1981, it has a current staff of about 1,800 people and facilities covering 54,000 m². It incorporates the rifle factory, which dates from 1912.

## QATAR (State of)

Population (estimate in 1984): 0.276 million. Ground forces: regulars, ca. 5,000; reserves, unknown.

**HANDGUNS:**
- *Cal.:* 9 x 17mm
  *Common Name:* HK4 pistol

*Remarks:* Heckler & Koch (HK) GmbH origin. Used by police organizations.

- *Cal.:* 9 x 29mmR
  *Common Name:* .38 Smith & Wesson revolver

*Remarks:* US origin. In 1978 the Qatar police obtained through direct purchase 610 S&W .38 caliber revolvers. They also bought a mixed lot of 26 revolvers (.357, .44, and .45) in 1978 from S&W.

- *Cal.:* 9 x 29mmR
  *Common Name:* .38 Colt revolver

*Remarks:* US origin. 10 Colt revolvers were delivered to a government customer in 1977.

**SUBMACHINE GUNS:**
- *Cal.:* 9 x 19mm Parabellum
  *Common Name:* MP5

*Remarks:* UK origin. Royal Small Arms Factory (RSAF), Enfield.

- *Cal.:* 9 x 19mm Parabellum
  *Common Name:* MK IV Sterling submachine gun

*Remarks:* Sterling Armament Co., UK.

**RIFLES:**
- *Cal.:* 5.56 x 45mm
  *Common Name:* M16A1 (Model 613) rifle and M16A1 (Model 653) carbine

*Remarks:* Colt, US. Approx. 6,000 (about equally divided in number between rifles and carbines). These weapons were acquired between 1981 and 1983. The Model 653 carbines are used by the police.

- *Cal.:* 7.62 x 39mm
  *Common Name:* M62 and M76 assault rifles

*Remarks:* Valmet, Finland.

- *Cal.:* 7.62 x 39mm
  *Common Name:* AK47 assault rifle

*Remarks:* East Bloc origin.

- *Cal.:* 7.62 x 51mm NATO
  *Common Name: Gewehr 3*

*Remarks:* HK design, but manufactured at RSAF.

- *Cal.:* 7.62 x 51mm NATO
  *Common Name:* FAL assault rifle

*Remarks:* FN origin?

**SHOTGUNS:**
- *Cal.:* 18.5 x 59mm
  *Common Name:* 12 gage Mossberg Model 500 shotgun

*Remarks:* Mossberg, US.

**MACHINE GUNS:**
- *Cal.:* 5.56 x 45mm
  *Common Name:* M16A1 (Model 611) heavy barrel automatic rifle

*Remarks:* Colt, US. Approx. 700.

- *Cal.:* 7.62 x 39mm
  *Common Name:* M62 LMG

*Remarks:* Valmet, Finland.

- *Cal.:* 7.62 x 51mm NATO
  *Common Name:* FN MAG

*Remarks:* Belgian origin. *Infanterie Standard* (60-20), T14 with nondisintegrating link; *Aviation* (60-30), M.O.32 B.A.C.; *Coaxial* (60-40), CAFL38.

- *Cal.:* 7.62 x 51mm NATO
  *Common Name:* HK21 LMG

*Remarks:* HK design, but manufactured at RSAF.

- *Cal.:* 12.7 x 99mm
  *Common Name:* .50 M2 HB HMG

*Remarks:* US origin. Ca. 500 with the Army and about 20+ with the police. Ramo, Inc. delivered 855 guns, spares, accessories, and mounts 1978–80. Included in these orders were 50 truck pedestal mounts. Disposition of these guns is not known.

**AUTOMATIC CANNON:**
- *Cal.:* 20 x 102mm
  *Common Name:* M693 automatic cannon

*Remarks:* French origin. It is not clear if these are the model 20mm guns that are mounted on their Vosper-Thorneycroft large patrol craft.

**GRENADE LAUNCHERS:**
- *Cal.:* 40 x 46mmSR
  *Common Name:* M203 grenade launcher attached to M16A1

*Remarks:* Colt, US. Approx. 200 in service.

## ROMANIA (Socialist Republic of)

Population (estimate in 1984): 22.68 million. Ground forces: regulars, ca. 150,000 (conscripts, 95,000); reserves, *Patriotic Guard* (established 1968), ca. 500,000 to 600,000. In addition there are two major paramilitary forces: the Internal Security Troops (ca. 20,000) and the Frontier Guards (ca. 20,000). There is also a militia of some 700,000 members.

## HANDGUNS:

- *Cal.:* 9 x 18mm
  *Common Name:* Copy of Soviet Pistolet Makarov

  *Remarks:* Romanian origin.

- *Cal.:* 7.62 x 25mm
  *Common Name:* TT33 Tokarev pistol

  *Remarks:* Romanian origin.

## SUBMACHINE GUNS:

- *Cal.:* 9 x 19mm Parabellum
  *Official Name: Pusca Automata Usoarm Orita M41*
  *Common Name:* Orita submachine gun

  *Remarks:* Romanian design made at Cugir Arsenal, 1941-44. Obsolescent, reserve units only.

- *Cal.:* 7.62 x 25mm
  *Common Name:* vz.24 and vz.26 submachine guns

  *Remarks:* Czechoslovakian origin.

## RIFLES:

- *Cal.:* 7.62 x 39mm
  *Common Name:* AK47 assault rifle

  *Remarks:* Origin uncertain. Obsolescent, reserves only?

- *Cal.:* 7.62 x 39mm
  *Common Name:* AKM assault rifle

  *Remarks:* Romanian origin. FOM 1005-12-2-7.62-1.

- *Cal.:* 7.62 x 54mmR
  *Common Name:* FPK sniper rifle

  *Remarks:* Domestic design built on AKM receiver. Similar external configuration to Soviet Dragunov. FOM 1005-12-2-7.62-5.

## SHOTGUNS:

## MACHINE GUNS:

- *Cal.:* 7.62 x 39mm
  *Common Name:* RPD LMG

  *Remarks:* Soviet origin. Reserves only.

- *Cal.:* 7.62 x 39mm
  *Common Name:* RPK LMG

  *Remarks:* Romanian origin.

- *Cal.:* 7.62 x 54mmR
  *Common Name:* SGM series of MGs

  *Remarks:* East Bloc origin. The ground guns are believed to be used only by reserve forces. The vehicle SGMT is believed to be still in service on older tanks.

- *Cal.:* 7.62 x 54mmR
  *Common Name:* DP series of MGs

  *Remarks:* Soviet origin. The ground guns are believed to be used only by reserve forces. The vehicle DT may still be in service on older tanks.

- *Cal.:* 7.62 x 54mmR
  *Common Name:* PKB, PKS, PKT GPMGs

  *Remarks:* Soviet origin.

- *Cal.:* 7.92 x 57mm
  *Common Name:* ZB26/30 LMG

  *Remarks:* Czechoslovakian origin. OBSOLETE.

- *Cal.:* 12.7 x 108mm
  *Common Name:* DShK38/46 HMG

  *Remarks:* Soviet origin.

- *Cal.:* 12.7 x 108mm
  *Common Name:* NSVT HMG

  *Remarks:* Soviet origin. Mounted on newer tanks.

**AUTOMATIC CANNON:**

- *Cal.:* 14.5 x 114mm
  *Common Name:* KPV HMG

  *Remarks:* Soviet origin.

- *Cal.:* 23 x 152mmB
  *Common Name:* ZU23 automatic
  cannon

  *Remarks:* Soviet origin. Several versions, including the ZSU-23-4 self-propelled AA system.

## RWANDA (Republic of)

Population (estimate in 1984): 5.84 million. Ground forces: regulars (Army called National Guard), ca. 5,000; paramilitary, Police Nationale Rwandaise (which supports the National Guard), ca. 1,200.

**HANDGUNS:**

- *Cal.:* 7.65 x 17mm Browning
  *Common Name:* FN Browning
  Mle. 1910 pistol

  *Remarks:* FN origin.

- *Cal.:* 7.65 x 20mm
  *Common Name:* Mle. 1935 pistol

  *Remarks:* French origin.

- *Cal.:* 9 x 19mm NATO
  *Common Name:* MAB PA-15

  *Remarks:* French origin. Manufacture d'Armes de Bayonne (MAB).

**SUBMACHINE GUNS:**

- *Cal.:* 9 x 19mm Parabellum
  *Common Name:* Vigneron M2
  submachine gun

  *Remarks:* Societe Anonyme Precision Liegeoise, Belgium.

- *Cal.:* 9 x 19mm Parabellum
  *Common Name:* Uzi submachine
  gun

  *Remarks:* Origin uncertain.

**RIFLES:**

- *Cal.:* 7.5 x 54mm
  *Common Name:* MAS36 bolt
  action rifle

  *Remarks:* Manufacture Nationale d'Armes de St. Etienne (MAS).

- *Cal.:* 7.5 x 54mm
  *Common Name:* MAS49/56 rifle

  *Remarks:* MAS.

- *Cal.:* 7.62 x 51mm NATO
  *Common Name:* FN FAL

  *Remarks:* FN origin.

**SHOTGUNS:**

**MACHINE GUNS:**

- *Cal.:* 7.62 x 51mm NATO
  *Common Name:* FN MAG

  *Remarks:* Belgian origin. MAG Coaxial (60-40), Panhard AML60 version using US M13 disintegrating links.

- *Cal.:* 12.7 x 99mm
  *Common Name:* .50 M2 HB
  HMG

  *Remarks:* US origin.

**AUTOMATIC CANNON:**

## ST. VINCENT AND THE GRENADINES

Population (estimate in 1984): 0.138 million. Ground forces: regulars, unknown; paramilitary, St. Vincent Police ca. 480. Defense is supported by UK forces.

**HANDGUNS:**

**SUBMACHINE GUNS:**

**RIFLES:**
• *Cal.:* 5.56 x 45mm                    *Remarks:* Origin unknown.
  *Common Name:* M16A1 rifle

• *Cal.:* 7.62 x 51mm NATO               *Remarks:* Origin unknown.
  *Common Name:* L1A1 rifle

**SHOTGUNS:**

**MACHINE GUNS:**
• *Cal.:* 7.62 x 51mm NATO               *Remarks:* Origin unknown.
  *Common Name:* M60 GPMG

**AUTOMATIC CANNON:**

**GRENADE LAUNCHERS:**
• *Cal.:* 40 x 46mmSR                    *Remarks:* Origin unknown.
  *Common Name:* M79 grenade
  launcher

## SAO TOME ET PRINCEPE

Population (estimate in 1984): 0.089 million. Ground forces: regulars, ca. 300; paramilitary, *Guardia Nacionale,* ca. 160; *Policia da Ordem Publica,* ca. 250. There are about 500 Cuban military security personnel in-country advising local forces. There are also Angolan troops stationed in Sao Tome, ca. 1,000.

**HANDGUNS:**

**SUBMACHINE GUNS:**
• *Cal.:* 7.62 x 25mm                    *Remarks:* East Bloc origin.
  *Common Name:* PPS 43

**RIFLES:**
• *Cal.:* 7.62 x 39mm                    *Remarks:* East Bloc origin.
  *Common Name:* SKS carbine

• *Cal.:* 7.62 x 39mm                    *Remarks:* East Bloc origin.
  *Common Name:* AK 47 assault
  rifle

**SHOTGUNS:**

**MACHINE GUNS:**
• *Cal.:* 7.62 x 51mm NATO               *Remarks:* Source unknown.
  *Common Name:* MG3 GPMG

- *Cal.:* 7.62 x 54mmR
  *Common Name:* DP and RP46 LMGs

  *Remarks:* Soviet origin.

- *Cal.:* 7.62 x 54mmR
  *Common Name:* SGM series MGs

  *Remarks:* Soviet origin.

- *Cal.:* 7.62 x 54mmR
  *Common Name:* PK series GPMGs

  *Remarks:* Soviet origin.

- *Cal.:* 12.7 x 108mm
  *Common Name:* DShKM HMG

  *Remarks:* Soviet origin.

**AUTOMATIC CANNON:**
- *Cal.:* 14.5 x 114mm
  *Common Name:* KPV HMG

  *Remarks:* Soviet origin.

## SAUDI ARABIA (Kingdom of)

Population (estimate in 1984): 19.79 million. Ground forces: regulars, ca. 45,000; paramilitary (National Guard, 35,000, and Border Security Force, ca. 6,500), militia, 15,000.

**HANDGUNS:**
- *Cal.:* 9 x 19mm Parabellum
  *Common Name:* 9mm Smith & Wesson pistols (model unspecified)

  *Remarks:* US origin. Saudi Ministry of Interior purchased 500 9mm pistols from S&W in 1978.

- *Cal.:* 9 x 19mm Parabellum
  *Common Name:* FN Mle. 1935 high power pistol

  *Remarks:* FN origin. These pistols are used by the Saudi National Guard.

- *Cal.:* 9 x 19mm Parabellum
  *Common Name:* H&K P9S pistol

  *Remarks:* Heckler & Koch (HK) GmbH.

- *Cal.:* 9 x 29mmR
  *Common Name:* .38 Smith & Wesson revolvers

  *Remarks:* US origin. Saudi Arabia has been one of the major overseas purchasers of Smith & Wesson revolvers in the post-1960 period. They have bought their revolvers from FMS and MAP and directly from Smith & Wesson. The military acquired the following unspecified .38 caliber revolvers in recent years: 4,600 in 1968, 39,450 in 1981, 15,000 in 1983 from MAP. FMS delivered 2,000 M10 military & police revolvers (1005-00-937-5839) before 1974 and 10,174 in 1976, an additional 1,000 M10s (1005-00-937-5840) before 1974, and 3,312 in 1976. The Saudi Ministry of Interior Special Security Forces purchased the following revolvers directly from S&W: 3,200 in 1976; 50 in 1977; 10,500 in 1978. Other revolver purchases included 50 .357s in 1978 for the Ministry of the Interior and 20 .38s for the Chief of Public Safety in Riyadh in 1976.

- *Cal.:* 9 x 29mmR
  *Common Name:* .38 Colt revolvers

  *Remarks:* US origin. Acquired the Police Positive model with 127mm barrel in the early 1960s through the German arms firm Merex. For example, the Public Security Forces purchased 1,000 of these revolvers in 1966–67.

- *Cal.:* 11.43 x 23mm
  *Common Name:* .45 M1911A1 pistols

  *Remarks:* US origin. About 6,300 delivered by FMS before 1974.

**SUBMACHINE GUNS:**
- *Cal.:* 9 x 19mm Parabellum
  *Common Name:* MPi69

  *Remarks:* Steyr-Daimler-Puch (SDP), Austria.

- *Cal.:* 9 x 19mm Parabellum
  *Common Name:* M12 submachine gun

  *Remarks:* Beretta, Italy. Public Security Department acquired 40,000 in 1972.

- *Cal.:* 9 x 19mm Parabellum
  *Common Name:* MK5 Sterling submachine gun

  *Remarks:* UK origin. Obtained in 1984. Used by the National Guard. Some Sten guns may still be held in reserve.

- *Cal.:* 9 x 19mm NATO
  *Common Name:* MP5, all variants of this submachine gun

  *Remarks:* The Saudi armed forces have acquired these weapons from HK and the Royal Small Arms Factory (RSAF), Enfield; currently they manufacture it in-country.

- *Cal.:* 9 x 19mm Parabellum
  *Common Name:* Smith & Wesson M76 submachine gun

  *Remarks:* Smith & Wesson, US. This was the only export sale of this weapon. Apparently, the Saudi armed forces decided to purchase MP5s when they could no longer get M76s from S&W.

- *Cal.:* 9 x 19mm Parabellum
  *Common Name:* Ingram MAC 10 submachine gun

  *Remarks:* Military Armament Company, US.

- *Cal.:* 11.43 x 23mm
  *Common Name:* .45 M3 and M3A1 submachine guns

  *Remarks:* US origin. FMS delivered 2,137 M3 SMGs in 1976; 4,537 M3A1 SMGs before 1975. An unspecified 4,871 .45 caliber SMGs were provided by MAP before 1975.

**RIFLES:**
- *Cal.:* 5.56 x 45mm
  *Common Name:* AUG

  *Remarks:* SDP. Between 50,000 and 100,000 are reported to have been acquired, but this has not been confirmed. First deliveries were made in 1980.

- *Cal.:* 7.62 x 51mm NATO
  *Common Name:* G3 rifle series

  *Remarks:* The West German government arranged for the creation of a production facility at the Al-Khardj Arsenal. This factory production line was established by the government-owned firm Fritz Werner. The Saudi armed forces have also purchased completed rifles from HK and RSAF.

- *Cal.:* 7.62 x 51mm NATO
  *Common Name:* FAL

  *Remarks:* Origin unknown.

- *Cal.:* 7.62 x 51mm NATO
  *Common Name:* SSG sniper rifle

  *Remarks:* SDP.

- *Cal.:* 7.62 x 33mm
  *Common Name:* M1 carbine

  *Remarks:* US origin. MAP provided 2,000 before 1975. These are still used by some public safety organizations.

- *Cal.:* 7.62 x 63mm
  *Common Name:* M1 rifle

  *Remarks:* US origin. MAP provided 34,530 before 1975. These rifles were used by the Army and have been replaced by the G3A3.

- *Cal.:* 7.62 x 63mm
  *Common Name:* M1918A2 Browning automatic rifle

  *Remarks:* US origin. MAP provided 1,000 before 1975.

- *Cal.:* 7.97 x 57mm
  *Common Name:* FN Mauser carbine

  *Remarks:* FN. FN Model 1924.

**SHOTGUNS:**
- *Cal.:* 18.5 x 59mm
  *Common Name:* 12 gage Mossberg Model 500 shotgun

  *Remarks:* Mossberg, US.

**MACHINE GUNS:**
- *Cal.:* 7.62 x 51mm NATO
  *Common Name:* MG3 GPMG

  *Remarks:* German design. The Saudis have bought MG3s from Rheinmetall of West Germany, SDP, Santa Barbara of Spain, and Beretta-Motofidies Whitehead of Italy.

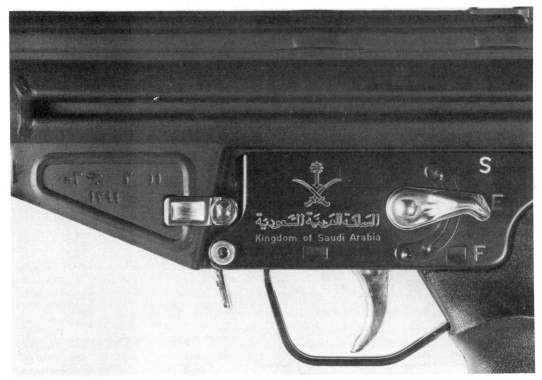

**Receiver markings on a Saudi-manufactured *Gewehr 3*. This particular G3 was a presentation model, which had several gold-plated parts. (Smithsonian; Eric Long)**

• *Cal.:* 7.62 x 51mm NATO
 *Common Name:* M73 armor MG

*Remarks:* US origin. Mounted on M60A3 tanks.

• *Cal.:* 7.62 x 51mm NATO
 *Common Name:* M219 armor MG

*Remarks:* US origin. Mounted on M60A3 tanks. FMS provided 32 in 1976 and MAP provided 5 in 1979.

• *Cal.:* 7.62 x 51mm NATO
 *Common Name:* FN MAG GPMG

*Remarks:* FN. *Infanterie Standard* (60-20), T1 and T1 without bipod on Cadillac Gage V150 APCs; *Coaxial* (60-40), V150 Cadillac Gage, AIFV 60-417 (P92S), Sanke AIFV, and T3 (MAG 58). The Saudis acquired 95 Cadillac V-150s in 1979.

• *Cal.:* 7.62 x 51mm NATO
 *Common Name:* M60 GPMG

*Remarks:* US origin. FMS delivered 10 before 1975.

• *Cal.:* 7.62 x 51mm NATO
 *Common Name:* M240 AMG

*Remarks:* US origin. FMS delivered 55 in 1979; 55 in 1980.

• *Cal.:* 7.62 x 63mm
 *Common Name:* .30 M1918A2 BAR

*Remarks:* US origin. FMS delivered 1,000 before 1975.

• *Cal.:* 7.62 x 63mm
 *Common Name:* .30 M1919A4 LMG

*Remarks:* US origin. FMS delivered 3,363 before 1975. Merex of West Germany also sold surplus *Bundeswehr* M1919s to the Saudis in the mid-1960s.

• *Cal.:* 7.62 x 63mm
 *Common Name:* .30 M37 AMG

*Remarks:* US origin. FMS delivered 704 before 1975.

- *Cal.:* 12.7 x 99mm
  *Common Name:* .50 M2 HB
  HMGs

  *Remarks:* US and Belgian origin. FMS delivered 2,300 M2HBs before 1975; 333 in 1975; 1,153 in 1976; 259 in 1979; 26 in 1980. Since that time the Saudis have bought M2 HBs from Ramo Manufacturing Company, Saco Defense Systems, and FN. Ramo alone delivered 840 guns in 1979–82 for the Frontier Forces. In addition, FMS has delivered M2s for the M1 cupola: 24 in 1975; 25 in 1976; 12 in 1978; 56 in 1979.

- *Cal.:* 12.7 x 99mm
  *Common Name:* .50 M85 armor
  MG

  *Remarks:* US origin. Mounted on M60A3 tanks. FMS provided 117 in 1979.

**AUTOMATIC CANNON:**
- *Cal.:* 20 x 102mm
  *Common Name:* 20mm M168 Vulcan automatic cannon on M167 Vulcan Air Defense System (VADS)

  *Remarks:* US origin. Approx. 50 SP M167A1s VADS in service. Approx. 150 towed M163A1s VADS in service.

- *Cal.:* 20 x 139mm
  *Common Name:* M693 automatic cannon

  *Remarks:* French origin.

**GRENADE LAUNCHERS:**
- *Cal.:* 40 x 46mmSR
  *Common Name:* M79 grenade launcher

  *Remarks:* US origin. FMS provided 80 M79s in 1980.

- *Cal.:* 40 x 46mmSR
  *Common Name:* HK69 A1 grenade launcher

  *Remarks:* HK GmbH origin.

## SENEGAL (Republic of) Also see entry for Gambia

Population (estimate in 1984): 6.54 million. Ground forces: regulars, ca. 8,500; paramilitary, ca. 2,500.

**HANDGUNS:**
- *Cal.:* 7.65 x 17mm Browning
  *Common Name:* Walther PP

  *Remarks:* Walther design made by Manurhin of France.

- *Cal.:* 9 x 29mmR
  *Common Name:* .357 Manurhin MR-73 revolver

  *Remarks:* Manurhin design made by Manurhin.

- *Cal.:* 9 x 29mmR
  *Common Name:* .38 Smith & Wesson revolver

  *Remarks:* US origin. The Dakar Police purchased 8 S&W revolvers directly from the manufacturer in 1979.

**SUBMACHINE GUNS:**
- *Cal.:* 7.65 x 20mm
  *Common Name:* MAS Model 38 submachine gun

  *Remarks:* French origin. Manufacture Nationale d'Armes St. Etienne (MAS).

- *Cal.:* 9 x 19mm Parabellum
  *Common Name:* MAT 49 submachine gun

  *Remarks:* Manufacture Nationale d'Armes de Tulle (MAT).

- *Cal.:* 5.56 x 45mm
  *Common Name:* HK53 submachine gun

  *Remarks:* Origin unknown.

**RIFLES:**
- *Cal.:* 5.56 x 45mm
  *Common Name:* HK33A1 rifle

- *Cal.:* 5.56 x 45mm
  *Common Name:* FAMAS rifle

- *Cal.:* 5.56 x 45mm
  *Common Name:* M16 rifle

- *Cal.:* 7.5 x 54mm
  *Common Name:* MAS 36/51 rifle

- *Cal.:* 7.5 x 54mm
  *Common Name:* MAS 49/56 rifle

- *Cal.:* 7.62 x 51mm NATO
  *Common Name: Gewehr 3*

**SHOTGUNS:**

**MACHINE GUNS:**
- *Cal.:* 7.5 x 54mm
  *Common Name:* MAC Mle 24/29 LMG

- *Cal.:* 7.5 x 54mm
  *Common Name:* AA 52 GPMG

- *Cal.:* 7.62 x 51mm NATO
  *Common Name:* HK21 GPMG

- *Cal.:* 12.7 x 99mm
  *Common Name:* .50 M2 HB HMGs

**AUTOMATIC CANNON:**
- *Cal.:* 20 x 139mm
  *Common Name:* 20mm M693 automatic cannon

*Remarks:* Heckler & Koch (HK) design, manufactured by MAS. These rifles are used by the Marine Commandos.

*Remarks:* MAS, Groupment Industriel des Armements Terrestres (GIAT), France. About 250 purchased in 1983.

*Remarks:* US origin. Ca. 50 in use.

*Remarks:* MAS.

*Remarks:* MAS.

*Remarks:* HK design, manufactured by MAS.

*Remarks:* French origin. Manufacture Nationale d'Armes de Chatellerault (MAC).

*Remarks:* French origin. Groupment Industriel des Armements Terrestres (GIAT).

*Remarks:* Heckler & Koch (HK) design, manufactured by MAS.

*Remarks:* US origin. Ramo, Inc. delivered M2 HBs in 1980. Government sought to purchase more M2s in 1983. Also via France? Observed mounted on trucks.

*Remarks:* French origin. GIAT.

## SEYCHELLES

Population (estimate in 1984): 0.066 million. Ground forces: regulars, People's Defense Force, ca. 1,000; reserves, unknown; paramilitary (police), 900. In recent years, North Korean and Tanzanian advisors have been assisting the military of the Seychelles.

**HANDGUNS:**
- *Cal.:* 7.65 x 17mm Browning
  *Common Name:* Walther PP

- *Cal.:* 9 x 20mmR
  *Common Name:* .38 Enfield No. 2 revolver

- *Cal.:* 9 x 20mmR
  *Common Name:* .38 Webley MK 4 revolver

- *Cal.:* 9 x 29mmR
  *Common Name:* .38 Manurhin MR 73 revolver

*Remarks:* Walther design made by Manurhin of France.

*Remarks:* UK origin.

*Remarks:* UK origin.

*Remarks:* French origin.

- *Cal.:* 9 x 29mmR
  *Common Name:* .38 Smith & Wesson revolver

*Remarks:* US origin. Bought 15 in 1976 for police use.

**SUBMACHINE GUNS:**
- *Cal.:* 9 x 19mm Parabellum
  *Common Name:* MAT 49 submachine gun

*Remarks:* Manufacture Nationale d'Armes de Tulle (MAT).

**RIFLES:**
- *Cal.:* 5.56 x 45mm
  *Common Name:* SG540 rifle

*Remarks:* Manurhin-made SIG rifle.

- *Cal.:* 7.62 x 39mm
  *Common Name:* SKS carbine

*Remarks:* East Bloc origin.

- *Cal.:* 7.62 x 39mm
  *Common Name:* AK47 assault rifle

*Remarks:* East Bloc origin. Exact variants used not presently known.

- *Cal.:* 7.5 x 54mm
  *Common Name:* MAS 36 bolt action rifle

*Remarks:* French origin. Manufacture Nationale d'Armes de St. Etienne (MAS).

- *Cal.:* 7.5 x 54mm
  *Common Name:* MAS 49/56 rifle

*Remarks:* French origin. MAS.

**SHOTGUNS:**

**MACHINE GUNS:**
- *Cal.:* 7.5 x 54mm
  *Common Name:* MAS Mle. 1924/ 29 LMG

*Remarks:* MAS.

- *Cal.:* 7.5 x 54mm
  *Common Name:* AAT52 GPMG

*Remarks:* MAT.

- *Cal.:* 7.62 x 51mm NATO
  *Common Name:* FN MAG

*Remarks:* UK origin. The L7A1 version from the Royal Small Arms Factory (RSAF), Enfield, is presently used.

- *Cal.:* 7.62 x 51mm NATO
  *Common Name:* L4 series Bren guns

*Remarks:* UK origin. From the RSAF. Some older .303 (7.7 x 56mmR) caliber Brens may also still be in the inventory.

- *Cal.:* 7.62 x 39mm
  *Common Name:* RPD LMG

*Remarks:* East Bloc origin.

- *Cal.:* 7.62 x 39mm
  *Common Name:* RPK LMG

*Remarks:* East Bloc origin.

- *Cal.:* 7.62 x 54mmR
  *Common Name:* RP46 company machine gun

*Remarks:* East Bloc origin. Some older DP LMGs may still be in the inventory.

- *Cal.:* 7.62 x 54mmR
  *Common Name:* PK series GPMG

*Remarks:* East Bloc origin.

- *Cal.:* 12.7 x 108mm
  *Common Name:* DShK38/46 HMG

*Remarks:* East Bloc origin. Both Soviet DShKs and Chinese Type 54s are presently in service.

**AUTOMATIC CANNON:**
- *Cal.:* 14.5 x 114mm
  *Common Name:* KPV HMG

*Remarks:* East Bloc origin.

## SIERRA LEONE (Republic of)

Population (estimate in 1984): 3.81 million. Ground forces: regulars, ca. 3,000; paramilitary, National Police Force, 3,500; Sierra Leone Constabulary, 1,000; auxiliary police, 400. There are about 150 Cuban civilian technicians stationed in-country. Small arms used have generally followed the American pattern in the past, but this has changed in recent years.

**HANDGUNS:**
- *Cal.:* 9 x 19mm
  *Common Name:* FN Mle. 1935 GP pistol

  *Remarks:* Belgian origin.

- *Cal.:* 9 x 20mmR
  *Common Name:* .38 Webley MK 4 revolver

  *Remarks:* UK origin.

- *Cal.:* 7.62 x 25mm
  *Common Name:* TT33 Tokarev pistol

  *Remarks:* East Bloc origin.

**SUBMACHINE GUNS:**
- *Cal.:* 9 x 19mm Parabellum
  *Common Name:* Sterling Mark 4 submachine gun

  *Remarks:* Sterling Armament Co., UK.

- *Cal.:* 9 x 19mm Parabellum
  *Common Name:* Sten submachine gun

  *Remarks:* UK origin.

- *Cal.:* 7.62 x 25mm
  *Common Name:* PPSh41 submachine gun

  *Remarks:* East Bloc origin.

- *Cal.:* 7.62 x 25mm
  *Common Name:* PPS43 submachine gun

  *Remarks:* East Bloc origin.

**RIFLES:**
- *Cal.:* 7.62 x 51mm NATO
  *Common Name:* L1A1 rifle

  *Remarks:* UK origin.

- *Cal.:* 7.62 x 39mm
  *Common Name:* SKS carbine

  *Remarks:* East Bloc origin.

- *Cal.:* 7.62 x 39mm
  *Common Name:* AK47 and AKM assault rifle

  *Remarks:* East Bloc origin.

**SHOTGUNS:**

**MACHINE GUNS:**
- *Cal.:* 7.62 x 39mm
  *Common Name:* RPD LMG

  *Remarks:* East Bloc origin.

- *Cal.:* 7.62 x 51mm NATO
  *Common Name:* FN MAG

  *Remarks:* FN origin?

- *Cal.:* 7.7 x 56mmR
  *Common Name:* .303 Mark 1 Bren LMG

  *Remarks:* UK origin.

- *Cal.:* 7.7 x 56mmR
  *Common Name:* .303 Vickers MMG

  *Remarks:* UK origin.

• *Cal.:* 12.7 x 108mm
*Common Name:* DShK38/46
HMG

*Remarks:* East Bloc origin.

**AUTOMATIC CANNON:**

# SINGAPORE (Republic of)

Population (estimate in 1984): 2.53 million. Ground forces: regulars, ca. 45,000; reserves, ca. 150,000; paramilitary, 7,500; Home Guard Force 30,000.

**HANDGUNS:**

• *Cal.:* 9 x 19mm NATO
*Common Name:* FN Mle. 1935 GP
pistol

*Remarks:* Belgian origin.

• *Cal.:* 9 x 19mm NATO
*Common Name:* HK P7 M8 pistol

*Remarks:* Heckler & Koch (HK), GmbH.

• *Cal.:* 9 x 29mmR
*Common Name:* .38 S&W revolver

*Remarks:* US origin. Direct acquisitions include: Singapore Police, 1976–77, 1,622; Singapore Customs, 1976–78, 37; Central Narcotics Bureau, 1976, 90; Singapore Prisons, 1977, 26.

**SUBMACHINE GUNS:**

• *Cal.:* 9 x 19mm NATO
*Common Name:* Sterling Mark 4
submachine gun

*Remarks:* Sterling Armament Co., UK.

• *Cal.:* 9 x 19mm NATO
*Common Name:* HK MP5 and
MP5SD submachine guns

*Remarks:* HK, GmbH.

**RIFLES:**

• *Cal.:* 5.56 x 45mm
*Common Name:* M16 (Model
614-S) rifle without bolt assist

*Remarks:* Chartered Industries of Singapore made these rifles under license from Colt. Approx. 18,000 Model 614-S rifles were purchased from Colt prior to CIS production. Total CIS production estimated at 150,000 to 180,000.

• *Cal.:* 5.56 x 45mm
*Official Name:* Singapore Assault
Rifle 80
*Common Name:* SAR80 assault
rifle

*Remarks:* A CIS evolutionary development and improvement of the AR-18 rifle. These rifles will be used by Singapore forces alongside M16A1. They have been exported.

• *Cal.:* 7.62 x 51mm NATO
*Common Name:* L1A1 rifle

*Remarks:* Commonwealth Small Arms Factory, Lithgow, Australia. Obsolescent. Reserve stocks only. Some used by the Singapore Police Force.

• *Cal.:* 7.7 x 56mmR
*Common Name:* .303 No. 5 rifle

*Remarks:* Obsolescent. Reserve stocks only. FOM 1005-35-2-7.7-4.

**SHOTGUNS:**

**MACHINE GUNS:**

• *Cal.:* 5.56 x 45mm
*Common Name:* M16A1 (Model
611) heavy barrel automatic rifle

*Remarks:* Colt, US. Approx. 2,300 of these weapons were acquired directly from Colt before 1970.

- *Cal.:* 7.62 x 51mm NATO
  *Common Name:* L2A1 automatic rifle

*Remarks:* Lithgow. Obsolescent.

- *Cal.:* 7.62 x 51mm NATO
  *Common Name:* L7A1 GPMG

*Remarks:* Royal Small Arms Factory (RSAF), Enfield. From FN, Herstal, they have also acquired the following MAG models: *Infanterie Standard* (60-20), T7 (L7A2); *Coaxial* (60-40), T3 (MAG 58), L7A2 (P806), and M240 (US model). Currently being made in limited numbers without a license by Ordnance Development & Engineering Company of Singapore (Pte.), Ltd.

- *Cal.:* 5.56 x 45mm
  *Common Name:* Ultimax 100, Mark II w/ fixed barrel and 100-shot drum magazine

*Remarks:* Domestic CIS SAW design, which has been adopted by the Singapore Armed Forces. It is likely that this weapon will replace M16A1 HBAR.

- *Cal.:* 5.56 x 45mm
  *Common Name:* M134 Minigun (Gatling)

*Remarks:* US origin. Made by General Electric. Provided by FMS; 69 in 1979 and 6 in 1984.

- *Cal.:* 7.7 x 56mmR
  *Common Name:* .303 Bren LMG

*Remarks:* Service status unknown. Probably obsolescent and held in reserve stocks.

- *Cal.:* 12.7 x 99mm
  *Common Name:* .50 M2 HB HMG

*Remarks:* US origin.

**AUTOMATIC CANNON:**
- *Cal.:* 20 x 128mm
  *Common Name:* 20mm Oerlikon; model unknown

*Remarks:* Oerlikon-Buhrle of Switzerland.

**GRENADE LAUNCHERS:**
- *Cal.:* 40 x 46mmSR
  *Common Name:* M203 grenade launcher attached to M16 rifle

*Remarks:* Colt, US. Approx. 300 were acquired directly from Colt 1978–81.

## SOMALIA (Democratic Republic of)

Population (estimate in 1984): 6.39 million. Ground forces: regulars, ca. 60,000; paramilitary, ca. 30,000 (Somali Police Corps, ca. 8,000; Border Guards, ca. 1,500; Pioneers of Victory [*Gulwadayaasha*], a volunteer Home Guard of ca. 20,000).

**HANDGUNS:**
- *Cal.:* 7.62 x 25mm
  *Common Name:* TT33 Tokarev pistol

*Remarks:* East Bloc origin.

- *Cal.:* 7.62 x 25mm
  *Common Name:* vz.52 pistol

*Remarks:* Czechoslovakian origin.

- *Cal.:* 9 x 18mm
  *Common Name:* Makarov pistol

*Remarks:* East Bloc origin.

- *Cal.:* 9 x 20mmR
  *Common Name:* .38 Enfield No. 2 revolver

*Remarks:* UK origin. OBSOLETE.

## SUBMACHINE GUNS:

- *Cal.:* 9 x 19mm Parabellum
  *Common Name:* Sterling Mark 4 submachine gun

  *Remarks:* Sterling Armament Co., UK.

- *Cal.:* 9 x 19mm Parabellum
  *Common Name:* Uzi submachine gun

  *Remarks:* Israeli Military Industries (IMI), Israel.

- *Cal.:* 9 x 19mm Parabellum
  *Common Name:* Beretta M12 submachine gun

  *Remarks:* Beretta, Italy.

- *Cal.:* 9 x 19mm Parabellum
  *Common Name:* Beretta M38 submachine gun

  *Remarks:* Beretta, Italy.

- *Cal.:* 9 x 9mm Parabellum
  *Common Name:* vz.23 and vz.25 submachine gun

  *Remarks:* Czechoslovakian origin.

- *Cal.:* 7.62 x 25mm
  *Common Name:* PPS43 submachine gun

  *Remarks:* East Bloc origin.

- *Cal.:* 7.62 x 25mm
  *Common Name:* PPSh41 submachine gun

  *Remarks:* East Bloc origin.

## RIFLES:

- *Cal.:* 5.56 x 45mm
  *Common Name:* SAR80 rifle

  *Remarks:* Chartered Industries of Singapore reportedly have provided 20,000 SAR80s 1982–83.

- *Cal.:* 5.56 x 45mm
  *Common Name:* M16A1 rifle

  *Remarks:* US origin. FMS delivered 3,000 of these rifles in 1980.

- *Cal.:* 7.62 x 33mm
  *Common Name:* .30 M1 and M2 carbines

  *Remarks:* US origin.

- *Cal.:* 7.62 x 39mm
  *Common Name:* AK47 and AKM assault rifles

  *Remarks:* East Bloc origin. Specifically, Hungarian and Romanian versions of the AKM appear in news photos. Yugoslavian M70AB2 models are also in service.

- *Cal.:* 7.62 x 39mm
  *Common Name:* SKS45 carbine

  *Remarks:* East Bloc origin.

- *Cal.:* 7.62 x 39mm
  *Common Name:* vz.52 rifle

  *Remarks:* Czechoslovakian origin.

- *Cal.:* 7.62 x 39mm
  *Common Name:* vz.58 assault rifle

  *Remarks:* Czechoslovakian origin.

- *Cal.:* 7.62 x 51mm NATO
  *Common Name:* M14 rifle

  *Remarks:* US origin, but transfer path unclear.

- *Cal.:* 7.62 x 51mm NATO
  *Common Name:* BM59 rifle

  *Remarks:* Beretta design. News photographs have shown these weapons in the hands of antigovernment fighters.

- *Cal.:* 7.62 x 51mm NATO
  *Common Name:* Gewehr 3

  *Remarks:* Heckler & Koch (HK), Germany.

- *Cal.:* 7.7 x 56mmR
  *Common Name:* .303 SMLE MK III and Enfield No. 4 rifles

  *Remarks:* UK origin.

- *Cal.:* 7.92 x 33mm
  *Common Name:* Sturmgewehr 44

  *Remarks:* East German origin. Surplus World War II weapons.

- *Cal.:* 7.92 x 57mm
  *Common Name:* SAFN rifle

  *Remarks:* FN origin.

- *Cal.:* 7.92 x 57mm
  *Common Name:* Mauser 98K rifle

  *Remarks:* Mausers of World War II German origin.

**SHOTGUNS:**

**MACHINE GUNS:**

- *Cal.:* 7.62 x 39mm
  *Common Name:* RPD LMG

  *Remarks:* East Bloc origin. These LMGs were observed in 1987 news photographs.

- *Cal.:* 7.62 x 39mm
  *Common Name:* RPK LMG

  *Remarks:* East Bloc origin.

- *Cal.:* 7.62 x 51mm NATO
  *Common Name:* M73 armor MG

  *Remarks:* US origin. Mounted on US M60A3 tanks.

- *Cal.:* 7.5 x 54mm
  *Common Name:* AAT52 GPMG

  *Remarks:* Manufacture Nationale d'Armes de Tulle (MAT).

- *Cal.:* 7.62 x 54mmR
  *Common Name:* RP46 company machine gun

  *Remarks:* East Bloc origin.

- *Cal.:* 7.62 x 54mmR
  *Common Name:* DP series MGs

  *Remarks:* East Bloc origin. Mounted on older vintage Soviet tanks and APCs.

- *Cal.:* 7.62 x 54mmR
  *Common Name:* SGM series MGs

  *Remarks:* East Bloc origin. Mounted on Soviet tanks and APCs.

- *Cal.:* 7.62 x 54mmR
  *Common Name:* PKT armor MG

  *Remarks:* Soviet origin. Mounted on T62 tanks.

- *Cal.:* 7.62 x 54mmR
  *Common Name:* Type 67 GPMG

  *Remarks:* Chinese origin.

- *Cal.:* 7.7 x 56mmR
  *Common Name:* .303 Mark 1 Bren LMG

  *Remarks:* UK origin.

- *Cal.:* 7.92 x 57mm
  *Common Name:* MG34

  *Remarks:* World War II German origin. Some of these guns have fallen into the hands of antigovernment forces.

- *Cal.:* 7.92 x 57mm
  *Common Name:* MG42

  *Remarks:* World War II German origin.

- *Cal.:* 12.7 x 99mm
  *Common Name:* .50 M2 HB HMG

  *Remarks:* US origin. Ramo, Inc. guns are in the inventory, but path of delivery unknown.

- *Cal.:* 12.7 x 99mm
  *Common Name:* .50 M85 armor MG

  *Remarks:* US origin. Mounted on M60A3 tanks.

- *Cal.:* 12.7 x 108mm
  *Common Name:* DShK38/46 HMG

  *Remarks:* East Bloc origin.

**AUTOMATIC CANNON:**

- *Cal.:* 14.5 x 114mm
  *Common Name:* KPV HMG

  *Remarks:* East Bloc origin. Both the ZPU-2 and ZPU-4 versions are in service.

- *Cal.:* 20 x 102mm
  *Common Name:* 20mm M168 automatic cannon

  *Remarks:* US origin. Both the M163A1 and M167 Vulcan Air Defense Systems (VADS) are in service.

- *Cal.:* 20 x 139mm
  *Common Name:* 20mm M693
  automatic cannon

  *Remarks:* French origin. Mounted on the Centaure AA system.

- *Cal.:* 23 x 152mmB
  *Common Name:* ZU23 automatic
  cannon

  *Remarks:* East Bloc origin. The ZSU-23-4 self-propelled AA system is in service.

**GRENADE LAUNCHERS:**
- *Cal.:* 40 x 46mmSR
  *Common Name:* M79 grenade
  launcher

  *Remarks:* US origin. FMS provided 150 in 1984.

# SOUTH AFRICA (Republic of)

Population (estimate in 1984): 31.70 million. Ground forces: regulars, ca. 67,400 (ca. 40,000 conscripts); paramilitary, South African Police, 17,000 whites and 20,000 blacks and Asians; National Intelligence Service (NIS), ca. 5,000; reserves, ca. 360,000. There is also an active reserve, the Citizen Force, of ca. 140,000.

**HANDGUNS:**
- *Cal.:* 9 x 19mm Parabellum
  *Common Name:* FN Mle. 1935 GP
  pistol

  *Remarks:* Belgian origin. No longer in service.

- *Cal.:* 9 x 19mm Parabellum
  *Common Name:* Star Model B
  pistol

  *Remarks:* Spanish origin. Star Bonafacio Echeverria y Cia.

- *Cal.:* 9 x 20mmR
  *Common Name:* .38 Webley MK4
  revolver

  *Remarks:* UK origin. OBSOLETE.

- *Cal.:* 9 x 20mmR
  *Common Name:* .38 Enfield No. 2
  revolver

  *Remarks:* UK origin. OBSOLETE.

**SUBMACHINE GUNS:**
- *Cal.:* 9 x 19mm Parabellum
  *Common Name:* Sana 77 semi-
  automatic carbine

  *Remarks:* Domestic design. Formerly used by paramilitary forces.

- *Cal.:* 9 x 19mm Parabellum
  *Common Name:* Uzi submachine
  gun

  *Remarks:* Purchased directly from Israeli Military Industries (IMI) and manufactured domestically under license. Adopted in 1961.

- *Cal.:* 9 x 19mm Parabellum
  *Common Name:* vz.23 and vz.25
  submachine guns

  *Remarks:* Captured from rebel forces and incorporated into the South African inventory.

- *Cal.:* 9 x 19mm
  *Common Name:* L2A2 submachine gun

  *Remarks:* Origin unknown.

- *Cal.:* 9 x 19mm
  *Common Name:* MAC 10 submachine gun

  *Remarks:* Presumably of US origin.

This South African modified 9 x 19mm Uzi submachine gun, being demonstrated by a Special Forces member, has a special long barrel so it can be used by riot police to launch tear gas and other chemical munitions. (Gander)

**RIFLES:**

• *Cal.:* 7.62 x 51mm NATO
  *Official Name:* R1
  *Common Name:* FN FAL

*Remarks:* Licensed manufacture at Lyttelton Engineering Works (LEW) of the state-owned Armaments Development and Production Corporation of South Africa (ARMSCOR). Adopted 1960.

• *Cal.:* 7.62 x 51mm NATO
  *Official Name:* R2
  *Common Name:* FN FAL

*Remarks:* Licensed manufacture at LEW, ARMSCOR. Lightweight version of the R1.

• *Cal.:* 7.62 x 51mm NATO
  *Common Name:* Gewehr 3

*Remarks:* Captured rifles of Portuguese manufacture (from Angola), which have been issued to paramilitary forces.

• *Cal.:* 5.56 x 45mm
  *Official Name:* R4
  *Common Name:* IMI Galil rifle

*Remarks:* Made at LEW, ARMSCOR.

• *Cal.:* 5.56 x 45mm
  *Official Name:* R5
  *Common Name:* IMI Galil with
    330mm barrel

*Remarks:* Made at LEW, ARMSCOR. This weapon is 1kg lighter than the R4. It is replacing the R2, just as the R4 is replacing the R1.

• *Cal.:* 5.56 x 45mm
  *Common Name:* M16A1 rifle

*Remarks:* Origin unknown. Used by mine and factory security police.

**SHOTGUNS:**

**MACHINE GUNS:**

- *Cal.:* 7.62 x 51mm NATO
  *Official Name:* L1
  *Common Name:* Vickers MMG

  *Remarks:* UK-reworked .303 Vickers.

- *Cal.:* 7.62 x 51mm NATO
  *Official Name:* L3
  *Common Name:* .30 M1919A4
  LMG converted to 7.62mm
  NATO

  *Remarks:* Converted to 7.62mm NATO at LEW, ARMSCOR. The converted weapon incorporates a new barrel, open bolt firing, and an improved feed system.

- *Cal.:* 7.62 x 51mm NATO
  *Official Name:* L4
  *Common Name:* L4A1 Bren gun

  *Remarks:* UK-reworked Bren. Observed in news photographs (1987).

- *Cal.:* 7.62 x 51mm NATO
  *Official Name:* L7 and L8
  *Common Name:* FN MAG

  *Remarks:* UK L7A1 and L8 versions from FN. These weapons were adopted in 1960.

- *Cal.:* 7.62 x 51mm NATO
  *Common Name:* SS-77 GPMG

  *Remarks:* Domestic design. Developed at LEW, ARMSCOR 1977–86. Series production began 1987.

- *Cal.:* 7.92 x 57mm
  *Common Name:* MG 34 GPMG

  *Remarks:* Germany, World War II. Captured from SWAPO forces about 1985.

- *Cal.:* 12.7 x 99mm
  *Official Name:* L4
  *Common Name:* .50 M2 HB
  HMG

  *Remarks:* US origin.

**South African troops accompany a Ratel Infantry Fighting Vehicle (mounting a French 20mm F2 automatic cannon). The man in the left foreground has a 7.62mm FN MAG, while his companion to the right has a 5.56mm R4 (copy of the Israeli Galil). (South Africa via JODD)**

South African efforts to gain self-sufficiency in armaments include this new 7.62 x 51mm NATO general purpose machine gun (the SR-77) that is being made by ARMSCOR. (Gander)

**AUTOMATIC CANNON:**
- *Cal.:* 20 x 128mm
  *Common Name:* KAA (204GK) automatic cannon

  *Remarks:* Oerlikon-Buhrle. Naval use only.

- *Cal.:* 20 x 128mm
  *Common Name:* KAB-001 (10ILa/5TG) automatic cannon

  *Remarks:* Oerlikon-Buhrle. On the GAI-B01 mount. Naval use only.

- *Cal.:* 20 x 139mm
  *Common Name:* KAD (HS820) automatic cannon

  *Remarks:* Oerlikon-Buhrle. Used on the GAI-C01 single AA mount.

- *Cal.:* 20 x 139mm
  *Common Name:* GIAT M693 (F2) automatic cannon

  *Remarks:* Groupment Industriel des Armements Terrestres (GIAT), France. Manufactured in South Africa as armament for the RATEL 20 and 60 IFVs and the RATTLER helicopter mount.

- *Cal.:* 23 x 152mmB
  *Common Name:* ZU 23 automatic cannon

  *Remarks:* Captured twin towed AA guns (ZSU-23-2) are being used by South African forces. These guns were captured in Angola.

**GRENADE LAUNCHERS:**
- *Cal.:* 30 x 29mm
  *Common Name:* AGS-17

  *Remarks:* South African forces have captured between 30 and 40 of the latest version of the Soviet AGS-17 automatic grenade launcher together with substantial stocks of ammunition. These weapons have been issued to some South African combat forces.

- *Cal.:* 37mm
  *Common Name:* 37mm Stopper riot control weapon

  *Remarks:* LEW, ARMSCOR.

- *Cal.:* 40 x 46mmSR
  *Common Name:* MGL-6

  *Remarks:* Domestic design. Used by the special forces.

The African National Congress (ANC), a Marxist antiapartheid revolutionary organization, has chosen the Kalashnikov as a symbol of its struggle against the current government of South Africa. This cover is taken from the ANC's March 1986 magazine *Sechaba*. *Umkhonto we Sizwe* is the ANC motto meaning "Spear of the Nation."

## SPAIN (State)

Population (estimate in 1984): 38.44 million. Ground forces: regulars, ca. 240,000 (170,000 conscripts); paramilitary, *Guardia Civil,* between 63,000 and 66,000 and the *Policia Nacional,* ca. 47,000; reserves, in excess of 500,000.

**HANDGUNS:**
* *Cal.:* 9 x 19mm Parabellum
  *Common Name:* Llama M-82 DA pistol

  *Remarks:* Gabilondo y Cia., Vitoria. Adopted by the Spanish Army.

* *Cal.:* 9 x 19mm Parabellum
  *Common Name:* Super Star pistol

  *Remarks:* Star-Bonifacio Echeverria, SA, Eibar. FOM 1005-24-1-9-3.

* *Cal.:* 9 x 19mm Parabellum
  *Common Name:* Star 30M pistol

  *Remarks:* Star-Bonifacio Echeverria, SA, Eibar. Used by the *Guardia Civil.*

* *Cal.:* 9 x 19mm Parabellum
  *Common Name:* Star 30PK pistol

  *Remarks:* Star-Bonifacio Echeverria, SA, Eibar. Used by the *Policia Nacional* and the *Cuerpo Superior de Policia.*

* *Cal.:* 9 x 19mm Parabellum
  *Common Name:* HK P9S pistol

  *Remarks:* Heckler & Koch (HK) origin. The Spanish Special Forces (GEO) use these weapons.

**SUBMACHINE GUNS:**
* *Cal.:* 9 x 19mm Parabellum
  *Common Name:* Z-45 submachine gun

  *Remarks:* Star.

* *Cal.:* 9 x 19mm Parabellum
  *Common Name:* Z-62 submachine gun

  *Remarks:* Star. FOM 1005-24-3-9-5.

* *Cal.:* 9 x 19mm Parabellum
  *Common Name:* Z-70-B submachine gun

  *Remarks:* Star.

* *Cal.:* 9 x 19mm Parabellum
  *Common Name:* Z-84 submachine gun

  *Remarks:* Star. This weapon has been bought by the Spanish Navy underwater demolition teams (UDT) since its introduction in 1984. This weapon has both 25- and 30-shot magazines.

* *Cal.:* 9 x 19mm Parabellum
  *Common Name:* HK MP5 submachine gun

  *Remarks:* HK origin. GEO uses these weapons. Gabilondo and HK have been negotiating a possible license for the manufacture of the MP5 in Spain.

**FIRING PORT WEAPONS:**
* *Cal.:* 7.62 x 51mm NATO
  *Official Name: Arma Automatica CETME Modelo R*
  *Common Name:* CETME-derived firing port weapon for APCs

  *Remarks:* Fabrica de Armas de Oviedo of the Empresa Nacional Santa Barbara de Industrias Militares, SA.

**RIFLES:**
* *Cal.:* 7.62 x 51mm NATO
  *Official Name: Fusil del asalto, CETME*
  *Common Name:* CETME assault rifle

  *Remarks:* Fabrica de Armas de Oviedo. FOM 1005-24-2-7.62-2.

* *Cal.:* 5.56 x 45mm
  *Official Name: Modelo L*
  *Common Name:* CETME Model L rifle

  *Remarks:* Fabrica de Armas de Oviedo. The government ordered 14,000 in 1984. Current plans call for about 20,000 to be purchased per year until sufficient (undefined) are available for the armed forces. By early 1987, 59,033 rifles were on order. The Modelo L-1-003 has been adapted to use standard M16 magazines. This latter weapon appears to be intended for export sale. FOM 1005-24-2-5.56-1.

The 7.62 x 51mm NATO Model R Firing Port Weapon was developed for use in APCs by CETME. Note the barrel fitting that allows the weapon to be attached to the ball mount, the relocated cocking handle, and the butt cap used in place of the stock assembly. (Gander)

Receiver markings on a Spanish 7.62 x 51mm Modelo C CETME assault rifle captured by the Israeli Defense Forces during "Operation Peace in Galilee." This rifle is marked "F.A.-CETME-C Cal.7,62mm. E.T.*71014*." The logo is that of the Empressa Nacional Santa Barbara de Industrias Militares, SA. (Smithsonian; Eric Long)

- *Cal.:* 5.56 x 45mm
  *Official Name: Modelo LC*
  *Common Name:* CETME Model
  LC rifle

  *Remarks:* Fabrica de Armas de Oviedo. Shortened barrel and collapsible stock.

- *Cal.:* 5.56 x 45mm
  *Common Name:* HK 33 rifle

  *Remarks:* HK origin. Used by the *Guardia Civil.*

- *Cal.:* 7.62 x 51mm NATO
  *Common Name:* Model 1943
  Mauser bolt action rifle

  *Remarks:* OBSOLETE.

- *Cal.:* 7.62 x 51mm NATO
  *Official Name: Fusil de Precision
  CETME*
  *Common Name:* CETME sniper
  rifle

  *Remarks:* Fabrica de Armas de Oviedo.

**SHOTGUNS:**
- *Cal.:* 18.5 x 59mm
  *Common Name:* 12 gage Moss-
  berg Model 500 shotgun

  *Remarks:* US origin. In service with the *Guardia Civil* and the *Cuerpo Superior* security forces.

**MACHINE GUNS:**
- *Cal.:* 5.56 x 45mm
  *Official Name: AMELI*
  *Common Name:* Ameli LMG/82

  *Remarks:* Fabrica de Armas de Oviedo. Being tested by the Spanish armed forces. Has been adopted for special operations troops.

- *Cal.:* 7.62 x 51mm NATO
  *Common Name:* MG42/59
  GPMG

  *Remarks:* Fabrica de Armas de Oviedo.

- *Cal.:* 7.62 x 51mm NATO
  *Common Name:* MG1A3 and 3S
  GPMGs

  *Remarks:* Fabrica de Armas de Oviedo.

- *Cal.:* 7.62 x 51mm NATO
  *Common Name:* NF-1 version of
  AAT52

  *Remarks:* Groupment Industriel des Armements Terrestres (GIAT), France.

- *Cal.:* 7.62 x 51mm NATO
  *Common Name:* FN MAG

  *Remarks:* FN origin. *Infanterie Standard* (60-20), T9.

- *Cal.:* 7.62 x 51mm NATO
  *Common Name:* M73 armor MG

  *Remarks:* US origin. Mounted on M60A3 tanks. FMS provided 19 guns before 1975.

- *Cal.:* 7.62 x 51mm NATO
  *Common Name:* M134 minigun

  *Remarks:* US origin. FMS provided 12 guns before 1975 and 8 more in 1982.

- *Cal.:* 7.62 x 51mm NATO
  *Common Name:* M1919A4E1
  LMG

  *Remarks:* US origin converted to 7.62mm NATO by the Fabrica de Armas de Oviedo. Mounted on M48A5 tanks.

- *Cal.:* 12.7 x 99mm
  *Common Name:* .50 M2 HB
  HMG

  *Remarks:* US origin. Used singly as a flexible gun and in the AA role on the quad AA M55 trailer mount. Approx. 130 M55 AA systems in service. The M2 HB is also used on M48A5 and AMX-30 tanks. FMS provided 195 of these guns before 1975; 19 in 1975; 1 in 1976; and 10 in 1978. In the early 1980s FN and CETME converted about 700 M3 aircraft guns to the M2 HB configuration.

- *Cal.:* 12.7 x 99mm
  *Common Name:* .50 M85 armor
  MG

  *Remarks:* US origin. Mounted on M60A3 tanks.

**AUTOMATIC CANNON:**
- *Cal.:* 20 x 102mm
  *Common Name:* 20mm M61 Vulcan

- *Cal.:* 20 x 102mm
  *Common Name:* 20mm *Meroka* multibarrel close-in weapon system

- *Cal.:* 20 x 128mm
  *Common Name:* 20mm KAA-001 (Type 204GK) automatic cannon

- *Cal.:* 20 x 128mm
  *Common Name:* 20mm KAB-001 (10La/5TG) automatic cannon

- *Cal.:* 20 x 139mm
  *Common Name:* 20mm Rh202 automatic cannon

- *Cal.:* 20 x 139mm
  *Common Name:* 20mm M693 automatic cannon

- *Cal.:* 25 x 137mm
  *Common Name:* Gun, automatic, 25mm M242 (Bushmaster)

**GRENADE LAUNCHERS:**
- *Cal.:* 40 x 46mmSR
  *Common Name:* M79 grenade launcher

*Remarks:* US origin. FMS provided 6 of these guns before 1975.

*Remarks:* Fabrica de Armas de Oviedo. This 12-barrel weapon is provided for missile defense on Spanish Navy ships such as the new *Oliver Hazard Perry*-class frigate *Santa Maria.*

*Remarks:* Oerlikon-Bührle.

*Remarks:* Oerlikon-Bührle. On the GAI-B01 mount.

*Remarks:* Rheinmetall, Germany.

*Remarks:* GIAT, France. On the 76T1 mount.

*Remarks:* McDonnell-Douglas Helicopters, Inc. Santa Barbara will build a total of 208 guns and turrets at a rate of about 50 per year. Manufacture will be carried under licenses obtained early in 1987. These guns will be mounted in OTO Melara turrets on the Spanish-built BMR-VEC-625 Cavalry Scout Vehicle, deliveries of which began in April 1987.

*Remarks:* US origin. MAP provided 80 before 1975.

# SRI LANKA (Democratic Socialist Republic of)

Population (estimate in 1984): 15.93 million. Ground forces: regulars, ca. 14,000; reserves, ca. 14,000; auxiliaries, about 3,000 to 5,000 part-time and generally unarmed (Home Guard); paramilitary, ca. 14,000 police. The opposition forces of the Tamil Tigers appear to have received new manufacture 7.62 x 39mm AKMs, the source of which is unknown.

**HANDGUNS:**
- *Cal.:* 7.62 x 25mm
  *Common Name:* Type 50 pistol

- *Cal.:* 9 x 19mm
  *Common Name:* FN Mle. 35 GP pistol

**SUBMACHINE GUNS:**
- *Cal.:* 9 x 19mm NATO
  *Common Name:* H&K MP5A3 submachine gun

*Remarks:* Chinese-made variant of the Soviet Tokarev.

*Remarks:* Origin unknown.

*Remarks:* Origin unknown.

• *Cal.:* 9 x 19mm NATO
  *Common Name:* Sterling submachine gun

*Remarks:* Seen in news photos of Sri Lankan government forces.

**RIFLES:**
• *Cal.:* 5.56 x 45mm
  *Common Name:* FNC 80 light
  rifle

*Remarks:* Belgian origin. Quantity unknown. Illustrated in news photographs during summer of 1986.

• *Cal.:* 5.56 x 45mm
  *Common Name:* SAR 80 rifle

*Remarks:* Singapore origin. A few hundred of these Chartered Industries of
Singapore rifles have been purchased from that Singapore firm.

• *Cal.:* 5.56 x 45mm
  *Common Name:* M16A1 rifle

*Remarks:* US origin.

• *Cal.:* 5.56 x 45mm
  *Common Name:* M16A2 carbine
  (Model 723 w/ 3-shot burst and
  376mm barrel)

*Remarks:* US origin. About 300 purchased in 1984 for the Police Special
Task Force, which is being trained by former British SAS personnel.

• *Cal.:* 7.62 x 39mm
  *Common Name:* SKS carbine

*Remarks:* East Bloc origin.

• *Cal.:* 7.62 x 39mm
  *Common Name:* Type 56 assault
  rifle

*Remarks:* Chinese-made AK47s and AKMs of both the folding and solid
stock varieties.

• *Cal.:* 7.62 x 51mm NATO
  *Common Name:* L1A1 SLRs

*Remarks:* In the mid-1980s (1984-85), Chartered Industries of Singapore sold
5,000 refurbished Australian L1A1 (FN FALS) to the Sri Lankan government. These are believed to be primarily used by police organizations.

• *Cal.:* 7.7 x 56mmR
  *Common Name:* .303 No. 4
  Enfield bolt action rifle

*Remarks:* UK origin via India? Used by local police.

**SHOTGUNS:**
• *Cal.:* 18.5 x 59mm
  *Common Name:* 12 gage Reming-
  ton shotguns

*Remarks:* Various models used by the police and guard units.

**MACHINE GUNS:**
• *Cal.:* 5.56 x 45mm
  *Common Name:* FN Minimi

*Remarks:* FN origin.

• *Cal.:* 7.62 x 39mm
  *Common Name:* Chinese Type 56
  (RPD)

*Remarks:* Chinese origin.

• *Cal.:* 7.62 x 51mm NATO
  *Common Name:* FN MAG (L7A1)
  GPMG

*Remarks:* FN origin?

• *Cal.:* 7.62 x 51mm NATO
  *Common Name:* HK11 LMG

*Remarks:* Origin uncertain. May be from the Royal Small Arms Factory
(RSAF), Enfield.

• *Cal.:* 7.62 x 51mm NATO
  *Common Name:* HK21E1 LMG

*Remarks:* Origin uncertain. May be from the RSAF.

• *Cal.:* 7.62 x 63mm
  *Common Name:* M1919A4
  Browning MGs

*Remarks:* Mounted on light armored vehicles. Reportedly these machine
guns were supplied (sold) by South African sources. May have been converted to 7.62 x 51mm NATO. Illustrated in news photographs during summer of 1986.

**AUTOMATIC CANNON:**

**GRENADE LAUNCHERS:**
- *Cal.:* 40 x 46mmSR      *Remarks:* Heckler & Koch (HK) GmbH origin.
  *Common Name:* HK69A1 grenade launcher

- *Cal.:* 40 x 46mmSR      *Remarks:* US origin.
  *Common Name:* M203 grenade launcher

### Antigovernment Forces

There are as many as 23 Tamil terrorist/separatist groups residing in Sri Lanka. The best known are the Tamil Eelam Liberation Army and the Tamil Eelam Army. The various groups currently field about 1,000 guerrilla fighters. Weapons seen in their hands include the 9 x 19mm FN Browning High Power and Czechoslovakian CZ 75 pistols; 9 x 19mm Parabellum Sterling, 9 x 19mm Parabellum Sten, and Beretta M12 submachine guns; 5.56 x 45mm M16A1 rifles with M203 grenade launchers; 5.56 x 45mm FNCs, and 5.56 x 45mm SAR80s; 7.62 x 39mm AKMs (sources unknown); Czech 7.62 x 39mm vz.52/57s modified to take AK magazines; 7.62 x 51mm FALs and G3s; 7.62 x 54mmR Romanian FPK sniper rifles; 7.62 x 54mmR PK GPMGs. Machine guns used include 7.62 x 51mm NATO M60 GPMGs and 7.62 x 51mm NATO FN MAGs. The government has brought in former Special Air Service and Israeli Shin Bit personnel to train their counter-terrorist forces. For additional background see: Penelope Tremayne and Ian Gelgard, *Tamil Terrorism: Nationalist or Marxist?* (Institute for the Study of Terrorism: London, 1986).

## SUDAN (Democratic Republic of)

Population (estimate in 1984): 21.10 million. Ground forces: regulars, ca. 53,000; paramilitary, ca. 7,500 (National Guard, 500; Republican Guard, 500; Border Guard, 2,500; Sudanese Police, 4,000). Since 1981, the People's Republic of China has been a primary supplier of small caliber weapons. Although there is no domestic manufacturing of small arms, the Sudanese do produce their own small caliber ammunition.

**HANDGUNS:**
- *Cal.:* 9 x 19mm Parabellum      *Remarks:* Heckler & Koch (HK), GmbH, West Germany.
  *Common Name:* HK P9S pistol

- *Cal.:* 9 x 19mm Parabellum      *Remarks:* Egyptian origin. This is the Beretta M951 Brigadier pistol as made
  *Common Name:* Helwan pistol      by the Maadi Military & Civil Industries Company.

- *Cal.:* 9 x 19mm Parabellum      *Remarks:* FN origin.
  *Common Name:* FN Mle. 35GP pistol

**SUBMACHINE GUNS:**
- *Cal.:* 9 x 19mm Parabellum      *Remarks:* Source uncertain. May have been German government military
  *Common Name:* Uzi submachine gun      assistance. Acquired in the mid-1960s.

- *Cal.:* 9 x 19mm Parabellum      *Remarks:* Beretta, Italy.
  *Common Name:* M12 submachine gun

- *Cal.:* 9 x 19mm Parabellum      *Remarks:* Beretta, Italy.
  *Common Name:* M38/49 submachine gun

- *Cal.:* 9 x 19mm Parabellum
  *Common Name:* MP5 submachine gun

  *Remarks:* Source uncertain. Probably from the Royal Small Arms Factory (RSAF), Enfield.

- *Cal.:* 9 x 19mm Parabellum
  *Common Name:* MK4 Sterling submachine gun

  *Remarks:* Sterling Armaments, Co., Ltd., UK.

- *Cal.:* 9 x 19mm Parabellum
  *Common Name:* Sten submachine gun

  *Remarks:* UK origin.

- *Cal.:* 9 x 19mm Parabellum
  *Common Name:* Super Sola submachine gun

  *Remarks:* Société Luxembourgeoise d'Armes, S.A., Ettlebruck, Luxembourg.

**RIFLES:**
- *Cal.:* 7.62 x 39mm
  *Common Name:* SKS carbine

  *Remarks:* East Bloc origin.

- *Cal.:* 7.62 x 39mm
  *Common Name:* AK47 assault rifle

  *Remarks:* East Bloc origin. Early AK47s w/ folding stocks have been observed in the hands of Sudanese antigovernment forces.

- *Cal.:* 7.62 x 39mm
  *Common Name:* AMD assault rifle

  *Remarks:* Hungarian-made AKM assault rifles have been observed in the hands of Sudanese antigovernment forces.

- *Cal.:* 7.62 x 51mm NATO
  *Common Name: Gewehr 3*

  *Remarks:* HK.

- *Cal.:* 7.61 x 51mm NATO
  *Common Name:* AR-10 rifle

  *Remarks:* Artillerie-Inrichtingen, Netherlands. OBSOLETE; few probably remain in active service.

**SHOTGUNS:**

**MACHINE GUNS:**
- *Cal.:* 7.62 x 39mm
  *Common Name:* RPK LMG

  *Remarks:* East Bloc origin.

- *Cal.:* 7.62 x 39mm
  *Common Name:* RPD LMG

  *Remarks:* East Bloc origin.

- *Cal.:* 7.62 x 51mm NATO
  *Common Name:* MG1A3 GPMG

  *Remarks:* Rheinmetall, Germany.

- *Cal.:* 7.62 x 51mm NATO
  *Common Name:* HK11 GPMG

  *Remarks:* RSAF.

- *Cal.:* 7.62 x 51mm NATO
  *Common Name:* FN MAG GPMG

  *Remarks:* FN Aviation (60-30), T1 (M.032 right-hand and left-hand feed).

- *Cal.:* 7.62 x 51mm NATO
  *Common Name:* AA-52 GPMG

  *Remarks:* Groupment Industriel des Armements Terrestres (GIAT), France. These machine guns are mounted on the Panhard M-3 armored cars.

- *Cal.:* 7.62 x 51mm NATO
  *Common Name:* M60 GPMGs

  *Remarks:* US origin.

- *Cal.:* 7.62 x 51mm NATO
  *Common Name:* M73/M219 armor MGs

  *Remarks:* US origin. Mounted on M60A3 tanks.

- *Cal.:* 7.62 x 51mm NATO
  *Common Name:* M240 armor MGs

  *Remarks:* US origin. Mounted on M60A3 tanks. FMS provided 20 in 1982.

**A Sudanese and an American soldier examine their M16A1 rifles during "Bright Star 83" activities in Sudan. (USAF)**

- *Cal.:* 7.62 x 63mm
  *Common Name:* .30 M1919A4E1 AMG

  *Remarks:* US origin. Mounted on US M41 tanks.

- *Cal.:* 7.62 x 63mm
  *Common Name:* .30 Lewis LMG

  *Remarks:* Origin unknown. OBSOLETE.

- *Cal.:* 7.62 x 54mmR
  *Common Name:* SG43 and SGMT

  *Remarks:* Soviet origin. Some of the vehicle versions are mounted on Soviet tanks and APCs.

- *Cal.:* 7.62 x 54mmR
  *Common Name:* PK series of MGs

  *Remarks:* Soviet origin.

- *Cal.:* 7.62 x 54mmR
  *Common Name:* RP46 series MGs

  *Remarks:* Soviet origin.

- *Cal.:* 7.62 x 54mmR
  *Common Name:* Type 59T

  *Remarks:* Chinese origin. Mounted on Chinese Type 62 and 62LT tanks.

- *Cal.:* 7.7 x 56mmR
  *Common Name:* .303 Bren guns

  *Remarks:* UK origin?

- *Cal.:* 7.92 x 57mm
  *Common Name:* Type D FN BAR

  *Remarks:* Belgian origin. OBSOLETE.

- *Cal.:* 12.7 x 99mm
  *Common Name:* .50 M2 HG HMG

  *Remarks:* US origin. Mounted on US M41 tanks and M113 APCs.

- *Cal.:* 12.7 x 99mm
  *Common Name:* .50 M85 armor MG

  *Remarks:* US origin. Mounted on US M60A3 tanks. FMS provided 20 in 1982.

- *Cal.:* 12.7 x 108mm
  *Common Name:* DShK38/46 HMG

  *Remarks:* East Bloc origin. Both Soviet DShKs and Chinese Type 54 HMGs are in use. News photographs (1987) have shown this weapon in the hands of the antigovernment Sudanese People's Liberation Army.

**AUTOMATIC CANNON:**

- *Cal.:* 14.5 x 114mm
  *Common Name:* KPV HMG

  *Remarks:* East Bloc origin.

- *Cal.:* 20 x 102mm
  *Common Name:* 20mm M168 Vulcan automatic cannon on Vulcan Air Defense System (VADS)

  *Remarks:* US origin. Both the M163 SP and the M167-towed M167 VADS are in service. In 1985 the Sudanese had 24 M163 systems on order.

- *Cal.:* 20 x 139mm
  *Common Name:* 20mm M693 automatic cannon

  *Remarks:* French origin. These 20mm guns are mounted on the Panhard M-3 armored cars.

- *Cal.:* 23 x 152mm
  *Common Name:* ZU23 automatic cannon

  *Remarks:* East Bloc origin. Some ZSU-23-2 systems have been observed in news photographs from the Sudan.

**Antigovernment Forces**

The Southern People's Liberation Movement has about 3,000 fighters in its Sudan People's Liberation Army (SPLA). The latter is being supplied by the Ethiopian government, because the Sudanese government is allegedly supplying Eritrean and Tigrean rebels. Recent news photos show the SPLA fighters with AKMs of undetermined model and Hungarian AMD-65 assault rifles with folding stock.

# SURINAM

Population (estimate in 1983): 0.370 million. Ground forces: regulars, 1,800; reserves, unknown; paramilitary, ca. 1,000.

**HANDGUNS:**
- *Cal.:* 9 x 19mm Parabellum
  *Common Name:* FN Mle. 35GP pistol

  *Remarks:* FN origin.

- *Cal.:* 9 x 29mmR
  *Common Name:* .38 Smith & Wesson revolver

  *Remarks:* US origin. Smith & Wesson delivered 129 .38 caliber revolvers for police use 1977–79.

**SUBMACHINE GUNS:**
- *Cal.:* 9 x 19mm Parabellum
  *Common Name:* Uzi submachine gun

  *Remarks:* Origin unknown.

- *Cal.:* 11.43 x 23mm
  *Common Name:* .45 M3A1 submachine gun

  *Remarks:* US origin.

A Surinamese soldier conducts a search. He is armed with a .30 M1 carbine. (De Caro)

**RIFLES:**
- *Cal.:* 7.62 x 33mm
  *Common Name:* .30 M1 carbine

  *Remarks:* Origin unknown.

- *Cal.:* 7.62 x 39mm
  *Common Name:* AKM

  *Remarks:* East Bloc origin.

- *Cal.:* 7.62 x 51mm NATO
  *Common Name:* FN FAL

  *Remarks:* FN origin?

**SHOTGUNS:**

**MACHINE GUNS:**
- *Cal.:* 7.62 x 51mm NATO
  *Common Name:* FN MAG

  *Remarks:* FN origin?

- *Cal.:* 7.7 x 56mmR
  *Common Name:* .303 Bren LMG

  *Remarks:* UK origin.

**AUTOMATIC CANNON:**

## SWAZILAND (Kingdom)

Population (estimate in 1980): 0.651 million. Ground forces: regulars, unknown; reserves, unknown.

**HANDGUNS:**
- *Cal.:* 8.13 x 15.2mm
  *Common Name:* .32 Smith & Wes-
  son revolver

  *Remarks:* US origin. Two of these revolvers were acquired by Commissioner of Police in 1976.

**SUBMACHINE GUNS:**
- *Cal.:* 9 x 19mm Parabellum
  *Common Name:* Sterling Mark 4
  submachine gun

  *Remarks:* Sterling Armament Co. UK.

- *Cal.:* 9 x 19mm Parabellum
  *Common Name:* Uzi submachine
  gun

  *Remarks:* Israeli Military Industries (IMI) origins.

**RIFLES:**
- *Cal.:* 5.56 x 45mm
  *Common Name:* SG540 rifle

  *Remarks:* Manurhin-made SIG rifle.

- *Cal.:* 5.56 x 45mm
  *Common Name:* Galil rifle

  *Remarks:* IMI origin.

- *Cal.:* 5.56 x 45mm
  *Common Name:* AR-18 rifle

  *Remarks:* Sterling Armament Co.

- *Cal.:* 7.62 x 51mm NATO
  *Common Name:* FN FAL

  *Remarks:* Origin uncertain. Believed to be from FN.

**SHOTGUNS:**

**MACHINE GUNS:**
- *Cal.:* 7.62 x 51mm NATO
  *Common Name:* L4A4 Bren LMG

  *Remarks:* Royal Small Arms Factory (RSAF), Enfield. There are also some .303 (7.7 x 56mmR) caliber Bren guns still in service.

• *Cal.:* 7.62 x 51mm NATO
  *Common Name:* L7A1 GPMG

*Remarks:* RSAF.

**AUTOMATIC CANNON:**

# SWEDEN

Population (estimate in 1984): 8.34 million. Ground forces: regulars, ca. 47,000 (37,000 conscripts); reserves, between 500,000 and 750,000 for all services.

**HANDGUNS:**
• *Cal.:* 9 x 19mm Parabellum
  *Official Name: automatisk re-peterpistol m/40*
  *Common Name:* M1940 Lahti pistol

*Remarks:* Husqvarna Vapenfabrik.

• *Cal.:* 9 x 19mm Parabellum
  *Official Name: automatisk re-peterpistol m/39*
  *Common Name:* Walther P38 pistol

*Remarks:* About 10,000 were purchased from Walther, Zella Mehlis, Thuringia, in 1939.

• *Cal.:* 9 x 17mm Browning
  *Official Name: automatisk re-peterpistol*
  *Common Name:* Walther PP

*Remarks:* These Walther model pistols are in service with the Army in limited numbers.

**SUBMACHINE GUNS:**
• *Cal.:* 9 x 19mm Parabellum
  *Official Name: kulsrutepistol m/45*
  *Common Name:* Model 1945 (Carl Gustav) submachine gun

*Remarks:* Forenade Fabrikverken (FFV) Ordnance, Eskiltuna. Both the standard and silenced versions are in service. The models include: m/45, first model, which used the 50-round Suomi magazine; m/45 B, second model, which used a 36-round magazine has improved retaining system for breech cap; m/45 C, second model with provision for mounting bayonet; and m/45, silenced model.

**RIFLES:**
• *Cal.:* 7.62 x 51mm NATO
  *Official Name: automatkarbin 4 (ak4)*
  *Common Name: Gewehr 3*

*Remarks:* FFV Ordnance licensed copy of G3. Heckler & Koch (HK) identification number 224042.

• *Cal.:* 5.56 x 45mm
  *Official Name: automatkarbin 5 (ak5)*
  *Common Name:* FN FNC

*Remarks:* FFV Ordnance licensed copy of the FN FNC. In 1984 the government ordered 80,000 FNCs with deliveries starting in 1986. The apparent goal was to acquire about 240,000 FNCs. The first FNCs came directly from FN with FFV subsequently picking up production. The Swedish model does not have the 3-shot burst feature.

• *Cal.:* 6.5 x 55mm
  *Official Name: 6.5mm auto-matgevar m/42B or Ag m/42B*
  *Common Name:* Ljungman rifle

*Remarks:* Husqvarna Vapenfabrik. The Swedes "materielnummer" for this rifle is M4800-612420 with magazine and M4800-612421 with magazine and accessories *(tillbehor).*

• *Cal.:* 6.5 x 55mm
  *Official Name: 6.5mm gevar m/96*
  *Common Name:* Model 1896 Swedish Mauser rifle

*Remarks:* Husqvarna Vapenfabrik; Carl Gustav Stads Gevarfaktori, Eskiltuna; and Mauser, Oberndorf an Neckar. The m/38 version with a 120mm shorter barrel is still used by some Home Guard forces.

**A Swedish soldier outfitted for combat carries his 7.62 x 51mm NATO ak4 (G3) made by FFV Ordnance. (Armemuseum)**

**SHOTGUNS:**

**MACHINE GUNS:**
• *Cal.:* 7.62 x 51mm NATO
  *Official Name: kulspruta 58* (Ksp 58)
  *Common Name:* FN MAG


• *Cal.:* 7.62 x 51mm NATO
  *Official Name: kulspruta M42B*
  *Common Name:* M1919A6 in 7.62mm NATO

*Remarks:* FFV licensed production. In 1982 the Swedish Armed Forces purchased about 1,000 to 1,200 more MAG 58s from FFV. Three of the guns are mounted on each Strv 103B main battle tanks. In 1958 the first FN MAGs were in 6.5 x 55mm caliber. Sweden was the first country to acquire this weapon, and Swedish Ordnance influenced its final design. Sweden converted over to the 7.62mm NATO caliber in 1962.

*Remarks:* FFV rework of the 6.5mm Browning LMG. These guns are designated FOM 1005-19-4-6.5-6 for the 6.5mm version.

A Swedish 7.62 x 51mm NATO MAG58 with a special winter sled mount attached to the bipod. This GPMG is made by FFV Ordnance. (Armemuseum)

- *Cal.:* 7.62 x 51mm NATO
  *Official Name: kulspruta M36B*
  *Common Name:* M1917A1 in
  7.62mm NATO

  *Remarks:* FFV rework of the 6.5mm Browning MMG.

- *Cal.:* 7.62 x 51mm NATO
  *Common Name:* HK21A1 GPMG

  *Remarks:* Origin unknown.

- *Cal.:* 8 x 63mm
  *Official Name: M36llv ekl & dbl*

  *Remarks:* Carl Gustav Factory. Still used by Home Guard for antiaircraft.

- *Cal.:* 12.7 x 99mm
  *Common Name:* .50 M2 HB
  HMG

  *Remarks:* US origin. Approx. 50 of the M55 quad gun (AKan M45) AA systems are in service. AKan = *Avtomat Kannone.*

**AUTOMATIC CANNON:**
- *Cal.:* 20 x 110mm
  *Common Name:* HS804 auto-
  matic cannon

  *Remarks:* Oerlikon-Buhrle.

- *Cal.:* 20 x 145mm
  *Common Name:* M40 Bofors

  *Remarks:* AB Bofors, Sweden.

## Swedish Police Handguns

In March 1986 FFV Ordnance announced that the Swedish Police were looking to purchase the 9 x 19mm SIG Sauer P225 or "similar pistol" as a new police sidearm. The initial order would be for between 150 and 1,000 pistols and then 400 to 1,000 pistols per year for the next 15 years. Delivery was desired to start in May through December 1986. These pistols were to be marked on the left side of the frame "tillhor polisen."

## SWITZERLAND (Confederation of)

Population (estimate in 1984): 6.48 million. Ground forces: regulars, 18,500 (annual group of conscripts, 15,000); and a quickly mobilized reserve force of ca. 580,000.

### HANDGUNS:
- *Cal.:* 9 x 19mm Parabellum
  *Official Name:* Modell 75 Pistole; Pistolet 9mm 1975
  *Common Name:* M75/P220 pistol; Pist 9mm 75

  *Remarks:* Schweizerische Industrie Gesellschaft (SIG) an Rheinfalls. Serial number series begins at A 100 0011. NSA 1005-671-7600. FOM 1005-18-1-9-3.

- *Cal.:* 9 x 19mm Parabellum
  *Official Name:* Modell 49 Pistole; Pistolet 9mm 1949
  *Common Name:* M49/P210 pistol Pist 9mm 49

  *Remarks:* SIG. FOM 1005-18-1-9-1. Gradually being phased out of service. These pistols bear the serial numbers A 100 001 to A 213 110, and they were purchased 1949–54.

- *Cal.:* 7.65 x 19mm Parabellum
  *Official Name:* Modell 06/29 Pistole; Pistolet 7.65mm 1949
  *Common Name:* Model 06/29 Luger pistol; Pist 7.65mm 06/29

  *Remarks:* Eidg. Waffenfabrik + Bern. OBSOLETE.

- *Cal.:* 7.65 x 17mm
  *Common Name:* 7.65mm PP and PPK pistols

  *Remarks:* Walther pistols for local police and military pilots.

- *Cal.:* 7.65 x 17mm
  *Common Name:* 7.65mm SIG P230 pistol

  *Remarks:* SIG. Used by local police.

- *Cal.:* 9 x 19mm Parabellum
  *Common Name:* 9mm SIG P225 and P226 pistols

  *Remarks:* SIG. Used by local and other police organizations.

### SUBMACHINE GUNS:
- *Cal.:* 9 x 19mm Parabellum
  *Common Name:* MP310 submachine gun

  *Remarks:* SIG. Police organizations.

- *Cal.:* 9 x 19mm Parabellum
  *Official Name:* Maschinenpistole 43/44; La Mitraillette 43/44
  *Common Name:* MP43/44 submachine gun; Mte. 9mm 43/44

  *Remarks:* Hispano Suiza version of Finnish Suomi. Used by some field medical personnel.

- *Cal.:* 9 x 19mm Parabellum
  *Common Name:* MP5 submachine gun

  *Remarks:* Heckler & Koch (HK). Used by Swiss airport police and other police organizations.

### RIFLES:
- *Cal.:* 5.6 x 45mm
  *Official Name:* Sturmgewehr 5.6mm 90; Le Fusil d'Assaut 5.6mm 90
  *Common Name:* SG 550 rifle; StG 90; F. ass. 90

  *Remarks:* SIG. New standard Swiss military rifle. Approx. 600,000 will be built 1985–2005. Each new recruit class will be issued the StG. 90 starting the late 1980s. This will be the individual soldier's rifle for the rest of his life.

A Swiss infantryman aims his 7.5 x 55.4mm *Sturmgewehr 57.* This SIG-made assault rifle can in fact be used as a light machine gun. (Swiss Defense Ministry)

- *Cal.:* 7.5 x 55.4mm
  *Official Name: Sturmgewehr 7.5mm 57; Le Fusil d'Assaut 5.6mm 90*
  *Common Name:* SG510-0 rifle; StG 57; F. ass. 57

- *Cal.:* 7.5 x 55.5mm
  *Official Name: Zilefernrhor Karabiner 55; Le Mosqueton a lunette 55*
  *Common Name:* Zf Kar 55; Mq lu 55

- *Cal.:* 5.56 x 45mm
  *Common Name:* HK33 SG1 rifle

*Remarks:* SIG and Waffenfabrik + Bern. The latter factory made some components and assembled some rifles. Approx. 600,000 were built 1957–1983. The StG. 57 will remain a standard Swiss military rifle throughout the lifetime of the soldiers equipped with it. NSA 1005-670-6800. The standard optical sight *(lunette pour fusil d'assaut 7.5mm 57)* is NSA 1240-670-7910, and the standard infrared sight *(lunette infrarouge d'observation et de pointage pour fusil d'assaut 7.5mm 57)* is NSA 5850-655-1205.

*Remarks:* Sniper rifle; also called the M31/55.

*Remarks:* HK. Used by Swiss airport police in special mount on APCs.

**SHOTGUNS:**

**A Swiss paratrooper with his 5.6 x 45mm *Sturmgewehr 90*. Note that the stock is folded to make it more compact for jumping. This SIG-made assault rifle is replacing the *Sturmgewehr 57*. (Braunschweig)**

**MACHINE GUNS:**

• *Cal.:* 7.5 x 55.5mm
  *Official Name: Maschinengewehr 7.5mm 1951; La Mitrailleuse 7.5mm 1951*
  *Common Name:* MG51; Mitr. 51

• *Cal.:* 7.62 x 51mm NATO
  *Official Name: Maschinengewehr 7.62mm 1987; La Mitrailleuse 7.62mm 1987*
  *Common Name:* MG87; Mitr. 87

• *Cal.:* 7.62 x 51mm NATO (?)
  *Common Name:* FN MAG

• *Cal.:* 7.5 x 55.5mm
  *Official Name: Leichtes Maschinengewehr 7.5mm 1925; Le Fusil Mitrailleur 7.5mm 1925.*
  *Common Name:* MG25 LMG; fm. et Fmt. 25

*Remarks:* MG51 GPMG. Waffenfabrik + Bern. In addition to use as an infantry gun, the MG51 is also mounted on several armored fighting vehicles as a coaxial machine gun without a stock (PZ 55; PZ55/60; PZ 57; PZ57/60) and externally as a commander's gun on PZ55 and PZ57 (w/ stock). Also externally mounted on PZ61. FOM 1005-18-4-7.5-3. Can be fitted w/ the Z00 L/R1 infrared sight.

*Remarks:* MG87 Armor MG. Waffenfabrik + Bern. This variant of the MG51 was specially adapted for installation of the fighting compartments of armored fighting vehicles. It is presently used on PZ87 (Leopard 2) main battle tank. It has a special mounting sleeve, butt cap (in place of a shoulder stock), and a special electric trigger mechanism.

*Remarks:* FN. Infanterie Standard (60-20), T1; and Aviation (60-30), P.935 both left- and right-feed.

*Remarks:* Waffenfabrik + Bern. OBSOLETE. FOM 1005-18-4-7.5-1.

**Swiss infantrymen ready with their 7.5 x 55.4mm** *Maschinengewehr 51.* **This Waffenfabrik + Bern-made GPMG is related in mechanical design to the German MG3. (Swiss Defense Ministry)**

• *Cal.:* 12.7 x 99mm
*Official Name: Maschinengewehr
12.7mm 64; La Mitrailleuse
12.7mm 1964*
*Common Name:* .50 M2 HB
HMG; Mg 64 and Mitr 64

*Remarks:* US origin. The Swiss purchased 207 M2s from FMS in 1980. They acquired 390 AN-M3 aircraft guns from FMS in 1964. This gun is used on *Truppetransportpanzer Typ M 113* (US M113) and *Panzerhaubitze Typ M 109* (US M109 self-propelled howitzer).

**AUTOMATIC CANNON:**
• *Cal.:* 20 x 110mm
*Official Name: Flab Kanone
20mm 43/57 Drilling* and *SPz
Kanone 20mm 48/73*
*Common Name:* HS804 automatic cannon

*Remarks:* Hispano Suiza/Oerlikon. OBSOLETE. FOM 1005-18-4-20-2.

• *Cal.:* 20 x 128mm
*Official Name: Flab. Kanone
20mm 1954; Le Canon DCA
20mm 1954*
*Common Name:* Type 204GK
(KAA) automatic cannon

*Remarks:* Oerlikon-Buhrle. This belt-fed AA cannon *(Gusten Kanone* = GK) was adopted in 1954. Subsequently this weapon's design was evolved into the vehicle-mounted 5TG. FOM 1005-18-4-20-5. Employed in single and twin towed AA mounts.

**A Swiss gun crew ready with their 20mm *Flab Kanone 54*. (Swiss Defense Ministry)**

**A Swiss gun crew mans their triple (drilling) 20mm *Flab Kanone 43/57.* (Swiss Defense Ministry)**

• *Cal.:* 20 x 128mm
  *Official Name: Pz Kanone 20mm 1961; Le Canon Char. 20mm 1961*
  *Common Name:* Type 10La/5TG (KAB-001) automatic cannon

• *Cal.:* 20 x 139mm
  *Common Name:* Type HS820L85 (KAD) automatic cannon

*Remarks:* Oerlikon-Buhrle. Vehicle version of the Type 204 GK. FOM 1005-18-4-20-3. There are approximately 250 of the GAI B01 AA systems in the Swiss service.

*Remarks:* Hispano Suiza/Oerlikon. FOM 1005-18-4-20-1.

## Swiss Police Handgun Usage Listed by Model

| | |
|---|---|
| Walther 7.65mm PP | Appenzell (OD*); Basel-Land; Basel-Stadt (OD); Bern (OD); Graubunden; Nidwalden (OD); Obwalden; Tessin; Wallis; Zug; Zurich (OD). |
| Walther 7.65mm PPK | Geneva; Glarus (OD); Neuenburg; Zurich (OD). |
| Parabellum 7.65mm | Schwyz; Wallis; Zurich. |
| FN 7.65mm | Waalt. |

*OD – off-duty sidearm.

| Astra 2000 7.65mm | Schaffhausen (OD). |
| SIG P210 series 7.65mm | Schaffhausen; Zurich. |
| SIG P210 series 9mm | Appenzell; Basel-Stadt; Glarus; Nidwalden; St. Gallen; Solothurn; Thurgau; Uri; Zurich. |
| SIG/Sauer P6 9mm | Fribourg; Zurich. |

Since 1977–78, there has been a trend toward adoption of the new generation of SIG pistols (P220–P225 and P230).

Several SIG-originated small caliber weapons have been exported. The FOM numbers for these weapons are as follows:

| 5.56 x 45mm | SG540 rifle | FOM 1005-18-2-5.56-1. | Made by Manurhin in France. |
| 5.56 x 45mm | SG543 rifle | FOM 1005-18-2-5.56-2. | Made by Manurhin. |
| 7.62 x 51mm NATO | SG542 rifle | FOM 1005-18-2-7.62-4. | Made by Manurhin. |
| 7.62 x 51mm NATO | SG710-1 MG | FOM 1005-18-4-7.62-2. | Made by SIG. |

## SYRIA (Arab Republic)

Population (estimate in 1984): 10.07 million. Ground forces: regulars, ca. 240,000; reserves, 460,000 (of which ca. 175,000 are active); paramilitary: gendarmerie, 8,000; Desert Guard (Frontier Force), 1,800; and Detachments for the Defense of the Regime estimated between 5,000 and 25,000. Small arms are of the Soviet and East Bloc pattern. In recent years, arms have been received new, directly from the factories of the Warsaw Pact. Those listed are confirmed as being in service.

**HANDGUNS:**
- *Cal.:* 7.62 x 25mm
  *Common Name:* TT33 Tokarev pistol

  *Remarks:* East Bloc origin.

- *Cal.:* 9 x 18mm
  *Common Name:* Makarov pistol

  *Remarks:* East Bloc origin.

- *Cal.:* 9 x 19mm Parabellum
  *Common Name:* FN Mle. 35 GP pistol

  *Remarks:* Belgian origin. Acquired before 1950.

- *Cal.:* 9 x 29mmR
  *Common Name:* .38 Smith & Wesson revolver

  *Remarks:* US origin. In the mid-1970s the Command of Interior Security purchased 72 miscellaneous .38 caliber revolvers.

**SUBMACHINE GUNS:**
- *Cal.:* 9 x 19mm Parabellum
  *Common Name:* vz.23 and vz.25 submachine guns

  *Remarks:* Czechoslovakian origin.

**RIFLES:**
- *Cal.:* 7.62 x 39mm
  *Common Name:* AK47 and AKM assault rifles w/ and w/o folding stock

  *Remarks:* East Bloc origin.

The Syrian national emblem as placed on Syrian FALs by FN. (FN)

- *Cal.:* 7.62 x 51mm NATO
  *Common Name:* FN FAL

  *Remarks:* Belgian origin. Adopted in 1956.

- *Cal.:* 7.62 x 51mm NATO
  *Common Name:* Steyr SSG sniper
  rifle

  *Remarks:* Steyr-Daimler-Puch (SDP), Austria. Acquired about 4,500 in mid-1980s.

- *Cal.:* 7.92 x 57mm
  *Common Name:* M98K Mauser
  rifle

  *Remarks:* A wide variety of World War II Mausers, plus rifles purchased from Czechoslovakia, East Germany, and Yugoslavia in the 1950s. Many recently sold off to the US civilian market.

## SHOTGUNS:

## MACHINE GUNS:
- *Cal.:* 7.62 x 39mm
  *Common Name:* RPK LMG

  *Remarks:* East Bloc origin.

- *Cal.:* 7.62 x 54mmR
  *Common Name:* PK series GPMG

  *Remarks:* East Bloc origin. These guns include PKTs on vehicles.

- *Cal.:* 7.62 x 54mmR
  *Common Name:* SGM vehicle
  MGs

  *Remarks:* East Bloc origin.

- *Cal.:* 7.62 x 54mmR
  *Common Name:* DT vehicle MGs

  *Remarks:* East Bloc origin.

- *Cal.:* 12.7 x 108mm
  *Common Name:* DShK38/46
  HMG

  *Remarks:* East Bloc origin.

- *Cal.:* 12.7 x 108mm
  *Common Name:* NSVT HMG

  *Remarks:* Soviet origin on newer model tanks.

## AUTOMATIC CANNON:
- *Cal.:* 14.5 x 114mm
  *Common Name:* KPV HMG

  *Remarks:* East Bloc origin. The ZPU-1, ZPU-2, and ZPU-4 AA systems all are in service.

- *Cal.:* 20 x ???mm

  *Remarks:* Huge numbers of unspecified 20mm cannon are employed for antiaircraft roles.

- *Cal.:* 23 x 152mmB
  *Common Name:* ZU23 automatic
  cannon

  *Remarks:* East Bloc origin. Both the twin towed and the quad self-propelled AA systems are in service.

- *Cal.:* 25 x 218mm
  *Common Name:* 2-M-3 and 2-M-8
  automatic cannons

  *Remarks:* Soviet automatic cannon mounted on minesweepers.

## TANZANIA (United Republic of)

Population (estimate in 1984): 21.02 million. Ground forces: regulars, ca. 38,500; reserves, ca. 36,000; paramilitary: Police Field Force, 1,400; Citizen's Militia, 50,000; Tanzania Police, ca. 8,000.

### HANDGUNS:

- *Cal.:* 7.62 x 25mm
  *Common Name:* vz.52 pistol

  *Remarks:* Czechoslovakian origin.

- *Cal.:* 9 x 18mm
  *Common Name:* Stechkin machine pistol

  *Remarks:* Soviet origin.

- *Cal.:* 9 x 19mm Parabellum
  *Common Name:* FN Mle. 1935 GP pistol

  *Remarks:* FN origin.

- *Cal.:* 9 x 20mmR
  *Common Name:* .38 Webley MK IV revolver

  *Remarks:* UK origin.

- *Cal.:* 9 x 29mmR
  *Common Name:* .357 Smith & Wesson

  *Remarks:* US origin. The Tanzanian Executive Protection Division of the Security Forces purchased 2 .357 Magnum revolvers in 1978.

### SUBMACHINE GUNS:

- *Cal.:* 9 x 19mm Parabellum
  *Common Name:* Sterling Mark 4 submachine gun

  *Remarks:* Sterling Armament Corp., UK.

- *Cal.:* 9 x 19mm Parabellum
  *Common Name:* vz.23 and vz.25 submachine guns

  *Remarks:* Czechoslovakian origin.

- *Cal.:* 7.62 x 25mm
  *Common Name:* PPSh 41 submachine gun

  *Remarks:* East Bloc origin.

### RIFLES:

- *Cal.:* 5.56 x 45mm
  *Common Name:* HK33 rifle

  *Remarks:* Origin unknown. Used by Citizen's Militia.

- *Cal.:* 7.62 x 39mm
  *Common Name:* SKS carbine

  *Remarks:* East Bloc origin.

- *Cal.:* 7.62 x 39mm
  *Common Name:* AK47 and AKM assault rifles

  *Remarks:* East Bloc origin. Chinese Type 56-1 rifles and Hungarian AMDs have been observed in the hands of troops.

- *Cal.:* 7.62 x 39mm
  *Common Name:* vz.58 assault rifle

  *Remarks:* Czechoslovakian origin.

- *Cal.:* 7.62 x 39mm
  *Common Name:* vz.52/57 rifle

  *Remarks:* Czechoslovakian origin.

- *Cal.:* 7.62 x 51mm NATO
  *Common Name:* Gewehr 3

  *Remarks:* Origin uncertain.

- *Cal.:* 7.62 x 51mm NATO
  *Common Name:* FN FAL

  *Remarks:* FN origin.

- *Cal.:* 7.7 x 56mmR
  *Common Name:* .303 SMLE MK III bolt action rifles

  *Remarks:* UK origin.

### SHOTGUNS:

**MACHINE GUNS:**
- *Cal.:* 7.62 x 39mm
  *Common Name:* RPD LMG

  *Remarks:* East Bloc origin.

- *Cal.:* 7.62 x 39mm
  *Common Name:* RPK LMG

  *Remarks:* East Bloc origin.

- *Cal.:* 7.62 x 51mm NATO
  *Common Name:* FN MAG

  *Remarks:* Belgian origin. *Infanterie Standard* (60-20), T10 using nondisintegrating links.

- *Cal.:* 7.62 x 54mmR
  *Common Name:* RP46 company machine gun

  *Remarks:* East Bloc origin.

- *Cal.:* 7.62 x 54mmR
  *Common Name:* PK series GPMGs

  *Remarks:* East Bloc origin. Both vehicle and infantry models are in service.

- *Cal.:* 7.62 x 54mmR
  *Common Name:* SGM vehicle MGs

  *Remarks:* East Bloc origin. SG43s have been observed in use on the ground-wheeled Siderenko-Malinovski mount.

- *Cal.:* 7.62 x 54mmR
  *Common Name:* PRC Type 67 GPMG

  *Remarks:* Chinese origin.

- *Cal.:* 7.62 x 54mmR
  *Common Name:* PRC Type 59T AMG

  *Remarks:* Chinese origin. Mounted on Chinese Type 62 and 62LT tanks.

- *Cal.:* 7.62 x 54mmR
  *Common Name:* vz.59 GPMG

  *Remarks:* Czechoslovakian origin.

- *Cal.:* 12.7 x 108mm
  *Common Name:* DShK38/46 HMG

  *Remarks:* East Bloc origin. Both Soviet version and the Chinese Type 54 HMG.

**AUTOMATIC CANNON:**
- *Cal.:* 14.5 x 114mm
  *Common Name:* KPV HMG

  *Remarks:* East Bloc origin. Both the ZPU-2 and ZPU-4 are in service.

- *Cal.:* 23 x 152mm
  *Common Name:* ZU23 automatic cannon

  *Remarks:* East Bloc origin. About 40 units of unspecified type are reported to be in service.

# THAILAND (Kingdom of)

Population (estimate in 1984): 51.72 million. Ground forces: regulars, ca. 160,000; reserves, ca. 500,000; paramilitary: Metropolitan Police, ca. 8,000; Provincial Police, ca. 40,000; Border Patrol Police, 15,000 to 20,000; Marine Police, 1,750; Special Action Force, 3,800. There is also a Volunteer Defense Corps of about 33,000 members.

**HANDGUNS:**
- *Cal.:* 9 x 29mmR
  *Common Name:* Variety of .38 Colt and Smith & Wesson revolvers

  *Remarks:* US origin. Mostly in police service. Before 1975, MAP provided 87 S&W M10 (1005-00-937-5859) .38 caliber revolvers, and 165 Colt Detective Special (1005-00-726-5786) .38 caliber revolvers to military organizations. Thai police forces acquired 23 S&W .357 Magnum and 6 S&W .44 Magnum revolvers in 1976. The Police Cadet Academy acquired 527 S&W .357 Magnum revolvers in 1977. The Bangkok police acquired 146 S&W .38 revolvers in 1979.

- *Cal.:* 9 x 19mm Parabellum
  *Common Name:* FN Mle. 35 GP pistol

  *Remarks:* FN origin. Acquired after 1962.

- *Cal.:* 9 x 19mm Parabellum
  *Common Name:* Glock P80

  *Remarks:* Glock origin. Police usage.

- *Cal.:* 11.43 x 23mm
  *Common Name:* .45 M1911A1 pistol

  *Remarks:* US origin. Before 1975 MAP provided 3,895 M1911A1s. In 1975 they provided 970, and in 1980 FMS delivered 8,681.

**SUBMACHINE GUNS:**

- *Cal.:* 9 x 19mm Parabellum
  *Common Name:* Madsen M46, M50, and M53 submachine guns

  *Remarks:* Danish origin.

- *Cal.:* 9 x 19mm Parabellum
  *Common Name:* Uzi submachine gun

  *Remarks:* Israeli Military Industries (IMI), Israel.

- *Cal.:* 9 x 19mm Parabellum
  *Common Name:* MP5 submachine gun

  *Remarks:* Heckler & Koch (HK), GmbH, West Germany.

- *Cal.:* 9 x 19mm Parabellum
  *Common Name:* MAC 10 submachine gun

  *Remarks:* Origin unknown.

- *Cal.:* 11.43 x 23mm
  *Common Name:* .45 M3 and M3A1 submachine guns

  *Remarks:* US origin. Before 1975 MAP provided 511 M3s and 1,436 M3A1s.

- *Cal.:* 11.43 x 23mm
  *Common Name:* .45 M1A1 submachine gun

  *Remarks:* US origin.

**RIFLES:**

- *Cal.:* 5.56 x 45mm
  *Common Name:* M16A1 (Model 613) rifle

  *Remarks:* Colt, US. Approx. 55,000 purchased direct from Colt since 1975. Others provided by US government through MAP include: 61,084 before 1975; 14,546 in 1975; 2,262 in 1976; 2,020 in 1977; 6,058 in 1981. FMS provided 2,822 before 1975.

- *Cal.:* 5.56 x 45mm
  *Common Name:* M16 (Model 614) rifle

  *Remarks:* Chartered Industries of Singapore. Approx. 30,000 delivered in about 1973–74.

- *Cal.:* 5.56 x 45mm
  *Common Name:* M16A1 (Model 653) carbine

  *Remarks:* Colt, US. Few hundred in early 1980s.

- *Cal.:* 5.56 x 45mm
  *Common Name:* Domestic design rifle

  *Remarks:* Looks very much like the Czechoslovakian vz.58 rifle.

- *Cal.:* 5.56 x 45mm
  *Common Name:* HK33 rifle

  *Remarks:* HK. Approx. 30,000 assembled from German components in Thailand during early 1970s.

- *Cal.:* 5.56 x 45mm
  *Common Name:* FNC rifle

  *Remarks:* Reported but not confirmed.

- *Cal.:* 7.62 x 33mm
  *Common Name:* .30 M1 and M2 carbines

  *Remarks:* US origin. MAP provided 48,421 M1 carbines before 1964; 15,339 M1s and 9,130 M2s before 1975; and 49 M1s in 1975. Sherwood International sold 270 M1 carbines to the Bangkok police in 1979.

- *Cal.:* 7.62 x 51mm NATO
  *Common Name:* FN FAL

  *Remarks:* Belgian origin. Adopted in 1961.

- *Cal.:* 7.62 x 63mm
  *Common Name:* .30 M1 rifle

  *Remarks:* US origin. MAP provided 7,924 M1 rifles before 1975. Earlier (before 1964), MAP provided 37,133 unspecified Model .30 caliber rifles. These are presumed to have been M1s.

- *Cal.:* 7.62 x 63mm
  *Common Name:* .30 M1D sniper rifle

  *Remarks:* US origin. MAP provided 30 M1D sniper rifles before 1975.

**SHOTGUNS:**

- *Cal.:* 18.5 x 59mm
  *Common Name:* 12 gage Mossberg Model 500 shotgun

  *Remarks:* US origin. Navy acquired these shotguns 1976–86 for use aboard ship and ashore. The Army acquired large numbers 1984–86 for issue to village volunteer forces.

- *Cal.:* 18.5 x 59mm
  *Common Name:* 12 gage Ithaca Model 37 shotgun

  *Remarks:* US origin. Acquired 1983.

- *Cal.:* 18.5 x 59mm
  *Common Name:* 12 gage Stevens Model 77E shotgun

  *Remarks:* US origin. MAP provided 3,146 M77Es before 1975.

- *Cal.:* 18.5 x 59mm
  *Common Name:* 12 gage Stevens Model 520A shotgun

  *Remarks:* US origin. MAP provided 6 M520As before 1975.

- *Cal.:* 18.5 x 59mm
  *Common Name:* 12 gage Winchester Model 1200 shotgun

  *Remarks:* US origin. MAP provided 28 M1200s before 1975.

**MACHINE GUNS:**

- *Cal.:* 7.62 x 51mm NATO
  *Common Name:* M73 and M219 AMGs

  *Remarks:* US origin. Mounted on M48A5 tanks. MAP delivered 23 M219s in 1974, and FMS provided 15 in 1979; 35 in 1980; and 5 in 1982.

- *Cal.:* 7.62 x 51mm NATO
  *Common Name:* M60 GPMG

  *Remarks:* US origin. MAP delivered 2,395 prior to 1975. Another 956 were delivered in 1976 and 172 in 1977. FMS delivered 2,614 M60s 1976–82.

- *Cal.:* 7.62 x 51mm NATO
  *Common Name:* M60D ACMG

  *Remarks:* US origin. MAP delivered 31 1972–78.

- *Cal.:* 7.62 x 51mm NATO
  *Common Name:* FN MAG

  *Remarks:* FN. Models used include MAG *Infanterie Standard* (60-20), T6 (L7A2); MAG *Infanterie Aviation* (60-30), P935 RH and LH feed; and *MAG Coaxial* (60-40) Cadillac Gage armored car version.

- *Cal.:* 7.62 x 63mm
  *Common Name:* .30 M1918A2 BAR

  *Remarks:* US origin. MAP delivered 397 before 1967.

- *Cal.:* 7.62 x 63mm
  *Common Name:* .30 M1919A4 LMG

  *Remarks:* US origin. MAP delivered 47 before 1967. An unspecified 1,351 .30 LMGs were delivered before 1953.

- *Cal.:* 7.62 x 63mm
  *Common Name:* .30 M1919A6 LMG

  *Remarks:* US origin. MAP delivered 224 1969–75.

- *Cal.:* 12.7 x 99mm
  *Common Name:* .50 M2 HB HMG

  *Remarks:* US origin. MAP delivered 68 1965–75. FMS delivered 90 1977–82. Used as a ground gun, armor gun, and in the M55 quad gun AA mount; 18 of the M55 AA systems were delivered in 1967. Ramo delivered 80 M2 HBs 1980–82. MAP also delivered 100 .50 AN-M3 aircraft guns in 1972.

**AUTOMATIC CANNON:**

- *Cal.:* 20 x 102mm
  *Common Name:* 20mm M168 Vulcan automatic cannon in the M167 Vulcan Air Defense System (VADS)

  *Remarks:* US origin.

- *Cal.:* 20 x 102mm
  *Common Name:* 20mm M39A2 automatic cannon

  *Remarks:* US origin. MAP provided 10 left-hand feed guns and 7 right-hand feed guns 1969–77.

**GRENADE LAUNCHERS:**

- *Cal.:* 40 x 46mmSR
  *Common Name:* M79 grenade launcher

  *Remarks:* US origin. MAP delivered 1,589 M79s 1964–75. FMS delivered 1,203 M79s 1977–79.

- *Cal.:* 40 x 46mmSR
  *Common Name:* M203 grenade launcher attached to M16A1

  *Remarks:* MAP delivered 2,520 M203s 1974–78. FMS delivered 1,260 M203s 1977–82. Colt has delivered approx. 1,900 directly since 1978.

## TOGO (Republic of)

Population (estimate in 1984): 2.54 million. Ground forces: *Forces armees togolaises regulars,* ca. 4,000; paramilitary, *Gendarmerie nationale togolaise, ca. 1,500.*

**HANDGUNS:**

- *Cal.:* 7.65 x 17mm Browning
  *Common Name:* Walther PP

  *Remarks:* Walther PP copy Manufacture de Haut Rhin (Manurhin).

- *Cal.:* 7.65 x 17mm Browning
  *Common Name:* P230 pistol

  *Remarks:* SIG pistol made by J. P. Sauer & Sohn, West Germany.

- *Cal.:* 7.65 x 20mm French
  *Common Name:* MAS Mle. 1935S pistol

  *Remarks:* Manufacture Nationale d'Armes de St. Etienne (MAS), France.

- *Cal.:* 9 x 19mm Parabellum
  *Common Name:* MAC Mle. 50 pistol

  *Remarks:* Manufacture Nationale d'Armes de Chatellerault (MAC).

- *Cal.:* 9 x 19mm Parabellum
  *Common Name:* MAB PA-15 pistol

  *Remarks:* Manufacture d'Armes de Bayonne (MAB).

- *Cal.:* 9 x 19mm Parabellum
  *Common Name:* FN Mle. 1935 GP pistol

  *Remarks:* Belgian origin. Both the 1950 and 1968 vintage models.

- *Cal.:* 9 x 29mmR
  *Common Name:* .357 Manurhin MR-73 revolver

  *Remarks:* Manurhin, France.

- *Cal.:* 9 x 29mmR
  *Common Name:* .38 Smith & Wesson M10 M&P revolver

  *Remarks:* US origin.

**SUBMACHINE GUNS:**

- *Cal.:* 9 x 19mm Parabellum
  *Common Name:* Uzi submachine gun

  *Remarks:* Israeli Military Industries (IMI), Israel.

- *Cal.:* 9 x 19mm Parabellum
  *Common Name:* MAT Mle. 49
  submachine gun

*Remarks:* Manufacture Nationale d'Armes de Tulle (MAT).

**RIFLES:**
- *Cal.:* 5.56 x 45mm
  *Common Name:* SG540 rifle

*Remarks:* Manurhin-made SIG rifle.

- *Cal.:* 7.62 x 39mm
  *Common Name:* AK47 assault
  rifle

*Remarks:* PRC Type 56 and North Korean Type 68 rifle. There may be other East Bloc origin AKs. Several hundred East German MPiKMS72 assault rifles were captured from antigovernment forces in 1986.

- *Cal.:* 7.62 x 39mm
  *Common Name:* Type 68 rifle

*Remarks:* PRC origin.

- *Cal.:* 7.62 x 51mm NATO
  *Common Name: Gewehr 3*

*Remarks:* Approx. 1,000 acquired from the Federal Republic of Germany, of Heckler & Koch (HK) origin. MAS-made guns may also be in service.

- *Cal.:* 7.62 x 51mm NATO
  *Common Name:* SSG sniper rifle

*Remarks:* Steyr-Daimler-Puch (SDP), Austria.

- *Cal.:* 7.5 x 54mm
  *Common Name:* MAS Mle. 36
  bolt action rifle

*Remarks:* MAS manufacture.

- *Cal.:* 7.5 x 54mm
  *Common Name:* MAS Mle. 49
  and 49/56 rifles

*Remarks:* MAS manufacture.

- *Cal.:* 7.92 x 57mm
  *Common Name:* Hakim rifle

*Remarks:* Maadi, Egypt.

**SHOTGUNS:**

**MACHINE GUNS:**
- *Cal.:* 7.62 x 39mm
  *Common Name:* RPD LMG

*Remarks:* East Bloc origin. North Korean version?

- *Cal.:* 7.5 x 54mm
  *Common Name:* MAC Mle. 24/29
  LMG

*Remarks:* MAC, France.

- *Cal.:* 7.5 x 54mm
  *Common Name:* AAT52 GPMG

*Remarks:* MAT, France.

- *Cal.:* 7.62 x 51mm NATO
  *Common Name:* MG3 GPMG

*Remarks:* German origin? Also MG 42 versions?

- *Cal.:* 7.62 x 54mmR
  *Common Name:* RP46 company
  machine gun

*Remarks:* East Bloc origin.

- *Cal.:* 12.7 x 99mm
  *Common Name:* .50 M2 HB
  HMG

*Remarks:* US origin.

- *Cal.:* 12.7 x 108mm
  *Common Name:* DShK38/46
  HMG

*Remarks:* East Bloc origin.

**AUTOMATIC CANNON:**
- *Cal.:* 14.5 x 114mm
  *Common Name:* KPV HMG

*Remarks:* East Bloc origin. At least 38 North Korean ZPU-4 towed AA systems in service.

## TONGA (Kingdom of)

Population (estimate in 1984): 0.106 million. Ground forces: regulars, unknown; reserves, unknown. Tonga Police Force, ca. 300.

**HANDGUNS:**
• *Cal.:* 9 x 29mmR                    *Remarks:* US origin.
  *Common Name:* .38 Smith &
  Wesson revolvers; models not
  known

**SUBMACHINE GUNS:**
• *Cal.:* 9 x 19mm Parabellum          *Remarks:* UK origin.
  *Common Name:* Sten gun

**RIFLES:**
• *Cal.:* 5.56 x 45mm                  *Remarks:* FN origin.
  *Common Name:* FNC 80 rifle

• *Cal.:* 7.7 x 56mmR                  *Remarks:* UK origin.
  *Common Name:* .303 Lee Enfield
  rifle

**SHOTGUNS:**

**MACHINE GUNS:**
• *Cal.:* 7.7 x 56mmR                  *Remarks:* UK origin.
  *Common Name:* .303 Bren LMG

• *Cal.:* 7.7 x 56mmR                  *Remarks:* UK origin.
  *Common Name:* .303 Vickers
  MMG

• *Cal.:* 12.7 x 99mm                  *Remarks:* US origin? Mounted on patrol boats.
  *Common Name:* .50 M2 HB
  HMG

**AUTOMATIC CANNON:**


## TRINIDAD AND TOBAGO

Population (estimate in 1984): 1.17 million. Ground forces: regulars, ca. 1,200; reserves, ca. 1,500. This nation has a defense agreement with the United Kingdom.

**HANDGUNS:**
• *Cal.:* 9 x 19mmR                    *Remarks:* US origin. State Department licensed sale of 7 .38 caliber S&W
  *Common Name:* .38 Smith & Wes-     revolvers in 1976 for the Prison Security forces in Trinidad.
  son revolver

**SUBMACHINE GUNS:**
• *Cal.:* 9 x 19mm Parabellum          *Remarks:* Sterling Arms Company, UK.
  *Common Name:* Sterling MK 4
  submachine gun

**RIFLES:**
• *Cal.:* 5.56 x 45mm                  *Remarks:* US origin. The police and Defense Forces have about 100 M16A1s
  *Common Name:* M16A1 rifle          in service.

• *Cal.:* 5.56 x 45mm
  *Common Name:* Galil rifle

*Remarks:* Israeli origin. Israeli Military Industries (IMI) are reported to have sold about 1,000 to 2,000. If true, the lower number is more apt to be correct given the small size of the regular forces.

• *Cal.:* 7.62 x 51mm NATO
  *Common Name:* L1A1 rifle

*Remarks:* British origin.

**SHOTGUNS:**

**MACHINE GUNS:**
• *Cal.:* 7.62 x 51mm NATO
  *Common Name:* M60 GPMG

*Remarks:* US origin.

**AUTOMATIC CANNON:**

## TUNISIA (Republic of)

Population (estimate in 1984): 7.20 million. Ground forces: regulars, *Armée Nationale Tunisienne* ca. 30,000 (26,000 conscripts); paramilitary, *Gendarmerie Nationale Tunisienne,* 6,000; National Guard, 3,500; *Surete Nationale,* 5,000. Some older French and some newer East Bloc small arms may also be in service.

**HANDGUNS:**
• *Cal.:* 7.65 x 17mm Browning
  *Common Name:* Mle. 1934/84 pistol

*Remarks:* Beretta, Italy.

• *Cal.:* 9 x 19mm Parabellum
  *Common Name:* Mle. 1951 pistol

*Remarks:* Beretta, Italy.

• *Cal.:* 9 x 19mm Parabellum
  *Common Name:* MAB P-15 pistol

*Remarks:* French origin. Manufacture d'Armes de Bayonne (MAB).

• *Cal.:* 9 x 29mmR
  *Common Name:* .38 Smith & Wesson revolver

*Remarks:* US origin. The US State Department licensed the sale of 190 .38 S&W revolvers to the Tunisian National Guard in 1977; 2,000 .38 S&W revolvers to the Ministry of the Interior in 1978; and 175 .38 S&W revolvers to the Palace Guard force in 1979. The 1977 and 1979 sales were through the US firm Fargo International; the 1978 sale was made directly by Smith & Wesson. In November, 1985, the Ministry of Defense requested quotations from vendors on 2,000 102mm barrel .38 caliber revolvers and 200 76mm barrel .357 Magnum revolvers.

• *Cal.:* 11.43 x 23mm
  *Common Name:* .45 M1911A1 pistol

*Remarks:* US origin. FMS and MAP delivered 92 M1911A1s 1964–71. Another 2,070 pistols (presumed to be M1911A1s) were delivered before 1964.

**SUBMACHINE GUNS:**
• *Cal.:* 9 x 19mm Parabellum
  *Common Name:* Beretta Model 12S submachine gun

*Remarks:* Beretta, Italy.

• *Cal.:* 9 x 19mm Parabellum
  *Common Name:* Beretta Model 38/49 Mod. 4 submachine gun

*Remarks:* Beretta, Italy.

• *Cal.:* 9 x 19mm Parabellum
  *Common Name:* Sterling Mark 4 SMG

*Remarks:* Sterling Armament Corp., UK.

- *Cal.:* 9 x 19mm Parabellum
  *Common Name:* Uzi submachine gun

  *Remarks:* Source unknown.

- *Cal.:* 9 x 19mm Parabellum
  *Common Name:* MPi69 submachine gun

  *Remarks:* Austrian origin. Steyr-Daimler-Puch (SDP).

- *Cal.:* 11.43 x 23mm
  *Common Name:* .45 M3A1 SMG

  *Remarks:* US origin. MAP provided 1,708 1964–74. Another unspecified 11,139 .45 caliber submachine guns were delivered before 1964.

**RIFLES:**
- *Cal.:* 5.56 x 45mm
  *Common Name:* AUG

  *Remarks:* Austrian origin. SDP. Deliveries began in 1978, with various estimates of quantities given. Largest estimate is 70,000.

- *Cal.:* 5.56 x 45mm
  *Common Name:* M16A1 rifle

  *Remarks:* US origin. Source unknown.

- *Cal.:* 7.62 x 33mm
  *Common Name:* .30 M1 and M2 carbines

  *Remarks:* US origin. MAP activities provided these weapons, including 2,160 M1s and 781 M2s before 1975. FN has also supplied M2 carbines.

- *Cal.:* 7.5 x 54mm
  *Common Name:* MAS Mle. 36 bolt action rifle

  *Remarks:* French origin. Manufacture Nationale d'Armes de St. Etienne (MAS).

- *Cal.:* 7.5 x 54mm
  *Common Name:* MAS Mle. 49/56 rifle

  *Remarks:* French origin. MAS.

- *Cal.:* 7.62 x 39mm
  *Common Name:* AK47 and AKM assault rifles

  *Remarks:* Origin unknown.

- *Cal.:* 7.62 x 51mm NATO
  *Common Name:* SSG sniper rifle

  *Remarks:* Austrian origin. SDP.

- *Cal.:* 7.62 x 51mm NATO
  *Common Name:* M21 sniper rifle

  *Remarks:* US origin. Source unknown.

- *Cal.:* 7.62 x 51mm NATO
  *Common Name:* FN FAL

  *Remarks:* FN.

- *Cal.:* 7.62 x 63mm
  *Common Name:* .30 M1 rifle

  *Remarks:* US origin. MAP activities provided 6,796 of these weapons before 1975.

**SHOTGUNS:**
- *Cal.:* 18.5 x 59mm
  *Common Name:* Remington Model 870 shotgun 12 gage

  *Remarks:* US origin.

- *Cal.:* 18.5 x 59mm
  *Common Name:* Winchester Model 1100 shotgun 12 gage

  *Remarks:* US origin.

**MACHINE GUNS:**
- *Cal.:* 5.56 x 45mm
  *Common Name:* AUG SAW

  *Remarks:* SDP AUG w/ heavy barrel for sustained fire squad automatic weapon role.

- *Cal.:* 7.5 x 54mm
  *Common Name:* MAC Mle. 1924/29 LMG

  *Remarks:* French origin. Manufacture Nationale d'Armes de Chatellerault (MAC).

- *Cal.:* 7.62 x 51mm NATO
  *Common Name:* M73 armor MG

  *Remarks:* US origin. Mounted on M48A5 and M60A3 tanks.

- *Cal.:* 7.62 x 51mm NATO
  *Common Name:* FN MAG

*Remarks:* FN. Models in use include the MAG *Aviation* (60-30) Pod Marchetti (P.904) and helicopter versions; and the MAG Coaxial (60-40) mounted on the Scimitar (ranging machine gun) and on the Brazilian EE-11 Urutu. The latter vehicle issued by the Ministry of the Interior.

- *Cal.:* 7.62 x 51mm NATO
  *Common Name:* MG3 (MG74) armor MG

*Remarks:* Austrian origin. Mounted on the Steyr Jagdpanzer SK105.

- *Cal.:* 7.62 x 51mm NATO
  *Common Name:* M240 armor MG

*Remarks:* US origin. MAP delivered 27 in 1982. Also MAG 58?

- *Cal.:* 7.62 x 54mmR
  *Common Name:* PKT armor MG

*Remarks:* Soviet origin. Mounted on Soviet T62 tanks.

- *Cal.:* 7.62 x 63mm
  *Common Name:* .30 M1918A2 BAR

*Remarks:* US origin. MAP activities provided 260 of these weapons before 1975.

- *Cal.:* 7.62 x 63mm
  *Common Name:* .30 M1919A6 LMG

*Remarks:* US origin. MAP activities provided 5,325 of these weapons 1964–74. MAP provided 426 .30 caliber LMGs of unspecified type before 1964 and 52 M1919A4s 1964–74.

- *Cal.:* 12.7 x 99mm
  *Common Name:* .50 M2 HB HMG

*Remarks:* US origin. MAP activities provided 187 of these weapons before 1964; 48 1964–74; 8 in 1979; 30 in 1980. Mounted on M48A5 series tanks. Six M55 AA systems were delivered before 1975.

- *Cal.:* 12.7 x 99mm
  *Common Name:* .50 M85 armor MG

*Remarks:* US origin. Mounted on the over 50 M60A3 tanks.

- *Cal.:* 12.7 x 108mm
  *Common Name:* DShK38/46 HMG

*Remarks:* Soviet origin. Mounted on Soviet T62 tanks.

**AUTOMATIC CANNON:**
- *Cal.:* 20 x ???
  *Common Name:* 20mm AA cannon on patrol boats

*Remarks:* Type and source unknown.

# TURKEY (Republic of)

Population (estimate in 1984): 50.21 million. Ground forces: regulars, ca. 500,000 (200,000 conscripts); reserves, ca. 700,000; paramilitary gendarmerie *(Jandarma),* estimated between 120,000 and 125,000.

**HANDGUNS:**
- *Cal.:* 9 x 17mm Browning
  *Official Name: 9mm Capinda Tabanca*
  *Common Name:* MKE pistol

*Remarks:* Copy of Walther PP. Also made in 7.65 x 17mm Browning by the Makina ve Kimya Endustrsi Kurumu (MKE) in Ankara. This state factory was previously called the Kirikkale Tufek Fabricular (or Fabrikasi) (Government Rifle Factory at Kirikkale). FOM 1005-39-1-9-1 is assigned to the 9 x 17mm version.

- *Cal.:* 9 x 29mmR
  *Common Name:* .38 Smith & Wesson revolver

*Remarks:* US origin. The National Police purchased 3,000 S&W .38 caliber revolvers 1977–79. In 1980 the government acquired another 70,000 S&W .38 caliber Model 10 revolvers. Another 50,000 are reported to have been ordered.

- *Cal.:* 11.43 x 23mm
  *Common Name:* .45 M1911A1 pistol

*Remarks:* US origin. MAP delivered 42,533 before 1975.

## SUBMACHINE GUNS:
- *Cal.:* 11.43 x 23mm
  *Common Name:* .45 M1A1 submachine gun

- *Cal.:* 11.43 x 23mm
  *Common Name:* .45 M3A1 submachine gun

- *Cal.:* 9 x 19mm NATO
  *Common Name:* Model 1968 submachine gun

- *Cal.:* 9 x 19mm NATO
  *Common Name:* MP5 SMG

## RIFLES:
- *Cal.:* 5.56 x 45mm NATO
  *Common Name:* M16A2 rifle (Model 711) and M16A2 carbine

- *Cal.:* 7.62 x 51mm NATO
  *Official Name:* G3 Otomatik Piyade Tufegi
  *Common Name:* Gewehr 3 (G3A7)

- *Cal.:* 7.62 x 51mm NATO
  *Official Name:* G1 Otomatik Piyade Tufegi
  *Common Name:* FN FAL G1-type

- *Cal.:* 7.62 x 33mm
  *Common Name:* .30 M1 carbine

- *Cal.:* 7.62 x 63mm
  *Common Name:* .30 M1 rifle

## SHOTGUNS:
- *Cal.:* 18.5 x 59mm
  *Common Name:* Model 500 Mossberg shotgun 12 gage

## MACHINE GUNS:
- *Cal.:* 7.62 x 51mm NATO
  *Official Name:* MG3 Makinali Tufek (Tam Otomatik)
  *Common Name:* MG3 GPMG

- *Cal.:* 7.62 x 51mm NATO
  *Common Name:* M73 armor MG

- *Cal.:* 7.62 x 51mm NATO
  *Common Name:* M134 high rate of fire Minigun

- *Cal.:* 7.62 x 63mm
  *Common Name:* .30 M1918A2 BAR

- *Cal.:* 7.62 x 63mm
  *Common Name:* .30 M1919A6 LMG

*Remarks:* US origin. MAP delivered 6,013 before 1975. Still used by the gendarmerie.

*Remarks:* US origin. MAP delivered 37,471 M3A1s before 1975. MAP also delivered 1,188 M3s before 1975.

*Remarks:* Turkish origin. This weapon is derived from the Swiss Rexim-Favor submachine gun. While it is no longer in production, it is still in service.

*Remarks:* Heckler & Koch (HK) and licensed production at MKE.

*Remarks:* US origin. Direct purchase from Colt by the Turkish Security Forces.

*Remarks:* HK and licensed production at MKE. HK stock number 224040.

*Remarks:* FN. Provided to Turkey by the German government as military aid.

*Remarks:* US origin. MAP delivered 450 before 1964.

*Remarks:* US origin. MAP delivered 136,670 before 1975. Another 175,762 .30 calibers of undisclosed type had been delivered before 1964. These are presumed to have been .30 M1 rifles as well.

*Remarks:* US origin. Acquired by the Turkish National Police in 1984–85.

*Remarks:* Rheinmetall and licensed production at MKE. Some finished parts imported from Santa Barbara in Spain.

*Remarks:* US origin. Mounted on M48 tanks.

*Remarks:* US origin. FMS delivered 368 in 1984.

*Remarks:* US origin. MAP delivered 6,289 before 1975.

*Remarks:* US origin. MAP delivered 8,650 .30 LMGs of an unspecified type before 1964.

**Two views of the 7.62 x 51mm NATO G3 as manufactured at MKE in Turkey. Note the distinctive Turkish retractable stock and the fact that this weapon has a phosphated finish. Most licensed G3s have a phosphated finish covered with a protective lacquer. (Smithsonian: Long).**

• *Cal.:* 12.7 x 99mm
  *Common Name:* .50 M2 HB
  HMG

*Remarks:* US origin. MAP delivered 318 before 1964; FMS delivered 152 1964–74. Approx. 160 M55 quad gun AA systems in service; most were delivered 1964–74.

**AUTOMATIC CANNON:**
• *Cal.:* 20 x 102mm
  *Common Name:* 20mm M61 cannon

*Remarks:* US origin. FMS provided 90 1964–74. MAP provided 1 in that same period.

- *Cal.:* 20 x 102mm
  *Common Name:* 20mm
  M39A2RH cannon

  *Remarks:* US origin. MAP provided 2 1964–74.

- *Cal.:* 20 x 110mmRB
  *Common Name:* 20mm US MK4
  Oerlikon (Type S) automatic
  cannon

  *Remarks:* US origin.

- *Cal.:* 20 x 139mm
  *Common Name:* 20mm Oerlikon
  automatic cannon

  *Remarks:* Swiss origin. Also MKE has license to manufacture these guns in Turkey. Exact model unknown.

**GRENADE LAUNCHERS:**
- *Cal.:* 40 x 46mmSR
  *Common Name:* M79 grenade
  launcher

  *Remarks:* US origin. MAP provided 1,275 1964–74.

- *Cal.:* 40 x 46mmSR
  *Common Name:* M203 grenade
  launcher

  *Remarks:* US origin. Colt delivered directly for the Turkish Security Forces.

## UGANDA (Republic of)

Population (estimate in 1984): 14.82 million. Ground forces: regulars, ca. 21,000; reserves, unknown. Effectiveness of Ugandan army unclear. Uganda has police forces equalling about 2,500 men. Variety of older Soviet small arms may still be available in serviceable condition. In early 1987 there were 250 Cuban troops assigned to Uganda.

**HANDGUNS:**
- *Cal.:* 9 x 19mm Parabellum
  *Common Name:* FN Mle. 35 GP
  pistol

  *Remarks:* FN origin.

- *Cal.:* 9 x 20mmR
  *Common Name:* .38 Enfield No. 2
  revolver

  *Remarks:* UK origin.

- *Cal.:* 7.62 x 25mm
  *Common Name:* Tokarev pistol

  *Remarks:* East Bloc origin.

- *Cal.:* 11.43 x 21.7mmR
  *Common Name:* .455 Webley revolver

  *Remarks:* UK origin.

**SUBMACHINE GUNS:**
- *Cal.:* 7.65 x 17mm Browning
  *Common Name:* vz.61 (Skorpion)
  machine pistol

  *Remarks:* Czechoslovakian origin.

- *Cal.:* 9 x 19mm Parabellum
  *Common Name:* L2A3 submachine gun

  *Remarks:* UK origin. Still seen in news photos (1987).

- *Cal.:* 9 x 19mm Parabellum
  *Common Name:* Uzi submachine
  gun

  *Remarks:* Israeli origin. Seen in several 1986 news photographs.

- *Cal.:* 9 x 19mm Parabellum
  *Common Name:* MKIV Sten submachine gun

*Remarks:* UK origin.

**RIFLES:**
- *Cal.:* 5.56 x 45mm
  *Common Name:* M16A1 heavy
  barrel rifle

*Remarks:* Source unknown.

- *Cal.:* 7.62 x 39mm
  *Common Name:* SKS carbine

*Remarks:* East Bloc origin.

- *Cal.:* 7.62 x 39mm
  *Common Name:* AK47 and AKM
  assault rifles

*Remarks:* East Bloc origin. Romanian and East German models appear to predominate as observed in news photographs. German models include AK47s and AKMs. During 1986, for example, the MPiKMS w/ wire folding stock was seen in numerous photographs of Museveni's National Resistance Army (NRA) troops. Some Yugoslavian M59166 and M64A AK-type weapons also seen in news photographs.

- *Cal.:* 7.62 x 39mm
  *Common Name:* Type 63 rifle

*Remarks:* People's Republic of China (PRC) origin. Seen in news photos of the antigovernment Ugandan People's Democratic Army.

- *Cal.:* 7.62 x 51mm NATO
  *Common Name:* Gewehr 3

*Remarks:* Heckler & Koch (HK), Germany or MAS, France?

- *Cal.:* 7.62 x 51mm NATO
  *Common Name:* FAL assault rifle

*Remarks:* FN origin? News photographs illustrate FALs in the hands of NRA forces.

- *Cal.:* 7.7 x 56mmR
  *Common Name:* .303 Lee Enfield
  No. 4 rifles

*Remarks:* UK origin.

**SHOTGUNS:**

**MACHINE GUNS:**
- *Cal.:* 7.62 x 39mm
  *Common Name:* RPD LMG

*Remarks:* East Bloc origin. Also used by NRA forces.

- *Cal.:* 7.62 x 39mm
  *Common Name:* RPK LMG

*Remarks:* East Bloc origin.

- *Cal.:* 7.62 x 51mm NATO
  *Common Name:* FN MAG

*Remarks:* FN. MAG Infanterie Standard (60-20), T14 using nondisintegrating link belt.

- *Cal.:* 7.62 x 51mm NATO
  *Common Name:* HK21A1 GPMG

*Remarks:* HK?

- *Cal.:* 7.62 x 51mm NATO
  *Common Name:* M60 GPMG

*Remarks:* US origin.

- *Cal.:* 7.62 x 51mm NATO
  *Common Name:* L4A1 Bren gun

*Remarks:* UK origin. Some .303 Bren guns are reported to be in service as well.

- *Cal.:* 7.62 x 54mmR
  *Common Name:* PK GPMG

*Remarks:* East Bloc origin.

- *Cal.:* 7.62 x 54mmR
  *Common Name:* SG43-type MG

*Remarks:* East Bloc origin. Seen in use by NRA as a ground gun.

- *Cal.:* 7.62 x 54mmR
  *Common Name:* DP LMG

*Remarks:* East Bloc origin.

- *Cal.:* 7.62 x 54mmR
  *Common Name:* RP46 LMG

*Remarks:* East Bloc origin.

- *Cal.:* 7.62 x 54mmR
  *Common Name:* Type 58 LMG

*Remarks:* Chinese origin.

- *Cal.:* 12.7 x 108mm
  *Common Name:* DShK38/46
  HMG

  *Remarks:* East Bloc origin. PRC Type 54 HMGs are also in service.

**AUTOMATIC CANNON:**
- *Cal.:* 14.5 x 114mm
  *Common Name:* KPV HMG

  *Remarks:* East Bloc origin.

- *Cal.:* 23 x 152mmB
  *Common Name:* ZU23 automatic
  cannon

  *Remarks:* East Bloc origin.

# UNION OF SOVIET SOCIALIST REPUBLICS

Population (estimate in 1984): 274.86 million. Ground forces: regulars, ca. 1,840,000 (1,400,000 conscripts), 16,000 Marine infantry; reserves, (all services), ca. 25,000,000; paramilitary, 675,000 (of which the *Komitet Gosudarstvennoy Bezopastoni* [Committee for State Security] or KGB has ca. 225,000 armed troops and the *Ministerstvo Vnutrennikl Del* [Ministry of Internal Affairs] MVD has about 300,000 armed troops). The general police organization—*Militsiya* (Militia)—is of unknown size. There is also a paramilitary defense organization—*Dobrovolne Obschestvo Sodeisviviya Armii, Aviatsii i Flotu* (Voluntary Society for the Support of the Army, Air Force, and Navy) or DOSAAF—which has an estimated membership in excess of 80 million. This society is the leading shooting sports sponsor in the USSR.

**HANDGUNS:**
- *Cal.:* 5.45 x 17.5mm
  *Official Name: Pistolet Samoza-ryadnyi Malogbaritnyi* (PSM)
  *Common Name:* Pistol, self-loading, small; PSM

  *Remarks:* Small caliber variant of the Makarov design. The purpose of this handgun has not been determined. FOM 1005-2-1-5.45-2. The 5.45mm PMT cartridge is assigned FOM 1305-2-5.45-3-1.

- *Cal.:* 9 x 18mm
  *Official Name: Pistolet Makarova* (PM)
  *Common Name:* Makarov pistol

  *Remarks:* Standard Soviet sidearm; derived from the Walther PP. Standardized in early 1950s. Made at state weapons factories. FOM 1005-2-1-9-1.

- *Cal.:* 9 x 18mm
  *Common Name:* Silenced pistol

  *Remarks:* A new silenced pistol, evolved from the PM, has appeared in Afghanistan and the Middle East. Made at state weapons factories, this weapon has a 2-part silencer: an internal silencer element around the barrel and an external element that attaches with a bayonet lock. When not in use, the external element is carried in a special pouch attached to the holster. Some sources refer to it as the P6.

- *Cal.:* 9 x 18mm
  *Official Name: Avtomaticheskiy Pistolet Stechkina*
  *Common Name:* Stechkin machine pistol

  *Remarks:* Obsolescent. Standardized in 1947. Made at state weapons factories. This fully automatic pistol is the closest weapon to a submachine gun still used by the Soviets. There were silenced versions of this weapon manufactured as well. FOM 1005-2-1-9-2.

- *Cal.:* 7.62 x 25mm
  *Official Name: Pistolet obrazets 1930–33g; Tulskiy-Tokarev* (TT30–33)
  *Common Name:* Tokarev pistol

  *Remarks:* OBSOLETE. Was made at the state weapons factories. Tens of thousands have been exported as military aid. Originally adopted in 1930; modified in 1933. FOM 1005-2-1-7.62-1.

**SUBMACHINE GUNS:** (No longer a standard class of weapons in the Soviet Army; replaced by the assault rifle — Avtomat.)

* Cal.: 7.62 x 25mm
  *Official Name: Pistolet-Pulemet Sudayeva obrazets 1943g* (PPS43)
  *Common Name:* PPS43 submachine gun

  *Remarks:* OBSOLETE. Made at state weapons factories. Standardized in 1943. Exported as military aid. FOM 1005-2-3-7.62-4.

* Cal.: 7.62 x 25mm
  *Official Name: Pistolet-Pulemet Shpagina obrazets 1941g* (PPSh41)
  *Common Name:* PPSh41 submachine gun

  *Remarks:* OBSOLETE. Made at state weapons factories. Standardized in 1941. Thousands have been exported as military aid. FOM 1005-2-3-7.62-1.

**RIFLES:**

* Cal.: 7.62 x 54mmR
  *Official Name: Karabina obrazets 1944g*
  *Common Name:* M1944 Mosin-Nagant carbine

  *Remarks:* OBSOLETE. Made at state weapons factories. Standardized in 1944; production continued until the late 1940s. This weapon has been exported by the thousands as military aid. FOM 1005-2-2-7.62-15.

* Cal.: 7.62 x 54mmR
  *Official Name: Vintovka obrazets 1891/30g*
  *Common Name:* Model 1891/30 Mosin Nagant rifle

  *Remarks:* OBSOLETE. Made at state weapons factories. FOM 1005-2-2-7.62-3.

* Cal.: 7.62 x 39mm
  *Official Name: Samozaryadinyi Karabina Simonova 1945g* (SKS45)
  *Common Name:* SKS; SKS46; Simonov carbine

  *Remarks:* OBSOLETE except for some formal ceremonial purposes. Made at state weapons factories. Exported in large numbers as military aid. Standardized in 1944. FOM 1005-2-2-7.62-16.

* Cal.: 7.62 x 39mm
  *Official Name: Avtomat Kalashnikova obrazets 1947g* (AK47)
  *Common Name:* AK; AK47; Kalashnikov assault rifle, "Kalach"

  *Remarks:* This older model is probably secondary standard. Made at several state weapons factories. Standardized in 1947 and made to 1959. At least three variants of weapon called AK47. See *Small Arms of the World* (12th ed.), pp. 36–39ff. FOM 1005-2-2-7.62-12 is the second model with the machined steel receiver and the special dovetail fitting for the butt stock. FOM 1005-2-2-7.62-6 is the third model, generally called the AK47.

* Cal.: 7.62 x 39mm
  *Official Name: Avtomat Kalashnikova Skladyvayushchimsya prikladom obrazets 1947g*
  *Common Name:* AK47 with folding stock

  *Remarks:* FOM 1005-2-2-7.62-12-1.

* Cal.: 7.62 x 39mm
  *Official Name: Modernizirovannyi Avtomat Kalashnikova* (AKM)
  *Common Name:* AKM

  *Remarks:* Standard since 1959. Made at several state weapons factories. FOM 1005-2-2-7.62-21-2.

* Cal.: 7.62 x 39mm
  *Official Name: Modernizirovannyi Avtomat Kalashnikova Skladyvayushchimsya prikladom* (AKMS)
  *Common Name:* AKMS

  *Remarks:* Standard. Used as a firing port weapon in BMP and other APCs. FOM 1005-2-2-7.62-21-5.

• *Cal.:* 5.45 x 39mm
*Official Name: Avtomat Kalashnikova obrazets 1974g* (AK74)
*Common Name:* AK74

*Remarks:* Standard since 1974. Made at state weapons factories, using AKM operating mechanism as basis of the design. FOM 1005-2-2-5.45-2.

• *Cal.:* 5.45 x 39mm
*Official Name: Avtomat Kalashnikova Skladyvayushchimsya prikladom obrazets 1974g* (AKS74)
*Common Name:* AKS74

*Remarks:* FOM 1005-2-2-5.45-1. The suffix "N" in the cryllic alphabet with the AK74 family denotes the weapon is fitted with a mount for a night vision sight. The standard infrared NSP-2 and light intensification NSP-3 night vision sights are probably used with the AK74. Sometimes called "Kallikov" by non-Soviet sources.

• *Cal.:* 5.45 x 39mm
*Official Name: Avtomat Kalashnikova samokhodnaya ustanovka*
*Common Name:* AKSU

*Remarks:* "Armored-vehicle automat Kalashnikov." Standard since late 1970s. This much altered submachine version of the AK74 is apparently issued to armored vehicle crews and other personnel who require a more compact weapon. The AKSU has a modified top cover and large muzzle device for control of blast and flash. This weapon is 720mm overall w/ stock extended and 480mm w/ stock folded. Sometimes called AKR and "Krinkov."

• *Cal.:* 7.62 x 54mmR
*Official Name: Samozariyadnyi Vintovka Dragunova.* Also called *Snayperskaya Vintovka Dragunova* (SVD)
*Common Name:* Dragunov sniper rifle

*Remarks:* Standard sniper rifle since 1963. Made at state weapons factories. FOM 1005-2-2-7.62-2.

• *Cal.:* 7.62 x 54mmR
*Official Name: Snayperskaya Vintovka 1891/30g*
*Common Name:* M1891/30 sniper rifle

*Remarks:* OBSOLETE. FOM 1005-2-2-7.62-12.

**SHOTGUNS:**
None known to be in military service.

**MACHINE GUNS:**
*Squad Automatic Weapons:*
• *Cal.:* 7.62 x 39mm
*Official Name: Ruchnoi Pulemet Degtyareva* (RPD)
*Common Name:* RPD and RPDM

*Remarks:* OBSOLETE. Entered service in 1947. There are 5 main variants:
*First model* — cup-type gas piston; no dust cover; many modified to look like later guns by modifying gas system and adding dust cover.
*Second model* — plunger-type gas piston; no dust covers; straight reciprocating charging handle; left-hand windage knob. Some 2d model guns have add-on sliding dust cover; others have riveted bracket to accept a nonreciprocating charging handle; may fold upward or forward.
*Third model* (also PRC Type 56) — similar to 2d model, but has dust covers on feed mechanism and folding nonreciprocating charging handle.
*Fourth model* (RPDM) — same as 3d model, but has longer gas cylinder; additional roller on piston; and buffer in butt stock.
*Fifth model* (also PRC Type 56-1) — similar to 4th model, but has folding drum bracket/dust cover and sectional cleaning rod stored in the butt stock. Large quantities of RPDs were exported as military aid. FOM 1005-2-4-7.62-15 assigned to 1st and 2d versions. FOM 1005-2-4-7.62-15-1 assigned to 3d model. FOM 1005-2-4-7.62-15-2 assigned to the RPDM.

• *Cal.:* 7.62 x 39mm
*Official Name: Ruchnoi Pulemet Kalashnikova* (RPK)
*Common Name:* RPK

*Remarks:* Standard since 1964. Made at state weapons factories. FOM 1005-2-4-7.62-17.

- *Cal.:* 7.62 x 39mm
  *Official Name: Ruchnoi Pulemet Kalashnikova prikladom* (RPKS)
  *Common Name:* RPKS with side folding stock

*Remarks:* Standard since late 1960s. Made at state weapons factories. FOM 1005-2-4-7.62-17-1.

- *Cal.:* 5.45 x 39mm
  *Official Name: Ruchnoi Pulemet Kalashnikova obrazets 1974g* (RPK74)
  *Common Name:* RPK74

*Remarks:* Standard since 1974. Made at state weapons factories. The suffix "N" in the cyrillic alphabet with the RPK74 family denotes the weapon is equipped with a mount for a night vision sight.

- *Cal.:* 5.45 x 39mm
  *Official Name: Ruchnoi Pulemet Kalashnikova Skladyvayush-chimsya prikladom obrazets 1974g* (RPKS74)
  *Common Name:* RPKS74 with side folding stock

*Remarks:* Standard since the mid-1970s. Made at state weapons factories. FOM 1005-2-2-5.45-1.

**Soviet troops on military exercises. The infantryman in the foreground has a 7.62 x 54mmR PK GPMG with fluted barrel. (Weeks)**

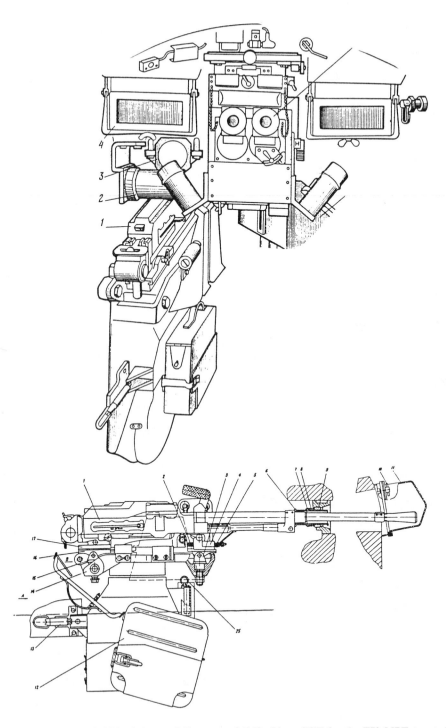

**Two views (from the rear and side) of the coaxially mounted 7.62 x 54mm PKT for the T72 MBT turret. Note the solenoid trigger at the rear of the gun. (USSR)**

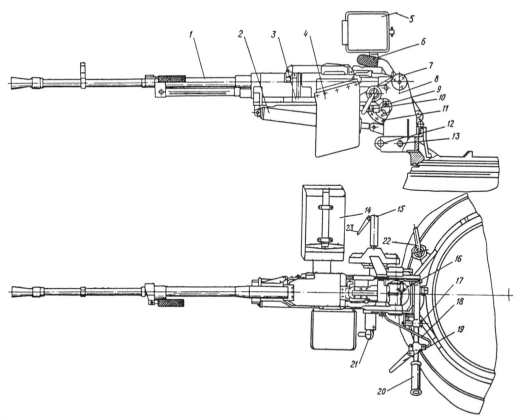

**Two views (from the top and side) of the antiaircraft-mounted 12.7 x 108mm NSVT machine gun for the T72 MBT commander's hatch. (USSR)**

*Medium Machine Guns (GPMG):*

• *Cal.:* 7.62 x 54mmR
  *Official Name: Rotniy Pulemet obrazets 1946g* (RP46)
  *Common Name:* RP46 company machine gun

• *Cal.:* 7.62 x 54mmR
  *Official Name: Stankovyi Pulemet obrazets* 1943 (*Stankovyi Goryunova* – SG43)
  *Common Name:* SG43 vehicle mounted machine gun

*Remarks:* OBSOLETE. Made at state weapons factories. Belt-fed version of World War II Degtyarev machine guns. FOM 1005-2-4-7.62-14. Older Degtyarev machine guns have the following FOM identifiers: DP is FOM 1005-2-4-7.62-4; DT is FOM 1005-2-4-7.62-7; DTM is FOM 1005-2-4-7.62-8; DPM is FOM 1005-2-4-7.62-16.

*Remarks:* First models standardized in 1943. Variants described in *Small Arms of the World* (12th ed.), p. 724ff. Briefly the different models are: SG 43 – smooth barrel, no dust covers, charging handle between spade grips. SG 43M – SGMB-type barrel lock, dust covers. SGM – splined barrel, micrometer barrel lock, no dust covers, charging handle on right side. SGMT – armor version of SGM, solenoid fired. SGMB – SGM w/ dust covers on feed ports, feed slide, ejection port. Modified lower received for vehicular mounts.

All SG machine guns are now OBSOLETE for Soviet forces, but still widely used by forces supplied by the Soviet Union. FOM 1005-2-4-7.62-13. Other SG variants have the following FOM identifiers: SGM is FOM 1005-2-4-7.62-13-1; SGMT is FOM 1005-2-4-7.62-18; SG43M is FOM 1005-2-4-7.62-13-2; SGMB is FOM 1005-2-4-7.62-19.

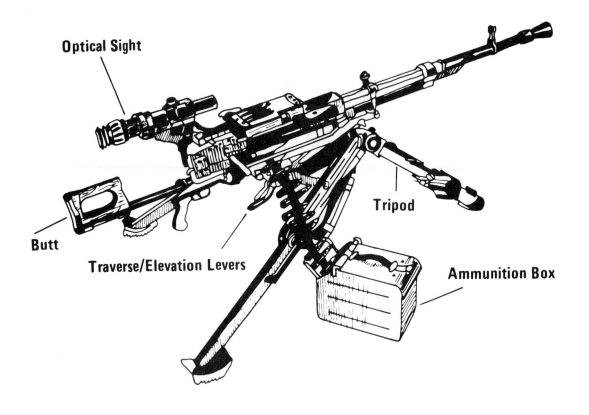

**Optical Sight**

**Butt**

**Traverse/Elevation Levers**

**Tripod**

**Ammunition Box**

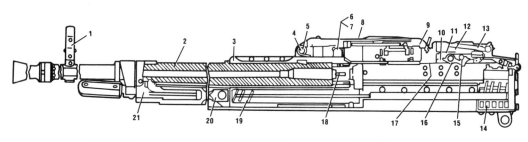

1. FRONT SIGHT
2. BARREL
3. RECEIVER
4. FEED TRAY COVER PIN
5. COVER SPRING
6. FEED TRAY RETAINING PIN
7. FEED TRAY RETAINING PIN WASHER

8. FEED TRAY COVER
9. FEED TRAY
10. TRIGER ASSEMBLY RETAINING PIN
11. TRIGGER ASSEMBLY
12. SIGHT LEAF SPRING
13. SIGHT LEAF
14. DRIVE SPRING ASSEMBLY

15. SAFETY
16. SEAR
17. FEED TRAY COVER CATCH
18. BREECHBLOCK
19. BREECHBLOCK CARRIER
20. GAS PISTON RETAINING SCREW
21. GAS REGULATOR

Two drawings illustrating the new Soviet 12.7 x 108mm NSV heavy machine gun. This gun is used both on ground mounts and on armored vehicles as a flexible air defense gun. This weapon is a further exploitation of the Kalashnikov bolt and bolt carrier system used in the Kalashnikov rifles and machine guns. (US Army)

- *Cal.:* 7.62 x 54mmR
  *Official Name: Pulemet Kalashnikova* (PK)
  *Common Name:* PK

*Remarks:* Standard since early 1960s. Made at state weapons factories. There are several variants. See below.

- *Cal.:* 7.62 x 54mmR
  *Official Name: Pulemet Kalashnikova Stankovyi* (PKS)
  *Common Name:* PKS

*Remarks:* Tripod mounted GPMG.

- *Cal.:* 7.62 x 54mmR
  *Official Name: Pulemet Kalashnikova na bronetransportere* (PKB)
  *Common Name:* PKB; for armored vehicles

*Remarks:* Flexibly mounted on a variety of vehicles, with spade grips. FOM 1005-2-4-7.62-20-2.

- *Cal.:* 7.62 x 54mmR
  *Official Name: Pulemet Kalashnikova Tankovyi* (PKT)
  *Common Name:* PKT

*Remarks:* Coaxially mounted on tanks and APCs. FOM 1005-2-4-7.62-21.

- *Cal.:* 7.62 x 54mmR
  *Official Name: Moderniziroyannyi Pulemet Kalashnikova* (PKM)
  *Common Name:* PKM

*Remarks:* Product-improved version of the basic PK. All PK variants are also found in the PKM series. FOM 1005-2-4-7.62-20-3.

*Heavy Machine Guns:*

- *Cal.:* 12.7 x 108mm
  *Official Name: Stankovyi Pulemet DShK (Degtyareva-Shpagina Krupnokalibernyi) obrazets 1938g* (DShK38)
  *Common Name:* DShK38

*Remarks:* Standardized in 1938. OBSOLETE in Soviet service. Replaced by DShK38/46 (DShKM), which has a much simplified feed mechanism. DShK 38 and the modernized version use different nondisintegrating metallic feed belts.

- *Cal.:* 12.7 x 108mm
  *Official Name: Stankovyi Pulemet DShKM (Modernizirovannyi)*
  *Common Name:* DShK38/46 and DShKM

*Remarks:* This product improved model was standardized in 1946. Made at state weapons factories. FOM 1005-2-4-12.7-3.

- *Cal.:* 12.7 x 108mm
  *Official Name: Stankovyi Pulemet NSV*
  *Common Name:* "UTES"

*Remarks:* Standardized ca. 1974. Made at state weapons factories. This weapon was designed by Nikitin-Sokolov-Volkov. It is used both as a ground gun and as a flexible gun on tanks. FOM 1005-2-4-12.7-6.

- *Cal.:* 12.7 x 108mm
  *Common Name:* 4-barrel, high-rate-of-fire machine gun

*Remarks:* Soviet design similar in concept to US Gatling guns. This gun is gas operated; blank cartridges are used to charge the gun and make it ready for firing (there is no external power source as in American Gatlings); it has a 4,000 shots per minute rate of fire.

## AUTOMATIC CANNON:
- *Cal.:* 14.5 x 114mm
  *Official Name: Krupnokalibernyi Pulemet Vladimironva* (KPV); there are two variants of the KPV that are usually called the early and later models by the Soviets
  *Common Name:* KPV

*Remarks:* Standardized ca. 1955. (ZPU — *Zenitnaya Pulemetnaya Ustanovka* or "antiaircraft machine gun installation.") Made at state weapons factories. FOM 1005-2-4-14.5-5 identifies the KPV automatic cannon by itself. FOM 1005-2-4-14.5-3 identifies the twin gun ZPU-2 AA version. FOM 1005-2-4-14.4-2 identifies the quad gun — ZPU-4. A 2-wheel AA version is FOM 1005-2-4-14.5-9. There is also a KPVT vehicle version w/o sights and solenoid trigger. The KPVT-1 is w/o sights and has a manual trigger.

- *Cal.:* 23 x 152mmB
  *Official Name:* ZU 23

*Remarks:* Made at state weapons factories. FOM 1005-2-4-23-6.

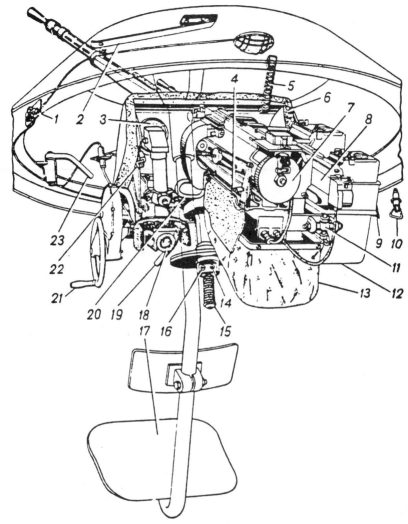

**Interior view of the turret-mounted 14.5 x 114mm KPVT automatic cannon for the BTR60 armored personnel carrier. (USSR)**

**GRENADE LAUNCHERS:**
- *Cal.:* 30 x 29mm
  *Official Name: Avtomatischeskyi Granatmyot Stankovyi 17* (AGS17)
  *Common Name:* AGS17

- *Cal.:* 40mm
  *Common Name:* BG-15 grenade launcher

*Remarks:* Made at state weapons factories.

*Remarks:* This 40mm grenade launcher attachment for the AK74 appeared in Afghanistan in the mid-1980s. It is believed to have a maximum range of 420 meters and an effective range of 300 meters. It fires a projectile that has an integral self-contained propellant charge.

## Soviet Weapons Factories

There are three major small arms factories in the Soviet Union. In order of establishment these are Tula, Sestroretsk, and Izhevsk (renamed Ustinov—after Marshall Dmitry Ustinov who died in 1984). The *Tulski Oruzheiny Zavod,* located approximately 200 kilometers south of Moscow, was formally established as a weapons factory in 1712. A dozen years later, in 1724, one of the metal-working establishments near St. Petersburg (now Leningrad) was converted to a small arms factory and became the *Sestroretski Oruzheiny Zavod.* Being so close to the western border of the nation, Sestroretsk was always the most vulnerable factory being overrun during the Napoleonic invasion of Russia, occupied during the Bolshevik revolution and threatened during World War II. Appreciating the exposed position of the *Sestroretski* weapons factory, the Russian government in 1805–07 established the *Izhevski Oruzheiny Zavod,* 900 kilometers east of Moscow at Ustinov in the heart of the Ural mountains. The latter factory has been the location of the Kalashnikov design bureau since the late 1940s, and thus has been the wellspring of new Soviet small arms during the past 35 years.

# UNITED ARAB EMIRATES

Population (estimate in 1984): 1.52 million. Ground forces: regulars, ca. 25,000; reserves, no formal reserves. The UAE was formed from seven sheikdoms: Abu Dhabi, Ajman, Dhubai, Fujaira, Ras al-Khaimah, Sharjah, and Umm al-Qaiwain.

**HANDGUNS:**
- *Cal.:* 6.35 x 15mm
  *Common Name:* Astra pistol

  *Remarks:* Specific model unknown.

- *Cal.:* 9 x 19mm Parabellum
  *Common Name:* HK P7M13 pistol

  *Remarks:* Heckler & Koch (HK), GmbH? Used by UAE Ministry of the Interior.

- *Cal.:* 9 x 20mmR
  *Common Name:* .38 Webley revolver

  *Remarks:* UK origin. Used only in Abu Dhabi.

- *Cal.:* 9 x 29mmR
  *Common Name:* .38 Smith & Wesson revolvers

  *Remarks:* US origin. The State Department licensed the sale of 130 to the Dhubai Police in 1979.

- *Cal.:* 9 x 29mmR
  *Common Name:* .38 Ruger revolvers

  *Remarks:* US origin. The State Department licensed the sale of Ruger revolvers to the Internal Security Forces.

**SUBMACHINE GUNS:**
- *Cal.:* 9 x 19mm Parabellum
  *Common Name:* Mark 4 submachine gun

  *Remarks:* Sterling Armaments Co., UK.

- *Cal.:* 9 x 19mm Parabellum
  *Common Name:* MP5 submachine gun

  *Remarks:* Source uncertain.

- *Cal.:* 5.56 x 45mm
  *Common Name:* HK53 submachine gun

  *Remarks:* HK GmbH design with Enfield markings.

**RIFLES:**

- *Cal.*: 5.56 x 45mm
  *Common Name:* M16A1 (Model 613) rifle and M16A1 (Model 653) carbine

  *Remarks:* Colt origin. Total less than 500 of both models before 1985.

- *Cal.*: 5.56 x 45mm NATO
  *Common Name:* M16A2 rifle (Model 703) and carbine (Model 727)

  *Remarks:* Colt origin. In 1985, 30,000 (without the 3-shot burst fire feature) were ordered from Colt. In 1987 Abu Dhabi ordered 20,000 M16A2 heavy barrel carbines (Model 727) with 368mm barrel. Very similar to US XM4 carbine.

- *Cal.*: 5.56 x 45mm
  *Common Name:* Mini-14 w/ folding stock

  *Remarks:* Sturm, Ruger and Co., US. Used by the UAE Customs police.

- *Cal.*: 5.56 x 45mm
  *Common Name:* FAMAS

  *Remarks:* Groupment Industriel des Armements Terrestres (GIAT), France. Reportedly delivered in 1983.

- *Cal.*: 5.45 x 39mm
  *Common Name:* AK74 assault rifle

  *Remarks:* East German origin. Ca. 2,000 were delivered for issue to the body guards of individual sheiks.

- *Cal.*: 7.62 x 39mm
  *Common Name:* AK47 assault rifle

  *Remarks:* East Bloc origin.

- *Cal.*: 7.62 x 51mm NATO
  *Common Name:* Gewehr 3 (G3)

  *Remarks:* Saudi Arabian origin? Some made in England at Royal Small Arms Factory (RSAF), Enfield have been reported. Used by Dubai and Abu Dhabi.

- *Cal.*: 7.62 x 51mm NATO
  *Common Name:* FN FAL

  *Remarks:* FN origin. Used by Dubai.

**SHOTGUNS:**

- *Cal.*: 18.5 x 59mm
  *Common Name:* 12 gage Mossberg Model 500 shotgun

  *Remarks:* Acquired by UAE military forces in 1984.

**MACHINE GUNS:**

- *Cal.*: 5.56 x 45mm
  *Common Name:* HK23E LMG

  *Remarks:* HK design with Enfield markings.

- *Cal.*: 5.56 x 45mm
  *Common Name:* FN Minimi LMG

  *Remarks:* FN origin.

- *Cal.*: 7.62 x 51mm NATO
  *Common Name:* FN MAG

  *Remarks:* FN. MAG *Infanterie Standard* (60-20), T6; and MAG *Coaxial* (60-40), L7A2, Type p.806 and L7A2 for OTO Melara mount in Dubai.

- *Cal.*: 7.62 x 63mm
  *Common Name:* .30 M1919A4 LMG

  *Remarks:* US origin.

- *Cal.*: 12.7 x 99mm
  *Common Name:* .50 M2 HB HMG

  *Remarks:* US and FN origin. The FN guns have a quick change barrel.

**AUTOMATIC CANNON:**

- *Cal.*: 20 x 139mm
  *Common Name:* M693 automatic cannon

  *Remarks:* GIAT.

- *Cal.:* 20 x 139mm
  *Common Name:* 20mm Hispano-Oerlikon, HS820/L85 (KAD-B-13-3)

*Remarks:* Oerlikon-Buhrle, Switzerland. These guns are mounted on the French SP AA M3VDA. At least 42 units are in service.

**GRENADE LAUNCHERS:**
- *Cal.:* 40 x 46mmSR
  *Common Name:* M203 grenade launcher

*Remarks:* Colt origin.

## UNITED KINGDOM OF GREAT BRITAIN AND NORTHERN IRELAND

Population (estimate in 1984): 56.02 million. Ground forces: regulars, ca. 162,000; reserves, 141,000; territorial army, 75,000.

**HANDGUNS:**
- *Cal.:* 5.6 x 16mmR
  *Official Name:* Pistol, Automatic 0.22 in. (Walther) L66A1
  *Common Name:* Walther .22 target pistol

*Remarks:* A Walther design, made by Manuhrin of France. NSN 1005-99-964-6300.

- *Cal.:* 9 x 19mm NATO
  *Official Name:* Pistol Automatic 9mm L9A1
  *Common Name:* FN Mle. 35 GP pistol

*Remarks:* FN origin. NSN 1005-13-010-0478. Issued with accessories as Automatic Pistol Kit, 9mm L11A1: NSN 1005-99-961-6088.

- *Cal.:* 9 x 29mmR
  *Common Name:* .38 Smith & Wesson Model 64 revolver (stainless steel Military & Police, 50.8mm barrel)

*Remarks:* US origin. Acquired for London Metropolitan Police. Total of 350 of these Smith & Wesson revolvers were acquired in 1984. These revolvers will replace the currently used S&W Model 36 (Chief Special).

- *Cal.:* 9 x 29mmR
  *Common Name:* .38 Smith & Wesson Model 10 revolver (102mm barrel)

*Remarks:* US origin. Acquired for London Metropolitan Police.

- *Cal.:* 7.65 x 17mm Browning
  *Official Name:* Pistol, Automatic 7.65mm L47A1
  *Common Name:* Walther PP

*Remarks:* Made by Manuhrin of France. NSN 1005-99-964-1256 (NSN 1005-12-159-3025).

**SUBMACHINE GUNS:**
- *Cal.:* 9 x 19mm NATO
  *Official Name:* Submachine gun 9mm L2A3
  *Common Name:* Military version of Sterling Mark 4

*Remarks:* Sterling Armament Co. and other government contractors. NSN 1005-99-960-0029.

- *Cal.:* 9 x 19mm NATO
  *Official Name:* Submachine gun 9mm L34A1
  *Common Name:* Silenced version of L2A3; similar to Sterling Mark 5

*Remarks:* Sterling Armament Co. and other government contractors. NSN 1005-99-961-4083. Used by Special Boat Squadron and other special operations units. Also used by the stay-behind Forward Artillery Observation parties of the Royal Artillery.

A British corporal aims his 9 x 19mm L34A1 silenced submachine gun. (Gander)

- *Cal.:* 9 x 19mm NATO
  *Common Name:* MP5A3 submachine gun

*Remarks:* UK origin from the Royal Small Arms Factory (RSAF), Enfield. The MP5A3s are used by the SAS, which also uses the MP5K (NSN 1005-99-966-2749) and MP5SD versions. MP5s are also used by the London Metropolitan Police firearms specialists and the counter-terrorist squad, and the Hong Kong Police.

- *Cal.:* 5.56 x 45mm
  *Common Name:* HK53 submachine gun

*Remarks:* Enfield origin. SAS use?

**RIFLES:**
- *Cal.:* 5.6 x 16mmR
  *Official Name:* Rifle, .22 in. No. 8, Mark 1
  *Common Name:* .22 LR target rifle

*Remarks:* RSAF. This is a single shot rifle. It is made w/ 3 different stock lengths. Long butt is NSN 1005-99-961-9008. Normal butt is 1005-99-961-9009. Short butt is 1005-99-961-9010.

- *Cal.:* 5.56 x 45mm NATO
  *Official Name:* Individual Weapon, 5.56mm L85A1
  *Common Name:* Enfield Weapon System

*Remarks:* RSAF. NSN 1005-99-966-6470. Enfield delivered the first small lot of this new rifle on 2 October 1985. The first order for 170,000 rifles is scheduled to be completed by 1989. These weapons are going to Infantry, Royal Marines, and RAF regiments first. Total production of L85A1 anticipated to be about 400,000 for British forces.

- *Cal.:* 5.56 x 45mm NATO
  *Official Name:* Rifle, 5.56mm Cadet General Purpose, L98A1
  *Common Name:* Modified Enfield Weapon System, manual operation only

*Remarks:* RSAF. NSN 1005-99-967-4825. Enfield created this manually operated version of the L85A1 for use by teenage cadets, because of the worry about issuing self-loading rifles to local armories where they might fall into the hands of terrorists or criminals.

**British soldier sighting the new 5.56 x 45mm L85A1 rifle developed by Royal Ordnance Small Arms, Enfield. Prior to adoption it was called the Individual Weapon of the Enfield Weapon System and the SAA80. (UK MOD)**

**A British Territorial Para trots forward with his 7.62 x 51mm NATO L1A1 rifle at the ready. (Gander)**

A British Commando and an American Marine exchange thoughts during joint exercises. The Commando has a 7.62 x 51mm NATO L1A1 rifle, while his American counterpart has a 5.56 x 45mm M16A1. (NATO)

**Accuracy International, Limited developed the 7.62 x 51mm NATO L96A1 sniper rifle for the British Army. Two variants are shown.** *Top,* **the standard L96A1 with a Schmidt & Bender 6 x 42 telescope;** *bottom,* **the SAS "moderated" variant with an integral silencer. (UK MOD)**

• *Cal.:* 5.56 x 45mm
  *Official Name:* Rifle, 5.56mm
    (AR.15 Model 01)
  *Common Name:* M16 (Model 614)
    rifle

*Remarks:* Colt, US. Some 750+ were purchased before 1970. NSN 1005-99-962-3493. Some men of the Edinburgh Royal Regiment, in Northern Ireland (1984), carried AR-15/M16 rifles with early style open flash hiders. The M16 has also been popular with Royal Marine and SAS men. The latter used the weapon in Borneo and Oman, and SAS unit commanders used AR-15s during the 1982 South Atlantic War. A few Model 613 rifles and Model 653 carbines were acquired in recent years. One Falkland photograph shows Hugh McNamara, RA (Naval Gunfire Forward Observer) with a Model 653.

• *Cal.:* 7.62 x 33mm
  *Common Name:* .30 M1 and M2
    carbines

*Remarks:* US origin. FMS sold 175,404 carbines to the British before 1964. Many are still used for police work by organizations such as the Royal Ulster Constabulary (RUC).

• *Cal.:* 7.62 x 51mm NATO
*Official Name:* Rifle 7.62mm L1A1; semiautomatic fire only
*Common Name:* English version of FN FAL

*Remarks:* RSAF and the Birmingham Small Arms Company. A .22 caliber LR conversion kit for the L1A1, NSN 6920-12-147-6954 is made by Heckler & Koch GmbH. The British assign 5 NSNs to the different models of their L1A1s: Long Butt – 1005-99-960-0000; Normal Butt – 1005-99-960-0001; Short Butt – 1005-99-960-0002; Extra Long Butt – 1005-99-960-0877; Rifle, Pooled (i.e., made from parts) – 1005-99-962-5831.

The L1A1 can be fitted with either the Sightunit, L2A1 Infantry Trilux (NSN 1240-99-963-0650) or the Weaponsight, Image, Intensified, L1A1 (NSN 5855-99-962-6868).

• *Cal.:* 7.62 x 51mm NATO
*Official Name:* Rifle 7.62mm L1A1, DP
*Common Name:* Drill version of the L1A1

*Remarks:* RSAF. Training rifle that will not fire.

• *Cal.:* 7.62 x 51mm NATO
*Official Name:* Rifle Instructional 7.62mm, L25A1
*Common Name:* Training version of the L1A1

*Remarks:* RSAF. Training rifle that will not fire. NSN 1005-99-960-8194.

• *Cal.:* 7.62 x 51mm NATO
*Official Name:* Rifle Instructional 7.62mm, L26A1
*Common Name:* Training version of the L1A1

*Remarks:* RSAF. Training rifle that will not fire. NSN 1005-99-960-8193.

• *Cal.:* 7.62 x 51mm NATO
*Official Name:* Rifle 7.62mm L39A1 (Target)
*Common Name:* No. 4 rifle converted to 7.62mm NATO from .303

*Remarks:* RSAF. Various NSNs. These rifles are used for competition shooting. NSN 1005-99-962-3089. It and the L42A1 are fitted w/ the "Telescope, Straight, Sighting, L1A1," which is assigned NSN 1240-99-963-2063.

• *Cal.:* 7.62 x 51mm NATO
*Official Name:* Rifle 7.62mm L42A1 (Sniper)
*Common Name:* No. 4 rifle converted to 7.62mm NATO from .303; used as a sniper rifle

*Remarks:* RSAF. NSN 1005-99-965-2387 and 1005-99-963-3786.

• *Cal.:* 7.62 x 51mm NATO
*Official Name:* Rifle 7.62mm L81A1 (Cadet Target Rifle)
*Common Name:* Single shot bolt action rifle developed from the Parker Hale 1200TX target rifle and M82 sniper

*Remarks:* Parker Hale, UK. This sniper/target-type rifle is built around a standard Mauser-type rifle action. This rifle will eventually be replaced by the L98A1 cadet rifle. NB: Large numbers of 7.7 x 56mmR (.303) No. 4 MK 1 Enfield rifles are still carried (but rarely fired) by Air Training Corps (ATC) and other cadet units. These ATC would be used by RAF ground crews for local defense in any emergency.

• *Cal.:* 7.62 x 51mm NATO
*Official Name:* Rifle 7.62mm L96A1 (Sniper)
*Common Name:* Accuracy International Sniper Rifle Model "PM"

*Remarks:* Accuracy International, Ltd., Portsmouth, Hampshire, UK. The Infantry version has both iron sights (to 700 meters) and a Schmidt & Bender 6x 42 telescope. The SAS uses a "moderated" variant that has a silencer and that fires subsonic ammunition.

• *Cal.:* 7.62 x 63mm
*Official Name:* Rifle, .30 in. (Garand)
*Common Name:* .30 M1 rifle

*Remarks:* US origin. NSN 1005-00-674-1426. OBSOLETE, but still carried in the small arms census.

**SHOTGUNS:**
- *Cal.:* 18.5 x 59mm
  *Official Name:* 12 Bore, Pump Action, L74A1 riot gun
  *Common Name:* Remington Model 870, riot-type shotgun (Wingmaster)

  *Remarks:* US origin. NSN 1005-99-966-0459. Wooden butt stock, with 4-shot magazine tube and 508mm barrel.

- *Cal.:* 18.5 x 59mm
  *Official Name:* 12 Bore, Pump Action, L74A1 riot gun, with folding butt stock and magazine extension
  *Common Name:* Remington Model 870, riot-type shotgun (Wingmaster)

  *Remarks:* US origin. NSN 1005-99-965-9060. This model has a folding metal stock, with 7-shot magazine tube and 508mm barrel.

- *Cal.:* 18.5 x 59mm
  *Official Name:* 12 Bore, Shotgun L32A1 Automatic Loading FN Browning Riot Gun
  *Common Name:* FN Browning auto-loading riot shotgun

  *Remarks:* Belgian origin. NSN 1005-99-960-8114.

- *Cal.:* 18.5 x 59mm
  *Official Name:* 12 Bore, Automatic Loading Winchester Riot Gun
  *Common Name:* 12 gage Winchester Model 1200 riot shotgun

  *Remarks:* US origin. NSN 1005-00-921-5483. The UK acquired 200 Winchester Model 1200s in 1971 from FMS to be used on Gibralter.

**MACHINE GUNS:**
- *Cal.:* 5.56 x 45mm NATO
  *Official Name:* Machine Gun, 5.56mm L86A1
  *Common Name:* Enfield light support weapon

  *Remarks:* RSAF.

- *Cal.:* 5.56 x 45mm NATO
  *Common Name:* Minimi SAW

  *Remarks:* FN. Used by the SAS.

- *Cal.:* 7.62 x 51mm NATO
  *Official Name:* Machine Gun 7.62mm L7A1
  *Common Name:* English version of FN MAG. "Jimpy"

  *Remarks:* RSAF and the Birmingham Small Arms Company. NSN 1005-13-010-0506.

- *Cal.:* 7.62 x 51mm NATO
  *Official Name:* Machine Gun 7.62mm L7A2
  *Common Name:* Modified L7A1

  *Remarks:* RSAF and other government contractors. NSN 1005-13-103-2524, and 1005-99-963-0959.

- *Cal.:* 7.62 x 51mm NATO
  *Official Name:* Machine Gun 7.62mm TK L8A1
  *Common Name:* Armor version of L7 series

  *Remarks:* RSAF and other contractors. NSN 1005-99-960-6851.

- *Cal.:* 7.62 x 51mm NATO
  *Official Name:* Machine Gun 7.62mm TK L8A2
  *Common Name:* Product improved version of L8A1

  *Remarks:* RSAF. NSN 1005-99-966-0656.

**Antiaircraft version of the 7.62 x 51mm NATO L4A4 Bren series as used on general purpose ground vehicles. (Gander)**

• *Cal.:* 7.62 x 51mm NATO
  *Official Name:* Machine Gun
    7.62mm L20A1 and L20A2
  *Common Name:* Helicopter versions of L7 series

*Remarks:* RSAF.

• *Cal.:* 7.62 x 51mm NATO
  *Official Name:* Machine Gun
    7.62mm L37A1
  *Common Name:* Armor version of L8 series that can be used in the infantry role by vehicle crew

*Remarks:* RSAF. NSN 1005-99-962-0645.

• *Cal.:* 7.62 x 51mm NATO
  *Official Name:* Machine Gun
    7.62mm L37A2
  *Common Name:* Improved version of L37A1

*Remarks:* RSAF. NSN 1005-99-966-0655.

• *Cal.:* 7.62 x 51mm NATO
  *Official Name:* Machine Gun
    7.62mm L41A1
  *Common Name:* Drill (instructional model) version of L8; inoperable

*Remarks:* RSAF. NSN 1005-99-964-3230.

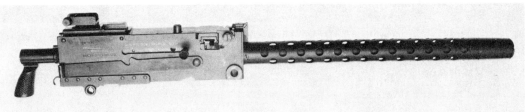

Vehicle version of 7.62 x 33mm US M1919A4, called the L3A2 (FLEX), as used by the British Army. Note the swivel-type safety that holds the bolt open when cocked and ready to fire. (RSAF, Enfield)

• *Cal.:* 7.62 x 51mm NATO
  *Official Name:* Machine Gun 7.62mm L43A1
  *Common Name:* L7 used as ranging gun for Scorpion AFV

*Remarks:* RSAF. NSN 1005-99-964-2619.

• *Cal.:* 7.62 x 51mm NATO
  *Official Name:* Machine Gun 7.62mm L44A1
  *Common Name:* Helicopter gun, Royal Navy

*Remarks:* RSAF.

- *Cal.:* 7.62 x 51mm NATO
  *Official Name:* Machine Gun
  7.62mm L45A1
  *Common Name:* Drill version of
  L37A1

*Remarks:* RSAF. NSN 1005-99-964-3231.

- *Cal.:* 7.62 x 51mm NATO
  *Official Name:* Machine Gun
  7.62mm L46A1 DP (Skeleton)
  *Common Name:* Drill version of
  L7

*Remarks:* RSAF. NSN 1005-99-964-3232.

- *Cal.:* 7.62 x 51mm NATO
  *Official Name:* Machine Gun
  7.62mm L4A2
  *Common Name:* 7.62mm version
  of Bren gun

*Remarks:* RSAF. NSN 1005-99-961-8595.

- *Cal.:* 7.62 x 51mm NATO
  *Official Name:* Machine Gun
  7.62mm L4A4
  *Common Name:* 7.62mm version
  of Bren gun

*Remarks:* RSAF. NSN 1005-99-963-8595.

- *Cal.:* 7.62 x 51mm NATO
  *Official Name:* Machine Gun
  7.62mm L4A6
  *Common Name:* 7.62mm version
  of Bren gun

*Remarks:* RSAF. OBSOLETE. NSN 1005-99-963-9584.

- *Cal.:* 7.62 x 51mm NATO
  *Official Name:* Machine Gun
  7.62mm L4A9, with GPMG
  dovetail
  *Common Name:* 7.62mm version
  of Bren gun

*Remarks:* RSAF. NSN 1005-99-965-4269.

- *Cal.:* 7.62 x 51mm NATO
  *Official Name:* Machine Gun
  7.62mm L55A1 DP
  *Common Name:* 7.62mm DP version of L4A4 Bren gun

*Remarks:* RSAF. NSN 1005-99-964-6286.

- *Cal.:* 7.62 x 51mm NATO
  *Common Name:* M60 GPMG

*Remarks:* US origin. FMS sold 4,483 to British in 1979. Possibly acquired for use elsewhere.

- *Cal.:* 7.62 x 51mm NATO
  *Official Name:* Machine Gun,
  Chain, 7.62mm (Long) L94A1
  *Common Name:* Hughes 7.62mm
  EX34 chain gun for new genera-
  tion of AFVs

*Remarks:* Being built by the RSAF. Fitted to Warrior Section Vehicle and Warrior Command Vehicle. NSN 1005-99-967-1658.

- *Cal.:* 7.62 x 51mm NATO
  *Official Name:* Machine Gun
  7.62mm TK L95A1
  *Common Name:* Hughes 7.62mm
  EX34 chain gun for new genera-
  tion of AFVs

*Remarks:* To be built by the RSAF.

- *Cal.:* 7.62 x 63mm
  *Official Name:* Machine Gun .30
  L3A1, Flexible
  *Common Name:* .30 Browning
  M1919A4 (flexible)

*Remarks:* US origin. Catalog no. C2/MG32GA.

- *Cal.:* 7.62 x 63mm
  *Official Name:* Machine Gun .30 L3A2, Flexible
  *Common Name:* .30 Browning M1919A4 (flexible) with rear sear arrangement

  *Remarks:* US origin. NSN 1005-99-964-5039. (Catalog no. C2/MG33GA).

- *Cal.:* 7.62 x 63mm
  *Official Name:* Machine Gun .30 L3A3, Fixed
  *Common Name:* .30 Browning M1919A4 (fixed) with modified rear sear arrangement

  *Remarks:* US origin. NSN 1005-99-960-5555.

- *Cal.:* 7.62 x 63mm
  *Official Name:* Machine Gun .30 L3A4, Flexible
  *Common Name:* .30 Browning M1919A4 (flexible) with modified rear sear

  *Remarks:* US origin. NSN 1005-99-5554.

- *Cal.:* 7.62 x 63mm
  *Official Name:* Machine Gun .30 L33A2, DP
  *Common Name:* .30 Browning M1919A4

  *Remarks:* US origin. NSN 1005-99-961-6098.

- *Cal.:* 7.62 x 63mm
  *Official Name:* Machine Gun .30 L56, DP
  *Common Name:* .30 Browning M1919A4

  *Remarks:* US origin. NSN 1005-99-964-8026 and 1005-99-964-8027.

**MOUNTS FOR 7.62mm MACHINE GUNS:**

*Official Name:* Mounting, Machine Gun, L7A1

*Remarks:* NSN 1005-99-960-8323.

*Official Name:* Mounting, Tripod, 7.62mm, MG, L4A1

*Remarks:* NSN 1005-99-960-4473.

*Official Name:* Mounting Tripod, 7.62mm, MG, L5A1

*Remarks:* NSN 1005-99-960-8922.

*Official Name:* Mounting Tripod, MG, .30 in. L2A1

*Remarks:* NSN 1005-99-961-9277.

*Official Name:* Mounting Tripod, MG, .30 in. L3A3

*Remarks:* NSN 1005-99-960-5555.

*Official Name:* Mounting Tripod, MG, .30 in. L3A4

*Remarks:* NSN 1005-99-960-5554.

*Official Name:* Mounting Tripod, MG, .30 in. M2

*Remarks:* NSN 1005-00-650-7052.

*Official Name:* Mounting Machine Gun DISA, Mk 400 (for L7 GPMG and L4 LMG)

*Remarks:* NSN 1005-99-839-4263.

**HEAVY MACHINE GUNS:**

- *Cal.:* 12.7 x 99mm
  *Official Name:* Machine Gun 12.7mm L1A1
  *Common Name:* .50 M2 HB HMG with UK-made barrel

  *Remarks:* US origin.

• *Cal.:* 12.7 x 99mm
*Official Name:* Machine Gun
12.7mm L2A1
*Common Name:* .50 M2 HB drill;
also L30A1

*Remarks:* L30A1 DP NSN is 1005-99-960-8812.

• *Cal.:* 12.7 x 99mm
*Official Name:* Machine Gun
12.7mm Ranging, L6A1 (Centurion)
*Common Name:* .50 M2 HB ranging; also L11A1, L21A1; and X16E1; L6A1 is ranging gun for 105mm tank gun

*Remarks:* RSAF. NSN 1005-99-960-6173. OBSOLETE; no longer used.

• *Cal.:* 12.7 x 99mm
*Official Name:* Machine Gun
12.7mm Ranging, L21A1
(Chieftan)
*Common Name:* Ranging gun for 120mm tank gun; L21A1 has a barrel 152mm longer than L6A1

*Remarks:* RSAF. NSN 1005-99-960-6819. OBSOLETE; very few left in service.

• *Cal.:* 12.7 x 99mm
*Official Name:* Machine Gun
12.7mm X17E1
*Common Name:* .50 M85

*Remarks:* US origin. Tested experimentally as a ranging machine gun. Both the X17E1 and the X17E2 were trial guns. These M85s were fitted with special UK-made barrels. No longer employed.

• *Cal.:* 12.7 x 77mm
*Official Name:* Ranging Gun
12.7mm L40A1
*Common Name:* .50 spotting rifle, M8C

*Remarks:* US origin. Used with UK WOMBAT antitank weapon. NSN 1005-00-511-9042 and 1005-99-962-9374. OBSOLETE. Withdrawn.

**AUTOMATIC CANNON:**
• *Cal.:* 20 x 128mm
*Common Name:* 20mm KAB-001
(Type 10La/5TG) on GAM-B01
AA mounts

*Remarks:* These guns are made by the British Manufacture and Research Company, Ltd., a division of the Swiss firm Oerlikon-Buhrle. 20mm cannon are being placed on British destroyers, frigates, and patrol craft to provide close antiaircraft defense after the South Atlantic War demonstrated need for such guns.

• *Cal.:* 20 x 128mm
*Common Name:* 20mm KAA-001
(Type 204GK)

*Remarks:* British Manufacture and Research Company, Ltd., a division of Oerlikon-Buhrle. Used on some British naval craft.

**GRENADE LAUNCHERS:**
• *Cal.:* 37mm
*Official Name:* Gun Riot 1.5 in
L48A1 Also L48A2.

*Remarks:* RSAF. NSN 1005-99-964-1262.

• *Cal.:* 37mm
*Official Name:* Gun Riot 1.5 in.
L67A1

*Remarks:* RSAF. NSN 1005-99-965-4038.

• *Cal.:* 37mm
*Official Name:* Arwen 37mm anti-riot system, XL76

*Remarks:* RSAF. NSN not yet assigned.

• *Cal.:* 37mm?
*Official Name:* Grenade Discharger, L1A1, Hand-Held
*Common Name:* Domestic design

*Remarks:* NSN 1095-99-964-2438. Never issued.

- *Cal.:* 40 x 46mmSR
  *Official Name:* Launcher, Grenade M79, 40mm
  *Common Name:* M79 grenade launcher

  *Remarks:* US origin. NSN 1010-00-691-1382. Approx. 425 sold by FMS 1975-79. NAPCO delivered 120-200 newly made M79s from J. C. Manufacturing of Spring Lake Park, Minnesota.

- *Cal.:* 40 x 46mmSR
  *Common Name:* M203 grenade launcher, attached to M16A1 (Model 613) rifle

  *Remarks:* Colt, US. Approx. 200 in past three years.

### British serial number prefixes

In recent years, the British have used two letters to designate the manufacturer of their small caliber weapons. These include:

| | |
|---|---|
| BL | FN, Herstal, Belgium. |
| UB | Birmingham Small Arms Company, Birmingham. |
| UE | Royal Small Arms Factory, Enfield. |
| UF | Royal Ordnance Factory, Fazakerley. |
| US | Sterling Armaments Company, Dagenham. |

## UNITED STATES OF AMERICA

Population (census in 1981): 226.50 million. Ground forces: regulars, 780,000+ ; reserves, 476,000 (248,300 in Army reserve units; 219,800 with individual ready reserve status; and 8,000 individual mobilization augmentees); and National Guard, 417,000.

### HANDGUNS:
- *Cal.:* 5.6 x 16mmR
  *Official Name:* Pistol, Caliber .22, Automatic, Colt Ace
  *Common Name:* Conversion kit mounted on .45 frame

  *Remarks:* NSN 1005-00-726-5662. The Colt .22 conversion unit is NSN 1005-00-897-8449 and 1005-00-319-7787.

- *Cal.:* 5.6 x 16mmR
  *Official Name:* Pistol, Caliber .22, Automatic, Colt Woodsman

  *Remarks:* Target Model—NSN 1005-00-859-0457.
  Match Target—NSN 1005-00-591-8045 with 165mm barrel.
  Match Target—NSN 1005-00-166-2877 with 114mm barrel.
  Standard—NSN 1005-00-726-5663.
  Super—NSN 1005-00-726-6494.

- *Cal.:* 5.6 x 16mmR
  *Official Name:* Pistol, Caliber .22, Automatic, Colt Huntsman

  *Remarks:* NSN 1005-00-860-7633.

- *Cal.:* 5.6 x 16mmR
  *Official Name:* Pistol, Caliber .22, Automatic, High Standard, Supermatic
  TOU—Tournament; CIT—Citation; TRO—Trophy; STOU—Super Tournament; SCIT—Super Citation; SPK—Sport King

  *Remarks:*
  Model 102TOU w/ 171mm barrel—NSN 1005-00-317-2474.
  Model 102TOU w/ 171mm barrel—NSN 1005-00-738-8042.
  Model 102TOU w/ 171mm barrel—NSN 1005-00-976-9231, w/o equipment.
  NSN 1005-00-317-2474 w/ equipment.
  Model 102CIT w/ 171mm barrel—NSN 1005-00-003-7495.
  Model 102TOU w/ 171mm barrel—NSN 1005-00-003-7496.
  Model 102-4.5TOU w/ 114mm barrel—NSN 1005-00-166-2755.
  Model 102-6TOU w/ 152mm barrel—NSN 1005-00-166-2759.
  Model 102-8TRO w/ 203mm barrel—NSN 1005-00-166-2793.
  Model 102-8CIT w/ 203mm barrel—NSN 1005-00-897-8448.

A comparative view of the US .45 caliber 11.43 x 23mm M1911 pistol (top) adopted in 1911 and the US 9 x 19mm M9 (Beretta Model 92SBF) adopted in 1982. The Colt .45 had a magazine capacity of 7, while the Beretta has a capacity of 15. (Smithsonian: Long)

Model 102-10TRO w/ 254mm barrel—NSN 1005-00-166-2794.
Model 102-10CIT w/ 254mm barrel—NSN 1005-00-166-2795.
Model 102-10CIT w/ 203mm barrel—NSN 1005-00-166-2804.
Model 103TRO w/ 190mm barrel—NSN 1005-00-602-0898.
Model 103-8 w/ 203mm barrel—NSN 1005-00-003-7497.
Model 103TOU w/ 172mm barrel—NSN 1005-00-003-7546.
Model 103TOU w/ 172mm barrel—NSN 1005-00-003-7555.
Model 103CIT w/ 172mm barrel—NSN 1005-00-005-2236.
Model 103SPK w/ 172mm barrel—NSN 1005-00-166-2817.
Model 104CIT w/ 140mm bull barrel—NSN 1005-00-083-5778.
Model 104 w/ 140mm barrel—NSN 1005-00-003-7544.
Model 106TRO w/ 171mm barrel—NSN 1005-00-166-2792.
With 171mm tapered barrel—NSN 1005-00-179-9181.
Model 107 w/ 197mm barrel—NSN 1005-00-003-2269.
Model 107SCIT—NSN 1005-00-148-6525.
Model 107STOU—NSN 1005-00-148-6526.
Model 107STOU—NSN 1005-00-148-6527.
Model 107STOU w/ 172mm barrel—NSN 1005-00-179-9181.
Model 107 single shot deluxe—NSN 1005-00-042-5358.
Other NSNs assigned to this series include 1005-00-630-7148; and 1005-00-630-7228. NSNs 1005-00-630-7229; 1005-00-630-7162 are associated with the High Standard Olympic Model.

- *Cal.:* 5.6 x 16mmR
  *Official Name:* Pistol, Caliber .22, Automatic, High Standard, Model B

*Remarks:* Training grade with 165mm barrel—NSN 1005-00-690-3220 w/ equipment. NSN 1005-00-726-5654 w/o equipment.

- *Cal.:* 5.6 x 16mmR
  *Official Name:* Pistol, Caliber .22, Automatic, High Standard, Model HD

*Remarks:* HD—NSN 1005-00-726-5665.
HD Military—NSN 1005-00-908-2386.

- *Cal.:* 5.6 x 16mmR
  *Official Name:* Pistol, Caliber .22, Automatic, Ruger Mark I

*Remarks:*
Target Model w/ 175mm barrel—NSN 1005-00-736-7841.
Target Model w/ 175mm barrel—NSN 1005-00-508-7874.
Target Model w/ 175mm barrel—NSN 1005-00-630-7263.
Target Model w/ 175mm barrel—NSN 1005-00-166-2780.
Target Model w/ 133mm barrel—NSN 1005-00-166-2776.
Target Model w/ 140mm barrel—NSN 1005-00-166-2781.
Target Model w/ 140mm barrel—NSN 1005-00-974-5359.

- *Cal.:* 5.6 x 16mmR
  *Official Name:* Pistol, Caliber .22, Automatic, Ruger Mark II

*Remarks:* Target Model—NSN 1005-01-171-4851.

- *Cal.:* 5.6 x 16mmR
  *Official Name:* Pistol, Caliber .22, Automatic, Smith & Wesson, Model 41

*Remarks:* 187mm barrel w/ grooves for counter-weights—NSN 1005-00-532-3025.
140mm heavy-weight barrel—NSN 1005-00-965-0698.
127mm heavy-weight barrel—NSN 1005-00-166-2754.
127mm barrel w/ grooves for counter-weights—NSN 1005-00-166-2753. US Air Force.
171mm heavy-weight barrel—NSN 1005-00-936-1158.

- *Cal.:* 5.6 x 16mmR
  *Official Name:* Pistol, Caliber .22, Automatic, Smith & Wesson, Model 46

*Remarks:* NSN 1005-00-831-1267.
127mm barrel—NSN 1005-00-166-2752.
127mm heavy barrel—NSN 1005-00-166-2775. US Air Force.

- *Cal.:* 9 x 19mm
  *Official Name:* Pistol, Semiautomatic, 9mm, M9
  *Common Name:* Beretta Model 92SB-F

*Remarks:* NSN 1005-01-118-2640. This handgun was adopted in January 1982 as the standard side arm for the US armed forces: US Army, US Navy, US Air Force, US Marine Corps, and the US Coast Guard. The first 5-year contract calls for the acquisition of 315,930 M9s. This pistol will replace the M1911A1 pistol and many different revolver types.

- *Cal.:* 11.43 x 23mm
  *Official Name:* Pistol, Caliber .45 Automatic, M1911
  *Common Name:* M1911; Colt's government Model

*Remarks:* Made by Colt, Remington, and other contractors. Standardized in 1911 and converted to M1911A1 in mid-1920s. Standard F. NSN 1005-00-575-0004, w/o equipment and NSN 1005-00-673-7955 w/ equipment. US Navy M1911 is 1005-00-344-6205.

- *Cal.:* 11.43 x 23mm
  *Official Name:* Pistol, Caliber .45 Automatic, M1911A1
  *Common Name:* M1911A1; Colt's government model

*Remarks:* Standardized in 1926 and still Standard A. NSN 1005-00-726-5655, w/o equipment, and 1005-00-673-7965 w/ hip holster and equipment. With shoulder holster and equipment it is NSN 1005-00-561-2003.

- *Cal.:* 11.43 x 23mm
  *Official Name:* Pistol, Caliber .45 Automatic, M1911A1 National Match (NM)
  *Common Name:* National Match .45

*Remarks:* Accurized M1911A1 for Match competition. Standard A. w/ adjustable rear sight and equipment NSN 1005-00-994-9512.

- *Cal.:* 11.43 x 23mm
  *Official Name:* Pistol, Caliber .45 Automatic, M1911A1 National Match (NM), w/ 1956 improvements
  *Common Name:* National Match .45

- *Cal.:* 11.43 x 23mm
  *Official Name:* Pistol, Caliber .45 Automatic, M1911A1 National Match (NM), w/ 1957 improvements
  *Common Name:* National Match .45

- *Cal.:* 11.43 x 23mm
  *Official Name:* Pistol, Caliber .45 Automatic, M1911A1 Match Grade
  *Common Name:* Match Grade .45

- *Cal.:* 11.43 x 23mm
  *Official Name:* Pistol, Caliber .45 Automatic, M1911A1 Target
  *Common Name:* Target Grade .45

- *Cal.:* 11.43 x 23mm
  *Official Name:* Pistol, Caliber .45 Automatic, M1911A1 Hard Ball Match
  *Common Name:* Hard Ball Match .45

- *Cal.:* 11.43 x 23mm
  *Official Name:* Pistol, Caliber .45 Automatic, M1911A1 National Match (NM), w/ 1961 improvements
  *Common Name:* National Match .45

- *Cal.:* 11.43 x 23mm
  *Official Name:* Pistol, Caliber .45 Automatic Colt National Match
  *Common Name:* .45 Colt Gold Cup

- *Cal.:* 11.43 x 23mm
  *Official Name:* Pistol, Caliber .45 Automatic Colt
  *Common Name:* .45 Colt Gold Cup for wadcutter ammo

- *Cal.:* 11.43 x 23mm
  *Official Name:* Pistol, Caliber .45 Automatic Colt National Match
  *Common Name:* .45 Colt National Match

*Remarks:* Accurized M1911A1 for Match competition. Standard A. NSN 1005-00-345-6124.

*Remarks:* Accurized M1911A1 for Match competition. Standard A. Issued with 3 magazines, each inscribed with gun's serial number. NSN 1005-00-588-3114.

*Remarks:* Model A—NSN 1005-00-148-6528.
Model B—NSN 1005-00-148-6530.
Model C—NSN 1005-00-148-6531.

*Remarks:* NSN 1005-00-166-2991.

*Remarks:* Accurized M1911A1 for Match competition, w/ adjustable rear sight—NSN 1005-00-972-1337.

*Remarks:* Accurized M1911A1 for Match competition. Standard A. The 1961 model w/ adjustable rear sight is NSN 1005-00-738-3026; and w/ fixed rear sight, NSN 1005-00-345-6121.

*Remarks:* Commercial equivalent of M1911A1NM. Standard A. NSN 1005-00-591-8046.

*Remarks:* Match pistol with fixed rear sight, NSN 1005-00-166-2891; w/ adjustable rear sight, NSN 1005-00-972-1563.

*Remarks:* NM reworked for Match shooting. NSN 1005-00-950-6304.

- *Cal.:* 11.43 x 23mm
  *Official Name:* Pistol, Caliber .45 Automatic, M1911A1, Inert model
  *Common Name:* M1911A1; Colt's government model

  *Remarks:* NSN 1005-01-042-4113. Nonfiring mode.

- *Cal.:* 11.43 x 23mm
  *Official Name:* Pistol, Caliber .45 Automatic, M15 General Officer
  *Common Name:* XM15 pistol

  *Remarks:* Reduced size M1911A1 pistol for issue to US Army general officers. Standard A, but no longer issued. NSN 1005-00-106-7788. Will be replaced by the M9.

- *Cal.:* 9 x 29mmR
  *Official Name:* Pistol, Caliber .38 Automatic Colt
  *Common Name:* .38 Special Colt mid-range Gold Cup

  *Remarks:* Commercial Match pistol. NSN 1005-00-173-4130, 1005-00-726-5661, and 1005-00-897-8447. All shoot rimmed .38 Special cartridges.

- *Cal.:* 9 x 29mmR
  *Official Name:* Pistol, Caliber .38 Automatic Colt AMU
  *Common Name:* .38 Special Colt pistol

  *Remarks:* Army Marksmanship Unit Match pistol. NSN 1005-00-166-2836.

- *Cal.:* 9 x 29mmR
  *Official Name:* Pistol, Caliber .38 Automatic Colt National Match
  *Common Name:* .38 Special Colt Gold Cup

  *Remarks:* Commercial Match pistol. Standard A. NSN 1005-00-859-0458 and 1005-00-897-8449.

- *Cal.:* 9 x 29mmR
  *Official Name:* Pistol, Caliber .38 Super Automatic Colt
  *Common Name:* .38 Special Colt Gold Cup

  *Remarks:* Commercial Match pistol. NSN 1005-00-166-2890, 1005-00-166-2892, and 1005-00-817-6117.

- *Cal.:* 9 x 29mmR
  *Official Name:* Pistol, Caliber .38 Automatic Smith & Wesson Model 52
  *Common Name:* .38 Special Smith & Wesson Model 52

  *Remarks:* Commercial Match grade pistol. Standard A. NSN 1005-00-971-5039 and 1005-00-858-5830. The same pistol for .38 caliber mid-range wadcutter ammunition is NSN 1005-00-166-2756.

- *Cal.:* 9 x 17mm
  *Official Name:* Pistol, Caliber .380 Automatic Colt
  *Common Name:* .380 ACP Colt 1903 pocket model pistol

  *Remarks:* OBSOLETE; replaced by the M15 as the pistol for general officers. NSN 1005-00-317-2468.

- *Cal.:* 7.65 x 17mm
  *Official Name:* Pistol, Caliber .32 Automatic Colt
  *Common Name:* .32 ACP Colt 1903 pocket model pistol

  *Remarks:* OBSOLETE; replaced by M15. NSN 1005-00-317-2469. Also 1005-00-166-2906.

- *Cal.:* 9 x 19mm NATO
  *Common Name:* Heckler & Koch P9S

  *Remarks:* Heckler & Koch (HK) P9S. Used by US Navy SEAL teams. LSN 1005-LL-HDK-N483. Some of the more recent P9S pistols have been equipped with special barrels that mount Qualatech silencers.

- *Cal.:* 9 x 19mm
  *Official Name:* Pistol, Mark 22, Mod 0 and suppressor kit
  *Common Name:* Hush Puppy

  *Remarks:* Predecessor to Smith & Wesson commercial Model 59 pistol made during the Vietnam War for the US Navy SEALS. NSN 1005-00-021-5137.

*Revolvers* — There is a wide variety of revolvers currently being used by US military police and federal police forces. The following are listed to aid in the identification of such handguns. Only those with a "Standard" indication are currently issued to US armed forces personnel. See note at end of the US section for more detail on the Smith & Wesson handgun numbering system.

• *Cal.:* 5.6 x 16mmR
  *Common Name:* Revolver, Caliber .22 Smith and Wesson, K22 Masterpiece, Model 17

*Remarks:* NSN 1005-00-831-0234 w/ 152mm barrel. NSN 1005-00-166-2758 w/ 152mm barrel. NSN 1005-00-166-2757 w/ 213mm barrel.

• *Cal.:* 5.6 x 16mmR
  *Common Name:* Revolver, Caliber .22 Smith and Wesson, K22 Combat Masterpiece, Model 18

*Remarks:* NSN 1005-01-076-8438 w/ 101mm barrel.

• *Cal.:* 5.6 x 16mmR
  *Common Name:* Revolver, Caliber .22 Colt Official Police

*Remarks:* NSN 1005-00-166-2898 w/ 152mm barrel.

• *Cal.:* 9 x 29mmR
  *Common Name:* .38 Colt Detective Special, square butt

*Remarks:* OBSOLETE. w/ 51mm barrel, NSN 1005-00-910-8752; w/ hip holster, NSN 1005-00-840-7302; and w/ shoulder holster, NSN 1005-00-699-1678.

• *Cal.:* 9 x 29mmR
  *Common Name:* .38 Colt Detective Special, round butt

*Remarks:* Standard A. W/ 51mm barrel. NSN 1005-00-726-5786.

• *Cal.:* 9 x 29mmR
  *Common Name:* .38 Colt Official Police

*Remarks:* Standard A. W/ 51mm barrel, NSN 1005-00-726-5666, NSN 1005-00-214-0933, and w/ shoulder holster NSN 1005-00-699-1679.
W/ 102mm barrel, NSN 1005-00-726-5687; w/ hip holster, NSN 1005-00-214-0934; and w/ shoulder holster, NSN 1005-00-699-1680. Formerly called the Commando.
W/ 127mm barrel, NSN 1005-00-166-2837.
W/ 152mm barrel, NSN 1005-00-166-2844.

• *Cal.:* 9 x 29mmR
  *Common Name:* .38 Colt Police Positive

*Remarks:* Standard A. W/ 51mm barrel, NSN 1005-00-166-2888. W/ a 102mm barrel, NSN 1005-00-166-2845. W/ a hip holster, the NSN is 1005-00-716-2938 or NSN 1005-00-691-1288; w/ a shoulder holster, NSN 1005-00-317-2464.

• *Cal.:* 9 x 29mmR
  *Common Name:* .38 Colt Agent

*Remarks:* W/ a 51mm barrel, NSN 1005-00-166-2907.

• *Cal.:* 9 x 29mmR
  *Common Name:* .38 Colt Cobra

*Remarks:* W/ a 51mm barrel, NSN 1005-00-166-2774 and NSN 1005-00-052-7467.

• *Cal.:* 9 x 29mmR
  *Common Name:* .38 Colt Cobra

*Remarks:* W/ a 76mm barrel, NSN 1005-00-468-0138.
W/ a 102mm barrel, NSN 1005-00-186-9926.

• *Cal.:* 9 x 29mmR
  *Common Name:* .38 Colt Officers Model National Match

*Remarks:* OBSOLETE. W/ a 152mm barrel, NSN 1005-00-690-3762; w/ adjustable sights, NSN 1005-00-682-4705.

• *Cal.:* 11.43 x 32.1mmR
  *Common Name:* .45 Colt New Service

*Remarks:* OBSOLETE. NSN 1005-00-166-2899 for target model with 140mm barrel.

• *Cal.:* 11.43 x 32.1mmR
  *Common Name:* .45 Colt single action Army

*Remarks:* NSN 1005-01-190-3373.

• *Cal.:* 11.43 x 23.1mmR
  *Common Name:* .45 Colt Model 1917

*Remarks:* OBSOLETE. With a 140mm barrel, NSN 1005-00-726-5656 w/o equipment. NSN 1005-00-214-0935 w/ equipment.

- *Cal.:* 9 x 29mmR
  *Common Name:* .38 M10 S&W
  round butt (called the military
  & police model)

*Remarks:* Standard A. W/ a 51mm barrel, NSN 1005-00-937-5840; w/ hip holster and lanyard loop, NSN 1005-00-840-7303; w/ shoulder holster and lanyard loop, NSN 1005-00-699-1683.
Standard A. W/ 102mm barrel, NSN 1005-00-213-0934. Standard A. W/ 102mm barrel, NSN 1005-00-840-7304 w/o equipment. Standard A. W/ 102mm barrel, NSN 1005-00-699-1686 w/ equipment.

- *Cal.:* 9 x 29mmR
  *Common Name:* .38 M10-2 S&W

*Remarks:* W/ a 51mm barrel, NSN 1005-00-166-2821.

- *Cal.:* 9 x 29mmR
  *Common Name:* .38 M10-5 S&W

*Remarks:* W/ a 127mm barrel, NSN 1005-00-166-2820.

- *Cal.:* 9 x 29mmR
  *Common Name:* .38 M10 S&W
  adjustable sights and square
  butt

*Remarks:* Standard A. With a 102mm barrel, NSN 1005-00-214-0934; w/ hip holster and lanyard loop; w/ shoulder holster and lanyard loop, NSN 1005-00-699-1685.

*In addition the following NSNs were previously assigned to Smith & Wesson short action Model 10 revolvers:*

51mm w/ hip holster and equipment — NSN 1005-00-840-7306
51mm w/ shoulder holster and equipment — NSN 1005-00-699-1684
102mm w/ hip holster and equipment — NSN 1005-00-840-7307
102mm w/ shoulder holster and w/o equipment — NSN 1005-00-699-1681
127mm w/ shoulder holster and equipment — NSN 1005-00-840-7305

- *Cal.:* 9 x 29mmR
  *Common Name:* .38 M12 S&W

*Remarks:* W/ a 51mm barrel NSN 1005-00-166-2762.

- *Cal.:* 9 x 29mmR
  *Common Name:* .38 M14 S&W

*Remarks:* OBSOLETE. This handgun was widely purchased by the US armed forces, but it was never officially type-classified. W/ a 152mm barrel and adjustable rear sight, NSN 1005-00-830-2947. NSN 1005-00-568-8704 w/ equipment. This match grade revolver also called K38 Masterpiece.

- *Cal.:* 9 x 29mmR
  *Common Name:* .38 M14 S&W

*Remarks:* W/ a 152mm barrel and fixed rear sight, NSN 1005-00-953-1234. NSN 1005-00-166-2773. Target model w/ a 213mm barrel and adjustable rear sight.

- *Cal.:* 9 x 29mmR
  *Common Name:* .38 M15 S&W

*Remarks:* W/ a 51mm barrel, NSN 1005-00-166-2767. Also NSN 1005-00-079-1147. Formerly called Combat Masterpiece.
W/ a 102mm barrel, NSN 1005-00-052-7452. Also NSN 1005-00-973-2058.
W/ a 102mm barrel and adjustable rear sight, NSN 1005-00-835-9773.

- *Cal.:* 9 x 29mmR
  *Common Name:* .38 M15-2 S&W

*Remarks:* W/ a 102mm barrel, NSN 1005-00-726-5687.
W/ a 127mm barrel, NSN 1005-01-003-7494.
W/ a 152mm barrel, NSN 1005-01-003-7493.

- *Cal.:* 9 x 29mmR Magnum
  *Common Name:* .357 Magnum
  M19 S&W

*Remarks:* W/ a 64mm barrel, NSN 1005-01-071-8293. NSN 1005-01-061-2349 is also used for an unspecified version. Also called the Combat Magnum.
W/ a 102mm barrel, NSN 1005-01-166-2768.

- *Cal.:* 11.18 x 33mmR Magnum
  *Common Name:* .44 Magnum
  Model 29 S&W

*Remarks:* NSN 1005-00-853-7087.

- *Cal.:* 11.43 x 23mm Auto Rim
  *Common Name:* .45 Model 1917
  S&W

*Remarks:* NSN 1005-00-214-0936 w/ equipment and 1005-00-726-5653 w/o equipment.

- *Cal.:* 9 x 20mmR
  *Common Name:* .38 S&W M32
  S&W

*Remarks:* W/ a 51mm barrel, NSN 1005-00-166-2771. Also called the Terrier.

- *Cal.:* 9 x 20mmR
  *Common Name:* .38 S&W M33
  S&W

*Remarks:* W/ a 51mm barrel, NSN 1005-00-166-2764. Also called the Regulation Police.

- *Cal.:* 9 x 29mmR
  *Common Name:* .38 M36 S&W

- *Cal.:* 9 x 29mmR
  *Common Name:* .38 M36-OSI
  S&W

- *Cal.:* 9 x 29mmR
  *Common Name:* .38 M37 S&W

- *Cal.:* 9 x 29mmR
  *Common Name:* .38 M38 S&W

- *Cal.:* 9 x 29mmR
  *Common Name:* .38 M66 S&W

- *Cal.:* 9 x 29mmR
  *Common Name:* .38 Mod 108
  Ruger

- *Cal.:* 9 x 29mmR
  *Common Name:* .38 Mod 108
  Ruger

- *Cal.:* 9 x 29mmR Magnum
  *Common Name:* .357 Magnum
  Ruger Military Model DA
  GS32-N

- *Cal.:* 11.18 x 33mmR Magnum
  *Common Name:* .44 Magnum
  Ruger Super Blackhawk

- *Cal.:* 9 x 29mmR Magnum
  *Common Name:* .357 Magnum
  Dan Wesson revolver with
  102mm barrel

**SUBMACHINE GUNS:**
- *Cal.:* 11.43 x 23mm
  *Official Name:* Submachine gun
  Caliber .45, M3
  *Common Name:* M3 grease gun

- *Cal.:* 11.43 x 23mm
  *Official Name:* Submachine gun
  Caliber .45, M3A1
  *Common Name:* M3A1 grease gun

- *Cal.:* 11.43 x 23mm
  *Official Name:* Submachine gun
  Caliber .45, M1
  *Common Name:* Thompson SMG

- *Cal.:* 11.43 x 23mm
  *Official Name:* Submachine gun
  Caliber .45, M1A1
  *Common Name:* Thompson SMG

- *Cal.:* 11.43 x 23mm
  *Official Name:* Submachine gun
  Caliber .45, M1928A1
  *Common Name:* Thompson SMG

*Remarks:* W/ a 51mm barrel, NSN 1005-00-166-2765. Also called the Chief's Special. The Model 36-2 w/ 51mm barrel is 1005-00-005-2312.

*Remarks:* W/ 51mm barrel, NSN 1005-01-003-7471. Also a version w/ NSN 1005-01-196-6086.

*Remarks:* Chief's Special Airweight with 51mm barrel, NSN 1005-00-089-7741. With 76mm barrel, NSN 1005-00-133-9280.

*Remarks:* Airweight w/ 51mm barrel, NSN 1005-00-005-2312.

*Remarks:* US Navy use. Stainless steel revolver, NSN 1005-01-088-1107.

*Remarks:* W/ 102mm barrel and w/o lanyard loop, NSN 1005-01-040-8989. Ruger catalog no. SDA-84G. Also called Police Service Six, with square butt and blue finish. Formerly NSN 1005-01-M10-5819. The round butt model is NSN 1005-01-094-7045, with Ruger catalog no. SDA-84L (NSN 1005-01-M10-5820).

*Remarks:* W/ 102mm barrel and lanyard loop, NSN 1005-01-040-8990. Used by US Navy Investigative Services agents and USMC embassy guards. These are result of recent contracts in which Ruger was low bidder. Square butt revolver with blue finish. Ruger catalog number SS-84L.

*Remarks:* NSN 1005-01-073-2465, w/o lanyard loop. US Navy Investigative Services.

*Remarks:* NSN 1005-01-011-9017.

*Remarks:* NSN unknown. Used by National Archives guard force.

*Remarks:* Standardized in 1943. Used by armored vehicle crews. Standard B. NSN 1005-00-672-1767.

*Remarks:* Standardized in 1944. Still used by armored vehicle crews. Standard B. NSN 1005-00-672-1771.

*Remarks:* OBSOLETE. NSN 1005-00-672-1754.

*Remarks:* OBSOLETE. NSN 1005-00-672-1755.

*Remarks:* OBSOLETE. NSN 1005-00-672-1740.

**A US M60 tank crewman checks his .45 caliber (11.43 x 23mm) M3A1 submachine gun during the NATO 1983 "Autumn Forge" exercise in the Netherlands. (US Army: Sutter)**

- *Cal.:* 9 x 19mm NATO
  *Official Name:* Submachine gun
    Ingram MOD 10
  *Common Name:* MAC-10 SMG

  *Remarks:* Obsolescent. US Navy. NSN 1005-01-061-2477.

- *Cal.:* 9 x 19mm NATO
  *Official Name:* Submachine gun
    Mark 24, MOD 0
  *Common Name:* S&W Model 76

  *Remarks:* Obsolescent. US Navy. NSN 1005-01-013-6050.

- *Cal.:* 9 x 19mm NATO
  *Common Name:* IMI Uzi SMG

  *Remarks:* LSN 1005-LL-HDK-N426. Special purchase for Naval Investigative Services.

- *Cal.:* 9 x 19mm NATO
  *Common Name:* IMI Mini-Uzi
    SMG

  *Remarks:* LSN 1005-LL-HDH-B308. US Navy special buy.

- *Cal.:* 9 x 19mm NATO
  *Common Name:* HK MP5

  *Remarks:* NSN-NA. Used by US Army Special Forces, Rangers, SEALS, Air Force Commandos, and other special operations units. In service since 1979. Also used by the Department of Energy, Coast Guard, Secret Service, Customs, FBI, and several other US federal police organizations.

- *Cal.:* 9 x 19mm NATO
  *Common Name:* HK MP5SD

  *Remarks:* NSN—not known. Silenced version of MP5. Rangers and other special operations units. Special purchase since 1980.

- *Cal.:* 9 x 19mm NATO
  *Common Name:* HK MP5A5

  *Remarks:* New version of MP5 w/ 3-shot shot burst feature and tritium sights. Acquired by US Navy SEALS. No NSN.

- *Cal.:* 9 x 19mm NATO
  *Common Name:* HK MP5SD5

  *Remarks:* Silenced variant of MP5A5 for SEALS.

- *Cal.:* 9 x 19mm NATO
  *Common Name:* HK MP5KA4

  *Remarks:* New version of MP5K as above for SEALS.

- *Cal.:* 5.56 x 45mm
  *Official Name:* Submachine gun 5.56mm, XM177
  *Common Name:* Colt Commando. Colt Model 610

  *Remarks:* NSN 1005-00-933-7672. Shortened version of the M16 w/ 254mm barrel, telescoping stock, and no forward assist. OBSOLETE; some may still be in service.

- *Cal.:* 5.56 x 45mm
  *Official Name:* Submachine gun 5.56mm, XM177E1
  *Common Name:* Colt Commando. Colt Model 609

  *Remarks:* NSN 1005-00-930-5595. Basically the same as the XM177, but has forward bolt assist. OBSOLETE, but some may still be in service.

- *Cal.:* 5.56 x 45mm
  *Official Name:* Submachine gun 5.56mm, XM177E2
  *Common Name:* Colt Commando. Colt Model 629

  *Remarks:* OBSOLETE. 292mm barrel. NSN 1005-00-021-2429.

- *Cal.:* 5.56 x 45mm
  *Official Name:* Submachine gun
  *Common Name:* Colt CAR-15 Commando

  *Remarks:* US Air Force. OBSOLETE.

- *Cal.:* 5.56 x 45mm
  *Official Name:* Submachine gun 5.56mm, GAU-5/A/A
  *Common Name:* Colt Commando; Colt Model 649

  *Remarks:* US Air Force version of XM177. Obsolescent. This is the same as GAU-5/A except has 274mm barrel. NSN 1005-00-973-5685.

- *Cal.:* 5.56 x 45mm
  *Official Name:* Submachine gun 5.56mm, GAU-5/A/B
  *Common Name:* Colt Commando; Colt Model 630

  *Remarks:* USAF version of XM177E1. OBSOLETE.

- *Cal.:* 5.56 x 45mm
  *Official Name:* Submachine gun 5.56mm, GAU-5/P
  *Common Name:* Colt Commando; Colt Model 610

  *Remarks:* USAF. W/ 368mm barrel, NSN 1005-01-042-9820.

**FIRING PORT WEAPONS:**
- *Cal.:* 5.56 x 45mm
  *Official Name:* Firing Port Weapon 5.56 x 45mm, M231

  *Remarks:* US Army design evolved from M16A1, which is made by Colt for M2 Bradley Fighting Vehicle—6 per vehicle. Standard A since 1979. NSN 1005-01-081-4582.

**TRAINING RIFLES,** Caliber .22 Long Rifle
- *Cal.:* 5.6 x 16mmR
  *Official Name:* Rifle, Caliber .22, US M1

  *Remarks:* NSN 1005-00-575-0085 w/ sling, 1005-00-726-5704 w/o.

- *Cal.:* 5.6 x 16mmR
  *Official Name:* Rifle, Caliber .22, US M2

  *Remarks:* NSN 1005-00-575-0086 w/ equipment; 1005-00-726-5705 w/o equipment. M2A1 is NSN 1005-00-674-4001 w/ equipment.

- *Cal.:* 5.6 x 16mmR
  *Official Name:* Rifle, Caliber .22, US M1922

*Remarks:* NSN 1005-00-448-4796.

- *Cal.:* 5.6 x 16mmR
  *Official Name:* Rifle, Caliber .22, M12: Winchester Model 52

*Remarks:* Model 52 w/ standard barrel — NSN 1005-00-317-2473 (PN 8415034).
Model 52 w/ heavy barrel — NSN 1005-00-317-2472, (PN 8415033).
Model 52B — NSN 1005-00-736-7845.
Model 52C — NSN 1005-00-829-6785.
Model 52C, Air Force? — NSN 1005-00-630-7163.
Model 52C w/ glass bedded action; heavy floating barrel. Air Force? — NSN 1005-00-166-2835.
Model 52D — NSN 1005-00-999-1187.
Model 52D w/ 711mm heavy barrel and telescopic sight — NSN 1005-00-166-2832.
Model 52D w/ 711mm heavy barrel and shoulder hook butt plate — NSN 1005-00-166-2833.
Model 52D w/ 403mm barrel — NSN 1005-00-468-0121.

- *Cal.:* 5.6 x 16mmR
  *Official Name:* Rifle, Caliber .22, Model 12 Remington, Model 40X series

*Remarks:* 40X-H1, Match Grade — NSN 1005-00-694-4123.
40X-S1, Match Grade, w/ 539mm barrel NSN 1005-00-694-4121 and the US Navy model 40X-S1, NSN 1005-00-630-7238.
40X-B1, w/ 711mm barrel — NSN 1005-00-887-8983.
40X-HB, w/ 711mm barrel — NSN 1005-00-087-0571.
40X, Rangemaster — NSN 1005-00-080-4032.

- *Cal.:* 5.6 x 16mmR
  *Official Name:* Rifle, Caliber .22, M13: Remington, Model 513T

*Remarks:* M513T Matchmaster NSN 1005-00-840-3758.
M513T Matchmaster NSN 1005-00-726-5684.
M513TR Matchmaster NSN 1005-00-826-8741.
C513TR Matchmaster NSN 1005-00-575-0083.

- *Cal.:* 5.6 x 16mmR
  *Official Name:* Rifle, Caliber .22, M12: Harrington & Richardson

*Remarks:* NSN 1005-01-108-4973.

- *Cal.:* 5.6 x 16mmR
  *Official Name:* Rifle, Caliber .22, M13: Mossberg, Model 144

*Remarks:* NSN 1005-00-183-5957.

- *Cal.:* 5.6 x 16mmR
  *Official Name:* Rifle, Caliber .22, M13: Stevens, Model 416-2

*Remarks:* NSN 1005-00-317-2470 (PN 8415031).
NSN 1005-00-228-3064.
NSN 1005-00-726-5680.

- *Cal.:* 5.6 x 16mmR
  *Official Name:* Rifle, Caliber .22, XM17, Semiautomatic

*Remarks:* NSN 1005-00-921-5056.

- *Cal.:* 5.6 x 16mmR
  *Official Name:* Rifle, Caliber .22, Remington, Model 514T

*Remarks:* NSN 1005-00-220-3063.

- *Cal.:* 5.6 x 16mmR
  *Official Name:* Rifle, Caliber .22, Junior Marksman Training Grade, Remington, Model 521T

*Remarks:* NSN 1005-00-957-4401 (PN 7791632).

- *Cal.:* 5.6 x 16mmR
  *Official Name:* Rifle, Caliber .22, Target, Winchester M75

*Remarks:* NSN 1005-00-887-8982. W/ 711mm barrel — NSN 1005-00-317-2471 (PN 8415032). NSN 1005-00-166-2763. NSN 1005-00-726-5683.

- *Cal.:* 5.6 x 16mmR
  *Official Name:* Rifle, Caliber .22, Target, Winchester M79

*Remarks:* NSN 1005-00-335-9773. NSN 1005-00-222-0447.

- *Cal.:* 5.6 x 16mmR
  *Official Name:* Rifle, Caliber .22, Target, Stevens M65

  *Remarks:* W/ 559mm barrel—NSN 1005-00-166-2822. NSN 1005-00-187-0454.

- *Cal.:* 5.6 x 16mmR
  *Official Name:* Rifle, Caliber .22, Target, H&R M65

  *Remarks:* NSN 1005-00-100-5657.

- *Cal.:* 5.6 x 16mmR
  *Official Name:* Rifle, Caliber .22, Target, Mossberg M44

  *Remarks:* M44—NSN 1005-00-344-6078 reconditioned. M44B—NSN 1005-00-726-5865. M44B—NSN 1005-00-726-5866. US Navy.

- *Cal.:* 5.6 x 16mmR
  *Official Name:* Rifle, Caliber .22, Ruger 10/22

  *Remarks:* NSN 1005-01-079-02074. US Navy.

- *Cal.:* 5.6 x 16mmR
  *Official Name:* Rifle, Caliber .22 Winchester Magnum, Marlin

  *Remarks:* NSN 1005-01-089-81264. US Navy.


**COMBAT RIFLES:**

- *Cal.:* 5.56 x 45mm
  *Official Name:* Rifle 5.56mm, M16
  *Common Name:* Colt M16; M16; Colt Model 604; AR-15

  *Remarks:* Standard B. NSN 1005-00-856-6885. This weapon is still the standard US Air Force rifle. While still the AR-15 it was assigned NSN 1005-00-983-6877; some early M16s were assigned NSN 1005-00-994-9136.

- *Cal.:* 5.56 x 45mm
  *Official Name:* Rifle 5.56mm, M16A1
  *Common Name:* Colt M16; M16A1; Colt Model 603; Formerly XM16E1

  *Remarks:* Standard A since Feb. 1967. NSN 1005-00-073-9421. While the XM16E1, this weapon was assigned NSN 1005-00-930-0584. "Rifle Training Simulator M16A1" w/ plugged barrel is assigned NSN 6920-01-092-7735. Other M16A1-based training aids have the following NSNs: "M16A1 Nonfiring Training Aid"—1005-00-126-5836; "M16A1 Demil Training Aid"—1005-01-061-2469.

- *Cal.:* 5.56 x 45mm
  *Official Name:* Rifle 5.56mm, M16A1
  *Common Name:* Colt M16; M16A1; Colt Model 603

  *Remarks:* When this weapon is fitted w/ the XM148 grenade launcher the NSN is 1005-00-832-8898. The 40mm XM148 grenade launcher is 1010-00-912-3014.

- *Cal.:* 5.56 x 45mm
  *Official Name:* Rifle 5.56mm, M16A1 Demil
  *Common Name:* Colt M16; M16A1

  *Remarks:* Nonfiring training aid. NSN 1005-01-061-2469.

- *Cal.:* 5.56 x 45mm
  *Official Name:* Rifle 5.56mm, MK 4 MOD 0
  *Common Name:* Stoner rifle

  *Remarks:* US Navy NSN 1005-00-102-8649.

- *Cal.:* 7.62 x 51mm NATO
  *Official Name:* Rifle 7.62mm, M14
  *Common Name:* M14 rifle

  *Remarks:* Standard A since 1957, but issued on a very limited basis except for the US Navy. NSN 1005-00-589-1271 w/o equipment; 1005-00-599-1271 w/ equipment. When fitted w/ telescope M84 the M14 is 1005-00-937-8777. M2 bipod is NSN 1005-00-711-6202. M76 grenade launcher is NSN 1005-00-722-3098 and 1005-00-778-8812. M6 bayonet is NSN 1005-00-722-3097. In prototype form (T44E4) it was 1005-00-799-9073.

- *Cal.:* 7.62 x 51mm NATO
  *Official Name:* Rifle 7.62mm, M15
  *Common Name:* M15 automatic rifle

  *Remarks:* OBSOLETE. Standardized in 1957 to replace the M1918A2 BAR, but never manufactured in any real quantities. NSN 1005-00-600-1461. M14A1 later developed to fill the role of the M15 automatic rifle.

US Marines of the 24th Marine Amphibious Unit use their vehicle as cover while preparing to return fire during an ambush drill near their positions in Beirut, Lebanon, in September 1983. (US Marine Corps)

Research Armament Prototypes' Convertible Long Range Rifle system has two barrels 7.62 x 51mm NATO and a new cartridge 8.58 x 71mm. The latter cartridge is based upon the .416 Rigby hunting cartridge necked down to .338. To convert the rifle from one caliber to another, it is only necessary to change the barrel, bolt head, and magazine. The Model 300 has a 9 power Leupold telescopic sight. Without the scope the rifle weighs 6.3 kg. (RAP)

Research Armament Prototypes' Model 300 disassembled. (RAP)

## BALLISTICS DATA

| RANGE (METERS) | VELOCITY (FT./SEC.) | | ENERGY (FT.-LBS.) | |
|---|---|---|---|---|
| | 8.58x71mm | 7.62mm | 8.58x71mm | 7.62mm |
| MUZZLE | 3000 | 2620 | 5000 | 2745 |
| 100 | 2894 | 2375 | 4651 | 2252 |
| 200 | 2790 | 2143 | 4219 | 1832 |
| 300 | 2701 | 1924 | 4005 | 1481 |
| 400 | 2583 | 1721 | 3706 | 1184 |
| 500 | 2482 | 1530 | 3424 | 941 |
| 600 | 2383 | 1368 | 3155 | 723 |
| 700 | 2299 | 1230 | 2902 | 605 |
| 800 | 2189 | 1121 | 2663 | 503 |
| 900 | 2095 | 1042 | 2438 | 435 |
| 1000 | 2001 | 983 | 2163 | 386 |
| 1100 | 1928 | 934 | 2028 | 348 |
| 1200 | 1823 | 893 | 1844 | 319 |
| 1300 | 1736 | 857 | 1675 | 286 |
| 1400 | 1654 | 824 | 1520 | 272 |
| 1500 | 1575 | 794 | 1378 | 252 |

**7.62mm NATO w/180 grain boat-tail bullet**
**8.58x71mm w/250 grain boat-tail bullet**

Ballistics data comparing the performance of the 7.62 x 51mm NATO and 8.58 x 71mm cartridges. (RAP)

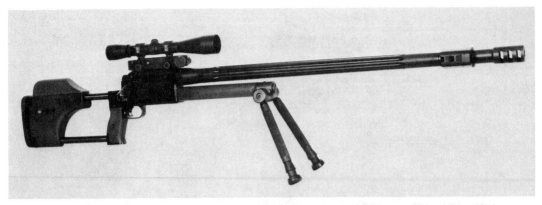

Research Armament Prototypes' Model 500 12.7 x 99mm Long Range Stand Off Weapon. This 14.7 kg rifle has many features of the smaller Model 300. It has the adjustable cheekpiece, and the length of the distance from the pistol grip to the butt plate is adjustable. To make the weapon controllable, a special muzzle device has been added to reduce recoil. Despite the fact that it fires the potent .50 Browning cartridge, the perceived recoil is about that of a 12-gage shotgun. (RAP)

- *Cal.:* 7.62 x 51mm NATO
  *Official Name:* Rifle 7.62mm, M14A1
  *Common Name:* Prototype called M14E2

*Remarks:* SAW version of M14. Standard A since mid-1960s to fill role of M15 automatic rifle, which was not manufactured. Issued on very limited basis. NSN 1005-00-072-5011.

- *Cal.:* 7.62 x 51mm NATO
  *Official Name:* Rifle 7.62mm, M14 National Match (NM)

*Remarks:* Accurized and glass bedded match rifle. Not selective fire, semi-automatic only. Standard A. NSN 1005-00-678-9828 and NSN 1005-00-678-9829.

- *Cal.:* 7.62 x 51mm NATO
  *Official Name:* Rifle, Dummy Drill 7.62mm, M14

*Remarks:* Demilitarized for ROTC units. NSN 1005-00-283-7695.

- *Cal.:* 7.62 x 51mm NATO
  *Official Name:* Rifle, Demil (Navy) 7.62mm, M14

*Remarks:* Demilitarized for Navy ceremonial units. NSN 1005-01-140-6968.

- *Cal.:* 7.62 x 51mm NATO
  *Official Name:* Rifle 7.62mm, M14(M)

*Remarks:* Standard M14 with welded dummy selector button to prevent full automatic fire. OBSOLETE. NSN 1005-00-678-9829.

- *Cal.:* 7.62 x 51mm NATO
  *Official Name:* Rifle, Sniper, 7.62mm M21
  *Common Name:* The M21 uses the ART (Adjustable Ranging Telescope) w/ 3 to 9 X magnification

*Remarks:* Sniper version of M14. Standard since 1975. Standard B. Issued on a very limited basis. NSN 1005-00-179-0300. Only 1,435 M21 sniper rifles were made from Match grade M14s. Scope matched to the M118 NATO Match cartridge.

- *Cal.:* 7.62 x 51mm NATO
  *Official Name:* Rifle, Sniper, 7.62mm M14 (Navy)

*Remarks:* Navy sniper version of M14. NSN 1005-01-106-8975.

• *Cal.:* 7.62 x 51mm NATO
*Official Name:* Rifle, EOD, 7.62mm M14
*Common Name:* The EOD M14 uses a wide field of view telescope

*Remarks:* This version of M14 is used by EOD personnel to shoot at and destroy suspected explosive devices; NSN 1005-01-235-3311. Issued with a padded carrying case.

• *Cal.:* 7.62 x 51mm NATO
*Official Name:* Rifle, Sniper, 7.62mm M24; of M24 Sniper Weapon System
*Common Name:* The M24 uses the 10 X Leupold M3 telescope

*Remarks:* Standard A. Remington Arms Company chosen in the fall of 1987 to supply the US Army with its new sniper weapon. The first 500 M24 SWS had a unit cost of $4,995. There were only two weapons in the XM24 competition, the Remington rifle and the Steyr SSG. Out to 500 meters they were comparable, but the Remington shot better at 700–800 meters.

• *Cal.:* 7.62 x 51mm NATO
*Official Name:* Rifle 7.62mm, caliber Mark 2 MOD 2
*Common Name:* 7.62mm M1; M1E14; earlier Army prototype called T35

*Remarks:* US Navy 7.62mm version of .30 caliber M1 rifle. These rifles were rebarreled for US Navy forces under BUWEPS ORDALT 5592. Obsolescent. NSN 1005-00-923-9070 w/ chrome plated bore. Unplated barrel model 1005-00-781-5547. Mark 2 MOD 0 is 1005-00-923-9071.
Match Grade A with glass bedded stock is 1005-00-148-6532.
Match Grade B with glass bedded stock is 1005-00-148-6524.
Standard glass bedded stock is 1005-00-256-8296.

• *Cal.:* 7.62 x 51mm NATO
*Common Name:* HK *Gewehr* 3

*Remarks:* NSN 1005-12-140-9436. Used by US Navy SEALS since 1980 and by US Army Rangers since mid-1970s.

• *Cal.:* 7.62 x 51mm NATO
*Common Name:* HK G3SG/1 sniper rifle

*Remarks:* Used by special operations teams since 1980. NSN 1005-12-181-2400.

• *Cal.:* 7.62 x 51mm NATO
*Official Name:* Rifle, Sniper 7.62mm, M40
*Common Name:* Remington Model 700

*Remarks:* USMC bolt action sniper rifle w/ 610mm barrel and Redfield 3 to 9 X telescope. Adopted April 1966. NSN 1005-00-166-2760 (Model 700M); also NSNs 1005-00-089-3739 and 1005-00-999-8807. The telescope is NSN 1240-00-937-0825; its mount is 1240-00-937-0826.

• *Cal.:* 7.62 x 51mm NATO
*Official Name:* Rifle, Sniper 7.62mm, M40A1
*Common Name:* Remington Model 700

*Remarks:* USMC bolt action sniper rifle with 610mm stainless steel barrel, fiberglass stock, and rubber butt plate. NSN 1005-01-030-8020 w/o equipment; NSN 1005-01-035-1674 w/. The issue equipment includes a molded plastic carrying case, telescope, telescope mount, sling, and cleaning equipment.

• *Cal.:* 7.62 x 51mm NATO and 8.58 x 71mm
*Common Name:* Convertible long range rifle system; Model 300 sniper rifle

*Remarks:* Research Armament Industries, Rogers, Arkansas. Special small scale production sniper rifle adopted by undisclosed special operations units. LSN 1005-LL-HDN-Q830.

• *Cal.:* 12.7 x 99mm
*Common Name:* Model 500 sniper rifle

*Remarks:* Research Armaments Industries. Special operations units. LSN 1005-LL-L99-4800.

• *Cal.:* 7.62 x 63mm
*Official Name:* Rifle, Caliber .30, M1

*Remarks:* Standardized 1936. Now class S. NSN 1005-00-674-1425. M7A2 grenade launcher, NSN 1005-00-317-2476. M7A3 grenade launcher, NSN 1005-00-317-2477. M5 bayonet, NSN 1005-00-726-6558. M5A1 bayonet, NSN 1005-00-336-8568.

• *Cal.:* 7.62 x 63mm
*Official Name:* Rifle, Sniper, Caliber .30, M1C
*Common Name:* M81 and M82 telescope

*Remarks:* Class S. NSN 1005-00-674-1430. M81 telescope is NSN 1240-00-759-7767, as is the M82 telescope.

- *Cal.:* 7.62 x 63mm
  *Official Name:* Rifle, Sniper, Caliber .30, M1D
  *Common Name:* M84 telescope

  *Remarks:* Class S. NSN 1005-00-674-1431. M84 telescope is NSN 1240-00-759-7774 w/o equipment, and NSN 1240-00-678-4690 w/ equipment.

- *Cal.:* 7.62 x 63mm
  *Official Name:* Rifle, Caliber .30, M1, National Match

  *Remarks:* OBSOLETE. NSN 1005-00-726-6476.

- *Cal.:* 7.62 x 63mm
  *Official Name:* Rifle, Caliber .30, M1, National Match, Coast Guard Model

  *Remarks:* OBSOLETE. NSN 1005-00-605-4651.

- *Cal.:* 7.62 x 63mm
  *Official Name:* Rifle, Caliber .30, M1, National Match

  *Remarks:* OBSOLETE. NSN 1005-00-974-5372. W/ glass bedded stock.

- *Cal.:* 7.62 x 63mm
  *Official Name:* Rifle, Dummy Drill, Caliber .30, M1

  *Remarks:* Demilitarized for ROTC units. Class S. NSN 1005-01-113-3767.

- *Cal.:* 7.62 x 63mm
  *Official Name:* Rifle, Training Aid, Caliber .30, M1

  *Remarks:* Demilitarized, barrel plugged for instructional use. Class S. NSN 1005-01-061-2456.

- *Cal.:* 7.62 x 63mm
  *Official Name:* Rifle, Inert, Caliber .30, M1

  *Remarks:* Demilitarized, barrel plugged for US Air Force instructional use. Class S. NSN 1005-00-599-3289.

- *Cal.:* 7.62 x 63mm
  *Official Name:* Rifle, Ceremonial, Caliber .30, M1

  *Remarks:* Single-shot version developed for the American Legion and the Veterans of Foreign Wars for ceremonial uses. Class S. NSN 1005-01-095-0085.

- *Cal.:* 7.62 x 63mm
  *Official Name:* Rifle, Caliber .30, M1903A3
  *Common Name:* M1903A3 Springfield

  *Remarks:* OBSOLETE. NSN 1005-00-674-1518. The NSN assigned to DCM issued M1903s is 1005-00-004-1282.

- *Cal.:* 7.62 x 63mm
  *Official Name:* Rifle, Caliber .30, M1903A3 National Match

  *Remarks:* OBSOLETE. NSN 1005-00-317-2478.

- *Cal.:* 7.62 x 63mm
  *Official Name:* Rifle, Sniper, Caliber .30, M1903A4

  *Remarks:* Class S. NSN 1005-00-674-1521. The M73B1 telescope is NSN 1240-00-757-9931. It was the standard scope in World War II, but other scopes were fitted during wartime. In the 1970s the rifle was fitted w/ the M84 telescope.

- *Cal.:* 7.62 x 63mm
  *Official Name:* Rifle, Dummy Drill, Caliber .30, M1903A3

  *Remarks:* Class S. NSN 1005-01-081-1400. This weapon is demilitarized by plugging the barrel with a steel rod. The rod is welded in place by cutting through the barrel approximately 40mm ahead of the receiver.

- *Cal.:* 7.62 x 63mm
  *Official Name:* Rifle, Training Aid, Caliber .30, M1903A3

  *Remarks:* Demilitarized, barrel plugged for instructional use. Class S. NSN 1005-01-061-2457.

- *Cal.:* 7.62 x 63mm
  *Official Name:* Rifle, Caliber .30, M1903A3 National Match

  *Remarks:* OBSOLETE. NSN 1005-00-317-2478.

- *Cal.:* 7.62 x 63mm
  *Official Name:* Rifle, Sniper, Caliber .30, M1903A4
  *Common Name:* M73B1 telescope was the standard sight, but other scopes fitted during wartime

*Remarks:* Class S. NSN 1005-00-674-1521. The M73B1 telescope is NSN 1240-00-757-9931. In the 1970s M1903A4 rifle was fitted with M84 telescope.

- *Cal.:* 7.62 x 63mm
  *Official Name:* Rifle, Dummy Drill, Caliber .30, M1903A3

*Remarks:* Class S. NSN 1005-01-081-1400.

*Other rifles assigned NSNs but not generally used by US armed forces:*

- *Cal.:* 5.56 x 45mm
  *Official Name:* Rifle, Test, 5.56mm
  *Common Name:* Remington Model 700

*Remarks:* Ammunition testing. NSN 1005-01-054-7146.

- *Cal.:* 7.62 x 51mm NATO
  *Common Name:* Remington Model 700

*Remarks:* NSN 1005-00-999-8807.

- *Cal.:* 7.62 x 51mm NATO
  *Common Name:* Ruger Model 77

*Remarks:* NSN 1005-01-114-0054.

- *Cal.:* 7.62 x 51mm NATO
  *Common Name:* .308 Winchester Model 70 Benchrest rifle

*Remarks:* NSN 1005-00-166-2834. 711mm barrel.

- *Cal.:* 7.62 x 63mm
  *Common Name:* .30-06 Winchester Model 70 Target rifle

*Remarks:* NSN 1005-00-166-2761. 610mm barrel.

- *Cal.:* 7.62 x 63mm
  *Common Name:* .30-06 Winchester Model 70 rifle (Special Match Grade)

*Remarks:* NSN 1005-00-322-9736.

- *Cal.:* 7.62 x 72mm
  *Common Name:* .300 Holland & Holland Winchester Model 70 rifle

*Remarks:* NSN 1005-00-694-4257.

- *Cal.:* 7.62 x 51mm NATO
  *Common Name:* Remington 40XB Target

*Remarks:* NSN 1005-01-080-4032.

**CARBINES:**

- *Cal.:* 5.56 x 45mm NATO
  *Official Name:* Carbine 5.56mm, M4
  *Common Name:* Modified M16A2; product-improved M16

*Remarks:* New version of the old XM177 submachine-gun-type weapon being tested by the US Marine Corps and the US Army. This weapon has M16A2 upper and lower receivers with a 368mm barrel, slightly larger diameter M16A2-style round front hand guards, and a M16A2-style pistol grip. Unlike the aluminum construction sliding butt stock of the older XM177 guns, the XM4 has the same stock fabricated from plastics to further reduce weight. Since the XM4 carbine is derived from a standard weapon, the US Army Test and Evaluation Command (TECOM) went directly into a Development Test/Operational Test II (DT/OT II) program in April of 1986. The US Marine Corps has standardized the M4; the Army has not yet made a decision. The Air Force and the Navy use some of the Colt M16A1-based Model 653 carbines from which the XM4 has evolved. The Navy designates it NSN 1005-01-029-3866; the Air Force calls it NSN 1005-01-042-9820.

- *Cal.:* 7.62 x 33mm
  *Official Name:* Carbine, Caliber .30 M1
  *Common Name:* M1 carbine

- *Cal.:* 7.62 x 33mm
  *Official Name:* Carbine, Caliber .30 M1 (inert)
  *Common Name:* M1 carbine

- *Cal.:* 7.62 x 33mm
  *Official Name:* Carbine, Caliber .30 M1A1
  *Common Name:* M1A1 carbine. Paratroop model

- *Cal.:* 7.62 x 33mm
  *Official Name:* Carbine, Caliber .30 M2 Carbine
  *Common Name:* M2 carbine

- *Cal.:* 7.62 x 33mm
  *Official Name:* Carbine, Caliber .30 M3 Carbine
  *Common Name:* M3 carbine

**SHOTGUNS:**
- *Cal.:* 18.5 x 59mm
  *Common Name:* Mossberg 12 gage ATP8SPL. Milsgun; Model 500

- *Cal.:* 18.5 x 59mm
  *Official Name:* Shotgun, 12 gage, Riot-type, Model 870 MK 1
  *Common Name:* Remington Model 870 pump shotgun

*Remarks:* OBSOLETE. NSN 1005-00-670-7672. The M4 bayonet is assigned NSN 1005-00-716-2787. The M7 bayonet is assigned NSN 1005-00-992-6645.

*Remarks:* OBSOLETE. NSN 1005-00-599-3289. This inert weapon was used for training purposes.

*Remarks:* OBSOLETE. NSN 1005-00-670-7670.

*Remarks:* OBSOLETE. NSN 1005-00-670-7675 w/ equipment; w/o equipment it is NSN 1005-00-575-0057.

*Remarks:* OBSOLETE. NSN 1005-00-658-0064 and NSN 1005-00-726-5697. This weapon was equipped w/ the infrared snooper scope.

*Remarks:* Standard A. NSN 1005-01-1032. This 508mm barrel gun is the first pump shotgun to be made to a MILSPEC. Used by the US Coast Guard and the US Navy.

*Remarks:* Standard A. NSN 1005-01-065-8989. This 533mm barrel 8-shot shotgun was developed for the US Marine Corps. A standard Model 870 is NSN 1005-00-973-5645.

*Miscellaneous shotguns with NSN identifiers.* Most are no longer issued for combat, but may still be in military and federal police inventories.

- *Cal.:* 18.5 x 59mm
  *Official Name:* Shotgun, 12 gage, riot-type, M1897 with bayonet lug assembly
  *Common Name:* Winchester Model 1897 pump shotgun

- *Cal.:* 18.5 x 59mm
  *Official Name:* Shotgun, 12 gage, trap-type, M1897
  *Common Name:* Winchester Model 1897 pump shotgun

- *Cal.:* 18.5 x 59mm
  *Official Name:* Shotgun, 12 gage, riot-type, Model 1912
  *Common Name:* Winchester Model 1912 pump shotgun. Model 12 pump

- *Cal.:* 18.5 x 59mm
  *Official Name:* Shotgun, 12 gage, Model 1912, with bayonet lug
  *Common Name:* Winchester Model 1912 pump shotgun

*Remarks:* OBSOLETE. NSN 1005-00-677-9145. This weapon has a 508mm barrel. The M1917 bayonet is assigned NSN 1005-00-716-2787.

*Remarks:* OBSOLETE. This weapon has a 711mm barrel. NSN 1005-00-051-8435.

*Remarks:* OBSOLETE. This weapon has a 508mm barrel. NSN 1005-00-677-9150.

*Remarks:* OBSOLETE. This weapon has a 508mm barrel. NSN 1005-00-731-2036.

- *Cal.:* 18.5 x 59mm
  *Official Name:* Shotgun, 12 gage,
  skeet-type, Model 1912
  *Common Name:* Winchester
  Model 1912 pump shotgun

- *Cal.:* 18.5 x 59mm
  *Official Name:* Shotgun, 12 gage,
  riot-type, M11 w/o bayonet lug
  assembly
  *Common Name:* Remington
  Model 11 autoloading shotgun

- *Cal.:* 18.5 x 59mm
  *Official Name:* Shotgun, 12 gage,
  riot-type, M11-48R
  *Common Name:* Remington
  Model 11 autoloading shotgun

- *Cal.:* 18.5 x 59mm
  *Official Name:* Shotgun, 12 gage,
  riot-type, M31 w/ bayonet lug
  assembly
  *Common Name:* Remington
  Model 31 pump shotgun

- *Cal.:* 18.5 x 59mm
  *Official Name:* Shotgun, 12 gage,
  M32
  *Common Name:* Remington
  Model 32 superposed shotgun

- *Cal.:* 18.5 x 59mm
  *Official Name:* Shotgun, 12 gage,
  trap-type, M32
  *Common Name:* Remington
  Model 32 superposed shotgun

- *Cal.:* 18.5 x 59mm
  *Official Name:* Shotgun, 12 gage,
  riot-type, M37 w/ bayonet lug
  assembly
  *Common Name:* Ithaca Model 37
  pump shotgun

- *Cal.:* 18.5 x 59mm
  *Official Name:* Shotgun, 12 gage,
  riot-type, M37 w/o bayonet lug
  assembly
  *Common Name:* Ithaca Model 37
  pump shotgun

- *Cal.:* 18.5 x 59mm
  *Official Name:* Shotgun, 12 gage,
  skeet-type, M58
  *Common Name:* Remington
  Model 58

- *Cal.:* 18.5 x 59mm
  *Official Name:* Shotgun, 12 gage,
  riot-type, M77E w/o bayonet
  lug assembly
  *Common Name:* Stevens Model
  77 pump shotgun

*Remarks:* OBSOLETE. This weapon has a 660mm barrel. NSN 1005-00-617-9151.

*Remarks:* OBSOLETE. Still in service. NSN 1005-00-677-9126.

*Remarks:* OBSOLETE. This weapon has a 508mm barrel. NSN 1005-00-933-1230.

*Remarks:* OBSOLETE. This weapon has a 508mm barrel. NSN 1005-00-9125.

*Remarks:* NSN 1005-00-892-4865. This weapon has a 711mm barrel.

*Remarks:* NSN 1005-00-892-4866. This weapon has a 711mm barrel.

*Remarks:* NSN 1005-00-214-0397.

*Remarks:* NSN 1005-00-973-2138.

*Remarks:* NSN 1005-00-892-4289. This weapon has a 661mm barrel.

*Remarks:* NSN 1005-00-952-4063. This weapon has a 508mm barrel.

- *Cal.:* 18.5 x 59mm
  *Official Name:* Shotgun, 12 gage,
  M162
  *Common Name:* High standard
  Model 162 shotgun

*Remarks:* NSN 1005-01-073-2368. This weapon has a 610mm barrel.

- *Cal.:* 18.5 x 59mm
  *Official Name:* Shotgun, 12 gage,
  riot-type, M520A w/ bayonet
  lug assembly
  *Common Name:* Stevens Model
  520-30 pump shotgun

*Remarks:* NSN 1005-00-677-9130. Standard A. This weapon has a 508mm
barrel.

- *Cal.:* 18.5 x 59mm
  *Official Name:* Shotgun, 12 gage,
  riot-type, M620, w/ bayonet lug
  assembly
  *Common Name:* Stevens Model
  620 pump shotgun

*Remarks:* NSN 1005-00-677-9135. This weapon has a 508mm barrel.

- *Cal.:* 18.5 x 59mm
  *Official Name:* Shotgun, 12 gage,
  riot-type, M620A, w/ bayonet
  lug assembly
  *Common Name:* Stevens Model
  620A pump shotgun

*Remarks:* NSN 1005-00-677-9140. Standard A. This weapon has a 508mm
barrel.

- *Cal.:* 18.5 x 59mm
  *Official Name:* Shotgun, 12 gage,
  riot-type, M720 w/o bayonet
  lug assembly
  *Common Name:* Savage Model
  720 autoloading shotgun

*Remarks:* NSN 1005-00-677-9107. This weapon has a 508mm barrel.

- *Cal.:* 18.5 x 59mm
  *Official Name:* Shotgun, 12 gage,
  skeet-type, M720
  *Common Name:* Savage Model
  720 autoloading shotgun

*Remarks:* NSN 1005-00-003-2267. This weapon has a 711mm barrel.

- *Cal.:* 18.5 x 59mm
  *Official Name:* Shotgun, 12 gage,
  riot-type, M1200, w/ bayonet
  lug
  *Common Name:* Winchester
  Model 1200 pump shotgun

*Remarks:* NSN 1005-00-921-5483. Standard A. This weapon has a 508mm
barrel; w/o bayonet lug, NSN 1005-00-926-9307.

- *Cal.:* 15.6 x 59mm
  *Official Name:* Shotgun, 12 gage
  *Common Name:* Remington
  Model 1100 autoloading shot-
  gun

*Remarks:* NSN 1005-00-934-1404.

- *Cal.:* 18.5 x 59mm
  *Official Name:* Shotgun, 12 gage,
  riot-type, M37 w/o bayonet lug
  assembly
  *Common Name:* Ithaca Model 37
  pump shotgun

*Remarks:* NSN 1005-00-973-2138.

- *Cal.:* 18.5 x 59mm
  *Official Name:* Shotgun, 12 gage,
  skeet-type, M58
  *Common Name:* Remington
  Model 58

*Remarks:* NSN 1005-00-892-4289. This weapon has a 661mm barrel.

- *Cal.:* 18.5 x 59mm
  *Official Name:* Shotgun, 12 gage, riot-type, M77E w/o bayonet lug assembly
  *Common Name:* Stevens Model 77 pump shotgun

*Remarks:* NSN 1005-00-952-4063.

- *Cal.:* 18.5 x 59mm
  *Official Name:* Shotgun, 12 gage, M162
  *Common Name:* High standard Model 162 shotgun

*Remarks:* NSN 1005-01-073-2368. This weapon has a 610mm barrel.

- *Cal.:* 18.5 x 59mm
  *Official Name:* Shotgun, 12 gage, riot-type, M520A w/ bayonet lug assembly
  *Common Name:* Stevens Model 520-30 pump shotgun

*Remarks:* NSN 1005-00-677-9130. Standard A. This weapon has a 508mm barrel.

- *Cal.:* 18.5 x 59mm
  *Official Name:* Shotgun, 12 gage, riot-type, M620, w/ bayonet lug assembly
  *Common Name:* Stevens Model 620 pump shotgun

*Remarks:* NSN 1005-00-677-9135. This weapon has a 508mm barrel.

- *Cal.:* 18.5 x 59mm
  *Official Name:* Shotgun, 12 gage, riot-type, M620A, w/ bayonet lug assembly
  *Common Name:* Stevens Model 620A pump shotgun

*Remarks:* NSN 1005-00-677-9140. Standard A. This weapon has a 508mm barrel.

- *Cal.:* 18.5 x 59mm
  *Official Name:* Shotgun, 12 gage, riot-type, M720, w/o bayonet lug assembly
  *Common Name:* Savage Model 720 autoloading shotgun

*Remarks:* NSN 1005-00-677-9107. This weapon has a 508mm barrel.

- *Cal.:* 18.5 x 59mm
  *Official Name:* Shotgun, 12 gage, skeet-type, M720
  *Common Name:* Savage Model 720 autoloading shotgun

*Remarks:* NSN 1005-00-003-2267. This weapon has a 711mm barrel.

- *Cal.:* 18.5 x 59mm
  *Official Name:* Shotgun, 12 gage, riot-type, M1200
  *Common Name:* Winchester Model 1200 pump shotgun

*Remarks:* NSN 1005-00-921-5483. Standard A. This weapon has a 508mm barrel.

- *Cal.:* 15.6 x 59mm
  *Official Name:* Shotgun, 20 gage
  *Common Name:* Remington Model 1100 autoloading shotgun

*Remarks:* NSN 1005-01-5543.

- *Cal.:* 14 x 59mm
  *Official Name:* Shotgun, 28 gage
  *Common Name:* Remingtom Model 1100 autoloading shotgun

*Remarks:* NSN 1005-01-110-5544.
The .410 gage model is NSN 1005-01-110-5543.
The 16 gage model is NSN 1005-01-113-1432.

- *Cal.:* 18.5 x 59mm
  *Official Name:* Shotgun, 12 gage, trap-type
  *Common Name:* Browning Trap shotgun, Broadway Grade 1

*Remarks:* NSN 1005-00-984-2273. This shotgun has a 813mm barrel.

- *Cal.:* 16.8 x 59mm
  *Official Name:* Shotgun, 16 gage
  *Common Name:* Browning

*Remarks:* NSN 1005-01-075-3147.

**SURVIVAL GUNS:**
- *Cal.:* 5.6 x 35.6mmR
  *Official Name:* Rifle, survival, .22 (Hornet) M4, (T38)

*Remarks:* NSN 1005-00-575-0070.

- *Cal.:* 5.6 x 16mmR/10.4mm
  *Common Name:* Rifle-Shotgun, survival, Caliber .22/.410 gage, M6 (T39)

*Remarks:* NSN 1005-00-575-0073.

- *Cal.:* 5.6 x 16mmR/5.6 x 35.6mmR
  *Official Name:* MA1 survival rifle, .22LR and .22 Hornet

*Remarks:* NSN 1005-00-516-7968.

**Two American airborne military policemen stand guard duty during "Bright Star 82." The driver has a 5.56 x 45mm M16A1 with a 40mm M203 grenade launcher. The trooper standing has a 7.62 x 51mm M60 GPMG on an M31A1 pedestal truck mount. (DOD)**

• *Cal.:* 5.6 x 16mmR
*Official Name:* AR-7 survival rifle
*Common Name:* Charter Arms
AR-7 survival rifle

*Remarks:* NSN 1005-01-060-4838.

## MACHINE GUNS:
• *Cal.:* 5.56 x 45mm NATO
*Official Name:* Squad Automatic
Weapon 5.56mm, M249
*Common Name:* FN Minimi

*Remarks:* NSN 1005-01-127-7510. Standard A since 1982. The US Army originally planned to acquire 49,979 between 1982 and 1991, while the US Marine Corps was to acquire 9,974 between 1982 and 1988. This schedule was changed on 23 August 1985 when the Under Secretary of the US Army temporarily suspended production pending fixes of deficiencies discovered w/ the M249 in early field use.

• *Cal.:* 5.56 x 45mm
*Official Name:* Machine Gun
5.56mm, MK23 MOD 0
*Common Name:* Stoner 63 machine gun. US Army designation XM207E1

*Remarks:* NSN 1005-01-018-7071. Still used in limited numbers by the US Navy SEAL Teams. Made by Cadillac Gage Corporation, Warren, Michigan.

**PFC Charles McConnell, 2nd Reconnaissance Battalion, US Marine Corps, guards access to the beach area during the relief of the 32nd Marine Amphibious Unit by the 24th Marine Amphibious Unit, Beirut, Lebanon, November 1982. (USMC)**

The product-improved M60E3 GPMG adopted by the US Marine Corps in 1983. This lighter version of the M60 GPMG will reduce the weight of the weapon by 25 percent. (Saco)

• *Cal.:* 7.62 x 51mm NATO
  *Official Name:* Machine Gun
  7.62mm, M60

*Remarks:* NSN 1005-00-605-7710 w/ equipment and NSN 1005-00-713-9823 w/o. Standard A since 1957. Basic tripod for the M60 GPMG is Mount, Tripod M122 — NSN 1005-00-710-5599. Mount, M142 assigned NSN 1005-00-854-4463. Saco Defense Systems Division, Maremont Corp., Saco, Maine.

• *Cal.:* 7.62 x 51mm NATO
  *Official Name:* Machine Gun
  7.62mm, M60C fixed

*Remarks:* NSN 1005-00-973-0375. Standard A. Helicopter gun fired by solenoid. Saco Defense Systems.

• *Cal.:* 7.62 x 51mm NATO
  *Official Name:* Machine Gun
  7.62mm, M60CA1

*Remarks:* NSN 1005-00-906-6313. Standard B. Aircraft.

• *Cal.:* 7.62 x 51mm NATO
  *Official Name:* Machine Gun
  7.62mm, M60D

*Remarks:* NSN 1005-00-909-3002. Standard A. Flexible gun w/ spade grips and modified trigger. Helicopter door gun. Saco Defense Systems. There are four current mounts for this gun: MG Mount, Door, Lightweight, M23 for UH-1D and UH-1H NSN 1005-00-907-0720; MG Mount, Door, Lightweight, M24 for CH-47 NSN 1005-00-763-1404; MG Mount, Ramp, Lightweight, M41 for CH-47 NSN 1005-00-087-2046; and MG Mount, Door, Lightweight, M144 for UH-60 NSN 1005-01-193-4878.

• *Cal.:* 7.62 x 51mm NATO
  *Official Name:* Machine Gun
  7.62mm, M60E2

*Remarks:* Armor machine gun used in US Marine Corps M60A1 tanks as coaxial gun. Standard A since 1977. NSN 1005-00-000-0061. Saco Defense Systems.

**A US Navy gunner aboard the USS Fox (CG-33) mans his .50 caliber M2 HB Browning machine gun (on a MK 26, MOD 15 soft mount) during a 1987 tour of duty in the Persian Gulf. (US Navy: Pixler)**

• *Cal.:* 7.62 x 51mm NATO
  *Official Name:* Machine Gun 7.62mm, M60E3
  *Common Name:* M60 lightweight

*Remarks:* Adopted by USMC in 1983. In 1985 the Marines converted all of their M60s to the "Echo 3" configuration, and they have purchased 4,630 new guns from Saco Defense Systems, a move that will allow them to supplement the 1,650 conversion kits and 977 rebuilt guns ordered. The Marines will convert their M60 machine guns at their own weapons repair facilities. The US Navy planned purchases of 1,384 M60E3s in 1986, plus 1,807 in 1987 and 257 in 1988. NSN 1005-01-169-7019.

• *Cal.:* 7.62 x 51mm NATO
  *Official Name:* Machine Gun 7.62mm, M240
  *Common Name:* FN MAG. Left-side feed

*Remarks:* Armor machine gun to replace M73, M73A1, and M219 machine guns. Made by FN, Herstal, Belgium, and FN Manufacturing Inc. (FNMI), Columbia, SC. Standard A since 1977. NSN 1005-01-025-8095.

• *Cal.:* 7.62 x 51mm NATO
  *Official Name:* Machine Gun 7.62mm, M240C
  *Common Name:* FN MAG. Right-side feed

*Remarks:* FNMI. NSN 1005-01-085-4758.

• *Cal.:* 7.62 x 51mm NATO
  *Official Name:* Machine Gun 7.62mm, M240E1
  *Common Name:* FN MAG. Flexible gun for use on USMC and US Army vehicles

*Remarks:* FNMI. Fitted with spade grips and rear-mounted trigger mechanism. DoD announced contract for 739 M240E1s (for $4 million) in October 1987 for delivery in 1988.

**417**

**Two US M1 Abrams tank crewmen change the barrel of the commander's .50 caliber (12.7 x 108mm) M2 HB machine gun during the NATO 1984 "Autumn Forge" exercise in West Germany. (US Army: Waite)**

- *Cal.:* 7.62 x 51mm NATO
  *Official Name:* Armor Machine Guns 7.62mm, M73, M73A1, and M219

*Remarks:* M73 standardized in 1959; M219 in 1970. Made at General Electric and Rock Island Arsenal. Being replaced by M240 and M60E2. All of these machine guns will continue to be standard until replaced. M73 w/o flash suppressor is NSN 1005-00-869-8816; w/ flash suppressor it is NSN 1005-00-679-6763. M73A1 is NSN 1005-00-937-7323. M219 is NSN 1005-00-077-2354.

- *Cal.:* 7.62 x 51mm NATO
  *Official Name:* Machine Gun 7.62mm, M73C

*Remarks:* Ground version of M73. OBSOLETE. Very few of these weapons were actually made. Some saw use in Vietnam. NSN 1005-00-791-3378.

- *Cal.:* 7.62 x 51mm NATO
  *Official Name:* Machine Gun 7.62mm, Six barrels M134
  *Common Name:* Minigun

*Remarks:* NSN 1005-00-903-0751. Used in several aircraft and ground vehicle applications, such as the "Armament Pod, Aircraft, 7.62mm Machine Gun M134" (1005-00-832-7498).

- *Cal.:* 7.62 x 51mm NATO
  *Official Name:* Machine Gun 7.62mm, MK 21, MOD 0

*Remarks:* US Navy conversion of the M1919A4 LMG.

- *Cal.:* 7.62 x 51mm NATO
  *Official Name:* Machine Gun 7.62mm, High Rate XM196
  *Common Name:* Minigun

*Remarks:* NSN 1005-00-104-8907.

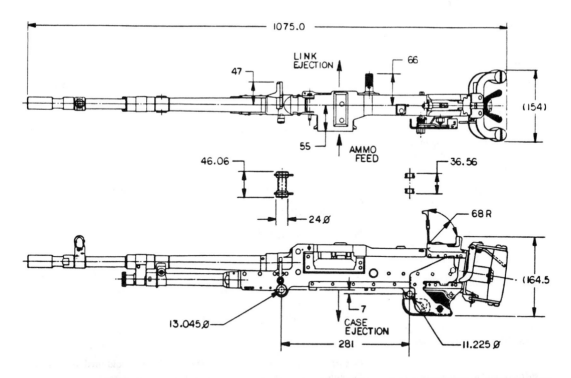

The 7.62 x 51mm NATO M240E1 flexible machine gun is being used on US Marine Corps Light Armored Vehicles (LAV) and some other tactical vehicles. Indicated dimensions are metric. (FN, Herstal)

- *Cal.:* 7.62 x 51mm NATO
  *Official Name:* Gun Automatic 7.62mm, GAU-2B/A
  *Common Name:* Minigun

  *Remarks:* NSN 1005-00-912-3987.

- *Cal.:* 7.62 x 63mm
  *Official Name:* Machine Gun, Caliber .30, M37 w/o sight

  *Remarks:* Standard A. NSN 1005-00-856-7528. Used in fixed and flexible mounts on tanks. Retracting bar as on the M1919A4E1.

- *Cal.:* 7.62 x 63mm
  *Official Name:* Machine Gun, Caliber .30, M37 w/ sight
  *Common Name:* T153

  *Remarks:* Standard B. NSN 1005-00-716-2946.

- *Cal.:* 7.62 x 63mm
  *Official Name:* Machine Gun, Caliber .30, M37C

  *Remarks:* OBSOLETE. NSN 1005-00-525-1365. Remotely charged and solenoid fired. Used in the Armament, Subsystem, Helicopter, .30 Caliber Machinegun, XM1 and XM1E1.

- *Cal.:* 12.7 x 99mm
  *Official Name:* Machine Gun, Caliber .50, M2 Heavy Barrel; flexible.
  *Common Name:* .50 Browning M2 HB

  *Remarks:* Standard A. W/ equipment. NSN 1005-00-322-9715.

- *Cal.:* 12.7 x 99mm
  *Official Name:* Machine Gun, Caliber .50, M2 HB Vehicular

  *Remarks:* Standard A. NSN 1005-00-726-5636.

- *Cal.:* 12.7 x 99mm
  *Official Name:* Machine Gun, Caliber .50, M2 HB for Cupola, M1

  *Remarks:* Standard B. NSN 1005-00-693-4854. Solenoid-fired w/ left-side charging chain.

- *Cal.:* 12.7 x 99mm
  *Official Name:* Machine Gun, Caliber .50, M2 HB for Cupola, M13.

  *Remarks:* Standard B. NSN 1005-00-606-8412. Solenoid-fired w/ right-side charging chain.

- *Cal.:* 12.7 x 99mm
  *Official Name:* Machine Gun, Caliber .50, M2 HB, M45
  *Common Name:* This series was used with the M45, M45C, M45D, and M45F quad mounts for the M55 trailer AA mount

  *Remarks:* Standard B. NSN 1005-00-602-2105. Solenoid firing w/ standard cocking handle. M45C used in M55 trailer antiaircraft mount. M55 mount is NSN 1005-00-673-4750.

- *Cal.:* 12.7 x 99mm
  *Official Name:* Machine Gun, Caliber .50, M2 HB for M48 Tank

  *Remarks:* Standard A. NSN 1005-00-957-3893. Left-side charging chain and standard trigger (Chrysler mount).

- *Cal.:* 12.7 x 99mm
  *Official Name:* Machine Gun, Caliber .50, M2 HB for XM26 Commander's Cupola

  *Remarks:* Standard A. NSN 1005-00-013-6944. Solenoid-fired with right-side charging chain.

- *Cal.:* 12.7 x 99mm
  *Official Name:* Machine Gun, Caliber .50, AC, Flexible Modified, Pintel Mounted, XM 213

  *Remarks:* NSN 1005-00-179-6526. Used on the Aircraft Armament Subsystem XM59. (Modified AN-M2 aircraft machine gun.)

• *Cal.:* 12.7 x 99mm
*Official Name:* Machine Gun, Caliber .50, AC, Flexible XM 218

*Remarks:* NSN 1005-00-165-4561. Used on the CH-47 helicopter.

• *Cal.:* 12.7 x 99mm
*Official Name:* Machine Gun, Caliber .50, M85

*Remarks:* Standard A. Cupola gun on the M60 series tanks. NSN 1005-00-690-2790.

• *Cal.:* 12.7 x 99mm
*Official Name:* Machine Gun, Caliber .50, M85C

*Remarks:* OBSOLETE. Ground version of M85. NSN 1005-00-791-3379.

**MOUNTS for 7.62mm and 12.7mm MACHINE GUNS:**

*Official Name:* Mount, Tripod, Machine Gun, Caliber .50, M3

*Remarks:* Standard A. NSN 1005-00-322-9716.

*Official Name:* Mount, Gun, Truck,
Pedestal, M31C

*Remarks:* Standard A. General NSN is 1005-00-706-9767. NSN 1005-00-317-2441 for M2 HB on M38A1. NSN 1005-00-317-2442 for the M1919A4E1.

*Official Name:* Mount, Gun, Pedestal, M4

*Remarks:* Standard A. NSN 1005-00-419-7041 for M151 series truck [jeep].

*Official Name:* Mount, Gun, Truck,
Pedestal, M31A1

*Remarks:* Standard A. General NSNs for this mount are 1005-00-736-0400 and NSN 1005-00-317-2442. For M2 HB on M38 vehicles NSN 1005-00-854-4463. NSN 1005-00-973-2831 for M60 on M38. NSN 1005-00-973-2832 for M60 on M38A1. NSN 1005-00-973-2833 for M60 on M151 vehicle series.

*Official Name:* Mount, Gun, Ring,
Caliber .50, M36

*Remarks:* Standard A. NSN 1005-00-317-2425.

*Official Name:* Mount, Gun, Ring,
Caliber .50, M36A1

*Remarks:* Standard A. NSN 1005-00-317-2427.

*Official Name:* Mount, Gun, Ring,
Caliber .50, M36A2

*Remarks:* Standard A. NSN 1005-00-317-2428.

*Official Name:* Mount, Gun, Ring,
Caliber .50, M49 Series

*Remarks:* Standard A. M49 is NSN 1005-00-655-4500. M49C is NSN 1005-00-711-5031. M49A1 is NSN 1005-00-732-3017.

*Official Name:* Mount, Trailer Multiple [4], Caliber .50, M55

*Remarks:* Standard F. NSN 1005-00-673-4750.

*Official Name:* Mount, Antiaircraft,
Machine Gun, Caliber .50, M63

*Remarks:* Standard A. NSN 1005-00-673-3246.

*Official Name:* Mount, Antiaircraft,
Twin Pedestal, Machine Gun,
Caliber .50, M65

*Remarks:* OBSOLETE. NSN 1005-00-324-9432.

*Official Name:* Mount, Gun, Ring,
Caliber .50, M66

*Remarks:* Standard A. NSN 1005-00-890-2610.

*Official Name:* Mount, Gun, Ring,
Caliber .50, M68 Series

*Remarks:* Standard A. M68 is NSN 1005-00-702-8676. M68E1 is NSN 1005-00-797-6451. M68E1 w/ supports is NSN 1005-00-797-6450.

*Official Name:* Mount, Gun, Ring,
Caliber .50, M81

*Remarks:* Standard A. NSN 1005-00-219-8135.

*Official Name:* Mount, Machine
Gun, M48 Tank Cupola

*Remarks:* Standard A. NSN 1005-00-736-4875 and 1005-00-834-6119.

**OBSOLETE MACHINE GUNS:**

• *Cal.:* 7.62 x 63mm
*Official Name:* Browning Auto-
matic Rifle, Caliber .30,
M1918A2

*Remarks:* OBSOLETE. NSN 1005-00-674-1309 and 1005-00-726-5703. The 7.62 x 51mm NATO caliber conversion is NSN 1005-00-930-3462.

• *Cal.:* 7.62 x 63mm
*Official Name:* Machine Gun, Water Cooled, Caliber .30, M1917A1
*Common Name:* M1917A1 Browning MMG

*Remarks:* OBSOLETE. NSN 1005-00-672-1640.

• *Cal.:* 7.62 x 63mm
*Official Name:* Machine Gun, Caliber .30, M1919A4
*Common Name:* M1919A4 Browning LMG

*Remarks:* OBSOLETE. W/ equipment, NSN 1005-00-672-1643 metal links only. NSN 1005-00-672-1644 uses both fabric belts and metal links. W/o equipment, NSN 1005-00-714-2393.

• *Cal.:* 7.62 x 63mm
*Official Name:* Machine Gun, Caliber .30, M1919A4E1

*Remarks:* OBSOLETE. NSN 1005-00-716-2922. This gun was used as an armor machine gun by the US Marine Corps and has a bar-type extension on the cocking handle.

• *Cal.:* 7.62 x 63mm
*Official Name:* Machine Gun, Caliber .30, M1919A6
*Common Name:* M1919A6 Browning LMG

*Remarks:* OBSOLETE. NSN 1005-00-611-6005 (PN 8429944), w/ chrome-plated trunnion block, w/ equipment. NSN 1005-00-672-1649 for older model w/ equipment.

• *Cal.:* 12.7 x 99mm
*Official Name:* Machine Gun, Caliber .50, M2 Water Cooled

*Remarks:* OBSOLETE. NSN 1005-00-672-1690.

• *Cal.:* 12.7 x 99mm
*Official Name:* Machine Gun, Caliber .50, M3

*Remarks:* OBSOLETE. NSN 1005-00-077-1658.

• *Cal.:* 12.7 x 99mm
*Official Name:* Machine Gun, Caliber .50, AN-M2

*Remarks:* OBSOLETE. NSN 1005-00-726-5644.

• *Cal.:* 12.7 x 99mm
*Official Name:* Machine Gun, Caliber .50, AN-M3

*Remarks:* OBSOLETE. NSN 1005-00-726-5650.

**AUTOMATIC CANNON:**

• *Cal.:* 20 x 110mmRB
*Official Name:* Cannon, Automatic 20mm, M3

*Remarks:* OBSOLETE. This gun is a variant of the Hispano-Suiza HS 404 automatic cannon. NSN 1005-00-672-4911.

• *Cal.:* 20 x 102mm
*Official Name:* Canon, automatic 20mm, M24A1

*Remarks:* Standard ? This is the Air Force version of the M3. It uses electrically primed ammunition. NSN 1005-00-723-8297.

• *Cal.:* 20 x 110mmRB
*Official Name:* Cannon, automatic 20mm, MK16, MOD 4

*Remarks:* Standard US Navy deck gun is derived from the HS404. This cannon is a rework of 1940s era 20 x 110 M3 aircraft cannon. This air-cooled weapon has been slowed down from 800 shots per minute to the 600 to 650 s.p.m. range. In addition, its percussion-primed ammunition is lubricated by a special oiler mechanism that has been added to the deck-mounted version. The MOD 4 gun has an electrical trigger mechanism (altered AN-M4).

• *Cal.:* 20 x 110mmRB
*Official Name:* Cannon, automatic 20mm, MK16, MOD 5

*Remarks:* This standard US Navy deck gun is basically the same as the MOD 4 gun, except that it has a hand-pulled, stepped mechanical trigger. About 5,000 of the MK 16 series guns were delivered for patrol boat and other use in Vietnam. It is also the standard 20mm deck gun for the US Coast Guard, and the conversion program continues to support Navy and Coast Guard requirements. In recent years, the US Navy has been cannabalizing M24 aircraft guns (from which 90% of the parts can be used) for their continuing program to convert M3 AC guns to MK 16 cannon. Both the MOD 4 and the MOD 5 use the M6 (modified) charger; the M2E7 (LH or RH) feed mechanism; and the M8 or M10 link. Both weapons fire the M99 series of ammunition, which includes the M95 APT; the M96 INC; M97 HEI, and M99 TP.

- *Cal.:* 20 x 102mm
  *Official Name:* Cannon, automatic 20mm, M39A2
  *Common Name:* M39 revolver gun

*Remarks:* Standard ? Right-hand feed is NSN 1005-00-566-0044. Left-hand feed is NSN 1005-00-723-0045.

- *Cal.:* 20 x 102mm
  *Official Name:* Cannon, automatic 20mm, M39A3

*Remarks:* Standard ? NSN 1005-00-930-7786.

- *Cal.:* 20 x 102mm
  *Official Name:* Gun, automatic 20mm, M61, electrically driven
  *Common Name:* Vulcan/Gatling; T171E3

*Remarks:* Standard A. NSN 1005-00-520-2620. Manufactured by the Armaments Division of General Electric.

- *Cal.:* 20 x 139mm
  *Official Name:* Cannon, automatic 20mm, M139

*Remarks:* Standard A. NSN 1005-00-999-0896. This gun is the US version of HS820 cannon (Oerlikon KAD-B13-3).

- *Cal.:* 20 x 102mm
  *Official Name:* Gun, automatic 20mm, M168, electrically driven

*Remarks:* Standard A. NSN 1005-00-895-3726. Made by General Electric. Used in the M167A1 towed and M163A1 self-propelled Vulcan Air Defense Systems (VADS). The M167 system, NSN 1005-00-999-4391. The M167E1 system, NSN 1005-01-014-0837. The M167A1 system, NSN 1005-01-177-9237.

- *Cal.:* 20 x 102mm
  *Official Name:* Gun, automatic 20mm, M195, electrically driven
  *Common Name:* Gatling

*Remarks:* NSN 1005-00-133-8215. General Electric.

- *Cal.:* 20 x 102mm
  *Official Name:* Gun, automatic 20mm, M197E1, electrically driven
  *Common Name:* 3-barrel Gatling

*Remarks:* Standard A. NSN 1005-00-409-9483. General Electric.

- *Cal.:* 25 x 137mm
  *Official Name:* Gun, automatic 25mm, M242
  *Common Name:* Hughes Chain Gun; 25mm Bushmaster

*Remarks:* Standard A. NSN 1005-01-086-1400. Basic armament for the Bradley M2 Infantry Fighting Vehicle. This weapon is also used by the US Marine Corps (vehicles) and the US Navy (ships). Made by McDonnell-Douglas Helicopters, Inc. (successor to Hughes Helicopters). By early 1987, over 3,500 had been delivered to US services. The Spanish government ordered about 200 of these guns in 1987.

**GRENADE LAUNCHERS:**
- *Cal.:* 40 x 46mmSR
  *Official Name:* Grenade Launcher 40mm, M79

*Remarks:* Standard A. NSN 1010-00-691-1382.

- *Cal.:* 40 x 46mmSR
  *Official Name:* Grenade Launcher 40mm, XM148

*Remarks:* OBSOLETE. NSN 1010-00-912-3014. Attached to the M16 rifle.

- *Cal.:* 40 x 46mmSR
  *Official Name:* Grenade Launcher 40mm, M203

*Remarks:* Standard A since 1969. NSN 1010-00-179-6447. Made by Colt. Attaches to M16 rifle.

- *Cal.:* 40 x 53mmSR
  *Official Name:* Grenade Launcher, Aircraft, 40mm, M75

*Remarks:* Standard A. NSN 1010-00-738-5810. The Armament Subsystem, Helicopter, 40mm, grenade launcher M5 is NSN 1010-00-953-9073.

- *Cal.:* 40 x 53mmSR
  *Official Name:* Grenade Launcher, Aircraft, 40mm, M129

*Remarks:* Standard A. NSN 1010-00-781-9953. Externally powered, belt-fed helicopter weapon.

- *Cal.:* 40 x 53mmSR
  *Official Name:* Grenade Launcher 40mm, M182

  *Remarks:* Class S. NSN 1010-00-133-8377.

- *Cal.:* 40 x 53mmSR
  *Official Name:* Machine Gun, Grenade Launching, 40mm MK 19 MOD 0

  *Remarks:* OBSOLETE. NSN 1010-00-124-8610.

- *Cal.:* 40 x 53mmSR
  *Official Name:* Machine Gun, Grenade Launching, 40mm MK 19 MOD 3

  *Remarks:* Standard A since 1983. NSN 1010-01-126-9063. Made by the Naval Ordnance Station, Louisville, Kentucky, and Saco Defense Systems Division.

- *Cal.:* 40 x 53mmSR
  *Official Name:* Machine Gun, Grenade Launching, 40mm MK 20

  *Remarks:* OBSOLETE. NSN 1010-00-130-6351.

**Smith & Wesson Handgun Model Numbering System**

(All models are revolvers unless noted as being for a self-loading pistol.)

| MODEL | YEAR INTRODUCED | YEAR DISCONTINUED | FRAME MARKING | FRAME SIZE | CALIBER | DESCRIPTIVE NOTES |
|---|---|---|---|---|---|---|
| 10 | 1899 | | | K | .38 SPL | Originally called the Military & Police model. Frame numbering system started in 1957. |
| 10HB | 1960 | | | K | .38 SPL | Frame numbering system started in 1957. |
| 10 | 1959 | | 10-1 | K | .38 SPL | Designation for heavy barrel. |
| 10 | 1961 | | 10-2 | K | .38 SPL | Changed extractor rod from right-hand thread to left-hand thread on standard-barrel model. |
| 10 | 1961 | | 10-3 | K | .38 SPL | Same as above on heavy-barrel model and front sight changed from .254mm to .317mm. |
| 10 | 1962 | | 10-4 | K | .38 SPL | Screw in front of trigger eliminated. |
| 10 | 1962 | | 10-5 | K | .38 SPL | Front sight changed from .254mm to .317mm on standard barrel model. |
| 10 | 1962 | | 10-6 | K | .38 SPL | Screw in front of trigger eliminated on heavy-barrel model. |
| 10 | 1977 | | 10-7 | K | .38 SPL | Change to put gas ring from yoke to the cylinder. |
| 10 | 1977 | | 10-8 | K | .38 SPL | Change to put gas ring from yoke to the cylinder on heavy-barrel model. |
| 11 | 1938 | 1965 | | K | .38 S&W | Military & Police. No dash numbers. |
| 12 | 1953 | 1986 | | KA | .38 SPL | Military & Police airweight. This revolver was used by the US Air Force as the M13 – "Air Crewman." This revolver had an aluminum alloy frame. Frame numbering system started in 1957. |
| 12 | 1962 | | 12-1 | KA | .38 SPL | Changed extractor rod from right-hand thread to left-hand thread, and eliminated screw in front of trigger guard. |
| 12 | 1962 | | 12-2 | KA | .38 SPL | Front sight changed from .254mm to .317mm on standard barrel model. |
| 12 | 1977 | | 12-3 | KA | .38 SPL | Change to put gas ring from yoke to the cylinder. |

## Smith & Wesson Handgun Model Numbering System (continued)

| MODEL | YEAR INTRODUCED | YEAR DISCONTINUED | FRAME MARKING | FRAME SIZE | CALIBER | DESCRIPTIVE NOTES |
|---|---|---|---|---|---|---|
| (All models are revolvers unless noted as being for a self-loading pistol.) | | | | | | |
| 12 | 1984 | | 12-4 | KA | .38 SPL | Change frame thickness to same as all K frames. |
| 13 | 1974 | | 13-1 | K | .357 Mag | .357 Magnum Military & Police. No designation used to avoid confusion with the USAF Model 13 Air Crewman. Originally marked 13-1 upon introduction. |
| 13 | 1977 | | 13-2 | K | .357 Mag | Changed to have gas ring on the cylinder. |
| 13 | 1982 | 1982 | 13-3 | K | .357 Mag | Elimination of cylinder counterbore. |
| 14 | 1946 | | | KT | .38 SPL | K-38 Masterpiece. Frame numbering system started in 1957. |
| 14 | 1959 | | 14-1 | KT | .38 SPL | Change right-hand to left-hand thread. |
| 14 | 1961 | | 14-2 | KT | .38 SPL | Cylinder stop changed; hole in front of trigger guard eliminated. |
| 14 | 1967 | | 14-3 | KT | .38 SPL | Relocation of rear sight leaf screw. |
| 14 | 1977 | | 14-4 | KT | .38 SPL | Change from gas ring on yoke to cylinder. |
| 15 | 1949 | | | KT | .38 SPL | K-38 Combat Masterpiece. Frame numbering system started in 1957. Dash system follows same pattern as the M14. |
| 16 | 1947 | 1973 | | KT | .32 S&W | .32 S&W Long. K-32 Masterpiece. Frame numbering system started in 1957. Dash system follows same pattern as the M14. |
| 17 | 1946 | | | KT | .22 LR | .22 Long Rifle. K-22 Masterpiece. Frame numbering system started in 1957. Dash system follows same pattern as the M14. |
| 18 | 1949 | 1986 | | KT | .22 LR | .22 Long Rifle. K-22 Combat Masterpiece. Frame numbering system started in 1957. Dash system follows same pattern as the M14. |
| 19 | 1955 | | | KT | .357 Mag | .357 Combat Magnum. Frame numbering system started in 1957. Dash system follows same pattern as the M14, with the exception of the 19-5 in which the counterbore was eliminated. |

| | | | | | | |
|---|---|---|---|---|---|---|
| 20 | 1930 | 1966 | | N | .38 S&W SPL | .38/44 Heavy Duty. Frame numbering begins in 1957. Dash numbers 1 to 3 follow pattern of the M14. |
| 21 | 1908 | 1966 | | N | .44 S&W SPL | .44 S&W Special. Also called the 1950 Model .44 Military. Dash numbers 1 to 3 follow pattern of the M14. The Dash 3s introduced in 1982 eliminated the counterbore on the Magnum models only. |
| 22 | 1917 | 1966 | | N | .45 ACP | Also called the Model 1917 S&W revolver by the US military and later the 1950 Model .45 Military by S&W. Dash numbers 1 to 2 follow pattern of the M14. |
| 23 | 1931 | 1966 | | NT | .38 S&W SPL | .38/44 Outdoorsman. Dash numbers 1 to 2 follow pattern of the M14. |
| 24 | 1908 | 1966 | | NT | .44 S&W SPL | 1950 Model .44 Target. Dash numbers 1 to 2 follow pattern of the M14. |
| 25 | 1955 | 1983 | | NT | .45 ACP | 1955 Model .45 Target. Dash numbers 1 to 2 follow pattern of the M14. |
| 25 | 1977 | 1977 | 25-3 | NT | .45 Colt | 125th Anniversary Commemorative. |
| 25 | 1977 | 1977 | 25-4 | NT | .45 Colt | 125th Anniversary Deluxe Commemorative. |
| 25 | 1978 | 1978 | 25-5 | NT | .45 Colt | The Dash 5 indicates the .45 Colt caliber. |
| 26 | 1950 | 1966 | | NT | .45 ACP | 1950 Model .45 Target Light Barrel. Follows frame numbering scheme of Model 20 after 1957. |
| 27 | 1935 | | | NT | .357 Mag | .357 Magnum. Follows frame numbering scheme of Model 20 after 1957. |
| 28 | 1954 | | | NT | .357 Mag | .357 Highway Patrolman. Follows frame numbering scheme of Model 20 after 1957. |
| 29 | 1955 | | | NT | .44 Mag | .44 Magnum. Follows frame numbering scheme of Model 20 after 1957. |
| 30 | 1896 | 1976 | | I&J | .32 S&W | .32 S&W Long. .32 Hand Ejector. |
| 31 | 1917 | | | I&J | .32 S&W | .32 S&W Long. .32 Regulation Police. |
| 32 | 1936 | 1974 | | I&J | .38 S&W | .38 Terrier. |
| 33 | 1917 | | | I&J | .38 S&W | .38 Regulation Police. |
| 34 | 1936 | | | I&J | .22 LR | .22/32 Kit Gun with 102mm barrel. |
| 35 | 1911 | 1973 | | I&J | .22 LR | .22/32 Target with 153mm barrel. |

## Smith & Wesson Handgun Model Numbering System (continued)

(All models are revolvers unless noted as being for a self-loading pistol.)

| MODEL | YEAR INTRODUCED | YEAR DISCONTINUED | FRAME MARKING | FRAME SIZE | CALIBER | DESCRIPTIVE NOTES |
|---|---|---|---|---|---|---|
| 36 | 1950 | | | J | .38 S&W SPL | .38 Chief Special. |
| 37 | 1952 | | | JA | .38 S&W SPL | .38 Chief Special Airweight. |
| 38 | 1955 | | | JAC | .38 S&W SPL | .38 Bodyguard. |
| 39 | 1954 | 1981 | Automatic pistol | | 9 x 19mm | 9mm Parabellum automatic pistol. |
| 39-1 | 1960 | 1960 | Automatic pistol | | .38 AMU | More commonly called the M-52A. Has an aluminum frame. Only 87 manufactured. |
| 39-2 | 1971 | | Automatic pistol | | 9 x 19mm | 9mm Parabellum. Pistol had a new extractor. |
| 40 | 1952 | 1974 | | JS | .38 S&W SPL | Centennial. |
| 41 | 1957 | | | Automatic | .22 LR | .22 Semiautomatic. |
| 41-1 | 1960 | 1972 | | Automatic | .22 Short | .22 Short Semiautomatic. |
| 42 | 1953 | 1974 | | JSA | .38 S&W SPL | Centennial Airweight. |
| 43 | 1954 | 1974 | | JAT | .22 LR | .22/32 Chief Special Target. |
| 44 | 1954 | 1959 | | Automatic | 9mm | 9 x 19mm Parabellum single action automatic. |
| 45 | 1936 | 1965 | | K | .22 LR | .22 Military & Police. |
| 46 | 1959 | 1968 | | Automatic | .22 LR | .22 Semiautomatic. |
| 47 | | | Experimental number used on several handguns. | | | |
| 48 | 1959 | 1986 | | KTM | .22 WMRF | K-22 Masterpiece MRF. |
| 49 | 1959 | | | JC | .38 S&W SPL | Bodyguard Steel Frame. |
| 50 | 1955 | 1975 | | JT | .38 S&W SPL | Chief Special Target. |
| 51 | 1960 | 1974 | | JTM | .22 WMRF | .22/32 MRF Kit Gun. |
| 52 | 1961 | | | Automatic | .38 S&W SPL | .38 Master. |
| 52-1 | 1963 | | | Automatic | .38 S&W SPL | Single-action only. |
| 52-2 | 1971 | | | Automatic | .38 S&W SPL | New extractor. |
| 52-A | | | See Model 39-1. | | | |
| 53 | 1961 | 1974 | | KTC | .22 Jet | .22 Center Fire Magnum. |
| 54-55 | | | Neither number used. | | | |

| Model | Year | Year | Frame | Caliber | Description |
| --- | --- | --- | --- | --- | --- |
| 56 | 1962 | 1963 | KT | .38 S&W SPL | KTX 38 – Became Model 15 with 50.8mm barrel. |
| 57 | 1964 | 1978 | NT | .41 Magnum | |
| 58 | 1964 | 1981 | N | .41 Magnum | |
| 59 | 1971 | | Automatic | 9 x 19mm | 9mm Parabellum w/ 14-shot magazine. No dash numbers used. |
| 60 | 1965 | 1970 | J | .38 S&S SPL | .38 Chief Special Stainless. |
| 61 | 1973 | 1970 | Automatic | .22 LR | .22 Escort. |
| 61-1 | 1973 | 1970 | Automatic | .22 LR | .22 Escort, w/ magazine safety. |
| 61-2 | 1973 | 1970 | Automatic | .22 LR | .22 Escort, w/ barrel nut. |
| 61-3 | 1973 | 1970 | Automatic | .22 LR | .22 Escort, w/ forged aluminum frame. |
| 62 | | | | | Experimental not assigned to a production model. |
| 63 | 1977 | | JT | .22 LR | 1977 .22/32 Kit Gun Stainless. |
| 64 | 1970 | | K | .38 S&W SPL | .38 Military & Police Stainless. |
| 64 | 1971 | | K | .38 S&W SPL | .38 Military & Police Stainless w/ heavy-weight barrel. |
| 64 | 1977 | | K | .38 S&W SPL | .38 Military & Police Stainless w/ 50.8mm barrel and change of gas ring from yoke to cylinder. |
| 64 | 1977 | | K | .38 S&W SPL | .38 Military & Police Stainless w/ 50.8mm heavy barrel and change of gas ring from yoke to cylinder. |
| 65-1 | 1974 | | K | .357 Mag | .357 Magnum Military & Police Stainless. |
| 65-2 | 1977 | | K | .357 Mag | .357 Magnum Military & Police Stainless w/ change of gas ring from yoke to cylinder. |
| 65-3 | 1982 | | K | .357 Mag | .357 Magnum Military & Police Stainless w/ cylinder counterbore eliminated. |
| 66 | 1971 | | KT | .357 Mag | .357 Magnum Combat Magnum Stainless. |
| 66-1 | 1977 | | KT | .357 Mag | .357 Magnum Combat Magnum Stainless w/ change of gas ring from yoke to cylinder. |
| 66-2 | 1982 | | KT | .357 Mag | .357 Magnum Combat Magnum Stainless w/ cylinder counterbore eliminated. |
| 67 | 1972 | | KT | .38 S&W SPL | .38 Combat Masterpiece Stainless. |
| 67-1 | 1977 | | KT | .38 S&W SPL | .38 Combat Masterpiece Stainless with change of gas ring from yoke to cylinder. |

**Smith & Wesson Handgun Model Numbering System (continued)**

(All models are revolvers unless noted as being for a self-loading pistol.)

| MODEL | YEAR INTRODUCED | YEAR DISCONTINUED | FRAME MARKING | FRAME SIZE | CALIBER | DESCRIPTIVE NOTES |
|---|---|---|---|---|---|---|
| 68 | 1976 | 1976 | 68 | KT | .38 S&W SPL | .38 Combat California Highway Patrol Stainless. |
| | | | 69 to 75 used only on experimental models. | | | |
| 76 | 1968 | 1974 | | SMG | 9 x 19mm | 9mm Parabellum submachine gun. |
| | | | 77 to 80 used only for air guns. | | | |
| 147-A | 1979 | 1979 | 147-A | Automatic | 9 x 19mm | 9mm automatic, 14-shot, double action steel frame Model 59 pistol. |
| 439 | 1980 | | 439 | Automatic | 9 x 19mm | 9mm automatic, 8-shot, double action pistol. Alloy frame. Note that the "4" indicates alloy frame; a "5" indicates blued steel frame; and a "6" indicates a stainless steel frame. |
| 459 | 1980 | | 459 | Automatic | 9 x 19mm | 9mm automatic, 14-shot, double action pistol. |
| 469 | 1983 | | 469 | Automatic | 9 x 19mm | 9mm automatic, 12-shot, double action pistol. |
| 520 | 1980 | | 520 | N | .357 Mag | |
| 539 | 1980 | | 539 | Automatic | 9 x 19mm | 9mm automatic, 8-shot, double action pistol. Alloy frame. Note that the "4" indicates alloy frame; a "5" indicates blued steel frame; and a "6" indicates a stainless steel frame. |
| 547 | 1980 | 1985 | 547 | K | 9 x 19mm | |

| Model | 1980 | 1983 | Action | Caliber | Description |
|---|---|---|---|---|---|
| 559 | 1980 | 1983 | Automatic | 9 x 19mm | 9mm automatic, 14-shot, double action pistol. |
| 581 | 1980 | | L | .357 Mag | .357 Distinguished Service Magnum. |
| 586 | 1980 | | L | .357 Mag | .357 Distinguished Combat Magnum. |
| 624 | 1985 | 1986 | NT | .44 S&W SPL | 1985 .44 Target Stainless. |
| 629 | 1979 | 1986 | NT | .44 Mag | .44 Magnum Stainless. |
| 639 | 1982 | | Automatic | 9 x 19mm | 9mm automatic, 8-shot, double action pistol. |
| 645 | 1985 | | Automatic | .45 ACP | .45 double action. |
| 649 | 1985 | | JC | .38 S&W SPL | .38 Bodyguard Stainless. |
| 650 | 1982 | | JM | .22 WMRF | .22 WMRF Service Kit Gun Stainless. |
| 651 | 1982 | | JTM | .22 WMRF | .22 WMRF Target Kit Gun Stainless. |
| 659 | 1982 | | Automatic | 9 x 19mm | 9mm automatic, 14-shot, double action pistol. |
| 669 | 1985 | | Automatic | 9 x 19mm | 9mm automatic, 12-shot, double action pistol. |
| 681 | 1980 | | L | .357 Mag | .357 Distinguished Service Magnum. |
| 686 | 1980 | | L | .357 Mag | .357 Distinguished Combat Magnum. |

*Notes*

Frame sizes: 
I — Original small .32 caliber frame
K — Medium frame
J — Small caliber frame
L — Large frame, K grip size
N — Large frame
KTC — Medium frame target center fire Magnum (.22 Jet)

A — Aluminum alloy
C — Shrouded hammer
S — Concealed hammer
T — Target
M — Magnum rim fire

The frame numbering system began in 1957. If a Smith & Wesson handgun does not have a frame number, it was manufactured before 1957.

*Sources:* Adapted from Roy G. Jinks, "Smith & Wesson Model Numbers," *American Rifleman* (July 1986), 41–43, and Roy G. Jinks, *History of Smith & Wesson* (North Hollywood, Cal.: Beinfeld Publishing, Inc., 1977).

## UPPER VOLTA (Republic of) Now called Burkina Faso

Population (estimate in 1984): 6.73 million. Ground forces: regulars, ca. 3,900; paramilitary gendarmerie, ca. 1,900.

**HANDGUNS:**
- *Cal.:* 7.65 x 17mm Browning
  *Common Name:* Walther PP

  *Remarks:* Manurhin-made copy.

- *Cal.:* 9 x 19mm NATO
  *Common Name:* MAB PA-15

  *Remarks:* Manufacture d'Armes de Bayonne (MAB).

- *Cal.:* 9 x 29mmR
  *Common Name:* .357 Manurhin
  MR-73 revolver

  *Remarks:* Manurhin-made

**SUBMACHINE GUNS:**
- *Cal.:* 7.65 x 20mm
  *Common Name:* MAS Mle. 38
  submachine gun

  *Remarks:* Manufacture Nationale d'Armes de St. Etienne (MAS).

- *Cal.:* 9 x 19mm NATO
  *Common Name:* MAT Mle. 49
  submachine gun

  *Remarks:* Manufacture Nationale d'Armes de Tulle (MAT).

- *Cal.:* 9 x 19mm NATO
  *Common Name:* Beretta Model 12
  submachine gun

  *Remarks:* Beretta, Italy.

**RIFLES:**
- *Cal.:* 5.56 x 45mm
  *Common Name:* SG540 rifle

  *Remarks:* Manurhin-made SIG rifle.

- *Cal.:* 5.56 x 45mm
  *Common Name:* AR70/223 rifle

  *Remarks:* Beretta, Italy.

- *Cal.:* 7.5 x 54mm
  *Common Name:* MAS Mle. 36
  bolt action rifle

  *Remarks:* MAS, France.

- *Cal.:* 7.5 x 54mm
  *Common Name:* MAS Mle. 49/56
  rifle

  *Remarks:* MAS.

- *Cal.:* 7.62 x 51mm NATO
  *Common Name: Gewehr 3*

  *Remarks:* Heckler & Koch (HK) design made at MAS in France.

**SHOTGUNS:**

**MACHINE GUNS:**
- *Cal.:* 7.5 x 54mm
  *Common Name:* AAT52 GPMG

  *Remarks:* MAT, France. Reportedly the AAT 52s mounted on the Panhard AML 60 and AML 90 APCs are 7.62mm NATO.

- *Cal.:* 7.5 x 54mm
  *Common Name:* MAC Mle. 24/29
  LMG

  *Remarks:* Manufacture Nationale d'Armes de Chatellerault (MAC).

- *Cal.:* 7.62 x 51mm NATO
  *Common Name:* FN MAG

  *Remarks:* FN origin?

- *Cal.:* 12.7 x 99mm
  *Common Name:* .50 M2 HB
  HMG

  *Remarks:* US origin.

**AUTOMATIC CANNON:**

## URUGUAY (Oriental Republic of)

Population (estimate in 1984): 2.93 million. Ground forces: regulars, between 20,000 and 23,000; reserves, ca. 120,000; paramilitary: gendarmerie, 2,200; Republican Guard, 520; Metropolitan Guard, 650; National Police, 22,000.

### HANDGUNS:

• *Cal.:* 9 x 17mm Browning
*Common Name:* HK-4 pistol

*Remarks:* Heckler & Koch (HK), GmbH. A few hundred purchased and issued to Army officers as an off-duty side arm.

• *Cal.:* 9 x 17mm Browning
*Common Name:* Model 84 pistol

*Remarks:* Beretta, Italy. Issued to Army officers as an off-duty side arm.

• *Cal.:* 9 x 19mm Parabellum
*Common Name:* FN Mle. 1935 GP pistol

*Remarks:* Argentine origin. Made at the Fabrica Militar de Armas Portatiles "Domingo Matheu," Rosario, Argentina (FMAP "DM"). Used by Army, Navy, and Air Force officers.

• *Cal.:* 9 x 19mm Parabellum
*Common Name:* Walther P38

*Remarks:* Postwar commercial. Used only by Army officers.

• *Cal.:* 9 x 19mm Parabellum
*Common Name:* SIG P220

*Remarks:* Schweizerische Industrie Gesellschaft/Rheinfalls (SIG)-Sauer origin. Used only by Navy officers.

• *Cal.:* 9 x 19mm Parabellum
*Common Name:* HK P7M8 pistol

*Remarks:* HK GmbH. Marked ROUMI (Republica Oriental de Uruguay Ministerio de Interior).

• *Cal.:* 9 x 29mmR
*Common Name:* Smith & Wesson M10 revolver

*Remarks:* Smith & Wesson, US. Marked ROUMI (Republica Oriental de Uruguay Ministerio de Interior).

• *Cal.:* 9 x 29mmR
*Common Name:* .38 Colt Detective Special revolver

*Remarks:* MAP delivered 375 revolvers before 1974 with round butt and 51mm barrel. NSN 1005-00-726-5655.

• *Cal.:* 9 x 29mmR
*Common Name:* .38 Caliber S&W Model 15 revolver

*Remarks:* MAP delivered a total of 43 units in 1974 w/102mm barrel. NSN 1005-00-973-2058.

• *Cal.:* 11.43 x 23mm
*Common Name:* .45 M1911A1 pistol

*Remarks:* MAP before 1974. Ca. 1,500 units.

### SUBMACHINE GUNS:

• *Cal.:* 9 x 19mm Parabellum
*Common Name:* FMK 3 (PAM 3 DM) submachine gun

*Remarks:* FMAP "DM" origin. Used by Army. Reported to be scheduled for disposal.

• *Cal.:* 9 x 19mm Parabellum
*Common Name:* MP5 and MP5SD submachine guns

*Remarks:* HK GmbH. Used by the *Servicio de Informacion de Defensa* (Defense Intelligence Service).

• *Cal.:* 9 x 19mm Parabellum
*Common Name:* Mini-Uzi submachine gun

*Remarks:* Israeli Military Industries (IMI), Israel. 14 purchased to arm guards who protect the senior generals. The Mini-Uzi replaces a similar number of 9 x 17mm MAC-10 submachine guns.

• *Cal.:* 9 x 19mm Parabellum
*Common Name:* Star Z45 submachine gun

*Remarks:* Star Bonafacio Echeverria, S.A., Spain.

• *Cal.:* 11.43 x 23mm
*Common Name:* .45 M3 and M3A1 submachine guns

*Remarks:* MAP before 1974. Ca. 150 M3 and 5,421 M3A1. Used by Navy and Air Force.

• *Cal.:* 11.43 x 23mm
*Official Name:* .45 M1928 and M1
Thompson submachine guns

*Remarks:* MAP. Used by Navy and Air Force.

## RIFLES:

• *Cal.:* 5.56 x 45mm
*Common Name:* M16A1 rifle

*Remarks:* Captured former Communist Party members who had ca. 600 M16A1 rifles from Vietnamese sources.

• *Cal.:* 7.62 x 33mm
*Common Name:* .30 M1 and M2 carbines

*Remarks:* MAP and FMS before 1974. MAP: Ca. 8,000 M1 and 1,000 M2. FMS: 23,349 M2. Some may still be used by the Navy; others are in reserve stocks. Also a very small number of M1A1 carbines.

• *Cal.:* 7.62 x 51mm NATO
*Common Name:* FN FAL II

*Remarks:* FMAP "DM," Argentine origin. Army also purchases the HK .22 long rifle adapter kit for training with this rifle.

• *Cal.:* 7.62 x 63mm
*Common Name:* .30 M1 rifle

*Remarks:* MAP before 1974. Ca. 8,000 units.

• *Cal.:* 7.62 x 63mm
*Common Name:* .30 M1C sniper rifle

*Remarks:* MAP before 1974. Ca. 36 units.

• *Cal.:* 7.62 x 63mm
*Common Name:* .30 M1D sniper rifle

*Remarks:* MAP before 1974. Ca. 525 units.

• *Cal.:* 7.62 x 63mm
*Common Name:* .30 M1903A4 sniper rifle

*Remarks:* MAP.

## OBSOLETE RIFLES:

• *Cal.:* 7 x 57mm
*Common Name:* M1908 Mauser rifles

*Remarks:* DWM, Germany. These and all other 7 x 57mm rifles have been withdrawn from service. Many were sold to Waffen-Frankonia of West Germany, ca. 1984. Remainder will probably be surplussed in the near future.

• *Cal.:* 7 x 57mm
*Common Name:* Mauser Model 1924 bolt action rifle

*Remarks:* Pre-1945 Czechoslovakia. Sold to Waffen-Frankonia.

• *Cal.:* 7 x 57mm
*Common Name:* Mauser Model 1927 bolt action rifle

*Remarks:* Fabrica de Armas de Oviedo, Spain. Sold?

## SHOTGUNS:

• *Cal.:* 18.5 x 59mm
*Common Name:* 12-gage Remington Model 870 automatic shotgun

*Remarks:* Remington, US. Both wooden and folding stock models are in use. Some 700 are marked with the Uruguayan national crest. More recently 18-inch and 20-inch barrel models have been purchased by the Republica Oriental de Uruguay Ministerio de Interior (marked ROUMI).

• *Cal.:* 18.5 x 59mm
*Common Name:* 12-gage Winchester Model 12 shotgun

*Remarks:* MAP delivered ca. 120 units before 1974.

• *Cal.:* 18.5 x 59mm
*Common Name:* 12-gage Winchester Model 1200 automatic shotgun

*Remarks:* MAP before 1974. Ca. 12 units.

• *Cal.:* 18.5 x 59mm
*Common Name:* 12-gage Stevens M77E shotgun

*Remarks:* MAP before 1974. Ca. 50 units.

**MACHINE GUNS:**
- *Cal.:* 7.62 x 51mm NATO
  *Common Name:* FAP

*Remarks:* FMAP "DM," Argentine origin.

- *Cal.:* 7.62 x 51mm NATO
  *Common Name:* FN MAG

*Remarks:* Belgian origin. MAG *Infanterie Standard* (60-20), T9; MAG *Aviation* (60-30), P.935 right-hand and left-hand feed; MAG *Coaxial* (60-40), T3 (MAG 58). The latter is used on the FN-made 4RM/62F AB light armored car.

- *Cal.:* 7.62 x 63mm
  *Common Name:* .30 M1918A2 BAR

*Remarks:* MAP. Ca. 1,200 units before 1975.

- *Cal.:* 7.62 x 51mm NATO
  *Common Name:* .30 M1919A1 LMG

*Remarks:* MAP. Sent to FN, Herstal, and converted to 7.62mm NATO.

- *Cal.:* 7.62 x 51mm NATO
  *Common Name:* .30 M1919A4 LMG

*Remarks:* MAP. Sent to FN, Herstal, and converted to 7.62mm NATO for armored vehicles.

- *Cal.:* 7.62 x 51mm NATO
  *Common Name:* M1919A6 LMG

*Remarks:* MAP. Sent to FN, Herstal, and converted to 7.62mm NATO.

- *Cal.:* 7.62 x 63mm
  *Common Name:* .30 Madsen LMG

*Remarks:* Danish origin.

- *Cal.:* 12.7 x 99mm
  *Common Name:* .50 M2 HB HMG

*Remarks:* MAP. Used in ground, vehicle, and ship mounts.

**OBSOLETE MACHINE GUNS:**
- *Cal.:* 7 x 57mm
  *Common Name:* Hotchkiss LMGs and HMGs

*Remarks:* OBSOLETE, but held in reserve pending disposal.

- *Cal.:* 7 x 57mm
  *Common Name:* ZB30 LMG

*Remarks:* OBSOLETE, but held in reserve pending disposal.

**AUTOMATIC CANNON:**
- *Cal.:* 20 x 102mm
  *Common Name:* 20mm Vulcan automatic cannon on the M167 Vulcan Air Defense System (VADS)

*Remarks:* USA and Korean origin. About 6 of these AA units in service.

## VANUATU (Republic of) Formerly the New Hebrides

Population (estimate in 1984): 0.130 million. Ground forces: regulars, unknown; reserves, unknown; paramilitary, unknown.

**HANDGUNS:**

**SUBMACHINE GUNS:**

**RIFLES:**

**SHOTGUNS:**

**MACHINE GUNS:**
* *Cal.:* 7.62 x 51mm NATO        *Remarks:* FN, Herstal, Belgium.
  *Common Name:* FN MAG

**AUTOMATIC CANNON:**

## VENEZUELA (Republic of)

Population (estimate in 1984): 18.55 million. Ground forces: regulars, ca. 28,000 plus 4,250 Marine infantry; paramilitary Guardia Nacional, between 18,000 and 20,000.

**HANDGUNS:**
* *Cal.:* 9 x 17mm Browning
  *Common Name:* HK-4 pistol

  *Remarks:* Heckler & Koch (HK), GmbH. A few hundred purchased in 1984.

* *Cal.:* 9 x 19mm Parabellum
  *Common Name:* FN Mle. 1935 GP pistol

  *Remarks:* FN origin.

* *Cal.:* 9 x 19mm Parabellum
  *Common Name:* Smith & Wesson automatic pistols; models unknown

  *Remarks:* US origin. State Department licensed sales include 50 revolvers to the Military State Police; and 300 to the Traffic Police.

* *Cal.:* 9 x 29mmR
  *Common Name:* .38 Smith & Wesson revolvers; models unknown

  *Remarks:* US origin. State Department licensed sales include 1,000 revolvers to the Military State Police; 1,000 for the Judicial Police; 2,000 for the Traffic Police in the Ministry of Commerce; 123 for the Governacion State Police; and 133 for the Trujillo Police in 1976. In 1977, 1,500 revolvers to the Military State Police. In 1978, the Ministry of Defense acquired 200 revolvers.

* *Cal.:* 9 x 29mmR
  *Common Name:* .357 Smith & Wesson revolvers; models unknown

  *Remarks:* US origin. State Department licensed sales include 2 revolvers to the Governacion State Police in 1976.

* *Cal.:* 9 x 29mmR
  *Common Name:* .38 Colt revolvers; models unknown

  *Remarks:* US origin. State Department licensed sales include in 1976, 50 revolvers; in 1977, 1,336 revolvers; and in 1978, 330 revolvers for the Judicial Police.

* *Cal.:* 11.43 x 23mm
  *Common Name:* .45 M1911A1 Colt government model

  *Remarks:* US origin. State Department licensed sales include in 1977, 100 pistols; and in 1978, 330 pistols for the Judicial Police.

**SUBMACHINE GUNS:**
* *Cal.:* 9 x 19mm Parabellum
  *Common Name:* Uzi submachine gun

  *Remarks:* Israeli Military Industries (IMI) and FN origin.

* *Cal.:* 9 x 19mm Parabellum
  *Common Name:* Model 12 submachine gun

  *Remarks:* Beretta, Italy.

* *Cal.:* 9 x 19mm Parabellum
  *Common Name:* Walther MP-K submachine gun

  *Remarks:* Walther, Germany.

* *Cal.:* 9 x 19mm Parabellum
  *Common Name:* Model 46 and Model 53 submachine guns

  *Remarks:* Madsen, Denmark.

- *Cal.:* 9 x 19mm Parabellum
  *Common Name:* MP5 submachine gun

- *Cal.:* 9 x 19mm Parabellum
  *Common Name:* Model 10 Ingram submachine gun

- *Cal.:* 9 x 19mm Parabellum
  *Common Name:* ZK 583 submachine gun

**RIFLES:**
- *Cal.:* 7.62 x 51mm NATO
  *Official Name: Fusil Automatico Livano*
  *Common Name:* FN FAL

- *Cal.:* 7.62 x 51mm NATO
  *Common Name:* M14 rifle

- *Cal.:* 7 x 57mm
  *Common Name:* FN SAFN 49 rifle

- *Cal.:* 7.62 x 63mm
  *Common Name:* Model unknown

- *Cal.:* 5.56 x 45mm
  *Common Name:* Ruger Mini-14 rifle

**SHOTGUNS:**
- *Cal.:* 18.5 x 59mm
  *Common Name:* 12 gage Mossberg Model 500 shotgun

- *Cal.:* 18.5 x 59mm
  *Common Name:* 12 gage Smith & Wesson police shotgun; model unknown

**MACHINE GUNS:**
- *Cal.:* 7.62 x 51m NATO
  *Official Name: Fusil Automatico Pesado*
  *Common Name:* FN FALO

- *Cal.:* 7.62 x 51mm NATO
  *Common Name:* M60C AC MG

- *Cal.:* 7.62 x 51mm NATO
  *Common Name:* M60D Door MG

- *Cal.:* 7.62 x 51mm NATO
  *Common Name:* FN MAG

- *Cal.:* 7.62 x 63mm
  *Common Name:* .30 M1919 LMG

*Remarks:* HK? The silenced MP5SD is also reported in service.

*Remarks:* RPB, Inc., US. State Department licesned sale of 60 in 1977 and 30 in 1978 for the Judicial Police.

*Remarks:* Czechoslovakian origin.

*Remarks:* Belgian and domestic origin. First 5,000 purchased in 1954 were 7 x 49.15mm. These were later converted to 7.62mm NATO. Ground forces FALs marked *Fuerzas Armadas de Venezuela.* Navy FALs marked *Fuerzas Navales de Venezuela.* In 1974 the National Guard purchased 10,000 FAL PARAs (50-63) with the super-short 436mm barrel without a bolt hold-open device or carrying handle. Made by C. A. Venezolana de Industrias Militares (CAVIM) under license from FN, Herstal.

*Remarks:* US origin. Ca. 6,700 US M14 rifles in country. Venezuela purchased 2 M14A1 rifles from the US in 1980. This may indicate plans to convert existing M14s to a squad automatic version.

*Remarks:* Belgian origin. Most of these have been sold as surplus to collectors.

*Remarks:* Prior to 1975, the US Military sold 55,671 .30 caliber rifles to Venezuela. It is believed that most of these were M1 rifles.

*Remarks:* Sturm, Ruger and Co., US.

*Remarks:* Official riot gun since 1981. Used by police and the National Guard.

*Remarks:* US origin. State Department licensed sale of 5 in 1976 for the State Police.

*Remarks:* FN origin. Some locally manufactured by CAVIM.

*Remarks:* US origin. FMS provided 62 in 1975.

*Remarks:* US origin. FMS provided 673 in 1975.

*Remarks:* FN origin. MAG *Infanterie* (60-20), T11 with M13 links.

*Remarks:* US origin. The US provided 18,740 .30 caliber machine guns through MAP before 1975.

• *Cal.:* 12.7 x 99mm
  *Common Name:* .50 M2 HB
  HMG

*Remarks:* US origin. This includes 139 before 1975 for the M1 Cupola.

**AUTOMATIC CANNON:**
• *Cal.:* 20 x 139mm
  *Common Name:* 20mm M693
  automatic

*Remarks:* Groupment Industriel des Armements Terrestres (GIAT), France. These guns are twin mounted on the French M3 VDA SP AA system. About a dozen of these systems are in service.

## VIETNAM (Socialist Republic of)

Population (estimate in 1984): 59.03 million. Ground forces: regulars, ca. 1,000,000; reserves (mixture of militia and various paramilitary organizations). The most important paramilitary organizations include: People's Self-Defense Force, 1,000,000; Armed Youth Assault Force, up to 1,500,000; People's Regional Militia Force, ca. 500,000; Border Defense Force, 60,000; Internal Security Force, ca. 70,000. Vietnam maintains the third largest army in Asia after the People's Republic of China and the Republic of India.

**HANDGUNS:**
• *Cal.:* 7.62 x 25mm
  *Common Name:* TT33 Tokarev
  pistol

*Remarks:* Soviet origin.

• *Cal.:* 7.62 x 25mm
  *Common Name:* Type 68, a variant of the TT33 pistol

*Remarks:* Domestic origin?

**SUBMACHINE GUNS:**
• *Cal.:* 7.62 x 25mm
  *Common Name:* Modified MAT
  49 submachine gun

*Remarks:* Domestic alteration of the MAT 49 that fires the 7.62 x 25mm cartridge. Receiver stamped on top rear with large "K" denoting alteration. FOM 1005-9-3-7.62-2.

• *Cal.:* 7.62 x 25mm
  *Common Name:* Modified PRC
  Type 50 submachine gun

*Remarks:* Domestic alteration of the Type 50 (PPSh41). Major changes included the elimination of wood butt stock and addition of MAT 49-type sliding wire stock and Type 56 (AK47) pistol grip. Forward end of barrel jacket eliminated to reduce weapon weight. Called K50M. FOM 1005-9-3-7.62-1.

**RIFLES:**
• *Cal.:* 7.62 x 39m
  *Common Name:* SKS carbine

*Remarks:* East Bloc origin.

• *Cal.:* 7.62 x 39mm
  *Common Name:* AK47 and AKM
  assault rifles

*Remarks:* East Bloc origin. Largely Soviet and People's Republic of China (PRC).

• *Cal.:* 7.62 x 54mmR
  *Common Name:* SVD sniper rifle

*Remarks:* East Bloc origin.

**SHOTGUNS:**

**MACHINE GUNS:**
• *Cal.:* 7.62 x 39mm
  *Official Name:* TUL-1
  *Common Name:* RPK-type
  weapon built from AK47

*Remarks:* Vietnamese adaptation of PRC Type 56 (AK47).

- *Cal.:* 7.62 x 39mm
  *Common Name:* RPD LMG

  *Remarks:* Soviet and PRC origin.

- *Cal.:* 7.62 x 54mmR
  *Common Name:* DPM LMG

  *Remarks:* Soviet and PRC Type 53.

- *Cal.:* 7.62 x 54mmR
  *Common Name:* SG43 and SGM
  vehicle MGs

  *Remarks:* Soviet origin.

- *Cal.:* 7.62 x 54mmR
  *Common Name:* Type 67 LMG

  *Remarks:* PRC origin.

- *Cal.:* 7.62 x 54mmR
  *Common Name:* PK series
  GPMGs

  *Remarks:* Soviet origin. Mounted on Soviet T62 tanks.

- *Cal.:* 12.7 x 108mm
  *Common Name:* DShK38/46
  HMG

## AUTOMATIC CANNON:

- *Cal.:* 14.5 x 114mm
  *Common Name:* KPV HMG

  *Remarks:* East Bloc origin. All models in use.

- *Cal.:* 23 x 152mmB
  *Common Name:* ZU23 automatic
  cannon

  *Remarks:* East Bloc origin. ZSU-1, ZSU-2, and self-propelled ZSU-23-4.

## United States Military Assistance Grant in Aid to the Republic of South Vietnam, 1950–75

| Weapon Type | 1950–64 | 1965 | 1966 | 1967 | 1968 | 1969 | 1970 | 1971 | 1972 | 1973 | 1974 | 1975 | Total |
|---|---|---|---|---|---|---|---|---|---|---|---|---|---|
| **HANDGUNS:** | | | | | | | | | | | | | |
| .38 Colt and S&W revolvers | 2,115 | | 70 | 1,278 | 29 | 1,293 | 4,016 | 1,397 | 2,250 | 82 | 10 | | 12,543 |
| .45 Cal. M1911A1 and other pistols | 20,789 | 4,056 | 3,284 | 5,278 | 10,064 | 29,248 | 515 | 9,447 | 7,839 | 10,493 | 644 | 2,200 | 104,867 |
| Subtotal | | | | | | | | | | | | | 117,410 |
| **SUBMACHINE GUNS:** | | | | | | | | | | | | | |
| M3 and M3A1, including 15 M1A1s in 1970, | 127 | 2 | 520 | 52 | 3 | | 103 | | 149 | 114 | | | 1,070 |
| 5.56mm XM177 and XM177E2 | | | | | | | | 64 | 83 | 157 | | | 304 |
| Subtotal | | | | | | | | | | | | | 1,374 |
| **RIFLES:** | | | | | | | | | | | | | |
| .30 M1/M2 carbines | 346,726 | 61,256 | 100,101 | 23,230 | 2,000 | 30 | 247,390 | 3,528 | 6,260 | 3,503 | | | 794,094 |
| .30 M1 rifle | 124,726 | 2,257 | 74,201 | 16,553 | 2,518 | | | 4 | | 37 | | | 220,302 |
| .30 M1C and M1D sniper rifles | 16 | 255 | 73 | 20 | 148 | 1 | | | | 7 | | | 520 |
| 5.56mm M16A1 including 6,145 M16s in 1972 | | | 126,862 | 2,052 | 3,265 | 516,464 | 83,762 | 38,468 | 77,417 | 82,446 | 5,435 | 7,819 | 943,989 |
| .30 M1818A2 BARs | 4,685 | 5,441 | 10,671 | 18 | 4,432 | | | | | | | | 25,247 |
| Subtotal | | | | | | | | | | | | | 1,984,152 |
| **SHOTGUNS:** | | | | | | | | | | | | | |
| 12 gage shotguns of various models | 54,670 | | | | | 52 | 35 | 134 | 31 | 248 | | | 55,018 |
| Subtotal | | | | | | | | | | | | | 55,018 |

MACHINE GUNS, GRENADE LAUNCHERS, MORTARS, AND RECOILLESS RIFLES

| Item | | | | | | | | | | | | Total |
|---|---|---|---|---|---|---|---|---|---|---|---|---|
| **MACHINE GUNS:** | | | | | | | | | | | | |
| .30 Cal. M1919A4, M1919A6 and M37 machine guns | 6,770 | 2,616 | 819 | 779 | 992 | 4 | 6 | 6 | 309 | 79 | | 9,772 |
| 7.62mm M60 machine gun, including M60C and M60D | | | 2,872 | 10,329 | 1,377 | 995 | 5,045 | 1,864 | 218 | 653 | | 23,853 |
| .50 Cal. M2 Browning machine guns | 9 | 12 | 2 | 21 | 392 | 867 | 403 | 578 | 759 | 16 | | 3,059 |
| Subtotal | | | | | | | | | | | | 36,684 |
| **GRENADE LAUNCHERS:** | | | | | | | | | | | | |
| 40mm M79 grenade launcher | 1,017 | 486 | 6,922 | 1,830 | 16,807 | 12,384 | 10,596 | 6,819 | 5,585 | 7,408 | 747 | 70,601 |
| 40mm XM148 grenade launcher (M203s in 1973–74) | | | | | 52 | | 43 | 164 | 13 | 63 | | 335 |
| 40mm MK 20 grenade launcher | | | | | | 20 | 100 | | | | | 120 |
| Subtotal | | | | | | | | | | | | 71,056 |
| **MORTARS:** | | | | | | | | | | | | |
| 60mm M2 mortars | 2,659 | 652 | 44 | 28 | 75 | 1,295 | 315 | 190 | 232 | 1,472 | 58 | 7,020 |
| 60mm M19 mortars | 26 | 273 | 263 | 158 | 16 | | | | 23 | | | 759 |
| Subtotal | | | | | | | | | | | | 7,779 |
| **RECOILLESS RIFLES:** | | | | | | | | | | | | |
| 57mm M18A1 recoilless rifle | 102 | 8 | 116 | 129 | 117 | 200 | 2 | 238 | 70 | 185 | 12 | 1,179 |
| Subtotal | | | | | | | | | | | | 1,179 |

## United States Military Assistance Grant in Aid to Laos, 1950–75

| Weapon Type | 1950–64 | 1965 | 1966 | 1967 | 1968 | 1969 | 1970 | 1971 | 1972 | 1973 | 1974 | 1975 | Total |
|---|---|---|---|---|---|---|---|---|---|---|---|---|---|
| **HANDGUNS:** | | | | | | | | | | | | | |
| .38 Colt Detective Special 2-inch revolver | | | 50 | 50 | | | | | | 129 | | | 229 |
| .45 Cal. M1911A1 pistol | 3,774 | 102 | 10 | 318 | 116 | 116 | | 995 | 1,116 | 161 | 14 | | 6,592 |
| Subtotal | | | | | | | | | | | | | 6,821 |
| **SUBMACHINE GUNS:** | | | | | | | | | | | | | |
| M3 and M3A1 | 11,333 | 375 | | | | | | | | | | | 11,708 |
| Subtotal | | | | | | | | | | | | | 11,708 |
| **RIFLES:** | | | | | | | | | | | | | |
| .30 M1/M2 carbines | 50,974 | 1,568 | 11,800 | 5,726 | 1,429 | | 1,450 | 1,140 | 500 | | | | 74,587 |
| .30 M1 rifle | 25,795 | 615 | 334 | 9,521 | | | | | | | | | 36,267 |
| 5.56mm M16A1 | | | | | 1,400 | 4,042 | 16,162 | 18,880 | | 43,185 | 4,800 | | 88,469 |
| .30 M1818A2 BARs | 88 | 235 | 424 | 299 | | | | | | | | | 1,046 |
| Subtotal | | | | | | | | | | | | | 200,369 |
| **MACHINE GUNS:** | | | | | | | | | | | | | |
| .30 Cal. M1919A4, M1919A6 machine guns | 1,330 | 172 | 47 | | 169 | 106 | | 32 | 57 | | | | 1,913 |
| 7.62mm M60 machine gun | | | | | | | | | 268 | 887 | 118 | | 1,273 |
| .50 Cal. M2 Browning machine guns | 245 | | | | | | | 10 | 9 | | | | 264 |
| Subtotal | | | | | | | | | | | | | 3,450 |
| **GRENADE LAUNCHERS:** | | | | | | | | | | | | | |
| 40mm M79 grenade launcher | 100 | | 5 | 115 | 514 | 338 | 165 | 218 | 1,257 | | | | 2,712 |
| Subtotal | | | | | | | | | | | | | 2,712 |
| **MORTARS:** | | | | | | | | | | | | | |
| 60mm M2 mortars | 989 | 102 | 55 | 113 | 125 | 38 | 38 | 199 | 334 | 203 | | | 2,176 |
| Subtotal | | | | | | | | | | | | | 2,176 |
| **RECOILLESS RIFLES:** | | | | | | | | | | | | | |
| 57mm M18A1 recoilless rifle | | | | 107 | 74 | | | | 27 | 57 | | | 265 |
| Subtotal | | | | | | | | | | | | | 265 |

## United States Military Assistance Grant in Aid to Cambodia, 1950–75

| Weapon Type | 1950–64 | 1965 | 1966 | 1967 | 1968 | 1969 | 1970 | 1971 | 1972 | 1973 | 1974 | 1975 | Total |
|---|---|---|---|---|---|---|---|---|---|---|---|---|---|
| **HANDGUNS:** | | | | | | | | | | | | | |
| .38 Colt Detective Special 2-inch revolver | | | 134 | | | | | 350 | 134 | | | | 618 |
| .45 Cal. M1911A1 pistol | 930 | | | | | | | 5,845 | 9,632 | 58 | 295 | | 16,430 |
| Subtotal | | | | | | | | | | | | | 17,048 |
| **SUBMACHINE GUNS:** | | | | | | | | | | | | | |
| Unknown | 2,853 | | | | | | | 239 | | | | | 3,092 |
| Subtotal | | | | | | | | | | | | | 3,092 |
| **RIFLES:** | | | | | | | | | | | | | |
| .30 M1/M2 carbines | 20,431 | | | | | | 25,925 | 64,809 | | | 5,403 | | 116,668 |
| .30 M1 rifle | 25,426 | | | | | | | 23,000 | | | | | 48,426 |
| 5.56mm M16A1 | | | | | | | 3,376 | 99,022 | 70,497 | 3,449 | 2,527 | 2,101 | 180,972 |
| 7.62mm AK47 | | | | | | | 1,549 | 3,775 | | | | | 5,324 |
| 7.5mm MAS unknown | | | | | | | | 198 | | | | | 198 |
| .30 M1818A2 BARs | | | | | | | 76 | 6,118 | | | | 12 | 6,206 |
| Subtotal | | | | | | | | | | | | | 257,794 |
| **MACHINE GUNS:** | | | | | | | | | | | | | |
| .30 Cal. M1919A4, M1919A6 machine guns | 487 | | | | | | 401 | 3,487 | 1,908 | 176 | 120 | 12 | 6,104 |
| 7.62mm M60 machine gun | | | | | | | 18 | | 1,185 | 245 | 65 | 4 | 1,517 |
| 7.5mm French unknown | | | | | | | 34 | | | | | | 34 |
| 7.62mm Type 56 PRC | | | | | | | | 257 | | | | | 257 |
| .50 Cal. M2 Browning and Type 56 machine guns | 18 | | | | | | | 55 | 82 | 278 | 211 | 78 | 722 |
| Subtotal | | | | | | | | | | | | | 7,962 |
| **GRENADE LAUNCHERS:** | | | | | | | | | | | | | |
| 40mm M79 grenade launcher | | | | | | | 1,260 | 10,052 | 9,803 | 472 | 150 | 55 | 21,792 |
| Subtotal | | | | | | | | | | | | | 21,792 |
| **MORTARS:** | | | | | | | | | | | | | |
| 60mm M2/M19 mortars, and 75 PRC Type 31s | 214 | | | | | | 272 | 947 | 1,908 | | | | 3,341 |
| Subtotal | | | | | | | | | | | | | 3,341 |

In 1971 the United States provided 562 RPG-2 and 99 RPG-7 launchers to Cambodian forces as part of a program to reutilize overhauled captured enemy materiel.

### United States Small Arms Abandoned in Vietnam in 1975

When the government of the Republic of South Vietnam collapsed in April 1975, substantial quantities of US-supplied materiel were left behind. During the past decade, the current government of Vietnam has been supplying some of these arms to allied countries and to the revolutionary and terrorist organizations in other countries, such as Chile, Colombia, El Salvador, Guatemala, Honduras, and Uruguay. The following is an abbreviated listing of the weapons left behind in Vietnam and Cambodia.

|                            | *Vietnam* | *Cambodia* | *Total*   |
|----------------------------|-----------|------------|-----------|
| .45 M1911A1 pistol         | 90,000    | 24,000     | 114,000   |
| 5.56mm M16A1 rifle         | 791,000   | 155,000    | 946,000   |
| Mixed other rifles         | 857,580   | 104,000    | 961,580   |
| 7.62mm M60 GMPG            | 15,000    | 320        | 15,320    |
| 40mm M79 grenade launcher  | 47,000    | 18,500     | 65,500    |
| Total                      | 1,800,580 | 301,820    | 2,102,400 |

No data are available for 7.62mm M73 and M37 armor MGs or 12.7mm (.50) M2 HB HMGs. These weapons were generally associated with APCs and AFVs, and the quad M55 trailer mount for the M2 HMG was also used in Vietnam. In addition, 63,000 M72 66mm light antitank weapons (LAW); 14,900 mortars (60 and 81mm); 200 90mm M67 recoilless rifles; 1,607 pieces of artillery (105mm, 155mm, and 175mm); 1,381 M113 APCs; and 550 tanks (M41A3 and M48A3). In excess of 150,000 tons of ammunition was abandoned to the North Vietnamese. It is obvious that these weapons will continue to be seen around the world for the next several decades.

## YEMEN (Arab republic of — North)

Population (estimate in 1984): 5.90 million. Ground forces: regulars, ca. 35,000; paramilitary: tribal levies, ca. 20,000; Ministry of National Security Force, ca. 5,000. Variety of British, Italian, American, and Soviet small arms. Soviet weapons were supplied from 1956, increasing in 1962, and ending in 1978–79. American support with materiel began in 1979. Confirmed details are limited.

**HANDGUNS:**

**SUBMACHINE GUNS:**

- *Cal.:* 9 x 19mm Parabellum
  *Common Name:* Beretta Model 38/49 Mod. 4 submachine gun

  *Remarks:* Beretta, Italy.

- *Cal.:* 7.62 x 25mm
  *Common Name:* PPS43 submachine gun

  *Remarks:* East Bloc origin.

- *Cal.:* 7.62 x 25mm
  *Common Name:* PPSh41 submachine gun

  *Remarks:* East Bloc origin.

**RIFLES:**

- *Cal.:* 5.56 x 45mm NATO
  *Common Name:* M16A2 rifle

  *Remarks:* In 1986 the armed forces acquired 6 M16A2 sample rifles. This may be the prelude to a larger acquisition.

- *Cal.:* 7.62 x 39mm
  *Common Name:* SKS rifle

  *Remarks:* East Bloc origin.

- *Cal.:* 7.62 x 39mm
  *Common Name:* vz.52 rifle

  *Remarks:* Czechoslovakian origin.

- *Cal.:* 7.62 x 39mm
  *Common Name:* AK47 assault
  rifle

  *Remarks:* East Bloc origin. Large numbers of these weapons are in private hands.

- *Cal.:* 7.62 x 51mm NATO
  *Common Name:* Gewehr 3

  *Remarks:* Some years ago, the armed forces received G3s from Saudi Arabia.

- *Cal.:* 7.62 x 54mmR
  *Common Name:* Mosin Nagant
  1891/30 and M44 rifles

  *Remarks:* East Bloc origin.

- *Cal.:* 7.92 x 57mm
  *Common Name:* HAKIM rifle

  *Remarks:* Egyptian origin.

- *Cal.:* 7.92 x 57mm
  *Common Name:* SAFN rifle

  *Remarks:* FN origin.

**SHOTGUNS:**

**MACHINE GUNS:**
- *Cal.:* 7.62 x 39
  *Common Name:* RPD LMG

  *Remarks:* East Bloc origin.

- *Cal.:* 7.62 x 51mm NATO
  *Common Name:* M73 armor MG

  *Remarks:* US origin. Mounted on M60A3 tanks.

- *Cal.:* 7.62 x 51mm NATO
  *Common Name:* M240 armor MG

  *Remarks:* US origin. Mounted on M60A3 tanks. FMS delivered 432 in 1979.

- *Cal.:* 7.62 x 54mmR
  *Common Name:* SGMT armor
  MG

  *Remarks:* Soviet origin.

- *Cal.:* 7.62 x 63mm
  *Common Name:* .30 M1918 BAR

  *Remarks:* US origin.

- *Cal.:* 7.62 x 63mm
  *Common Name:* .30 M1919A6

  *Remarks:* US origin. MAP delivered 889 before 1964.

- *Cal.:* 12.7 x 99mm
  *Common Name:* .50 M2 HB
  HMG

  *Remarks:* US origin. FMS delivered 50 before 1975 and an additional 50 in 1979.

- *Cal.:* 12.7 x 99mm
  *Common Name:* .50 M85 armor
  MG

  *Remarks:* US origin. FMS delivered 32 in 1979. Mounted on M60A3 tanks.

- *Cal.:* 12.7 x 108mm
  *Common Name:* DShK38/46
  HMG

  *Remarks:* Soviet origin.

**AUTOMATIC CANNON:**
- *Cal.:* 14.5 x 114mm
  *Common Name:* KPV HMG

  *Remarks:* East Bloc origin.

- *Cal.:* 20 x 102mm
  *Common Name:* 20mm M168 Vulcan automatic cannon on M167
  and M163 VADS

  *Remarks:* US origin. There are about 70 M167 VADS and at least 72 M163 VADS in service.

• *Cal.:* 23 x 152mmB
  *Common Name:* ZU23 automatic
  cannon

*Remarks:* East Bloc origin. About 40 ZSU-23-4 SP AA systems are in
service.

### GRENADE LAUNCHERS:
• *Cal.:* 40 x 46mmSR
  *Common Name:* M79 grenade
  launcher

*Remarks:* US origin. FMS delivered 200 in 1979.

## YEMEN (People's Democratic Republic — South)

Population (estimate in 1984): 2.15 million. Ground forces: regulars, ca. 24,000; People's Militia, 30,000; paramilitary, between 15,000 and 30,000. Public security forces equal about 30,000. Soviet pattern small arms predominate.

### HANDGUNS:

### SUBMACHINE GUNS:
• *Cal.:* 9 x 19mm
  *Common Name:* MKIV Sterling
  submachine gun

*Remarks:* Sterling Armament Company, UK.

• *Cal.:* 9 x 19mm
  *Common Name:* Port Said submachine gun

*Remarks:* Egyptian origin.

### RIFLES:
• *Cal.:* 7.62 x 39mm
  *Common Name:* PRC Type 56
  (SKS) carbine

*Remarks:* Chinese origin. Seen in the hands of ceremonial troops.

• *Cal.:* 7.62 x 39mm
  *Common Name:* AK47 assault
  rifle

*Remarks:* East Bloc origin.

• *Cal.:* 7.62 x 54mmR
  *Common Name:* M44 carbine

*Remarks:* East Bloc origin.

### SHOTGUNS:

### MACHINE GUNS:
• *Cal.:* 7.62 x 54mmR
  *Common Name:* SGMT armor
  MG

*Remarks:* Soviet origin.

• *Cal.:* 7.62 x 54mmR
  *Common Name:* PKT armor MG

*Remarks:* Soviet origin. Mounted on Soviet T62 tanks.

• *Cal.:* 12.7 x 108mm
  *Common Name:* DShK38/46
  HMG

*Remarks:* Soviet origin.

**AUTOMATIC CANNON:**

• *Cal.:* 14.5 x 114mm
*Common Name:* KPV HMG

*Remarks:* East Bloc origin.

• *Cal.:* 23 x 152mmB
*Common Name:* ZU23 automatic
cannon

*Remarks:* East Bloc origin.

# YUGOSLAVIA (Socialist Federal Republic of)

Population (estimate in 1984): 22.99 million. Ground forces: regulars, ca. 191,000 (140,000 conscripts); reserves/paramilitary, 500,000–1,000,000 (Frontier Guards, 15,000–20,000; Territorial Defense Force, variously estimated from 1,000,000 to 3,000,000). The police *(Milicija)* has about 160,000 officers. Yugoslav Border Police 8-man squads have been observed with the following mix of weapons: four AKs, two M1 Thompson SMGs; one K98 sniper rifle; and one DP LMG.

**HANDGUNS:**

• *Cal.:* 7.62 x 25mm
*Official Name:* M57
*Common Name:* TT33 Tokarev
pistol

*Remarks:* Yugoslavian copy made at the state factory Zavodi Crvena Zastava
(ZCZ), Kragujevac.

• *Cal.:* 9 x 19mm Parabellum
*Official Name:* M70(d)
*Common Name:* 9mm version of
TT33

*Remarks:* Made at ZCZ.

• *Cal.:* 7.65 x 17mm Browning
*Official Name:* M70
*Common Name:* Domestic pocket
pistol

*Remarks:* Made at ZCZ.

• *Cal.:* 9 x 17mm Browning
*Official Name:* M70(k)
*Common Name:* Same as 7.65mm
M70 in .380 ACP

*Remarks:* Made at ZCZ.

• *Cal.:* 9 x 19mm Parabellum
*Common Name:* FN Mle .35 GP
pistol

*Remarks:* Belgian origin. Purchased before 1950 and after 1962.

**SUBMACHINE GUNS:**

• *Cal.:* 7.62 x 25mm
*Official Name:* M49/57
*Common Name:* Variant embodying design elements from
PPSh41 and PPD SMGs

*Remarks:* Made at ZCZ. OBSOLETE. FOM 1005-14-3-7.62-1.

• *Cal.:* 7.62 x 25mm
*Official Name:* M56
*Common Name:* This submachine
is a simplified version of the
German MP40

*Remarks:* Made at ZCZ. FOM 1005-14-3-7.62-2.

- *Cal.:* 9 x 19mm
  *Common Name:* HK MP5 submachine gun

- *Cal.:* 7.65 x 17mm
  *Official Name:* M61(j)
  *Common Name:* Yugoslavian ver-
  sion of Czechoslovakian vz.61
  Skorpion

**RIFLES:**
- *Cal.:* 7.62 x 39mm
  *Official Name: Poluautomatiska
  Puska M59/66*
  *Common Name:* Yugoslavian ver-
  sion of SKS carbine

- *Cal.:* 7.62 x 39mm
  *Official Name: Automat M64*
  *Common Name:* AK47 assault
  rifle

- *Cal.:* 7.62 x 39mm
  *Official Name: Automat M64A*
  *Common Name:* Grenade launch-
  ing version of M64

- *Cal.:* 7.62 x 39mm
  *Official Name: Automat M64B*
  *Common Name:* Grenade launch-
  ing version w/ folding stock

- *Cal.:* 7.62 x 39mm
  *Official Name: Automat M70*
  *Common Name:* Improved M64

- *Cal.:* 7.62 x 39mm
  *Official Name: Automatic M70A*
  *Common Name:* W/ folding stock

- *Cal.:* 7.62 x 39mm
  *Official Name: Automat M70AB1*
  *Common Name:* AKM version of
  M70 w/ fixed wood stock

- *Cal.:* 7.62 x 39mm
  *Official Name: Automat M70AB2*
  *Common Name:* AKM version of
  M70 w/ folding stock

- *Cal.:* 7.62 x 51mm NATO
  *Official Name: Automat M77B1*
  *Common Name:* M70AB1 in
  7.62mm NATO

- *Cal.:* 7.92 x 57mm
  *Official Name: M76*
  *Common Name:* Semiautomatic
  M70AB1 for sniping

- *Cal.:* 7.92 x 57mm
  *Official Name: Puska M48*
  *Common Name:* Mauser 98 rifle

**SHOTGUNS:**

*Remarks:* Heckler & Koch (HK), Germany. Used by selected police organizations.

*Remarks:* Made at ZCZ.

*Remarks:* Made at ZCZ. FOM 1005-14-2-7.62-1-1. Integral rifle grenade
sight.

*Remarks:* Made at ZCZ. This weapon has an integral rifle grenade sight.

*Remarks:* Made at ZCZ. This weapon has an integral rifle grenade sight.

*Remarks:* Made at ZCZ. FOM 1005-14-2-7.62-2.

*Remarks:* Made at ZCZ. FOM 1005-14-2-7.62-3.

*Remarks:* Made at ZCZ. This weapon has an integral rifle grenade sight.

*Remarks:* Made at ZCZ.

*Remarks:* Made at ZCZ.

*Remarks:* Export model made at ZCZ. All models of the Yugoslav AK47s
and AKMs have been exported in substantial numbers. Also in 5.56 x 45mm.

*Remarks:* Made at ZCZ.

*Remarks:* Made at ZCZ. FOM 1005-14-2-7.92-1.

**MACHINE GUNS:**

• *Cal.:* 7.62 x 39mm
  *Official Name: Puskomitrajez M65A*
  *Common Name:* LMG version of M64 assault rifle w/ fixed barrel

  *Remarks:* Made at ZCZ.

• *Cal.:* 7.62 x 39mm
  *Official Name: Puskomitrajez M65B*
  *Common Name:* Same as M65A w/ quick change barrel

  *Remarks:* Made at ZCZ.

• *Cal.:* 7.62 x 39mm
  *Official Name: Puskomitrajez M72B1*
  *Common Name:* LMG version of M70 series w/ fixed wood stock and fixed barrel

  *Remarks:* Made at ZCZ.

• *Cal.:* 7.62 x 39mm
  *Official Name: Puskomitrajez M72AB1*
  *Common Name:* LMG version of M70 series w/ folding stock and fixed barrel

  *Remarks:* Made at ZCZ.

• *Cal.:* 7.62 x 39mm
  *Official Name: Puskomitrajez M77B1*
  *Common Name:* NATO caliber M70 for export sales

  *Remarks:* Made at ZCZ. Also available in 5.56 x 45mm for export sales.

• *Cal.:* 7.62 x 54mmR
  *Official Name: Mitrajez M80*
  *Common Name:* Model 80 GPMG

  *Remarks:* Made at ZCZ. Developmental General Purpose Machine Gun (GPMG) closely following the design of the Soviet PK series.

• *Cal.:* 7.92 x 57mm
  *Official Name: Mitrajez M53*
  *Common Name:* SARAC (MG42) GPMG

  *Remarks:* Made at ZCZ. Copy of German MG42.

• *Cal.:* 7.62 x 54mmR
  *Common Name:* PKT armor MG

  *Remarks:* Soviet origin. Mounted on Soviet T62 tanks.

• *Cal.:* 7.62 x 54mmR
  *Common Name:* SGMT armor MG

  *Remarks:* Soviet origin. Mounted on older Soviet tanks.

• *Cal.:* 7.62 x 54mmR
  *Common Name:* DP and DTM LMGs

  *Remarks:* Soviet origin. Mounted on older Soviet tanks.

• *Cal.:* 7.62 x 63mm
  *Common Name:* .30 Browning LMG

  *Remarks:* The US provided 2,889 .30 LMGs through MAP before 1964.

• *Cal.:* 12.7 x 99mm
  *Common Name:* .50 M2 HB HMG

  *Remarks:* US origin.

• *Cal.:* 12.7 x 108mm
  *Common Name:* DShK38/46 HMG

  *Remarks:* Soviet origin. Domestic production?

**AUTOMATIC CANNON:**

- *Cal.:* 20 x 110mm
  *Official Name:* M55
  *Common Name:* Yugoslavian cannon based on HS804

*Remarks:* Made at ZCZ. Commonly found in 3-gun 20/3mm M55 A2 AA gun mount. Other gun mounts include the M55 A3 B1, M55 A4 B1, 20/1mm M75 single AA gun mount.

- *Cal.:* 23 x 152mmB
  *Common Name:* ZSU-23-4 self-propelled AA system

*Remarks:* Soviet origin.

### Yugoslavian Arms Industry

In recent years the Yugoslavian arms industry has been very active in providing small caliber weapons to the Middle East. In addition, that industry has also provided technical assistance to governments, such as that of Iraq, which has helped those governments establish a domestic manufacturing capability for small arms. Currently, the Iraquis produce Yugoslavian-type AKMs and sniper rifles in factories established for them by the Yugoslavs. The recent decision to manufacture 9 x 18mm (Makarov) pistol ammunition led the Yugoslavians to acquire additional cartridge-making machinery from Manuhrin of France.

Ammunition is made by the following factories: Privi Partizan, in Titovo (founded 1928); Unis, in Sarejevo (founded 1948); Igman, in Kontic, and Pobjeda, in Gorazde. All of these factories use modern machinery from Manurhin, Fritz Werner, and other well-known machinery makers including domestic machine tool companies. Propellant for all ammunition is made by the Milan Blagojevic Powder Factory. In addition to extruded propellants, they have been making ball-type powder since 1985 under a license from Olin, US.

### ZAIRE (Republic of)

Population (estimate in 1984): 32.16 million. Ground forces: regulars, ca. 22,000; paramilitary *(Gendarmerie Nationale du Zaire),* ca. 35,000. Older Belgian small arms still predominate, but in recent years there has been an influx of Soviet patterns, some of which have been supplied by the Israelis as part of their military aid program.

**HANDGUNS:**

- *Cal.:* 9 x 19mm Parabellum
  *Common Name:* FN Mle .35 pistol

*Remarks:* FN. Post-1958 purchase.

- *Cal.:* 9 x 19mm Parabellum
  *Common Name:* P7 pistol

*Remarks:* Heckler & Koch (HK), GmbH, West Germany.

**SUBMACHINE GUNS:**

- *Cal.:* 9 x 19mm Parabellum
  *Common Name:* Uzi submachine gun

*Remarks:* Israeli Military Industries (IMI), Israel.

- *Cal.:* 9 x 19mm Parabellum
  *Common Name:* MP5 submachine gun

*Remarks:* Source unknown.

- *Cal.:* 9 x 19mm Parabellum
  *Common Name:* MP40 submachine gun

*Remarks:* Germany, World War II.

- *Cal.:* 9 x 19mm Parabellum
  *Common Name:* LF-57 submachine gun

  *Remarks:* Luigi Franchi, Italy.

- *Cal.:* 9 x 19mm Parabellum
  *Common Name:* Vigneron submachine gun

  *Remarks:* Societe Anonyme de Precision Liegeoise, Herstal, Belgium.

- *Cal.:* 11.43 x 23mm
  *Common Name:* .45 M3 submachine gun

  *Remarks:* US origin.

**RIFLES:**
- *Cal.:* 7.62 x 51mm NATO
  *Common Name:* FN FAL

  *Remarks:* FN origin. Adopted in 1956.

- *Cal.:* 7.62 x 39mm
  *Common Name:* AK47 and AKM assault rifles

  *Remarks:* East Bloc origin, but may be via Israel. Chinese Type 56-1 rifles have been observed.

- *Cal.:* 5.56 x 45mm
  *Common Name:* M16A1 rifle

  *Remarks:* US origin. Ca. 20,000 in the inventory. About 1,000 were delivered by FMS in 1976. There may also have been some deliveries via Israel. It is anticipated that Zaire will purchase M16A2 rifles.

- *Cal.:* 5.56 x 45mm
  *Common Name:* Galil assault rifle

  *Remarks:* IMI, Israel.

- *Cal.:* 5.56 x 45mm
  *Common Name:* FNC assault rifle

  *Remarks:* FN, Herstal, Belgium.

- *Cal.:* 7.62 x 51mm NATO
  *Common Name:* Gewehr 3

  *Remarks:* HK design made at the Royal Small Arms Factory (RSAF), Enfield.

- *Cal.:* 7.62 x 51mm NATO
  *Common Name:* CETME Mod. 58 assault rifle

  *Remarks:* Made at Santa Barbara in Spain.

- *Cal.:* 7.62 x 51mm NATO
  *Common Name:* SIG-510-4 assault rifle

  *Remarks:* Made at Schweizerische Industrie Gesellschaft/Rheinfalls (SIG), Switzerland.

- *Cal.:* 7.92 x 57mm?
  *Common Name:* SAFN semiautomatic rifle

  *Remarks:* Belgian origin. OBSOLETE.

- *Cal.:* 7.92 x 57mm or 7.62 x 51mm NATO
  *Common Name:* Mauser 98K bolt action rifle

  *Remarks:* Manufacture unknown. These may be in 7.62mm NATO caliber from Israeli surplus. OBSOLETE?

- *Cal.:* 7.7 x 56mmR
  *Common Name:* .303 Enfield No. 4 bolt action rifle

  *Remarks:* Made at the RSAF, Enfield.

**SHOTGUNS:**
- *Cal.:* 18.5 x 59mm
  *Common Name:* 12 gage Model 12 shotguns

  *Remarks:* US origin. MAP delivered 100 before 1964.

**MACHINE GUNS:**
- *Cal.:* 5.56 x 45mm
  *Common Name:* M16A1 heavy barrel automatic rifle

  *Remarks:* Reported, but origin unknown.

- *Cal.:* 5.56 x 45mm
  *Common Name:* FN Minimi

  *Remarks:* FN origin.

- *Cal.:* 7.62 x 39mm
  *Common Name:* RPD LMG

  *Remarks:* East Bloc origin.

- *Cal.:* 7.62 x 51mm NATO
  *Common Name:* AA 52 GPMG

  *Remarks:* Groupment Industriel des Armements Terrestres (GIAT), France.

- *Cal.:* 7.62 x 51mm NATO
  *Common Name:* FN MAG

  *Remarks:* FN. MAG *Infanterie Standard* (60-20), T5 with nondisintegrating link belt and MAG *Infanterie Standard* (60-20), T8 with nondisintegrating link belt.

- *Cal.:* 7.62 x 51mm NATO
  *Common Name:* M60 GPMG

  *Remarks:* US origin. FMS delivered 20 in 1976.

- *Cal.:* 7.62 x 54mmR
  *Common Name:* RP46 company machine gun

  *Remarks:* East Bloc origin.

- *Cal.:* 7.62 x 54mmR
  *Common Name:* SGMT armor MG

  *Remarks:* Soviet origin. Mounted on older model Soviet tanks.

- *Cal.:* 7.62 x 54mmR
  *Common Name:* Type 56 GPMG

  *Remarks:* Chinese origin.

- *Cal.:* 7.62 x 54mmR
  *Common Name:* Type 59 T armor MG

  *Remarks:* Chinese origin. Mounted on Chinese T62 light tanks.

- *Cal.:* 7.62 x 54mmR
  *Common Name:* Type 64 GPMG

  *Remarks:* North Korean origin.

- *Cal.:* 7.92 x 57mm
  *Common Name:* FN Type D BAR

  *Remarks:* FN origin.

- *Cal.:* 12.7 x 99mm
  *Common Name:* .50 M2 HB HMG

  *Remarks:* US origin. FMS delivered 21 in 1976.

- *Cal.:* 12.7 x 108mm
  *Common Name:* DShK38/46 HMG

  *Remarks:* East Bloc origin. Also Chinese Type 54 version.

**AUTOMATIC CANNON:**

- *Cal.:* 14.5 x 114mm
  *Common Name:* KPV HMG

  *Remarks:* East Bloc origin.

- *Cal.:* 23 x 152mmB
  *Common Name:* ZU23 automatic cannon

  *Remarks:* East Bloc origin.

## ZAMBIA (Republic of)

Population (estimate in 1984): 6.55 million. Ground forces: regulars, ca. 13,000; paramilitary, 2,000 including a police paramilitary unit of about 500 men. There were about 200 Cuban troops in-country at the end of 1987. Armed forces generally carry older British-pattern small arms.

## HANDGUNS:
- *Cal.:* 7.62 x 25mm
  *Common Name:* TT33 Tokarev pistol

  *Remarks:* East Bloc origin.

- *Cal.:* 7.62 x 25mm
  *Common Name:* vz.52 pistol

  *Remarks:* Czechoslovakian origin.

- *Cal.:* 9 x 18mm
  *Common Name:* Stechkin (APS) machine pistol

  *Remarks:* Soviet origin.

## SUBMACHINE GUNS:
- *Cal.:* 9 x 19mm Parabellum
  *Common Name:* Sterling Mark 4 submachine gun

  *Remarks:* Sterling Armament Corp., UK.

- *Cal.:* 9 x 19mm Parabellum
  *Common Name:* MP5 submachine gun

  *Remarks:* Heckler & Koch (HK), design from the Royal Small Arms Factory (RSAF), Enfield.

## RIFLES:
- *Cal.:* 7.62 x 51mm NATO
  *Common Name:* FN FAL

  *Remarks:* FN origin?

- *Cal.:* 7.62 x 51mm NATO
  *Common Name:* Gewehr 3

  *Remarks:* HK design from the RSAF, Enfield.

- *Cal.:* 7.62 x 39mm
  *Common Name:* AK47 and AKM assault rifles

  *Remarks:* East Bloc origin.

- *Cal.:* 7.7 x 56mmR
  *Common Name:* .303 MK III and No. 4 Enfield bolt action rifles

  *Remarks:* UK origin.

## SHOTGUNS:

## MACHINE GUNS:
- *Cal.:* 7.62 x 54mmR
  *Common Name:* SGM MG series

  *Remarks:* East Bloc origin, including the SGMT.

- *Cal.:* 7.62 x 54mmR
  *Common Name:* PK GPMG series

  *Remarks:* East Bloc origin.

- *Cal.:* 7.62 x 54mmR
  *Common Name:* PRC Type 67 GPMG

  *Remarks:* Chinese origin.

- *Cal.:* 7.62 x 51mm NATO?
  *Common Name:* MG42-type GPMG

  *Remarks:* Have been observed in news photographs, but variant and caliber unknown.

- *Cal.:* 12.7 x 108mm
  *Common Name:* DShK38/46 HMG

  *Remarks:* East Bloc origin.

## AUTOMATIC CANNON:
- *Cal.:* 14.5 x 114mm
  *Common Name:* KPV HMG

  *Remarks:* East Bloc origin.

## ZIMBABWE

Population (estimate in 1984): 8.33 million. Ground forces: regulars, variously estimated from 15,000 to 50,000; paramilitary, estimated up to 50,000 (National Militia ca. 20,000; Zimbabwe Republic Police Force, 10,000; police support unit, 3,000). Formerly, Southern Rhodesia with some older British patterns, but largely equipped with Warsaw Pact small arms at present. Although the government has plans to create a domestic small arms manufacturing industry, they have been receiving large quantities of small arms from their North Korean advisors/allies since 1981.

**HANDGUNS:**
- *Cal.:* 9 x 19mm Parabellum
  *Common Name:* FN Mle. 1935 GP pistol

  *Remarks:* FN origin?

- *Cal.:* 9 x 20mmR
  *Common Name:* .38 Enfield No. 2 Mark 1 revolver

  *Remarks:* UK origin. FOM 1005-35-1-9-4.

- *Cal.:* 9 x 29mmR
  *Common Name:* .38 Colt Cobra with 76mm barrel

  *Remarks:* US origin.

- *Cal.:* 11.43 x 21.7mmR
  *Common Name:* .455 Webley No. 1 Mark VI revolver

  *Remarks:* UK origin. FOM 1005-35-1-11.43-2.

- *Cal.:* 11.43 x 23mm
  *Common Name:* .45 M1911A1 pistol

  *Remarks:* US origin.

- *Cal.:* 7.62 x 25mm
  *Common Name:* TT33 Tokarev pistol

  *Remarks:* East Bloc origin.

**SUBMACHINE GUNS:**
- *Cal.:* 9 x 19mm Parabellum
  *Common Name:* Sterling Mark 4 submachine gun

  *Remarks:* Sterling Armament Corp., UK.

- *Cal.:* 9 x 19mm Parabellum
  *Common Name:* Walther MP-K submachine gun

  *Remarks:* Walther, Germany.

- *Cal.:* 9 x 19mm Parabellum
  *Common Name:* Uzi submachine gun

  *Remarks:* Israeli Military Industries (IMI), Israel.

- *Cal.:* 9 x 19mm Parabellum
  *Common Name:* Star Z45 submachine gun

  *Remarks:* Star, Bonafacio Echeverria y Cia., Spain.

- *Cal.:* 9 x 19mm Parabellum
  *Common Name:* Madsen M50 submachine gun

  *Remarks:* Madsen, Denmark.

- *Cal.:* 9 x 19mm Parabellum
  *Common Name:* Sanna semiautomatic carbine

  *Remarks:* South African origin. Another semiautomatic carbine called the LDP is reported in service, but information very sketchy.

- *Cal.:* 9 x 19mm Parabellum
  *Common Name:* Sten Mark II submachine gun

  *Remarks:* UK origin. OBSOLETE.

## RIFLES:

- *Cal.:* 5.56 x 45mm
  *Common Name:* R4 rifle

  *Remarks:* South African origin.

- *Cal.:* 5.56 x 45mm
  *Common Name:* AR70/223

  *Remarks:* Beretta, Italy. Used by the Air Force.

- *Cal.:* 7.62 x 51mm NATO
  *Common Name:* FN FAL/R1

  *Remarks:* Belgian and South African origin.

- *Cal.:* 7.62 x 51mm NATO
  *Common Name:* M14 rifle

  *Remarks:* US origin.

- *Cal.:* 7.62 x 51mm NATO
  *Common Name:* Gewehr 3

  *Remarks:* Heckler & Koch (HK) design of Portuguese manufacture.

- *Cal.:* 7.62 x 51mm NATO
  *Common Name:* AR-10 Rifle

  *Remarks:* Ex-Angolan issue rifles made by A-I of the Netherlands.

- *Cal.:* 7.62 x 39mm
  *Common Name:* AK47 and AKM assault rifles

  *Remarks:* East Bloc origin. Some Chinese Type 56 AKMs have been reported.

- *Cal.:* 7.62 x 39mm
  *Common Name:* Type 68 rifle

  *Remarks:* People's Republic of China.

## SHOTGUNS:

## MACHINE GUNS:

- *Cal.:* 5.56 x 45mm
  *Common Name:* Ultimax 100 LMG

  *Remarks:* Chartered Industries of Singapore, Republic of Singapore.

- *Cal.:* 7.62 x 51mm NATO
  *Common Name:* L7A1 GPMG (FN MAG)

  *Remarks:* FN, Herstal, Belgium. MAG *Infanterie Standard* (60-20), T9. Some of these guns provided previously by the Republic of South Africa.

- *Cal.:* 7.7 x 56mmR
  *Common Name:* .303 Mk 1 Bren LMG

  *Remarks:* UK origin. Service status uncertain. Some of these guns in 7.62mm NATO provided previously by the Republic of South Africa.

- *Cal.:* 7.7 x 56mmR
  *Common Name:* .303 Mk 1 Vickers MMG

  *Remarks:* UK origin. Service status uncertain.

- *Cal.:* 7.62 x 63mm
  *Common Name:* .30 M1917A1 MMG

  *Remarks:* US origin. Service status uncertain.

- *Cal.:* 7.62 x 63mm
  *Common Name:* .30 M1919A4 LMG

  *Remarks:* US origin. Some of these guns provided previously by the Republic of South Africa. Standard, but obsolescent.

- *Cal.:* 7.62 x 39mm
  *Common Name:* RPD LMG

  *Remarks:* East Bloc origin.

- *Cal.:* 7.62 x 39mm
  *Common Name:* RPK LMG

  *Remarks:* East Bloc origin.

- *Cal.:* 7.62 x 54mmR
  *Common Name:* PK GPMG

  *Remarks:* East Bloc origin.

- *Cal.:* 7.62 x 54mmR
  *Common Name:* DP LMG

  *Remarks:* Soviet origin.

- *Cal.:* 7.62 x 54mmR
  *Common Name:* RP46 company
  machine gun

  *Remarks:* Soviet origin.

- *Cal.:* 7.62 x 54mmR
  *Common Name:* PRC Type 67
  GPMG

  *Remarks:* PRC origin.

- *Cal.:* 8 x 50.5mmR (Steyr)
  *Common Name:* M1907/12 MMG
  Schwarzlose

  *Remarks:* Austrian origin. Reported in service, but likely OBSOLETE.

- *Cal.:* 12.7 x 99mm
  *Common Name:* .50 M2 HB
  HMG

  *Remarks:* US origin. Some of these guns provided previously by the Republic of South Africa.

- *Cal.:* 12.7 x 108mm
  *Common Name:* DShK38/46
  HMG

  *Remarks:* Soviet origin.

**AUTOMATIC CANNON:**

- *Cal.:* 14.5 x 114mm
  *Common Name:* KPV HMG

  *Remarks:* Soviet origin.

- *Cal.:* 23 x 152mmB
  *Common Name:* ZU23 automatic
  cannon

  *Remarks:* Soviet origin.

# Small Arms Ammunition Since 1939

*with the assistance of*
*Peter Labbett*

As with small caliber weapons, World War II represented a watershed for the development of small arms ammunition. That war was fought for the greater part with small arms mechanisms originally designed decades before the war. The ammunition fired in these weapons generally was created in the early years of the century. To this general pattern there were some notable exceptions. The United States entered the war with the self-loading .30 M1 rifle. Still, this weapon fired the 7.62 x 63mm cartridge, which had been introduced in 1903. Both Germany and the Soviet Union also introduced self-loading rifles that fired the standard rifle cartridge. The German MP43/Stg.44 began a new pattern, because it incorporated a new class of cartridge, the 7.92 x 33mm *kurz*. That shortened round—the standard Mauser rifle cartridge was 7.92 x 57mm—set a significant design trend after the war. The 7.92 x 33mm *kurz* was, in effect, the first assault rifle cartridge.

After the shooting stopped in 1945, there was little immediate change in standard issue small arms. The early postwar period was one of reevaluation and research. These studies led to the new generation of cartridges that appeared in the 1950s. Since then the major powers have standardized around seven "international" calibers. These include for rifles and light machine guns the following: the Soviet 5.45 x 39mm; the US 5.56 x 45mm; the Soviet 7.62 x 39mm; the NATO 7.62 x 51mm; and the Soviet 7.62 x 54mmR. For heavy machine guns there are two basic calibers: the 12.7 x 99mm Browning and the 12.7 x 108mm Degtyarev. The world of automatic cannon calibers is a little more complicated. In the East Bloc, the 14.5 x 114mm and the 23 x 152mmB are the basic cartridges. In the West, particularly in NATO, there are several types of 20mm ammunition, including: the US 20 x 102mm; the Swiss 20 x 110mm; the Swiss 20 x 128mm; and the 20 x 139mm Hispano-Suiza, which is used in both US and German automatic cannons. The 25 x 137mm is issued in both US and Swiss armored vehicle guns.

A new class of cartridges introduced since 1945 is found in the shoulder-fired and automatic grenade launchers that are currently gaining wider usage. In the West, there are two basic 40mm grenade cartridges – the low velocity shoulder-fired 40 x 46mmSR and the automatic grenade launcher cartridge, the high velocity 40 x 53mmSR. Both of these rounds embody the high-low pressure system for generating the necessary launching pressures. In the Warsaw Pact, the Soviets introduced their 30 x 29mm cartridge for their AGS-17 grenade launching machine gun. They have also introduced a 40mm caseless grenade round for their rifle mounted launcher. In early 1988, the People's Republic of China announced a new 35mm automatic grenade launcher. It will compete with the 30mm Soviet AGs-17 and the US Mark 19.

This chapter provides a quick summary of small arms ammunition developments since 1945.

## Developmental Ammunition
## Since 1945

When World War II ended there were two major groups that undertook the development of new small caliber ammunition. In the first were grouped the major contestants, who had survived the war with their military establishments intact. In the second were those nations who had sat out the war, but who had drawn some conclusions about the type of calibers and cartridges that would be needed in the future. Active in the second group were Switzerland and Spain. The majority of the experimentation in the years following the war concentrated on the creation of new rifle cartridges. There was less emphasis on the development of pistol/submachine gun ammunition or on heavy machine gun ammunition.

### *Soviet Union*

Soviet historians state that work was begun on the development of a new rifle cartridge in 1939. This round was intended for use in a new self-loading rifle. As is so often the case, the sudden start of the war interrupted the preparations for that conflict. Thus the basic Soviet rifle and machine gun cartridge continued to be the Model 1891 7.62 x 54mm rimmed cartridge. Soviet records go on to say that work on a new intermediate and

rimless cartridge was restarted in 1943. This new 7.62 x 39mm cartridge – styled the Model 1943 cartridge – is very similar in concept to that of the 7.92 x 33mm German ammunition. The exact linkage between the two cartridges has never been fully determined. Soviets attribute their cartridge to N. M. Elizarov and B. V. Semin. They claim that the Model 1943 cartridge was first used in the Simonov self-loading carbine (SKS45) on the first Byelorussian front before the end of the 1939–45 war. Whatever is actual fact, this cartridge and rifle did not enter full-scale Soviet service until some years after the war.

After 40 years, the 7.62 x 39mm M43 cartridge is still standard issue in the armed forces of the Soviet Union, the Warsaw Pact nations, and dozens of other nations that have adopted this caliber. In recent years the Soviets have developed a new and smaller caliber ammunition based on the 1943 cartridge case. The 5.45 x 39mm M1974 cartridge is used in the modified AKM and RPK, which have been redesignated the AK74 and RPKS74. This caliber and these weapons at present seem confined to Soviet ground forces and to special elite units of allied armed forces.

Another area in which the Soviets have been active is the development of handgun ammunition. Among the major powers only the Soviets have thought it necessary to introduce a new caliber – the 9 x 18mm Makarov cartridge. This new round – not interchangeable with the 9 x 19mm Parabellum/NATO – is fired with the now obsolete Stechkin machine pistol (APS) and the Makarov pistol, both of which date from 1952. In the West, a 9 x 18mm cartridge has been marketed as a police cartridge. It is not identical to the Makarov, nor has it been very successful. This round is called the 9mm Ultra and the 9mm Police.

### *United Kingdom*

Britain and her Commonwealth nations fought World War II armed with variants of the Lee Enfield rifle and a family of machine guns chambered to fire the .303 cartridge – 7.7 x 56mmR. An interwar attempt to change calibers had been thwarted by economics. In 1945 the British knew that they needed a new cartridge. To determine the correct caliber, the British army established the

"Small Arms Caliber Panel" in 1945. After two years of intensive study, the panel reported on its experimentation with cartridges ranging in caliber from 6.5mm to 8.38mm (.256 to .33). The panel of experts concluded that desired effects could be obtained from a smaller diameter, shorter length, and lighter cartridge, and they recommended a 6.86mm projectile (.27 caliber). As a direct consequence of this study, design of two cartridges was commenced — 6.86mm (.270) and 7mm (.276). The latter was redesignated .280 for political purposes.

The British intended that their work would be the basis of a standard caliber for the newly established North Atlantic Treaty Organization (1949). Unknown to the British, the Americans were secretly working on a new cartridge of their own in 7.62mm (.30). Eventually, competitive trials were arranged in the United States in mid-1950. Three weapons were fired during these experiments — the British EM.2, the US T25, and the Belgian FN FAL. The British cartridge by this time had the same base diameter as the American T65 series to reduce the problem of choice to just one of caliber. It was now called the .280/30. American ordnance experts objected to the British cartridge because of a whole series of features. The argument boiled down to the simple fact that it was not 7.62mm (.30).

Attempts to solve this vexing controversy were to no avail. The result was that the Americans had their way, and in 1953 the T65E3 case was adopted as the 7.62 x 51mm NATO cartridge case. As field experience has subsequently demonstrated, the 7.62mm NATO round was far too powerful for the lightweight rifles in which it was intended to be used. The controversy over rifle cartridge size and power begun in the mid-1940s continues unabated four decades later.

In the late 1960s the British carried out another assessment of the proper caliber for a military rifle. During the intervening years, some of the tactical and technical considerations that had held sway in the late 1940s had been significantly modified. After some examination of 6.25mm cartridges, the British engineers shifted their emphasis to 4.85mm projectiles in 1971. This shift reflected lessons learned in the US ammunition development program — especially Project

SALVO — and tactical and other considerations laid down by the small arms people at NATO Headquarters in Brussels. The initial British 4.85mm cartridge had a case length of 44mm and bore a close resemblance to the US M193 5.56 x 45mm case. Once bullet seating problems were discovered, the British shifted to a 48.75mm long case. This cartridge had a 3.63 gram (56 grain) projectile with a published muzzle velocity in the new rifle of 900 m/s (2953 f.p.s.) and 930 m/s (3051 f.p.s.) from the longer barreled light machine gun. After the NATO small caliber trials of 1977–79, the British decided once again to abandon their preferred caliber for the one selected by the alliance. Thus they standardized on the 5.56 x 45mm NATO cartridge that fired the 4 gram (63 grain) Belgian SS109 projectile.

### United States of America

Before the end of the Second World War, Americans began to think seriously about development of a light automatic rifle. While many individuals had been impressed with the German *Sturmgewehr,* US Army Ordnance officials preferred a full power rifle cartridge to the 7.92 x 33mm *kurz.* The initial approach was to shorten the 7.62 x 63mm cartridge by using improved propellants, which took less space in the cartridge case. By the end of 1944, initial firing tests were being conducted with an experimental cartridge based upon the commercial .300 Savage sporting round. In the next year a new case, called the T65, was evolved. Starting with this case, which was 47.4mm long, the US ordnance engineers progressed through a series of cases until they settled on the 51mm T65E3 case. That case became the basis for all subsequent light rifle experiments in the United States.

In many respects, the T65E3 cartridge was simply a shortened 7.62 x 63mm. Its ballistic characteristics were very similar. The chamber pressures were 50,000 p.s.i. and 52,000 p.s.i., respectively. Instrumented velocity at 23.7 meters from the muzzle was 838 m/s (2,750 f.p.s.) for the T65E3 and 835 m/s (2,740 f.p.s.) for the .30 M2 (7.62 x 63mm) cartridge. Late in 1953, after years of heated debate, the North Atlantic Treaty Organization standardized the T65E3 as the

7.62 x 51mm NATO cartridge. This round had the FN SS77 9.3 gram (145 grain) projectile.

Subsequent to the adoption of the 7.62mm NATO ammunition family, the ordnance engineers in the United States sponsored additional research projects of considerable consequence. One of these, Project SALVO, grew out of wound ballistics studies conducted by the Operations Research Office (ORO) of the Johns Hopkins University. As a result of examining wounds and the manner in which they were inflicted, ORO investigators discovered that the rifle was a very poor vehicle for cost-effective wounding or killing of an enemy soldier. An individual's chances of being hit by a consciously aimed projectile were no greater than being struck by a random fragment or projectile. Thus to improve hit probability, the soldier needed to fire more projectiles. It was preferable that these projectiles had a random distribution around the point of aim. SALVO studies also indicated that the rifle was seldom effective at ranges greater than 300 meters because of aiming errors and the obscuring effect of terrain features.

During the early years of Project SALVO, a series of cartridges and bullet types were tested. By the mid-1950s there was a general agreement that a small caliber high velocity projectile fired from a high rate of fire rifle would produce improved hit and kill probabilities. From this conclusion came the 5.56 x 45mm cartridge and the M16 rifle. This weapon might have been passed over and experimentation continued if it had not been selected for use in Vietnam. With that decision the United States and subsequently NATO became committed to smaller caliber rifles and later to small caliber machine guns.

Concurrent with the later development of the 5.56 x 45mm weapons, the US Army experimented with even higher velocity lightweight projectiles called flechettes. This was one ammunition component of the Special Purpose Individual Weapon (SPIW) project. The other element was the 40 x 46mmSR grenade launcher. Although various weight flechettes were tried, the 0.5 to 0.65 (10 grain) version was typical. These flechettes — finned steel darts — were carried down the smooth bore barrel of the SPIW by a 0.45 gram (7 grain) fiberglass or nylon sabot.

Typically, a flechette's muzzle velocity was about 1,400 m/s (4,590 f.p.s.), and since these darts tended to buckle when they hit the human target, their residual kinetic energy was dumped directly into the target. This made the flechette potentially a very effective wounding agent. These projectiles proved very effective when fired in large numbers from an artillery shell. However, the single SPIW fired flechette was difficult to control because of problems with stripping the sabot from the dart. Serious experimentation with singly fired flechettes was halted in the early 1970s. Flechette technology was revived in the early 1980s. There are still dedicated supporters in the US military establishment.

At about the time flechettes passed from favor, US Army research and development personnel began to look for a smaller caliber cartridge for a squad level machine gun — the Squad Automatic Weapon (SAW). Some believed that a cartridge about halfway between the 7.62mm NATO and the 5.56mm rounds would be ideal. The result was the 6mm SAW project. As noted in chapter 2 of the 12th edition of *Small Arms of the World*, the 6 x 45mm SAW cartridge was short-lived. There was just not sufficient reason to adopt a third infantry caliber. The result was the creation of a project to improve the long distance terminal effects of the 5.56 x 45mm cartridge. In the United States this became the XM777 series, and in Belgium it became the FN SS109 project.

Both of these 5.56mm developments involved the use of penetrator core elements to defeat body armor and helmets. At the end of the 1977–79 NATO small caliber trials, some members of the alliance decided to adopt the SS109 projectile in the 5.56 x 45mm case as the 5.56 x 45mm NATO cartridge. Since that time the US government has adopted the M855 projectile series, essentially an Americanization of the SS109. Olin Corporation in the United States has developed their own proprietary 62 grain 5.56mm Penetrator round. They claim that this round is superior in armor penetration to the SS109. In the decades to come the improved 5.56 x 45mm projectiles are going to be very popular, and the sale of this ammunition is going to be big business for ammunition companies such as Olin and FN.

With the reentry into the military ammunition development business with their 62 grain Penetrator round, Olin has also become involved in other projects to enhance the performance of existing cartridges. One of the most promising is the 7.62 x 51mm and 12.7 x 99mm saboted light armor penetrator (SLAP) rounds. Both involve the use of tungsten subcaliber projectiles carried down the weapon barrel by a nylon sabot. These projectiles are expected to lend new life to the 7.62mm and 12.7mm machine guns when used against lightly armored vehicles such as armored personnel carriers. In another mid-1980s development, Olin is manufacturing the MK211 MOD 0 Armor Piercing Incendiary cartridge (replacing the M8 API); an Americanized version of the Norwegian Raufoss Multipurpose high explosive round. All of these cartridges will extend the useful life of the very popular Browning .50 (12.7mm) heavy machine guns.

### Belgium

Fabrique Nationale (FN) has conducted an extensive small caliber ammunition development program since World War II. They were intimately involved in the development of the 7.62mm NATO cartridge, and they have experimented with a variety of other types and calibers of cartridges. Of these the most important is the SS109 projectile with its steel penetrator, which rides in front of the larger lead core. The projectile weight of the SS109 is 4 grams (63 grains), and it has a muzzle velocity of 915 m/s (3,000 f.p.s.). It is designed to be fired from a barrel with a 1 in 178mm (1 in 7 inch) twist as compared with the older US M193 3.5 gram (55 grain) bullet, which is fired from a 1 in 305mm (1 in 12 inch) twist barrel. The SS109, because of the increased spin, is more stable for longer ranges but is less lethal than the M193. The latter tends to tumble when it hits the human body.

### West Germany

When the Germans joined NATO, the 7.62 x 51mm NATO was a *fait accompli*. German military authorities have no great affection for the 7.62mm NATO cartridge, because it was too powerful for an assault rifle. Recent events demonstrate that they are not very keen on the 5.56 x 45mm cartridge either. After several experimental projects, the Germans have cast their lot with the development of a caseless ammunition rifle system. Currently this project is being conducted for the *Bundeswehr* by Heckler & Koch and Dynamit Nobel. German authorities anticipate that the *Gewehr 11* project will yield a rifle and ammunition system that can be fielded in the mid-1990s. This high rate of fire weapon (see pp. 66–73 of the 12th edition of *Small Arms of the World*) has also been entered by these German firms into the US Advanced Combat Rifle (ACR) project. The fate of the American project is uncertain because there are other contractors (AAI, Inc.; ARES; Colt; McDonnell-Douglas; and Steyr-Daimler-Puch) and because the Americans may choose to adapt the German technology to their own design. An American design could blend elements borrowed from the concepts of both contractors, or it could be the result of an in-house development. In any case, caseless ammunition will be a development to watch during the next few years.

### France

The French used a wide variety of military small arms during World War II. They found themselves with an equally wide variety of cartridges at the end of the war. Out of a series of experiments—some of which were supported by engineers from the former Mauser factory in Germany—the French military concluded that it was best to standardize on the 7.5 x 54mm Model 1929 cartridge. There was an irony about their decision not to adopt the 7.62 x 51mm NATO cartridge. For many years, it had been argued that France needed the new cartridge before they adopted a new rifle. In the 1970s the French have switched to 7.62mm NATO for their vehicle mounted machine guns.

In 1970 the French adopted the FAMAS F3 5.56 x 45mm assault rifle. This weapon fires the US M193-type 5.56 x 45mm ammunition as does the SG540 rifle, a SIG design made by Manurhin. The French are now fully committed to 5.56mm as their infantry rifle caliber.

### Czechoslovakia

Following the Second World War, the Czechoslovakian army standardized on the 7.92 x 57mm caliber as an interim step. As this process got underway, the General Staff directed their ordnance people to develop an intermediate power 7.62mm cartridge. After experimenting with case lengths, ordnance engineers settled on the Z-50 7.62 x 45mm case. A family consisting of a rifle and a light machine gun (both designated the vz.52) was adopted in 1952 to fire that cartridge. Subsequently, in 1957, under growing pressure from the Warsaw Pact, the Czechoslovakian General Staff made the switch to the Soviet M43 7.62 x 39mm cartridge. All service rifles and machine guns were modified to fire the Soviet cartridge, and they were redesignated the vz.52/57. When the Czechoslovakian army adopted an assault rifle, the vz.58, it was chambered from the beginning for the 7.62 x 39mm round. Both before and after 1957, the Czechoslovakian government exported large quantities of their small caliber weapons. As a result, both vz.52 and vz.52/57 versions will be found in national inventories around the world.

### Switzerland

Although the Swiss sat out the Second World War as a neutral, they followed the development of the assault rifle in Germany with keen interest. From the mid-1940s to the early 1950s, the Swiss military experimented with a 7.5 x 52.7mm case and with a 8 gram (123.4 grain) ball projectile. The reported muzzle velocity of this bullet was 670 m/s (2,198 f.p.s.). Ultimately, the Swiss decided to keep their full power 7.5 x 55.5mm cartridge, which has been the standard Swiss rifle cartridge since 1889. This was the ammunition used with the *Sturmgewehr 57*.

During the 1970s the Swiss military experimented with a variety of 5.6mm and 6.0mm cartridges. They finally settled on a round that has a case very similar to the US 5.56 x 45mm case, but with a bullet of Swiss origin. This cartridge is the one that is used in the new *Sturmgewehr 90* (SG541).

### Spain

In the early postwar years, the Spanish military benefitted from the technical expertise of former Mauser engineers who moved to Spain where they worked at the government *Centro de Estudios Technicos y Materiales Especiales* (CETME). Out of this partnership came the CETME assault rifle, the design ancestor of the *Gewehr 3,* and a series of special assault rifle cartridges. These experimental cartridges included 7.62 x 41mm and 7.92 x 40.4mm versions. After NATO adopted the 7.62 x 51mm NATO round, the Spanish military followed suit, and they subsequently replaced their older 7.92 x 57mm rifles and machine guns with ones designed to fire the NATO round.

### Ammunition in Service Since 1945

As noted at the outset of this section, there has been an attempt on the part of the major powers to reduce the number of calibers used by their armed forces. The desire to simplify the supply system has been a universal one. The following provides a brief look at the basic cartridges in service today.*

### 7.62 x 39mm (USSR Model 1943)

This cartridge has seen incredibly widespread service since its adoption four decades ago. It is a standard infantry cartridge in the Soviet army, the armies of the Warsaw Pact, the People's Republic of China, and a host of other countries both allied and neutral in their relations with the East Bloc. The standard USSR ball projectile, the Type PS, is boat-tailed, has a mild steel core, and weighs 7.97

---

*Since only limited space is available to describe ammunition in use, readers are referred to two volumes prepared by the US Army Foreign Science and Technology Center: *Small-Caliber Ammunition Identification Guide,* volume 1, *Small-Arms Cartridges up to 15mm* (DST-1160G-514-81-Vol 1) and volume 2, *20-mm to 40-mm Cartridges* (DST-1160G-514-78-Vol 2). Both volumes are unclassified and are available commercially.

grams (123 grain). Some countries manufacture a flat base, lead core projectile of approximately the same weight. The PS projectile has an average velocity of 710 m/s (2,330 f.p.s.). Tracer (Type T45) Armor Piercing Incendiary (Type BZ), and Incendiary (Type ZP) are also available in the 7.62 x 39mm cartridge family. Cartridge cases of brass and steel have been used for the 7.62 x 39mm ammunition, with steel being the basic material used by East Bloc countries. These steel cases will be found either with a copper plating or green to brown lacquer.

The following countries manufacture or have manufactured 7.62 x 39mm ammunition:

| | |
|---|---|
| Algeria | Korea (North) |
| Austria | Korea (South) |
| Belgium (FN) | Netherlands (NWM) |
| Brazil | Norway (Plastic training) |
| Bulgaria | Pakistan |
| China (PRC) | Poland |
| Cuba | Portugal |
| Czechoslovakia | Romania |
| Egypt | South Africa |
| Finland | Sudan |
| (Lapua & | Sweden |
| Sako) | Syria |
| France | Union of Soviet Socialist |
| Germany (East) | Republics |
| Germany (West) | United States (Lake City |
| Hungary | Army Ammunition |
| Indonesia | Plant) |
| Iraq | Yugoslavia |
| Israel | |

### 7.62 x 51mm (7.62mm NATO)

In addition to the NATO armies, the middle eastern nations of CENTO and the nations of SEATO also adopted this cartridge. Many African and South American states followed this path and adopted either the FN FAL or the Heckler & Koch G3. Predominant projectiles are the lead core (SS77 or US M59) and the mild steel core (US M80). They average 9.3 grams (145 grains) with an expected muzzle velocity of about 837 m/s (2,745 f.p.s.). The most common case material is brass, but steel and aluminum cases are occasionally encountered.

The following countries manufacture or have manufactured 7.62 x 51mm NATO ammunition:

| | |
|---|---|
| Argentina | Malaysia |
| Australia | Mexico |
| Austria | Morocco |
| Belgium | Nepal |
| Brazil | Netherlands |
| Bulgaria | New Zealand |
| Burma | Nigeria |
| Cameroons | Norway |
| Canada | Pakistan |
| Chile | Paraguay |
| China (PRC) | Peru |
| Colombia | Philippines |
| Czechoslovakia | Portugal |
| Denmark | Saudi Arabia |
| Dominican Republic | Singapore |
| Ecuador | South Africa |
| Finland | Spain |
| France | Sudan |
| Germany (West) | Sweden |
| Greece | Syria |
| Hungary | Taiwan (ROC) |
| India | Thailand |
| Indonesia | Turkey |
| Iran | United Kingdom |
| Ireland | United States of America |
| Israel | Upper Volta |
| Italy | Venezuela |
| Japan | Yugoslavia |
| Korea (South) | |

### 5.56 x 45mm (.223 Remington)

This cartridge has a rimless bottlenecked case 44.5mm long, but it is called 45mm in standard terminology. Cases may be Berdan or Boxer primed, and will be found made of brass, steel, and, less frequently, of aluminum. Until the adoption of the 5.56 x 45mm NATO, the standard reference 5.56mm cartridge was the USA M193 (FN SS 92) ball round, which has a lead core boat-tailed 3.56 gram (55 grain) projectile. Nominal muzzle velocity for the M193 is 966 m/s (3,170 f.p.s.). The new SS109 projectile, of the 5.56 x 45mm NATO, weighs 4 grams (63 grains) and has a nominal muzzle velocity of 915 m/s (3,000 f.p.s.).

The following countries manufacture or have manufactured 5.56 x 45mm-type cartridges:

| | |
|---|---|
| Argentina | Malaysia |
| Australia | Netherlands |
| Austria | Norway |
| Belgium | Philippines |
| Brazil | Portugal |
| Canada | Singapore |
| China (PRC) | South Africa |
| Finland | Spain |
| France | Sweden |
| Germany (West) | Switzerland |
| Guatemala | Taiwan (ROC) |
| Indonesia | Thailand |
| Israel | United Kingdom |
| Italy | United States of America |
| Japan | Yugoslavia |
| Korea (South) | |

For ease of reference, we have included cartridge data from an FN ammunition catalog for some of the most popular cartridges. More detailed information can be found in the FSTC documents cited earlier in the footnote.

---

**NATO**
**9mm**
**(9 x 19)**

---

**USE**
Automatic pistols.
Submachine guns.

**TECHNICAL DATA**
- **Cartridge:**   length:   29.70 mm.
                   weight:   12.05 g.
- **Projectile:**  weight:    8    g.

**9 x 19mm NATO (also called Parabellum and Luger).**

**BALLISTIC DATA**
**Meet all NATO requirements.**
- **Muzzle velocity:** 356 m/s.
- **Velocity at 12.5 m:** 336 m/s.
  (with a FN HP 35 pistol, barrel length: 122 mm).
- **Chamber pressure:** max. 2,856 bars.
- **Muzzle energy:** 507 J.

**COMPONENTS**
- **Primer:** "oxyless" non-corrosive.
- **Case:** brass.
- **Full metal jacketed projectile:** core: lead, jacket: brass.
- **Powder:** single or double base.

**PACKING**
- **Type:**
  In bulk: SPP 25 plastic boxes.
  Pallet of 74,250 rounds in 27 CM01 metallic cases of 2,750 rounds.
- **Weight of one case:** 40 kg.
- **Volume of one case:**
  315 x 295 x 189 mm = 18 dm$^3$.

**SPECIAL FEATURES**
**Performance:**
- At 15 m, can pierce 5 mild steel 1 mm thick plates, situated at 5 cm one from the other.

---

**5.56 x 45**
**(.223)**
**SS 92 (M193)**

---

**USE**
Automatic individual weapon (FNC with a 12″ RT barrel).

Light support weapon (MINIMI with a 12″ RT barrel).

**TECHNICAL DATA**
- **Cartridge:**   length:   57    mm.
                   weight:   12    g.
- **Projectile:**  weight:    3.56 g.

## BALLISTIC DATA
- **Velocity:** (at 25 m) 965 m/s.
  (with a 508 mm long barrel).
- **Chamber pressure** (piezo):
  max. 380 MPA.
- **Energy at 25 m:** 1,660 J.

## COMPONENTS
- **Primer:** "oxyless" non-corrosive.
- **Case:** brass.
- **Projectile:** core: lead, jacket: brass.
- **Powder:** double base.

## PACKING
- **Type:**
  1. In bulk: CTN 60 cardboard boxes. Pallet of
     63,180 rounds in 27 CM 01 metallic cases of
     2,340 rounds.
- **Weight of one case:** 34 kg.
- **Volume of one case:**
  315 x 295 x 189 mm = 18 dm³.
  2. On FN-M27 links: 200-round belts.
     Pallet of 54,000 rounds in 27 metallic CM 01
     cases of 2,000 rounds.
- **Weight of one case:** 34 kg.
- **Volume of one case:**
  315 x 295 x 189 mm = 18 dm³.
  3. On clips.
     Pallet of 51,840 rounds in 27 metallic CM 01
     cases of 1,920 rounds.
- **Weight of one case:** 32 kg.
- **Volume of one case:**
  315 x 295 x 189 mm = 18 dm³.

## SPECIAL FEATURES
**Performances:**
- Optimum performances of the bullet are obtained with 12″ RT barrels.

---

### 5.56 x 45
### (.223)
### SS 109 (M855)

---

## USE
Automatic individual weapon (FNC).
Light support weapon (MINIMI).

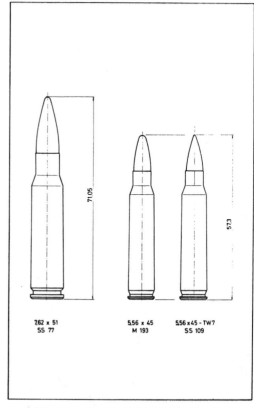

5.56 x 45mm. M193 is US designation for SS 92.

## TECHNICAL DATA
- **Cartridge:** length:  57  mm.
  weight: 12.50 g.
- **Projectile:** weight:  4  g.

## BALLISTIC DATA
**Meet all NATO requirements.**
- **Velocity:** (at 25 m) 915 m/s.
  (with a 508 mm long barrel).
- **Chamber pressure** (piezo): max. 380 MPA.
- **Energy at 25 m:** 1,700 J.

## COMPONENTS
- **Primer:** "oxyless" non-corrosive.
- **Case:** brass.
- **Projectile:** core: steel + lead, jacket: brass.
- **Powder:** double base.

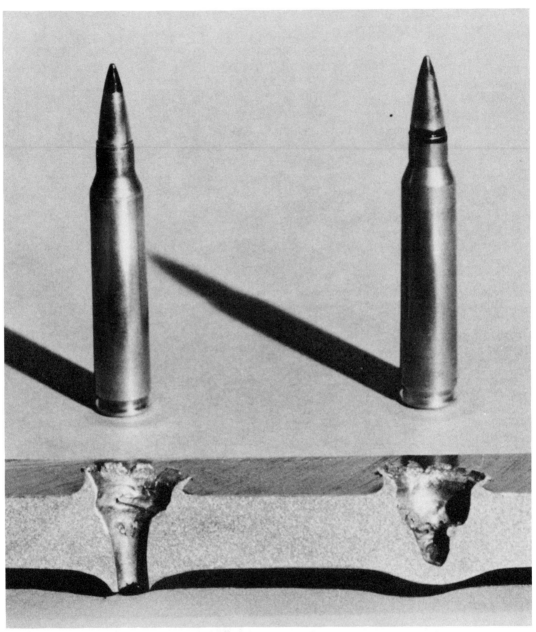

5.56 x 45mm NATO Penetrator Ammunition. The new 5.56mm penetrator rounds, with their steel insert in the tip, have significantly improved the armor perforation of this small caliber ammunition. The target plate illustrated is SAE 1010 hot-rolled 10mm steel plate. These side-by-side shots were fired at a range of 240 meters at zero degrees obliquity. The Winchester 62 grain Penetrator round is illustrated on the left, and the Fabrique Nationale SS109 is illustrated on the right.

## PACKING
- **Type:**
    1. In bulk: CTN 60 cardboard boxes.
       Pallet of 63,180 rounds in 27 CM 01 metallic cases of 2,340 rounds.
- **Weight of one case:** 35 kg.
- **Volume of one case:**
  315 x 295 x 189 mm = 18 dm³.
    2. On FN-M27 links: 200-round belts.
       Pallet of 54,000 rounds in 27 metallic CM 01 cases of 2,000 rounds.
- **Weight of one case:** 35 kg.
- **Volume of one case:**
  315 x 295 x 189 mm = 18 dm³.
    3. On clips.
       Pallet of 51,840 rounds in 27 metallic CM 01 cases of 1,920 rounds.
- **Weight of one case:** 32 kg.
- **Volume of one case:**
  315 x 295 x 189 mm = 18 dm³.

## SPECIAL FEATURES
**Performance:**
- When fired at an angle of 90° in relation to the plate, the ball projectile must perforate completely an SAE 1010 or SAE 1020 mild steel plate, of a hardness situated between 100 and 123 HB, 3.5 mm nominal thickness, located at 615 m from the weapon muzzle. The test must be made under 20° C ambient temperature.
- Optimum performances of the bullet are obtained in 7″ RT barrels.

---

### 7.62 x 39 M43 ball

---

## USE
Automatic individual weapon.
Light support weapon.

**7.62 x 39mm Soviet M43 series.**

## TECHNICAL DATA
- **Cartridge:** length: 55.7 mm.
  　　　　　　　weight: 18.20 g.
- **Projectile:** weight: 8 g.

## BALLISTIC DATA
- **Velocity:** (at 25 m) 695 m/s.
  (cal. 7.62 x 39 rifle, barrel length: 418 mm).
- **Chamber pressure:** max. 3,335 bars.
- **Energy at 25 m:** 1,904 J.

## COMPONENTS
- **Primer:** "oxyless" non-corrosive.
- **Case:** brass.
- **Projectile:** core: lead, jacket: brass.
- **Powder:** double base.

## PACKING
- **Type:**
  In bulk: CTN 50 cardboard boxes.
  Pallet of 48,600 rounds in 27 CM 01 metallic cases of 1,800 rounds.
- **Weight of one case:** 39 kg.
- **Volume of one case:**
  315 x 295 x 189 mm = 18 dm³.

---

### 7.62 x 51 NATO
### SS 77/1

---

## USE
Automatic individual weapon (LAR).
Light support weapon.
Medium support weapon (GPMG).

## TECHNICAL DATA
- **Cartridge:** length: 71.12 mm.
  　　　　　　　weight: 23.95 g.
- **Projectile:** weight: 9.30 g.

## BALLISTIC DATA
**Meet all NATO requirements.**
- **Velocity:** (at 25 m) 837 m/s.
  (with a 560 mm long barrel).
- **Chamber pressure:** < 3,360 bars.
- **Energy at 25 m:** 3,180 J.

## COMPONENTS
- **Primer:** "oxyless" non-corrosive.
- **Case:** brass.
- **Projectile:** core: lead, jacket: brass.
- **Powder:** single or double base.

## PACKING
- **Type:**
  1. In bulk: CTN 50 cardboard boxes.
     Pallet of 32,400 rounds in 27 CM 01 metallic cases of 1,200 rounds.
- **Weight of one case:** 34.5 kg.
- **Volume of one case:**
  315 x 295 x 189 mm = 18 dm³.
  2. Linked: 250-round belts.
     (Ratio at choice).
     Pallet of 27,000 rounds in 27 CM 01 metallic cases of 1,000 rounds.
- **Weight of one case:** 34.5 kg.
- **Volume of one case:**
  315 x 295 x 189 mm = 18 dm³.
  3. On 5-round clip and CTN 20 cardboard cases.
     Pallet of 34,560 rounds in 27 CM 01 metallic cases of 1,280 rounds.
- **Weight of one case:** 39 kg.
- **Volume of one case:**
  315 x 295 x 189 mm = 18 dm³.

---

### 12.7 x 99
### (.50 Browning)

---

## USE
M2 and M3 Browning and machine guns.
M85 General Electric.

## TECHNICAL DATA
- **Cartridge:** length: 138.4 mm.
  　　　　　　　weight: 112 g.
- **Projectile:** weight: 43 g.

## BALLISTIC DATA
- **Velocity:** (at 25 m) 910 m/s.
  (Browning machine gun with 45″ barrel).
- **Chamber pressure:** max. 3,770 bars.
- **Energy:** (at 25 m) = 18,040 J.

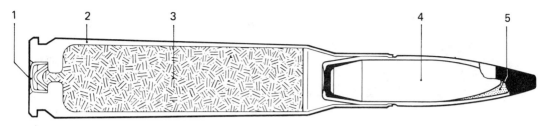

1    2    3              4    5

**12.7 x 108mm Armor Piercing.**

## COMPONENTS
- **Primer:** "oxyless" non-corrosive.
- **Case:** brass.
- **Propulsive powder:** single or double base.
- **Projectile:** body: steel. Jacket: brass.
- **Incendiary material:** non phosphorous.

## PACKING
- **Type:**
  1. In bulk, on 25-round tray.
     Pallet of 7,200 rounds in 36 AX "No-nail" cases of 200 rounds.
- **Weight of one case:** 26 kg.
- **Volume of one case:**
  340 x 270 x 190 mm = 18 dm³.
  2. Linked, 100-round belt.
     (Ratio at choice).
     Pallet of 4,500 rounds in 45 M2 A1 metallic cases of 100 rounds.
- **Weight of one case:** 16 kg.
- **Volume of one case:**
  305 x 155 x 190 mm = 9 dm³.
  3. Linked, 100-round belt.
     (Ratio at choice).
     Pallet of 5,400 rounds in 27 wirebound cases of 200 containing 2 metallic M2 A1 cases.
- **Weight of one wirebound case:** 33 kg.
- **Volume of one wirebound case:**
  366 x 314 x 198 mm = 32 dm³.

## FEATURES
**Performances:**
- At 200 m, the projectile can pierce a chromium-nickel 15 mm thick steel plate, Brinell hardness 450 minimum.

- At 100 m, ignites wood chips soaked in petrol or kerosene and located behind a 5 mm thick mild steel plate.

**Note:**
- Ballistically, the API M8 bullet is equivalent to the M33 bullet.

---

### 20 x 102
### (20mm FN 142)

---

## USE
Ground-air.

This round has been specifically designed for A.A. defense and in particular for the protection of airports against low-flying aircraft. Indeed, when used for A.A. defense the projectiles which do not hit their target fall down with a sufficiently important velocity which could cause its functioning and so damage personnel, buildings, materiel, etc.; incorporating a tracer–self-destruction device to the projectile avoids this drawback and eases the direct firing against aircraft without a reduction of efficiency.

## TECHNICAL DATA
- **Cartridge:**    length:  168 mm.
                    weight:  257 g.
- **Projectile:**   weight:  101 g.

## BALLISTIC DATA
- **Velocity:** (at 25 m) 1,030 m/s.
- **Chamber pressure:** max. 4,170 bars.
- **Muzzle energy:** = 53,575 J.

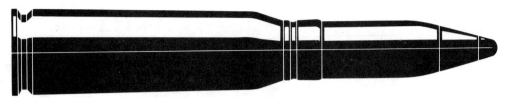

20 x 102mm M50 series.

## COMPONENTS
- **Primer:** electrical, with conducting compound.
- **Case:** brass.
- **Projectile:** body: steel.
  head: head fuze with instant percussion.
- **Driving band:** copper.
- **Tracer:** pyrotechnical material with strontium base giving a red coloration. After the round is ignited, the trace remains visible during 3.1 s. minimum (1,525 m range).
- **Propulsive powder:** single or double base.
- **Pyrotechnical material:** explosive and incendiary load.

## PACKING
- **Type:**
  Linked, 100-round belt.
  Pallet of 2,000 rounds in 20 metallic cases type M 548, each case containing a belt of 100 rounds mounted on M14 A2 metallic disintegrating links.
- **Weight of one case:** 41.5 kg.
- **Volume of one case:**
  472 x 371 x 211 mm = 37 dm³.

**Note:**
These ammunition can be delivered in bulk, in M548 metallic case of 200 rounds.

## OBSERVATIONS
1. **Functioning** (sensitivity): The fuze functions at 100% when fired at 200 m against a 1 mm thick dural plate.
2. **Beginning of trajectory safety:** It has been increased compared to the original ammunition. The fuze does not function against a 2 mm thick dural plate at a distance inferior or equal to 6 m.

3. **Incendiary effects:** The projectile ignites kerosene or wood chips soaked in alcohol or kerosene located 10 cm from a 1 mm thick aluminum plate placed at 100 m from the muzzle of the weapon.
4. **Self-destruction:** Self-destruction occurs between 3.1 and 7 seconds. To prevent a round which did not hit the target from damaging at impact on the ground, the self-destruction provokes the fragmentation of the projectile.
   - The ammunition meet the concept for the safety imposed by U.S. MIL. STD and NATO STANAG, as well as the U.S. functional characteristics concerning the ammunition of M50, M150, and M246 series.
   - They can be mounted on M14A2 or M12 (for U.S. M39 gun) metallic links and form a continuous disintegrating belt.

---

### 20 x 110
### (20mm Hispano-Suiza FN 92)

---

## USE
For HS 404 and HS 804 guns.

For air-to-air, for anti-aircraft defense, or against ground targets.

On request, a model is available for the Mk V British gun.

## TECHNICAL DATA
- **Cartridge:**  length: 183 mm.
  weight: 258 g.
- **Projectile:**  weight: 130 g.

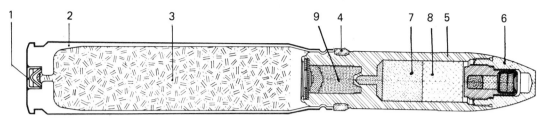

20 x 110mm.

## BALLISTIC DATA
- **Velocity:** (at 25 m) 845 m/s.
- **Chamber pressure:** max. 3,800 bars.
- **Energy at 25 m:** = 46,412 J.

## COMPONENTS
- **Primer:** "oxyless," non-corrosive.
- **Case:** brass.
- **Propulsive powder:** single or double base.
- **Driving band:** copper.
- **Projectile:** body: semi-hard steel.
- **Fuze:** single action, instantaneous, without firing pin.
- **Incendiary material.**
- **Load:** high explosive.
- **Tracer:** red, visible during 3 s. minimum.

## PACKING
- **Type:**
  On 12-round trays.
  Pallet of 3,240 cartridges in 27 CM 02 metallic cases of 120 rounds.

- **Weight of one case:** 38 kg.
- **Volume of one case:**
  315 x 295 x 300 mm = 28 dm³.

## FEATURES
### Performances:
- The projectile bursts on contact with a 1 mm thick mild steel plate, located at 100 m from the muzzle of the weapon.
- After having exploded, the projectile has to ignite jerrycans or wood chips soaked in petrol or alcohol, located at 30 cm behind the plate.
- The self-destruction can occur at the end of the trace. No self-destruction can occur before 1 second of time of flight.

### Note:
- Concordance of trajectory with TP ammunition at 550 m.

# Selected Bibliography

Andrade, John. *World Police & Paramilitary Forces.* London: Macmillan Publishers Ltd., 1985.

*Arms Production in Developing Countries: An Analysis of Decision Making.* Edited by James Everett Katz. Lexington, Mass., and Toronto: Lexington Books, D. C. Heath and Company, 1984.
  Summarizes the evolution of defense manufacturing in 14 nations.

Dupuy, T. N.; Andrews, A. C.; and Hayes, Grace P. *The Almanac of World Power.* 4th edition. London and Sydney: Jane's Publishing Company, 1980.

English, Adrian J. *Armed Forces of Latin America: Their Histories, Development, Present Strength and Military Potential.* London: Jane's Publishing Inc., 1984.

Ezell, Edward C. *Small Arms of the World: A Basic Manual of Small Arms.* 12th revised edition of the classic work by W. H. B. Smith. Harrisburg, Pa.; Stackpole Books, Inc., 1983.
  Contains descriptions of the infantry weapons below 14.5mm listed in the country-by-country inventories of *Small Arms Today.* Very helpful for understanding the operation and disassembly of contemporary small arms.

Gabriel, Richard A. *Fighting Armies: Nonaligned, Third World, and Other Ground Armies: A Combat Assessment.* Westport, Conn., and London: Greenwood Press, 1983.

————. *Fighting Armies: NATO and Warsaw Pact: A Combat Assessment.* Westport, Conn., and London: Greenwood Press, 1983.

————. *Fighting Armies: Antagonists in the Middle East: A Combat Assessment.* Westport, Conn., and London: Greenwood Press, 1983.

Gerber, Major General Johannes. *Taschenbuch fur Logistik.* Bonn-Duisdorf: Wehr & Wissen, 1977.

International Institute for Strategic Studies. *Arms to Developing Countries, 1945-1965,* by John L. Sutton and Geoffrey Kemp. London: International Institute for Strategic Studies, 1966. (Adelphi Papers no. 28).

———. *The Military Balance, 1984-1985.* London: International Institute for Strategic Studies, 1984.

This annual publication is most useful for tracking tanks, armored vehicles, and other equipment that is larger than infantry weapons.

Jaffee Center for Strategic Studies, *The Middle East Military Balance, 1983,* Mark Heller, ed. Tel Aviv, Israel: Tel Aviv University, 1983.

Klare, Michael T. *American Arms Supermarket.* Austin, Tex.: University of Texas Press, 1984.

Klare, Michael T., and Arnson, Cynthia. *Supplying Repression: U.S. Support for Authoritarian Regimes Abroad.* 2d edition. Washington, D.C.: Institute for Policy Studies, 1981.

Klieman, Aaron S. *Israel's Global Reach: Arms Sales as Diplomacy.* Washington *et al.:* Pergamon-Brassey's International Defense Publishers, 1985.

Pierre, Andrew J. *The Global Politics of Arms Sales.* Princeton, N.J.: Princeton University Press, 1982.

United States Arms Control and Disarmament Agency. *World Military Expenditures and Arms Transfers, 1972-1982.* Washington, D.C.: Government Printing Office, April 1984.

———. *World Military Expenditures and Arms Transfers, 1987,* edited by Daniel Gallik. Washington, D.C.: Government Printing Office, March 1988.

United States Central Intelligence Agency. *The World Fact Book, Nineteen Hundred and Eighty-Four.* Washington, D.C.: Government Printing Office, 1984.

United States Department of State. *Conventional Arms Transfers in the Third World, 1972-81.* Special Report 102. Washington, D.C.: Bureau of Public Affairs, State Department, August 1982.

———. *Status of the World's Nations.* Publication No. 8735. Washington, D.C.: Bureau of Intelligence and Research, June 1983.

*World Armies.* Edited by John Keegan. 2d edition. Detroit, Mich.: Gale Research Company, 1983.

# Index

**Wanted: New Information**
**for Future Editions**
**of *Small Arms Today***

If you have additional information that should be included or changes that should be made, please send it to us in the following format at the address listed below.

**COUNTRY:** _____

**WEAPON TYPE:** (Check one)

Handgun ___ SMG ___ Rifle ___ Shotgun ___ MG ___ Auto Cannon ___ Grenade Launcher ___

Caliber      Official Nomenclature      Common Name      Remarks
_____

Send to: Edward C. Ezell
        Institute for Research on Small Arms in International Security
        Suite 4
        1847 Vernon Street, N.W.
        Washington, DC 20009

Quality Printing and Binding by:
R.R. Donnelly & Sons Company
1400 Kratzer Road
Harrisonburg, VA 22801 U.S.A.